Web Development: Full Stack

F. Max Coller

Australia • Brazil • Canada • Mexico • Singapore • United Kingdom • United States

Web Development: Full Stack First Edition
F. Max Coller

SVP, Higher Education Product Management: Cheryl Constantini

VP, Product Management and Marketing, Learning Experiences: Thais Alencar

Senior Portfolio Product Director: Mark Santee

Portfolio Product Director: Rita Lombard

Portfolio Product Manager: Tran Pham

Learning Designer: Mary Convertino

Content Manager: Ethan Wheel

Associate Digital Project Manager: John Smigielski

Technical Editor: Matthew Beecher

Developmental Editor: Lisa Ruffolo

VP, Product Marketing: Jason Sakos

Director, Product Marketing: April Danaë

Portfolio Marketing Manager: Mackenzie Paine

Content Acquisitions Analyst: Ann Hoffman

Vendor Project Manager: Anjali Kambali

Production Service: Straive

Senior Designer: Erin Griffin

Cover Image Source: shutterstock.com

For product information and technology assistance, contact us at
Cengage Customer & Sales Support, 1-800-354-9706
or support.cengage.com.

For permission to use material from this text or product, submit all requests online at **www.copyright.com.**

Library of Congress Control Number: 2023905455

ISBN: 9780357673850

Cengage
200 Pier 4 Boulevard
Boston, MA 02210
USA

Cengage is a leading provider of customized learning solutions with employees residing in nearly 40 different countries and sales in more than 125 countries around the world. Find your local representative at **www.cengage.com.**

To learn more about Cengage platforms and services, register or access your online learning solution, or purchase materials for your course, visit **www.cengage.com.**

Notice to the Reader

Publisher does not warrant or guarantee any of the products described herein or perform any independent analysis in connection with any of the product information contained herein. Publisher does not assume, and expressly disclaims, any obligation to obtain and include information other than that provided to it by the manufacturer. The reader is expressly warned to consider and adopt all safety precautions that might be indicated by the activities described herein and to avoid all potential hazards. By following the instructions contained herein, the reader willingly assumes all risks in connection with such instructions. The publisher makes no representations or warranties of any kind, including but not limited to, the warranties of fitness for particular purpose or merchantability, nor are any such representations implied with respect to the material set forth herein, and the publisher takes no responsibility with respect to such material. The publisher shall not be liable for any special, consequential, or exemplary damages resulting, in whole or part, from the readers' use of, or reliance upon, this material.

Printed at CLDPC, USA, 04-23

About the Author

F. Max Coller is a Distinguished Business Systems Analyst at the University of Wisconsin–Madison and a Senior Instructor at the Madison Area Technical College. He lives near Madison, Wisconsin with a family of Bobs, to whom he is forever grateful for tolerating his dad jokes, culinary experiments, and obsession with collecting rusty tractors. He wrote his first GOTO statement in 1988 and starting teaching at the technical college level in 1999, so he's been at this technology stuff for a while if you do the math.

Brief Contents

v

Contents

Chapter 3

HTML and CSS: Page Layout and Content   61

Chapter 4

Mobile Development and Responsive Design   99

Chapter 5

JavaScript Programming   137

Chapter 6

JavaScript Libraries   177

Chapter 7

Scripting Frameworks: An Overview and Comparative Exploration   207

Chapter 8

Content Management Systems: An Overview   233

Chapter 9

WordPress Security, Themes, and Plug-Ins   265

Chapter 10

Building Dynamic Webpages with PHP 295

Chapter 11

Database Basics with MySQL 325

Chapter 12

Building a Dynamic Webpage with a MySQL Database   365

Preface for the Instructor

This book is written with an audience of the author's own students in mind. It draws from experiences and instructional materials the author has gathered as both a full stack web developer and technical college instructor for more than two decades. The intent of this text is to present important technical material in an approachable manner while answering a question that students inevitably ask: "Why is this important for me to know?"

The students this book is written for are not computer science majors, but instead are technically adept students with an interest in web development. The course progresses from a common starting point of understanding how the web works to the peak of creating a dynamic web application using PHP and MySQL. Along the way, the text notes many technological waypoints and cites common mistakes.

The objective of this text is to provide a broad overview of the technologies in a full stack web application. To accommodate a typical 16-week course, the book takes a brisk pace through a breadth of coverage rather than a deeper dive into any single technology.

Organization of the Text

The text is organized to progress from basic to more advanced web development concepts and techniques. Chapter 1 establishes a common understanding of how the web works and explains why that knowledge sets the foundation for the rest of the book. Chapter 2 starts the technical content, introducing students to the first and fundamental building block of every webpage, HTML.

Chapter 3 covers creating webpage content and layout using HTML and CSS, while Chapter 4 discusses how to develop for mobile platforms and apply responsive web design. Chapter 5 introduces programming with JavaScript, and Chapter 6 explains how to use JavaScript libraries, jQuery in particular. Chapter 7 explores other scripting frameworks, including Angular, Vue, and React. Chapter 8 provides an overview of content management systems and demonstrates how to use WordPress to create a webpage. Chapter 9 continues examining WordPress and its security features, themes, and plug-ins. Chapter 10 explains how to use PHP to build interactive webpages. Chapter 11 introduces MySQL and basic database concepts, while Chapter 12 combines MySQL, PHP, and other web technologies to create a dynamic web application.

Each chapter contains a tutorial that guides students through the how and why of using the new technology successfully. The end-of-chapter projects give students the chance to apply what they learned to a new challenge. The exercises ask students to use critical thinking skills to explore the important topics introduced in the chapter.

Features of the Text

This first edition of this textbook has been developed around a clearly established set of learning objectives. Each chapter begins with a list of objectives to prepare the student for the chapter content and help them organize their learning experience. Objectives are clearly aligned to the major headings of the chapter and to the end-of-chapter questions, exercises, and projects.

Note | The Note feature provides additional information to supplement the chapter content—for example, helpful tips or background information on a chapter topic.

Common Mistakes

The Common Mistakes feature highlights missteps and errors that a new developer might make with the tasks and concepts introduced in the chapter and provides suggestions for locating and fixing those errors.

Quick Checks

Quick Check self-assessments are placed throughout the reading to allow learners to increase understanding of new concepts in-the-moment. In the online reader, these assessments are auto graded and help instructors to confirm student understanding as new material is presented.

Review Questions

Review Questions test student comprehension of the major ideas and techniques presented throughout the chapter. Each question is aligned directly with a learning objective so students can track their learning and review supporting content as needed.

Programming Exercises

Programming Exercises provide opportunities to apply concepts. These exercises allow students to explore each major programming concept presented in the chapter. Supporting data files are provided in the Cengage resource site when required.

Projects

Projects synthesize multiple learning objectives and concepts within the chapter and allow students to take their skills to the next level by applying new concepts and problem-solving skills in more complex activities. These activities mirror real-world tasks that students are likely to encounter in full stack web development positions.

Chapter Summaries

Chapter Summaries recap the concepts and techniques covered in the chapter and provide students with a bulleted list from which to review content.

Key Terms

Key Terms are identified and defined throughout the chapter and listed again at the chapter's completion. A glossary at the end of the book lists all key terms in alphabetical order along with their working definitions.

Ancillary Package

Additional instructor resources for this product are available online. Instructor assets include an Instructor Manual, Educator's Guide, PowerPoint® slides, and a test bank powered by Cognero®. Sign up or sign in at www.cengage.com to search for and access this product and its online resources.

Instructor Manual: The Instructor Manual follows the text chapter by chapter to assist in planning and organizing an effective, engaging course. The manual includes learning objectives, chapter overviews, lecture notes, ideas for classroom activities, and additional resources.

PowerPoint Presentations: This text provides PowerPoint slides to accompany each chapter. Slides are included to guide classroom presentations and can be made available to students for chapter review or to print as classroom handouts.

Solution and Answer Guide (SAG): Solutions and rationales to review questions, exercises, and projects are provided to assist with grading and student understanding.

Data Files: Data files necessary to complete some of the steps and projects in the course are available.

Educator's Guide: The Educator's Guide provides an overview of the features of the text and resources available on the instructor resource site.

Complete List of Learning Objectives: A complete list of all objectives addressed in the textbook is available to help instructors plan and manage their course.

Test Bank®: Cengage Learning Testing Powered by Cognero is a flexible, online system that allows you to:

- author, edit, and manage test bank content from multiple Cengage Learning solutions,
- create multiple test versions in an instant, and
- deliver tests from your LMS, your classroom, or anywhere you want.

Acknowledgments

Although there is one name on the front of the book, a work of this size and scope is never the product of one person working alone. I've had the good fortune to work with an amazingly patient team of remarkably talented people who have provided guidance, encouragement, and weekly meetings with completely derailed agendas because it's so much more fun to talk about the other things. (Sorry, Ethan, for hijacking most of your carefully crafted agendas with my non sequiturs and tangents.)

Lisa Ruffolo has been instrumental in patiently and repeatedly transforming my first draft of Jackson Pollock–esque abstract impressionism word spatters into the coherent masterpiece of realism that you hold in your hands. Perhaps with some classical music quietly playing in the background while she does so. At least, that's my mental image of her word artistry skills in action. She probably listens to Metallica or Slayer for all I know.

Matthew Beecher has been generous with his technical wisdom while finding and correcting the many "undocumented features," technical oversights, and outright mistakes I made in the code written for this text. I appreciate his advice and counsel, willingness to dive into debugging something I assumed would just work, and honesty about his own biases relative to technology.

Mary Convertino, Tran Pham, and Ethan Wheel have been indispensable in helping to navigate the complexities of putting a book together. I would also like to thank Maria Garguilo for the initial invitation to attempt this project and Nicole Spoto for testing and verifying each chapter with precision.

Clay Hess, Northcentral Technical College, and Thomas Brown, Forsyth Tech Community College, reviewed the chapters and provided valuable insights and suggestions for shaping the content to fit today's students.

Preface to the Student

If you are reading this section, it most likely means that (a) you are a student who actually reads the Preface to the Student section in your textbooks and (b) this book was selected by someone else for you to use as part of a class you are taking so you can learn about full stack web development.

Don't worry, though—I wrote this book for you. My assumption is that you are comfortable using technology, but you don't currently regard yourself as a computer programmer. I've had many students in my classes over the past several decades in your exact situation.

This book begins with a refresher on the basics of how webpages are loaded from a web server into a web browser. Even if this is content you already know, please read Chapter 1 with patience because each chapter that follows adds more complexity and detail to your understanding of the technology and the processes. By the final chapter, you will be writing PHP code that interacts with a MySQL database to compose dynamic webpages.

My intent with this book is to share what I have learned over my many years of making innumerable mistakes both as a full stack web developer and instructor of future full stack web developers. If you read between the lines, you can sense my impatience with the jargon-oriented intellectual competitions littering the field of computer programming. Learning these secret code words is necessary to communicate with other programmers, but once you can get past the verbiage, I believe the concepts are straightforward and understandable.

My advice to you is not to apologize for asking questions. In fact, question everything, including all the contents of this book. If you were sitting in one of my classes, I would want you to pay the most attention to this advice. You could probably ignore the part where I tell you, "No food or drink in the lab."

I tell my students to get their money's worth out of the tuition they paid by asking questions whenever they don't understand something. Ask every question that occurs to you—without feeling like you should apologize for doing so first.

Chapter 1

How Does the Web Work?

Learning Objectives

When you complete this chapter, you will be able to:

1.1 Explain how a web browser connects to the Internet to retrieve a webpage.

1.2 Explain how a search engine returns search results.

1.3 Explain how a static HTML page is rendered from a remote server to a web browser.

1.4 Explain how a dynamic webpage is composed on a remote server and loaded into a web browser.

1.5 Describe a basic path of construction from concept to delivery of a website.

1.6 Describe the similarities and differences among at least three types of full stack web development.

1.1 How Does a Browser Work?

It is difficult to imagine a world in which the contents of the Internet aren't available at all times. You wake up in the morning and check your smartphone for the most recent updates from the local news and the score to last night's sportsball game or to see what a friend posted on social media while you were asleep. Before leaving for work or school, you may ask a smart speaker for the day's forecast to make sure you're dressed appropriately for the weather. When you remember that you ran out of a household staple while you are at work or school, you check prices and order from an online retailer who ships to your door. Looking up the menu of a nearby restaurant on your phone, you order food online and pick it up on the way home. All these interactions occur over the Internet and most through a **web browser**, a software application used to access, search, and interact with the Internet. But how does that software actually work? What does it connect to so that nearly the entire world is available to you at any moment?

The Web Browser

A web browser is so common that it's easy to disregard it as nothing more than a utility, yet it performs the following five highly technical and amazing tasks when you open it:

1. Presents a **user interface (UI)**, the space where users interact with software; in a web browser, you interact with the UI to ask a question or start a search for information using the following tools:
   - A menu containing options similar to those in other applications but specific to the browser functions
   - A text box for entering the webpage address, which is also known as the **Uniform Resource Locator (URL)**
   - Back, forward, and reload buttons
   - Space reserved for webpage content
2. Translates the URL into the encoded text of a **fetch request**, a message that asks to retrieve information—in this case, the webpage at the specified URL—and sends the request to a web server
3. Receives the encoded response from the web server and buffers a decoded response until it is complete enough to begin composing the requested webpage
4. Renders the response from the web server into a webpage with text, images, and other content you can click, scroll, or listen to with an auditory reader
5. Stores certain pieces of information for future use and reloading efficiency

The Mozilla Foundation, which produces the Firefox web browser, has provided helpful documentation for how their web browser performs these tasks. Go to https://developer.mozilla.org/ and search for "how the web works" to read more about how the Firefox browser handles these steps.

The Browser User Interface

Step 1, presenting a UI, is the task you are most familiar with. In fact, you may be reading this text online in your browser's UI on a laptop or on a phone.

The common features of a web browser have been in place since Tim Berners-Lee created the first web browser using a **graphical user interface (GUI)** in 1989 while working at CERN (*Conseil Européen pour la Recherche Nucléaire*), which he called the World Wide Web. (A GUI is a visual way of interacting with a computer using objects such as windows, icons, and buttons.) Prior to his browser, it was possible to navigate the early Internet, but only from a command line using text-based commands. Berners-Lee's GUI allowed users to click buttons and links or type a webpage address directly into the URL text box. CERN recreated an online version of this browser in 2019 that is fully functional in a modern browser.

Figure 1-1 shows the browser in use.

The next significant milestone in the evolution of web browsers was created in 1993 at the University of Illinois' National Center for Supercomputing Applications (NCSA) by a team of students, who called it Mosaic (https://www.ncsa.illinois.edu/research/project-highlights/ncsa-mosaic/). Mosaic was the first browser for Microsoft Windows and had a simplified UI that is recognizable as the template for almost all screen-based browsers you might use today. See **Figure 1-2**.

The software kernel at the core of Mosaic evolved into Netscape Navigator, which led to Mozilla Firefox, which is still in use today. Search online for the "history of the Mozilla project" to learn more about its ongoing evolution.

URL Fetch Request

Step 2, sending a fetch request to a web server, is where browser tasks become more complicated and interesting. If you click a link in Google search results or type a website address (like www.google.com) directly into the URL text box, the browser connects to the nearest **Domain Name System (DNS)** server to translate that text into an Internet Protocol (IP) address.

Figure 1-1   World Wide Web, the first web browser with a GUI

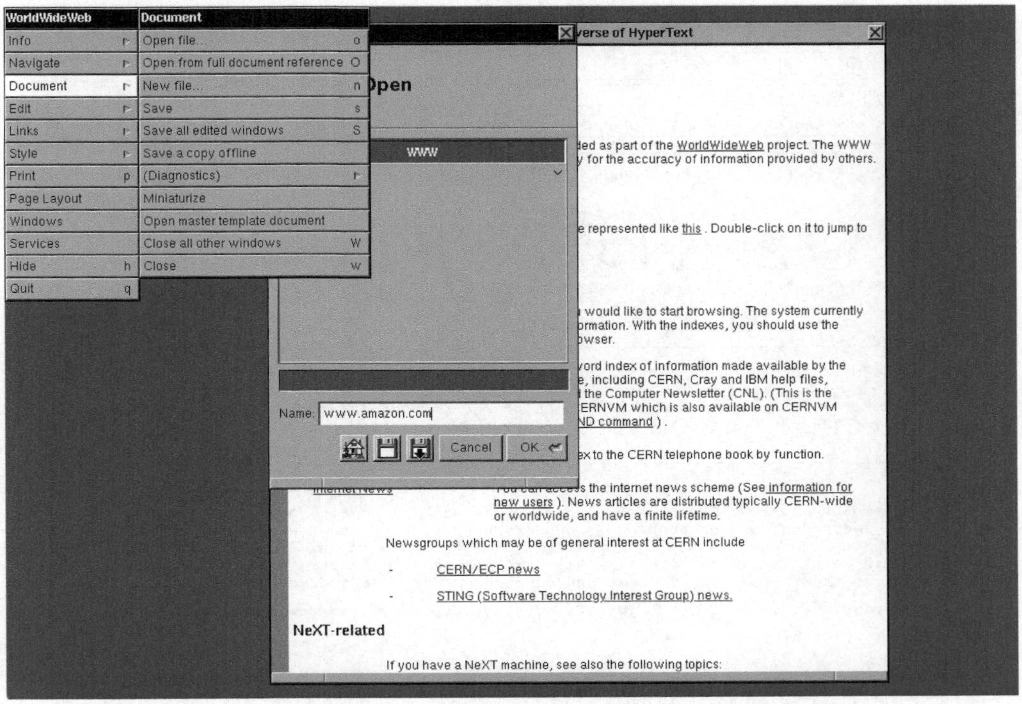

The DNS is a global network of servers, each with a copy of the database of all known human-friendly web addresses like www.google.com and their corresponding IP addresses to return to the browser. The database updates at least daily, so any new URLs published to one DNS server become available to the rest of the Internet in less than a day.

IP addresses are like the phone numbers of the web. Each is a unique value that corresponds to a server, listening for incoming requests and responding with appropriate return data. Using the simple standard for IP addresses, you can use the ping command-line utility to find servers by typing a command such as the following:

```
ping 8.8.8.8
```

This command tests the network connectivity between your local machine and the server listening at the IP address 8.8.8.8, which is actually a Google server. The server then returns a small payload of data in the form of a "Yes, I'm still here" message if the ping is successful in reaching the server. Similarly, you can ping www.google.com and receive a set of responses from the Google server.

However, the browser's **Hypertext Transfer Protocol (HTTP)** fetch request is more than merely asking if the server is listening. (HTTP is the networking language browsers use to communicate with web servers.) It is typically a **GET request**, which asks the web server at the IP address provided by the DNS to return the webpage it has for the URL in the initial request.

For example, if you click a link to www.bbc.com in Google search results, your browser heads to the nearest DNS server, resolves the bbc.com URL to the IP address 151.101.0.81, and uses a GET request to ask the server responding at IP address 151.101.0.81 for its home or index page. **Figure 1-3** summarizes this request–response path.

On the server, the response can follow a number of paths, which are covered in greater detail in the next two sections on static **Hypertext Markup Language (HTML)** pages and dynamic webpage composition. (HTML is the code that makes up webpages.) If the browser calls for a single **static webpage**, the web server's response is to return that text file. If the web server needs to build a **dynamic webpage** by adding page content from a database and incorporating it into the page at request time, the server does so using code a developer has deployed. In short, a static webpage is the

Figure 1-2 Mosaic, the first web browser built for Microsoft Windows

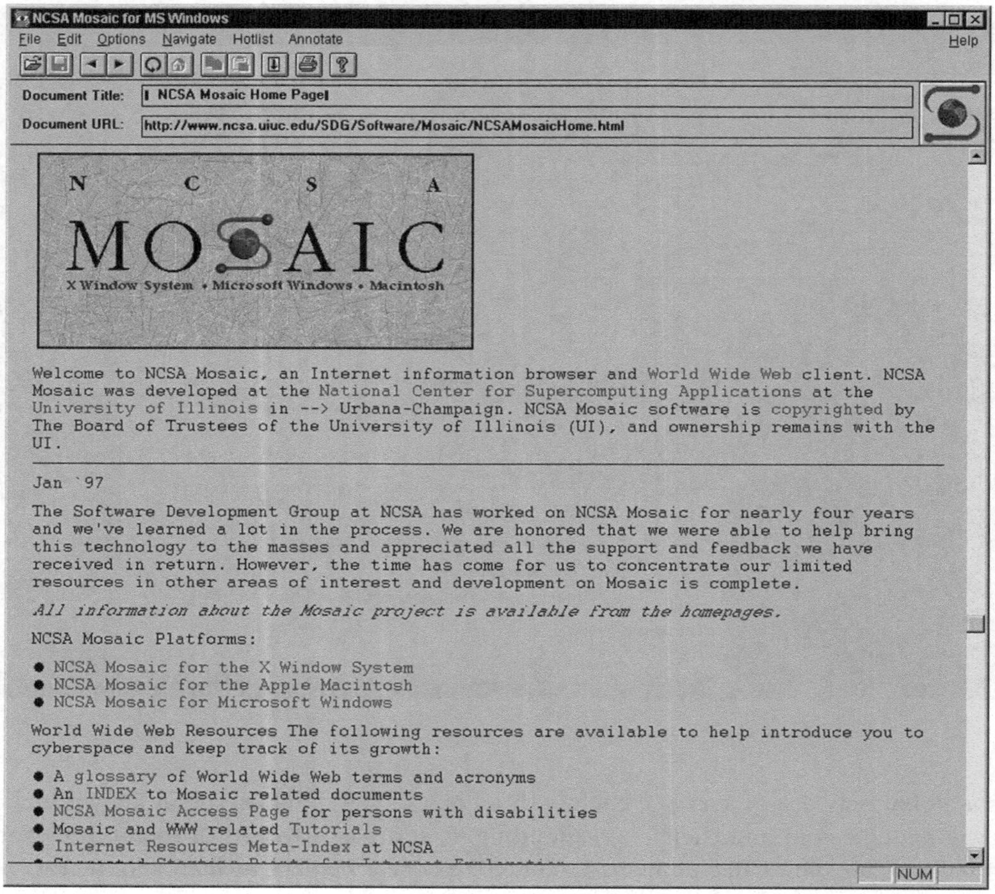

https://www.ncsa.illinois.edu/research/project-highlights/ncsa-mosaic/

same each time your web browser displays it, whereas the appearance and behavior of a dynamic webpage depends on the user or situation. Regardless of the path of the server response, a complete webpage is returned to the calling browser in a series of smaller pieces called **data packets**.

Browser Response Reception

Step 3, when the browser receives the web server's response, occurs after the web server has composed a webpage. After making the request in step 2, the browser waits for the web server to respond. The entire webpage is not returned to the web browser in one large file but is instead broken into data packets. The browser reassembles them as they arrive.

Occasionally with a slow web connection or web server response, you can watch the webpage reassemble. The browser builds the page from top to bottom, with missing content filling in the blank spaces on the page as new chunks of content arrive. You might also observe HTML text appear as unformatted and then become styled as the browser's rendering engine works through the HTML code and searches any **Cascading Style Sheets (CSS)** for directions on how to present the content of the HTML document. This is what happens in step 4.

Document Tree Building

Step 4, rendering the response from the web server, begins during step 3. The browser's **rendering engine** fashions the text, images, and other content for display as a webpage. It tries to be efficient in translating the raw HTML code into a form the user can see or hear in the browser, so it builds the webpage as individual data packets arrive.

Figure 1-3   How a web browser retrieves a page from a web server

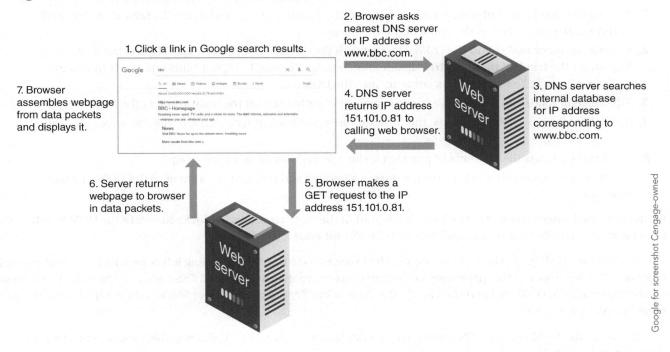

1. Click a link in Google search results.

2. Browser asks nearest DNS server for IP address of www.bbc.com.

3. DNS server searches internal database for IP address corresponding to www.bbc.com.

4. DNS server returns IP address 151.101.0.81 to calling web browser.

5. Browser makes a GET request to the IP address 151.101.0.81.

6. Server returns webpage to browser in data packets.

7. Browser assembles webpage from data packets and displays it.

Google for screenshot Cengage-owned

As the browser is translating the HTML code into webpage contents, it may encounter links to additional supporting files (such as files for CSS or **JavaScript**, a programming language for creating interactive effects in web browsers). When it does, the browser sends requests to the server for those supporting files. The browser uses the HTML **Document Object Model (DOM)** to reconstruct the webpage. The HTML DOM is like the running version of the code in other programming languages, and the browser uses this to "run" or develop the webpage that the web developer has created.

Figure 1-4 shows the text of a simple HTML page.

Figure 1-4   Raw HTML code of a simple webpage

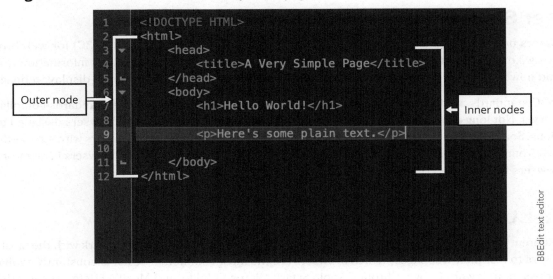

```
1   <!DOCTYPE HTML>
2   <html>
3       <head>
4           <title>A Very Simple Page</title>
5       </head>
6       <body>
7           <h1>Hello World!</h1>
8
9           <p>Here's some plain text.</p>
10
11      </body>
12  </html>
```

Outer node

Inner nodes

BBEdit text editor

When the browser loads this page, it follows an orderly sequence:

1. The browser finds the outermost node, or object, the pair of `<html>` and `</html>` tags at the top and bottom of the code. This is the trunk of the DOM tree.
2. It loads the inner nodes into the DOM, starting with the `<head>...</head>` tags. This is the first branch off the trunk of the DOM tree. Inside the `<head>...</head>` tags, it finds and loads the pair of `<title>...</title>` tags and its contents into the DOM.
3. The browser loads the `<body>...</body>` tags, another branch off the main trunk of the tree.
4. Inside the `<body>...</body>` tags, the browser finds and loads the contents of the `<h1>...</h1>` and `<p>...</p>` tags.
5. The browser loads the contents of any tags inside the previously mentioned tags.
6. The browser repeats these steps until it parses all nodes and text and adds them to the DOM in a tree structure.

In this way, the browser recreates the logic and layout of the page structure in blocks to create the DOM tree that can then be styled via CSS code or manipulated with JavaScript code.

To style the HTML page shown in Figure 1-4, the browser uses the default styling it has for a limited set of example objects. If the developer of this page were more ambitious or creative and created CSS styles for the page, the browser would construct the DOM tree and then apply the **Cascading Style Sheets Object Model (CSSOM)** to make the page more visually interesting.

Similar to the DOM tree, the CSSOM creates a matching tree structure. Following the CSSOM tree, the rendering engine styles the DOM tree using the CSS code that the web developer created.

Data Storage

Step 5, storing information, may occur during the loading or parsing of a page or after the page is displayed. Browsers are designed to make efficient use of network resources by creating a cached copy of some webpage content such as images, HTML, CSS, and other items not likely to change. A cache is short-term storage space with an expiration deadline. Browsers store some items in the cache so they do not have to make repeated trips across the network to retrieve the same content. Additionally, cookies and other persistent data are stored in memory that the operating system has allocated to the browser.

Browser Standards

Most browsers now use the standards set out by the **World Wide Web Consortium (W3C)** for web browsers (see https://www.w3.org/standards/). The W3C is the committee that makes the rules for how information travels on the Internet and how web servers and web browsers should communicate with each other to display webpages.

The W3C standards are the rules for how the Internet should work when using a standards-compliant browser and web server. Not long ago, several large technology companies created their own browsers designed to their own specifications. Some of these browsers were notorious for unexpected results and behaviors with standards-compliant web content from a web server. Users of the Internet stopped using those proprietary browsers in favor of more mainstream browsers that followed the W3C standards.

Browser Usage Statistics

Because different browsers show webpages differently, a full stack web developer must work with the most commonly used browsers to test their webpages. Which browsers are the most common? The list is constantly evolving, but the top four browsers today are Google Chrome, Apple Safari, Microsoft Edge, and Mozilla Firefox. It's worth looking for these usage statistics frequently since your users only tell you which browser they are using when they have trouble with your webpage. If you search for "Usage share of web browsers", you should see an updated percentage of market share for these browsers.

> **Note** | An interesting fact is that in November 2016, the number of webpages accessed by smartphone-based web browsers surpassed the number of desktop-laptop-based web browsers, a trend that has only accelerated. Responsive web design addresses this evolution by providing similar webpage content in different modes depending on the web browser and its rendering format.

What You Need to Know About Browsers

Unless you want to amaze your friends at parties with your extensive knowledge of otherwise useless web browser trivia, you only need to know how a browser *should* work when it *isn't* working. Each of the five steps in "The Web Browser" section is a potential source of failure for a page that isn't loading or rendering properly.

As a full stack web developer, it is often your responsibility to find the cause of a broken webpage and fix it if the fault is your responsibility. Some problems are deeper or more systemic than a full stack web developer can fix, however. If a user loses connectivity to the Internet, for example, or a web server is down due to a power outage, you are off the hook. Everything else is basically your problem to find, diagnose, and repair.

> ### Quick Check 1-1

1. What does a GET request from a web browser do?

   a. Asks Jeeves to search for information on the Internet
   b. Requests a webpage from a web server
   c. Requests that the web server start running
   d. Sends compatibility information about the user's operating system from the web browser to the web server

2. What does clicking a link in a list of results from a Google search do?

   a. Opens one of the many millions of webpages that Google has previously downloaded and stored in the cloud for faster retrieval
   b. Creates a new connection to the Google search engine to retrieve the webpage through a Google server
   c. Retrieves the webpage from a Google database of all of the webpages it can find
   d. Makes a fetch request to the server hosting the URL in the link after resolving the IP address through a DNS server

3. Why is responsive web design important?

   a. More people are using the web on their phones than on laptops or desktops.
   b. It is a legal requirement.
   c. Responsive web design is faster to load on smaller screen sizes.
   d. People like options and prefer to choose between large or small format webpages for themselves.

1) b. A GET request is a type of fetch command from a browser to a web server. **2) d.** Each click of a link creates a fresh trip to the DNS server followed by a fetch request to the web server. **3) a.** The tipping point happened in 2016 and use by mobile devices is now more common than larger screens.

1.2 How Does a Search Engine Work?

Many people begin an interaction with the Internet by using a **search engine**, which is a website that lists other websites categorized by search terms or keywords that users might type while looking for information. The basics of how a search engine works seem straightforward: a robust piece of software regularly searches or crawls the web for new pages and adds them to an index database owned by the search engine company. When users search for results, they filter the database for content similar to their search terms.

The details are more complex and shrouded in proprietary intellectual property and legal nondisclosure. So how does a search engine actually find all new pages, and why is it so important that it finds your amazing new site?

The second question is easier to answer than the first. If a search engine didn't crawl and index your new www .totallyawesomestuff.com site, nobody would find your exciting new product, Low-Fat Candy for Goldfish, which is why you created the site in the first place.

The first question is partially answered by reading the detailed documentation provided by the engineers who authored the search engine used by nearly 90 percent of the world when searching for healthy dessert options for goldfish: the "In-depth guide to how Google Search works." See https://developers.google.com/search/docs/advanced/ guidelines/how-search-works.

How Does Google Work?

The following is a summary of the TLDR (Too Long, Didn't Read) version of the documentation from Google:

- Google automates the task of discovering new webpages through software that searches for URLs it hasn't previously found and indexed. Google also accepts submissions of new website URLs from people who want their URLs to be found and indexed.

- Next, **Googlebots** crawl the webpages, reading through the contents of each new webpage and using a proprietary algorithm to determine what is most important or useful about the page. Googlebots are self-contained applications that use the desktop and mobile versions of Chrome to replicate how a human user would interact with the website.

- If Google finds that a webpage is unique, useful, and interesting, the page is indexed, or stored in a database. The search engine later queries this index database when someone is searching for information.

- When someone interested in tasty snacks for goldfish subsequently searches using Google, the index database is queried and all results are ranked by location and relevance, then returned to the user.

> **Note** | Is Google the only search engine people use? A quick search for "market share of search engines" reveals that almost nobody is currently using a search engine other than Google. This is important to know for a full stack web developer, since having Google index your site means it is visible to most Internet users.

Search Engine Optimization

Ensuring your web content is visible to the search engine and ranked as highly as possible in the index database is called **search engine optimization (SEO)**. A full stack web developer is responsible for building a website that follows the rules for webpages so they are successfully crawled and indexed. You should be familiar with those rules (discussed in the next section).

Later, you explore a **content management system (CMS)** called **WordPress**. A CMS is software used to create and update websites in an automated way, rather than writing the code manually. This system speeds up the website development cycle but also limits what is possible.

WordPress has automated some of the SEO tasks so that a site built on the WordPress platform has a reasonable chance of capturing the attention of Googlebots and web users. WordPress also ensures you follow the search engine rules so you are not downranked for breaking those rules.

The Rules According to Google

Google has published the set of rules it follows to determine which pages to rank in a search result set and how to rank them. Additionally, Google has published rules that, if broken, cause a page to fall lower in the ranking, or perhaps be removed from the index database entirely.

The TLDR version of those two sets of rules are as follows:

DO:

- Build useful pages composed of important content for humans to read or hear.
- Use valid HTML to create your content and test it in multiple browsers.
- Use webpage design best practices for people to interact with your pages, including the necessary features for users who will only hear your pages being read to them by a screen reader.
- Ask Google politely (and only once) to crawl your pages through their website URL submission form.

DO NOT:

- Try to game the system by tweaking your page content specifically for Googlebot crawling.
- Try to create artificial site popularity by asking your friends to create links unnecessarily to your site or by linking to it from external public pages.
- Create unnecessary pages filled with keywords or links to try to boost your page's relevance or ranking.

See https://developers.google.com/search/docs/advanced/guidelines/overview for best practices and https://developers.google.com/search/docs/advanced/guidelines/webmaster-guidelines#quality_guidelines for techniques to avoid.

Quick Check 1-2

1. What is the best way to get to the top of the Google search list?
    a. Pay Google to list your page first.
    b. Create a standards-compliant, user-friendly webpage with original content.
    c. Pay all of your friends to create links to your webpage from theirs.
    d. Refresh your page constantly so it shows a lot of page-loading activity in the browser.

2. How does Google find new pages to index?
    a. Nobody really knows, but they do a great job at it.
    b. Google uses automated web browsers to load all the pages on the web and then click the links in all those pages.
    c. Google pays thousands of people to surf the web looking for new pages to add to their index database.
    d. Google has added a URL-capture plug-in to Chrome that runs in the background and indexes all new pages that Chrome users open regularly.

(continues)

3. What is search engine optimization?

    a. Building webpages specifically to get to the top of the search results list

    b. Buying software designed to boost your search rankings

    c. Cheating the system to get your page boosted to the top of every search result

    d. Using web development best practices and checking your webpages to ensure they meet the criteria for search engine indexing

1) b. If you build a good website and ask Google to crawl it, it will be indexed. **2) b.** It's all about the Googlebots. **3) d.** Check to make sure your webpage can be indexed and follows the published rules. You can use software to automate this task.

1.3 How Does a Static HTML Page Load?

A static HTML page is just a text file downloaded from a web server to the browser. For that matter, so are CSS and JavaScript files. The web server hosting the website comprised of static webpages is only in the business of returning text files to web browsers.

Apache Web Server Overview

One type of web server is called the Apache web server (see https://httpd.apache.org). The open source Apache web server project began in 1995, early in the development of the Internet as you know it today. Apache was originally developed to run on the Linux/Unix operating systems, but current releases are available for Windows as well.

The Apache web server software accounts for nearly one in three web servers used today. It has been thoroughly documented by the developers of the project and by the web server administrators who use it. Moreover, the internal plumbing is similar enough to other web servers that it is a useful example to examine for delivering a static webpage to the user.

Common Mistakes

While installing and configuring the Apache web server software is well documented and straightforward, a significant number of security precautions must be taken to ensure that the web server hosting this software isn't compromised through a malicious attack, or hack.

You might be tempted to try to install and start a web server to see how it works and if you can make it work. However, these tasks are best left to server administrators who have the proper training and credentials, since a web server needs to be exposed to the Internet to be functional. In short—do not try this at home.

Web Server Function

Once installed and running, an Apache web server waits for incoming requests from the Internet. It responds to those requests by returning one or more files from the directories the server administrator allows it to use.

As with every operating system, the physical or virtual computer hosting the web server software has many files in many folders. A few folders hold the operating system and other important pieces of installed software. Users are granted full access to open, save, and delete files and folders in a few other directories such as their Desktop and Documents folders.

The Apache software is similarly granted access to only a few special folders as web-accessible directories. In each web-accessible directory, a file is designated as the default index or home page. That is, if you request a URL without specifying a page, the web server returns the default index or home page.

A Web Server Is Just a File Server

How does finding and retrieving a webpage actually work on the web server? A URL is like a file path. If you save a file on your Windows device at C:\Users\yourname\documents\templates\documentName.txt, you could find that file again by navigating that same file path while logged in to that same device. If you cannot access that computer again, however, you cannot access your file from any other computer because the folders on your Windows machine aren't made available across a network by default. The rules of the Internet solve the problem of file accessibility since the role of web servers is to function as file storage available to the Internet.

If you create an ordinary folder on your computer, install and configure the software that runs a web server, then tell that web server to listen to the network it is connected to for incoming HTTP requests for the files in that folder, you have basically recreated the technology of the Internet. That's nearly all there is to a web server. It is just a computer running software that grants access to a specific folder and its contents from anyone on its network or the Internet.

When the browser makes a GET request for the index or home page for a website (step 1 in **Figure 1-5**), the web server receives the incoming request from the network and then looks in the folder configured to store a page called index.html (step 2). If the web server finds the page (step 3), it returns the contents in a series of data packets to the requesting web browser (steps 4 and 5). This process is summarized in Figure 1-5.

Figure 1-5   How a web server finds and returns a static webpage to a browser

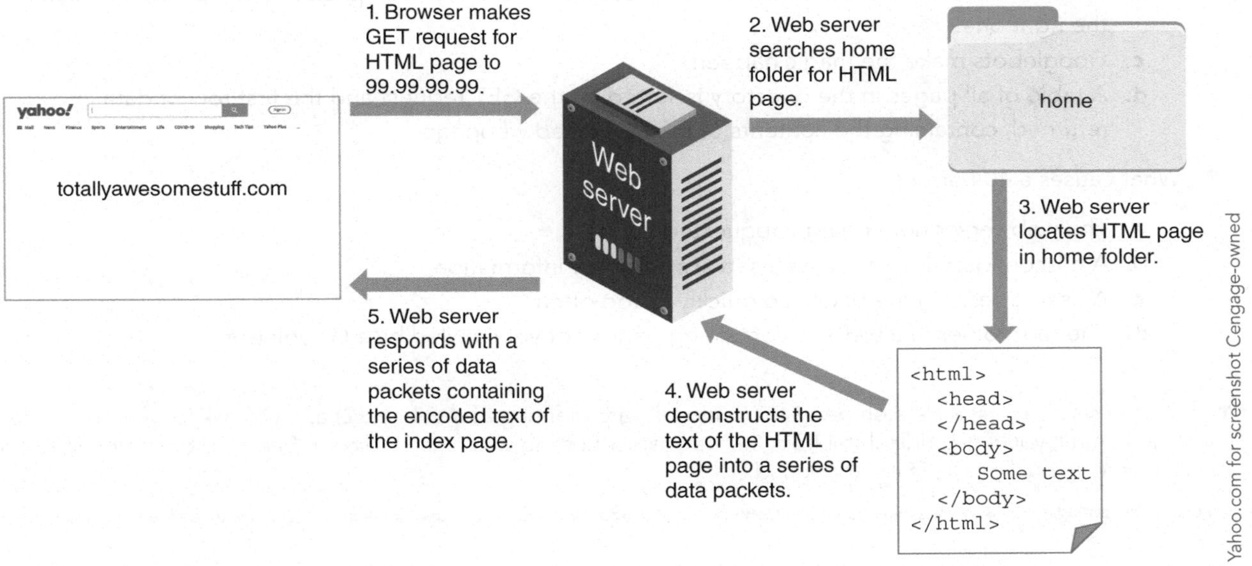

If the web server doesn't find the requested page, the web server can either return a **404 error** for a "File Not Found" error, or it can return the default file it is configured to return for all page requests it cannot find. If you follow a link to http://www.totallyawesomestuff.com/products/list.html, for example, the web server looks in the default folder for another folder called products, and then in the products folder for a file called list.html, which it would then return.

A web server dutifully tries to return any file a GET request from a web browser asks it to retrieve, as long as the administrator's configuration allows the server to return that type of file. It doesn't matter if the file has a .html, .png, .css, or .js extension—the web server is just a file retrieval engine.

Recall that the browser often makes multiple file retrieval requests as it loads a single webpage. First, it requests the page itself—index.html, for example—then any linked CSS files, and finally any JavaScript files. The web server is not responsible for composing that data into a sensible document. It merely returns the files to the browser, which handles the rendering of the webpage.

Contract Web Server Hosting

When you sign up for a web hosting service like GoDaddy, Wix, or Squarespace, you are renting a folder on one of their servers. You then load your website files into that folder. The web hosting service assigns you a URL and IP address that points to your folder. The web host also registers your domain name with the keepers of the directory of the Internet, InterNic (https://www.internic.net), to ensure your site has a unique address. However, you are really just renting storage space on a server for a folder with the plumbing of the Internet linked to it.

Quick Check 1-3

1. Which of these most closely resembles a web server?

   a. A database of webpages
   b. A desktop computer with a well-organized folder structure
   c. A network of computers all hosting different folders with files in them
   d. A file storage system with software installed to grant access to only specific folders

2. How does a web server know which webpage to return to the browser?

   a. The page is requested by file name from the browser.
   b. The browser uses the fetch command to retrieve a directory of all pages in the folder, then selects the right one.
   c. Googlebots make the magic happen.
   d. A table of all pages in the directory is sorted by the GET request and the first row of data is returned, containing the contents of the requested webpage.

3. What causes a 404 error?

   a. The web server not finding a requested file
   b. A misconfiguration of the web server's directory information
   c. A user refreshing the page too quickly or too often
   d. The root folder of a website containing pages not yet crawled by a Googlebot

1) d. A web server is just a file storage system with software granting accessibility. 2) a. If you ask for www.example .com/index.html, you'll get index.html from the web server hosting www.example.com. 3) a. This error, generated by the web server, usually says, "File Not Found."

1.4 How Does a Dynamic Webpage Load?

As with the static HTML page load process, the end product of the dynamic webpage loading process is a webpage delivered to the browser. The difference is what happens at the web server to compose the page prior to delivery.

Dynamic PHP Webpage Loading

PHP is a programming language designed for web development. Using PHP as an example of one way to create dynamic webpages, the initial browser request of a URL would look like this one:

https://www.totallyawesomestuff.com/products.php?id=243

That URL causes the browser to contact the server that resolves to https://www.totallyawesomestuff.com, making the connection to HTTPS on port 443 via the Secure Sockets Layer instead of the usual port 80, which is used for HTTP traffic.

> **Note**
>
> What is the difference between HTTP and HTTPS? You have probably seen the https prefix to a URL before. Perhaps it has made you feel more confident in making an online purchase, knowing that your personal information is "secure." But how is it more secure?
>
> HTTPS uses encryption to make it more challenging to read the text that is sent to or returned from a web server. Your birthday being sent in unencrypted, plain text over the Internet looks like this:
>
> ```
> Birthday=January-01-2005
> ```
>
> HTTPS encrypts your data and sends it over the Internet in a text hash, which might look like the following:
>
> ```
> QmlydGhkYXk9SmFudWFyeS0wMS0yMDA1
> ```
>
> The computers on each end of the transaction unencrypt that hash using an agreed-upon key and then use the unencrypted normal text internally.

Web Server Response Path

The Apache web server receives the request for the file products.php, but instead of returning the code in the file, the web server is configured to recognize that .php files require processing. The web server passes along to the PHP processor engine the requested page and the id variable, along with the value in that variable (243).

The PHP engine finds and executes the code in products.php, beginning from the top of the page and working downward. In that code, the following operations might be made:

- Create the top portion of a valid HTML page, including links to the CSS and the JavaScript documents.
- Create the start of the HTML body section.
- Open the connection to a database, such as a MySQL database, execute a query, and wait for the database to find and return the data for the record with the ID of 243 in the form of a hash or array of values.
- Loop through the values in the dataset returned from the database, adding them to the HTML it is composing along with the HTML tags that surround the data elements.
- Append the footer and closing HTML tags to the text response.
- Hand off the entire text file response to the Apache web server, which then returns it to the browser in a series of data packets.

This process is summarized in **Figure 1-6**.

Saving Form Data

The reverse of the process shown in Figure 1-6 is a trip back to the server from the browser with a payload of user-submitted data to save in the database. Typically, this is from an HTML form originally composed on the web server using the PHP engine to render the form with a unique field name and ID for each of the form elements.

For example, if you want to collect data from your users for a Best Goldfish Name contest, you can create a web form in PHP with a text box for the goldfish name, user name, and user email address. It might look like the form in **Figure 1-7**.

The PHP engine creates this HTML web form and then hands it off to the Apache web server, which returns it to the browser that requested the page. The user types the necessary data in the required fields and clicks the Submit button. This creates a **POST request**, which is how the browser sends the form data to the URL of the web server.

Figure 1-6 How a web server finds and builds a dynamic webpage before returning it to the browser

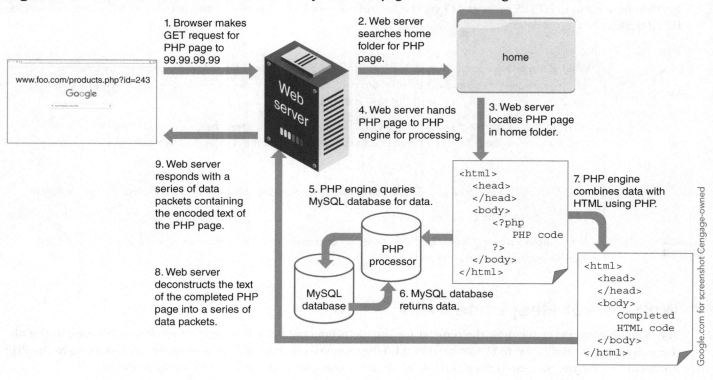

Figure 1-7 A sample web form

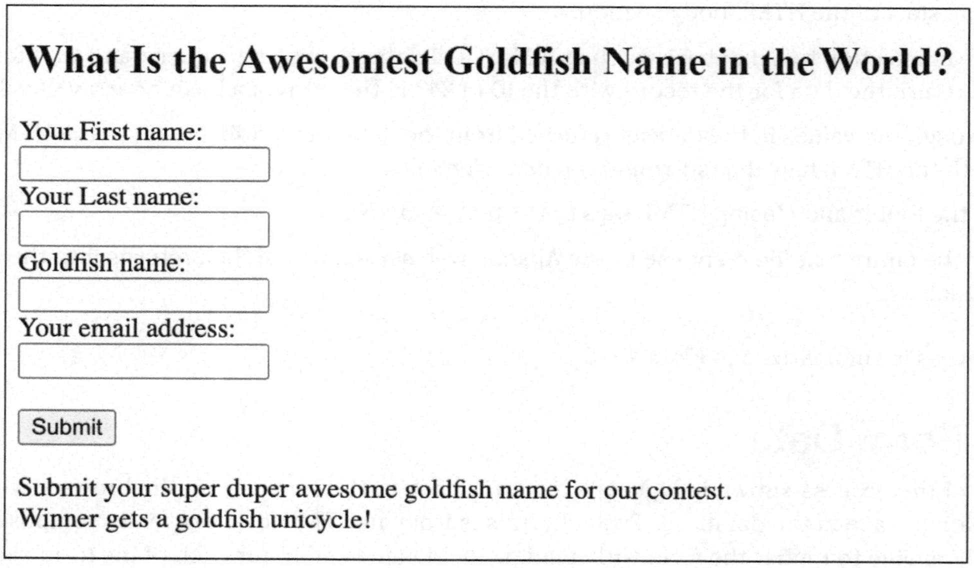

What Is the Awesomest Goldfish Name in the World?

Your First name:

Your Last name:

Goldfish name:

Your email address:

Submit

Submit your super duper awesome goldfish name for our contest.
Winner gets a goldfish unicycle!

As you recall, the GET request from a web browser asks for a webpage at a URL. The POST request tells the web server that a webpage at a URL has form data to process. The POST request contains the form data in a string of key-value pairs.

The PHP page contest.php contains the necessary variables to receive those user input data elements, process them, and store them in the database using code the PHP programmer has written.

You can read more about how Mozilla handles HTML POST data by searching for "Mozilla sending and retrieving form data," but all current web browsers use the same basic operations. When one person builds this complex layered technology, that person is performing the job of a full stack web developer. The full stack web developer builds the UI of a webpage, including the HTML, CSS, and JavaScript code. The developer also builds the back end—in this case, the PHP code and the MySQL database to hold the data that composes the pages.

Quick Check 1-4

1. What is the difference between a static and a dynamic webpage?

    a. Static webpages don't change, and dynamic pages always change.
    b. Static webpages are stored on a different type of server from dynamic webpages.
    c. Static webpages are stored in a database, and dynamic webpages are stored in a web server.
    d. Static webpages are basically text files, and dynamic webpages are built by the web server when the browser makes a fetch request.

2. What does a PHP processor do?

    a. Composes a response to a request from the web server for a PHP file
    b. Loads HTML pages into the PHP framework to return to the web server as text files
    c. Responds to fetch requests from the browser
    d. Runs a database on the web server

3. What is the difference between a GET and a POST request?

    a. A GET request is for a specific page on the web server, and a POST request sends information back to the default directory of the web server
    b. A GET request is made by the web browser, and a POST request is made by the user by clicking on the submit button in a web form
    c. A GET request is made from the browser to the web server, and a POST request is made from the web server to the browser
    d. A GET request asks the web server to return a webpage to the web browser, and a POST request tells the web server that the web browser has form data for it to process

1) d. Static webpages are just made up of HTML code, whereas dynamic pages use compiled or interpreted code to build the page each time it is requested. **2) a.** The PHP processor interprets PHP code, building a webpage as it works from the top to the bottom of the code. **3) d.** The GET request is made by the browser for a page the web server is hosting, but a POST request is made by the browser to tell the web server to process form data submitted by the user.

1.5 How Do I Get Started Building Webpages?

This is a trick question in the form of a heading. You are starting to build webpages at this very moment! The first step in building even the most complex of international e-commerce websites is doing research, asking questions, and gathering requirements for the project. That's what you are starting to do by reading this chapter. As you learn what is technically possible, you'll gain an appreciation of how webpages are built, then become ready to build your own international e-commerce platform.

Building Your Knowledge

More is involved in creating webpages, of course. As you work through the examples and projects in this course, you first build simple HTML pages, then more complex HTML with CSS and advanced page layout techniques. Next, you add JavaScript to give your pages interactive and dynamic in-page elements. You'll gain experience with WordPress, which is the most widely used CMS delivering website content to users.

Next, you learn about building dynamic websites that use data from a database to render pages on demand and store user-submitted data from HTML forms. This course uses PHP as the programming platform and MySQL as the database because they are a lightweight, well-documented, and mature technology stack that have the overwhelming percentage of market share.

Making Good Technology Choices

Having broad experience with multiple technologies helps you choose the right tool for the job when you are doing the business of web development. Making pragmatic and informed decisions based on project requirements, budgets, available tools, and support after launch will confirm the validity of the technology stack you chose.

Web development involves the workflow shown in **Figure 1-8**.

Figure 1-8   Building a website using the agile project management methodology

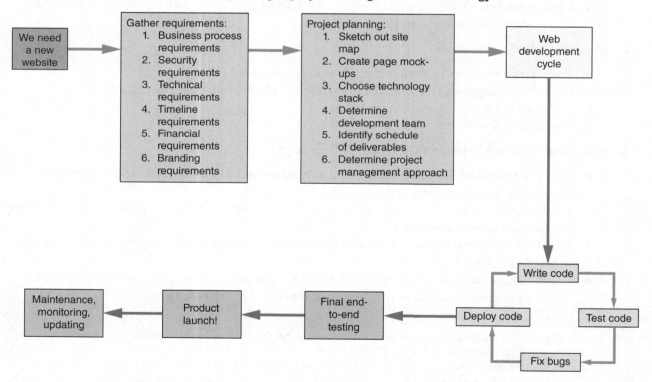

Whether you are your own customer or you are on a team of hundreds of full stack developers working for an international technology company, most projects follow the basic steps outlined in Figure 1-8.

As a full stack web developer, you might be tempted to begin writing code after receiving the request "We need a new website!" since writing code is the fun part of being a programmer. However, it's important to go through each project management step in order and be diligent about completing them.

Gathering requirements as the second step defines what the end product will do and who will use it. Planning the project properly as the third step saves many intellectual dead ends and mistaken false starts while encouraging the right people and technology to collaborate.

In the fourth step, Web development cycle, you cycle through short sprints. During each sprint, you build a block of software that corresponds to a single requirement gathered in the second step and planned in the third step. Completing the development in cycles speeds up the development–testing–fixing process loop. Following that loop, in which many smaller tests occur, a final end-to-end test should confirm success, leading finally to the product launch.

> **Note** | As you develop webpages, remember that not every user views your webpages on a screen. In fact, many users only listen to your webpages being read to them. For people who use screen readers and those who use home assistants and smart speakers like Amazon Alexa, Google Assistant, or Apple Siri, web content is heard rather than seen.

Roles of a Business Analyst and Project Manager

As a full stack developer, you may also need to assume the roles of both a **business analyst (BA)** and a **project manager (PM)** while working on a web development project. In larger organizations, these roles are often handled by different people to spread the workload. If you are building your own web project, you are the customer as well as the BA, PM, database administrator, and full stack developer. Your staff meetings will be more efficient with a 100 percent attendance rate when you show up.

A BA is a professional question-asker. The person in the role of a technical BA asks questions like the following:

- What is the problem this website or application will solve?
- How will users interact with this application?
- Who else will be using this application and the data that comes from it?
- What data elements do you need this application to report?
- What are the features the application absolutely must have?
- What are the features you would like to have?

Being a BA requires that you ask everyone who has a role in using the website for their opinion of the project. You then synthesize all those opinions into a cohesive set of documents that describe what a successfully completed project looks like when it is done. Additionally, a BA might use software such as Google Analytics to create documentation of current usage for a website or web application. This initial startup work helps the decision-makers on the project determine the most successful path by providing information that otherwise might be missing or incorrectly assumed to be true.

PMs serve as professional planners. They make sure everyone involved knows the project schedule, stays up to date on deliverables, and keeps to the project budget. PMs also facilitate meetings among groups and communicate the current project status to all involved. They often miss the fun that the actual project participants have such as writing code or testing and debugging. Instead, PMs solve problems, connect people with resources, and keep everyone on track to deliver the slate of promised outcomes at the agreed-upon time.

Styles of Project Management

The two basic styles of project management in common use today are waterfall and agile. In **waterfall project management**, the entire project is tested and then launched into production (or goes over the edge of the waterfall) only after all development is completed.

Waterfall can be successful with the following components:

- Small projects
- Small teams of developers
- Well-established processes that are constrained to a simple set of deliverables

Agile project management, on the other hand, is an incremental and iterative approach to building a technology solution. In this approach, the requirements gathering and planning phases are completed before beginning the development, as in the waterfall approach. However, the larger project is then broken into a series of sprints or development cycles.

Each sprint is a single unit of work the team can accomplish in a week or two weeks, with introduction, development, testing, and deployment completed before moving on to the next chunk of work. Software such as Jira and Trello (produced by the Atlassian Corporation) assist with agile project management. Search online for "Atlassian Agile Project Management" to read more about their software and ideas on the agile approach to project management. Agile is appropriate for the following:

- Large or complex projects
- Large development teams
- New software product development
- Customers who are still establishing their business processes or who need to test a solution to react to it on a regular schedule

Both waterfall and agile project management approaches have pros and cons, but most web development projects now use the agile approach. You can read more about the Manifesto for Agile Software Development at https://agilemanifesto.org. The 12 principles of agile project management are shown in **Figure 1-9**.

Quick Check 1-5

1. How do you start doing web development?

    a. Do research and ask questions.
    b. Just build whatever webpage you think is right to solve the problem.
    c. Get fancy business cards with your name on them telling people you are a web developer.
    d. Start your own Apache web server so you have a test platform for your websites.

2. What does a business analyst do?

    a. Asks a lot of questions and documents the answers
    b. Keeps a web development project on track and under budget
    c. Keeps the financial resources of the organization in good order
    d. Analyzes businesses, of course

3. What is agile project management?

    a. An approach to project management incorporating yoga and flexibility training
    b. A philosophical approach to project management that incorporates mental agility training
    c. Project management designed for indecisive customers and conflict-avoidant project managers
    d. An approach to project management where large tasks are broken down into many small subtasks, each of which is completed before moving on to the next one

1) a. Learning about web development is the best first step. **2) a.** A business analyst is a professional question-asker. **3) d.** Agile project management is designed to make large tasks more successful by dividing them into a series of smaller tasks, each of which is completed before the next one begins.

Figure 1-9 The principles of the Agile Manifesto

Principles behind the Agile Manifesto

We follow these principles:

Our highest priority is to satisfy the customer through early and continuous delivery of valuable software.

Welcome changing requirements, even late in development. Agile processes harness change for the customer's competitive advantage.

Deliver working software frequently, from a couple of weeks to a couple of months, with a preference to the shorter timescale.

Business people and developers must work together daily throughout the project.

Build projects around motivated individuals. Give them the environment and support they need, and trust them to get the job done.

The most efficient and effective method of conveying information to and within a development team is face-to-face conversation.

Working software is the primary measure of progress.

Agile processes promote sustainable development. The sponsors, developers, and users should be able to maintain a constant pace indefinitely.

Continuous attention to technical excellence and good design enhances agility.

Simplicity—the art of maximizing the amount of work not done—is essential.

The best architectures, requirements, and designs emerge from self-organizing teams.

At regular intervals, the team reflects on how to become more effective, then tunes and adjusts its behavior accordingly.

https://agilemanifesto.org/principles.html

1.6 What Is Full Stack Web Development?

A **technology stack** is a list of the software used to complete a process from start to finish. In web development, a technology stack is typically listed in order starting from the webpage that the end user interacts with.

A shorter stack might be composed of the HTML, CSS, and JavaScript files that make up the static webpage a user views in a browser, the Apache web server hosting those pages and sending them to the browser, and the Linux operating system that hosts the Apache web server.

From a web development perspective, the person building those static webpages is primarily creating the user interface, or the parts the user interacts with. These are called the front-end components, and the person building them is called the front-end developer.

While there are different flavors of full stack web development, the ingredients are similar—a web developer builds the front-end components of the user interface (i.e., the HTML, CSS, and JavaScript that make a webpage) as well as the back-end components (programming in a server-side language such as PHP, C#, or VB.NET) and creates a database (such as MySQL, MS SQL Server, or Oracle).

Additionally, full stack developers use project management software (such as Smartsheet, Jira, or Trello) to plan the project and keep it on track. They also use version control software (such as Git or Subversion) to store the source code for the project in a series of code milestones. Version control software is also advantageous for team-based development of an evolving product.

These technologies represent the five components of full stack web development: front-end, back-end, database, version control, and project management.

WordPress as a Full Stack Application

Some full stack developers prefer to use WordPress to expedite the user interface or front-end development of a website. WordPress is a web application installed on the web server used to host and build websites. Developers interact with WordPress on the web server through the website it is hosting. It's easy to get started using WordPress, and it has a large community of users who willingly exchange information and technology to help each other build websites.

Using WordPress reduces the level of effort in producing raw HTML and CSS since that code is automatically generated for you but increases the amount of time spent configuring WordPress, along with the themes and plug-ins you use to customize the site to fulfill the project requirements.

Determining whether WordPress works for a project is a pragmatic judgment call. For a web application with many static HTML pages, WordPress provides an efficiency of scale that creates a good return on the investment in time spent setting it up. When you build (or configure) your own WordPress plug-in to handle a database interaction, you are completing the full stack development process. In other words, WordPress is one way to accomplish full stack web development.

Interpreted Languages

Another way to build full stack webpages is to use an **interpreted programming language** such as PHP. An interpreted programming language is one that isn't compiled into executable machine code prior to running on the web server, but instead uses the processing power of the web server to execute the code directly from the webpage. An interpreted language is slower to run than executable machine code but is faster for web developers to write and modify.

The PHP processor on the web server, as you have read, retrieves and processes data from the database to compose an HTML page. It returns that page to the web server, which then returns it to the requesting browser. Additionally, the PHP processor can handle the key/value pairs it receives when an HTML form is submitted from the browser. The PHP processor is sent the file name of the webpage along with the form data from that webpage and interprets or executes the code in the webpage on the web server to process the data.

Using an Application Programming Interface

Some full stack development requires the use of an **Application Programming Interface (API)**. An API is software built to create an interaction point between the database and the dynamic webpages that need to pull data from or send data to the database.

Prior to the widespread adoption of APIs, all the code to interact with the database was included in the same code for building the dynamic webpage and for processing form data submitted by the user. As you might imagine, this created long pages of code. Additionally, modifications involved updating the entire body of code. Every part of a web application also had to be retested to ensure no new bugs were introduced when fixing or modifying the original code.

The API serves as an intermediary response layer between requests for data from the outside world and attempts to save datasets to the database storing that data. An API is like another webpage that handles only inbound and outbound text representation of the data in a database, not HTML for presentation to a webpage user.

An API is especially useful if you are going to use the same set of data to build multiple dynamic webpages. Instead of each of several pages making the same set of procedure calls to the database in the same way, you could build an API that performs this action and connect each webpage to the API. This is a notion of strategic efficiency known as Don't Repeat Yourself.

For example, if multiple pages on a website perform a GET request for the record with an ID of 834, the API call, or request, would be similar to the following:

GET: https://www.totallyawesomestuff.com/products.php?id=834

This looks familiar, right? It's like the GET request for a standard webpage over HTTPS. What is returned to the page requestor is the difference. Typically, the data returned from an API is in the form of **JavaScript Object Notation (JSON)** (see https://www.json.org/json-en.html).

The JSON dataset is the plain-text representation of the contents of a database, as in the following:

```
{"id":"834",
"product_category":"Tasty Snacks",
"product":"Low-Fat Candy for Goldfish",
"price":2.99,
"currency":"dollars",
"units_available":"199"}
```

While the data set includes some markup (the curly brackets and other punctuation), you can see the text form of the columns of data in the table—id, product_category, product, price, currency, and units_available. Also included is the data from the unique record 834 in key-value pairs separated by colons, such as "price":2.99.

Full stack web developers on smaller projects can be more efficient than dedicated front-end, API, and back-end development teams. If a sprint requires a new data structure, API call, and web component, the full stack developer can build each without waiting for anyone else to build their portion. However, for large or complex web development projects, teams of dedicated developers distributing the workload are significantly faster than the solitary developer.

Compiled Languages

One more way to build full stack web application is to use a **compiled programming language**. Compiled programming languages require the extra step of being compiled after the web developer writes the code and before the code is moved to the web server. Compiling the code translates it into machine language that runs faster on the server than interpreted languages do. For large corporations or international e-commerce platforms, the increased speed is worth the extra time and work it takes to compile a program.

Some web developers argue that true full stack development uses an integrated development environment (IDE) such as Microsoft Visual Studio to create the entire web project from HTML to the API, and then to produce compiled code from a language such as C#. Separate database software such as Microsoft SQL Server is used to create and maintain the back-end database. The compiled code is installed on a production server as an executable file, which is faster to run and provides greater command over the web server resources than interpreted code.

The same people might argue enthusiastically about whether there are more doors or wheels in the world (the answer is obviously doors). It is true that more complex full stack development can be done using an IDE to create compiled code. However, any time a developer is creating the entire path from the front end of the user experience to the back end of data storage, regardless of the technology stack, that developer is doing full stack development. Additionally, as stated in the Agile Manifesto, the most useful outcome is working code, regardless of the technology or platform.

More complex business processes sometimes do require more complex solutions. An adept full stack developer adopts the least complex solution appropriate to the problem being solved, as identified by the business analyst in response to Question Number One: "What is the problem this software will solve?"

Common Mistakes

Programming is fun. Writing code to see what works can be a fascinating and rewarding puzzle to solve. Writing code to see how complex a challenge you can leave for the next developer or writing code using only the tools you currently know how to work with creates obstacles for any future developers who have to fix your mistakes or modify your code.

Always be considerate of the next developer. Write simple, well-commented code that solves only the problems identified in the problem statement corresponding to the question, "What is the problem this software will solve?" When you inherit a project, you will thank the previous developer for following these principles, and you should pay it forward in return by doing the same.

Version Control

While you are writing code, you will undoubtedly repeatedly click the Save button on your text editor to store your most recent changes. You will probably also have a folder structure set up to save your files in an organized way. What happens if your hard drive fails or you need to share the development load with a team? What if the business process you're building software to support suddenly changes?

Adept full stack web developers need to use **version control** (also known as source control) software to ensure the availability of their code regardless of hardware failures, to respond to changes in project requirements, and to create a common space to develop in parallel with other members of the development team.

You can think of version control software as helpful "save draft" software that allows you to create a series of code milestones at convenient points during development. If the project requirements change or you realize you made a mistake, you can roll back the most recent set of changes to a previous milestone date associated with a better starting point to solve this new problem or correct your mistake. Additionally, version control software allows multiple developers to do this simultaneously so you can build different parts of the project at the same time.

Typical Technologies of Full Stack

In an ever-changing landscape of new technologies and programming languages, the full stack web development enterprise is no different from any other technology-based work. The ever-fickle flavor-of-the-month approach to choosing a technology for any of the five parts (project management, front-end, back-end, database, and version control) of full stack web development is enough to drive even the most ambitious developer to consider handing in their laptop for an Etch-A-Sketch. However, the market share for the most popular tool for each of these five components changes more slowly and has remained consistent for several years.

As a new full stack developer, you are well served to learn about the technologies and development tools with the largest market share for each of the five components. This chapter has mentioned some of them, including HTML, CSS, JavaScript, PHP, and MySQL. The products for each component are similar enough that if you are comfortable working in one, you can learn the nuances of another product when necessary.

Figure 1-10 shows a flow of ideas and information between the five full stack web development technologies. Each technology exists in an ecosystem with interactions between it and the others.

Figure 1-10 The process flow diagram for the five types of software used in full stack web development

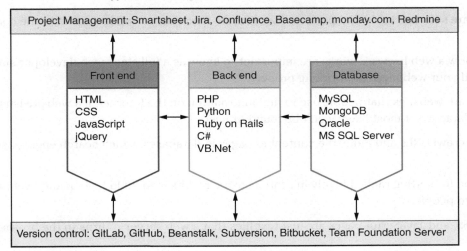

Typical technologies of full stack web development

Project Management: Smartsheet, Jira, Confluence, Basecamp, monday.com, Redmine

Front end	Back end	Database
HTML	PHP	MySQL
CSS	Python	MongoDB
JavaScript	Ruby on Rails	Oracle
jQuery	C#	MS SQL Server
	VB.Net	

Version control: GitLab, GitHub, Beanstalk, Subversion, Bitbucket, Team Foundation Server

Quick Check 1-6

1. What is full stack web development?

   a. An approach to mainframe programming that creates multiple layers of code stacked on top of each other adopted for use in web development
   b. When one developer builds the user interface, data processing, and database structure of a web application
   c. The adoption of an N-Tier architecture in web application development
   d. Web development intended to run on a full stack of technologies, including smartphones, tablets, laptops, desktops, and Internet appliances

2. What is an API?

   a. Automated programmatic interface
   b. A three-letter acronym added to the resumé of every full stack developer to ensure automated resumé screeners forward the resumé to the "interview" pile
   c. Administrative program interface
   d. Application programming interface

3. Why would a full stack developer create an API?

   a. Writing more code means greater job security
   b. To gain strategic efficiency
   c. It is in the BA documentation of the project requirements
   d. All of the cool kids are doing it

1) b. Full stack web development means one developer is responsible for the entire application from user interface to data processing to back-end database. **2) d.** API is an application programming interface. **3) b.** The basic idea behind Don't Repeat Yourself is strategic efficiency.

Summary

- Web browsers are software tools that perform five discrete functions to connect users to the contents of the Internet.

- The details of how a web browser works are important to know as a full stack web developer since that's how you will test to see if your webpages are working properly.

- Search engines are websites that people use to find information on the Internet. If a website isn't indexed in a search engine database, it most likely won't be found or used.

- Search engines crawl URLs and index the content of pages in databases, which search engine users then search for results.

- The best method for getting ranked highly in search engine results is to build high-quality webpages that present useful content to people.

- Static HTML, CSS, and JavaScript pages are just text files that a web server returns to the browser when asked for them by name.

- Dynamic webpages require additional processing by a code engine before the resulting HTML is returned to the browser.

- Saving web form data involves a return trip to the code of a dynamic webpage with a payload of data that a web developer has programmed the webpage to handle.

- Being a full stack web developer requires research, learning, and assuming the roles of programmer, business analyst, project manager, and database administrator.

- Five software components are used in full stack web development: project management, front-end development, back-end development, database administration, and version control.

Key Terms

404 error

Agile project management

Application Programming
    Interface (API)

business analyst (BA)

Cascading Style Sheets (CSS)

Cascading Style Sheets Object
    Model (CSSOM)

compiled programming language

content management
    system (CMS)

data packets

Document Object Model (DOM)

Domain Name System (DNS)

dynamic webpage

fetch request

GET request

Googlebots

graphical user interface (GUI)

Hypertext Markup
    Language (HTML)

Hypertext Transfer
    Protocol (HTTP)

InterNic

interpreted programming
    language

JavaScript

JavaScript Object
    Notation (JSON)

PHP

POST request

project manager (PM)

rendering engine

search engine

search engine
    optimization (SEO)

static webpage

technology stack

Uniform Resource
    Locator (URL)

user interface (UI)

version control

web browser

WordPress

World Wide Web
    Consortium (W3C)

waterfall project
    management

Review Questions

1. What does a DNS server do? (1.1)

   a. Translates IP addresses into URLs

   b. Hosts the database in a full stack web development environment

   c. Translates URLs into IP addresses

   d. Runs the software that serves webpages to browsers requesting them

2. What does HTML DOM stand for? (1.1)

   a. District Object Model

   b. Document Object Model

   c. Distinct Object Model

   d. Domain Object Model

3. Why is it important to understand how a search engine works? (1.2)

   a. To help users find your website when they use a search engine

   b. To guarantee you get to the top of the ranked list of search results

   c. Because Google keeps the details of its search engine technology wrapped in obscurity and nondisclo-sure agreements

   d. It's the only way to game the system to get ahead of everyone else in the rankings

4. What does SEO stand for? (1.2)

   a. Single enterprise operation

   b. Search engine operation

   c. Search engine optimization

   d. Search engine object

5. How can you guarantee Google will list your website at the top of its search results? (1.2)

   a. You can't. You can only build a good, standards-compliant website and ask Google to crawl it.

   b. Pay up front to get to the head of list.

   c. Pay a search engine optimization subcontractor to create links to your site.

   d. Use WordPress to ensure your website is standards-compliant.

6. How does a web server know which page to return to the browser making a GET request? (1.3)

   a. It searches the entire computer it is loaded on for any matching files.

   b. The file name is usually specified in the GET request.

   c. It uses artificial intelligence to find the file or page.

   d. It lets the browser connect with direct access to the default folder containing all of its files so the browser can choose.

7. How does a web server return an HTML page to a browser? (1.3)

   a. As a series of single lines of text from the file

   b. In data packets

   c. All at once in a simple text file

   d. Using JSON

8. What is the basic service a web hosting company offers? (1.3)

   a. Building your full stack webpages for you using your choice of programming language and database

   b. HTML, CSS, and JavaScript file version control

   c. Tech support for the full stack developers working on one of their sites

   d. Rental of a folder on one of their web servers and contacting InterNic to ensure your URL is unique

9. Why does a web server not just return the text of the PHP code in a dynamic webpage file like it does with an HTML page? (1.4)

    a. The PHP code is precompiled into machine language.

    b. A server administrator configures the web server to execute the PHP code in the dynamic webpage.

    c. The PHP code is encrypted to look like a set of random characters prior to moving into production.

    d. The web server can only return HTML, CSS, or JavaScript files.

10. How does the PHP engine build a dynamic webpage? (1.4)

    a. From top to bottom of the code on the page

    b. From the precompiled executable file on the server

    c. By assembling the component parts from code libraries stored in the code library database

    d. By traversing the HTML DOM tree from top to bottom and adding the CSS and JavaScript after it is done

11. How is data from a web form returned to the web server for processing? (1.4)

    a. As key-value pairs in the POST response from the browser

    b. As data packets in an HTML file sent back to the server from the browser

    c. In a UTF-8-encoded response file

    d. In a JavaScript POST response file

12. How does a full stack web developer choose the appropriate technology for a web project? (1.5)

    a. By doing research, using experience, and making judgments

    b. Using a project flowchart to determine best fit from ranked choices of available technologies

    c. Using cost-center accounting to determine which solution is least expensive in the near and far term

    d. Tracking the users of the current software using Google Analytics to determine which browser most of them are using, then choosing the best development tools to serve content to that browser

13. What does a project manager do? (1.5)

    a. Keeps the concurrent versions of the software being developed by different full stack developers from interfering with each other

    b. Starts a project off on the right foot with an all-staff meeting, then steps aside to observe the progress until the project is done

    c. Keeps a project on track and all key personnel accountable and informed of the project status

    d. Nobody really knows, but they make a lot of money doing it

14. What is an advantage of using the waterfall approach to project management? (1.5)

    a. All parts of the project are finished at the same time. The customers won't have a chance to change the project requirements mid-project.

    b. The developers will be able to concentrate on development without having unnecessary meetings.

    c. Waterfall is the project management strategy with the longest history.

    d. The customers can change the project requirements mid-project.

15. What are the five software components of full stack web development? (1.6)

    a. Front end, back end, database, version control, and project management

    b. Agile, waterfall, scrum, strategic, Kanban

    c. HTML, CSS, JavaScript, PHP, MySQL

    d. Front end, API, back end, CRUD data layer, database

16. What is an interpreted programming language? (1.6)

    a. One used in many countries that speak different languages
    b. The programming language written prior to being compiled into machine language
    c. The programming language used in the web browser to create a webpage to display in the user interface
    d. A programming language that is not compiled prior to running

17. What does version control software do? (1.6)

    a. Controls the version of the software being released into production
    b. Creates a series of code milestones while allowing multiple programmers to work on the same project
    c. Restricts the full stack programmers to specific tasks in the requirements documents so they aren't all working on the same part at the same time
    d. The same thing as source control software, but with numbered "versions" for easier organization

Programming Exercises

1. Research the top three current technologies or programming languages used for each of the five software components of full stack web development by market share. Add one new technology or programming language that is predicted to be the amazing new thing in the near future. Create a two-page report of your findings and cite your sources. (1.6)

2. For the years 1995, 2005, and 2015, find the top three most-used browsers by market share and research why the market shifted between each of these years. Then, make a prediction—what browser will be the most popular in 2030? Summarize your findings in a two-page report and cite your sources. (1.1)

Projects

1. Assume the role of a business analyst and research the use of Google Analytics (https://analytics.google.com/analytics/web/provision/#/provision). Write a two-page proposal to yourself as the customer arguing for or against using Google Analytics in your own website. (1.5)

2. Google is the undisputed leader of search engines, and yet many others are available. Using a search engine other than Google, investigate six alternative search engines. In your opinion, will any of these overtake Google? Summarize your findings in a two-page report, defend your opinion, and cite your sources. (1.2)

3. Research when the use of "full stack web development" began as a concept. How has it evolved since the initial idea? What programming languages or technologies have been used most often during this time? Make a prediction about the future direction of full stack web development. Summarize your research in a two-page report and cite your sources. (1.6)

Chapter 2

HTML and CSS: Building Blocks

Learning Objectives

When you complete this chapter, you will be able to:

2.1 Describe the tools used for building basic HTML pages.

2.2 Create a webpage using basic HTML tags.

2.3 Create links between two or more webpages.

2.4 Build a list of similar items using appropriately nested HTML tags.

2.5 Create the styling for a basic webpage.

2.6 Construct an external style sheet to modify the appearance of one or more webpages.

2.7 Explain the difference between class and ID references and when to use each.

2.1 HTML and CSS: Just Text in a Text File

As you now know, HTML starts as text in a text file. You can use any simple text editor to create an HTML page, but a few text editors have been proven through use to be easier and more user friendly than the rest. In addition, you need to determine a logical way to store files and which tools to use to do so.

Choosing a Text Editor

If you are using a Windows computer, you can choose from a few options for a simple text editor. Many full stack web developers use Notepad++ successfully. You can download it for free from the Notepad++ home page (https://notepad-plus-plus.org), but a donation is recommended to keep the development project funded and ensure future patches and upgrades.

Other options for Windows computers include TextPad (https://www.textpad.com/home), which is also available for free with a donation recommended to offset the cost of development and maintenance. Sublime Text (https://www.sublimetext.com) is available as a free download for a minimalist version with upgrades for an additional fee. Visual Studio Code (https://code.visualstudio.com) is another option available as a free multiplatform option from Microsoft.

If you are using a Mac, both Sublime Text and Visual Studio Code are viable options. Additionally, Bare Bones Edit, or BBEdit (https://www.barebones.com/products/bbedit/), is a robust text editor with a small footprint that is available with a free full-feature 30-day trial and an upgrade for a fee. Most figures in this text that show code examples use BBEdit.

On the Linux platform, Sublime Text and Visual Studio Code are available, but you can also use Atom (https://atom.io) for free.

Common Mistakes

The single most important criterion you should use for choosing a simple text editor to begin your HTML development is that it is actually simple. **What you see is what you get (WYSIWYG)** editors such as Microsoft Word, Dreamweaver, and Google Web Designer are not good options to begin working with HTML. These editors obscure the raw HTML you need to write and modify by creating a visual representation of the results instead of showing the text of the code.

You should also avoid using WordPress to start doing HTML development, since it leaps over many important web development milestones that you need to understand before diving into the world of WordPress web development.

Finally, while it is possible for you to use Notepad on a Windows machine, the way it saves files and other quirks means that for most web developers it is not a preferred option.

Choosing a File Storage Structure

After selecting a text editor, your next choice is how to store your HTML files. The simplest option for this course is to create one main folder to contain all of your work. The main folder can contain folders for each chapter, and each chapter folder can contain folders for individual projects. **Figure 2-1** shows an example of this organization.

Figure 2-1 A sample folder setup for the projects and exercises in the course

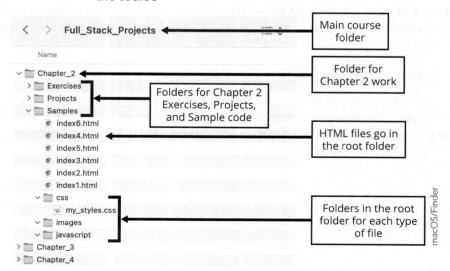

macOS/Finder

As you are completing these projects, using a folder structure on your computer such as the one shown in Figure 2-1 is sufficient. However, a backup location for storing files allows you to keep them safe from failures or loss of computer hardware.

One step you can take to protect your files is to store them in the cloud. **Cloud storage** is a way of using file space on a web server through websites such as Google Cloud, Microsoft Azure, and Amazon Web Services. You use the storage space as if it were your own local hard drive, without having access to a specific computer. Cloud storage is just a cloud of computers somewhere on the Internet.

Saving your files in Google Drive (https://www.google.com/drive/) ensures that they are available from any device you connect to the Internet. Other similar products include Box (https://www.box.com/home) and Dropbox (https://www.dropbox.com). The following are two distinct advantages of using (and in some cases paying for) these services:

1. You have access to your files regardless of the computer you are currently using.
2. You have backups to make sure your files are available.

For example, if you are interviewing for a web development job and a person on your interview panel asks if you've built a PHP API that returns JSON, you can say, "Yes, would you like to see my code? I wrote it for this awesome class I took on full stack web development and stored it in the cloud so I can open it from any computer with Internet access." You could then access your Google Drive on any available laptop and display your state-of-the-art knowledge.

You can also look back at files from previous projects to use and adapt for current projects. This code reuse is a way to build a personal code bank. Over time, you'll build enough blocks of code, or widgets, that any new project will involve composing a series of previously built widgets with modifications. Strategic efficiency at its most efficient.

However, to knock that interview question out of the park, you need to use what is recognized as the default standard for **version control**—Git (https://git-scm.com) and GitHub (https://github.com). Version control software tools are built to create a series of backup versions of the code in a repository of code. While the tools share the same starting three letters, they have a significant difference.

Using Git and GitHub

Git is open source software that runs on your local machine to keep track of the versions of your web development projects as you write them. When you use the Commit command in Git, you make a fresh copy of the files you're working on in a new folder with a date/time stamp.

Between each commit, you can save your changes locally without creating a new copy of the code. However, uncommitted changes may be lost if you have a hardware failure or you can't log in to the same machine where you were doing your initial development. It is up to you to remember to use Git to create backups at critical milestones during project development.

GitHub is a web application that provides cloud storage service and integrates with Git to give you a location to save all the time-stamped versions you create when you use the Commit command. In earlier version-control software, an administrator installed the application on a local network server used by the development team. GitHub is now more widely used than server-based solutions because direct access to a computer on the local network isn't necessary with a cloud-based solution. Additionally, the work of maintaining a server that requires substantial uptime with redundant backups is outsourced to a vendor.

The word count of this chapter would be quadrupled with a complete tutorial on Git and GitHub. For more information, refer to the free online documentation (https://git-scm.com/doc). Additionally, you can read the Hello World tutorial (https://docs.github.com/en/get-started/quickstart/hello-world) to help you get started with GitHub.

While you do not need to use Git and GitHub to successfully complete the chapters, projects, and exercises in this course, you are encouraged to use Git to store your files in a GitHub account. Your experience will be a useful line item to round out a full stack developer's resumé. You can download and install Git on your computer if you aren't using one of the text editors that comes bundled with Git already installed.

For the purposes of learning Git and GitHub, you would need to complete the following tasks:

1. Install Git on your local computer if your text editor doesn't already come bundled with Git or have a plugin that does.
2. Create a GitHub account.
3. Create a repo, or repository, for your code with GitHub.
4. Connect the repo to your text editor via plugin or a configuration setting.
5. Set up a main branch in your repo.
6. Begin editing files locally, saving them, and then committing those files to push them to your GitHub storage.
7. Pull your most recent changes down from GitHub, edit them if necessary, and recommit them to complete the cycle of version control.

This might seem like a lot of initial setup work, and it can be. However, the dividends you will enjoy include the following:

- Having date/time-stamped versions of your projects that you can access anywhere with an Internet connection
- Gaining useful experience with version control using Git and GitHub
- Having a secure, backed-up storage space in the cloud for your projects
- Learning about collaborating with other web developers on a single project using Git and GitHub
- Adding familiarity with Git and GitHub as a line item on your resumé

Quick Check 2-1

1. What is the most important part about choosing a text editor for HTML development?

   a. That it is a simple text editor
   b. That it offers HTML tag autocomplete and CSS autoformat options
   c. That it is a WYSIWYG editor
   d. That it is free

2. Why would a web developer choose to store files using a cloud service provider like Google Drive?

   a. Because the cloud then works as a free web hosting server
   b. Because this is a good way to gain valuable experience with web development
   c. Because the cloud works best with text files
   d. Because the files are backed up and available from any computer with Internet access

3. What is GitHub used for?

   a. Creating simple text files to be saved as HTML documents
   b. Storing repositories of code uploaded from Git
   c. Compiling the HTML code into the HTML DOM and CSS code into CSSOM
   d. Storing cached webpages to speed up the web browser

1) a. Simple text editors are the best way to learn HTML development and, for many developers, the fastest way to do it professionally. **2) d.** Cloud service providers regularly back up your data and provide access from a web interface. **3) b.** GitHub is a cloud storage provider for repositories of code that developers commit using Git.

2.2 Building the HTML Page Structure

If you started your full stack web development journey by reading Chapter 1, you have read one entire chapter, plus the first section of this chapter without writing any full stack web development code. Or any code, for that matter. This is a programming course, so it's time to change that and write some code.

Building Your First Webpage

Review the example of a simple webpage from Chapter 1, shown again in **Figure 2-2**.

Figure 2-2   Sample code for a simple webpage

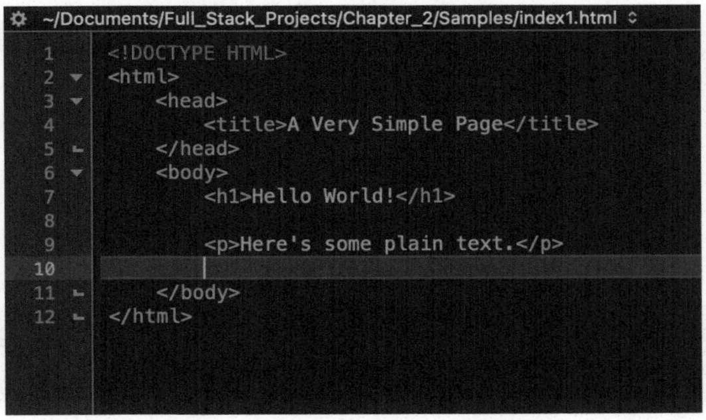

```
~/Documents/Full_Stack_Projects/Chapter_2/Samples/index1.html
1    <!DOCTYPE HTML>
2    <html>
3        <head>
4            <title>A Very Simple Page</title>
5        </head>
6        <body>
7            <h1>Hello World!</h1>
8
9            <p>Here's some plain text.</p>
10
11        </body>
12    </html>
```

BBEdit

1. Open your simple text editor and type the following code exactly as it appears here (and in Figure 2-2):

```
<!DOCTYPE HTML>
<html>
    <head>
        <title>A Very Simple Page</title>
    </head>
    <body>
        <h1>Hello World!</h1>

        <p>Here's some plain text.</p>

    </body>
</html>
```

2. Save the file as index1.html in the Samples folder for Chapter 2 in the folder structure you created in the first section of this chapter. If you didn't previously create that folder structure, now is a fantastic time to do so.

Note   If your simple text editor is in fact simple, you must type opening and closing tags for each of the paired HTML elements in the index1.html page. To keep track of tags and prevent unclosed tags (an opening tag without a paired closing tag), most developers do one of the following:
- Turn on the autocomplete feature in their text editor so it closes each opening tag automatically as they type it.
- Type the opening tag and immediately type the closing tag, then add some white space for the contents in the tags.

3. Open your favorite web browser, and then use the File menu to locate your new webpage. Depending on your choice of browser, Open or Open File should be available as an option on the File menu. If the File menu is not displayed in your browser, press Ctrl+O (Windows) or Cmd+O (Mac) to display the Open File dialog box.

4. Navigate to the folder where you stored your page (such as the Samples folder for Chapter 2), select index1 .html, and then open it. If all of your code is correct, you should see a webpage like that in **Figure 2-3**.

Figure 2-3   The index.html webpage

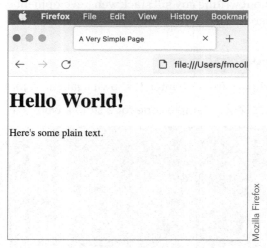

Mozilla Firefox

Common Mistakes

If your webpage does not open or look like the one in Figure 2-3, don't despair. Check and correct the following:

- Make sure your page is saved in the right location (the Samples folder for Chapter 2).
- Make sure your page is saved as index1.html.
- Double-check the HTML code you entered in your text editor. It has to be *exactly* the same as that shown in Figure 2-2, including the doctype declaration in the first line and all opening and closing tags.
- Ask for a second opinion. Because you are writing your own code, it is easy to overlook a mistake or omission. Asking another programmer to take a look at your code is humbling but helpful. A fresh set of eyes on your code almost always finds your mistake in seconds.

Deconstructing a Simple HTML Page

You just created a webpage that contains all the common parts of nearly every webpage on the Internet. HTML code is made up of tags and text. The tags tell the browser how to display the text, but the tags themselves don't appear on the screen—only the text (or images, videos, or other content) appears.

Starting from the top of the code in the index1.html file and working downward, you can see the following parts:

1. A doctype declaration that identifies the document type to the browser and directs it to render the page as HTML and not a PDF, Microsoft Excel spreadsheet, or some other file type
2. An opening <html> tag with a paired closing </html> tag at the bottom of the file that enclose all the text of the webpage
3. Opening and closing <head>...</head> tags
4. Opening and closing <body>...</body> tags

These parts are numbered in **Figure 2-4**, with the numbers corresponding to the preceding list.

Figure 2-4   Main parts of a webpage

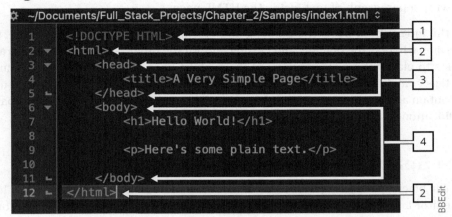

The <head>...</head> tags enclose webpage information that is included primarily for the browser. In index1.html, you can see a pair of <title>...</title> tags, with the title of the webpage (A Very Simple Page) between those tags. You can also see the title displayed in the browser. Later in this chapter, you use the <link> tag to add links to external files from the head section to make your page more functional, such as Cascading Style Sheets and JavaScript files.

The <body>...</body> tags enclose what is rendered as a webpage in the browser. Examining the contents between those tags, you can see the following:

5. An opening and closing pair of <h1>...</h1> tags

6. Some plain text inside a pair of <p>...</p> tags

7. White space for the human reader of the HTML

These parts are numbered in **Figure 2-5**.

Figure 2-5   White space and contents of the <body>...</body> tags

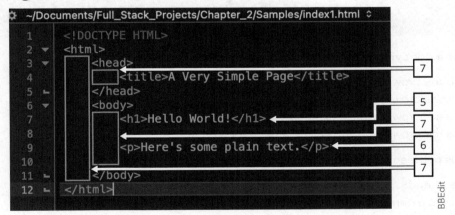

The <h1>...</h1> tags are HTML tags that the browser renders using its User Agent, or internal style sheet, as a first-level heading since this page includes no other styling information. (Later in this chapter, you will modify those tags by adding some styling.) A pair of tags and their content is called an HTML element. The <h1>...</h1> tags are useful to create headings, since they are **block-level elements**. (That is, they make space for themselves in the text display of a webpage from the left margin to the right, moving all other text out of the way.)

Note   The h1 element is used for heading 1 text—the largest heading with a default style in all browsers. There are also h2, h3, h4, and h5 headings available as block-level elements. These headings have been used by web developers since the dawn of the Internet and are still used on occasion today.

However, most web developers now use these heading tags sparingly and instead use <div>...</div> tags. The <div>...</div> tag set is a block-level element and accomplishes the same outcome without some of the constraints of the heading tags. The div element defines a division or section in an HTML document. Most developers use div elements extensively as containers of content.

The `<p>`...`</p>` tags are used to enclose plain text. The `<p>` tag stands for a paragraph, and you use a set of `<p>`...`</p>` tags to wrap a paragraph of text inside the HTML page.

Notice that in the index1.html page, the opening and closing tags for `<h1>`...`</h1>` and `<title>`...`</title>` appear on the same line, whereas the opening and closing tags for the other tags appear on separate lines. This format is an editorial choice to clarify the **containership** of those short lines of text. Containership means that the outer `<html>`...`</html>` tags contain the inner `<head>`...`</head>` and `<body>`...`</body>` tags **nested** inside them. Because those tags in turn contain additional tags and text, inserting the opening and closing tags on separate lines makes the future work of modification easier.

Using White Space for Nested HTML Tags

Using white space (or black space in Figure 2-5) to indent lines of code is helpful only to the human reader of the HTML. Both a text editor and a web browser would display this page appropriately if it were stored as a single, very long line of text. However, that would present significant problems to the person who has to read the HTML and figure out where the tags begin and end and what they contain.

The idea of containership can be visually represented by indenting each block of elements by the same amount of space from the left margin. Consistent indentation of nested HTML elements is one of the web development best practices you follow throughout this course.

> **Note** | Most text editors provide a setting or preference for converting tabs to spaces. This creates a more uniform experience and appearance across text editors, since each space is one character wide, whereas a tab can be from three to seven characters wide depending on the text editor. The actual number of spaces used is less critical than using them consistently, however.

Quick Check 2-2

1. What does a `doctype` declaration do?

    a. Tells the browser how to format the text of the page that follows
    b. Tells the browser what type of document follows the declaration
    c. Tells the browser which external style sheet to load for the screen size
    d. Tells the browser how to style the page for a printer

2. What goes between the `<body>`...`</body>` tags in an HTML page?

    a. The `<head>`...`</head>` tags
    b. Links to external CSS files
    c. The text of the external style sheet
    d. The text and other tags that make up the visible or audible webpage itself

3. What are nested tags?

    a. HTML tags that are styled to appear nested inside a webpage
    b. HTML tags that appear between other HTML tags
    c. A specific type of HTML tag used to create nested elements
    d. Special HTML tags used to signify that an HTML element is a nested element

1) b. The `doctype` declaration helps the browser determine what type of document follows the declaration.
2) d. The text, images, videos, or other media on a webpage that most users see or hear are enclosed within the `<body>` tags. **3) b.** Nested tags are HTML tags that occur between other HTML tags.

2.3 Creating Links in HTML

In the previous section, you created a complete webpage. However, that page is merely a text file displayed in a web browser as an HTML document. It is missing the most important part of the entire Internet ecosystem—links to other webpages.

Links differentiate webpages from online text documents. Without links, users of the Internet would need to know the file name of every page to access those files. Search engines would have to display the text of the full file names for you to copy and paste into the address bar of your browser. Links make the entire web work better.

Examining the HTML Link Syntax

Links displayed in a web browser are composed of a pair of `<a>`...`</a>` tags surrounding text in the HTML file, similar to the `<h1>`...`</h1>` tags that you used previously. However, the `<a>`...`</a>` tags need additional keyword components known as **attributes** to create the links. The attributes provide information the `<a>`...`</a>` tags need to do more than the `<h1>`...`</h1>` tags do. An example of the link syntax is as follows:

```
<a href="index.html">Click Here</a> to go to another page.
```

The link syntax begins with the opening of an `<a`, or anchor tag. The attribute is the additional code inside the `<a>` tag. The inner structure of the anchor tag has the following parts:

- The `href="index.html"` attribute is composed of an **attribute name** and the **attribute value**. The `href=` identifier in the attribute stands for hypertext reference. The text in quotations following the equal sign is the value, or destination, for the link. In this case, `index.html` is the actual hypertext reference, or webpage the browser will attempt to resolve if a click event occurs on this link. This pattern is repeated often throughout HTML—an attribute composed of a name and a value is added to the interior text of a tag. Tags can occasionally have more than one attribute.

- The `Click Here` text between the opening `<a>` tag and the closing `</a>` tag is the text displayed in the browser as a link. By default, browsers show links in a color different from other text and underlined, with the pointer changing from an arrow to a hand when moved over it.

You'll now create the first of two links in your current document.

1. Start by saving a second copy of the page you just created. Use the Save As command on the File menu of your text editor or copy and paste the file into the same folder using your favorite file-handling app, such as Finder or File Explorer.

2. Name the new file index2.html. (The file name is important—unless the file is named correctly, your links won't work.) Modify the text in the `<title>`...`</title>` and `<h1>`...`</h1>` tags so your new second page is obviously a different page. Add some new content.

Common Mistakes

The most common reason for a broken link is a file path naming error. Remember that the Internet is basically just a massive network file handling system, and a link is just a file path name passed to a web server hosting files by the browser when it makes a GET or POST request.

Computers do exactly what they are told, not always what you intend or hope they should do. If you include a link to a document that doesn't exist because you used the wrong or misspelled file name, even if you are just one letter off, the web browser still requests that page with one letter incorrect, and the web server tries to find that webpage with one letter incorrect. The server will then return a 404 error—File Not Found.

The server returns the same error if the file has been removed or never existed in the first place, though most often, the link is simply misspelled.

3. Open the index1.html file in your text editor, if necessary, and add the following HTML code between the `<body>` and `</body>` tags immediately after the "Here's some plain text" line:

```
<a href="index2.html">Click Here</a> to go to another page.
```

4. Add that same line to your index2.html webpage but update the text of the link and make the `href` target equal index1.html instead. Your completed link in index2.html will look like the following:

```
<a href="index1.html">Take me back</a> to the first page.
```

You can see an example of the updated index2.html in **Figure 2-6**.

Figure 2-6   The index2.html document with a link to index1.html

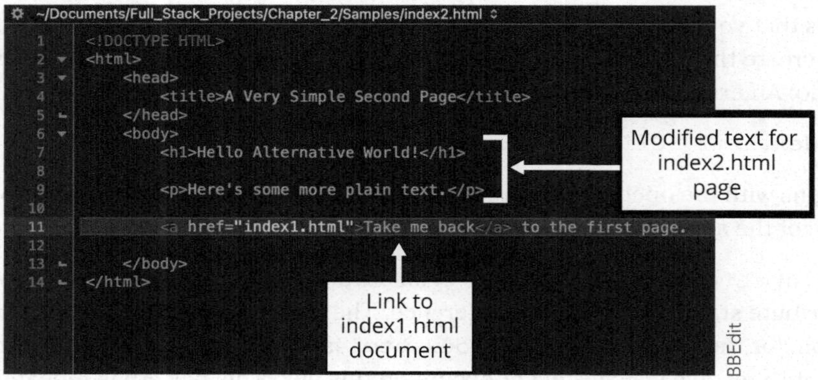

5. Make sure you save your changes to both pages, then reload index1.html in your web browser.
6. Click the "Click Here" link to open the second page, which has a link back to the first page.
7. Click the "Take me back" link to return to your original page.

You have now created webpages that have **relative links**, links that work only if the pages are in the same file system on the computer. In this case, the relative links to index1.html and index2.html include only the file names, not the path, because the files are stored in the same folder.

Creating HTML Links to External Websites

So far, you have created relative links between pages stored in the same folder in your file system. The power of the Internet is that you are not limited to linking between documents on one computer or web server, however. You can link to any webpage on any web server around the world using **absolute links**.

After the "Click Here" link in index1.html, add the following link to the BBC news site, which opens the site in a new window or tab and contains a `title` attribute:

```
<a href="https://www.bbc.com/" target="_blank" title="A link to the BBC
News.">BBC News</a>
```

The absolute link to the BBC site includes the following three new components:

1. You are creating a link using an `href` attribute pointing to the URL of an external page—in this case, https://www.bbc.com.
2. You are adding a `target` attribute for that link, which is either a new tab or a window, depending on the browser settings, as specified by the `_blank` value.
3. You are creating a `title` attribute for this link, which helps people who are hearing a webpage read to them by a screen reader or smart speaker identify the link and where it will take them.

Save your changes, and then reload your page in the browser. Click the link to the BBC News home page to open the site in a new tab or window.

The reason this is called an absolute link is that no matter what webpage you add it to, it works as long as you are connected to the Internet. It works because of the way it is written—it is the full file path to the webpage, including the server that hosts that page.

The relative links to index1.html and index2.html work as long as those two pages are stored in the same folder on the same server. The specified location of the linked file is relative to the HTML document that contains them. To make them absolute paths, you need to add the name of the web server or file system hosting the pages. You can see this in the web browser's address bar when you open each file. The absolute path to a file stored on the local machine looks something like this:

file:///Users/userName/Documents/Full_Stack_Projects/Chapter_2/Samples/index1.html

Quick Check 2-3

1. What is the difference between absolute and relative links?

   a. Absolute links always load a webpage; relative links only work if written correctly.
   b. Absolute links cause the browser to load a page absolutely, whereas relative links tell the browser to load the page relatively.
   c. Absolute links include a full URL like `https://whatever.org`, and relative links use the file path to a page on the same server like `detail/items.html`.
   d. Absolute links only work on pages hosted on a web server, whereas relative links will work anywhere.

2. What does `target="_blank"` tell the browser to do?

   a. Create a blank HTML document to load page content into.
   b. Refresh the current page in a new blank window.
   c. Open the page that the link references in a blank browser window or tab.
   d. Clear the browser window of cookies and other identity information to make space for a new webpage.

3. Why is it important to include a `title` in links?

   a. It contains the text displayed on the webpage.
   b. It creates the attribute used to create a site map.
   c. It displays the title of the webpage in the browser window.
   d. It helps people hearing the webpage being read to them know what the link is going to do.

1) c. Absolute links include the full name of a web server or drive letter in the URL to a specific file. **2) c.** The browser decodes the `_blank` value in the `target` attribute of a link to mean "open this link in a new browser window or tab." **3) d.** The `title` attribute provides additional information about a link to people using the webpage.

2.4 Building HTML Lists with Nested Tags

Now that you've mastered the complexities of creating simple webpages containing links, it's time to start creating more complex nested content within webpages. The following paragraphs provide two quick reminders before you get started on this new content.

First, use white space to help identify which tags are nested inside of others. Remember, white space in an HTML page is only there for the people who read the page, especially the next developer who has to figure out what you built. Customers might also want to examine the HTML code when they ask why their webpage is broken. The next developer might be you many months after you wrote the code. In each case, white space helps people read and interpret the HTML code.

Second, remember that for each opening tag you create, immediately create the closing tag before moving on to the next step. If your text editor does this for you, that's to your advantage, but if it does not, you should type these pairs manually.

Building HTML Lists

You've probably seen lists displayed in webpages. HTML provides three types of lists: **ordered lists**, **unordered lists**, and **description lists**. You can probably guess what an ordered list is—a series of items in a ranked order, like the steps in a recipe or the eras in geology.

An unordered list is also what the name suggests—a bulleted list of similar items that belong together but don't occur in any specific order like the ingredients in a recipe or life forms of a geologic era. Unordered lists are also useful for building menus for webpages.

Description lists are most often a series of key terms and their definitions. Though not as common as ordered and unordered lists, description lists are useful for creating content such as glossaries.

Examining the Ordered and Unordered List Syntax

You can create an ordered list and examine its syntax, which is similar to the syntax for an unordered list.

1. In your text editor, save a copy of index1.html as index3.html in the same folder.
2. Change the `title` text in index3.html to A More Complex Page.
3. Remove most of the contents of the `<body>`...`</body>` tags so they contain only the original `<h1>`...`</h1>` tags.
4. Change the text between the `<h1>`...`</h1>` tags to A List of My Favorite Colors.
5. Add the following content immediately below the pair of `<h1>` tags to rank your favorite colors in order of preference:

```
<ol>
    <li>Green</li>
    <li>Red</li>
    <li>Blue</li>
</ol>
```

You should end up with a page like that in **Figure 2-7**.

Figure 2-7   Adding a list to index3.html

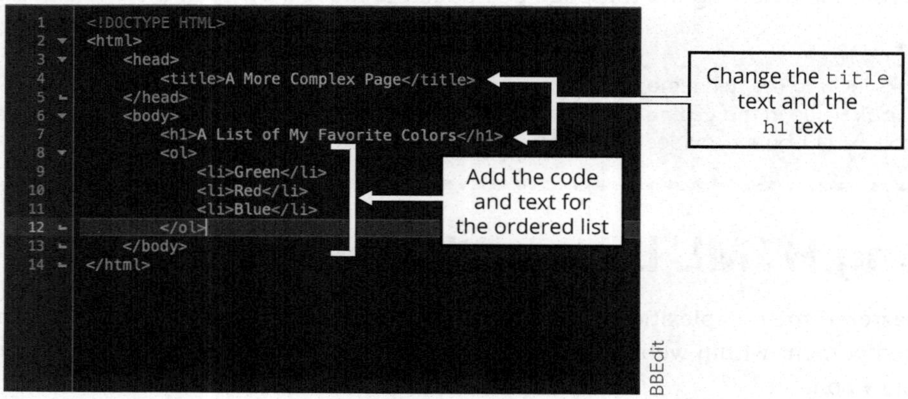

The `<ol>`...`</ol>` pair of tags tells the browser to create the structure for an ordered list. Each `<li>`...`</li>` tag pair creates a **list item**, which the browser then numbers sequentially in the webpage.

For strategic efficiency in this example, each list item appears in the code on a single line while the ordered list tags are stacked vertically on separate lines. This format makes the short list easier to read for the person who has to debug the list in the future. If the text of the list items were much longer, you could include the `<li>` tags on separate lines and indent the list text between them for readability.

Save the index3.html page, and then open it in your web browser. Your results should look like **Figure 2-8**.

Figure 2-8   Webpage with an ordered list

That's an HTML list! You are encouraged to customize the HTML list of your favorite colors—it's your webpage, you can do what you want with it.

The unordered list uses an identical format to the ordered list, with one text change. Instead of `<ol>...</ol>` tags, the unordered list uses `<ul>...</ul>` tags.

Reviewing the Description List Syntax

The description list is similar to the ordered and unordered lists in that it has an outer tag (`<dl>`), but the difference is that it has two inner tags—`<dt>` and `<dd>`—instead of `<li>`. You use `<dt>` for the term and `<dd>` for the description. The format for creating a proper description list is as follows:

```
<dl>
    <dt>Term</dt>
        <dd>Description of the Term</dd>
    <dt>Another Term</dt>
        <dd>Description of Another Term</dd>
</dl>
```

Description lists are not used as often as ordered or unordered lists. However, if you need to create a list of terms and definitions or items and descriptions, you can use this type of list.

Building Nested Ordered Lists

In the ordered list you created, you might want to include various shades of green. To list additional shades of green, you need a nested list. You can accomplish this variation by starting a new list inside the current list. The nested list also shows why proper tag nesting with white space enhances the readability of HTML.

Replace the interior of the `<li>Green</li>` list item with the following content:

```
<li>
    Green
    <ol>
        <li>Chartreuse</li>
        <li>Emerald</li>
        <li>Sage</li>
    </ol>
</li>
```

Notice that the outer <li>...</li> tags are now arranged vertically, or placed on separate lines, as is the inner ordered list. The opening and closing tags for the individual list items appear on the same line. This creates proper visual nesting of the inner list tags inside the outer list item. The completed code is shown in **Figure 2-9**.

Figure 2-9 The code for creating a nested list

```
1   <!DOCTYPE HTML>
2   <html>
3       <head>
4           <title>A More Complex Page</title>
5       </head>
6       <body>
7           <h1>A List of My Favorite Colors</h1>
8           <ol>
9               <li>
10                  Green
11                  <ol>
12                      <li>Chartreuse</li>
13                      <li>Emerald</li>
14                      <li>Sage</li>
15                  </ol>
16              </li>
17              <li>Red</li>
18              <li>Blue</li>
19          </ol>
20      </body>
21  </html>
```

Nested list

BBEdit

Save your changes and refresh the page in your browser. Note that you now have an outer numbered list with an inner numbered list. That's the desired outcome, except this doesn't look like a proper list of inner items within an outer list. Outlines like this usually have a first tier of numbered items followed by an interior secondary tier that uses lowercase alpha items. You will see how to follow that convention in the next section.

Examining the Ordered List Type Attribute

Using the `type` attribute, you can modify the inner list of items to use a different ranking format. For example, the ordered list can display numeric, alphabetic uppercase, or alphabetic lowercase values before each list item. Modify the inner ordered list to reflect the following code snippet:

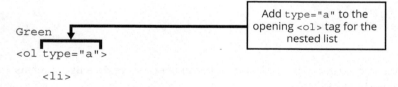

Add `type="a"` to the opening `<ol>` tag for the nested list

```
Green
<ol type="a">
    <li>
```

The `type` attribute used here changes the value displayed before the list items from the default of 1, 2, 3 to a, b, c. The name/value pair separated by an equal sign makes up the attribute. Save your changes to index3.html, and then refresh your webpage. You should now see a webpage like that shown in **Figure 2-10**.

Figure 2-10 Nested list with a different numbering scheme

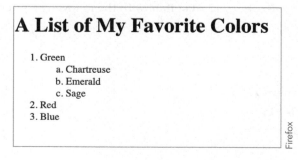

A List of My Favorite Colors

1. Green
    a. Chartreuse
    b. Emerald
    c. Sage
2. Red
3. Blue

Firefox

You can also use other features of the ordered list. For example, you could start numbering at a value other than 1 by using the `start` attribute. The format for this would look like the following code snippet:

```
<ol start="10">
```

As you have seen, attributes always occur after the opening tag name and are composed of either a single keyword or a set of name/value pairs. Some attributes, like the `href="url"` used with links, are required for an HTML tag to function properly, whereas others, like `start="10"`, are optional but add significant value.

If you want to amaze your friends at parties with your mad memorization skills, you can certainly memorize all of the available attributes for all HTML tags. If instead you want to maintain your friendships, you can search for "attributes of <tagname>" when you are using that tag in your code.

Quick Check 2-4

1. What does the `<ol>...</ol>` tag set create in HTML?

   a. An ordinary list with no specific order to the list items
   b. The outer framework for an ordered list of ranked list items
   c. An outer list, with another inner list nested inside of it
   d. An individual list item that appears inside an ordered list

2. What is a `<li>...</li>` tag set used for?

   a. Creating like items to group together inside a table
   b. Creating a large index for the heading text on a webpage
   c. Creating a list index for the web browser to render as numbers
   d. Creating a list item nested inside an ordered or unordered list

3. What value does the `type` attribute add to an ordered list item?

   a. Tells the browser what numbers or letters to use in the ordered list
   b. Tells the browser what type of HTML tag to use
   c. Tells the browser how to display style information about the list
   d. Tells the browser which type of items to apply the style to

1) b. The `<ol>...</ol>` tag set tells the browser to number or letter each of the inner list items incrementally.
2) d. The `<li>...</li>` tag set contains each list item inside an ordered or unordered list. 3) a. The `type` attribute tells the browser what type of ordered list to display—numeric, alphabetic uppercase, or alphabetic lowercase.

2.5 Using Inline Styles

The webpages you've created so far in this chapter use the default style built into each browser. All screen-based web browsers have a User Agent style sheet that displays h1 elements in a larger font size than h2 elements, for example, and links with an underline and blue text color. Creating webpages that default to this style results in generic-looking webpages, lacking in creative expression and, well, style. You are about to change that.

Create a new copy of index3.html and save it as index4.html. Leave the nested ordered lists and the `<h1>...</h1>` content as they are.

Creating an Inline Style for Color

Modify the list item for Green to reflect the following code snippet:

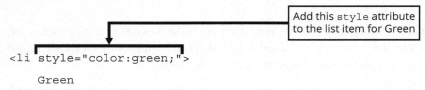

```
<li style="color:green;">

    Green
```

Looking at that code, you can see what the intended outcome should be. For this list item, the style information tells the browser that the color of the list item should be green. The syntax for an **inline style** is similar to other attributes you've worked with—an attribute (in this case, style) with a property and a value (color:green;) inside quotations separated by a colon and ending with a semicolon. The inline style provides styling information for the HTML tag it is written inside of, that is, inline with.

The style attribute tells the browser to display the contents of the HTML element in green. That is, since tags are not shown by a web browser, all of the text inside the pair of <li>...</li> tags will be green. The type attribute used with the ordered list has only a name (type) assigned a value (a) by an equal sign. In contrast, the style attribute has both a property and value separated by a colon after the name and equal sign. In the style example, the property is color and the value is green. You can add multiple styles to the style attribute by separating multiple property/value pairs with semicolons, as in the following example:

```
<li style="color:green; font-family:Tahoma;">
    Green
```

In index4.html, add the necessary style information to also modify the colors of the red and blue items, or whatever colors you've included as your favorites. Save your changes, open your new page in a web browser, and check the results. You should see a page that looks similar to that in **Figure 2-11**.

Figure 2-11   Results of adding color styles to an ordered list

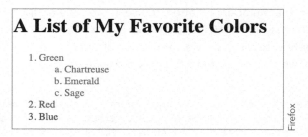

Modifying the Default Font Style

The <h1>...</h1> heading for this page also needs styling to move toward a more creative expression and away from the default font. In index4.html, modify the h1 element to include the following style attribute, save your changes, and refresh the page in your browser.

Add this style attribute to the opening h1 tag

```
<h1 style="font-family:Tahoma; font-size:1.5em;">
```

The style attribute includes the font-family property to specify a font (Tahoma) followed by a semicolon delimiter and a font-size declaration of 1.5 em units. **Em units** are the size of a capital letter *M* in the default display text size. In this case, the em unit is multiplied by 1.5 to make it one and a half times the size of a standard letter *M*. This is what is known as a **relative size**, which is useful in a proportional display for different sizes of screens or resolutions, a critical component of adaptive display.

Figure 2-12 shows the result of this most recent update.

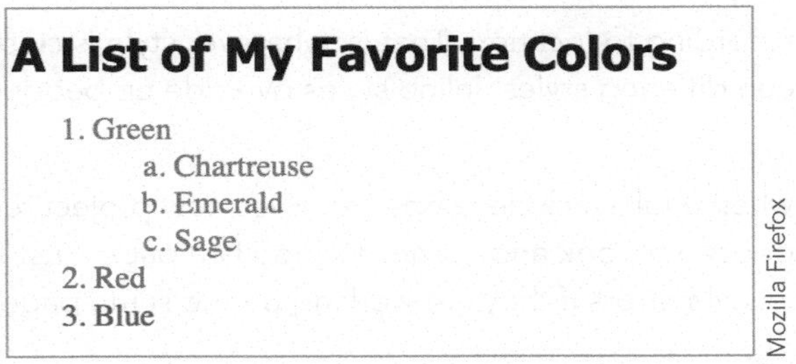

Figure 2-12   Updates to the `h1` heading
with a new font and font size

A List of My Favorite Colors

1. Green
     a. Chartreuse
     b. Emerald
     c. Sage
2. Red
3. Blue

Mozilla Firefox

You've now created four pages that contain `<h1>...</h1>` tags and content, all in the same folder. If these were pages from the same website, you would need to add the previous style declaration to each of those pages in each of those tags. Additionally, each time you need to update that style information to change from Tahoma to Times New Roman, for example, you must open each page again, find the `<h1>...</h1>` tags, and update the `style` attribute. This is a lot of cumbersome work. The following section explains a much better way to accomplish the same result.

Determining an HTML Style Storage Location

You can write webpage style information to style HTML in three places. You have just written examples of inline styles, those that are included in the text of the HTML tags themselves. An inline style is occasionally useful for rapid development or singleton cases where one HTML element is unique and needs a specific style that isn't used anywhere else in the page or website. However, an inline style is not an optimal solution because it applies only to the HTML element that contains the style and prevents reusing that style elsewhere.

Another place to store the styling information is between the `<head>...</head>` tags at the top of a webpage. This location allows you to use a single style in multiple locations but only on the same page. Styling information written in the top of the HTML page is known as using an **embedded style sheet** or **internal style sheet**. As with the inline styles, an embedded or internal style sheet is often used for rapid development or singleton cases. **Figure 2-13** shows the format for this type of style sheet.

Figure 2-13   HTML page with embedded style sheet

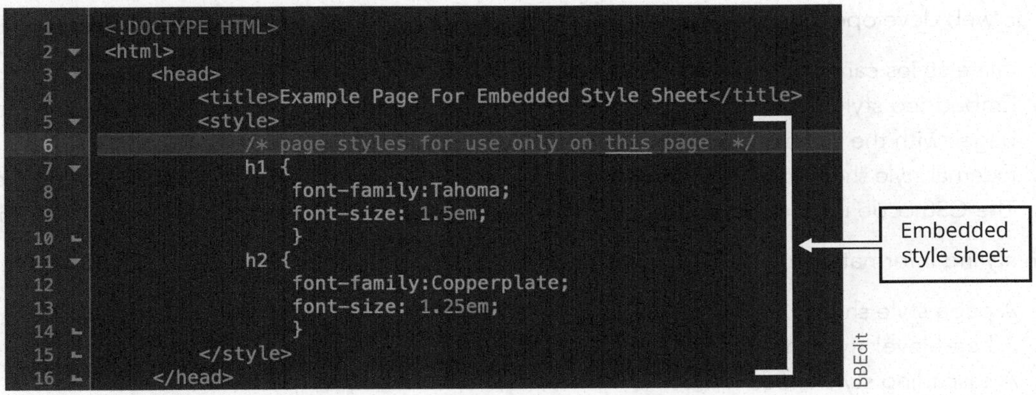

```
1    <!DOCTYPE HTML>
2    <html>
3        <head>
4            <title>Example Page For Embedded Style Sheet</title>
5            <style>
6                /* page styles for use only on this page  */
7                h1 {
8                    font-family:Tahoma;
9                    font-size: 1.5em;
10                   }
11               h2 {
12                   font-family:Copperplate;
13                   font-size: 1.25em;
14                   }
15           </style>
16       </head>
```

Embedded
style sheet

BBEdit

The fundamental problem with inline styles and embedded style sheets is that they don't provide a single, uniform location to store style information that spans multiple webpages in a website. To find where a specific HTML tag is being styled might mean looking through the HTML tags in the page, in the `<head>...</head>` section of the page, and in an **external style sheet**, which is a text file separate from the HTML files used to store all of the style information for a website. The best solution is to create one external style sheet for all the styling information to maintain consistency and simplicity.

The concept known as Don't Repeat Yourself is reflected in this approach. When you put your style information in a file separate from your HTML files, all of the HTML files can link to that style sheet. The common HTML elements in the pages like the header, menu, and footer can all use the same style information from the file. If you need to update a particular style, all of the webpages that use that style will show that update. This is strategic efficiency.

Common Mistakes

Style information is applied according to location. That is, whatever style is closest to the tag being styled is the winner in a conflict between differing styles. Inline styles override embedded styles, and embedded styles override external styles.

A style error can be created when a full stack developer receives new project requirements that fundamentally change the way a page is supposed to look and hurries to modify a page "just this once." Multiple developers can also introduce style errors if they are working on the same page and haven't agreed on a standard approach.

Style problems are difficult to diagnose and fix, especially when the code that makes up the CSS can be perfectly formatted and is not generating errors, but the browser is applying the style closest to the tag.

The best solution is to use a single, uniform approach to styling, which is most often a well-composed external style sheet with reader-friendly names for styles.

Quick Check 2-5

1. What is an inline style?

   a. A style declaration that lines up the HTML tags in the web browser for better visual flow
   b. A style declaration that ensures the list items in ordered and unordered lists align at the left side of the page
   c. A style declaration embedded in the HTML tag as an attribute
   d. A style declaration made inside the embedded style sheet in the `<head>`...`</head>` section of a webpage

2. Why do web developers discourage using inline styles?

   a. Inline styles cannot be reused without being repeated elsewhere in the page or website.
   b. Embedded style sheets accomplish the same thing as inline styles but are used to style multiple pages with the same code.
   c. External style sheets override the inline style if there is a conflict between duplicate HTML tag references.
   d. The CSS code in inline styles creates more errors than using embedded or external style sheets.

3. When styling information is included in the `<head>`...`</head>` section of a webpage, what is it called?

   a. A page style sheet
   b. A head-level style sheet
   c. A cascading style sheet
   d. An embedded or internal style sheet

1) c. Inline styles are written inside the HTML tag that they style. **2) a.** Inline styles are not reusable for any other tags in the same page or website and therefore break the Don't Repeat Yourself rule. **3) d.** Embedded or internal style sheets refer to CSS information stored in the `head` section of a webpage.

2.6 Using External Style Sheets

Most experienced web developers use an external style sheet for all styles, even for styling one unique tag or in rapid development use cases. External style sheets are preferred for functional and strategic efficiency reasons. From a functional perspective, you need to create style information somewhere. Writing it once and doing it right the first time in a central location makes for the greatest coding simplicity with the same amount of effort as creating an inline style or embedded style sheet.

To achieve strategic efficiency, a single style source in an external file follows the development philosophy of Don't Repeat Yourself. You can reuse or reapply a style stored in an external style sheet by linking to the external file from within the `head` element of each webpage in the site. Moreover, if you need to update that style, you update it in only one place. The updated style cascades down to all tags that use it across the entire breadth of the website.

Creating an External Style Sheet

To create an external style sheet, begin by creating a new plain text file in your text editor. Save it as my_styles.css inside the CSS folder that you created in your Samples folder. You specify this file location and file name when you create the link from your webpages to the external file. You could use a name other than my_styles.css as long as it has a .css file name extension.

Next, add the following CSS code to the my_styles.css file:

```css
/* page styles for sample exercises */


h1 {
    font-family: Tahoma;
    font-size: 1.5em;
}


h2 {
    font-family: Copperplate, "Copperplate Gothic";
    font-size: 1.25em;
}
```

Figure 2-14 shows the completed my_styles.css file.

Figure 2-14   The CSS code of an external style sheet, my_styles.css

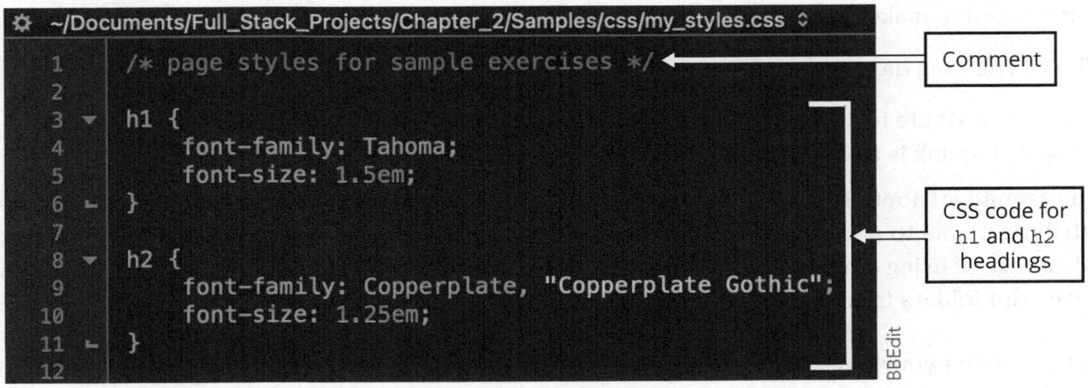

You may recognize the style information for the `h1` element in that first block of code, which you used previously in this chapter. There are subtle differences between how the external CSS code is written and how an inline style is composed, since the style definition is no longer an attribute of an HTML tag. The CSS properties are identical to those of the embedded or internal style sheet, however.

An external style sheet doesn't require the use of the opening and closing `<style>...</style>` tags like those in the HTML file, since the code appears in its own file and is not embedded between the `<head>...</head>` tags.

Examining the Cascading Style Sheet Syntax

The first line in Figure 2-14 is a comment. You can add your name, the date you created this file, and any other important information to a comment between the beginning and ending `/*...*/` delimiters. Comments provide information about the code or page to the person reading them. Browsers ignore the comments.

CSS code also uses white space to help people read the code. Each style declaration could actually be on one long line, similar to HTML. However, spaces between the elements in CSS are useful to identify where the logical blocks begin and end.

Also note that the text of an external style sheet is composed of property/value pairs contained in curly braces associated with an HTML element, also called a selector. Reading from the top down, the `h1` selector on line 3 in Figure 2-14 has a font family of Tahoma and a font size of 1.5 em. The `h2` selector on line 8 specifies the two font families of Copperplate and "Copperplate Gothic" with a font size of 1.25 em. The two font families are necessary to create the same appearance in browsers that support only one font or the other. Windows-based browsers will display "Copperplate Gothic" and Mac-based browsers will display the Copperplate font family. Though your webpages do not currently have any `h2` elements, you'll add them in the next section.

Adding a Reference to a Cascading Style Sheet

You've successfully created an external style sheet. It too is just a text file, similar to the HTML text files you've written. The browser creates the HTML Document Object Model (DOM) from the text of the HTML file. The CSS file will become the Cascading Style Sheet Object Model (CSSOM) and be incorporated into the web presentation once the browser combines the DOM and CSSOM. You just need to tell the browser where to find the CSS file.

Save a new copy of the index4.html page, naming it index5.html so you can make changes to a new page and see the difference between it and the previous index4.html.

To tell the browser to traverse the HTML DOM in the HTML file and apply the styles in the CSSOM, add a link to the my_styles.css file from your new index5.html page. Insert the code below on a new line after the `title` element and before the closing `</head>` tag. The code for the link is as follows:

```
<link rel="stylesheet" href="css/my_styles.css"/>
```

You add the `link` code to the `<head>...</head>` section of your webpage. The syntax of the `link` element is similar to other HTML tags, except without a closing tag. This is one of the rare HTML tags that is a **self-closing tag** or **void tag**, so you don't need an opening and a closing tag to complete the `link` element. You do need to include the slash at the end to make the tag self-closing. **Table 2-1** lists other self-closing tags.

The `<link>` tag has two attributes:

- The first attribute is the relationship type, abbreviated `rel`. The `rel="stylesheet"` attribute tells the browser the link is to a style sheet.

- The second attribute is the hypertext reference, abbreviated `href`. The `href="css/my_styles.css"` attribute points to a relative path from the current page to a folder (css) that contains a file (my_styles.css). The advantage of using a relative path is that you could move the folder containing the HTML pages and the css and javascript folders from one location to another and the link would still work.

Before saving your index5.html file and viewing it in the browser, remove the inline style information from the `<h1>...</h1>` tag pair so they are simple `<h1>...</h1>` tags in their original unstyled state: `<h1>A List of My Favorite Colors</h1>`. Right below the original `h1` element, add a new `<h2>...</h2>` tag set containing additional text such as the following: `<h2>This is just a test</h2>`.

Table 2-1   Self-closing or void HTML tags

Void element	Description
`<area/>`	Creates a geometric shape on an image used for links
`<base/>`	Creates an absolute link prefix for all relative links on a page
` `	Inserts a line break
`<col/>`	Creates a column reference in an HTML table
`<command/>`	Creates a command element in a web form
`<embed/>`	Includes external content such as videos
`<hr/>`	Inserts a horizontal rule
`<img/>`	Inserts a picture or graphic
`<input/>`	Includes a web form element to create input elements
`<keygen/>`	Includes a web form element to create a public/private key
`<link/>`	Links to a file outside the HTML page
`<meta/>`	Provides a header element for data about the webpage
`<param/>`	Provides a startup parameter for a plugin
`<source/>`	Specifies the source of an audio or video element
`<track/>`	Specifies the media track for audio or video elements
`<wbr/>`	Inserts a line break opportunity

The results will look like **Figure 2-15**.

Figure 2-15   An updated HTML page with a link to an external CSS file

```
1   <!DOCTYPE HTML>
2   <html>
3       <head>
4           <title>A More Complex Page</title>
5           <link rel="stylesheet" href="css/my_styles.css">
6       </head>
7       <body>
8           <h1>A List of My Favorite Colors</h1>
9           <h2> This is just a test </h2>
10          <ol>
```

Link to external style sheet

Inline style removed and new h2 element added

BBEdit

Save your changes then open the index5.html page in your web browser. If all is well, you should see no change to the h1 element compared to index4.html since the same style information is now in an external style sheet instead of stored inline. You should also see a new h2 element below the original h1 element. An example of the change is shown in **Figure 2-16**.

Figure 2-16   Webpage with new heading 2 text

A List of My Favorite Colors

THIS IS JUST A TEST

1. Green
   a. Chartreuse
   b. Emerald
   c. Sage
2. Red
3. Blue

Firefox

Common Mistakes

Note the `href` syntax in the link to a style sheet. You have seen the same syntax before when you created links between webpages. Those links were of the form shown in the following code snippet:

```
<a href="https://www.bbc.com/" target="_blank" title="A link to the BBC
News.">BBC News</a>
```

The a and `link` HTML elements are similar, but don't confuse them. Use the `<link>` tag in the `<head>`...`</head>` section of the webpage to create a link to an external style sheet. Use the `<a>` tag in the `<body>`...`</body>` section to create a visible link on a webpage.

Add the same `<link rel="stylesheet" href="css/my_styles.css"/>` element to your index1.html, index2.html, index3.html, and index4.html pages. Save those changes and open or refresh any of those pages. You should see a uniform set of `<h1>`...`</h1>` tags styled in each page. This is an illustration of the utility and power of using a single external style sheet for a multipage website.

The other component of strategic efficiency in this approach is that you can modify all of those pages with one change. For example, if you modified the h1 element in my_styles.css to a font size of 2em and saved that change, all five pages that use the one style sheet receive an update when you refresh them. That's strategic efficiency, in a nutshell.

Quick Check 2-6

1. What are comments in external style sheets used for?

   a. Anything the developer thinks a person would need to read to understand more about the purpose of the style sheet
   b. Creating CSS code that will be compiled when the external style sheet is published
   c. Creating the appropriate file name for a style sheet
   d. Adding links to the external CSS file

2. What is the difference between an embedded style sheet and an internal style sheet?

   a. Internal style sheets are written in the individual HTML tags, and embedded style sheets are written in the `<head>`...`</head>` section of the HTML page.
   b. Embedded style sheets are stored as files that are then embedded in the HTML code, and internal style sheets are saved inside the HTML page.
   c. Embedded style sheets are written inside the `<head>`...`</head>` section, and internal style sheets are written inside the `<body>`...`</body>` section.
   d. Nothing—these are two names for the same thing.

3. What does `href` stand for in the link to an external style sheet?

   a. HTML reference
   b. Hypertext reference
   c. HTML Referrer Enterprise Framework
   d. Hypertext Relational Entity Framework

1) a. Comments in code are used to provide information about the code or page to the web developer who is reading them. **2) d.** Different developers often refer to these by either name, but they both refer to a style in the `<head>`...`</head>` section of the webpage. **3) b.** The correct answer is hypertext reference.

2.7 Identifying Class and ID References

Not every `<h1>...</h1>` tag set in a website is identical. So far, you've applied styling information to all tags in all pages as if that were the case, but boring uniformity makes for boring websites. You need a way to describe two or more classes of `<h1>...</h1>` tags so that a website can show some interesting diversity. Fortunately, the `class` attribute and selector are intended for just this purpose.

Creating the Class Selector

In your external style sheet, you have a style for all instances of the `<h1>...</h1>` tag pair. It looks like the following code snippet:

```
h1 {
    font-family: Tahoma;
    font-size: 1.5em;
}
```

Suppose that style is fine for the main page of a website, but you want heading 1 text to appear with different formatting on the other pages. You need to describe two different versions, or classes, of the `<h1>...</h1>` tag set. You can create those versions by appending the **class selector** to the h1 style to create the two additional style definitions shown in the following code snippet:

```
h1.big {
    font-family: Tahoma;
    font-size: 2.5em;
    color: #000080;
}
h1.medium {
    font-family: "Times New Roman";
    font-size: 1.5em;
    color: #013220;
}
```

Figure 2-17 shows a completed version of this new file.

Figure 2-17   The completed style information for two class selectors

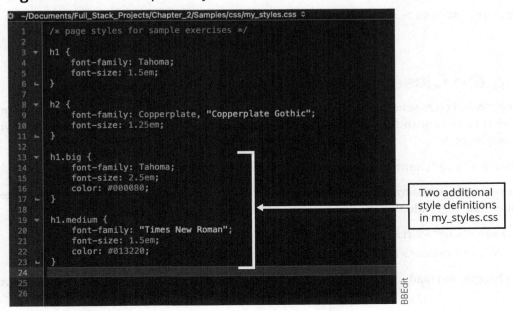

```
~/Documents/Full_Stack_Projects/Chapter_2/Samples/css/my_styles.css
1    /* page styles for sample exercises */
2
3    h1 {
4        font-family: Tahoma;
5        font-size: 1.5em;
6    }
7
8    h2 {
9        font-family: Copperplate, "Copperplate Gothic";
10       font-size: 1.25em;
11   }
12
13   h1.big {
14       font-family: Tahoma;
15       font-size: 2.5em;
16       color: #000080;
17   }
18
19   h1.medium {
20       font-family: "Times New Roman";
21       font-size: 1.5em;
22       color: #013220;
23   }
24
25
26
```

Two additional style definitions in my_styles.css

BBEdit

Complete that update, save your changes, and refresh the index5.html in your web browser. If nothing changes, you actually are successful since you haven't applied the new styles to your webpages yet.

Deconstructing the CSS code in the code snippet and Figure 2-17, you can see a dot or period followed by a class name appended to both of the h1 selectors. That syntax tells the browser to apply the style that follows (inside the curly braces) to any h1 element of the class big or medium.

Note	h1.big and h1.medium are not special class names. You could also use h1.frog and h1.toad or h1.aaa and h1.bbb with equal success. But you really shouldn't. Choosing a class name that is readable and self-descriptive is more helpful to the next developer who has to work with this code. Class names such as h1.large_green_heading and h1.small_blue_heading are more valuable and meaningful and will be appreciated by the next developer.

You shouldn't reuse HTML tag names like "small" or "sub" for your class names. The duplicate names will work in the webpage, but they might cause confusion. If you search for a list of all HTML tags, you can see a list of the names of the tags. It is a web development best practice to use unique self-descriptive class names that aren't already used as HTML tag names. |

The style declaration in the previous code snippet introduces additional details to unwrap. Each class includes a new color property with a specified **hexadecimal color** value. Hexadecimal color values are of the format #XXXXXX, with the first two Xs specifying the amount of red to use, the second two Xs specifying green, and the last two Xs specifying blue.

CSS often uses hexadecimal values for colors. The color chart of hexadecimal values offers far more variation than the previous use of "green," "red," and "blue." If you search for "hexadecimal color chart," you will find several useful color selection utilities, such as the color picker at https://htmlcolorcodes.com/color-picker/.

Next, notice that the font-family name in the second h1 style declaration is enclosed in quotation marks. Since the font name "Times New Roman" is more than one word, it needs to be enclosed in quotation marks.

Finally, the style declarations you added are associated specifically with an h1 element. However, you can also create a class for any HTML element by removing the first part of the selector that specified the HTML tag. For example, you can create the following class in your cascading style sheet and apply it to any valid HTML tag used anywhere in your website:

```
.big_blue_header {
    font-size: 3em;
    color: #000080;
}
```

Assigning the Class Attribute to an HTML Element

Now that you've created class selectors in your external style sheet, you need to add the class attribute to the HTML elements you want to paint with that style. Assigning a class attribute to an HTML element uses syntax similar to the following code snippet:

```
<h1 class="big">Heading Text</h1>
```

To use this new style, save any changes to your index5.html page, then save a new copy of it as index6.html. Below the h1 element of that page, add two h1 elements on new lines using the following code snippet:

```
<h1 class="big">This Is a Test of Big</h1>
<h1 class="medium">This Is Another Test of Medium</h1>
```

Save your changes and load index6.html in your browser. You should see a result like that in **Figure 2-18**.

Figure 2-18 Webpage with class attributes assigned to headings

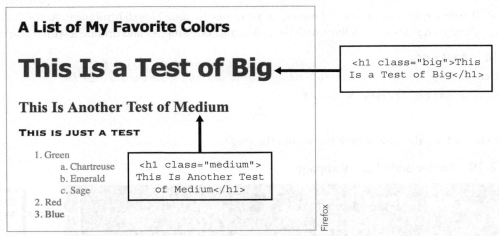

Creating the ID Selector

In addition to the class selector, you can use a more specific **ID selector**. Use class selectors to style more than one HTML element on the same page in the same way. Use ID selectors to style one element per page. These unique elements can be repeated on different pages, however.

For example, if each page on your website has a header and a footer (and of course, each page has only one header and one footer), you can use the ID attribute to style the header and footer. Logically, you wouldn't create a header class or footer class since there is only one of each on a page. You would use a header ID and a footer ID instead.

The syntax of an ID selector is similar to the class selector. It is reflected in the following code snippet:

```
#footer {
    font-size: .5em;
    color: #000080;
    text-align: center;
}
```

Add this code snippet to your my_styles.css file and save your changes. Refresh index6.html and, if nothing changes, you are successful. Since you haven't assigned the footer ID to any HTML element on your page yet, the style should not appear, nor should it break anything either.

> ## Common Mistakes

In the preceding paragraph, you were directed to make changes to a style sheet, save those changes, and then refresh your page. If nothing changed, that was a successful test. This is a type of incremental test that often helps to figure out why something that was working is no longer working after you save your changes.

The basic notion is to save early and often while making a series of small or incremental changes and testing after each change, rather than making all modifications, then testing. Since CSS selectors can override each other, finding and fixing a CSS error can be frustrating if you've made a long series of changes prior to testing again.

Assigning the ID Attribute to an HTML Element

After creating the ID selector for the `footer` element, add a footer to your index6.html page. At the bottom of the page, above the closing `</body>` tag, insert new lines with the following code snippet and update it with the appropriate values:

```
<div id="footer">
    Created by (your name) and copyright &copy; thereof. <br/>
    Last updated (today's date)
</div>
```

Figure 2-19 shows how the new footer fits within the page.

Figure 2-19   Footer added to a webpage

```
23     </ol>
24  ▼  <div id="footer">
25         Created by F. Max Coller and copyright &copy; thereof. <br/>
26         Last updated January 1, 2023
27     </div>
28   </body>
29 </html>
```

ID attribute assigned to `footer`

BBEdit

Save your changes and refresh the page in your browser. You should now see a page with a footer centered at the bottom like that in **Figure 2-20**.

Figure 2-20   Styled footer in the webpage

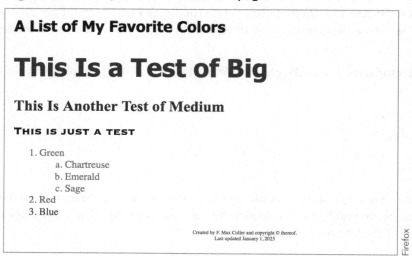

Recall that the `div` element defines a division or section in an HTML document—in this case, the footer section—and contains other HTML code, which you can style with CSS. The footer includes two additional features that have not previously been addressed. First, you can use special symbols in HTML. The code for many begins with the & symbol, as in `&copy;` for the copyright symbol. You can find other symbol codes by searching for "HTML symbols" using your favorite search engine.

Table 2-2 lists some HTML symbol codes.

Table 2-2   Some special symbols in HTML

Symbol	Character string	Description
©	`&copy;`	Copyright
®	`&reg;`	Registered trademark
€	`&euro;`	Euro currency
™	`&trade;`	Trademark
•	`&middot;`	Middle dot

Additionally, the `<br/>` tag creates a line break, or the equivalent of a return in a text editor. The `<br/>` tag is another self-closing or void HTML tag, so you don't need an opening and a closing tag to complete it. Include the slash at the end to make the tag self-closing. You can use two `<br/>` tags to move a block of text down the page by one blank line, although with some CSS styling on block-level elements, this isn't always necessary.

Using the ID and Class Selectors with HTML Tag Specifiers

Note that as with the class selector, it isn't necessary to use a specific HTML tag as a prefix for the ID selector, though it is helpful in certain circumstances. The syntax of the ID selector would be similar to the class selector, as in the following shortened snippet:

```
div#footer {...}
```

The code snippet tells the browser to find the `div` element that has the `id` of `footer`. Only that `div`, and no other HTML element with an `id` of `footer`, nor any other `div` element on the page, will have the style that follows the selector. This type of specificity is useful when a webpage has a unique instance of an HTML element like a `div` used as a footer or an `h2` with a different font size and font face from all of the other `h2` elements in the website.

Remember the general rule that the next developer who reads your code would appreciate more self-documenting help than less. Using the `element.class` syntax as in `h1.medium` or the `element#id` syntax as in `div#footer` in your CSS helps the next person know the purpose of a CSS selector by looking at it.

Note | Class and ID selectors have different syntaxes and different use cases. A mnemonic to recall these differences is that the # sign that starts the ID selector is also used for numbers, and the number of times you can use an HTML element with an ID style attribute in a webpage is one.

Quick Check 2-7

1. What is the difference between a class selector and an ID selector in a cascading style sheet?

   a. The class selector uses curly braces and the ID selector uses square brackets.

   b. The class selector starts with parentheses and the ID selector starts with curly braces.

   c. The class selector is indented three spaces and the ID selector is not indented.

   d. The class selector begins with a period and the ID selector begins with a pound symbol.

2. Is `.tiny` a good choice for a class name?

   a. No, because it is not descriptive enough to be helpful to the next developer.

   b. No, because `tiny` is a reserved word in HTML.

   c. No, because `.tiny` won't create the correct size of text in the HTML page.

   d. No, because `tiny` can only be used for ID selectors.

3. Why can't you use an ID selector more than once in a webpage?

   a. Because the web browser has a unique counter and the number of the ID elements in the DOM and CSSOM have to match

   b. Because that's what the ID selector is designed for—creating a style applied to one unique part of the DOM in a webpage.

   c. Because once an ID number is used, the page needs to be refreshed to use it again

   d. Because ID selectors can only be used with inline styles

1) d. The ID selector begins with a # symbol, which is helpful to remember the difference since the ID can be used only one time in a webpage. **2) a.** The class name `.tiny` is not descriptive enough to be a good choice, but something like `.tiny_footer_text` is. **3) b.** The purpose of an ID in CSS is to create a unique style for a single element on a webpage like a header or footer.

Summary

- Learning full stack web development begins with using a simple text editor.

- Creating a proper folder structure to hold webpages is an investment in organization.

- Storing files in the cloud is safer for file retention and backups than storing files on a local hard drive.

- Version control software is useful to create date/time-stamped backups of code under development.

- HTML pages are composed of tags and content such as text. The tags tell the browser how to present the content.

- HTML tags are nested inside the page structure. White space is used to show the nesting level of the tags.

- The `<head>...</head>` tags contain information for the browser. The `<body>...</body>` tags contain the webpage content displayed in the browser.

- Links in webpages are what makes the Internet work as a web. Links can be absolute or relative. Absolute links include a full file path, but relative links contain a shortened path describing how to get to the other file on the same computer from the current file.

- Attributes, with a name and a value, add information to an HTML tag to tell the browser how to perform tasks.

- HTML provides three kinds of lists: ordered, unordered, and description. Lists can be nested inside each other.

- You can modify the appearance of HTML elements by applying style attributes, such as font family, color, and size, in an inline style declaration, an embedded style sheet, or an external style sheet.

- Inline styles modify specific tags to change the appearance of the contents from the default style of the browser.

- Embedded or internal style sheets are stored in the `<head>...</head>` section of a webpage to modify HTML tags in the same page.

- External style sheets are stored as separate text files of style information that webpages link to. External style sheets are the best practice for storing style information in web development projects, since they maximize strategic efficiency and uphold the rule of Don't Repeat Yourself.

- CSS class selectors modify more than one element on the same page in the same way.

- CSS ID selectors modify one element on each webpage but can be reused on a different webpage in the same site to create uniformity between pages.

Key Terms

absolute links

attribute name

attribute value

attributes

block-level elements

class selector

cloud storage

comment

containership

description lists

em units

embedded style sheet

external style sheet

hexadecimal color

ID selector

inline style

internal style sheet

list item

nested

ordered lists

relative links

relative size

self-closing tag

unordered lists

version control

void tag

what you see is what you get
  (WYSIWYG)

Review Questions

1. What benefits does using version control software like Git have over other, simpler forms of file storage? What are the drawbacks of using Git? (2.1)

2. What is the difference between Git and GitHub? (2.1)

   a. Git is hosted on cloud servers and used for the code repository, and GitHub is installed and used on a web developer's local computer.

   b. Git is used on a web developer's computer to keep track of versions and send files to and retrieve files from the code repository on the GitHub cloud servers.

   c. Git is a web application and GitHub is an open source software project.

   d. There is no difference—they are just two different names for the same software package.

3. Why is code indenting, or white space, important in HTML? (2.2)

4. What are attributes in HTML tags? (2.3)

   a. The text of the name of the tag itself, like `title` or `h1`

   b. The text that appears between the opening and closing HTML tags

   c. The text after the equal sign in an HTML tag set

   d. The text in the tag after the tag name and a space that adds name/value pairs of modifiers to the tag

5. What is the most common source of broken links in HTML? (2.3)

6. What are the attributes of an ordered list used for? (2.4)

   a. Change the default start value or type

   b. Change the default starting tag name

   c. Change the default indent spacing

   d. Change the ordered list into an unordered or definition list

7. When should you use an inline style? (2.5)

   a. Rarely, and then only for single unique elements

   b. For repeated elements on different webpages in the same website

   c. When creating an external style sheet would take too much time or work

   d. When you are the only full stack developer of a webpage and nobody else will need to work on it

8. Why do most web developers prefer to use external style sheets for all styling information? (2.5)

9. What is the proper syntax for creating a link to an external style sheet? (2.6)

   a. `<stylesheet rel="link" href="css/my_styles.css"/>`

   b. `<a rel="stylesheet" href="css/my_styles.css"/>`

   c. `<a href="css/my_styles.css">stylesheet</a>`

   d. `<link rel="stylesheet" href="css/my_styles.css"/>`

10. What is the difference in usage and text between a class selector and an ID selector in HTML and CSS? (2.7)

11. What are self-closing HTML tags? (2.3)

    a. Tags that automatically generate a closing tag when the web developer creates the opening tag

    b. Tags that close any open tags used before them in the HTML code

    c. Tags that don't require an opening and a closing tag but instead have the closing slash at the end of the tag

    d. Shortened singular tags used by web developers who don't choose to follow the rule of including both an opening and a closing tag for their HTML elements

Programming Exercises

1. Using your text editor, create a well-formatted webpage with the following elements and content:

   a. A page title

   b. An h1 heading

   c. A 10-item description list from the key terms in this chapter:
      - A definition of each term in your own words based on web research
      - A link from each of those terms to a source you found on the web for that term definition

   d. A file name of key_terms.html (2.1–2.4)

2. Using your text editor, create a well-formatted webpage with the following elements and content:

   a. A page title

   b. An h1 heading

   c. An ordered list of the four major eras in the geology of the earth

   d. An unordered list nested inside each of the four eras containing five common life forms

   e. A link from each item in the ordered list to a relevant webpage you found when searching

   f. A file name of geologic_eras.html (2.1–2.4)

3. Using your text editor, create a well-formatted webpage with the following elements and content:

   a. A page title

   b. An h1 heading

   c. An ordered list of the outer categories of HTML, CSS, Browsers, and Etc

   d. An unordered list inside each item of the ordered list containing at least three useful links you find in your research on the topics presented in this chapter

   e. A file name of full_stack_research.html (2.1–2.7)

4. Research the "10 most useful" or "10 most commonly used" HTML tags. Using your text editor, create a well-formatted webpage with an example of each of those tags. Include a link to the page or pages you found on the web while doing your research. (2.1–2.4)

Projects

1. Using a text editor and the HTML tags that you've learned so far in this chapter, create a well-formatted resumé webpage named resume.html that documents your current skills and abilities. Include at least one each of the following:

   a. `<title>...</title>` tag

   b. `<h2>...</h2>` tag

   c. `<ul>...</ul>` tag

   d. `<li>...</li>` tag

   e. `<br/>` tag

   f. Plain text

   g. An external style sheet named resume.css with the following types of styles:
      - A font family
      - A font size
      - An ID (2.1–2.7)

2. Using a text editor and the HTML tags that you've learned so far in this chapter, create a sample three-page website for a new business that you or someone you know might want to start. You can also create the start to www.totallyawesomestuff.com page and advertise low-fat candy for goldfish.

To complete this project, you need to include the following:

    a. A home page named index.html

    b. An About Us page named about.html

    c. A products or details page named products.html

    d. Appropriate headers and footers on each page

    e. A horizontal menu under the header composed of short links and a middot symbol as a menu item separator

    f. An external style sheet named psf.css that all three pages use

    g. A page title for each page (2.1–2.7)

3. Using a text editor and the HTML tags that you've learned so far in this chapter, create a well-formatted webpage named boring.html that will win an award for the World's Most Boring Webpage. Include at least one each of the following:

    a. `<title>...</title>` tag

    b. `<h1>...</h1>` tag

    c. `<h2>...</h2>` tag

    d. `<ul>...</ul>` tag

    e. `<li>...</li>` tag

    f. `<br/>` tag

    g. 100 characters of plain text

    h. An external style sheet named boring.css with the following:

        • A font family

        • A font size

        • Two different ID selectors used in the HTML (2.1–2.7)

Chapter 3

HTML and CSS: Page Layout and Content

Learning Objectives

When you complete this chapter, you will be able to:

3.1 Build an HTML menu from an unordered list styled by CSS

3.2 Incorporate images into the contents of a website

3.3 Add videos to a website

3.4 Create an HTML table for a webpage

3.5 Create the style for an HTML table

3.6 Build an HTML form to gather user data from a webpage

3.1 Creating a Menu with HTML and CSS

With a few notable exceptions such as www.google.com, most websites have a menu to help users navigate the pages of the site and find the content they are looking for. The purpose of a menu is to summarize the website contents in a series of links to the pages in the site. Navigation is one of the first things visitors notice about the **user experience** of a website when they encounter a webpage, so you need to spend time designing a good navigational structure. The user experience of a site is the overall impression or emotion created by the site, including the look and feel, color scheme, navigation, fonts, and information presented.

> **Note**
>
> Users expect to find menus in one of two places on a webpage. Horizontal menus appear near the top of the page above or below the header, and vertical menus appear in the left margin of the page. It can be helpful to your users to add links in the footer of a page, but you should not use the footer menu as the primary navigation structure.
>
> Menu placement is not a formal World Wide Web Consortium (W3C), HTML, or Internet rule but rather a convention that has become accepted as standard practice over the years. Unorthodox menu placement as an expression of creativity confuses the user and creates obstacles to site navigation.
>
> If your website users can't easily find what they are looking for on your site, they will find another site that is more user friendly.

Designing a User-Friendly Menu

Before you start writing the code to create your menu, you need to document what your menu will contain and how users will interact with it. If you have a small website with three pages, for example, your menu will contain only three links to those pages. However, if the site has more than a few pages, you need to consider how to group your pages into an intuitive menu of similar items.

Consider the following guidelines in the design of your navigation menu:

- A user should be able to reach any content in your site in three clicks or less.
- The navigation structure and placement should be consistent across a website, although the home page can be different from the rest of the pages.
- Menu items can be links to pages (if you have a limited number of pages) or links to sub-menus (if you have a lot of pages organized by theme or category) but you shouldn't overwhelm the user with excessive options at any one time.
- Menu item text should be simple and self-descriptive, like Home, Products, and About Us.
- A search feature on or near the menu is helpful for complex or multipage sites.

Next time you encounter a new site or visit a familiar site, note the grouping of menu items by feature, content, theme, or logic. A well-designed and user-friendly menu takes a lot of planning to make it appear simple and functional.

Starting the Page Build

When HTML5 was introduced in 2014, its new tags included an acknowledgment that many websites contain a similar structure:

- Header across the top
- Navigation at the left or the top
- Content pane on the right taking up most of the screen
- Footer at the bottom

Web developers had been using generic HTML tags such as `<div>` and `<span>` to create this structure. Some had resorted to using `<table>` tags to create a page grid structure despite its accessibility and maintenance problems. The release of HTML5 introduced new tags specifically to address these common elements. The bare-bones structure of a page using these tags can be seen in **Figure 3-1**.

If you have not done so already, create a Chapter_3 folder with subfolders for Exercises, Projects, and Samples. Using your simple text editor, type the following code (also shown in Figure 3-1) into a new file and save it in your Chapter_3\Samples folder as index.html. Update the code to include your name, the date, and the current year.

Figure 3-1 The starting HTML code for the Chapter 3 webpages

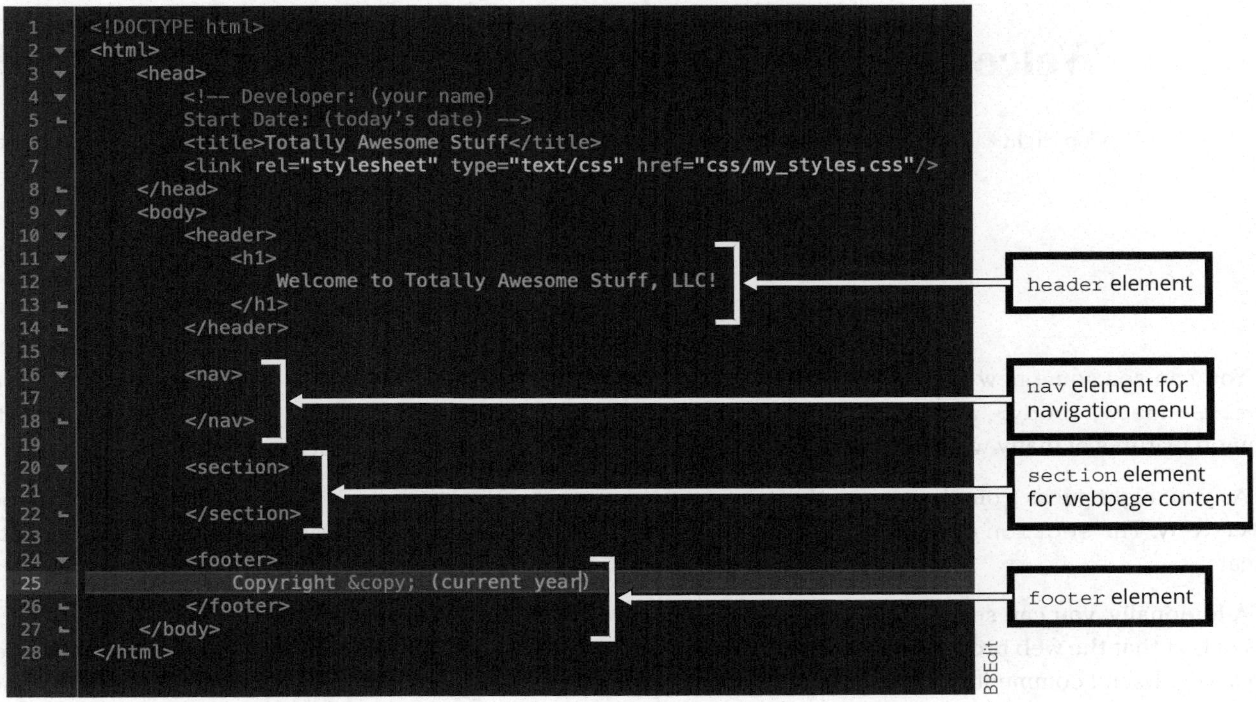

```html
<!DOCTYPE html>
<html>
    <head>
        <!-- Developer: (your name)
        Start Date: (today's date) -->
        <title>Totally Awesome Stuff</title>
        <link rel="stylesheet" type="text/css" href="css/my_styles.css"/>
    </head>
    <body>
        <header>
            <h1>
                Welcome to Totally Awesome Stuff, LLC!
            </h1>
        </header>
        <nav>
        </nav>
        <section>
        </section>
        <footer>
            Copyright &copy; 2023
        </footer>
    </body>
</html>
```

Save your changes and open the page in a web browser. The webpage should look like the one in **Figure 3-2**.

Figure 3-2 The initial webpage

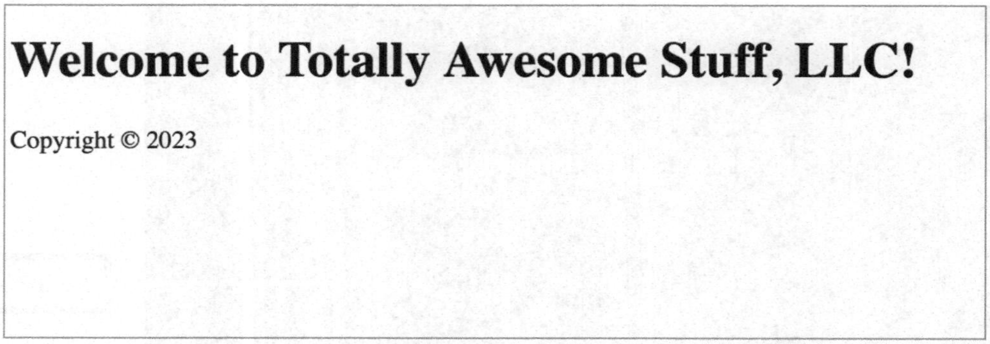

Welcome to Totally Awesome Stuff, LLC!

Copyright © 2023

You can see some new tags mixed in with the usual HTML tags that you have used previously. The standard `<html>`, `<head>`, `<body>`, and `<title>` tags remain. The new tags between the `<body>`...`</body>` tags reflect the common features of many webpages—the `<header>`, `<nav>`, `<section>`, and `<footer>` tags.

As you might guess from the names, these new tags are used for the header, navigation, page section, and footer, respectively. The `section` element is used for the large pane in the middle of the page where the primary contents appear.

Additionally, you can see an HTML comment starting on line 4 in Figure 3-1 and ending on line 5. These are two lines of text that the web browser ignores when rendering the page. The HTML comment begins with a `<!--` and ends with a `-->`. Useful comments contain author names, creation and/or last-updated dates, and other pieces of information that might be helpful for the next developer to know about the webpage.

Constructing a Menu

Inside the `<nav>`...`</nav>` tags, use the following code to add an unordered list along with the list items for each of the menu items and a link to the other pages you will soon be creating:

```
<ul>
    <li>
        <a href="index.html">Home</a>
    </li>
    <li>
        <a href="products.html">Products</a>
    </li>
    <li>
        <a href="about.html">About Us</a>
    </li>
</ul>
```

This is an unordered list with three list items, each containing a link to a webpage in the site you are building. Save your changes. Save two more copies of this webpage, one as products.html and the other as about.html, in the same folder as index.html. Open or refresh your page in your browser to see a page that looks like **Figure 3-3**.

This is almost a good menu, but for now remains just a bulleted list of links. Test the links in all three pages. You should be able to switch from any of the three pages to another page in the site.

This menu is functional but very plain. You can transform this into a true menu with some CSS, which you will do in the next section.

Figure 3-3 Unordered list as the starting webpage menu

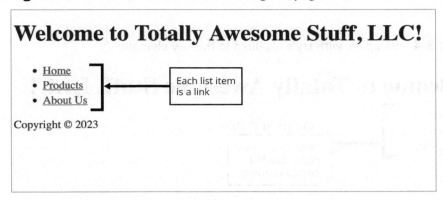

Styling an Unordered List Menu

The next step in constructing this website and menu is to add some serious styling to it. Create a new text file and save it as my_styles.css inside a css folder in your Chapter_3/Samples folder. While you are not required to have a css folder inside your root folder, it does help keep your contents organized and make individual files easier to find. It will also make the link that you created in the `<head>`...`</head>` section functional.

Add the following contents to my_styles.css, replacing "(your name)" with your first and last names and replacing "(today's date)" with the current date:

```
/* Created by (your name) on (today's date) */
/* Set the height of the body and html to 100% */
html, body {
    height: 100%;
}
/* Display HTML5 structural elements as blocks */
footer, header, section, nav {
    display: block;
}
```

The first two lines are CSS comments like those you have used previously.

The third line sets the height of the `<html>` and `<body>` elements to the full height of the screen, even if the content in the page is less than that. This becomes important to keep the footer at the bottom of the screen.

Following the next comment is a style declaration that begins with a comma-separated list of all of the elements that will be styled by the contents between the curly braces. In this case, the `footer`, `header`, `section`, and `nav` elements will be displayed as block-level elements.

Block-level elements make a space for themselves that other elements can't also occupy in a webpage. So, for example, the header will span the entire top of the page and move the `nav` and `section` elements down the page by an amount equal to its height.

Next, add some style to the unordered list that contains the menu items. Add the following code to my_styles.css:

```
/* Style for the nav element */
nav {
    width: 200px;
    float: left;
    margin-right: 10px;
    margin-top: -35px;
}
```

Save your changes then refresh the webpage in your browser. You should now have a page that looks like **Figure 3-4**.

Figure 3-4   Webpage with styles applied to the nav element

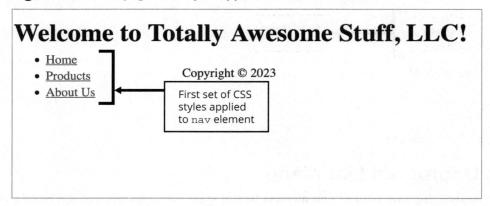

At this stage, the webpage in development looks a little worse than it did before, but that's to be expected. The footer text has moved up and is now intruding over the top of the content section because that's exactly what the float: left; style for the nav element told the browser to do. When you float an element to the left, the other elements flow around it, even the block-level elements like the footer. You will fix this in the near future.

The nav style includes the following four properties:

- The width property specifies how wide the block should be—in this case, 200 pixels.

- The float property tells the browser to move the nav element as far to the left as it can while keeping it at the same place vertically.

- The margin-right property creates 10 pixels of space to the right of the block, which is 10 pixels beyond the 200 pixels defined in the width property.

- The negative margin-top property moves the menu 35 pixels over the top of the block-level space of the header. This is actually about the same amount of space an unordered list normally creates in a page to separate itself from the rest of the page contents, so you just moved the menu up directly below the header where it belongs.

The unordered list still looks like a standard bulleted list and needs to look like a menu instead. Add the following code to the end of your CSS file to start to change the appearance:

```
nav ul {
    background-color: rgb(175,175,175);
    line-height: 2em;
    list-style-type: none;
    padding-left: 0px;
    text-indent: 5px;
    border-radius: 5px;
}
```

Notice the ul selector in that block of styling information. Since you might have other unordered lists in your website, you want this style to apply only to the unordered list in the nav element. The selector in the new CSS code, read from the curly brace to the left, tells the browser to apply this style only to a ul element that occurs inside the nav element. In other words, this style will apply only to the navigation menu.

The new CSS styles have the following effects:

- The `background-color: rgb(175,175,175);` property sets gray as the background color for the entire unordered list using the `rgb` specifier. This is the amount of red, green, and blue to use, similar to the hexadecimal color specification. RGB values fall in the range 0–255 for each color. If you search online for "RGB Color Chart," you can find examples of other colors that might work better for your site than the gray used in this tutorial. You are also encouraged to customize any of the color choices in this tutorial.

- The `line-height` property describes to the browser how tall to make each list item that contains a link in the menu. In this case, `2em` is the height of two capital letter *M*s, or about twice the height of the menu link text.

- The `list-style-type` property modifies the unordered list, with `none` meaning that no bullets should accompany the text. This property transforms a regular unordered list into an organized stack of textual elements that make up a menu.

- The `padding-left` value of `0` means that the unordered list contains no extra space. The individual list items will start just inside the left side of the margin for that element instead of indented as they would be if they were still bulleted.

- The `text-indent` value of `5px` indents the text of the unordered list items by 5 pixels, so the list doesn't start at the left margin but a smidge inside of that. The reason you didn't just use the `padding` property to accomplish this will become apparent in a future modification.

- Finally, for a polishing touch, the `border-radius` value is set to `5px`. This creates the rounded corners that make a menu look softer and more user friendly instead of the default square and blocky.

> **Note**
>
> The stylistic elements in this section of the chapter are being introduced as completed blocks of code for efficiency. If you want to test what each line does, you can "comment out" a line using a CSS comment. For example, to remove the background color from the style block for the nav ul selector, change the text to the following:
>
> ```
> /* background-color: rgb(175,175,175); */
> ```
>
> Save your changes and refresh the page. The menu should revert to a white background. If you prefer the gray background, restore the code by removing the beginning /* and ending */.

Adding Style to the List Items in the Menu

The next set of styles to add are applied to the individual list items in the menu. Add the following code to the end of your CSS file, save your changes, and then view the results in your refreshed webpage:

```
nav ul li:hover {
    background-color: rgb(148,51,62);
    border-radius: 5px;
}
```

If you see no changes when you refresh your page, then you have done everything correctly. Move your pointer over the top of the menu to change the background color of the menu item as in **Figure 3-5**.

This style uses what is known as the CSS `:hover` **pseudo-class** to create an effect only when the pointer hovers over a specific element. A pseudo-class is one that only exists when the element is in a conditional state, such as when the pointer is moved over it. This is different from a regular CSS class, which is used to modify the appearance or position of one or more HTML elements in the same way from the time they are rendered in the browser.

Figure 3-5 The menu after adding the `nav ul li:hover` style

Note the chain of selectors in `nav ul li:hover` that go into creating this effect. Reading from the inside out, or right to left, this declaration styles list items that are hovered over by the pointer, contained in an unordered list, and inside the nav section. Whew!

The two style elements are similar to those you've created elsewhere: a change of the background color and a border radius for the individual list item. The effect, however, is to create a menu that looks dynamic and still remains accessible to users who are having the page read to them by a screen reader or smart device.

Adding Style to the Links in the Menu

The last step of building the menu is to change the color of the menu text from the default the browser uses (usually blue and underlined) to a color that provides greater visual contrast. The following is the code used to accomplish this effect:

```
nav ul li a {
    color: rgb(255,255,0);
    font-weight: bold;
    text-decoration: none;
}
```

First, note the `nav ul li a` selector in this block of code. This style will apply only to `<a>` tags inside `<li>` tags that are inside of `<ul>` tags that are inside of the `<nav>` section of the webpage. That's another complex selector.

However, using such a specific selector is helpful to the next developer since this style will only be found and applied using that chain. For the browser, a simpler selector would work equally well. An example of that simpler selector would look like the following:

```
nav a { ...
```

This selector is not as descriptive as the longer one in the previous example. For a few extra keystrokes, it is significantly easier for you and other developers to see what the full path of the style is meant to apply to.

The style declaration contains the following two new elements:

- In the `font-weight` property, the `bold` attribute increases the thickness of the letters that make up the text in the `<a>` tag for greater visibility.

- In the `text-decoration` property, the `none` attribute removes the underline that the browser normally adds to links.

Save all of your changes, then refresh the page in your browser. The menu should look like the one in **Figure 3-6** when you move the pointer over a menu option.

Figure 3-6   The finished menu

Quick Check 3-1

1. How are HTML comments formatted?

    a. HTML comments start with `/*` and end with `*/`

    b. HTML comments start with `<!` and end with `!>`

    c. HTML comments start with `<!--` and end with `-->`

    d. HTML comments start with `<*` and end with `*>`

2. What does the style declaration `display: block;` do for an HTML tag?

    a. Tells the browser to show the tag and its contents in a grid of blocks like cells in a table

    b. Tells the browser to give the tag its own space on the webpage from one side of the page to the other

    c. Tells the browser to place the tag horizontally on the same line with the other tags in the page

    d. Tells the browser to display the tag with a block border

3. What is a pseudo-class in CSS?

    a. A CSS selector that will exist only in a temporary state such as when the user interacts with the website

    b. A CSS class that is created by the web developer and not normally included as part of the standard CSS

    c. A CSS selector that pretends to be a class but is actually an ID selector

    d. A CSS selector that works as a placeholder pointing to an actual class

1) c. HTML comments begin with `<!--` and end with `-->`. **2) b.** The `display: block;` declaration makes space for the HTML tag from one side of the page to the other. **3) a.** Pseudo-classes are used for creating user-interactive elements that change with user activity.

3.2 Embedding Images

Even if the website you are building isn't selling artistic pictures of cityscapes taken at night through rain-covered panes of glass (or, for that matter, adorable pictures of cats), adding images to your webpages is another crucial part of creating an engaging user experience. Appropriately sized and positioned images make a website more visually interesting than a plain-text website.

Coding the Image Tag

The code for adding an image to a website is similar to the code for adding other pieces of external content. You use the `<img>` HTML tag with attributes to specify information about the image such as the file path.

If necessary, create a new folder inside your Chapter_3 folder and call it images. Save the file splash_screen.png inside that images folder. Your website will still work if you do not create the images folder and store the website images in that folder. However, it is easier to maintain a website with organized contents in well-named folders than it is to have all of the files in one large folder.

Open the index.html file if you don't already have it open, and add the following code between the empty `<section>`…`</section>` tags:

```
<img id="home_page_img" src="images/splash_screen.png" alt="An image containing
    About Us, Our Products, and Causes We Care About images."/>
```

The `<img>` tag tells the browser to create the space for an image on the HTML page, and the `id` attribute uniquely names this image tag in the index.html page. The browser then retrieves the file specified after the `src=` code. In the new code, this is specified by a relative path to a folder called `images` containing a file named `splash_screen.png`.

The `alt` attribute is used to display the text shown on the screen if the image doesn't load due to an incorrect file path. Screen readers also use the `alt` text to describe the image to a person listening to the page contents being read to them, so you must include it.

Note that the `<img>` tag is self-closing; there is no such thing as a closing `</img>` tag. Save your changes and refresh the page in your browser. If you have everything right, you should see an oversized image that takes up too much of the page.

If you see a blank image placeholder with the text of the `alt` attribute, the path to your image file isn't working. This can be due to the file not being found in the images folder or a misspelling in the text of the path itself.

| Note | An image is a picture is a graphic is an image, right? Nope. Some image types work better on the web than others because browsers are built to handle those specific image types. **Table 3-1** lists the image types that standards-compliant browsers can render properly. You can find images in other formats, but those images should be converted using an application like Adobe Photoshop before being incorporated into a website. |

Table 3-1 Common file formats for webpage images

File extension	File type description
.apng	Animated Portable Network Graphics
.cur	Cursor file format for Microsoft Windows
.gif	Graphics Interchange Format
.ico	Icon file format for Microsoft Windows
.jfif	JPEG File Interchange Format
.jpg, .jpeg	Joint Photographic Experts Group
.pjpeg, .pjp	Progressive JPEG
.png	Portable Network Graphics
.svg	Scalable Vector Graphics

Resizing Images

The image provided for the splash screen is purposefully oversized since you are likely to encounter oversized images in your work as a web developer. This problem has two solutions, and you may need to employ both of them to make your webpage work.

The first solution is to resize the image using image-editing software such as Adobe Photoshop. The resized image has smaller dimensions that are closer to the target size for the screen resolution you are testing. Additionally, it will be a smaller file in terms of storage and transfer size, so it will be faster to load over a slow network.

The second solution is to use style information to make the image appear in a specific size in the page. This is often necessary even when the image has been resized with image-editing software to make the image fit with the rest of the contents of the webpage. Additionally, specifying an image size in the CSS code allows for greater control over the flow of the page contents.

It is better to have an image that is slightly larger than its container than to try to make a smaller image larger with CSS. Making a small image appear larger may result in images that are grainy or pixelated.

You need to downsize the splash_screen.png image supplied for this chapter using styling to make the image fit the containing `<section>...</section>` element on the page. Add the following style declaration to the end of my_styles.css:

```
/* Style for the home page image */
section img#home_page_img {
    width: 560px;
    height: 400px;
}
```

As in other style declarations, notice the selector. Only images inside the `section` element with an `id` of home_page_img will be styled with this information.

The other two properties are straightforward, specifying the width (560 pixels) and height (400 pixels) of the image. Save your CSS file and your HTML page and refresh the webpage in your browser. You should now see an image like that in **Figure 3-7**.

Figure 3-7   The home page with the image added to the `section` element

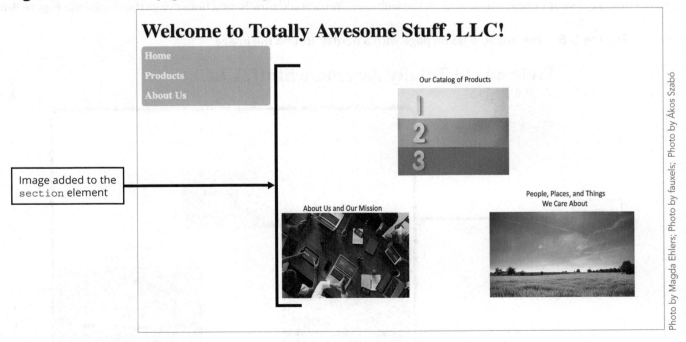

Photo by Magda Ehlers; Photo by fauxels; Photo by Ákos Szabó

Adding an Image Border

A border is one addition to an image that can significantly improve the user experience of a webpage. A border helps define the boundaries of the image so the user can more easily distinguish the image from the rest of the page. A border also makes the image look purposeful instead of added as an afterthought.

To add a border to your images, add the following code to your my_styles.css file:

```
/* General image styles */
.img_border {
    padding: 5px;
    margin: 5px;
    border-style: solid;
    border-color: rgb(175,175,175) rgb(200,200,200);
    background-color: black;
    border-radius: 20px;
}
```

This declaration will create a CSS class that can be applied to any of the images in the website. The `border-style` property is used to create a solid border, and the `border-color` property is used to create two shades of color for borders: dark gray and light gray. The first color is applied to the top and bottom of the image, and the second color is applied to the sides. The `background-color` of black fills in the space created by the `padding` property to add an image-matting effect—a border within the border. As with the menu, the `border-radius` property softens the corners, but this time with a larger radius to make the effect more pronounced on a larger rectangle.

Next, add the `.img_border` class to the `<img>` tag on your index.html page. The code snippet for that is as follows:

```
class="img_border"
```

You can type this new attribute anywhere within the `<img>` tag as long as you include a space before and after the class code. Save your changes then refresh the webpage. You should now have a home page that looks like **Figure 3-8**.

Figure 3-8   The updated home page with a border around the image

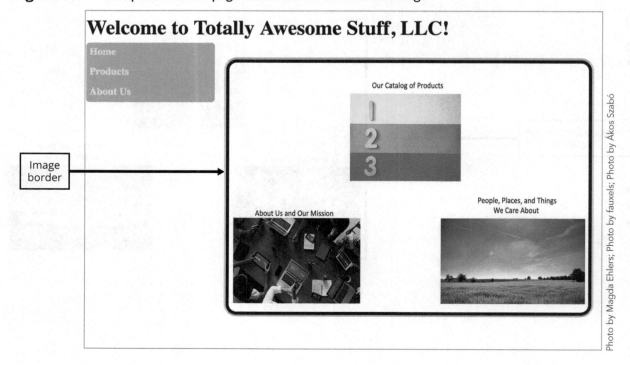

Creating Image Maps

The image you just added to the home page of totallyawesomestuff.com has three distinct components or areas. Each area could serve as a clickable region that would lead to another page. An **image map** creates another way for a user to navigate on a website, although it doesn't replace a site menu. The image map creates links to other webpages in specified shapes inside the image.

To create the image map, add the following code to the `<section>`...`</section>` area after the `<img>` tag:

```
<map name="home_page_map">
    <area shape="rect" coords="10,220,220,385" alt="About Us" href="about.html"/>
    <area shape="rect" coords="180,5,380,200" alt="Our Products" href="products
        .html"/>
    <area shape="rect" coords="370,220,570,385" alt="Causes We Support"
        href="causes.html"/>
</map>
```

This code creates an image map that can be applied to an image. The `name` attribute in the `map` element uniquely identifies the map so the `usemap` property added to an image can tell the browser which map to use for a specific image.

The three `<area>` tags in the `map` element each define a different clickable region. The parameters of an `<area>` tag include the `shape`, the upper-left and lower-right `coords` or coordinates (for rectangular shapes, in this case), and an `alt` attribute to display text to the user. Other values for the `shape` attribute include `default` to use the entire image, `circle` to create a circular region, and `poly` to create a polygon.

The `coords` attribute of the `area` element is defined in relation to the upper-left corner of the image, which has the coordinates 0,0. For the first area, this means the upper-left corner of rectangle will be 10 pixels in from the left margin and 220 pixels down from the top margin, and the lower-right corner will be 220 pixels in from the left margin and 385 pixels down from the top margin.

Update your `<img>` tag to include the `usemap` attribute pointing to the new image map, using the following code sample as a guide:

```
<img ... usemap="#home_page_map" ...
```

Save your changes and refresh your index.html page. You should see no change to the appearance of the page, but you should now be able to click the three graphics inside the larger image and open the page that corresponds to that graphic. Note that the causes.html page doesn't yet exist; you build it later in this chapter.

Common Mistakes

Just because it is possible to make your site navigation in an image map doesn't mean you should. For people using screen readers or text-based browsers, your site will become a single page without audible or text links. Image maps should supplement text-based site navigation rather than be the primary source of navigation.

Using Images Wisely

Following are rules and guidelines for using images in a website. First the rules:

1. Only use images that you have taken yourself or paid someone for. Do not copy and paste images from the Internet, as those are likely someone else's copyright-protected property.
2. Always add `alt` text to image tags in the HTML document that describe what the picture contains for a person who can't see the image.

3. Don't make your entire site out of images. Well-constructed sites are made up of text with images to supplement the text, not the reverse.

4. Don't make critical parts of your site such as menus out of images. Screen readers can only read the text of the `alt` tag, and text-based browsers don't show images. If important information or contents in your site are only located in images, some users won't be able to access any of your content.

Guidelines for using images wisely on a website include:

1. Size your images carefully. Large images overwhelm page content and slow your site down.

2. Add text descriptions or captions to your images, immediately above or below the image in the page, to help your users understand the contents of the image.

3. Take well-composed pictures using a high-quality camera. If you are using images to sell products, show multiple perspectives of the product.

> **Note** For additional information on using images wisely, search for "Google SEO image best practices" and read the content. Google engineers compiled this documentation to describe how they interpret images when crawling websites and what they recommend for using images in webpages.

To follow rule #2, use your favorite search engine to research "how to write good alt text for an image." Many resources and tutorials online can help you create this valuable addition to the image.

Given rule #3 to use images to supplement text, you need to add text to the home page for totallyawesomestuff. com. On a new line after the opening `<section>` tag, add the following code:

```
<h2>
    We are international purveyors of many fine examples of totally awesome stuff.
</h2>
```

Next, add a caption below the image map to help people understand what the picture is all about. To do so, first add a `<figure>` tag on a new line before the `<img>` tag and add a `</figure>` tag on a new line below the closing `</map>` tag to enclose the image and image map between the `<figure>`...`</figure>` tags. Add a blank line between the closing `</map>` tag and the closing `</figure>` tag, and then add the following figure caption and text:

```
<figcaption>
    Click any of the images above to see more details!
</figcaption>
```

The `figcaption` element provides the text describing the contents of the `figure` element. Save your changes and refresh the page in your browser. The h2 and `figcaption` elements need to be styled, since the h2 heading is plain and the `figcaption` text is too far to the left to work as a caption. Add the following two style declarations to the end of your CSS file:

```
/* Style for the h2 inside the section */
section h2 {
    font-family: Copperplate, "Copperplate Gothic", serif;
    max-width: 870px;
}

/* Style for the image caption */
section figcaption {
    text-align: center;
    max-width: 870px;
    font-family: Monaco, Consolas;
}
```

In the style declaration for the h2 heading inside the `section` element, `max-width` is a new property that you haven't used before. The `max-width` property sets the maximum width an element can take up before wrapping the text at the next available whitespace character. In this case, when the h2 heading reaches a width of 870 pixels, it wraps to the next line.

Another new addition to the font-family declaration is the comma-separated list of fonts. Because Copperplate is a Mac font and "Copperplate Gothic" is a Windows font, you need to include both to make the same font appear in the browser in both operating systems. The "serif" at the end of the list is applied if neither one of those fonts is available in the browser.

The `figcaption` style uses the same `max-width` property to align the heading text with the image in case the page is wider than the image. The `text-align` property of `center` centers the caption text below the image.

The completed HTML for the image map and caption is shown in **Figure 3-9**.

Figure 3-9   The HTML code for the image map and caption

```
36  ▼          <section>
37  ▼              <h2>
38                     We are international purveyors of many fine examples of totally awesome stuff.
39  ⌐              </h2>
40  ▼              <figure>
41                     <img id="home_page_img" class="img_border" src="images/splash_screen.png"
42                        usemap="#home_page_map" alt="An image containing About Us, Our Products, and Causes We Care About images."/>
43  ▼                 <map name="home_page_map">
44                        <area shape="rect" coords="10,220,220,385" alt="About Us" href="about.html"/>
45                        <area shape="rect" coords="180,5,380,200" alt="Our Products" href="products.html"/>
46                        <area shape="rect" coords="370,220,570,385" alt="Causes We Support" href="causes.html"/>
47  ⌐                 </map>
48  ▼                 <figcaption>
49                        Click any of the images above to see more details!
50  ⌐                 </figcaption>
51  ⌐             </figure>
52  ⌐         </section>
```
BBEdit

Now that you've successfully added styles for the h2 and `figcaption` elements, the header across the top and the footer at the bottom look lackluster. Add the following styles to the end of your my_styles.css to tidy up the header:

```
/* Style for the home page title */
header h1 {
    text-align: center;
    letter-spacing: 5px;
    text-shadow: 2px 2px 5px rgb(30,144,255);
    font-family: Garamond;
    margin: -10px -10px 20px -10px;
    background-image: linear-gradient(rgb(255,255,255),rgb(30,144,255));
}
```

The style definition includes a smattering of new properties. As you've seen, the `text-align` property is used to move the text to the center with `center`, but you can also use `text-align` to align the text left with the `left` value or right with the `right` value. Justify text with the `justify` value, which fills the full width of the container element (the `header` element) with the text evenly spaced out across it.

Two other new styles are also used to style the header. The `text-shadow` property does exactly what it sounds like it should—it creates a shadow effect with, in order, a horizontal length of 2px, a vertical length of 2px, and a radius of 5px to blur the effect behind the main text. The color specified (an rgb value, in this case) creates a blue shadow to match the rest of the site.

Next, four separate values are used with the `margin` declaration. These values are applied clockwise around the element, starting from noon, or top. That is, the margin for the top of the `header` element is first (`-10px`), then the right (`-10px`), bottom (`20px`), and finally left (`-10px`). This moves the element from where it would be on the page by default, creating a neater appearance. Negative margins move the element in the direction of whichever of the four values it is specified for, whereas positive values move it away.

The `background-image` property is used with a linear gradient to create a fading color from one specified shade (white) to the other (blue) across the full height of the `header` element.

Save your changes to the my_styles.css file, then refresh index.html. You should see some significant improvements to the header. The footer still looks dull. To change that, add the following style to the end of my_styles.css:

```
/* Style for the footer */
footer {
    text-align: center;
    font-size: .75em;
    font-family: Garamond;
    background-color: rgb(200,200,200);
    margin: 0px -10px 20px -10px;
}
```

The style applied to the footer includes properties you've used previously to center the footer; change its font size, font, and background color; and set its top, right, bottom, and left margins. Those styles set off the footer and make it appear as a proper footer.

Save all of your changes, then refresh your home page. You should now see a page like the one in **Figure 3-10**.

Figure 3-10   The completed home page

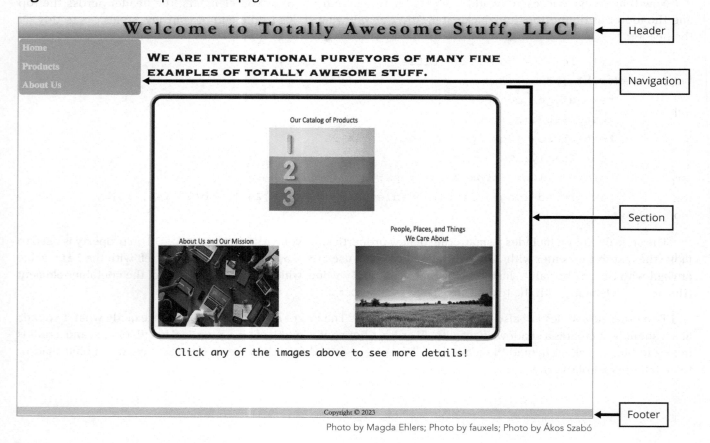

Photo by Magda Ehlers; Photo by fauxels; Photo by Ákos Szabó

Considering Images and Responsive Design

Not every user will be visiting your totally awesome webpage on a full-size screen like the one you are using to build and test the page. In fact, a majority of your users will be viewing your content on a mobile device.

Responsive design is an approach to building webpages that creates a flexible framework for webpage content. The webpages show and load different content and styles depending on the screen size of the device accessing the webpage.

To make your website usable, you must meet your users where they are, and the `<picture>` tag set creates an easy way to accomplish this when incorporating images. You will see more of this important aspect to full stack web development in the chapter devoted exclusively to responsive web design.

Make a copy of your about.html page and save it as wax.html. Add the following code between the `<section>`…`</section>` tags:

```
<picture>
    <source media="(min-width: 640px)" srcset="images/large_dapper_cat.png"/>
    <source media="(min-width: 460px)" srcset="images/medium_dapper_cat.png"/>
    <source media="(min-width: 320px)" srcset="images/small_dapper_cat.png"/>
    <img src="images/default_cat.png" alt="A picture of a black cat with tan
        spots and the markings of a mustache on her face."/>
</picture>
```

This tag set is a cascade of images wrapped inside the `<picture>`…`</picture>` tags. The first image file specified by the `<source>` tag in the `srcset` attribute (large_dapper_cat.png) is used if the `media` attribute applies to the browser loading this picture. That is, if the screen loading the webpage has a minimum width of 640 pixels, the browser shows the large_dapper_cat.png picture.

If the screen has a minimum width of 460 pixels, like a tablet or small laptop might, the second image (medium_dapper_cat.png) is used instead. If the screen has a minimum width of 320 pixels like a phone does, the third image (small_dapper_cat.png) is loaded instead. If none of those minimum screen widths apply, or the browser doesn't work with the `<picture>`…`</picture>` tag set, the final `<img>` tag is used to display the default_cat.png image file.

The last image is also the source of the `alt` text that will be displayed by default if none of the other images load or if a screen reader is reading the screen to the user.

Each of the first three images is typically a resized version of the same image, with the first being the largest in screen size (and file size) and the last before the default being the smallest. In this way, the most appropriately sized image will be the only one that loads for this page, improving load times.

Save your changes, save the images supplied with the course materials in your images folder so the file path will work, then open the webpage wax.html in your browser. You should see the large picture of the mustachioed cat in the main part of the page.

To test the automatic image reselection, drag the right margin of the browser window to the left until the medium image is displayed, then even further to the left until the small image is displayed. Dragging the right side of the browser window back to the right should load the appropriately sized images again in the same order.

Quick Check 3-2

1. What does the CSS `max-width` property of an element set?

    a. The number of pixels for the width of an image

    b. The maximum screen width for displaying a block-level element

    c. The maximum amount of screen space an element will expand to fill

    d. The number of em units an element will take up before the font size automatically becomes smaller

2. What is an image map?

    a. An image of a map included in a website

    b. An image used as the site map to show users how the website is laid out and how to move from page to page

    c. An image composed of two or more pictures assembled together by Adobe Photoshop or other image-editing software

    d. An image used as a source of navigation with places to click to open other pages or interact with the website

3. Why should you resize your images to fit the webpage and specify a size using CSS?

    a. To make sure the images are displayed the same in all browsers

    b. To make the images usable for people with screen readers

    c. To ensure that the image file loads completely before the CSS code can be applied to show it

    d. To reduce the file size to no larger than necessary and to ensure the image is displayed properly in the webpage on all screens

1) c. The `max-width` property is used to set the upper limit on how much screen width an HTML element can take up. **2) d.** An image map is an image with clickable links. **3) d.** Smaller file size and webpage layout are both important factors in using images wisely.

3.3 Embedding Videos

Adding a video to your website can make a big difference in user engagement, transforming casual visitors to your site into activated users interacting with your content. Videos providing customer testimonials, product demonstrations, or product assembly instructions are more engaging (and useful) when the user can start, pause, and replay parts of the videos. People like to click things that do stuff in webpages.

Common Mistakes

Be cautious about adding videos to your website. If you have important content in your videos (such as assembly instructions or product usage guidelines) you need to provide an alternative means for all users to access that content on a webpage.

To make your videos as accessible as possible, keep the following guidelines in mind:

- Use a media player that supports accessible content.
- Provide captioning for your videos.
- Create transcripts for your videos.

Fortunately, you don't have to guess how to make a video accessible to your users. The W3C has a guidance document that you can read for more information at www.w3.org/WAI/media/av/.

Creating the Video Tag Structure

If the web hosting contract with your commercial provider (such as GoDaddy or Wix) doesn't have a constraint for total folder content size or if you have only a few short videos, you can upload and host your own videos as if they were images. Similar to images, the videos are incorporated into the HTML code of the webpage using tags specific to videos.

Make a copy of products.html and save it as video.html. Add a new item to the navigation menu named Video that links to video.html, and then add this link to the other pages in your website so all pages have the same menu.

In your folder structure containing Chapter 3 materials (currently including the css and images folders), create a folder for your videos called, of course, videos, if necessary. Copy the clouds.mp4 video supplied as part of the course materials to the new videos folder. Next, you need to use the `<video>` tag to create a space in the webpage for the video. Add the tag structure necessary for the video between the `<section>`...`</section>` tags in video.html. Use the following code:

```
<video width="320" height="240" controls>
    <source src="videos/clouds.mp4" type="video/mp4" />
    Your browser does not support the video tag.
</video>
```

This `<video>` tag was introduced with HTML5. It tells the browser to use the browser-native video controls to play, pause, or fast-forward the video. The attributes for `width` and `height` control the size of the video as shown in the browser window. Between the `<video>`...`</video>` tags is another self-closing tag for the `<source/>`. This contains two attributes, one for the `src` file path to the video's storage location, and the other for the `type` of video format to tell the browser how to handle the content of the video.

The other item in the `video` element is a plain-text error message that will be displayed if the browser cannot support or play the video or if the browser cannot find the video because the file path is incorrect.

Save your changes, then open video.html in your browser. You should see a page like the one in **Figure 3-11**, and you should be able to play your video in the webpage.

Figure 3-11　The video.html webpage

Video by Alexander Lutkov

Embedding an Online Video

Many websites have videos that are hosted online but embedded in the website. Similar to using GitHub to store your source code, storing your videos on YouTube or Vimeo makes the concerns about storage space and server uptime a problem that the online host solves for you.

YouTube has documentation on how to create an account, upload videos, and embed videos. They also have a helpful "embed this video" menu option available in their media player. The following is a copy of the embed code supplied by YouTube:

```
<iframe width="640" height="480" src="https://www.youtube.com/embed/LLFhKaqnWwk"
title="Rick Astley - Never Gonna Give You Up" frameborder="0"></iframe>
```

That looks like a lot of HTML code to include in your webpage, and it is. The outer tags are `<iframe>...</iframe>` tags with attributes and values but no content. The `iframe` tags create a space for a webpage inside a different web-page. In this case, the `iframe` will show YouTube content inside the totallyawesomestuff.com webpage. The `src` element contains the URL of the inner page. The other attributes are similar to those you have seen in other HTML elements: `width`, `height`, `title`, and `border`.

A word of caution, however. Before you consider rickrolling your website users, add the code to your video.html webpage to test the YouTube link. Save your changes and refresh the page. Then, join in the disappointment. Adding a video to your webpage this way doesn't work because this video is copyrighted and only plays in the native YouTube site or for authorized users who own the copyrights. Unless you are Rick Astley, this video is unavailable to your webpages as an embedded video, just like every copyrighted video.

Creating a YouTube account is straightforward when you follow the instructions provided by YouTube, and upload-ing your own videos is similarly well documented. If you complete both tasks, you can use the example `iframe` code to link to your own YouTube videos from your website. You will be able to do this because you own the copyrights to all of your intellectual property. These tasks are outside of the scope of this textbook, however.

Quick Check 3-3

1. Where does the file path/name for an embedded HTML video tag appear?
   a. Inside the `<video>` tag using the `src` attribute
   b. Between the `<iframe>` and `</iframe>` tags
   c. Between the `<video>` and `</video>` tags in the `<src>` tag
   d. Between the `<video>` and `</video>` tags in the `<source>` tag

2. Why can't you use a video that someone else uploaded to YouTube on your own site?
   a. The videos on YouTube are someone else's intellectual property
   b. The videos on YouTube are the wrong format to be included in a website
   c. YouTube prevents all videos from being included in external websites
   d. YouTube videos have file size constraints that prevent webpages from loading them properly

3. Which of the following does adding videos to your website NOT create?
   a. Better user engagement with your website
   b. Easier and better product feature documentation
   c. More sales of products featured in videos
   d. Faster website load times on mobile devices

1) d. The file path for a video is saved in the `src` attribute of the `<source>` tag inside a `<video>...</video>` tag set. **2) a.** Copyrighted videos are someone else's intellectual property. **3) d.** One significant drawback to adding videos to a website is the increased load time for pages that contain them.

3.4 Building Tables

Tables, when used wisely, are useful to display content that needs to be organized and arranged in rows and columns. Tables can be styled to show borders or to create a borderless row-and-column format for words, pictures, or anything else on a webpage that would benefit from this type of structure. However, tables should not be used when you have other better options to create page structure such as using `divs`, `spans`, and the other block-level elements you have been using.

Creating the Table Structure

Earlier in this chapter, you created a mostly blank page called products.html as a clone of the home page of total-lyawesomestuff.com. Open the products.html page in your text editor if you don't still have it open and review the HTML code. Check to make sure all of the other content added to the cascading style sheet is working when you open products.html and view it in a browser.

To add a table to a webpage, you use the HTML table elements. These elements are arranged in rows and columns in the HTML code so a person doing the development can read them, but of course could all be on one line and still work in the browser.

> **Note**
>
> The W3C has published guidelines to follow when creating tables in HTML to ensure all users can access your rows and columns of important content.
>
> To make your tables accessible, use `<th>` tags for table headers and `<td>` tags for table data cells and avoid unnecessary complexity in spanning rows or columns.
>
> You can read more table guidelines in one of the W3C Web Accessibility Initiative tutorials at www.w3.org/WAI/tutorials/tables/.

The basic structure of the three-row, five-column table of products follows and is illustrated in **Figure 3-12**. Add this content to your products.html file between the `<section>...</section>` tags:

Figure 3-12   HTML code used to build a table of products

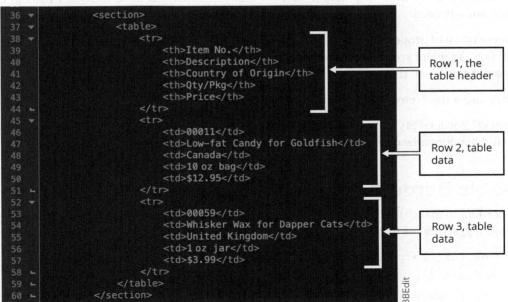

```
36      <section>
37          <table>
38              <tr>
39                  <th>Item No.</th>
40                  <th>Description</th>
41                  <th>Country of Origin</th>
42                  <th>Qty/Pkg</th>
43                  <th>Price</th>
44              </tr>
45              <tr>
46                  <td>00011</td>
47                  <td>Low-fat Candy for Goldfish</td>
48                  <td>Canada</td>
49                  <td>10 oz bag</td>
50                  <td>$12.95</td>
51              </tr>
52              <tr>
53                  <td>00059</td>
54                  <td>Whisker Wax for Dapper Cats</td>
55                  <td>United Kingdom</td>
56                  <td>1 oz jar</td>
57                  <td>$3.99</td>
58              </tr>
59          </table>
60      </section>
```

Row 1, the table header

Row 2, table data

Row 3, table data

BBEdit

```
<table>
    <tr>
        <th>Item No.</th>
        <th>Description</th>
        <th>Country of Origin</th>
        <th>Qty/Pkg</th>
        <th>Price</th>
    </tr>
    <tr>
        <td>00011</td>
        <td>Low-fat Candy for Goldfish</td>
        <td>Canada</td>
        <td>10 oz bag</td>
        <td>$12.95</td>
    </tr>
    <tr>
        <td>00059</td>
        <td>Whisker Wax for Dapper Cats</td>
        <td>United Kingdom</td>
        <td>1 oz jar</td>
        <td>$3.99</td>
    </tr>
</table>
```

This table structure begins with an opening `<table>` tag. Inside that tag, the first table row begins with the `<tr>` tag. Nested inside of that are five pairs of `<th>...</th>` tags, which are used to create table headers. These are column headings that identify the contents of each column. Some tables don't require column headings, so they are optional when building an HTML table.

The next table row contains the first set of five `<td>...</td>` tags containing the table data. These are required to define the cells of the table. Each row should have the same number of cells as the other rows in the table unless a special configuration is used.

Note the importance of proper indenting in the HTML code used to build the table. A table requires at least three layers of HTML tags, so white space is critical to the readability of the code. It is possible to create a table inside a table cell of a parent table, and that creates a doubly challenging code collection to keep organized.

Save these changes then refresh the products.html page in your browser.

What's missing? Borders! Style! This table of stuff appears to be floating in the middle of white space—in fact, it basically looks like semiorganized text, not really a table.

Adding Table Borders

Next, you add borders to make this table look more organized and easier to read. Add the following style declaration to the end of your my_styles.css file:

```
/* Styles for the products table */
section table {
    border: 2px solid black;
}
```

That adds a border 2 pixels wide to the table in the `section` element. Save your changes and refresh the products. html page. If you have everything right, the table is displayed with an outside border.

Your table still has no inside borders between the table cells because web browsers do exactly what you tell them to do, not what you actually mean. Only the `table` element was styled by this selector, not the `td` or the `th` elements that make up the inner contents of the table.

This table of items might look better with the thicker outside border you just created and thinner inside borders separating the cells. To accomplish this, add the following code after the table style declaration:

```
section table td, th {
    border: 1px solid rgb(175,175,175);
}
```

Note how this selector works—for the `td` and the `th` elements contained inside a `table` inside the `section`, apply a solid border 1 pixel thick that is the same shade of gray as the menu.

Save your changes, then refresh the page. The table should look similar to **Figure 3-13**.

Figure 3-13 The HTML table with outside and inside borders applied

Item No.	Description	Country of Origin	Qty/Pkg	Price
00011	Low-fat Candy for Goldfish	Canada	10 oz bag	$12.95
00059	Whisker Wax for Dapper Cats	United Kingdom	1 oz jar	$3.99

This is starting to look like a more organized table of data, except the inside borders should intersect with the outside border. Each cell has its own border because that's exactly what you told the browser to create. That is, each cell in the table is a unique element and has a style applied only to it.

Add the following lines of CSS code to the `section table` selector you created earlier:

```
border-collapse: collapse;
width: 80%;
```

The `border-collapse` property tells the browser to make adjoining borders into a single border, so the cell borders appear as intersecting gridlines. Specifying the `width` of `80%` makes the table wider so the contents are more readable.

Save your changes to the stylesheet and refresh the webpage, which now shows a proper table. Since it is the only one in this website, the `table` style selector in the CSS file can remain as it is, but if you had more than one table and each table had its own formatting, you would want to be more specific, creating separate classes for tables with thicker outer borders and gray inner borders and tables with all of the borders the same thickness and blue, for example.

Quick Check 3-4

1. What are `<th>` tags used for when building an HTML table?

   a. `<th>` tags create the rows in the table.
   b. `<th>` tags create the caption for the table.
   c. `<th>` tags create the column headings in the table.
   d. `<th>` tags create the title for the table.

2. When is it necessary to add borders to the `table` element?

   a. To show a grid with borders around the cells in a table
   b. To make sure a screen reader can read your table
   c. To display the table structure inside the `<table>...</table>` tags
   d. To display a line around the outer edges of the table

3. What does collapsing the borders in a table do?

   a. Collapsing transforms the individual `td` and `th` element borders into a single-line grid
   b. Collapsing shows only the outer borders of a `table` element by removing the inner borders of the `td` and `th` elements
   c. Collapsing shows the inner borders around the `th` and `td` elements
   d. Collapsing transforms a thick border into a thinner border around the table in mobile web browsers

1) c. You use `<th>` tags to create the column headers in a table. **2) d.** The borders of a `table` element appear only around the outside of the table, not the interior parts. **3) a.** Collapsing removes the space between each of the borders around the `td` and `th` elements.

3.5 Styling Tables

In the previous section, you created a table that contains the products offered by totallyawesomestuff.com. While tables are a useful way to present a grid of information, the bare-bones styling creates a less engaging user experience.

Adding Row Styles

For longer tables of data, an every-other-row shading scheme (called banded rows) will help your users follow a row of data across the width of the table. Add the following style declaration to the end of your stylesheet to create banded rows:

```
section table tr:nth-child(even) {
    background-color: rgb(240,248,255);
}
```

This style declaration uses the `tr:nth-child` pseudo-class with an `(even)` parameter to select the rows for this styling. The browser will apply this style to each even-numbered row (`tr`) by displaying a subtle shade of light blue in the background. Other possibilities for the parameter include `odd`, a number, or a formula to calculate which elements this style applies to.

You could use a less subtle shade of blue to create a more dramatic effect, but the intention is not to dominate the grid with flashy contrasting colors that might overwhelm your users.

Save your changes and refresh the webpage in your browser. The second row in the table should have a light blue background. The banded row effect will repeat when you add rows of data to the table in the Programming Exercises for this chapter.

Adding Column Styles

The first question your customers will probably ask themselves after finding the only source in the world for Low-Fat Candy for Goldfish is "How much does this amazing product cost?" You can help them answer this question by highlighting the last column in the table, which displays the Price values. Add the following HTML code to your table in the products.html file, right after the opening `<table>` tag:

```
<colgroup>
    <col class="details" span="4" />
    <col class="price" />
</colgroup>
```

Your code should now look like **Figure 3-14**.

Figure 3-14   The HTML table code with the `colgroup` element 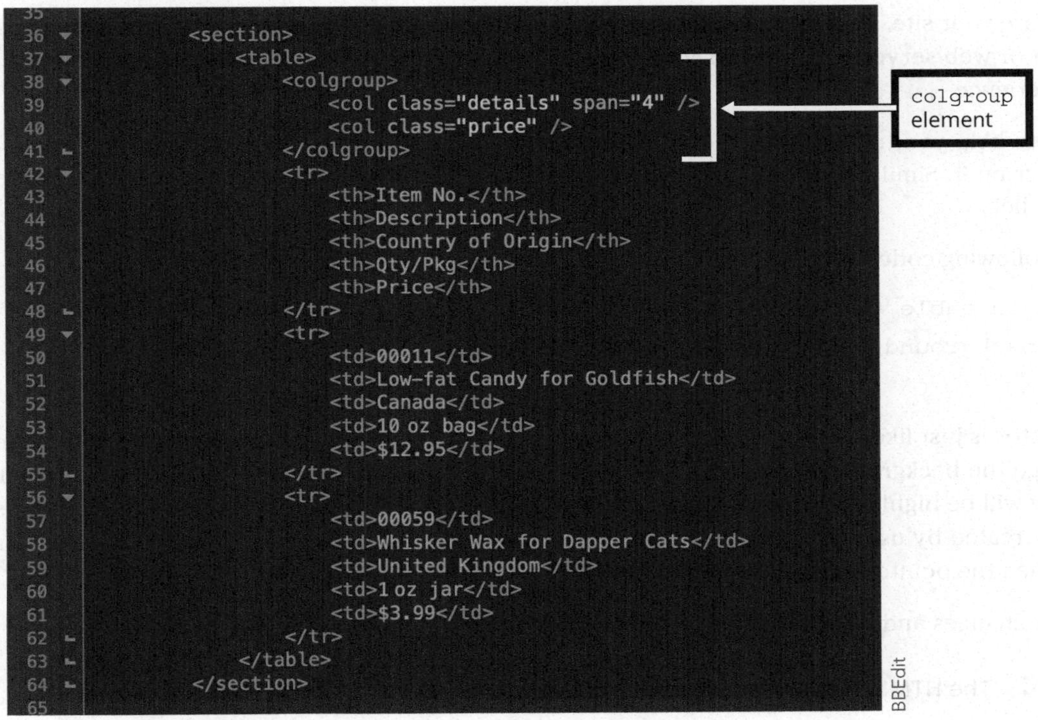

This HTML structure gives the browser additional information about the table. The `colgroup` element indicates that the browser should separate the table columns into two groups. The first `col` group spans the four columns starting at the left of the table. The second `col` group is the fifth table column containing the price information.

Now you need to add style information for the last `col` element with the `class="price"` identifier. Add the following to the end of my_styles.css:

```
section table col.price {
    background-color: rgb(255,255,224);
}
```

Save your changes, then refresh your page. You should now have a grid that looks like **Figure 3-15**.

Figure 3-15   The HTML table after styling the `colgroup` element to highlight the Price column

Welcome to Totally Awesome Stuff, LLC!				

Home
Products
About Us
Videos

Item No.	Description	Country of Origin	Qty/Pkg	Price
00011	Low-fat Candy for Goldfish	Canada	10 oz bag	$12.95
00059	Whisker Wax for Dapper Cats	United Kingdom	1 oz jar	$3.99

The Price column is now highlighted to direct your users to the information they want to know. Note that the new column style doesn't override the banded-row shading applied to the table, since that effect is applied directly to the table.

Creating an Interactive Table

As users explore your site, they will undoubtedly want to order its totally awesome products. While you don't have a shopping cart or web server set up yet to complete customer transactions, you can still create the starting point for that user experience.

One way to help your users select the product they want to order is to add a shading style to the line item that has the pointer on it. Similar to the menu that you created earlier, this visual indicator helps users identify the row they want to click.

Add the following code to the end of my_styles.css to create this effect for the table:

```
section table tr:hover {
    background-color: rgb(176,224,230);
}
```

This selector is just like the menu pseudo-class selector that you created previously. It uses the `:hover` pseudo-class to change the background color of a `tr` element inside a `table` in a `section`. When the pointer hovers over a row, the row will be highlighted with a shade of blue darker than the banded-row color. Additionally, since this is a pseudo-class created by user interactivity, the `:hover` style supersedes the banded-row styling but then reverts to the default when the pointer moves away from the row.

Save your changes and refresh the page. The finished table should look like **Figure 3-16**.

Figure 3-16   The HTML table with the `:hover` pseudo-class

Welcome to Totally Awesome Stuff, LLC!				

Home
Products
About Us
Videos

Item No.	Description	Country of Origin	Qty/Pkg	Price
00011	Low-fat Candy for Goldfish	Canada	10 oz bag	$12.95
00059	Whisker Wax for Dapper Cats	United Kingdom	1 oz jar	$3.99

Quick Check 3-5

1. What does a `tr:nth-child(odd)` selector do?

   a. Applies the style that follows to all of the odd-numbered rows in a table
   b. Applies the style that follows to all of the odd-numbered `td` or `th` elements inside a `tr` element
   c. Applies the style that follows to the first odd `tr` element in the `table`
   d. Creates a style that appears when the user moves the pointer over the odd-numbered rows in a table

2. Why do tables need to be styled?

   a. Without additional styling, the default borders in the table don't touch each other.
   b. Without additional styling, the table will look like a generic spreadsheet.
   c. Tables don't need to be styled to appear on an HTML page.
   d. Without additional styling, the table is made up of HTML elements that aren't visible in the webpage.

3. What does the selector `table#calendar col.weekend` indicate in a CSS file?

   a. Somewhere in the website is a table with an ID of `calendar` and a `col` value in a `th` element and a `weekend` value in the `td` element below it.
   b. Somewhere in the website is a table with an ID of `calendar` and a `colgroup` element that includes a `col` element with the class of `weekend`.
   c. Somewhere in the website is a table that contains a `col` element that has the ID of `weekend`.
   d. Somewhere in the website is a `td` element with an attribute of `weekend` inside a `tr` element with a class of `col` inside a table with an ID of `calendar`.

1) a. This selector applies the style that follows to all of the odd-numbered rows. **2) d.** By default, the tags that make up an HTML table don't show in a webpage. **3) b.** This selector only applies to a table with an ID of `calendar` containing column groups with at least one `col` element of class weekend.

3.6 Creating HTML Forms

An HTML form is a way to collect information from the users of the website and then do something more with that information. A form is composed of a collection of HTML tags, just like the other HTML tags you've been using in this chapter.

A number of form elements can be incorporated that you have probably seen or used before, such as text boxes, check boxes, radio buttons, and submit buttons. Similar to the HTML table you built in a previous section that contains inner elements like rows and cells, the HTML form is composed of an outer tag that contains the inner form elements.

Building the HTML Form

Create a new webpage by saving a copy of your products.html page as contact_us.html. Remove the table inside the `<section>...</section>` tags from this new page. Add another list item to the `<nav>...</nav>` unordered list menu with the text "Contact Us" and a link pointing to contact_us.html. Copy that list item and paste it into the menus of your other pages as well so that your menu is consistent on all pages.

Add the following content to the `section` element to create the first part of the form:

```
<form>
    <fieldset>
        <legend>Visitor Feedback Form</legend>
```

```
<label for="f_name">First name:</label>
<input type="text" id="f_name" name="f_name" required/>
<br/>
<label for="l_name">Last name:</label>
<input type="text" id="l_name" name="l_name" required/>
<br/>
<label for="email">Email:</label>
<input type="email" id="email" name="email" required/>
<br/>
```

Starting at the top of the tags in the `<form>` tag and working down, the first new tag is the `<fieldset>` tag. This tag isn't required for the form to function in the browser, but it improves the usability of the form. It creates a group around the form elements inside the `<form>` tags. By default, most browsers style a `fieldset` element with an outside border. Similarly, the next tag, the `<legend>`, creates a helpful title (Visitor Feedback Form) for this group of form elements.

The next set of tags are required to create an accessible form. The `<label>...</label>` tags contain the text that the user will see, and equally importantly hear, when using this form. For example, the first `label` element provides a "First name:" prompt. It is possible to use bare text before or after each `input` element as the prompt to the user. However, the `<label>` tag includes a `for` attribute that tells a screen reader to read the prompt between the `<label>...</label>` tags before selecting the form element for data entry. In this way, a person who is hearing the webpage read to them by a screen reader will know which form element they are using to enter data. This is one key to creating fully accessible websites.

The first two `<input>` tags are simple `type="text"` data entry fields, which create text boxes for entering the user's first and last names into the form. The `id` and `name` attributes included in an `input` element have the same value. For example, the first `input` element has `id` and `name` attributes of `f_name`. Each `name/id` pair, however, is unique in the form. You must include these attributes to differentiate the values submitted. These values will become the keys in the key/value pairs submitted to a web server, so each form element has to be uniquely identified.

Additionally, note the `required` attribute for each `input` element. The `required` attribute tells the web browser that a valid data entry needs to be made before the form can be submitted. The `required` attribute should be included on all of the form fields that need an answer in a valid form submission.

The last `input` element in this section of the form defines an email field. Email fields were introduced with HTML5, since collecting a user's email address had become so common on a web form and using a generic text box required extra work for data validation. The web browser form validation will automatically detect if anything other than a valid email address has been entered into an email field and prompt the user to enter a valid email address. Prevalidating user data helps to create more useable data in the database and prevents other errors.

Next, enter another `fieldset` element for the "How did you hear about us?" section of the form with check boxes for the responses:

```
<fieldset>
    <legend>How did you hear about us? Check all that apply:</legend>
    <input type="checkbox" id="google" name="google" value="Google"/>
    <label for="google">Google Search</label>
    <input type="checkbox" id="owl" name="owl" value="Owl"/>
    <label for="owl">An Owl Told Me</label>
    <input type="checkbox" id="skywriter" name="skywriter" value="Skywriter"/>
    <label for="skywriter">I Saw a Skywriter Message</label>
</fieldset>
<br/>
```

This `fieldset` element contains three check boxes. The `legend` element in this group serves the same purpose as the `<label>` tags for the first three form elements, in that the text between the `<legend>`...`</legend>` tags serves as the prompt to the user hearing this web form being read to them. Users select one of the three check boxes to respond to the prompt, "How did you hear about us? Check all that apply."

The check boxes are all uniquely named because each is a unique form element. However, they are grouped together for the user to choose zero or more check boxes. If only one was required, and only one selection allowed, radio buttons would be a better option.

Check boxes are useful for showing six or fewer options that correspond to a single question or prompt. If you need to have more than six options, use a selection list instead to keep your form from filling an entire screen.

Enter another `fieldset` element for the "Would you like to subscribe to our occasional newsletter?" section of the form with radio buttons for the responses:

```
<fieldset>
    <legend>Would you like to subscribe to our occasional newsletter?</legend>
    <input type="radio" id="yes_subscribe" name="subscribe" value="Yes"/>
    <label for="yes_subscribe">Yes</label>
    <input type="radio" id="no_subscribe" name="subscribe" value="No"/>
    <label for="no_subscribe">No</label>
</fieldset>
<br/>
```

This `fieldset` element groups radio buttons. Similar to the previous instances of the `fieldset` element, a `legend` element helps the user hear or see the prompt for the group of radio buttons. Note the `id` and `name` attributes in this radio button group. The `id` is different for each radio button, but the `name` has the same value.

Using the same `name` attribute tells the browser to treat the radio buttons as mutually exclusive. That is, you can choose one or the other of the radio buttons, but unlike the check boxes, you can't choose both. Clicking one radio button to indicate "on" automatically turns the other radio button "off." This can work for three or more radio buttons as well.

Next, add a third block for the "What is the nature of your inquiry?" section of the form with a drop-down box and text box for the responses:

```
<label for="nature">What is the nature of your inquiry?</label>
<select id="nature" name="nature" required>
    <option value="new_product">New Product Suggestion</option>
    <option value="question">Question About an Existing Product</option>
    <option value="just_lonely">I'm Just Lonely and Crave Human Interaction
        </option>
    <option value="other">Other</option>
</select>
```

This block of code follows the pattern of the `label` element used earlier. The `label` in this case is for the `select` type of form element, which creates a selection list. This is another way for a user to choose one of several options in a single convenient spot. As you can see, the outer `<select>` tag is the wrapper around four `option` elements. Each pair of `<option>`...`</option>` tags surround the text for that option. If the user selects an `option` element in the selection list, the value in its `value` attribute is what the browser sends to the web server when the form is submitted.

Enter the following code to complete the web form:

```
<textarea name="message" rows="10" cols="50" maxlength="400" placeholder="Type
    your message here" required></textarea>
```

```
            <input type="submit" value="Submit"/>
        </fieldset>
    </form>
```

The `<textarea>`…`</textarea>` tags create the last data input element. The `textarea` element has an opening and a closing tag with attributes and values but no content displayed to the user. Instead, the `textarea` element provides a space for the user to type a response of up to several sentences.

Read through the attributes, noting a few differences that the `textarea` element has that none of the other fields in this form share. First, the `textarea` element has attributes for `rows` and `columns`. They tell the browser how many characters to reserve for the width and height of the `<textarea>` on the page. The `maxlength` attribute sets the maximum number of characters the user can enter into this field. Setting a maximum helps a user write a brief response and prevents an error with an overly long database entry. Finally, the `placeholder` attribute provides a prompt to the user—in this case, "Type your message here." The `<input type="text">` tag can also use the `placeholder` attribute.

The final form element is the Submit button, created by the `<input type="submit">` tag. This button will be the trigger for the user to submit this form. However, since this form doesn't specify an action during or after submission, the form will only undergo the browser data validation and nothing more.

Figure 3-17 shows the completed code on the contact_us.html page.

Figure 3-17 The HTML code for a data-gathering form

```
<section>
    <form>
        <fieldset>
            <legend>Visitor Feedback Form</legend>
            <label for="f_name">First Name:</label>
            <input type="text" id="f_name" name="f_name" required/>
            <br/>
            <label for="l_name">Last name:</label>
            <input type="text" id="l_name" name="l_name" required/>
            <br/>
            <label for="email">Email:</label>
            <input type="email" id="email" name="email" required/>
            <br/>
            <fieldset>
                <legend>How did you hear about us?  Check all that apply:</legend>
                <input type="checkbox" id="google" name="google" value="Google"/>
                <label for="google">Google Search</label>
                <input type="checkbox" id="owl" name="owl" value="Owl"/>
                <label for="owl">An Owl Told Me</label>
                <input type="checkbox" id="skywriter" name="skywriter" value="Skywriter"/>
                <label for="skywriter">I Saw A Skywriter Message</label>
            </fieldset>
            <br/>
            <fieldset>
                <legend>Would you like to subscribe to our occasional newsletter?</legend>
                <input type="radio" id="yes_subscribe" name="subscribe" value="Yes"/>
                <label for="yes_subscribe">Yes</label>
                <input type="radio" id="no_subscribe" name="subscribe" value="No"/>
                <label for="no_subscribe">No</label>
            </fieldset>
            <br>
            <label for="nature">What is the nature of your inquiry?</label>
            <select id="nature" name="nature" required>
                <option value="new_product">New Product Suggestion</option>
                <option value="question">Question About An Existing Product</option>
                <option value="just_lonely">I'm Just Lonely And Crave Human Interaction</option>
                <option value="other">Other</option>
            </select>
            <textarea name="message" rows="10" cols="50" maxlength="400"
                placeholder="Type your message here" required></textarea>
            <input type="submit" value="Submit"/>
        </fieldset>
    </form>
</section>
```

BBEdit

This form has the parts necessary to help users give feedback to the owners of the site in an organized way. Rather than using a simple "Contact Us" email address, the form will help the site owners to create a database of user feedback to analyze in the future.

The code running on a web server needed to process this data and store it in a database is the code you will write in the chapters on PHP. However, you have just completed the front-end development of a web form! This is a significant step toward becoming a full stack developer.

Save all of your changes, then open the page in your web browser. You should see a web form that looks like the one in **Figure 3-18**.

Figure 3-18   The completed Visitor Feedback web form

HTML Form Elements

HTML has more form elements than you have seen in this brief tutorial. To provide backward compatibility, the W3C rarely removes an old HTML tag.

Instead, they occasionally declare a tag as **deprecated**, or no longer recommended for use. They also introduce new HTML tags to replace or improve the existing functionality. One tag that has been deprecated is the `<blink>` tag, which makes specified text flash slowly. Using animation and style information instead, web developers can still create annoying blinking text on a webpage, if they insist on doing so. However, the use of the `<blink>` tag has been discouraged, especially because it makes the blinking text less accessible to all users.

The `<input type="email">` tag is an example of the W3C introducing new web form tags that extend functionality. Web developers had been using the `<input type="text">` tag to gather email addresses. However, to validate the response data, developers had to include additional JavaScript code. The `<input type="email">` tag tells the browser that only data with the format of a standard email address is valid, and the user should be prompted with a "please enter a valid email address" message if the data entered was not in the valid format.

Table 3-2 lists the types of input and web form elements that are currently used. You may never use some of these in your full stack development, but you will use others in nearly every web form you build.

Table 3-2 HTML form input elements

Form input element	Description
`<button>`	Creates a button for a user to click
`<input type="button">`	Creates a button for a user to click
`<input type="checkbox">`	Creates a single check box
`<input type="color">`	Creates a color palette selector
`<datalist>`	Creates a list of options that appear in an input element
`<input type="date">`	Creates a calendar for a date selector
`<input type="datetime-local">`	Creates a calendar/time selector
`<input type="email">`	Creates a text box that accepts only email addresses
`<fieldset>`	Creates a group of input form elements
`<input type="file">`	Creates a file picker
`<input type="hidden">`	Creates a hidden form element to store values not displayed to the user of the form
`<input type="image">`	Creates a submit button out of an image
`<label>`	Creates a text element associated with another input element
`<legend>`	Creates a text space inside a fieldset
`<input type="month">`	Creates a month calendar selector
`<input type="number">`	Creates an input text box that allows only numbers
`<output>`	Creates a form element to display the output of a form operation such as a calculation
`<option>`	Creates one item in a list of options
`<optgroup>`	Creates a subgroup in a list of options in a selection list
`<input type="password">`	Creates a password input text box
`<input type="radio">`	Creates one radio button
`<input type="range">`	Creates a range slider input element
`<input type="reset">`	Creates a form reset button
`<input type="search">`	Creates a search text box
`<select>`	Creates the outer framework for a selection/drop-down list
`<input type="submit">`	Creates a button used to submit the form
`<input type="tel">`	Creates a text box that accepts only phone number input
`<input type="text">`	Creates a text box
`<textarea>`	Creates a multiline text box
`<input type="time">`	Creates an input element that shows a time picker and allows only valid times as input values
`<input type="url">`	Creates a text box that accepts only valid URLs as inputs
`<input type="week">`	Creates an input element that shows a calendar selector and allows only valid date inputs

Quick Check 3-6

1. What does the `<fieldset>` tag add to an HTML form?

    a. The outer HTML tag for the start and end of the web form

    b. A grouping of the HTML web form elements

    c. A border around each of the HTML form elements inside the `<fieldset>`

    d. A helpful prompt for the user to assist them with filling out the form

2. When should you use check boxes in a web form?

    a. To require the user to choose only one answer from a list

    b. To create a group of input elements that are associated with each other

    c. To allow the user to choose one or more options from a list

    d. To create an input element that allows the user to toggle between two or more values

3. Why would you use an `<email>` form element instead of `<input type="text">` to gather form data?

    a. To validate that users have entered only email addresses in the field

    b. To ensure only users with modern browsers are using your form

    c. To prevent users from saving their email address in your form

    d. To send email newsletters from the form to the user

1) b. The `fieldset` element is used to create both a logical and visual grouping of form elements inside a form.
2) c. Check boxes are used when users can choose multiple options from a list. **3) a.** The `<email>` form field tells the browser that only valid email addresses are allowed in it.

Summary

- User-friendly website navigation is a critical element of the user experience of the website.

- Creating a menu from an unordered list with style applied is one way to successfully manage website navigation.

- Incorporating images into a website creates a positive, engaging user experience.

- A necessary part of every image is the alt tag, which is the text description of what appears in the image. This text is read to users by a screen reader and appears in the placeholder space if an image can't be loaded.

- Images should appear at a size that fits the page and purpose of the image. Resize images with both image-editing software and CSS styles for the image element itself.

- Image maps can be used to create clickable regions within images so users can navigate from the image to another page or website, but image maps should not be the only source of navigation on a webpage.

- Including videos increases user engagement with the content of the website and can be done either with embedded videos or iframes of external videos like those stored in YouTube.

- Tables are useful for creating rows and columns of data. They should not be used to create a structure for the webpage, however.

- Tables can be built with column headers and different styles for banded rows or certain columns in the table to help users notice important details.

- Use HTML forms to gather input from users of the website in an organized manner. HTML has many types of input elements to gather information from users.

Key Terms

deprecated	pseudo-class	user experience
image map	responsive design	

Review Questions

1. Search for "bad website navigation examples" and review six of the search results. Identify common themes among the examples that would help you avoid recreating similar navigation menus in your own web development. Summarize the similarities and differences in a one-page report and include links to the pages you found in your search. (3.1)

2. Why is it important to have a text-based navigation on all of your webpages? (3.1)

   a. It is a W3C requirement to render the webpage in a web browser.
   b. To help Google find your webpage on the Internet
   c. Because older versions of web browsers can only handle text-based navigation
   d. To ensure all users can successfully navigate your website

3. Where is the best place to find images to use on your website? (3.2)

   a. The Internet, since you can just download and save all images you find
   b. Your own camera or purchased from a photographer
   c. From friends or acquaintances who take lots of pictures
   d. From competitors' websites since you are selling the same products

4. Search for "best image size for a website" using your favorite search engine. Read the top five results and summarize the opinions in a one-page report. Include links to the pages you found in your search. (3.2)

5. What does the `<iframe>` tag set do? (3.3)

   a. Creates an HTML form element that allows videos to play on a webpage
   b. Creates a space in a webpage to show the contents of a different webpage
   c. Creates a grouping of similar form elements inside a web form
   d. Creates a border around an HTML `<image>` tag set

6. Search for "should I add videos to my website" using your favorite search engine. Read the top seven returns, then summarize the opinions in a one-page report. Include links to the pages you found in your search. Add your own opinion in the conclusion. (3.3)

7. What does a `<td>` tag create in a webpage? (3.4)

   a. A cell inside of a row in an HTML table
   b. A column heading cell inside of a row in an HTML table
   c. The starting outer element of an HTML table
   d. A row inside of an HTML table

8. Search for "why don't tables make good websites" using your favorite search engine. Read the top 10 returns and, in a one-page report, summarize the most important parts that they have in common. Include links to the pages you found in your search. (3.4)

9. What does a `colgroup` element add to a table? (3.5)

    a. It designates columns that belong together for styling.

    b. It merges two or more columns into a single column.

    c. It shows the sum of the values in two or more columns of numerical data.

    d. It groups the columns in a table to create single borders between the table cells that make up those columns.

10. Why would website owners want to create a web form to gather data from the website users instead of just using an "email us" link? (3.6)

    a. To gather data in an organized way so it can be analyzed in a useful manner

    b. To make the website look more professional

    c. To dissuade users from providing potentially annoying feedback by making them fill out a form

    d. Because all of the cool kids are doing it these days

11. Why is prevalidation of form input elements necessary? (3.6)

    a. It helps the user who is hearing the form read to them while using the keyboard to navigate through the form elements.

    b. It prevents the user from submitting the form without providing an answer for all of the required elements.

    c. It ensures the form is valid HTML so it is displayed properly in all web browsers.

    d. It ensures the form follows W3C guidelines for appropriate `input` element usage.

12. When is an HTML tag deprecated? (3.6)

    a. When web developers stop using it to build HTML pages

    b. When mobile and tablet web browsers stop showing it and its contents

    c. When it expires after the usual HTML tag lifespan of 10 years

    d. When the W3C declares the HTML tag to be no longer supported in the web browser standards

Programming Exercises

1. Open the file for wax.html that you created earlier in the chapter. Add a border around the image. Above the image, use an `<h2>` tag to add an appropriate title for the page. Add a caption below the image. Add a link from the products.html table item description to this new page. Save your changes and refresh the products page. Test your link. (3.1–3.3)

2. Add the following two items to the products.html table. (3.4)

Item No.	Description	Country of Origin	Qty/Pkg	Price
00103	No-More-Snarls Shampoo and Conditioner for Curly Hedgehog Quills	South Africa	16 oz bottle	$19.95
00211	Revive-O-Possum Smelling Salts for Catatonic Marsupials	United States	144 individual packets	$13.99

3. Add a light blue background color to the form on the Contact Us page. (3.1, 3.6)

Projects

1. Create a new page named causes.html. Add bulleted lists for worthy causes, your favorite entertainment sites, and similar products. Style the page appropriately. Add a background color to the list. See **Figure 3-19** for a suggestion of the content you might include and how to format it. (3.2)

   Figure 3-19   The completed causes.html webpage

   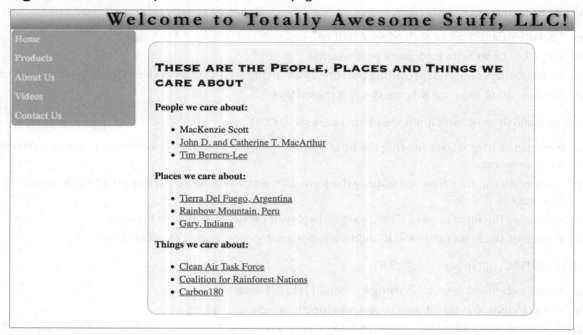

2. Open the page you created earlier called about.html. Add a paragraph to about.html describing the history of totallyawesomestuff.com. See **Figure 3-20** for a suggestion of content you might include and how to format it. (3.2)

3. Create a page for the product Low-Fat Candy for Goldfish using the wax.html page as a starting point. Update the text and images for the page. Create a link from the products.html table to this new page. (3.2)

4. Create a page for the product No-More-Snarls Shampoo and Conditioner for Curly Hedgehog Quills using the wax.html page as a starting point. Update the text and images for the page. Create a link from the products.html table to this new page. (3.2)

Figure 3-20   The completed about.html webpage

5. Create a page for the product Revive-O-Possum Smelling Salts using the wax.html page as a starting point. Update the text and images for the page. Create a link from the products.html table to this new page. (3.2)

Mobile Development and Responsive Design

Learning Objectives

When you complete this chapter, you will be able to:

4.1 Describe the important parts of responsive web design.

4.2 Describe how to test responsive webpages using browser-based emulators.

4.3 Create mobile-friendly style sheets for HTML pages.

4.4 Describe how to use images carefully when building a responsive website.

4.5 Create printer-friendly style sheets for HTML pages.

4.6 Describe how WordPress themes and CSS frameworks like Twitter Bootstrap help automate responsive design.

4.1 What Is Responsive Design?

To ensure a complete build and successful launch of a new website, you need to invest a significant amount of time in the planning stage of the web development process. You need to think about what content to include and how to display it. You should consider systemic questions like the following:

- What are the most critical contents and functions of your website?
- What interactions will your users have with those critical contents and functions?
- How many pages will you need to display your critical content in logical blocks?
- How will users navigate between those pages?
- What content on each page should receive the greatest amount of screen space?

These are important questions to ask yourself and the customers you are building the site for. However, since the majority of your Internet audience isn't available to answer these questions, you may only consider their perspective after you are done planning what you and your customers consider the most important parts of your website. This is a mistake.

What's the Problem?

The goal of a website is to engage users with your content in the easiest-to-use manner possible. As you've read previously, a website that isn't user-friendly will cause your visitors to move onto one that is. A website that is designed for, built on, and tested only on a laptop or desktop will have content wider than the screen of a mobile device. Vertical scrolling is an expected behavior in webpages, but horizontal scrolling is not.

Overly wide content forces users to move back and forth through that content. Horizontal scrolling in pages that are wider than the **viewport**, or default screen width on the device, hinders user interaction. Images that overwhelm the screen prevent users from reading the rest of the content and interacting with the important user input elements. Content that is too small or too large to be read easily prevents users from accessing it.

More than half of your website users will view your new webpages on a mobile device. At one time, early in the use of mobile devices to access the Internet, web developers would build two completely different websites in each web development project. One was intended for desktops and laptops, and the other was for mobile devices. The URLs for each site were different so users could tell which site to access on their device.

Building two websites was fantastic for the job security of the web developers responsible for keeping those sites up to date but problematic for both the content developers who wanted to only keep one site updated and the customers who had to pay double the development costs.

The problem only became worse as additional devices were connected to the Internet. Consider building different websites to show your webpage content on the following devices:

- Smartwatch
- Mobile phone
- Tablet
- Internet-connected refrigerator
- Dashboard display in a car
- Laptop or desktop screen
- Smart TV
- Large-screen projector
- Printed page

Keeping all those versions concurrent would be a lot of tedious work, and new devices are landing in the hands of Internet users every year. Fortunately, there is a solution.

What's the Solution?

A solution requires multiple parts to address a problem as complex as accommodating the ever-growing number of device types connected to the Internet. The first part of the solution is using a **mobile-first design**. When you plan a website with mobile-first design, you begin by identifying the site's most critical components so you can display those components on the small screen of a mobile device.

Navigation is near the top of this list, but page content should be included as well. Perhaps showing images of the products you are selling is the top priority. The ranked list of contents and functions that you identified in the planning stage will be your guide.

You should also consider the primary actions you want your users to take on each page when they interact with your most critical content, and make sure those actions occur near the middle of the screen. Buttons are easiest to click near the bottom-middle of the screen. Menus and a search function are easiest to use near the top-middle of the screen. Putting objects and content near the margins hinders usability.

After you've addressed the most critical features with your display requirements and considered how your users will interact with them, you can add content or display elements that work on a larger screen size. This is an additive approach rather than a reductionist approach. That is, you aren't taking away information or content from mobile users; you are adding stylistic or display elements for larger-display users.

The second part of the solution is to define **breakpoints** for screen widths. Breakpoints are the critical widths, measured in pixels, of the screen sizes for these devices. This means that you don't need to build separate webpages or style sheets for iPhones, Samsung Galaxy tablets, Tesla dashboards, and Dell monitors. Instead, you can write code that tells the browser that if the display is less than 480 pixels wide—which might be a phone screen, for example—the browser should show the page using the style you created for any device less than 480 pixels wide.

Each breakpoint tells the browser which style sheet to use to hide or show content and how to display the content it is showing. Instead of creating different webpage content, you create different style sheets to show the same content at, for example, widths less than 480 pixels, between 481 and 768 pixels, and greater than or equal to 769 pixels.

Using breakpoints also makes your website future-proof against a fantastic new device that is just about to hit the consumer electronics market. Perhaps it's a new smart dog collar, on which you can check your stock portfolio while your dog Bill gets some exercise and has his heart rate monitored. As long as the new device has a screen to render webpage contents, the browser used for that screen will have a display width defined in it, and your webpages will render properly if you've set up the website properly.

What's the Return on Investment?

This multifaceted approach to building webpages seems like a lot of extra work, and it does increase the complexity of web development. However, the benefits far outweigh the costs. When you design and build your webpages to respond to a user's device instead of assuming the user can view your preferred format, you flip the approach from a product you build to a consumable item your audience interacts with.

If you still aren't persuaded that the effort of creating breakpoints for a mobile-first design is worthwhile, consider this. When Google indexes your webpages, Googlebots are using the mobile version of Chrome and a simulated screen width of 375 pixels to assess your website. Webpage content that doesn't work with that resolution won't be ranked highly in the results returned from a Google search.

If your competitor also builds a new website selling products like Partially Hydrogenated Candy for Guppies and their page loads much faster than yours and is mobile-friendly, their website will be ranked higher in the Google search returns than yours.

If you search for "Google Mobile-Friendly Test," you will find a helpful Google page in which you enter the URL of your new website to run the same test that the Googlebots run when indexing your pages.

Note | One additional benefit to building your webpages with a responsive design is that it creates a scalable interface for users with visual impairments. Zooming in to enlarge the text size on the screen helps users overcome text readability issues, and a responsive design will dynamically compensate and scale up, since it is already built to accommodate a change in the viewport. In the United States, building a site that is accessible in this way is a legal requirement of the Americans with Disabilities Act. The European Union has a comparable Web Accessibility Directive.

How Do I Verify the Results?

As you will see in the next section, most of the common web browsers include utilities for web developers that show a screen similar to the most common mobile devices. These **mobile device emulators** show a webpage in a screen that is the same size (width and height) as the mobile device. You can test your work with these emulators without having to buy one of each device, which might quickly become prohibitively expensive.

When testing, it isn't necessary to anticipate each new device coming to the market, nor to even test with every available emulator. If you define your breakpoints to meet the most popular devices, you will serve all of the less widely used devices as well.

Quick Check 4-1

1. What is the problem mobile-first design is designed to solve?

    a. Most of your website users will be accessing the content on a mobile device.
    b. Job security for web developers is decreasing.
    c. Most websites are designed for developers to build easily, not for users.
    d. Webpage contents near the margins of the screen are not seen.

2. What does mobile-first design entail?

    a. Building websites that work well on mobile screens and having larger screen formats show the same mobile-friendly content in a larger space
    b. Building separate websites for mobile, tablet, and large-screen displays
    c. Adding style sheets to hide unnecessary content from mobile displays
    d. Building websites to fit mobile screens, then adding extra, less-critical content and function for larger screens

3. Why is mobile-friendly design so important?

    a. Google ranks fast, mobile-friendly sites that the mobile-screen Googlebots can access higher than slow, nonmobile-friendly sites.
    b. Users like the appearance of mobile-friendly sites more than standard screen displays.
    c. Web developers can add more creative content and write more interesting code for mobile-friendly sites.
    d. It's what all of the cool kids are doing these days.

1) a. Over half of website traffic occurs on a mobile device. **2) d.** Mobile-first design distills the contents of a webpage down to the most critical contents and functions, then adds extra details for larger screens. **3) a.** Because Google prioritizes mobile-friendly sites over nonadaptive-display sites in its rankings, mobile-friendly design is critical to a successful website.

4.2 Testing with Emulators

The process of testing your webpages across multiple devices could be a substantial (and expensive) challenge if you needed to have each targeted device in your hands. Fortunately, there's a much easier way.

Chrome, Firefox, Edge, and Safari each come bundled with a mobile device emulator that simulates the display for many specific devices along with generic screen sizes. The most difficult part of using these emulators is finding their location in the menu of the browser.

If you search for terms such as "Firefox responsive design mode" or "Chrome emulate device mode," you will find the most recent documentation for accessing the emulator utility for your browser of choice. The utility is typically associated with the Web Developer toolbar or Utilities menu. Most options have a keyboard command associated with them for faster access.

Getting Started

If you have not done so previously, create a new folder for Chapter 4. Then create folders for the Samples, Exercises, and Projects inside the Chapter_4 folder. Finally, create folders inside each of those to hold your Cascading Style Sheets (CSS) and image files. Download the starting files for Chapter 4 and put these files inside the appropriate folders in the Chapter_4\Samples folder. Store the starting HTML files in the root folder, CSS files in the css folder, and images in the images folder.

Open the starter files for Chapter 4 in your text editor and review the HTML in index.html and the CSS in my_styles.css. The webpage index.html was constructed in Chapter 3 but was designed from the perspective of a full-screen user. This webpage is a concrete example of a working webpage that you can now redesign using the mobile-first methodology. First, you need to find out what isn't working by testing this page with a mobile device emulator.

Using the Emulator

Start the mobile device emulator by following the directions you found in your previous search or when you were exploring the browser utilities.

You should see a screen like that in **Figure 4-1**, which is from Firefox on a Mac:

Figure 4-1 The starting index.html webpage designed for large screens

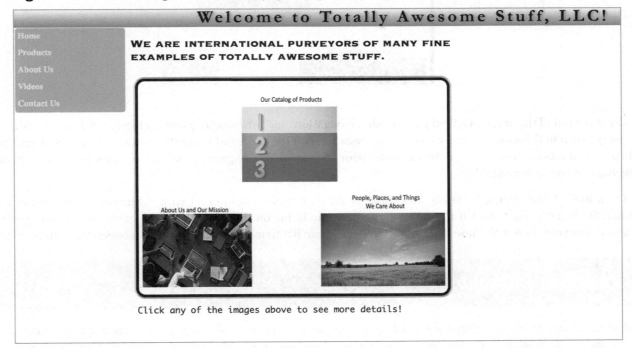

This page will be your control in the experiment of mobile-first design. It is working, but it is designed for large screens and the contents, navigation, and images are crowded and not mobile-friendly.

Since you are designing for three breakpoints instead of for a specific device, you will use those breakpoints as tests. Three screen widths at these breakpoints trigger a switch between style sheets: less than 480 pixels, 481 to 768 pixels, and greater than 769 pixels.

The first breakpoint to test is at 480 pixels wide for mobile devices. Set the device simulator width to 480 pixels. You can do this by typing the value in the page width text box or by dragging the simulated screen to that width. The page now looks like **Figure 4-2**.

Figure 4-2 Mobile emulator showing the page at a reduced width

The top third of the screen is filled with header, navigation, and introductory text. In Firefox, Safari, and Edge, the large image map in the `<section>...</section>` tags runs off the page and is nearly useless. The image does shrink in Chrome, but it does in only one of the big four major browsers. This page is not set up for mobile devices, although the navigation menu is available.

If you look at that menu, however, and think about how users will interact with it, the list items are too close together. Someone using their left thumb to click the menu items on their mobile phone could inadvertently click a menu item above or below the one they intend to use. Those list items need more space between them to be usable.

Common Mistakes

A word of caution about using the emulator included on your browser. If it appears you are zooming in on the content (that is, the webpage gets bigger instead of changing resolution in the simulated screen display size), then your simulator likely has a bug.

If you search for "Chrome Responsive Mode Bug" (or whatever browser you are using for testing) and review the results, you will find documentation of the various bugs that have been reported. Some have been fixed. One standard solution that seems to work is turning responsive mode off, then turning it back on before resuming your testing.

The Testing Process

As you have been doing previously, this tutorial instructs you to make one discrete change to the HTML or CSS code, save your page, then refresh the browser you are using to view your webpage.

Sometimes the change will make everything appear to break but still move the existing webpage closer to a mobile-friendly design; other times, the change will make things better. Be patient and make notes of what you have changed when you are creating a new webpage from scratch so you can try different scenarios. This is also where storing your files in a source control can be helpful, since you can roll back a series of changes to a last-known-good state if you go down a rabbit hole of lousy code or design.

In addition to testing the specific breakpoint for the targeted device, you should also test all the previously completed breakpoints, since a systemic style change or HTML update often has unintended consequences. Using an emulator makes this testing easier, since you can just drag the emulator to toggle the breakpoints. Testing regularly while you are making changes also makes adjusting these changes easier if you find that a change to your tablet resolution breaks the mobile or full-screen display, for example.

When you begin testing your mobile-first design on your own with a website that isn't constructed as part of tutorial like this one, you will use trial and error to find solutions. This chapter shortcuts through the week it took to transform the previous nonmobile-friendly design to a mobile-first webpage so that you can build a working mobile-friendly webpage quickly. As you gain experience, that process will speed up and you will know what works and what doesn't, but it will take time and patience.

Quick Check 4-2

1. What does a mobile device emulator do?

   a. Uses the operating system and screen settings of the mobile device to display webpages inside a browser window

   b. Shows webpage content in the browser at the same size screen as the mobile device being emulated

   c. Shows the web browser running as an app on the mobile device to recreate the screen size and settings

   d. Displays webpage content inside an iframe showing the device manufacturer's default screen size and resolution

2. How do you test screen size breakpoints using a mobile device emulator?

   a. Set the breakpoints in the HTML and test to see if the emulator will find them correctly.

   b. Set the breakpoints in the CSS and test to see if the emulator will find them correctly.

   c. Adjust the browser window size to each of the breakpoint values.

   d. Drag the screen size in the emulator to the value of the breakpoint or type the value manually.

3. Why should you test all of the breakpoints after making a major change to one display size?

   a. Changes to one style or HTML element can cause inadvertent changes to the display at another breakpoint.

   b. To find any mistakes you made in the other display size development.

   c. To order the selectors in the style sheets, ensuring that the style closest to the HTML element is the one that gets applied to that element.

   d. Showing additional content as you go up through the screen sizes in a mobile-first design will clutter the lower screen sizes.

1) b. The mobile device emulator shows the webpage inside a browser window at the same size as the device.
2) d. Emulators show the screen size as a text box input element and allow you to drag the simulated screen wider or narrower inside the browser window. **3) a.** Inadvertent overwriting of a portion of the style or HTML is a problem that is easier to fix after a small unit of change than at the end of a complete build.

4.3 Differentiating Style Sheets

Creating a responsive webpage begins with identifying which components of the webpage are most important to display to the users on the targeted screen sizes. With mobile-first design, you create a ranked list of the elements to display on a small screen, then add extra content and style to enrich the user experience as screen size allows.

The next step is creating a separate style sheet for each of the targeted breakpoints. In this way, the same HTML page will show, hide, or alter the display of the HTML elements depending on the display size of the device loading the page. Additionally, you will create a style sheet to contain your display-independent style themes, like fonts and colors that are used across all of the different breakpoints.

Because this course is designed and written to build your knowledge and understanding of the concepts of full stack web development as an incremental process, you were directed in previous chapters to create a simple webpage, then make it more complex, and finally add other webpages with a menu to navigate to each page. No assumption was made about your prior experience with technology, so you were guided through the building blocks of HTML and CSS from the most fundamental components.

In the real world, the mobile-first design process would begin with the concepts you'll find from this point forward in this chapter. However, you now know enough to recognize the critical steps in a technical design and the important HTML elements to assemble like building blocks in the mobile-first design and building of a webpage.

Mobile-First Design

Consider distilling the contents of the webpage index.html in the totallyawesomestuff.com website down into a list of the most important chunks of content. Everyone using this webpage needs the navigation to the subsequent pages since this page serves primarily as a welcome screen directing users to other pages with more detailed content. That means the navigation will need the most prominent screen real estate in an easy-to-use rendering on a mobile device.

The second most important part of this page is the content inside the `<section>...</section>` HTML tags. This content should occupy the balance of the smallest screen resolution you'll be targeting.

The header is the third most important component to this webpage since it provides the unique branding for the page. Users expect navigation near the top of the page, so you can integrate the header with the navigation for the mobile and tablet breakpoints.

Additional content to enrich the user experience will be added by using the different style sheets for midsize and large screens. However, the most critical components that make your site usable and user-friendly will need to be displayed on a mobile device with a screen less than 480 pixels wide.

The current style sheet for this page, my_styles.css, is adequate for screen sizes larger than 769 pixels wide (the standard minimum width of a laptop display or desktop monitor). However, for mobile devices, you'll need to create one style sheet for screen widths of 480 pixels or less and another style sheet for screen widths between 481 pixels and 768 pixels. These represent mobile devices ranging from small phones to tablets.

Make a backup copy of index.html and call it index2.html. Make a backup copy of my_styles.css and call it my_styles2.css. Update the link in index2.html to point to my_styles2.css so you have these files as a working reference to go back to if you need them. You will not update the index2.html and my_styles2.css files any further from this point on in the chapter.

> **Note** The screen sizes you are specifying as breakpoints are not arbitrary or randomly chosen. If you search for "common responsive design breakpoints," you'll find results from the most current datasets of devices connected to the Internet. The recommended breakpoints in your search results will include those chosen for this chapter.

Adding Meta and CSS Link Information

The first code to add to your index.html page is a **meta tag**. Meta tags are HTML tags that supply information to the browser about the HTML in the webpage that follows. Meta tags are not shown when the user views the webpage in a browser. Add the following meta tag to the `<head>...</head>` section of your webpage:

```
<meta name="viewport" content="width=device-width, initial-scale=1.0">
```

The `name` and `content` attributes of this meta tag differentiate it from other meta tags that might be included in the `<head>...</head>` section of a webpage. They provide the following information to the browser:

- The name in this case is `"viewport"`, which tells the browser that the visible parts of the webpage are described by the other attribute in this tag.
- The `content` attribute tells the browser that the webpage should have the `width` specified as the `device-width`. That is, it should fill the full width of the usable screen for the device showing it.
- The `initial-scale` attribute tells the browser not to zoom in on the page but instead leave it at the default scale of 1.0.

The next block of code to add between the `<head>...</head>` tags is a series of style sheets to use for the breakpoints chosen. The code is as follows:

```
<link rel="stylesheet" type="text/css" href="css/my_styles.css" media="screen" />
<link rel="stylesheet" type="text/css" href="css/full_screen.css" media="screen
    and (min-width:769px)" />
<link rel="stylesheet" type="text/css" href="css/tablet.css" media="screen and
    (max-width:768px) and (min-width:481px)" />
<link rel="stylesheet" type="text/css" href="css/mobile.css" media="screen and
    (max-width:480px)" />
```

These links are similar with some critical differences. The similarities are that each is a link to a style sheet, just like you have used previously. Those style sheets are stored in the css folder and relatively pathed to their respective file names: my_styles.css, full_screen.css, tablet.css, and mobile.css.

The new attributes in these links are the `media=` attribute and the values that follow that name. The tags provide the following information:

- In the first `<link>` tag, the media specified is for a `screen`. Note that no max or min width is specified for this style, unlike the other style sheets. This style sheet will be used for style declarations that apply to all screen widths, like the branding fonts and default settings. Using this style sheet will help to ensure you follow the web development principle of Don't Repeat Yourself.
- The next link is to the full_screen.css style sheet. It uses the `media="screen and (min-width:769px)"` attribute and value to separate itself from the rest of the style sheets. The `min-width:769px` breakpoint value ensures that the browser does not apply this style sheet to screens less than 769 pixels wide. A tablet screen typically does not display content properly on screen widths over 769 pixels, so this style sheet will be used for any screen larger than a tablet—like those on a laptop or desktop monitor.
- The third link is to tablet.css and has the most specific screen widths: `media="screen and (max-width:768px) and (min-width:481px)"`. This style sheet is applied to screens above the minimum width of 481 pixels and below the maximum width of 768 pixels. Because the link uses and to join the two specifications, both must be true to use this style sheet. Those breakpoints are typically the smallest and largest screen sizes for tablets, refrigerators, and car dashboards.
- The last link is to the mobile.css style sheet and should be used with most mobile devices. It has a `max-width:480px` set to ensure that it is applied only to screens less than 480 pixels wide. You will test as low as 320 pixels wide since that is about as narrow as mobile phones currently display content.

Create these three new style sheets—mobile.css, tablet.css, and full_screen.css—and save them inside the css folder in the Samples folder for Chapter 4. Add the standard comment block at the top of each file. Note that the names chosen for these files are not special. These style sheets could have been called small.css, medium.css, and large.css and work equally well.

> **Note**
>
> It is also possible to use the media and size specifications in a single style sheet. You would then put all of the default styles that apply to every page at the top of your style sheet, followed by the smallest screen size styles in a section, then the intermediate screen size selectors, then those for large screens. For simple websites, this can work, but for complex websites, this approach makes a long style sheet that becomes cumbersome to navigate and update.
>
> The next developer to pick up your code will appreciate your choice of a simpler approach like the one you are using here with unique style sheets and specific screen sizes for each breakpoint.

The Mobile Minimalism

With a mobile-first design and screen real estate at a premium, two major sections of the index.html page have been identified as the key areas to display—the nav and section elements. The current menu is set to be 200 pixels wide in the my_styles.css style sheet. The menu will fill nearly two-thirds of a 320-pixel-wide smartphone, leaving almost no space for other content. This is not optimal, since navigation to the other pages in the site is important but only when the user needs it.

One of the conventions of mobile-friendly webpages is to build a "hamburger menu" icon that users click to display more navigation options. While it is by no means a rule, most mobile users understand that the three-line equal sign (two buns and a patty between them) is a place to click to see more options on a menu. You will create a version of a hamburger menu to hide the navigation area until the user interacts with the webpage. **Figure 4-3** shows an example of two hamburger menus in the mobile display of the BBC World News Sport webpage, with the lower menu expanded.

Figure 4-3 Two hamburger menus on the BBC World News website

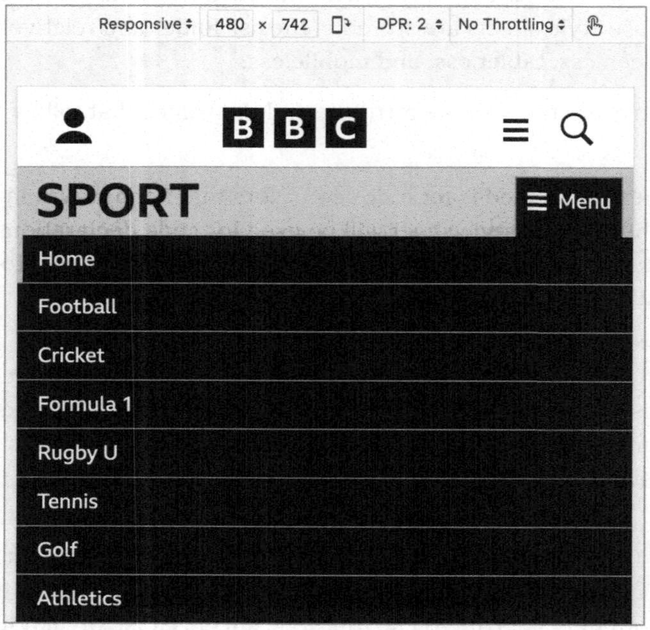

Source: bbc.com

> **Note**
>
> The lore of the Internet is that the hamburger menu you may have seen on many mobile websites was created by Norm Cox decades ago. If you search for "who created the hamburger mobile menu icon," you'll find pages describing the history of this iconic, well-known icon. It has been replicated often enough in numerous variations that it has become one of the default standards for mobile website navigation.

The hamburger icon and the slightly reduced site header can easily fit together on the first line of the smallest screen size you will target—a 320-pixel screen width. This design maintains the branding of the header while minimizing the footprint of the navigation until the user needs it. Then, with a click of the hamburger icon, the menu for the site will appear and occupy more screen space.

Building the Burger

To create the hamburger menu, you need to revise the index.html page. Since you are using a mobile-first design, move the `<nav>...</nav>` section inside the `<h1>...</h1>` tags in the header element.

The following shows the original header and nav elements:

```
<header>
    <h1>
        Welcome to Totally Awesome Stuff, LLC!
    </h1>
</header>


<nav>
...
</nav>
```

Combine the heading and the navigation into the header as follows:

```
<header>
    <h1>
        Welcome to Totally Awesome Stuff, LLC!
    </h1>
    <nav>
...
    </nav>
</header>
```

Add a blank line below the `<h1>...</h1>` tags and above the `<nav>...</nav>` tags, and then add the following HTML code:

```
<input class="menu-chkbx" type="checkbox" id="menu-chkbx" />
<label class="menu-burger" for="menu-chkbx">
    <span class="hamburger"></span>
</label>
```

When you are done, you will have a page of code that looks like **Figure 4-4**.

When you read the new HTML code, starting with the `<input class="menu-chkbx" type="checkbox" id="menu-chkbx" />` code, you may see something familiar but slightly out of context. A check box is typically associated with data-gathering forms for user input. The useful part about a check box is that it has exactly two states: checked and unchecked. This is similar to the menu in a mobile site, which is visible or not visible.

If you add a label to a check box, as in the next three lines of code, the label becomes part of the clickable region for that check box. That is, you can click the label to also check the check box. If the label contains a hamburger icon, the user will be checking the box by clicking the hamburger icon, toggling the menu to appear. Unchecking the box by clicking the hamburger icon again will hide the menu. The span element with the class of hamburger is the HTML element that contains this hamburger icon.

Figure 4-4 The HTML code for the first set of updates to the index.html webpage

```
1    <!DOCTYPE html>
2  ▼ <html>
3  ▼     <head>
4  ▼         <!-- Developer: (your name)
5  └            Start Date: (today's date) -->
6             <title>Totally Awesome Stuff</title>
7             <link rel="stylesheet" type="text/css" href="css/my_styles.css" media="screen,
   print" />
8             <link rel="stylesheet" type="text/css" href="css/full_screen.css" media="screen
   and (min-width:769px)" />
9             <link rel="stylesheet" type="text/css" href="css/tablet.css" media="screen and
   (max-width:768px) and (min-width:481px)" />
10            <link rel="stylesheet" type="text/css" href="css/mobile.css" media="screen and
   (max-width:480px)" />
11            <meta name="viewport" content="width=device-width, initial-scale=1.0" />
12 └        </head>
13 ▼        <body>
14 ▼            <header>
15 ▼                <h1>
16                     Welcome to Totally Awesome Stuff, LLC!
17 └                </h1>
18                 <input class="menu-chkbx" type="checkbox" id="menu-chkbx" />
19 ▼                <label class="menu-burger" for="menu-chkbx">
20                     <span class="hamburger"></span>
21 └                </label>
22 ▼                <nav>
23 ▼                    <ul>
24 ▼                        <li>
25                             <a href="index.html">Home</a>
26 └                        </li>
27 ▼                        <li>
28                             <a href="products.html">Products</a>
29 └                        </li>
30 ▼                        <li>
31                             <a href="about.html">About Us</a>
32 └                        </li>
33 ▼                        <li>
34                             <a href="video.html">Videos</a>
35 └                        </li>
36 ▼                        <li>
37                             <a href="contact_us.html">Contact Us</a>
38 └                        </li>
39 └                    </ul>
40 └                </nav>
41 └            </header>
42
```

To focus development on just the mobile design for this page, you need to temporarily remove all of the other styling supplied by my_styles.css. Make sure you have made a backup copy of this file (and named it my_styles2.css or similar) and then delete all of the styling information from my_styles.css so just the opening comment remains. Your site should now be completely unstyled when you view it in a web browser and look like **Figure 4-5**, which shows the webpage at a width of 362 pixels.

This is the starting point for your mobile-first redesign. Add the following CSS to your mobile.css file, pressing Tab to separate the words in the two lines before the closing curly bracket:

```
header {
    margin: -10px 0px 0px -10px;
    padding-left: 5px;
    display: grid;
    grid-template-areas:
        "hamburger   title   title"
        "nav         nav      nav";
}
```

Figure 4-5   The unstyled index.html webpage

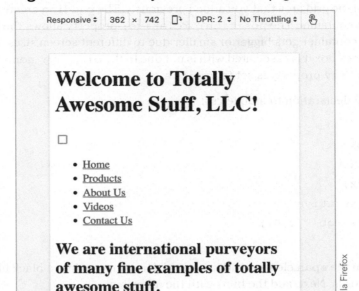

Source: Mozilla Firefox

You have used the `margin` and `padding` styles before—these are adjustments to the header position inside the browser window. The next two declarations are new, however. The `display: grid;` style tells the browser that the contents inside the `header` will use a grid layout, and the `grid-template-areas` declaration describes what those grid areas will be named and where they are positioned inside the header. This is similar to telling the browser to display these elements inside a table with rows and columns, then naming the cells inside those rows and columns, and finally assigning content to the named cells.

Based on those template area names, you can probably guess what content goes where—the hamburger icon will go on the upper-left and the title in the next two "cells." The navigation, when it is displayed, will occupy the rest of the header's second row.

Next on the menu is building the burger. The `<span>` you added earlier will be filled with this delicious content, yet it doesn't have any space inside an opening and closing tag. However, you can apply CSS magic sauce to the buns and patty.

Add the following to your mobile.css style sheet after the `header` declaration:

```
.menu-chkbx {
    display: none;
}
```

This will hide the check box that has a class of `.menu-chkbx`, since you are using the check box label rather than the check box itself. While you are using the check box for its checked or unchecked status, the users interacting with the site don't need to see it, so it isn't displayed. Next, add the following content:

```
.menu-burger {
    grid-area: hamburger;
    padding: 30px 20px 30px 0;
    position: relative;
    visibility: visible;
}
```

Working from the top down, the `grid-area` specified for where the menu-burger appears is the `hamburger` cell. That's the upper-left part of the grid area that you added previously. The `padding` creates space around the burger so it is not crowded inside its container. The `position: relative;` property allows the burger to move around relative to its container as the container gets bigger or smaller due to different screen sizes. Finally, the label needs to be visible, even though the check box it is associated with is not due to the `display: none;` added in the `.menu-chkbx` declaration, so the `visibility` property is set to `visible`.

Next, add the following declaration to mobile.css:

```css
.hamburger {
    display: block;
    height: 2px;
    width: 20px;
    position: relative;
    background: rgb(0,0,0);
}
```

This chunk of style will turn the `span` element with a `class` of `hamburger` into a black block 2 pixels tall by 20 pixels wide. The patty, in other words. Next, add the buns with the following:

```css
.hamburger:before {
    top: 5px;
}
.hamburger:after {
    top: -5px;
}
.hamburger:before, .hamburger:after {
    background: rgb(0,0,0);
    display: block;
    width: 100%;
    height: 100%;
    content: '';
    position: absolute;
}
```

These three declarations use the pseudo-classes `:before` and `:after` to create a **pseudo-element**, which is something that doesn't actually exist in the HTML. The first two declarations create space at the top of this phantom element of 5 pixels above and below the actual `.hamburger` element. The third declaration combines the style for the before and after pseudo-classes into one style declaration since the buns of the burger will be styled identically. Notice that the background color is the same as the patty and that these phantoms will be displayed as a block, but the `width` and `height` are both `100%` of the patty. This creates buns of the same dimensions as the patty, three lines of equal thickness and length. If the dimensions of the patty change, the buns will too, and the position will stay absolutely fixed to the patty as well. The `content` property is necessary to show these phantom elements, but the value is nothing (`' '`) since they specify only a background color.

Save your changes, then refresh your page in the browser emulator. You should now see a burger and have an alignment similar to that shown in **Figure 4-6**.

This is a good start, but if you click the hamburger icon, nothing happens and the menu items that are floating at the right of the page header don't change. This is because you haven't yet told the browser what to do when the check box is checked.

Figure 4-6 Hamburger menu icon and navigation menu moved into the header

Source: Mozilla Firefox

Add the following declaration to mobile.css:

```
.menu-chkbx:checked ~ .menu-burger .hamburger {
    background: transparent;
}
```

This CSS code combines three selectors into one style declaration. The first part, `.menu-chkbx: checked`, is the selector that tells the browser to apply the style only when the check box of the class `menu-chkbx` is in the checked state using the `:checked` pseudo-class. The tilde (~) tells the browser to apply the style that follows to the next HTML element that occurs within the same enclosing HTML element. This is known as a **sibling element**. A **parent element** is the one that contains the **child element**, but within the same parent element, more than one child element becomes sibling elements. To be more specific in the preceding code, the target for the `background: transparent;` style is the `span` HTML element with the `.hamburger` class element in the `<label>`...`</label>` tags, and the `menu-burger` class element inside the `<header>`...`</header>` tags that also contain the `<input>` tag with the class `.menu-chkbx`. The last two selectors in this chain are read in reverse, similar to other chained styles you have used previously.

The effect of this complex style is to hide the burger patty by making the background transparent instead of black. Next, you transform the buns by adding the following CSS code:

```
.menu-chkbx:checked ~ .menu-burger .hamburger:before {
    transform: rotate(-45deg);
}
.menu-chkbx:checked ~ .menu-burger .hamburger:after {
    transform: rotate(45deg);
}
```

These two selectors rotate the top and bottom buns (the before and after pseudo-elements) by 45 degrees. The top bun rotates down by 45 degrees and the bottom rotates up by 45 degrees. These will form an X—almost. One more piece is necessary to move them into position:

```
.menu-chkbx:checked ~ .menu-burger .hamburger:before,
.menu-chkbx:checked ~ .menu-burger .hamburger:after {
    top: 0;
}
```

When the top of both "buns" is set to 0, they are moved over each other to form the X. The intended effect is to change the hamburger icon to an X when the menu is opened, prompting the user to click the X to close the menu again. This selector combines the two element selectors with a comma since the same style is applied to both. Again—Don't Repeat Yourself.

Save your changes and refresh your webpage. You should now have a hamburger icon that, when you click it, transforms into an X, and then back to a hamburger when the check box is unchecked. While this is very neat, the only problem is that it doesn't do anything with the navigation on the page. You will change that next.

Now for Navigation

All of the display sizes on this website will use the same default style for the unordered list items that contain the navigation links. Add that universal style to my_styles.css with the following code:

```
nav {
    width: 200px;
    float: left;
}
nav ul {
    line-height: 2em;
    list-style-type: none;
    padding-left: 0px;
    text-indent: 5px;
    border-radius: 5px;
}
nav ul li {
    background-color: rgb(175,175,175);
    border-radius: 5px;
    width: 99%
}
nav a {
    color: rgb(255,255,0);
    font-weight: bold;
    text-decoration: none;
}
```

If the code looks familiar, it should since it is a partial copy of the previously used styles for totallyawesomestuff.com site navigation. The positioning elements like margins and padding that would incorrectly position the elements in the mobile and tablet display have been removed, but the rounded corners, background colors, and other stylistic elements that represent a common site theme remain.

Next, you need to style the mobile menu items uniquely for the mobile display. Add the following styles to the end of your mobile.css:

```
nav ul li {
    margin: 10px 0px 10px 0px;
    text-align: center;
    border: 1px solid rgb(0,0,0);
}
```

This set of styles will transform the list items into a large-format menu separated by a wide margin between each item. It also adds a border around each of the list items so that they look more like buttons in a menu.

Save all of your changes, then refresh your page. You should see a screen like that in **Figure 4-7**.

Figure 4-7   Continuing the mobile-first redesign of the index.html webpage

The page includes all the required parts, but the elements in the header need to be rearranged. To do this, add the menu class to your nav element in the index.html page with the following code:

```
<nav class="menu">
```

Next, add the following code to mobile.css:

```
.menu {
    grid-area: nav;
    display: flex;
    flex-direction: column;
    max-height: 0;
    overflow: hidden;
    margin: 0;
    padding: 0;
}
```

The first item in this stack assigns the menu to the nav cells in the grid you created earlier. These nav cells were in the second row, below the hamburger and header.

The `display: flex;` property tells the web browser that the elements in the HTML element being styled by this declaration (i.e., the list items inside the unordered list that has the class menu) will be displayed using the `flex-direction: column;` property, so when they are visible, they will appear stacked vertically, like a mobile menu should.

More generally, the `display: flex;` property tells the browser that the HTML element should be added to the **flexbox**. The flexbox is another flexible container used to show content that expands, contracts, and rearranges itself depending on the screen size. Flexbox containers are HTML elements that hold repeated elements inside them. Flexbox items are displayed in a row or a column that resizes and rearranges itself for different display sizes, and each item that is added to the flexbox with the addition of this style will become part of the flexible layout.

The `max-height` of 0 makes the menu and its items 0 pixels tall. That is, they will not be shown in this state. This is how the menu is hidden until the hamburger is clicked.

Save your changes, then refresh the page. The nav menu should disappear since it was assigned the `max-height` of 0 by the previous declaration. Clicking the hamburger changes it to an X but doesn't trigger a change to the menu. One more style is needed to change the `max-height` from 0 to something more. Add the following to your mobile.css:

```
.menu-chkbx:checked ~ .menu {
    max-height: 250px;
    position: absolute;
    margin-top: 62px;
    z-index: 1;
    border-radius: 5px;
    background-color: rgb(220,220,220);
}
```

This is the meal ticket to an expanding menu from the hamburger. When the check box is in the checked state, the maximum height of the menu becomes 250 pixels. When the check box is unchecked, the menu reverts to a height of 0 pixels. The `position: absolute;` and `z-index: 1;` properties move the menu over the top of the remaining page contents. The `border-radius` and `background-color` properties add the final polishing touches.

Save your changes, then refresh the page. Clicking the hamburger icon should now display the menu below the header and clicking the X should hide it.

Styling the Header

The rest of the mobile page needs some aesthetic updates to complete the mobile-friendly look. The my_styles.css style sheet will contain styles common to the other three style sheets. Since the pages use the same font and color for all display sizes, the first style belongs in my_styles.css. Add the following style to the beginning of the my_styles.css style sheet:

```
html, body {
    height: 100%;
    width: 100%;
}
header {
    width: 105%;
    margin: 0px -10px 0px -10px;
    background-color: rgb(240,248,255);
}
```

The first style declaration fills the full screen with the html and body elements, and the second sets the width and margins of the header to just over the full width of the screen so that the header fills the full width with the background color.

Next, add the following code to my_styles.css to modify the h1 element to match the theme of the original site.

```
header h1 {
    text-shadow: 2px 2px 5px rgb(30,144,255);
    font-family: Garamond;
    background-image: linear-gradient(rgb(255,255,255),rgb(30,144,255));
}
```

This is a slightly reduced set of the original styling, with only the common elements included. In mobile.css, add the following code after the header style set to apply a specific mobile-friendly style to the same h1 element:

```
header h1 {
    display: flex;
    grid-area: title;
    font-size: 20px;
    margin: 10px -10px 0px 0px;
    align-items: center;
    width: 100%;
}
```

The most important part of this code that hasn't been previously addressed is assigning the h1 via the display: flex; and grid-area: title; properties to the upper-right cells in the grid you created earlier. This header h1 style also reduces the font size to 20 pixels, a more appropriate value for mobile displays, and moves the header down and to the right by 10 pixels.

Save your changes, refresh the page in the browser, and click the hamburger icon. Your page should look like that in **Figure 4-8**.

Figure 4-8   The completed mobile menu displayed in the mobile screen emulator

If your page looks like Figure 4-8, congratulations, you have finished the first part of your first mobile-first design. That's a lot of firsts. This was also the most labor-intensive part of this project since you needed to start over completely. The tablet and full-screen displays will both use the common elements from this work, so you will have less work to do with them.

To the Tablet

The next screen size to target is that of the tablet. According to the specifiers in the `<link>` tag in the `head` section of the HTML page, a tablet-sized screen has breakpoints of a minimum of 481 pixels to a maximum of 768 pixels.

Open your tablet.css in your text editor if you don't already have it open and adjust the display screen size in the browser between 481 pixels and 768 pixels. You should see a screen that looks like that in **Figure 4-9**.

Figure 4-9 The initial tablet screen styling for index.html

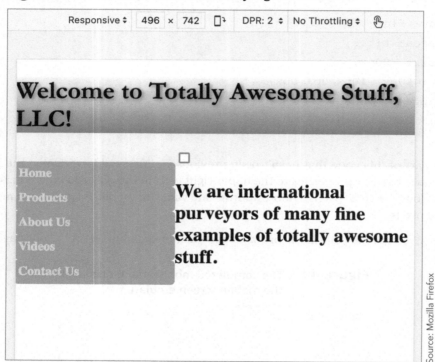

Source: Mozilla Firefox

That looks like a good start, but the page is still a composite of some features of the full-size site and the mobile site. The header and menu should be updated to fit the tablet screen size.

While you could reuse the hamburger, the navigation would look and function better as a horizontal array of buttons in this presentation. First, hide the hamburger icon and check box by adding the following style to your tablet.css:

```
.menu-burger, .menu-chkbx, .hamburger {
    display: none;
}
```

This declaration hides all three components of the hamburger icon with the single `display: none;` property because they are part of a comma-separated list.

Next, add the following code to tablet.css to make the `nav` element span the full height and nearly the full width of the allowed space and rearrange it slightly using the margins:

```
nav {
    margin: -15px 0px 0px 5px;
    width: 99%;
    height: 100%;
}
```

Now for the important part. Add the following code to your tablet.css:

```
nav ul {
    width: 95%;
    display: flex;
    flex-direction: row;
    justify-content: center;
    align-items: center;
}
```

This style declaration is where the first part of the tablet menu magic happens, but it is actually just the horizontal version of the `display: flex;` property you used in the mobile.css menu. The `flex-direction: row;` property tells the browser to display the list items inside the unordered list inside the nav HTML element in a row. In the mobile.css style sheet, these same elements were displayed in a column since a mobile device has more vertical screen space than horizontal space.

The `justify-content: center;` property goes with the `display: flex;` property to distribute the list item elements evenly across the navigation space. The `align-items: center;` property ensures that if the items become unequal in height, they will be centered vertically through their midlines.

The `nav ul` declaration styles the container for the list items, but not the list items themselves. They are already gray and have rounded corners due to the common styling in my_styles.css but need more polish to look good on a tablet. Add the following code to your tablet.css to style those list items:

```
nav ul li {
    flex: 1;
    margin: 0px;
    padding: 0px;
    border: 1px solid rgb(0,0,0);
    text-align: center;
}
```

The only new part to this declaration is the `flex: 1;` part. This tells the browser to keep all of the elements the same size as the display resolution changes.

Finally, the header could use additional work. Add the following style definition to your tablet.css to make the header look better in the midsized display:

```
header h1 {
    width: 100%;
    margin: -5px 0px 0px -10px;
    text-align: center;
    font-size: 22px;
}
```

This declaration is similar to the `header h1` style for the mobile display but with different margins and font size, which will make the header fit in a tablet rendering.

Save all of these changes, then refresh your page. You should now have a tablet-friendly webpage that looks like **Figure 4-10**.

Figure 4-10 The completed tablet header and menu for index.html

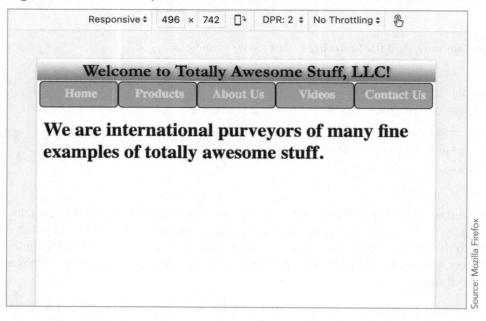

Finally the Full Screen

With the mobile-first and tablet-second designs completed, the full-screen presentation is the last screen size to address. However, you already have a completed build of this size in the starting files. The work now is primarily in adding the unique styles to full_screen.css that don't apply to mobile or tablet displays.

Expand the emulator to a width value more than 769 pixels, which is the lower breakpoint for the full_screen.css. You should see a screen like that shown in **Figure 4-11**.

Figure 4-11 The initial index.html webpage for full-screen displays

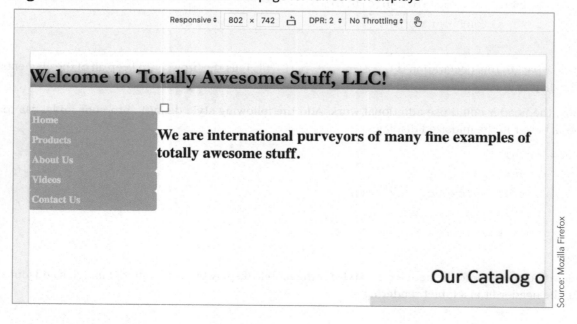

This is close to finished, but that pesky check box still appears and should not. You could add an identical block of CSS code to the one you created in tablet.css to hide the check box in full_screen.css, but that would break the Don't Repeat Yourself rule.

A better solution is to update my_styles.css. The common CSS styles for all of the display sizes are in my_styles. css, and if you add one extra block of code there, you can apply the style used to hide this selection to all screen widths greater than or equal to 480 pixels, the upper breakpoint for the mobile screens.

Cut the following block of CSS from tablet.css, which was used to hide the menu check box from tablet display sizes, and then add it to my_styles.css after the html, body style:

```
.menu-burger, .menu-chkbx, .hamburger {
    display: none;
    }
```

For all displays of 480 pixels or wider (i.e., everything except the mobile display), you can hide the hamburger menu and its check box by adding a display size constraint to a style sheet using the min-width: 480px; selector along with a media constraint. The code for that selector and constraint when used inside a style sheet is as follows:

```
@media screen and (min-width: 480px) {
}
```

Combined in the my_styles.css style sheet, the completed block looks like the following:

```
@media screen and (min-width: 480px) {
    .menu-burger, .menu-chkbx, .hamburger {
    display: none;
    }
}
```

The important parts of this style declaration are all components you've seen before, now combined into one block. Note the double curly braces, which are used to wrap the style declaration inside a media and screen size constraint.

Next, add the following to full_screen.css to complete the navigation style for that screen size:

```
nav {
    width: 200px;
    float: left;
    margin-right: 10px;
    margin-top: -35px;
}
nav ul {
    background-color: rgb(175,175,175);
}
nav ul li:hover {
    background-color: rgb(148,51,62);
    border-radius: 5px;
}
```

These are style declarations unique to the full-screen display that modify the nav section, copied from the previously completed CSS file.

Save your changes, then refresh the page. You need to make a few final changes to return the page to the original style. Add the following to your full_screen.css style sheet:

```
header h1 {
    width: 100%;
    margin: -5px 0px 20px -10px;
    text-align: center;
}
```

This block of CSS rearranges the h1 element inside the header to fit the largest screen display size you are targeting.

One last touch to add before declaring a partial victory is to incorporate the style for the h2 element into my_styles.css from the previously completed webpage. Add the following style declaration to my_styles.css:

```
section h2 {
    font-family: Copperplate, "Copperplate Gothic", serif;
    max-width: 870px;
}
```

Save your changes, and then refresh the page. You should now have a full-screen webpage that looks like **Figure 4-12**.

Figure 4-12 The completed header and menu for full-screen displays

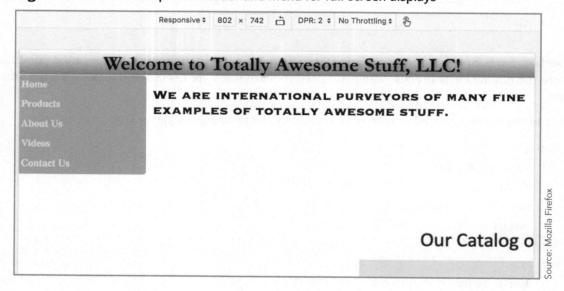

If you are willing to ignore the elephant-sized splash screen image lurking in the lower-right corner of the room, this display size and the other two display sizes targeted are now complete. Or nearly complete.

In the next section, you modify the splash screen image to make it more compatible with different screen sizes and return the footer to the webpage where you can see it again.

> ## Quick Check 4-3

1. How does a mobile-first design also show the same webpage contents on a full-screen display?

   a. By making the mobile-friendly page look larger in the full-screen display

   b. By zooming out on the webpage in the full-screen display

   c. By creating multiple webpages for each of the screen sizes, starting with the smallest mobile screen

   d. By changing the appearance of the HTML elements to take advantage of the larger screen size

2. Why are different style sheets necessary for each of the breakpoint targets?

   a. They aren't, but the next web developer to work on the website will appreciate using separate style sheets for each screen size corresponding to each of the breakpoints.

   b. This is the only way to make different screen sizes look different.

   c. Web browsers require different style sheets for the emulator to work properly.

   d. Googlebots will read the different style sheets and identify the website as mobile-friendly.

3. What does the z-index of 1 do to an HTML element when it is applied?

   a. Moves it to the front of the display on top of all of the other elements

   b. Moves it to the back of the display under all of the other elements

   c. Moves it all the way to the right of the display

   d. Moves it all the way to the left of the display

1) d. A mobile-first design uses styling to show additional content as the screen size gets bigger. **2) a.** All of the style information can go in one style sheet, but it becomes very large and difficult to maintain. **3) a.** The z-index property controls the depth of the HTML elements in the layout grid.

4.4 Using Images Wisely

The splash screen image used in the previous version of this webpage was designed only for a full-screen display to fill the `section` element. This is not optimal for a multimodal resolution like you have built so far in this chapter, since it is a large image and uses an image map to create links to the subsections of the website.

Each browser displays large images differently when the viewport is reduced in a mobile or tablet-sized display. Some browsers proportionally shrink the image while others add a horizontal scroll bar at the bottom of the page to continue to show the image at its original size. The effects are not universal, so large images used as image maps are not optimal for mobile-first design. The hotspots on the original image will no longer apply if the image shrinks with a smaller display size.

It might be possible to create a separate image size declaration for each style sheet that would modify the image and make it appear smaller from the default size, but that would still present a challenge for load times, since large images take longer to load. It would also be possible to create multiple image maps for each screen size and modify the corners of the map depending on the screen size, but this would create a lot of extra and unnecessary work.

Making Images Work

A better way to solve the problem is to create multiple smaller images that can move around as the screen size changes, similar to the way the menu changed from a vertical to horizontal orientation, then back to a vertical full-flavor presentation as the screen size changed from small to medium to large. Each of those smaller images can then serve as a link to the secondary content pages.

Open the images folder provided for this chapter and look at the files in it. The four smaller images—about_us.png, catalog.png, contact_us.png, and people_places.png—can be used to create the desired outcome along with the large original splash_screen.png image used for the image map.

In the index.html file, remove the `<figure>...</figure>` contents of the `<section>...</section>` area, leaving the `<h2>...</h2>` tags and content.

After the closing `</h2>` tag in index.html, add a span element with the class of `image-grid`, as in the following code:

```
<span class="image-grid"> </span>
```

Between the opening and closing `<span>...</span>` tags you just created, add four more sets of `<span>...</span>` tags. These will become the containers for the images that will move, depending on the display format.

Add a class to each of the four spans, assigning `class="img-top-l"` to the first span, `class="img-top-r"` to the second, `class="img-bot-l"` to the third, and `class="img-bot-r"` to the fourth. These will correspond to the template areas (top left, top right, bottom left, and bottom right) you used previously to display the header.

Inside each of the four spans you just completed, add the following code:

```
<a href=""><img class="four-square" src="" alt="" /></a>
```

Then, fill in the empty quotes with the filename values necessary to create a link to each of the pages suggested by the images, the file path to the image, and the appropriate alternative text. When you are done, you should have a page of the following HTML code, also shown in **Figure 4-13**.

Figure 4-13 HTML code for displaying four smaller images in a flex layout

```
43      <section>
44          <h2>
45              We are international purveyors of many fine examples of totally awesome
        stuff.
46          </h2>
47          <span class="image-grid">
48              <span class="img-top-l">
49                  <a href="causes.html">
50                      <img class="four-square" src="images/people_places.png" alt="An
        image of a green field with a blue sky." />
51                  </a>
52              </span>
53              <span class="img-top-r">
54                  <a href="about.html">
55                      <img class="four-square" src="images/about_us.png" alt="An image
        of a group of people working together around a table." />
56                  </a>
57              </span>
58              <span class="img-bot-l">
59                  <a href="products.html.html">
60                      <img class="four-square" src="images/catalog.png" alt="An image of
        a grid of products." />
61                  </a>
62              </span>
63              <span class="img-bot-r">
64                  <a href="contact_us.html">
65                      <img class="four-square" src="images/contact_us.png" alt="An image
        of a laptop with the words 'Contact Us!' on it." />
66                  </a>
67              </span>
68          </span>
69      </section>
```

Source: BBEdit

```
<span class="image-grid">
    <span class="img-top-l">
        <a href="causes.html"><img class="four-square" src="images/people_
            places.png" alt="An image of a green field with a blue sky." /></a>
    </span>
```

```
<span class="img-top-r">
    <a href="about.html"><img class="four-square" src="images/about_us.png"
        alt="An image of a group of people working together around a
        table." /></a>
</span>
<span class="img-bot-l">
    <a href="products.html"><img class="four-square" src="images/catalog.
        png" alt="An image of a grid of products." /></a>
</span>
<span class="img-bot-r">
    <a href="contact_us.html"><img class="four-square" src="images/contact_
        us.png" alt="An image of a laptop with the words 'Contact Us!' on
        it." /></a>
</span>
</span>
```

As you may have already guessed, you need to add some classes to the my_styles.css style sheet, since these styles will apply to all screen resolutions. First, add the following code to the end of my_styles.css:

```
.image-grid {
    width: 90%;
    justify-content: center;
    align-items: center;
    display: grid;
    grid-template-areas:
        "img-top-l    img-top-r"
        "img-bot-l    img-bot-r";
}
```

This style declaration follows the same pattern that you saw in the setup for the header. The `display: grid;` and `grid-template-areas:` properties are the keys to making the images appear correctly in all of the display sizes.

Next, you need to create a separate class for each span inside the span for the image-grid. To do so, add the following to the end of my_styles.css:

```
.img-top-l{
    display: flex;
    grid-area: img-top-l;
}
.img-top-r{
    display: flex;
    grid-area: img-top-r;
}
.img-bot-l{
    display: flex;
    grid-area: img-bot-l;
}
.img-bot-r{
    display: flex;
    grid-area: img-bot-r;
}
```

While those four style declarations repeat code, the alternative approach of listing the common `display: flex;` properties for four comma-separated class selectors, followed by four unique class selectors for each of the grid areas, is the same amount of work and CSS code. This is one time when repeating yourself and not repeating yourself are equal in terms of maintainability and effort.

Add the following to your my_styles.css:

```
img.four-square {
    width: auto;
    height: auto;
    max-width: 90%;
    padding: 5px;
    margin: 5px;
    border-style: solid;
    border-color: rgb(175,175,175) rgb(200,200,200);
    background-color: black;
    border-radius: 20px;
}
```

This style declaration puts a frame around the images just like the previous frame used for the single large image. Additionally, it uses the `width: auto;` and `height: auto;` properties to keep the images resized appropriately regardless of device width.

Save all of your changes, then refresh the page. You should now see a screen that looks like **Figure 4-14** in the full-screen display, with the image grid content shrinking and the menus changing as you resize to smaller displays.

Figure 4-14 The completed index.html webpage

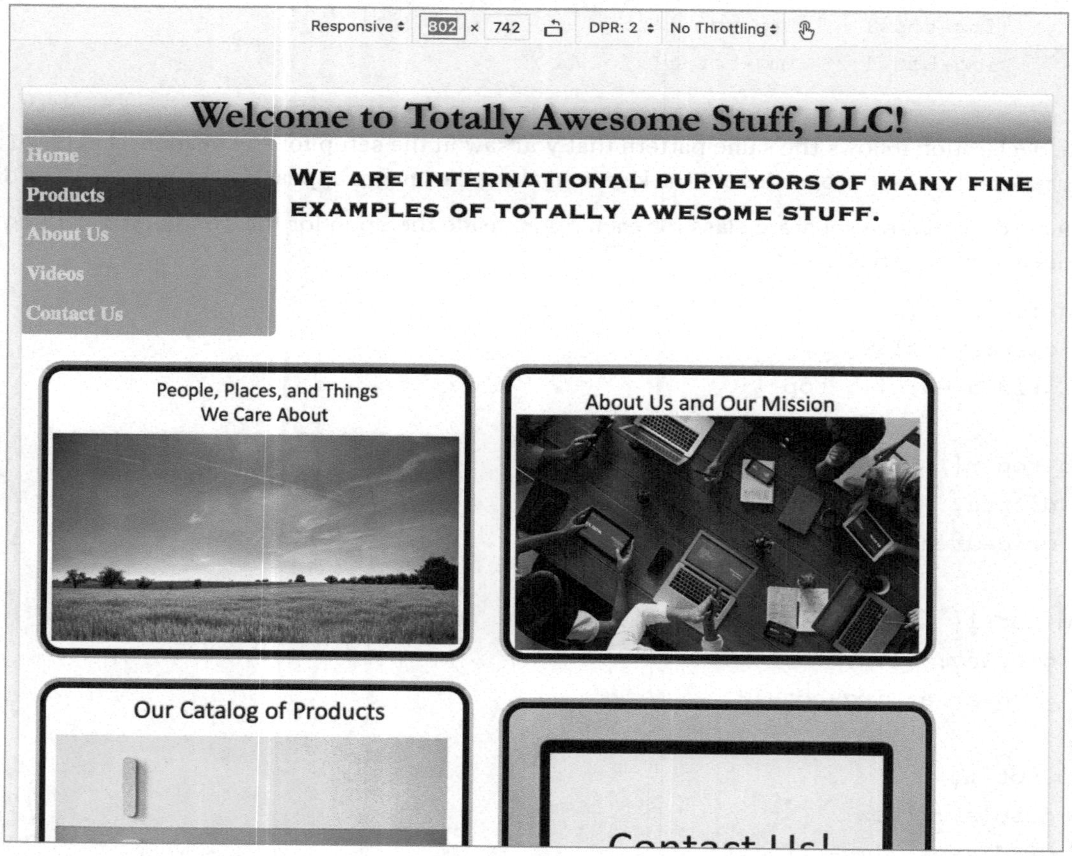

Source: Mozilla Firefox

You can make one last addition to complete the mobile-first webpage. Add the following to your my_styles.css file to style the footer:

```
footer {
    text-align: center;
    font-size: .75em;
    font-family: Garamond;
    background-color: rgb(200,200,200);
    margin: 0px -10px 20px -10px;
}
```

Image Sizes

Whenever possible, you should specify image sizes in terms of a percentage of the available container size instead of a specific number of pixels for the width and height. Using a percentage allows the browser to dynamically resize your images relative to the display size, as long as the HTML element that contains the image also has its size specified as a percentage of the total screen width.

To constrain the upper and lower bounds of an image size, you can use the max-width and min-width properties in your style sheet and specify the maximum and minimum number of pixels for an image. Combining the relative sizing and the size constraints makes your webpage contents fit the intended design instead of allowing them to be manipulated by the default settings on the browser.

You can see this effect in the tiles that make up the section content in index.html. If you drag the screen smaller than the target mobile screen resolution, the images are reduced to mere thumbnails since you didn't add a specific min-width. They effectively become unreadable dots at any display size under 250 pixels wide.

Since the images have a margin of 25 pixels on each side, together those margins use approximately 50 pixels of space around the images. That leaves 100 pixels for each image as a min-width. Add the following code to the img.four-square style declaration in your my_styles.css to make this happen:

```
min-width: 100px;
```

Save your changes and refresh the page. When you reduce the screen size below 250 pixels, a horizontal scroll bar appears and the images stay wider than the display window. While not optimal, this leaves your content usable even at the smallest screen size with a little horizontal scrolling.

Quick Check 4-4

1. Why should you not use specific image width and height parameters measured in pixels on a webpage?

   a. Because images already have a default size, and if you need to make the image smaller you should use image editing software

   b. Because images with a specific size won't load as fast as images with a dynamic size

   c. Because images with a specific size can't be reused on a different page

   d. Because images with a specific size won't resize with a smaller or larger display screen size

2. What are grid template areas used for?

   a. Creating the cells in a rows-and-columns layout of the webpage and its contents

   b. Creating mobile-friendly tables of tabular data

   c. Creating placeholders for menu and header items in a mobile style sheet

   d. Creating the style information for an unordered list used in a mobile-friendly design

(continues)

3. What is a challenge with using image maps in a mobile-first design?

    a. As the screen size changes, the number of pixels from the top-left corner of the image to the hotspot on the image also change, making the image map break.

    b. Image map links don't work on mobile-friendly pages.

    c. Image maps are too large and too slow to download on a mobile device.

    d. Image maps don't show the same image in different screen sizes, potentially confusing users.

1) d. Images that resize automatically are responsive by default. **2) a.** Grid templates are like tables used for the layout of flexible layouts, and the areas are the cells in the table. **3) a.** The image map hotspots are defined in the number of pixels from the top-left corner of the image, so if the image size changes, the image map breaks.

4.5 Making Printer-Friendly Webpages

While the use of printers has declined precipitously in the last few years, users will want to print some webpages to have a hard copy of the content. Users may want to print the instructions to a product that requires assembly or print a recipe to save or view while cooking. Whatever the reason, printing webpages creates a problem similar to showing webpages on multiple screen sizes. The content can be too big or too small, the columns misaligned, or the images obstructing the narrative.

Printer-Friendly Planning

The problem with printed pages is just like that created by displaying the same content on multiple screen sizes, and so is the solution. Until now, you've been using the `media="screen..."` attribute in your links to the mobile, tablet, and large-format CSS files. With one small change, you can incorporate a printer-friendly-format CSS file. Add the following link to the `<head>...</head>` section of your index.html page:

```
<link rel="stylesheet" type="text/css" href="css/print.css" media="print" />
```

Note that all the other links to style sheets have used the `media="screen"` attribute, so this print style sheet will be used when styling the webpages on the printer. You will also use the sitewide styles incorporated into my_styles.css, with one small but important addition.

Determining what is important on a printed page is similar to determining what to show on a small mobile screen. The screen, in this case, is most likely an 8.5 × 11-inch sheet of paper, although with a minimum of half-inch margins on each side. Thus, the "screen" size is effectively one inch less in width and height, making the dimensions 7.5 × 10 inches.

In the recipe example, the list of ingredients and the steps to follow are more important than the pages-long life story by the recipe author that precedes it.

Similarly, the navigation for a webpage doesn't serve a useful purpose on the printed page, but a **breadcrumb trail** might. The breadcrumb trail is a list of the navigation followed to get to the page being viewed and is typically included near the header. The header is useful for branding, but the footer is not critical. Pictures of the food use up printer resources without adding value to the actual recipe. These ideas inform which page contents to hide or show, resize as larger, or move off to the side.

Testing the Printer-Friendly Page

Most browsers provide a print preview that can serve as a printer emulator. If your browser has a File menu, choose Print on the File menu, and then find and select Print Preview. If your browser doesn't have a File menu, try pressing Ctrl+P in Windows or Cmd+P on a Mac, or search for "how to print with Konqueror on Ubuntu Linux" (or whatever your browser and operating system are).

The print preview window shows you what your page will look like on paper—without having to actually print the page. If you are doing iterative development, you could print dozens of pages before getting the display just right. With the print preview, you can view the on-screen version of your content even if you don't own a printer. It's like toggling the device emulator on and off again.

Using Firefox on a Mac, the print preview looks like **Figure 4-15** for the website in its current form.

Figure 4-15   The index.html page in the Print Preview window

Source: Mozilla Firefox

That check box has made a reappearance, and the navigation doesn't serve a useful purpose other than to take up space, so those are the two things you can eliminate from the printed page. This will give you more room to feature the `header` and `section` prominently, which is the same goal as you had in the mobile-first design.

Printer-Friendly CSS

Knowing that the `<section>...</section>` and the `<header>...</header>` content is the most important, you can begin building the new CSS file to style the webpage as it is shown on the printed page. Create a new file and save it as print.css inside your css folder. Add the standard comment block at the top of the file.

Next, hide the nav and footer for the pages with the following code:

```
nav {
    display: none;
}
```

Next, you need to hide the check box and the rest of the nav toggle HTML structure. Update the code at the beginning of my_styles.css to reflect the following change:

```
@media print, screen and (min-width: 480px) {
    .menu-burger, .menu-chkbx, .hamburger {
```

```
        display: none;
    }
}
```

The comma separating these selectors is effectively an "or," so the style applies to print or to screens with a minimum width of 480 pixels. By adding the `print` media attribute to the block of code you already wrote to hide the check box and menu toggle, this style is also applied when the page is printed.

You also need to update the link in the `<head>...</head>` section of the index.html page to include the print media type in the link to my_styles.css. That link should reflect the following:

```
media="screen, print"
```

The complete line is `<link rel="stylesheet" type="text/css" href="css/my_styles.css" media="screen, print" />`.

Next, notice that the `h1` header text is positioned to the left of the `h2` heading below it, and both are left-aligned on the page. It might look better if they were both centered on the page instead. Add the following code to your print.css to accomplish this:

```
header, section {
    text-align: center;
}
```

Save your changes, refresh the page, then do another print preview. You should now have a screen that looks like **Figure 4-16**.

Figure 4-16   The print preview of the completed printer-friendly styling of index.html

Source: Mozilla Firefox

That's the printer-friendly version of the home page for totallyawesomestuff.com.

> ## Quick Check 4-5

1. What does `media="print"` do in a `link` element?

    a. Directs the browser to print the page when it is opened

    b. Directs the browser to use the style sheet named in the link when the webpage is printed

    c. Directs the browser to open the print preview screen

    d. Adds a printer icon to the page to tell users the page is printer-friendly

2. What is an easy way to test a `media="print"` style sheet without actually printing the webpage?

    a. Use the browser's device emulator and choose the brand and model of printer you are targeting with your styles.

    b. Print the page to a PDF instead.

    c. Open the printer test page and copy and paste the webpage contents.

    d. Do a print preview.

3. How do you determine what content to show on a printed page?

    a. Show the entire webpage as it is on the screen so users aren't confused.

    b. Only show the HTML elements the user has selected.

    c. Show the largest screen size that will also fit on an 8.5 × 11-inch sheet of paper.

    d. The same way that you determine what content to show on the mobile screen—with a prioritized list of importance for each element.

1) b. The `media` property designates which style sheet to use for rendering the webpage contents. **2) d.** The print preview function lets you test print styles without actually printing a webpage. **3) d.** Printing is just another type of display, so a prioritized list of content is helpful to determine what to show to the webpage viewer.

4.6 Automating Responsive Design

While this course is designed to build your knowledge of HTML, CSS, and other languages to help you become a successful full stack web developer, many websites built by web developers don't involve typing one line of HTML or CSS code at a time as you are doing. These tasks are automated through the use of a content management system like WordPress or a **CSS framework** like Twitter Bootstrap to create the display of the HTML page in a mobile-first and responsive manner.

Mobile-First WordPress Themes

WordPress is a content management system built to compose content inside predefined themes made up of CSS styles, HTML structural elements, and JavaScript code to add dynamic functionality. When using WordPress, your work consists of choosing a theme and then incorporating your content into that theme. If you need to customize or extend the theme, the foundation in HTML and CSS that you are learning will help you add the necessary code.

WordPress themes are built by people who configure the HTML, CSS, and JavaScript to work with the user-supplied content. Most newer themes are designed with a mobile-first approach. However, some themes have proven more mobile-friendly than others.

If you search for "most popular mobile friendly WordPress themes," you will find numerous listicles (articles made up of lists) detailing the options available to you when you need to use WordPress for web development. Often, the better themes are retail themes. That is, you need to buy these themes prior to using them. Some themes are free for the default version but require you to pay for upgrades.

You could also try to create your own mobile-friendly WordPress theme, but you should crunch the numbers prior to doing so to determine if the return on investment is worthwhile. When you count your time as valuable, buying a premade theme might save you significantly on the total cost of a website, although it does limit the amount of fun you have writing code.

Mobile-Friendly WordPress Plug-Ins

If you are working on a website that has been built using an older WordPress theme that was not originally designed to be mobile-friendly or with a mobile-first approach, you can still update the site without starting over.

First, determine if the theme has an update to a mobile-first design that you can install over the current theme. This upgrade might be all that is necessary to have your site pass the Google Mobile-Friendly Test and boost your rank in the Google search results.

If your theme doesn't have an upgrade, many WordPress plug-ins can retrofit mobile-friendly design elements into an older large-screen theme. These work as a patch to make an older nonmobile-friendly theme conform to the standards of mobile-first design and to ensure your website passes the Google Mobile-Friendly Test.

If you search for "WordPress mobile-friendly plug-in," you will find more listicles detailing the authors' favorite WordPress plug-ins to adapt older content to the newer standards. You will need to check the documentation provided to make sure the plug-in works with the theme that was originally used on your site and verify the compatibility between the theme and the plug-in.

You will work in much greater depth with WordPress themes and plug-ins in the chapters on these subjects. Because this work is starting from the newest versions, you will use mobile-first versions of WordPress utilities.

Twitter Bootstrap

Web developers have used Twitter Bootstrap for over a decade to automate the task of creating uniform, mobile-friendly webpages. If you search for "most popular CSS frameworks," the consensus in the search results is that Bootstrap is one of the top choices for most web developers. With the addition of one CSS file, one JavaScript file, and some images, your website will be styled for you to be mobile-first by default.

In the Bootstrap documentation, you will find the key HTML tags, class and ID names, and HTML structure that Bootstrap expects to use to modify the display of your existing content. When using Bootstrap, you match your HTML code to the style declarations in the style sheets instead of the way you have been building your webpages, which is to match the CSS to the HTML.

The user community supporting Bootstrap is extensive, as is the documentation. Components to Bootstrap include all of the critical features that make up a robust website including navigation, master/detail pages, web form components, and tables. However, using Bootstrap takes you 90 percent of the way to complete, and the foundation in CSS and HTML that you are building here by working through the examples in the chapters will be necessary to finish the loose ends.

Quick Check 4-6

1. How do you choose a mobile-friendly theme for a WordPress site?

    a. Test the theme on each of the targeted devices.
    b. Use a WordPress mobile-friendly plug-in to test the theme.
    c. All themes are now mobile-friendly by default.
    d. Read the documentation for the theme.

2. When should you use a mobile-friendly plug-in to update your WordPress theme?

    a. After you determine that there isn't an update to the old theme to make it mobile-friendly.
    b. You should use both—a mobile-friendly theme and a mobile-friendly plug-in.
    c. Mobile-friendly plug-ins for WordPress are not necessary for making WordPress themes mobile-friendly.
    d. You should update any time that the WordPress theme is more than three years old.

3. What is an advantage of using a CSS framework like Twitter Bootstrap?

    a. Most of the display will be styled if you use the right HTML tags and attributes.
    b. You don't have to know anything about CSS to make your webpage look good.
    c. You can make your website look just like Twitter.
    d. Your webpage will look like a mobile app in all screen display sizes.

1) d. Reading through the documentation is always a good idea when choosing a WordPress theme. **2) a.** Many of the older, more commonly used WordPress themes have mobile-friendly updates. **3) a.** Bootstrap takes care of the layout and some stylistic elements if you label your HTML accordingly.

Summary

- Responsive design is the broad consideration of displaying the same webpage content in multiple screen sizes.

- Mobile-first design is one successful way of accomplishing the goal of responsive design. You design webpages for mobile screen sizes first and add or show other content as larger screen sizes allow.

- Breakpoints are critical screen widths, measured in pixels, that are the upper and lower bounds of displays on devices.

- Style sheets can be targeted to specific breakpoints so different styles are applied to different screen widths.

- Mobile device emulators are simulated screen displays incorporated into most browsers that allow web developers to test their webpages in one browser instead of on multiple devices.

- Displaying the navigation only when the user wants to see it is one way to allow more important contents to take up the limited screen space of a mobile device.

- Images that are flexible in size are responsive design elements that work with all screen sizes.

- Printer-friendly webpages use style sheets and the `print media` option to hide content that doesn't need to be included on the printed page and rearrange HTML elements to create a well-formatted printed page.

- CSS frameworks are an expedited, 90 percent solution to creating responsively designed pages, but you must match the HTML to the CSS in the framework.

- You can use mobile-friendly WordPress themes and plugins to speed up the development of responsive WordPress websites.

Key Terms

breadcrumb trail	flexbox	parent element
breakpoints	meta tag	pseudo-element
child element	mobile device emulators	sibling element
CSS framework	mobile-first design	viewport

Review Questions

1. Why is navigation near the top of the list of priorities for mobile-first design? (4.1)

   a. Users need to be able to move between the pages of the site regardless of the device they are using.

   b. Navigation is the most difficult to build in CSS, so web developers need the most time on it.

   c. Navigation is what makes the unique site branding different from other websites.

   d. Navigation takes up a significant amount of screen real estate and needs to be done right so it fits within the rest of the page.

2. How do you choose the breakpoints for testing with a mobile-first design? (4.1, 4.2)

   a. Determine what page contents look good on various widths of screens, then use those screen widths.

   b. Use the values that Googlebots are using when they are assessing mobile-friendliness.

   c. Research the established standard breakpoints for targeted device screen sizes.

   d. Use your best judgment as to how big the screen on your mobile phone looks in pixels.

3. Is a hamburger menu icon required for a successful mobile-first menu design? (4.3)

   a. No, but it sure does look tasty on the navigation menu and most users know how to use it successfully.

   b. Yes, this has become a W3C recommended best practice.

   c. No, creative web developers can use any menu structure that makes them feel creative and happy.

   d. Yes, the Googlebots look for this icon to open up the mobile menu.

4. What is a sibling element in HTML? (4.3)

   a. An HTML element inside of a parent HTML element

   b. The HTML element containing the parent HTML element

   c. An HTML element that doesn't have a parent HTML element

   d. An HTML element at the same level as another HTML element, both of which are inside a parent HTML element

5. What does adding the `display: flex;` style do to an HTML element? (4.3)

   a. Makes it into a menu item in a mobile display

   b. Makes it into a browser-friendly image in a mobile display

   c. Creates a mobile-friendly HTML node in the DOM

   d. Adds it to the flexbox if it is inside another container that is also using this style or creates the container if this is the outer HTML element with other flexible elements inside it

6. What does a `meta` element add to an HTML page? (4.3)

    a. Information for the user of the webpage

    b. Information for the browser showing the webpage

    c. Information for the web server hosting the webpage

    d. Information for the network transmitting the webpage

7. In a mobile-first designed website, what style information goes in the style sheet that isn't referenced by a specific screen size? (4.3)

    a. All of the style information that is necessary to print the page

    b. General style information that is applied to the website for all screen sizes

    c. Style information for the screen sizes larger than mobile and tablets

    d. Styles that don't apply to mobile, tablet, or full-screen displays

8. What is the best way to size images so they work with all screen sizes? (4.4)

    a. Use a specific `max-width` property in pixels for each style sheet depending on the targeted breakpoint for that style sheet.

    b. Save a different size of picture for each screen size.

    c. Use the `flex-image` style selector to create resizable images.

    d. Use the `width: auto;` property to make the images automatically resize to whatever the `html` element containing them will hold.

9. What are the `max-width` and `min-width` properties used for when displaying images in a responsive webpage? (4.4)

    a. To load different images depending on the screen size

    b. To show different versions of the same image depending on the screen size

    c. To show the same image the same way in different browsers and devices

    d. To keep the image from getting too big or too small in a responsive design

10. Is it necessary to have a printer-friendly CSS style sheet for your website? (4.5)

    a. No, nobody prints webpages anymore.

    b. Yes, somebody might print the webpage, so it is better to have your website prepared.

    c. No, the mobile-first design also shows only the important parts on the printed page.

    d. Yes, this is a browser requirement that is tested by the Googlebots for site indexing.

11. What is a disadvantage of creating your own mobile-friendly WordPress theme? (4.6)

    a. It takes a significant amount of time.

    b. It is more technically challenging than creating a mobile-friendly plug-in.

    c. You have to test it in multiple versions of WordPress.

    d. It requires specialized training that most people don't have.

12. Why is Twitter Bootstrap popular with many web developers? (4.6)

    a. There is a lot of documentation and help available for using it.

    b. Twitter is a popular application that many people like to emulate.

    c. It takes care of everything in the HTML code and style sheets for you—all you need to supply is the content.

    d. Because many web developers want to work for Twitter and try to use its product to create a line item in their resumé.

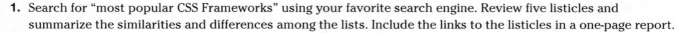

Programming Exercises

1. Search for "most popular CSS Frameworks" using your favorite search engine. Review five listicles and summarize the similarities and differences among the lists. Include the links to the listicles in a one-page report.

2. Search for "most popular mobile-friendly WordPress themes" using your favorite search engine. Review the results, then create a ranked list in a table of your top three free or freemium mobile-friendly themes and the top three of your favorite available-for-purchase mobile-friendly themes. In your table, include the strengths and weaknesses of each theme you chose to review.

3. Search for "problems with using Twitter Bootstrap" and "mistakes with using Twitter Bootstrap" using your favorite search engine. Write a letter to your future self describing what these articles suggest doing and not doing when using Twitter Bootstrap. Include at least three links to articles or reviews you found in your search in your letter.

Projects

1. Add comments to the mobile.css, tablet.css, full_screen.css, my_styles.css, and print.css files describing what each style declaration in each style sheet does. (4.3–4.5)

2. Update the other pages in the totallyawesomestuff.com site from the starting files you downloaded at the beginning of this chapter so that all of them are mobile-friendly. Test the pages using the navigation in each page in the mobile, tablet, and full-screen display sizes. Make sure the webpage content stays within the screen and is displayed inline with the other components of the page. Center the products table and the "about us" list in the mobile and tablet displays. (4.1–4.5)

3. Update the other pages in the totallyawesomestuff.com site to be printer-friendly. Center the products table and the "about us" list in the printed page. Test the pages using the print preview. (4.2–4.5)

JavaScript Programming

Learning Objectives

When you complete this chapter, you will be able to:

5.1 Explain what JavaScript is and the value that JavaScript adds to a webpage.

5.2 Create blocks of JavaScript code that add text into an HTML page.

5.3 Test and debug JavaScript with the web developer toolset in a browser.

5.4 Create JavaScript code that manipulates the HTML DOM.

5.5 Create JavaScript code to validate HTML form data.

5.1 What Is JavaScript?

In addition to HTML and Cascading Style Sheets (CSS), JavaScript is the third corner in the triangle of modern web development for the browser. If you have been working through the chapters in this course sequentially, you learned first about the functions of the browser, then the building blocks of HTML, and finally styling the HTML with CSS. JavaScript adds a dynamic element to webpages that creates user interaction with the webpage contents.

JavaScript has existed since early in the history of the modern Internet—1995, to be specific. It is the single most common programming language. Other web development languages such as PHP, Ruby, and C# are used to create code that runs on the web server to compose webpages and process data returned from users. The webpages built with those languages can also incorporate JavaScript to make them more interactive in the browser.

The words and logic in JavaScript code are close enough to a human language that it is a good first programming language. JavaScript doesn't require a specific development platform and can be written using a simple text editor. You don't need a separate **code debugger** to diagnose errors, or bugs in the code, since a debugger is included with most modern web browsers. Furthermore, you have probably used JavaScript without knowing it when you used an interactive webpage, so you have enough experience to know what is possible.

Programming languages called server-side programming languages run on a web server to build webpages before sending them to users. These programming languages use the raw processing power of web servers to run complex code before sending the resulting webpage to the browser or to handle the data returned from that webpage when the user submits a form.

JavaScript in the webpage is used for client-side programming, which is written to run in the web browser and to create interactivity and dynamic web elements. Code that runs in the web browser is more limited in scope and capabilities than server-side code, since the web browser running on a laptop or other personal device doesn't have the robust hardware capabilities of a server farm hosting massive web applications.

Note	JavaScript can also be used on the server in libraries like Node.js and Express, but this chapter focuses on the client-side use. The basic structure is the same in both instances, but client-side programming is easier to test and debug because you need only a web browser and simple text editor.

Executing Code in the Browser

JavaScript is an interpreted programming language, which means that it isn't compiled into an executable file before it is made available to users. It remains a text file loaded in the browser just like the CSS files you have worked with. Most modern browsers use a just-in-time complier to create the composite of the best features of an interpreted language (less processing power required by the computer running the browser) with those of a compiled language (faster to run after the code is optimized).

This compiler is also sometimes called the JavaScript engine in the browser. Different browsers have different names for their JavaScript engines, but all follow the same basic rules defined in the standards written by the World Wide Web Consortium (W3C). To read more about these standards, see https://www.w3.org/standards/webdesign/script.

If your JavaScript code runs only once, the JavaScript engine in the browser interprets the code. If the JavaScript code needs to run more than once, the interpreter hands the code to the compiler to try to optimize the code into a faster-executing block stored in the working memory of the browser. The downside to this optimization is that it takes longer the first time it runs, but the payoff is that each subsequent execution is significantly faster.

For more technical information about how Firefox handles JavaScript and uses its just-in-time complier, search for "Firefox JavaScript engine" and read the results. Other web browsers also have JavaScript processing engines, but Firefox and the Mozilla Foundation have some of the most extensive documentation of their engine, known as Spider-Monkey. You don't need to know how SpiderMonkey works behind the scenes to be a good JavaScript programmer, but it does help you gain an appreciation for the complexity of what you are building. To read more about SpiderMonkey, visit https://firefox-source-docs.mozilla.org/js/index.html.

The Basics of a Programming Language

All modern programming languages are similar in concepts and function. For example, all programming languages are learnable. A programming language that is impossible to learn or use won't have many users. Some programming languages are more difficult to learn than others because they use an unfamiliar syntax. The syntax is the logic and rules that make any type of language—spoken, written, or computer—understandable by a human.

For the syntax of a sentence written in English to make sense, it has to follow the rules of sentence structure, grammar, and spelling that are used by English speakers. Words are made up of groups of letters, but "asdf jkl;" is not two English words, nor is it a sentence expressing a thought, even though it has two groups of letters and a punctuation mark. "I am." is a valid sentence, with a subject and a verb, a beginning and an end, and a punctuation mark that denotes the conclusion of the sentence.

Most programming languages require units of code that perform discrete tasks known as functions. A function often contains at least one variable, which is a designated container of data in the memory of the computer that holds and processes information. Functions also include **logical operators** to test conditions like equal to, not equal to, greater than, or less than to create decision points in the code flow. This chapter includes examples of functions, variables, and logical operators in context.

What Is JavaScript Good For?

A webpage without JavaScript is just a fancy text document shown in a web browser. You can use JavaScript to modify the HTML DOM, which is the browser's in-memory structure of the webpage. Modifying the HTML DOM was the original purpose of JavaScript. Because JavaScript exists in the same space in the browser as the HTML and CSS code, it is allowed to modify both of those components in the webpage. You can use JavaScript to add and remove HTML or CSS code in a webpage.

You can also use JavaScript for creating the code that runs on a webpage. Interactive elements such as buttons can trigger **events**, which are actions that happen in a browser. For example, displaying a message and changing the color of an object are events. Some events occur because the user did something like clicking a button, and other events happen because the browser starts or completes a process. Buttons can also be used to create more complex user-interactive elements inside a webpage, like you do in the next section.

JavaScript is also useful for form validation, such as to ensure that the user filling out the form in a web browser supplies answers to all required questions. Finally, you can use JavaScript like any other programming language to calculate values or parse text strings.

Advanced users of JavaScript can create graphics and interactive games, but those are beyond the scope of this course.

Clever Code versus Maintainable Code

As with other types of programming, it is always possible to create a technical challenge to prove your intellectual superiority over the next programmer who has to then try to understand your underappreciated genius. This is not a good idea. Writing simple code that takes a few extra lines to achieve a result instead of leaving a complex puzzle to be solved by the next developer is a polite pay-it-forward way of being collaborative.

Professional programming is not a contest to see who can write the most complex or clever solution to a simple problem. Professional programmers who are secure in their own skills write simple solutions to simple problems and a series of simple solutions to solve complex problems.

The initial development of a webpage is merely the beginning of its life cycle. Most of the time a developer spends on a webpage is in maintaining, testing, and upgrading it after initial development and deployment. A simple solution is less expensive in terms of time and money because simple code is easier to read, fix, and test. In other words, simple code is easier to maintain, which is the most important quality of well-written code.

JavaScript versus Java

If you use your favorite search engine to search for "JavaScript vs Java," you will find a slate of results. To summarize the results, the two share no similarities other than the first four letters of the name and the fact that both are programming languages.

One theory for the origin of the name JavaScript is that the original developers of Netscape Navigator were supporting Java applets as small, precompiled units of code written in Java that could be embedded in webpages. JavaScript was supposed to be a scripting language embedded in the browser that would be easier to use and not require compilation since it would be interpreted by the browser.

Running Java applets in the web browser was eventually discovered to be a significant security vulnerability. Web developers adopted JavaScript as an easier, simpler, and more secure way to create interactive webpages. JavaScript as a client-side web application development platform has been the standard ever since.

Quick Check 5-1

1. What is JavaScript used for?

    a. Creating user-interactive components in a webpage

    b. Creating style information to modify the HTML in a webpage

    c. Building the page structure of an HTML page

    d. Merging the style from the CSS with the HTML building blocks to display a webpage

2. What is the syntax of a programming language?

    a. The executable file that results from compiling the source code

    b. The debugging system that helps developers fix problems in the code

    c. The text of the code written in the programming language

    d. The logic and rules that make code written in the language work as intended

3. How do buttons on a webpage cause JavaScript to run?

    a. By reloading the page in the web browser

    b. By triggering click events that the browser is waiting for and responds to

    c. By compiling the JavaScript code into an executable form

    d. It's a mystery, but it works pretty well, regardless

1) a. User-interactive elements in a webpage are often based on JavaScript. **2) d.** Syntax is like the grammar rules for a programming language. **3) b.** Buttons trigger click events when they are clicked, which the web browser is waiting for so it can run the JavaScript attached to those events.

5.2 Programming with Nouns and Verbs

JavaScript is a programming language made up of actions and targets for those actions. Like every other spoken, written, and programming language, these parts must agree for the sentence to clearly communicate its meaning.

The rules of the programming language, as you learned in the previous section, make up the syntax for the language. Each programming language is different from others in its rules, but nearly all languages share common themes.

All languages have symbols that stand for actual things. In English, these are nouns. The word *dog* is not actually a dog, but a series of letters that represent an animal with four legs that barks. *Bark* is the action the dog can take, so it is a verb that applies to the noun. Similarly, symbols stand for objects in a programming language and actions those objects can take.

Like learning any other new language, it takes time to learn what the symbols represent and how to use them properly. It is often easiest to learn in context of what you already know or have experience with, so that is the approach this chapter takes.

Getting Started

If you haven't already done so, copy the Chapter_5 folder to the folder you are using for this course.

Open calculator.html and my_styles.css in your text editor.

Looking through the HTML in calculator.html, you can see some familiar code. This HTML code is the framework for a JavaScript graphical calculator that performs mathematical operations. Inside the `section` element is an outer `div` element with an `id` of `calculator` that serves as the wrapper around the rest of the calculator elements. Inside the outer `div` elements are two inner `div` elements to divide the calculator into the display and the buttons.

Inside the display `div` are two `input` elements. The first is a text box that will function as the display in the calculator, and the second is a hidden element that will be used as the memory storage location.

The block of HTML input elements inside the keypad is composed of standard calculator buttons. The number buttons are straightforward, with the name, id, and value the same for each button. The mathematical operator buttons such as divide and multiply contain a different name from the value, since the operators contain symbols that have other possible values. The calculator also includes extra function buttons like $+/-$, C (for Clear), and M (for Memory).

If you have your files arranged properly, you should see a webpage that looks like **Figure 5-1** when you open calculator.html in your browser.

Figure 5-1 The starting point for the calculator.html webpage

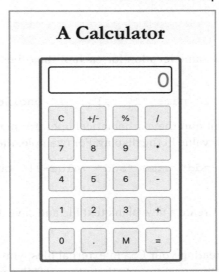

Beginning with the Buttons

The first task in building this calculator is having the numeric buttons send their value to the display. To do this operation, the buttons need an `onclick` event with a JavaScript function assigned to the event. Events, as you'll recall, are actions that happen in a webpage. For example, when a user interacts with a page by clicking a button, the user creates a click event in the browser. A function is composed of one or more lines of JavaScript code contained in an opening and closing declaration that performs a discrete task.

Add the following code to the 1 button before the closing > at the end of the `<input>` tag:

```
onclick="displayMe(this.value)"
```

This code is similar to other attributes you have added to HTML tags. In this case, the attribute adds an `onclick` event to the 1 button along with a process to follow when that click event happens. The logic of this code is similar to the way the full attribute reads from left to right. When this button is clicked, run the `displayMe` code using the value this button has. In this case, JavaScript is basically like super-nerdy English.

The completed button code looks like the following:

```
<input type="button" id="1" name="1" value="1" onclick="displayMe(this.value)">
```

The JavaScript code `displayMe()` represents the name of a JavaScript function with the parentheses containing the value to send to the function for processing. The content in parentheses is called a parameter. Instead of using a numeric value like 1 as the parameter, this code uses `this.value` to get the value from the button. For the 1 button, the attribute `value="1"` is accessed because `this` refers to the 1 button itself, and the 1 button has a `value` property of 1.

Note	JavaScript uses the keyword `this` to represent whatever object the code references. If a button is calling an `onclick` event, `this` would refer to the button. If a radio button group is calling for the code to run, `this` would refer to the radio button group. In other words, `this` is convenient shorthand for "whatever object is causing the action for starting the code execution."
	JavaScript is unique as a programming language in that the HTML entities that can start a JavaScript process in a webpage are often the target of the results of that same process. Sometimes, a form or the HTML DOM is the target for the results of the process. The buttons that users click are inside the form or DOM, allowing JavaScript to access or update the form or DOM using the `this` reference to the button.
	JavaScript often uses the `this` keyword to identify how a process started and the state of the associated object or element at the time.

Add the similar code snippets in the same location for each of the other numeric buttons. For example, the following is the code for the 2 button:

```
<input type="button" id="2" name="2" value="2" onclick="displayMe(this.value)">
```

Add similar code to the decimal point and the mathematical operator buttons as well (+, −, *, /, %). All of these buttons will do the same thing—put their value in the display. For example, the following is the code for the + button:

```
<input type="button" id="add" name="add" value="+" onclick="displayMe(this.
value)">
```

Save your changes to the HTML file. Create a new blank text file and save it as calculator.js in the javascript folder you created earlier.

Similar to the way you have been creating your CSS in external files, you add JavaScript code to an external file to keep your HTML page tidy and to create reusable code that other HTML pages can access via the same shared link in the `head` section.

Crafting the Code

Next, you need to create the code that retrieves the value from the clicked button and puts it in the display. The name of the function that you added to each button is `displayMe` but because programming languages are like geeked-up English, the code needs more than the function name. JavaScript has a format to follow to create proper code.

Add the following JavaScript code to your calculator.js file:

```
function displayMe(inVal)
{
    document.getElementById('display').value =
        document.getElementById('display').value + inVal;
}
```

The first line of code—`function displayMe(inVal)`—tells the JavaScript interpreter that a function named `displayMe` requires an input, which is the variable named `inVal` in the parentheses. Variables are containers for holding data that are assigned values while the interpreter runs the code.

Recall that the code `this.value` in the HTML document is used to send the value of the clicked button to the `displayMe` function. Because this function in the JavaScript code contains a variable in the parentheses, the value from the button is assigned to that variable at the beginning of the function.

The argument `inVal` is not a special variable name; it is just the name given to this variable for this lesson. Similar to class and ID names in CSS, variables can be named x or X or Bob, though those are less helpful to the next developer who has to read your code. A variable name like `inVal` describes an input value in a shorthand way, so it is easy to use properly in the rest of the code, whereas `Bob` would be more difficult to remember contextually. Additionally, `inVal` follows the camelCaseName convention, with no spaces between words, the first word in lowercase, and the first letter of each subsequent word capitalized for readability.

JavaScript has a few rules about variables:

- Variables must begin with a letter, dollar sign, or underscore, so 1 as a variable name will result in an error.

- JavaScript variable names are case sensitive, so `inVal` is not the same variable as `InVal`.

- You can't use JavaScript-reserved words for variables. A reserved word is one that has special meaning in JavaScript or any programming language. Calling a variable `this` or `function` would result in an error.

- JavaScript variables may not contain spaces or characters other than numbers, letters, and the dollar sign or underscore.

So far, the JavaScript code contains only the following line of executable code:

```
document.getElementById('display').value = document.getElementById('display').
value + inVal;
```

To make sense, the line needs to be read in reverse. At the end of the code is the variable `inVal` again, followed by a semicolon. The variable contains the value sent to this function by the clicked button. The semicolon is used to end a completed line of code, or **statement**, similar to the way a period ends a sentence.

Before the `inVal` variable is a plus sign. In JavaScript, the plus sign can be used to add numbers or **text strings** together. A text string is one or more characters. All inputs that come from the browser begin as text strings, so in this case, the string contained in the variable `inVal` is added, or appended, to the text string that `document.getElementById('display').value` retrieves.

Note the capitalization in the `getElementById` function. JavaScript is particular about uppercase and lowercase letters, so `getelementbyid` is not the same as `getElementById`.

The `document` in `document.getElementById('display')` refers to the HTML DOM created in memory by the browser when it loads the HTML page. The JavaScript application programming interface (API) function called `getElementById` searches the DOM for an element with the ID passed to it in the parentheses—in this case, `'display'`. The API is the JavaScript code included with the browser. You can use the functions in the API (as long as you spell them correctly) to perform standard tasks that are common to web browsers, like searching the DOM for one element that has a specific ID.

That specific ID was given to the input text box used to display the numbers and mathematical operators. Note that the single quotes surround the text of the ID `'display'` since it is a text string being sent to the function `getElementById()`.

In `document.getElementById('display').value`, the `value` operator is appended to the end of the `getElementById` function, asking the JavaScript interpreter to retrieve the value of the DOM element with the ID of `'display'`. The `value` for the input element `'display'` starts without any value; it is just a placeholder property that displays a default of 0. The first button clicked will replace this placeholder display with an actual value through the use of the block of code you are writing.

To the left of the equal sign is `document.getElementById('display').value`, which is a copy of nearly the same code to the right of the equal sign. These two chunks of code are the same because they are being used contextually. The code on the right of the equal sign retrieves a value, and the code on the left of the equal sign assigns the value. That is, when `document.getElementById('display').value` is used on the left of the equal sign, the JavaScript interpreter knows it will be assigning a value to the HTML element with the ID of `'display'` and, when it is used on the right of the equal sign, it will be used to retrieve the value from the HTML element with the ID of `'display'`.

> **Note** | In JavaScript, a single equal sign is used for assignment. That is, the value, variable, or object on the right of the equal sign is assigned to the variable or object on the left. You use two equal signs to test if two values, variables, or objects are the same, or equal to each other. Programming languages have different ways of handling this reuse of one symbol for both assignment and testing for equality or sameness.

Finally, notice the pair of curly brackets around the code to run as part of the `displayMe` function. The curly brackets enclose the code, marking the beginning and ending of the block. This bracket syntax is similar to CSS syntax, which wraps the individual style modifiers together into a block.

Reading the complete code from left to right, this block tells the JavaScript engine to find an element in the DOM with the ID of `display` and assign to it the value currently in the DOM element with the ID of `display` plus the string sent to this function by the button that was clicked to start the whole operation.

The result is that when a user clicks the 1 button, the click event starts the code running and sends its value (1) to the function called by that click event, `displayMe()`. The `displayMe()` function takes the 1 value the button has sent it, finds the display element, and retrieves its value, which is nothing if the display does not contain a value. The `displayMe()` function then appends the value sent to it to the value retrieved from the display and puts the resulting new value back into the display. If the display contained no value, appending 1 to nothing results in showing 1 in the display.

Connecting the Code File to the HTML Page

Between the `<head>...</head>` tags in calculator.html, add the following link to the external JavaScript file:

```
<script src="javascript/calculator.js"></script>
```

You are not required to separate the JavaScript code from the HTML document defining the button. In fact, you could write the following code into each button's `onclick` event:

```
<input type="button" id="1" name="1" value="1"
onclick="document.getElementById('display').value = document.
getElementById('display').value + this.value;">
```

However, the Don't Repeat Yourself rule means you should not do this! Every button would contain the same complete block of code. That's repetitious. And inefficient. The right thing to do is try to minimize the amount of repeated code as much as possible.

Save your changes to all the files and refresh the page. If you have everything right, you should now be able to click 123+321 and have the characters appear in the display. If that isn't working, skip ahead to the next section on debugging to figure out why your code isn't working properly.

Adding the Equal Sign

The next piece of this calculator to add is the equal sign. In normal calculators, the equal sign is understood to mean "process the two numbers using the mathematical operator between them." If you have the display working correctly in calculator.html, you can enter two numbers along with an operator between them. You can even enter several numbers and operators in the display.

To process these numbers and operators, you need another block of code and another `onclick` event for the equal button. To create the `onclick` event in calculator.html, add the following code to the end of the input tag for the equal button, just like you did with the numbers and mathematical operators:

```
onclick="calculate()"
```

Note the difference between the `calculate()` function and the `displayMe()` function. Obviously, the names of the functions are different. As with `displayMe()`, `calculate()` is a name chosen to describe what the function does. However, the parentheses that follow the function name do not contain a value because this function doesn't need anything from the equal button. The equal button will be the only one calling the `calculate()` function.

Next, you need to create another new function, just like you did for `displayMe()`. Add the following code to your calculator.js file:

```
function calculate()
{
    document.getElementById('display').value =
        eval(document.getElementById('display').value);
}
```

The code in this function is similar to the code in `displayMe()`, with one major difference. Notice the `eval()` function? That's a built-in JavaScript API function that takes a string and attempts to perform the operation it represents. So, if the display shows 3+3, the `eval()` function will take that text string and attempt to evaluate it as if it were a mathematical function—and it will be successful. If the display shows 10/0 (i.e., 10 divided by 0), the result will be NaN (Not a Number) or Infinity, since the result of evaluating that expression is infinity.

Common Mistakes

A word of caution about using `eval()` in JavaScript. If you search for "problems with using eval() in JavaScript," you will encounter cautionary articles about the intrinsic security flaws in using `eval()`. In fact, the Mozilla Foundation urges caution against ever using `eval()`.

These warnings are all true and accurate. The problem with using `eval()` is that malicious code can easily be added to the statement being evaluated, and JavaScript will dutifully attempt to evaluate (or run) that code just like the simple math calculations you are using here.

However, for the purposes of a standalone web calculator that needs very simple JavaScript as a stepping-stone toward understanding how JavaScript and programming works, the previous code using `eval()` will suffice.

If you do need to create a calculator like this one in a webpage that is exposed to the users of the Internet, you can use the following block of code instead:

```
document.getElementById('display').value =
Function("return " + document.getElementById('display').value)();
```

This code is safer but significantly more complex. You learn more about the syntax of this type of code later in this chapter.

Save your changes, then refresh the calculator.html page. Click 2+2 and then click the equal button. The display should show 4 since this is truly a competent calculator capable of adding two plus two.

Test the rest of your math operation buttons. You should be able to add, subtract, multiply, and divide. If you combine these operations, `eval()` will follow the proper mathematical order of operations. Again, if something is not working as you would expect, skip ahead to the next section on diagnosing JavaScript errors to work through the debugging process, then return here.

Other Calculator Buttons

The calculator is coming along, but several buttons do not have `onclick` events or code to run. The Clear button (named C in the calculator) is the first button in the first row, so it is next on the list. Since the display is holding the input and result values, the Clear button should clear the display. The following code accomplishes exactly that:

```
function clearMe()
{
    document.getElementById('display').value = '';
}
```

The code tells the JavaScript engine to find the element with the ID of `'display'` and assign no value (`' '`) to it. Computers do exactly what you tell them to do, so the display will show no value, though the input element will revert to the placeholder that shows a 0 when there is no value.

Add that code to calculator.js to clear the display. In calculator.html, add the click event that calls `clearMe()` to the end of the input element for the C button:

```
onclick="clearMe()"
```

Test this new functionality by clicking 123, then C. The display should revert to the placeholder value of 0. Again, if this is not working, start debugging the code using the directions given in the next section.

Next, you need to add code to the sign switcher button, traditionally labeled with a $+/-$. When clicked, this button changes the sign of whatever is in the display to the opposite. If you enter 21 and click the $+/-$ button, the calculator changes the value to –21. To accomplish this, multiply the display contents by –1 (negative one). Add the following code to calculator.js:

```
function switchSigns()
{
    document.getElementById('display').value =
        document.getElementById('display').value * -1;
}
```

This code combines functions you've already used. Only the multiply symbol (*) and the hard-coded -1 value are new.

In calculator.html, add the following `onclick` event to the $+/-$ button:

```
onclick="switchSigns()"
```

Save your changes, refresh the page, and clear the calculator display, if necessary. Click 2, then click the $+/-$ button. The display should change to -2.

The next button on the calculator is the % button. To make a percentage out of a number, you divide by 100. However, this operation is different from anything else on the calculator, so it deserves its own function. Add the following code to calculator.js:

```
function percentMe()
{
    document.getElementById('display').value =
        document.getElementById('display').value / 100;
}
```

Also add the `onclick` event to the % button in calculator.html and call the `percentMe()` function with it:

```
onclick="percentMe()"
```

Save your changes, refresh the page, and clear the calculator display. Click the 1, then click the % button, and the display should change to 0.01 or 1%.

The only button left is the M or Memory button, and this one is a doozy. Think for a minute about how the Memory button should work. If the Memory button is clicked and there is a value in the hidden HTML input element used for memory, then the value in memory should be appended to the display. If the memory element does not contain a value but the display does, the value in the display should be moved to the memory and the display should be cleared.

Writing this out in **pseudocode**, which is like almost programming without using an actual programming language, the memory function would look like this:

> If value in memory then
>
> > Display = display + memory
>
> Else if display is not empty
>
> > Memory = display
> >
> > Display = ''

Often when encountering a programming challenge like this one, writing the pseudocode first is useful to clarify the problem and think logically about the solution, without having to worry about getting the code syntax just right.

Add the following JavaScript code for this memory function, which is similar to the pseudocode:

```
function rememberMe()
{
    if(document.getElementById('memory').value)
    {
        displayMe(document.getElementById('memory').value);
    }
    else if (document.getElementById('display').value != '')
    {
        document.getElementById('memory').value =
            document.getElementById('display').value;
        document.getElementById('display').value = '';
    }
}
```

In this block of code, the `if()` and `else if()` functions are logical tests. They act like the equivalent in a spoken language: If it is raining, you should bring an umbrella. When should you bring an umbrella? When the test outlined with the `if` statement is true—it is raining. Otherwise, you don't need an umbrella.

Notice that the `if` and the `else if` lines do not end with a semicolon since they aren't complete programming sentences. The next step, which is what to do if the test is true, completes the programming sentence. If you end the `if` line with a semicolon, none of the rest of the code will run, since the semicolon ends the line, sentence, and thought.

For the `if()` test, the `document.getElementById('memory').value` code asks if the `memory` HTML element contains a value. It doesn't matter what the value is, just that it exists. The code does not retrieve the value and assign it to anything. It only checks to see if `memory` has a value.

The logical `if` test uses whatever code is in the parentheses as its **conditional**, which is an expression that resolves to true or false. As with the umbrella example, `if(there is a value in memory)` evaluates to true when there is a value in memory. The code that follows a true evaluation then runs.

In this case, if the conditional is true, JavaScript runs the `displayMe(document.getElementById('memory').value);` code. This code reuses the `displayMe()` function to append the `memory` value to the end of the display. If there is no value in `memory`, however, the next test in the chain is run, so the `else if` gets its turn:

```
else if (document.getElementById('display').value != '')
```

The `!=` in this code is a new comparison operator meaning not equal. In JavaScript, the equal sign doesn't test for equality; it is used for assignment. That is, the value, variable, or object on the right of the equal sign is assigned to the variable or object on the left, as you have seen. In this code, empty quotes follow the not equal operator to mean null or nothing. The condition translates to "if the `display` value does not equal an empty string." In other words, if the display value is anything other than nothing, run the code after the `else if` statement.

> **Note** | JavaScript has a number of comparison operators, as do all programming languages. These are summarized in **Table 5-1**.

Table 5-1   JavaScript comparison operators

Operator	Description
==	Equal to
===	Equal to (value and datatype)
!=	Not equal to
!==	Not equal to (value and datatype)
>	Greater than
<	Less than
>=	Greater than or equal to
<=	Less than or equal to
!	Logical "Not," or opposite

Why not write the `else if` statement to perform a positive test and check for anything in the `display` value? The reason is that "anything" is too broad a test. "Anything" could be a letter, a group of letters in a string, a number, a group of numbers, or an object like a button with all of its properties. Each type of "anything" would need to be included as valid in the test for "anything." On the other hand, "not nothing" is easy to test since any possible value, letter, number, or object will logically be "not nothing."

Another way to think about this is in terms a computer could understand. Recall that variables are containers of data. A variable can contain a value or not. So you can compare the variable to the empty string like this:

```
if (variable != '')
```

In this `if` statement, the computer has a simple logic test even it can get right. If the variable is not empty, that is, not nothing, then it will do something with the code that follows that test.

After the `else if` statement are the following two lines of code inside curly brackets:

```
document.getElementById('memory').value =
    document.getElementById('display').value;
document.getElementById('display').value = '';
```

They run when the `else if` statement is true (and the value in the display is not nothing). First, the value in the display is assigned to `memory`. Then, the value in the display is emptied (assigned to `''`, or no value), just like the pseudocode suggested.

Finally, note the indenting and whitespace. This entire function could work equally well if it were all on one line, but that would be challenging to read by a human. The indenting clarifies which parts are nested inside of other parts.

Add the onClick event that calls the rememberMe() function to the M button. Save your changes, refresh the page, and clear the display, if necessary. It's time to test the new functionality with a series of common-use steps:

1. Click the 123 buttons, then click the M button. The calculator should clear 123 and store it in the hidden `memory` element.
2. Click 789, followed by the + button, and then click the M button again. The display should show 789+123.
3. Click the = button to run this arithmetic problem through the calculator to find the result of 912.
4. Click the C button to clear the display, and then click the M button. The value 123 is displayed again.

This is a bug in the logic that needs a fix.

The C button should clear the memory, too, since the first test in the function `rememberMe()` is whether the memory has a value. If the C button doesn't clear the memory, it will always contain a value until you reload the webpage.

In calculator.js, add the following line of code to the body of `clearMe()`:

```
document.getElementById('memory').value = '';
```

Insert this line right after the corresponding display value is assigned to nothing in `document.getElementById('display').value = '';`. Now, the Clear button really does clean the slate in preparation for the next calculation.

Save all of your changes, refresh the page, and bask in the warm glow of your successful completion of a JavaScript calculator.

Quick Check 5-2

1. What is a JavaScript function?

   a. A symbol that JavaScript understands to be a container for data
   b. A unit of code made up of a single line of JavaScript
   c. The text file that contains the JavaScript code
   d. A block of JavaScript code that performs a discrete task

2. Why can't you name a JavaScript variable "this"?

   a. Because "this" is a reserved word in the JavaScript language
   b. Because variable names are case sensitive
   c. Because "this" is reserved for creating loops in JavaScript
   d. Because "this" is reserved for the browser to call internal API functions

3. Why is testing for "not nothing" more useful in JavaScript than testing for "anything"?

   a. Because computers are literal and would need to test "anything" against all possibilities like numbers, letters, and objects
   b. Because "not nothing" is a logical test that is faster to compute than "anything"
   c. Because "not nothing" is easier for humans to understand than "anything"
   d. Because the next programmer to pick up your code will appreciate the bawdy sense of humor that "not nothing" shows you have and want to subscribe to your podcast

1) d. A function is composed of one or more lines of JavaScript code contained inside an opening and closing declaration that performs a discrete task. **2) a.** "This" is a reserved word in JavaScript for self-referencing an object like a button or check box. **3) a.** "Anything" has too many possibilities to consider, but "not nothing" covers all of them.

5.3 Testing and Debugging JavaScript

When trying to determine why code doesn't work, most experienced developers follow a similar pattern of asking themselves yes or no questions to try to find what is broken. In medicine, this process is referred to as a differential diagnosis. If the patient is complaining of chest pain, examining the patient's toenails is not going to help determine the cause and solution to the chest pain. Focusing on the simplest reason for the chest pain first and working through other more obscure causes is a logical approach that is most often successful.

Mechanics use the same basic process to figure out what is wrong with a car. When the Check Engine light is on, they don't begin by looking in the headlights for dead insects. They instead plug the car into the code reader and retrieve the error code that the car is storing.

The logic of this operation is common to all professions that require problem assessment and solution refining. The simplest case is assessed first, then dismissed if it doesn't describe the symptoms or create a solution. One adept description for this approach to troubleshooting is "When you hear hoofbeats, think horses, not zebras," since horses are common and zebras are rare.

Categories of JavaScript Errors

If you are writing JavaScript on a new webpage and the code doesn't work, start with the simplest case first, repeating the process each time you encounter another error or when your solution doesn't solve the problem.

For example, did you remember to save the files after making your most recent change? If the answer is yes, move on to the next, slightly more complex question. Does your webpage link to the JavaScript file, if that's where you are storing your code? You can test this by viewing the source of the HTML page in the browser and clicking the link to the JavaScript file in the head element. That JavaScript file should also open in the browser. If the browser reports "File not found," then you have a broken path caused by a bad file name or folder path. Fix that, then retest your webpage.

If you have a valid link but the code doesn't appear to run, consider the following possible coding errors:

1. First, the code could contain fundamental coding errors that break the rules of the programming language, preventing the browser's JavaScript engine from executing the code. A bug of this type is known as a **syntax error**. Syntax errors show up when you load the page in the browser if you are looking at the right diagnostic tools like the JavaScript debugger.

2. Second, you could be calling a function or using a variable that doesn't exist due to a mistyped name. This is known as a **runtime error**. Runtime errors occur when you try to run the code.

3. Third, the code could be running, but not producing the expected output, or any output for that matter. This type of bug is known as a **logical error**. Though more common than syntax or runtime errors, logical errors are the most difficult to diagnose since the code follows the basic rules of the JavaScript language and does not include misspelled variables or functions.

A JavaScript debugger is useful in all three situations since JavaScript usually fails silently so it doesn't interrupt the rest of the browser user experience.

All widely used browsers come with JavaScript debugging tools but, as with the mobile display testing utility, finding them is a challenge. Using the JavaScript debugging tools in a helpful manner is another, sometimes bigger challenge. Firefox, Chrome, Safari, and Edge have a similar debugging toolset. The figures in this section are from Firefox on a Mac, but the display in your browser should be similar.

Browser Debugging Tools

Using your favorite search engine, search for "*your browser* JavaScript debugging tool" and find out how to open the JavaScript debugger. Open the debugger (and read the documentation in your search results). You should see a screen similar to the one in **Figure 5-2**, which is from Firefox, although some debuggers dock on the right side of the page instead of the bottom and all have slightly different displays for similar functionality.

Figure 5-2   JavaScript debugger for calculator.html

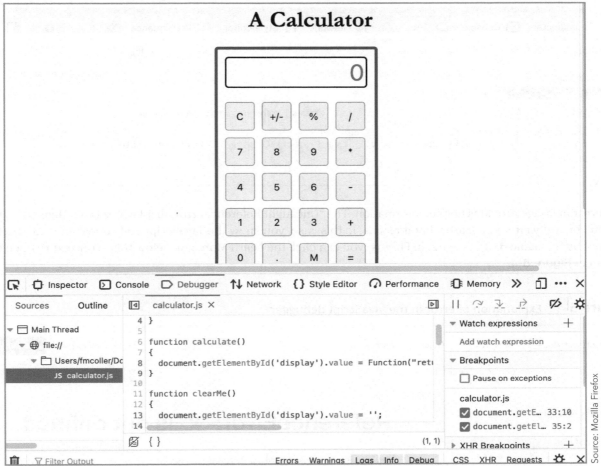

The JavaScript debugger is the starting point for determining why a block of JavaScript code is not behaving as expected. Assuming you completed the previous section successfully, you have a block of code you can break and then fix. If you are reading this section because you are trying to find your errors, follow the same basic differential diagnosis steps.

Runtime Errors

A good way to learn about runtime errors is to create them deliberately. In this way, when you encounter them in your actual programming, you will already have some experience in finding and fixing them. Create a runtime error as follows:

1. Start by changing the name in the `onclick` event of the 1 button in the calculator. In calculator.html, add a *z* to the end of `displayMe` so it is instead `displayMez`. Mistyping the name for a function or variable is a common coding error.

2. Save your changes, then refresh the browser. Nothing. No warnings, no errors. You broke something obvious, and yet, nothing. This JavaScript debugger isn't a genius solution after all that buildup.

3. Click the 1 button. Now things change! JavaScript isn't a compiled language, and it doesn't run until an event triggers it. In this case, an `onclick` event tied to the 1 button calls a function that doesn't exist because you changed its name. The error looks like **Figure 5-3**.

Figure 5-3 The error code for a misspelled function name

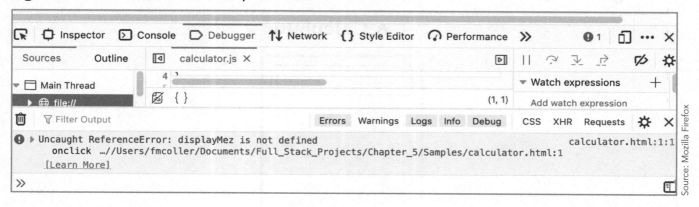

The error message provides helpful information. The "Uncaught ReferenceError: displayMez is not defined" is the most helpful, but only after you learn what it means. In this case, you know the JavaScript code does not contain a function defined by the name `displayMez`. In Firefox, you can click the Learn More link below this error text to open the page shown in **Figure 5-4**.

Figure 5-4 Explanation of error in the JavaScript debugger

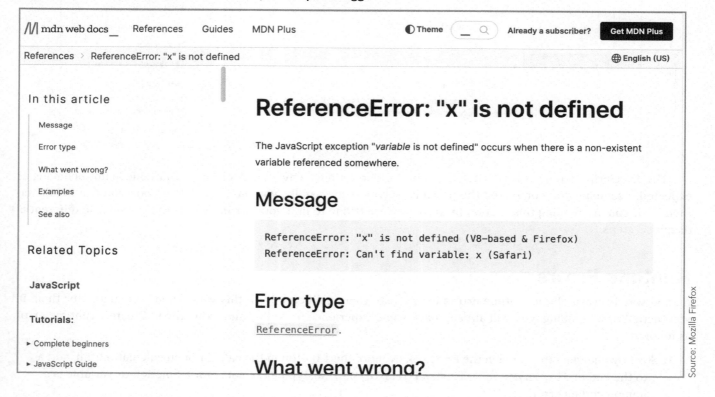

The text on this page describes an undefined variable rather than a function, but the idea is the same—something is misspelled or just plain missing. You could search the HTML document for the string "displayMez" to find the error. If the function name is correct in the HTML document, check your JavaScript page to make sure the function (or variable) is spelled exactly the same and uses the same case. Remember that a function named `calculateMe` is different from the function `CalculateMe`.

Syntax Errors

Syntax errors fundamentally break an important coding rule in JavaScript. Syntax errors include not closing every open curly bracket, missing a parenthesis, or using the wrong punctuation marks. The JavaScript engine catches these errors before the code is run, since the basic syntax of JavaScript is evaluated prior to any execution.

Correct the change you made earlier to calculator.html by changing `displayMez` to `displayMe`, then save your change and open calculator.js. Remove the inner closing curly bracket after the `else if` statement in the function `rememberMe()`. Save your changes, then refresh the browser. An error message appears as in **Figure 5-5**.

Figure 5-5   Syntax error in the JavaScript debugger

This error message appears prior to running the code because you created a syntax error. This code now breaks the basic rules of JavaScript—every opening curly bracket must have a closing curly bracket. Note too that "calculator. js: 41" on the right indicates the line number of the error, though that line number doesn't correspond to the actual missing curly bracket that you removed.

The browser reports that the curly bracket is missing on line 41 because calculator.js does not contain any more code or curly brackets after that line. The actual error isn't on line 41, but that's where the JavaScript engine precheck discovered that the file does not contain another bracket.

In general, syntax errors are easier to find and fix than other types of errors once you have some experience with JavaScript. Undo your previous change to calculator.js, save your change, then refresh the webpage in the browser. The page should be error-free for now.

Logical Errors

A lot of your early coding experience will involve searching the Internet for code samples. When you find code close to what you want to accomplish, you can copy and paste the working code.

Often, you'll need to update this code to fit your specific requirements, coding standards, or personal style. When you have more experience with JavaScript, you'll just write your own code from scratch. Both of these circumstances are where coding mistakes can be made, however.

In this course, you are given blocks of code that have been tested by the author and editors. Some of the bugs have even been fixed prior to publication. In the real world, you will often find many, many bugs in your code and the code of other developers.

To introduce a logical error in the function `rememberMe` in calculator.js, remove the exclamation point from the condition for the `else if` test. That is, change this:

```
else if (document.getElementById('display').value != '')
```

to this:

```
else if (document.getElementById('display').value = '')
```

This type of error is also common but much harder to diagnose and fix. The code is technically correct, in that the names of all of the parts are spelled correctly, and the operational parts are in the right order and place. From the JavaScript engine's perspective, this code can be executed successfully.

The problem here is one of code usage. What was a test of "not equal" is now an assignment operation. Recall that the equal sign in JavaScript is used both for assignment (when there is only one equal sign, the value on the right is assigned to the variable or function on the left) and for logic testing (the != is the "not equal to" operator).

Save your changes, then refresh the page. No syntax errors. Create a logical error in the calculator as follows:

1. Click 100.
2. Click the M button. The value 100 should now be in memory since the display emptied successfully.
3. Click 200.
4. Click the plus button.
5. Finally, click the M again, which should recall the last value stored in memory and append it to the end of the display, but does not.

No runtime errors occur but also no function appears to run. This is where the differential diagnosis begins. Ignore for a minute that you know what the problem is and think about how you would try to find out what it is.

You know the link to the JavaScript file from the HTML page is valid because other buttons still work. In fact, if you test them, every single button works except the M button when you try to recall a number from memory. No runtime error is generated, and the names of the functions must be the same because no syntax error appears. All of the easy options are exhausted, so this has to be an error in the logical operational code of the function.

Open the JavaScript file in the debugger of your web browser. You should see the code you wrote previously displayed in the window of the debugger. Click the line number at the left margin for the lines of code that correspond to lines 33 and 35 in **Figure 5-6**, which shows the Firefox debugger. Your line numbers may differ.

Figure 5-6 Breakpoints in the JavaScript debugger

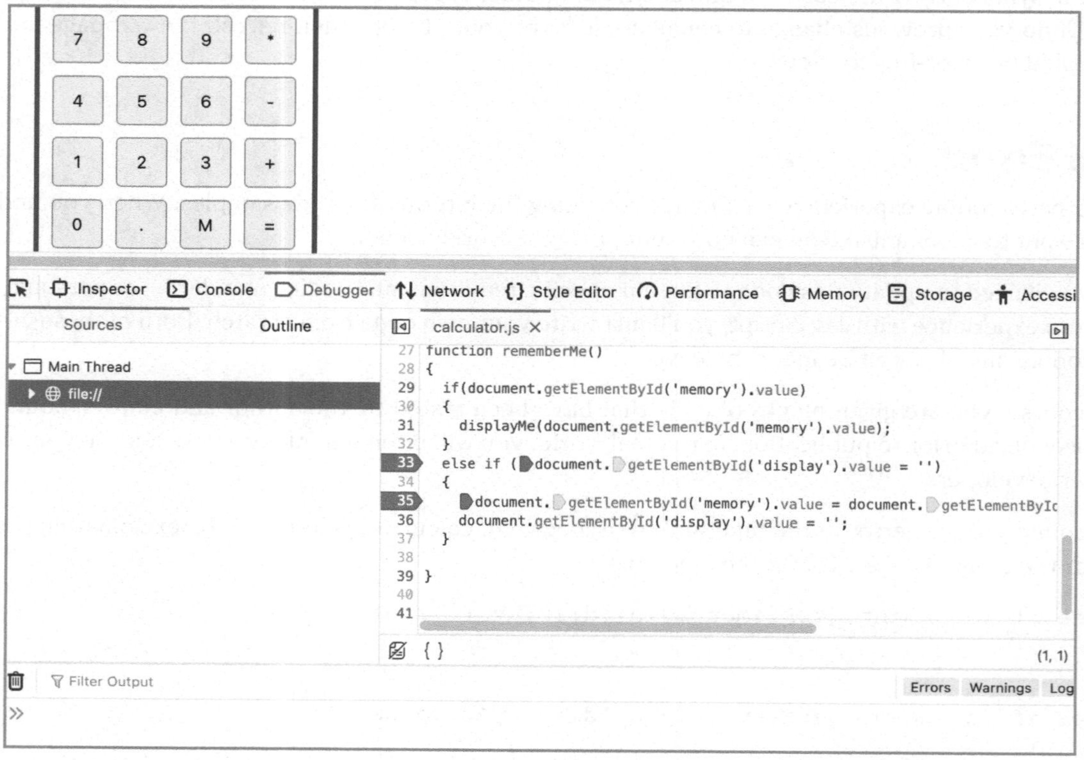

Source: Mozilla Firefox

Notice the two blue chevrons on the left side of lines 33 and 35 in the code. These are breakpoints that were added to the debugger by clicking the line number in the left margin. Breakpoints stop the code from running so you can see what is happening to the variables, functions, or processes in the code.

Your browser and debugging utility might provide other ways of adding breakpoints to the calculator.js file at those lines. If you search for "adding breakpoints to JavaScript for *your browser*," you should find results that help you do this.

To find out why the code isn't behaving as it should, you run it. In the calculator webpage, clear any previous values, click 100, and then click the M button. The code pauses at the first breakpoint on line 33, as shown in **Figure 5-7**.

Figure 5-7   Debugging with breakpoints

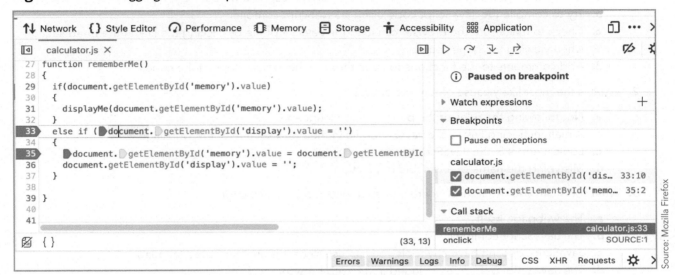

The "Paused on breakpoint" notification tells you that the code execution is awaiting your next step. Firefox includes four buttons above that notification: Pause, Step Over, Step Into, and Step Out. Click the Step Into button (the third one from the left in Firefox), which moves the code execution to the next operational step. Your debugger will have a Step Into button, though it may not be in this same location.

> **Note**
> What do those four buttons in the Firefox JavaScript debugger do? The following is a quick summary:
> - Pause/Play: Shows the pause symbol when the JavaScript debugger is paused on a breakpoint and clicking it toggles it to the Play button while resuming the normal code execution from the breakpoint forward.
> - Step Over: Moves the execution past the current line of code and resumes execution at the next line of executable code in the same function.
> - Step Into: Starts the execution of the current line of code, stepping through each part of the code in the line.
> - Step Out: Moves to the end of the function without running the rest of the code in the function.

Clicking the Step Into button should take the process to the second breakpoint, but it doesn't. Instead, the operation moves to the end of the function. It does so because the Else If condition isn't met, so the code inside the curly brackets never runs. This is exactly the behavior you have seen. Now you know the error is definitely in that Else If condition.

This is where the difficulty of being a web developer is also a fun challenge with interesting problems to solve. The code you are reviewing isn't completely wrong, but it also isn't working correctly. You've narrowed the problem to line 33 because the process never executes line 35. Your experience, which you will gather quickly as you write code and make mistakes, will help you read the code on line 33 and see that you didn't mean to use the JavaScript assignment operator inside a conditional test. In fact, you need to use the logical "not equal to" operator here.

Undo your change, then save your calculator.js again. Clear your breakpoints in the JavaScript debugger by clicking the line number again in the debugger or using the Clear Breakpoints tool. Refresh and retest your page to make sure it works correctly again.

Quick Check 5-3

1. What is a good first step in determining why new JavaScript code isn't working in a new webpage?

   a. Check all of your variables to make sure they aren't reserved words.
   b. Try to compile the JavaScript code using a JavaScript compiler.
   c. Check to make sure the browser can load the JavaScript file by clicking the link in the `head` section when viewing the page source.
   d. Add comments to the functions to trace through the logical steps of the code.

2. What is the most likely cause of runtime errors?

   a. Not following the rules of the programming language
   b. A malfunctioning link to the JavaScript file in the `head` section of the webpage
   c. Logical errors in the JavaScript code
   d. Mistyping the name of a variable or function

3. What tools can you use to find where errors are occurring in JavaScript?

   a. The webpage itself
   b. The JavaScript compiler
   c. JavaScript doesn't have any tools you can use since it is an interpreted language
   d. The JavaScript debugger included in the web browser

1) c. If the browser can't access the JavaScript file, it won't be able to execute the code in the JavaScript file.
2) d. Runtime errors are often caused by mistakes in spelling the name of a variable or function. **3) d.** The JavaScript debugger is a valuable tool used to determine where errors are occurring.

5.4 Manipulating HTML with JavaScript

JavaScript runs within the browser, so it has access to the HTML and CSS files related to the webpage. You can use JavaScript to modify both the HTML and the CSS in a webpage based on events that a user triggers.

Modifying the HTML Style

Open the starting files stoplight.html, light_style.css, and stoplight.js in a text editor, and then open stoplight.html in a browser. Review the existing code in each file, although reviewing stoplight.js will be easy because it doesn't yet contain any code.

As you might have guessed, you are going to build a stoplight in a webpage. Clicking the Red, Yellow, and Green buttons will turn on the red, yellow, and green lights. The goal is to learn how to use JavaScript to manipulate the HTML and CSS of a webpage based on user-triggered events.

Before writing any code, it is always a good practice to think through the process that the code will follow and write some pseudocode. For this stoplight, all three buttons will perform the same type of action when clicked. The pseudocode for that might look like the following:

Function make light lit

   Get light HTML element by ID, set background color to light color

End function

The `onclick` event for each button could then call the individual function for that button and light combination, so the red button turns on the red light, the yellow button turns on the yellow light, and the green button turns on the green light.

Looking further at the HTML, each of those "lights" has a unique ID so that will be helpful to this code. A sample of the JavaScript code then would look like this:

```
function makeGreenLight()
{
    document.getElementById("GreenLight").style.background = "green";
}
```

The code `getElementById("GreenLight")` is similar to the code you used previously to retrieve from the HTML DOM the display element modified in the calculator. The dot operator after the parenthesis appends a property selector for the `style` property. This is the style of the HTML element that has been accessed by ID from the DOM. Finally, the `background` property of the style for the `GreenLight` HTML element is set to `"green"`.

Add this code to your stoplight.js, then add two more copies of it for the red and yellow light functions. Modify each function name to refer to the correct color, and the element ID values in the functions to `RedLight` and `YellowLight`. Change the `style.background` property to `red` and `yellow` as appropriate.

Next, you need to add an `onclick` event to each button in stoplight.html. This will look just like the previous work you did with the calculator but customized to the stoplight. The following is the `onclick` event for the green button:

```
onclick="makeGreenLight()"
```

Add this attribute to the green button. Then add similar attributes to the red and yellow buttons as well, modifying the name of the function being called to the correct name for each button.

Save your changes, then refresh the HTML page. Click the green button, and you should see the green light come on as in **Figure 5-8**.

Figure 5-8   The initial stoplight.html

Click the red and yellow buttons. Each should turn on the right light. If this doesn't work, head back to Section 5.3 and work your way through the testing and debugging process.

Making the Code More Efficient

The stoplight code poses two fundamental challenges. First, though it is working, it contains so much redundancy that the Don't Repeat Yourself warning buzzer is going off. Each function is identical except for the light being changed and the color being set. When you think, "There has to be a better way to do this," you are probably right.

The second challenge is that the code works, but not like a real webpage stoplight should. The buttons turn on each light but the stoplight should show only one light at a time.

The first step in each light turning on should be shutting off all the others. This could be an independent function since it will be reused by each button. Then, the individual light that triggered the function call can be turned on by showing the background color. Meeting these two challenges will involve more complex code than you've used previously, but the payoff will be greater strategic efficiency in that code.

The pseudocode for the revised code looks like this:

Function make light lit (one light's ID)

   Reset lights function

   Change "one light's ID" background color to lit

End function

Function reset lights ()

   Loop through the lights, reset background color to blank

End function

Start by making copies of stoplight.html and stoplight.js. Save the new versions as stoplight2.html and stoplight2.js. Update the link in the `head` section of stoplight2.html to point to the new JavaScript file. This way, you can keep the old, working code as a reference as you refine the more efficient process. Save your changes, then open stoplight2.html in your browser. Test it to make sure it still works. You should still have a working webpage stoplight at this point.

Begin by removing the old functions from stoplight2.js. Then, create a new function using the following code:

```
function makeLight(inColor)
{
    clearLights();
    document.getElementById(inColor + "Light").style.background = inColor;
}
```

Reading this code, you can see some familiar parts and some new code, too. The name of the function is `makeLight` and it takes one parameter, the input color. The first line of code in this function calls the `clearLights()` function, which doesn't yet exist. This came directly from the pseudocode, which followed the logic of clearing the lights then turning on a new light.

The second line of code begins the same way as the old script but changes the selector. The `inColor` variable will contain the color passed into this function. The plus sign appends that color name to the text string `"Light"`, so the result will be `RedLight`, `GreenLight`, or `YellowLight`. Those are the IDs for the lights in the stoplight.

As in stoplight.js, the code selects the `style` property then the `background` property and assigns the value in `inColor` to the background of the element found in the DOM by its ID.

Next, you need to write that handy `clearLights()` function to reset the background colors of all three lights. Add the following code to stoplight2.js:

```
function clearLights()
{
    var lightsArr = document.getElementsByClassName("light");
    let ndx;
    for (ndx = 0; ndx < lightsArr.length; ndx++)
    {
        lightsArr[ndx].style.backgroundColor = "";
    }
}
```

This function contains two of the four ways to declare, or establish, a variable in JavaScript. The `var` command in the first line of code is one way to create a **variable declaration** in JavaScript. You use variable declarations like this to create the variable so the rest of the code can use it. Another term for this is **instantiation** since you are creating an instance of a variable when you declare it.

Other programming languages have specific types of variables for use with numbers, dates, or text strings, but JavaScript is not **strongly typed** in this manner. Instead, JavaScript uses variables as simple containers and determines what type of data is stored in the container based on the data itself.

Following the `var` command is the name of the variable, `lightsArr`. The variable is assigned the values found using the code to the right of the equal sign.

Previously, you've used the `getElementById` function, which tells JavaScript to search the HTML DOM for a specific ID and return the HTML element associated with it. The `getElementsByClassName` function searches the HTML DOM and returns an **array** of the elements in a specific class. An array is a single variable that holds multiple values, as long as they are all the same type. You might think of this like a row in a spreadsheet with different cells for each value or item. The first cell contains the first value in the array, and so forth.

This code is useful because searching the DOM for elements by a class name could find 0 or 500 HTML elements. Getting elements by an ID should always find only one element, since IDs need to be unique.

This code searches by class name because each of the three lights conveniently belong to the same CSS class named `light`. If you look at the HTML in stoplight2.html, you can see this class for each `div` element.

When the line of code containing `document.getElementsByClassName("light")` runs, three HTML elements are found (`GreenLight`, `YellowLight`, and `RedLight`) and placed in the array called `lightsArr`.

The next line of code is another variable declaration. Using the `let` command is the second of four ways to declare variables. In the code sample, `let ndx;` creates a variable named `ndx`. The name `ndx` isn't different from using a variable `x` or `counter`. However, `ndx` is shorthand for index, which is another term for the counter used inside loops.

Using both types of variable declarations in this example illustrates the different ways to declare variables. While `var` and `let` are different in subtle ways, which you can read about in the results of a search of the Internet for "javascript var or let," consistently using `let` for variables within a function is a good practice.

The third way to create variables is to use the `const` command, which creates a constant. Constants are variables that don't vary, like Pi. Constants are useful when you want to make sure that the contents of the variable are never updated or changed in the code.

The fourth way to declare variables is to just start using them without making a formal declaration. This is a sloppy coding practice that is strongly discouraged, since most developers look at the list of variables declared in the top of a function and can easily overlook variables you just started to use. This can cause difficult-to-diagnose errors that will haunt the next developer who has to pick up your code.

Common Mistakes

JavaScript is casual about variable declaration, so if you misspell a variable in your code, the JavaScript engine assumes you know what you are doing and allows that undeclared variable to be used from that point forward in the rest of the code. Sometimes this causes a runtime error, but often you will have a major debugging challenge of your own creation.

There is a simple solution to this major problem, however. If you add `"use strict"` (including the quotes) at the top of your JavaScript file, undeclared variables will cause an error that you can find in the debugger. This header tells the JavaScript engine that all variables must be declared before use, with one exception. Variables in the parentheses of a function name are considered declared, even though you don't include the `var`, `let`, or `const` variable type in front of the name. You should always add `"use strict"` as the first line in a JavaScript file.

The first line of code that follows the two variable declarations is a **for loop**. Looping in all programming languages is a way to repeat the same block of code for some number of times. The `for` loop is similar to the English language use of the word *for*. For the next 2 minutes, the microwave will be running. How long will the microwave be running? Two minutes. When will it stop? After it runs for 2 minutes.

How many times will the `for` loop run? Look again at the line of code containing the `for` loop:

```
for (ndx = 0; ndx < lightsArr.length; ndx++)
```

You can read this from left to right inside the parentheses. The first part sets up the starting conditions. The `ndx` variable is set to 0 to begin the loop. Why does `ndx` start at 0? Because the 0 element in the array is in the first counted position. This is one of the most difficult parts to remember about using arrays. An array containing one thing stores that thing in the cell of the row with the 0 column header. The second item will be in the cell that has the 1 column header, and so forth.

The middle chunk of the `for` loop contents is the condition under which the `for` loop will run. In this case, it runs while `ndx` is less than the length of the array that contains the HTML elements.

When you use an array to hold similar items, the array knows how many cells contain items. Because the stoplight has three lights, the array will hold three cells, each containing one light from the DOM. The cell with the 0 column header will contain the first light, so it will be updated by the code inside the `for` loop with `ndx` at 0. The second light will be updated when `ndx` is 1, and the third light will be updated when `ndx` is at 2.

The last part of the `for` loop causes `ndx` to increase in value to count the cells in the array. The `ndx++` command is shorthand for "take whatever value is currently in `ndx` and add one to it."

Note | The programming language C++ is so named due to the use of the ++ shorthand, since a previous programming language is named C and C++ was supposed to be one better than that.

Computer programmers are a hilarious bunch.

The last block of code runs each time through the loop:

```
lightsArr[ndx].style.backgroundColor = "";
```

This line shows the power and efficiency of an array. The array holds all of the elements with the class `light` in the HTML DOM. The `for` loop counts each item in the array and runs this line of code. The code updates the background color to nothing (`""`), one light at a time.

The first part (`lightsArr[ndx]`) accesses the contents of the cell in the array that `ndx` currently points to, starting with 0 and going up to 2. These contents are the HTML elements in the DOM, which the rest of the line of code then updates so the background color is empty.

This code is even more useful if you anticipate adding HTML elements of the class `light` to the webpage in the future. Perhaps the webpage stoplight will display a left turn arrow. This code is already written to take that into account, since a fourth HTML element (which will be found at array position 3) will just be added to the array and handled by the loop automatically.

Save your changes, then update the stoplight buttons in stoplight2.html to call the `makeLight()` function, passing to it the color of the light. For the red light, that call will look like this:

```
onclick="makeLight('Red')"
```

Note the combination of single and double quotes. Sending a text string to the function requires you to enclose the text string in quotes, but the `onclick` attribute requires you to enclose the property after the equal sign in quotes as well. The solution to this problem is to use double quotes on the outside and single quotes on the inside.

Update the `onclick` events for the green and yellow lights, changing the color name being sent to the `makeLight` function for each. Then save your changes. Refresh the webpage stoplight2.html, and if you have everything working properly, clicking the green button should turn on the green light with no other lights displayed. Clicking the yellow button should do the same for the yellow light, while also turning off the other lights. Test all three buttons. If you have any bugs, go back through the section on debugging to figure out why.

Using More Than Click Events

Users can trigger more events by interacting with a webpage in other ways. In addition to clicking buttons, a user could move their pointer over the lights and turn them on. Add the following code to the `div` elements that make the lights in the HTML page:

```
onmouseover="makeLight('Green')"
```

The completed green light `div` element will look like this:

```
<div class="light" onmouseover="makeLight('Green')" id="GreenLight"></div>
```

Reusing code like this is a fantastic way to practice strategic efficiency. Update the other two lights to reuse the `makeLight()` function for the yellow and red lights as well.

Save your changes, then refresh the webpage. You should be able to click any button or move your pointer on a light and switch the color. That's a pretty fantastic webpage stoplight you have right there.

Quick Check 5-4

1. What is pseudocode?

    a. Code that is the English-language equivalent of computer code

    b. Code that only exists when the user triggers an event in the browser

    c. Code that runs when a user triggers an event in the browser

    d. Code that hasn't yet been compiled into executable form

2. What is a variable declaration used for?

    a. To tell the JavaScript engine that a new variable exists and is ready to be used in the code

    b. To create the pseudocode for the variable

    c. To create space in the HTML document for the variable's input element

    d. To add the variable to the CSS list of variables

(continues)

3. What is a const variable used for?

    a. To call a different function that always returns the same value

    b. To hold a value that never changes

    c. To create a variable that holds a single number such as 1 or 9

    d. To create an array of variables of the same type

1) a. Pseudocode is the written, English version of what you want the code to do in logical steps. **2) a.** A variable declaration tells the JavaScript engine that the variable exists and is ready to be used. **3) b.** The const variable type holds a value that doesn't change.

5.5 Validating HTML Form Data with JavaScript

A third use case for JavaScript in a webpage is validating HTML form data in the browser before it is sent to the web server. Because JavaScript can capture user-triggered events like the form submission event before the trip to the web server begins, it can parse the data in the web form and prevent submitting the form if the user makes a mistake or attempts a malicious bit of hackery. Even before that, you can use CSS styling to help your users identify which fields in the form are required or invalid.

The idea for form validation is to make sure that you can gather required and reliable form data with as little annoyance for the users as possible. Form validation can also catch some malfeasance on the users' part, but it is not a complete security net.

Common Mistakes

Form validation with JavaScript in the browser can only prevent data that actually exists on the webpage from being submitted to the web server. This validation is faster than a full round trip of the data back to the web server for data validation in the page code that runs on the web server. That round trip would then conclude with a return to the browser with a set of errors to display to the user. The round trip takes extra time that an impatient user might find annoying.

A mildly adept hacker can still send malicious data back to the web server even with the most robust and thorough JavaScript browser form validation. Through the use of the debugging tools, a malicious script, or available website hacking utilities, the hacker can easily bypass your form validation.

Browser validation is the first step in data validation, but not the only step. It's like a prescreening to make validation the least annoying experience possible for the 99 percent of users who are just trying to do the right thing and fill out your form. Server-side validation of the submitted data is also critical to ensure malicious users aren't successful in their attempts to hack your full stack website. You learn more about this in the chapter on PHP server-side processing.

In the previous chapter, you created a data-gathering form used to collect input from the users of the website totallyawesomestuff.com. That webpage was called contact_us.html and can be found in the starting files for this chapter.

In a text editor, open contact_us.html and the required CSS files that are listed in its head section and then read the code. Open contact_us.html in your browser and click the Submit button without entering any data. A helpful hint should pop up pointing to the First Name field and reminding the user to "Please fill out this field" or similar message, depending on the browser you are using. The message appears because the required input elements include the required attribute.

Using this type of form validation with the browser's default settings to identify required fields, you can prescreen the form data before the user submits it. However, the user must submit the form to trigger the validation. That's an extra step toward annoying your users. With some work, you can show the users which fields are required even before they click the Submit button.

The First Pass: Helpful Highlighting

Before your users even begin filling out your form, it is helpful to identify which form fields are required. This prevents a frustrating user experience that you may have encountered. You enter your email address twice, your mother's maiden name, the name of your first pet, your home address, your phone number, and all the other data you want to add to the form, click all the images that contain stoplights, and then click the Submit button to submit the form.

After a few seconds, an alert pops up and tells you that you missed three fields—but doesn't tell you which ones. Or the alert says "Please fill out all required fields" but no notification indicates which fields are required. So you try again, adding more data that you think is right for the required fields, click all images that contain sailboats, and then click the Submit button again. A few more seconds go by and the same error pops up again with different information.

Annoying your users in this manner is never a good idea if you want them to keep using your website. The least painful and simplest web form with the clearest instructions is the goal of a data-gathering exercise. Happy users are engaged users who will return to your site.

All modern browsers alert users to missing form input elements if you use the `required` attribute on your form input fields. One additional piece of feedback that improves the overall user experience is to highlight the required fields. This can be accomplished using CSS.

Save my_styles.css as my_styles2.css. Add the following code to your my_styles2.css file:

```
/* form validation styles */
input:invalid, textarea:invalid {
    border: 2px solid orange;
    border-radius: 5px;
}
input:focus:invalid, textarea:focus:invalid {
    border: none;
}
```

This pair of styles works together by incorporating the `:invalid` and `:focus:invalid` pseudo-classes. The `:invalid` pseudo-class exists when the input element is in an invalid state, such as when a required field is missing data or the email field doesn't contain a valid email address. The concatenation of the `:focus` and `:invalid` pseudo-classes selects input elements that were in an invalid state and have been selected by clicking or pressing Tab to move between form fields.

The second style declaration toggles off the error highlighting when the user navigates through the form fields, but the first style is reapplied if the field remains in the invalid state.

Save your changes, then refresh the contact_us.html page. The required fields are highlighted in orange, but the first-time user would probably not know this. Click the Submit button without entering any data. The "Please fill out this field" prompt appears, so you know that's still working to prevent form submission without fully completing the required fields.

Add the following to contact_us.html above the `input` element for the Submit button:

```
<br/>
<span class='required'>Required input fields are highlighted in orange.</span>
<br/>
```

Add the `.required` class to the selectors for the comma-separated invalid group list in your my_styles2.css. Adding the `.required` class to this list means that if you change the highlight color from orange to purple, all of these elements will automatically be changed. The following is the first line of that selector:

```
input:invalid, textarea:invalid, .required {
```

Save your changes, then refresh the page. You should now have a form that looks like that in **Figure 5-9**.

Figure 5-9 Required fields highlighted in a form

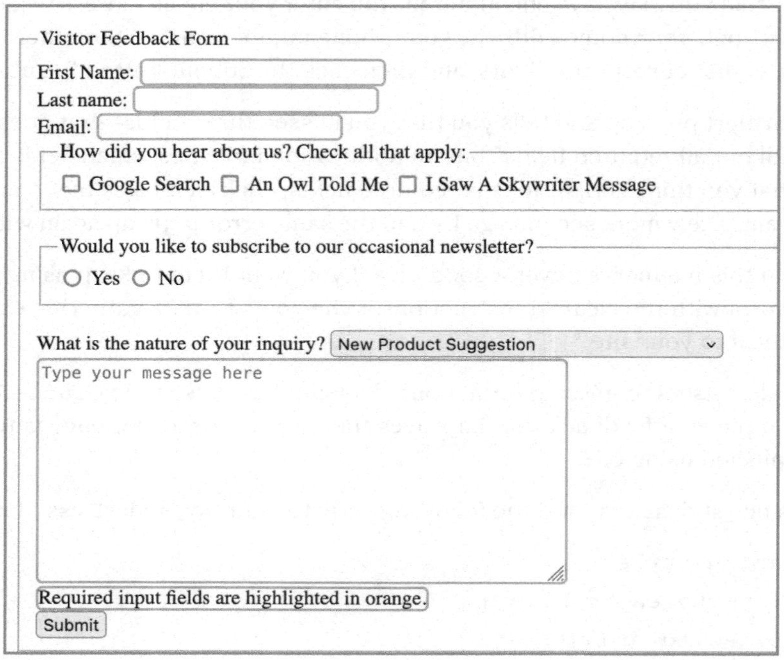

The orange highlighting and hint help the user identify which fields require data even before starting to fill out the form. This is the first notification that these fields require attention, and the user hasn't even clicked the Submit button yet.

Add data to the required fields in the form in your browser. The border is removed as soon as you meet the conditions. Try entering a single character in the email address, for example, and the field remains invalid. Only a valid email address removes the invalid condition.

This is the first step in making form validation as painless as possible for your users. But you aren't done yet.

The Second Pass: Counting the Missing Fields

For a long form with many fields, the user may want to know exactly how many web form entry errors are preventing submission. JavaScript provides a way to count the incomplete required fields.

Add the following `span` element to your contact_us.html page, right after the opening `<section>` tag and before the opening `<form>` tag:

```
<span class="form_errors"></span>
```

Then, add the same `span` element and a line break right above the code for the Submit button:

```
<span class="form_errors"></span>
<br/>
```

Note these two `span` elements contain only the `form_errors` class. You will use JavaScript to change that, dynamically updating both the content of the `span` element and the CSS `form_errors` class to inform the user about how many required fields are incomplete in the form.

To count the missing required form elements, consider the following pseudocode:

Select all form elements in an invalid state into an array variable

Set a variable X = the array length

Update the warning labels with text "You have X missing fields"

However, because two warning labels now appear, one at the top and the other at the bottom of the form, you can use the same select-by-class function that you used previously to collect both warning labels into an array, and then loop through both and use the same line of code to update their text and style.

For longer web forms, a warning label at both the top and bottom helps the user more easily find what is wrong with the form data without having to scroll to the bottom to find the count or back up once the bottom of the form is reached to see if all of the previous errors have been cleared. Once again, the more helpful (and less annoying) your form validation, the more likely it is that your users will be willing to fill out the form.

With only two warning labels for this small form, you are not violating the Don't Repeat Yourself rule. On the other hand, if you had a multipage form with warning labels on the top and bottom of each page, you could significantly minimize repetition by using this loop.

Create a new file named form_validation.js and store it in the javascript folder for Chapter 5. Enter `"use strict"` (including the quotes) as the first line in the file so that undeclared variables cause an error. Add a link from the head section of contact_us.html to form_validation.js.

Enter the following code, which is the function declaration and variable instantiation:

```
function validate_form(inForm)
{
    let warnArr = document.getElementsByClassName("form_errors");
    let ndx;
```

That is all code you have seen before, just updated to reflect the contact_us webpage and its contents. The function is named `validate_form` and the form itself is passed into this function so you can count the number of invalid form elements in it. Then, the `warnArr` variable is created and set to the results of `document.getElementsByClassName("form_errors")`, which will find all of the HTML elements with the CSS class of `form_errors`. Finally, an index variable named `ndx` is created.

Next, add the following block of code to your form_validation.js file. This code is more complex due to the operations it completes:

```
if (inForm.checkValidity() == false)
{
    let elementsArr = inForm.querySelectorAll(':invalid');
    let errCount = elementsArr.length;
    for (ndx = 0; ndx < warnArr.length; ndx++)
    {
        warnArr[ndx].innerHTML = "You are missing data in " +
            errCount + " fields in this form.";
        warnArr[ndx].classList.add("required");
    }
}
```

The `if` statement introduces a conditional test. If the form passed into this function is not valid, then the rest of the code will run. The JavaScript function `checkValidity()` is part of the web browser's API. The API, as you'll recall, is made up of all of the code used for JavaScript functions that a browser can perform.

The `checkValidity()` function is a browser function you can use to check whether a form is valid; you don't have to write it yourself. This function will return true or false, depending on the state of the form.

Recall from Table 5-1 that the == operator means "equals." If the form is invalid, `checkValidity()` is false. False equals false results in true. In other words, if the form is invalid, the rest of the code runs.

First, an array variable named `elementsArr` is used to count the number of form elements with an `:invalid` pseudo-class applied to them. These are the elements in an invalid state.

Next, a variable named `errCount` is created and set to the length of the array of elements in an invalid state.

Finally, a `for` loop cycles through the array of warning labels (`warnArr`) that have the CSS class `form_errors` and updates the text and style of each. The text is updated through the use of the `.innerHTML` property, and the style is updated by adding a new class (the `required` class) to the list of classes the HTML element has assigned to it.

In form_validation.js, after the block of code you just created for the `if` condition, enter the following block of code, which is the reverse of the previous one. It specifies the `else` part of the condition:

```
else
{
    for (ndx = 0; ndx < warnArr.length; ndx++)
    {
        warnArr[ndx].innerHTML = "";
        warnArr[ndx].classList.remove("required");
    }
}
```

This `else` code is the second half of two opposite parts. Either the form is invalid and the first part of the code runs, or the form is valid and the second part runs.

The second part also has a loop, but this loop sets the `innerHTML` property to nothing and removes the CSS `required` class from the warning labels. This cleans up the webpage as soon as the user fills out all of the required fields properly.

Finally, add one more closing curly bracket to end the `validate_form()` function.

The completed code looks like that in **Figure 5-10**.

Figure 5-10 Completed code for the `validate_form()` function

```
1    "use strict"
2
3    function validate_form(inForm)
4    {
5        let warnArr = document.getElementsByClassName("form_errors");
6        let ndx;
7
8        if (inForm.checkValidity() == false)
9        {
10           let elementsArr = inForm.querySelectorAll(':invalid');
11           let errCount = elementsArr.length-1;
12
13           for (ndx = 0; ndx < warnArr.length; ndx++)
14           {
15               warnArr[ndx].innerHTML = "You are missing data in " + errCount + " fields in this form.";
16               warnArr[ndx].classList.add("required");
17           }
18        }
19        else
20        {
21           for (ndx = 0; ndx < warnArr.length; ndx++)
22           {
23               warnArr[ndx].innerHTML = "";
24               warnArr[ndx].classList.remove("required");
25           }
26        }
27    }
```

The final puzzle to solve is when to call this function. Start by adding the `validate_form()` function to the form using an `onsubmit` event after the `<span class="form_errors"></span>` line in contact_us.html:

```
<form onsubmit = "return(validate_form(this));">
```

This code interrupts the normal form submission process by creating a custom path using the `onsubmit` event. When the form is submitted, the function `validate_form()` runs, taking the form itself as the variable passed to it via the `this` parameter that you have used previously. If the process in `validate_form()` is successful, the form is submitted via the `return()` function to the normal route in the browser form submission process.

Save the change, refresh the webpage, and submit the form without entering any data. The browser catches the action before the form is submitted and shows the "Please fill out this field" prompt, so the `onsubmit` event is actually too late in the process to be useful here. The users may still be annoyed. Remove this `onsubmit` event from the form element in contact_us.html since it doesn't create the desired result.

As an alternative, you could use each of the required fields to create an event that triggers the `validate_form()` function. In contact_us.html, add the following code to the First Name input element:

```
onblur="validate_form(this.form)"
```

The completed form input element looks like the following:

```
<input type="text" id="f_name" name="f_name" required
    onblur="validate_form(this.form)">
```

The `onblur` JavaScript event is triggered when the user clicks or tabs away from an input element. This event means the user is most likely done with that field and the code can run to check to see how many invalid fields remain—which is the goal of validating the form.

The `this.form` parameter is another use of the contextual `this`, which in this case refers to the input element. The input element is contained inside a form, so using `this.form` sends the entire form containing the input element to the `validate_form()` function. That function takes in a form and asks how many invalid elements it has.

Add the `onblur` code to the rest of the required form input elements (Last Name, Email, and "Type your message here" fields) so any will trigger the `validate_form()` function. Save your changes, refresh the webpage, then without entering any data in the form, click the First Name field then the Last Name field. You should see a custom error message like that in **Figure 5-11**.

However, there's still a problem, even though the `onblur` event works correctly. The code is working, but the function is incorrect. Count the number of required elements in the web form. There are four. The error message says you are missing five elements. Add data to the four elements, clicking to navigate from one to the next. After entering the last required field, the code changes from displaying "You are missing 2 required fields" to emptying the error message of text and removing the required class. What the what?

This is an opportunity to use the JavaScript debugger to figure out what is going on in the code as it is running. Refresh the page to reset the valid and invalid form fields. Open the JavaScript debugger in your browser and add a breakpoint on the following line of code in form_validation.js:

```
let elementsArr = inForm.querySelectorAll(':invalid');
```

This is the variable and line of code that loads the invalid input elements from the form and are the starting point for validation, so they need to be inspected in greater depth.

Click the First Name field, then click elsewhere to trigger the `onblur` event. The breakpoint stops the execution of the code. Move your pointer over each part of this line of code. Because it hasn't run yet, the variable `elementsArr` is undefined. The `inForm` property contains a list of the elements in the form. If you drill down by clicking each one, you can find the `valid` property for each element. That's a lot of work, so you can just run this line of code and stop at the next one to load the `elementsArr` with only the elements that are in an invalid state.

Figure 5-11 Warning labels identifying how many fields are missing in the web form

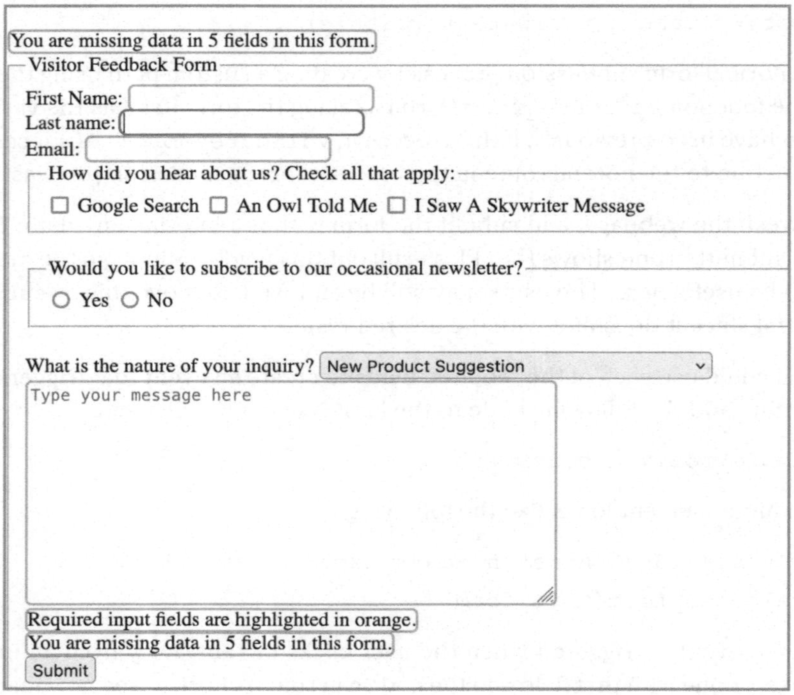

You are missing data in 5 fields in this form.

┌─ Visitor Feedback Form ─────────────────────────┐

First Name: [   ]
Last name: [   ]
Email: [   ]

┌─ How did you hear about us? Check all that apply: ─┐
│ ☐ Google Search ☐ An Owl Told Me ☐ I Saw A Skywriter Message │
└──┘

┌─ Would you like to subscribe to our occasional newsletter? ─┐
│ ○ Yes ○ No │
└──┘

What is the nature of your inquiry? [New Product Suggestion   ∨]

[Type your message here
                                                          ]

Required input fields are highlighted in orange.
You are missing data in 5 fields in this form.

[Submit]

To do this, click the Step Into button (or equivalent button). This button executes the current line of code and then pauses at the next. Move your pointer over elementsArr. You should see a pop-up window like that in **Figure 5-12**.

Figure 5-12 The array variable contents in the JavaScript debugger

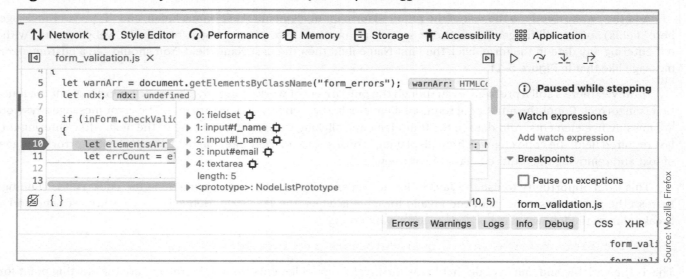

That's a helpful clue. The elementsArr array has five elements—the fieldset and the four anticipated input elements that are currently invalid and highlighted. This overcount by one is a quirk of the HTML form and fieldset properties.

A fieldset that contains an invalid input element is also invalid. So, a form always has one more invalid element than visible input elements that the user interacts with. You can modify the code with one small change and make the validation work properly, now that you know what is going wrong.

Note that using the fieldset is recommended for web accessibility, but it is not required. If your code doesn't include the fieldset, only the input fields are counted into your array of invalid form elements.

Update the following line of code in your form_validation.js to subtract one from the length of the array before telling the user how many more fields need to be filled out:

```
let errCount = elementsArr.length - 1;
```

Save your change, then refresh the page. You can remove the breakpoint from the code or run the check again to see if the output string gets the right value. Click the First Name field then click out of it. The warning label should say the form has four missing fields.

The Third Pass: Validating the Data with JavaScript

In addition to using the web browser's automated form validation and counting the missing form elements, a third helpful feature for both the user and administrator of a web form is validating the contents of the data gathered in the form.

This validation is more than testing whether a field contains an entry or a syntactically valid email address. Data validation screens the data for proper length, formatting, content, and other properties before the data is sent to the web server for further validation.

In the current form on the contact_us page, it is easy to bypass the browser validation. You can type the letter A repeatedly in the First Name and Last Name fields and use a@b.cc to create a valid email address. Adding the letter A will also satisfy the text area required-field validation.

Someone could enter the email address of a@b.cc, though an email server could not deliver the message since the protocol used by email servers known as Simple Mail Transfer Protocol (SMTP) requires at least two letters in each part of the address.

The next step in the validation is to prompt the user to confirm that an email address less than eight characters long is valid. You could use the following pseudocode for the first type of length validation:

Function checkLength(inField, fieldName, minLength)

    If length of the value of inField is greater than zero and less than the minLength

        prompt user "Are you sure your fieldName is inField.value?"

        If user says no, remove the text in the inField and let them reenter it

This pseudocode is abstracted from the requirements of the Email field so that it can be reused for any fields with a minimum length requirement. The JavaScript code for this validation is more complex than the pseudocode because Firefox has an idiosyncrasy with a part of it. Add the following code to the form_validation.js file:

```
function checkLength(inField, formField, fieldLength)
{
    if(inField.value.length > 0 && inField.value.length <
fieldLength)
    {
        if(confirm("Is your " + formField + " actually " +
inField.value + "? \n\n OK to confirm, Cancel to edit.")==false)
        {
            inField.value = '';
            setTimeout(function() { inField.focus(); }, 1);
        }
    }
}
```

This function starts with familiar code: `function checkLength(inField, formField, fieldLength)`. It includes a function name followed by three inbound variables.

The first line of code—the first `if` statement—is more complex. If a user hasn't typed any characters, the browser's "This field is required" message will appear, so you don't want to provide redundant messaging. This field should prompt the user with an OK/Cancel message only if the entry has at least one character and is less than the minimum length. This is why the first `if` statement has two tests separated by the `&&`, or AND operator. Both tests must be true for the `if` statement to evaluate to true.

| Note | The `&&` symbol in JavaScript represents a logical AND operator. **Table 5-2** lists other logical operators. |

Table 5-2 Javascript logical operators

Operator	Description
&&	And
||	Or
!	Not

The OR operator results in True if either test is true. The AND operator results in True only if both tests are true. The NOT operator makes a true operation false and the reverse.

Next is the `if` statement that uses the JavaScript `confirm()` function to create a pop-up confirmation message:

```
if(confirm("Is your " + formField + " actually " + inField.value + "? \n\n OK to
confirm, Cancel to edit.")==false)
```

The `confirm()` function provides OK and Cancel buttons. If the user clicks OK, true is returned from the message. Otherwise, if the user clicks Cancel, false is returned from the function, which returns a true result since `false ==` `false` is a true statement.

The following two lines of code run if the `if` statement returns a true result:

```
inField.value = '';
setTimeout(function() { inField.focus(); }, 1);
```

The first line of code clears the input field that was passed into the `confirm()` function, since the user has confirmed that the value entered is not correct.

The second line of code uses `function()` as an **anonymous function** to run the `setTimeout()` JavaScript API function, which causes a 1-second delay before moving the focus to the field that the user confirmed as containing bogus data. Anonymous functions are those that don't have a proper name like `doStuff()` or `validateInputs()`. They are useful to run a process that uses a JavaScript API function after a delay or to return results from that function.

This extra line of code is necessary because Firefox would otherwise put the focus on the next input field in its speedy processing of the JavaScript, rather than on the field that contains the bogus data.

Add the new validation function to the input email element list of `onblur` functions to run, using the following code:

```
checkLength(this,'Confirm Email',8);
```

The complete `onblur` function list looks like the following:

```
onblur="validate_form(this.form);checkLength(this,'Email',8);"
```

Save all of your changes, then refresh the page. Test again to confirm that the contact_us.html page is working as you would expect. If you encounter errors, go back through the section on testing and debugging again.

> **Note** | You can create a validation similar to the one for the minimum length of an input field by using the `minlength` attribute for the input field. However, the user will not be presented with an opportunity to bypass the form validation if their email address really is less than eight characters. Additionally, there would not be an opportunity to create a JavaScript `confirm()` function, which would make this tutorial in JavaScript less comprehensive.

Quick Check 5-5

1. When is an `onblur` event triggered?

   a. When the user minimizes the web browser to open another window
   b. When the web browser has to load an external file
   c. When the user clicks a button
   d. When the user clicks away from an active element

2. Is using the `required` attribute for input fields a robust enough form validation to ensure valid data from your users?

   a. No, users might make other mistakes that cause problems.
   b. Yes, that's just the right amount of prescreening to ensure quality data is returned from users without annoying them unnecessarily.
   c. No, using the `required` attribute isn't necessary to ensure valid data if you have clear, correct directions and proper CSS styling.
   d. Yes, malicious hackers can't bypass the attributes in form input elements, only the JavaScript code validation.

3. What does `confirm()` create in JavaScript?

   a. A yes/no pop-up message used to confirm or deny a choice from the user
   b. A validation procedure for an input element in a web form
   c. A dynamic input element in the HTML document body with OK and Cancel buttons
   d. An OK/Cancel pop-up message that returns true or false depending on which button the user clicks

1) d. The `onblur` event is triggered when focus is changed from an active element to elsewhere in the page. **2) a.** The `required` attribute is a good initial step, but more steps are necessary to ensure robust form validation. **3) d.** The JavaScript `confirm()` function creates a pop-up message with OK and Cancel buttons and returns true if the user clicks the OK button and false if the user clicks the Cancel button.

Summary

- JavaScript is the third of three technologies that make up the most common programming languages used in the web browser. The others are HTML and CSS.

- JavaScript is a client-side programming language that is interpreted by the JavaScript engine in the web browser.

- You can use JavaScript to create interactive components in a webpage, modify the HTML and CSS on a webpage, and validate user data.

- JavaScript is similar to other programming languages in that it uses a syntax made up of functions, variables, logical control structures, and other elements that form the rules for the language.

- JavaScript events are actions that happen in the browser and can trigger JavaScript code to run.

- JavaScript comparison operators are used to evaluate two expressions against each other, resulting in a true or false.

- The JavaScript logical operators And, Or, and Not are used to combine comparison operators.

- You can debug JavaScript code using the JavaScript debugger included with most modern browsers.

- Three types of JavaScript errors are runtime, syntax, and logical errors. Of the three, logical errors are the most difficult to find.

- Pseudocode is useful to map the logical flow of code before writing the JavaScript code.

- Client-side validation of web form data is a first step, but not the only step, in data validation.

- Validate form data so using the form is least annoying for users.

Key Terms

anonymous function	instantiation	strongly typed
array	just-in-time compiler	syntax
client-side	logical error	syntax error
code debugger	logical operators	text strings
conditional	pseudocode	variable
events	runtime error	variable declaration
for loop	server-side	
functions	statement	

Review Questions

1. What is the difference between client-side and server-side code? (5.1)

   a. Client-side code runs on the web server, and server-side code runs in the web browser.

   b. Client-side code runs in the web browser, and server-side code runs on the web server.

   c. Client-side code runs after it is compiled, and server-side code is interpreted.

   d. There is no difference; these are two names for the same code running in different locations.

2. Why is it important to write simple code? (5.1)

   a. Because the majority of a web developer's time with the code is spent maintaining it

   b. Because simple code runs faster in the web browser

   c. Because simple code is shorter than more complex code that does the same thing

   d. Because simple code works in all versions of the most popular web browsers

3. What does the keyword `this` represent in JavaScript? (5.2)

    a. The body of the JavaScript function code

    b. The object creating the start to the action that begins the code execution

    c. The JavaScript function being called by an event

    d. The properties of the object that an action will use in the JavaScript function

4. What are variables used for in JavaScript? (5.2)

    a. To create the names of executable blocks of code

    b. To follow the rules of the JavaScript language

    c. As shorthand for functions that make up the browser's JavaScript API

    d. As containers of data that are used in the JavaScript code

5. Why is the use of `eval()` discouraged in JavaScript? (5.2)

    a. It isn't; `eval()` is widely used in JavaScript.

    b. Because it can only be used in client-side code that runs in the web browser, not in server-side JavaScript

    c. Because it doesn't work in older browsers

    d. Because it can be used by hackers to run malicious code instead of the intended code

6. What causes syntax errors? (5.3)

    a. Mistyped variable or function names

    b. Logical errors in the code

    c. Incorrect links in the `head` section of the HTML page to the JavaScript file

    d. Code that doesn't follow the rules of the programming language

7. Why are logical errors the hardest to find and fix? (5.3)

    a. Because all parts of the code are correct but the logic in the code is incorrect

    b. Because logical errors are rare and most programmers don't have much experience with them

    c. Because the JavaScript debugger will step over logical errors by default

    d. Because logical errors are the most complex of the three types of errors

8. Why do programmers perform the extra step of writing pseudocode before writing the actual code? (5.4)

    a. For job security, since writing pseudocode adds an extra step to the process that they can get paid for

    b. To create the logical flow of the code, which makes the actual writing of the computer code easier and faster

    c. To create code that will get compiled into the actual executable code by the compiler

    d. To prevent syntax and runtime errors in the actual code that is eventually written

9. What does the code snippet `ndx++;` do? (5.4)

    a. Adds 1 to the value of the variable `ndx`

    b. Adds the variable `ndx` to whatever value it currently holds

    c. Adds the contents of the variable `ndx` to whatever value comes next in the code

    d. Adds the number stored in `ndx` back into `ndx`, twice

10. When should you add `"use strict"` to the top of a JavaScript file? (5.5)

    a. Always

    b. Never

    c. Only when you want to ensure your code will work in older browsers

    d. Only while you are writing the code, and after that you can remove it since it isn't useful anymore

11. What is the purpose of web form validation? (5.5)

    a. To prevent malicious hackers from entering corrupt data into the web form

    b. To annoy the users of the web form

    c. To help ensure users provide the necessary and correct data that you need to collect from them

    d. To make the form work properly in all browsers

12. What is an array used for? (5.4, 5.5)

    a. Creating a comma-separated list of the same type of values

    b. Storing a tab-delimited set of the same type of values

    c. Holding a row of data from a database in the code

    d. Creating a single variable that holds multiple instances of the same type of variable

Programming Exercises

1. Using your favorite search engine, search online for "common JavaScript form validation mistakes." Read through at least three of the references you find and summarize the commonalities in a one-page report. Include links to the pages you reviewed.

2. Using your favorite search engine, search for "most common uses of JavaScript in the browser." Read through five of the articles returned in the results and summarize the most common uses in a one-page report. Include links to the pages you reviewed.

3. Search for "common mistakes when using JavaScript" using your favorite search engine. Read five of the articles returned in the results and summarize the common themes of these articles in a one-page paper. Include links to the pages you reviewed.

Projects

1. Add a "blinking red stoplight" function to the stoplight webpage by doing the following (5.1–5.5):

    • This function will run only when the red light itself is clicked and leave the stoplight in a blinking-red state until another button is clicked to change the color of the light. You can use the CSS `animation` and `@keyframes` operators to create the blinking effect via a `.blink` class. Search for "css blinking background" and modify what you find to create your own version in the `.blink` class in light_style.css.

    • In stoplight2.js, use the `onclick` event for the red light `div` to call the `blink()` function. This function will add the `.blink` class to the red light.

    • Add another line of code to remove this class in the first line of `makeLight()` so any other button on the stoplight will still work properly.

2. Modify the contact_us webpage as follows (5.1–5.5):

    • In contact_us.html, add a second "Confirm Email Address" input element to the HTML web form and add the `required` attribute.

    • In form_validation.js, add the necessary JavaScript to compare the email addresses in both email address boxes and, if the values are different, create an alert that tells the user the email addresses must match.

    • In my_styles.css, add the style necessary to display this email input element as a required field. Also include the minimum length prescreen function that runs when the `onblur` event occurs.

3. Continue modifying the contact_us webpage as follows (5.1–5.5):

- In contact_us.html, add an `isMaxLength()` function call to the `textarea` that runs when the `onkeyup` event occurs.
- In form_validation.js, pass the `textarea` as a parameter to the corresponding function you need to write. The function should compare the `maxlength` attribute value from the `textarea` to the length of the value currently in the `textarea` and put the text "You have X characters remaining" in a `span` used as a warning label just to the right or just below the `textarea`.

JavaScript Libraries

Learning Objectives

When you complete this chapter, you will be able to:

6.1   Explain what JavaScript libraries are and why they are used.

6.2   Create a local copy of jQuery and link to it from within HTML pages.

6.3   Create JavaScript that implements jQuery functionality to manipulate the HTML DOM.

6.4   Create interactive webpages using jQuery.

6.5   Validate the data entered by a user in a web form using the jQuery Validation plug-in.

6.6   Extend the functionality of jQuery by incorporating the DataTables plug-in.

6.1   What Are JavaScript Libraries?

If you have been working through this book in sequential order of the chapters, you just completed a chapter that introduced you to programming with JavaScript. In that previous chapter, you learned about the basic syntax of JavaScript, along with the functions, variables, and events that make it work in the browser. If that chapter was your first exposure to web programming, it may have seemed like programming is complex and repetitive. It may also have felt like you needed to write a lot of code to accomplish a few discrete actions.

However, JavaScript can add so much functionality to the user experience that most new websites use JavaScript to enhance the experience. A lot of code can be written to make a website more interactive, but much of that code is redundant. Consider how many times you wrote `document.getElementById` in the previous chapter. After a few hundred times writing that as a full stack web developer, you might be tempted to listen to the voice that says, "There has to be a better way to do this."

There is.

Now that you know the basics of how to write simple JavaScript code longhand, you are ready to learn how to use a **JavaScript library** to bypass many mundane tasks that web browsers require of JavaScript to access and manipulate the DOM, modify the CSS of an element on a page, or perform webpage automations. A JavaScript library is a package of prebuilt JavaScript code that web developers can use to extend webpage functionality in the browser. A JavaScript library creates a layer of code that calls base JavaScript functions without requiring you to write the full text of the JavaScript code each time. JavaScript libraries also combine multiple basic JavaScript functions to complete and automate common tasks.

One of the early challenges you will encounter when using a JavaScript library is learning what possibilities the library offers. You will need to read the documentation provided by the developers of the original library to become familiar with its features, functions, and syntax. This chapter includes references to the documentation for features and functions, but more documentation is available than can be included in one chapter of a full stack web development textbook. You are encouraged to explore the documentation of the library you will be using and the two additional software packages related to it.

Flavors of JavaScript Libraries

If you use your favorite search engine to search for "most popular JavaScript libraries," you will see numerous pages citing many lists, some ranked by usage statistics and some by the author's preference for the most exciting technological flavors of the month.

The articles that cite JavaScript libraries by usage are more relevant to determine which libraries you should explore. The shiny new technology doesn't always become a preferred platform through usage.

Dozens of JavaScript libraries are uniquely suited to fill a specific niche in the full stack web development ecosystem. Some libraries focus on automations in the GUI, and others are written to manipulate the DOM. Other libraries are used to create online games, which require using complex graphics processing in the browser.

Most JavaScript libraries are similar enough that after you learn how to use your first library, it becomes easier to learn your second library. You still need to learn different coding patterns, syntax rules, and API functions, but the fundamental structure is similar.

Learning JavaScript libraries is like learning a second spoken language. If you are fluent in English, for example, learning another language in the Indo-European family of languages like French or Spanish is easier than learning a tonal language like Mandarin or Thai because the concepts and structure are similar.

The programming languages to learn and list on your resumé are those that are most widely adopted by employers in your field or specialty. The easiest JavaScript libraries to learn are those you should start with to create a foundation of understanding. The intersection between these two important factors—easy to learn and widely adopted for use—is filled by a few JavaScript libraries. jQuery is one of them.

Why jQuery?

Although jQuery was not the first JavaScript library, usage grew rapidly after it debuted until it became the most widely used library. One reason it grew so fast was that it was built to be platform independent. In the early days of the interactive web, each web browser had its own unique flavor of JavaScript. Code that you wrote, tested, and perfected for Firefox often created errors in Internet Explorer and didn't work at all in Opera or Safari.

The less-than-optimal solution was to maintain a separate body of JavaScript code for each major web browser and to detect the browser in the first step of each JavaScript function you called in your code. That detection included an if-then-else-if stack to run varieties of the same code for each browser.

jQuery finally solved this problem by providing a layer between the code the developer wrote and the API of each browser jQuery was documented to work with. A browser-specific translation was built into the jQuery library so that the same developer-built code could work with many browsers. The differing interpretations of how JavaScript should work in each browser isn't as much of a problem today, however, because proprietary web browser functionality has fallen out of favor with the creators of the major web browsers.

As you know, browsers still have quirks, so adopting a library that has been tested across all the popular browsers helps significantly with creating a seamless body of code that works with all of them. The documentation for each library identifies the browsers and operating systems the library has been tested on.

jQuery remains relevant today in spite of its age because so many developers used it to solve so many problems and add functionality to so many webpages. Employers are still seeking jQuery developers to keep those legacy pages updated and extend them to include new features. If you pursue a career path in full stack web development, you are likely to encounter jQuery in pages you are responsible for maintaining.

The other reason jQuery remains popular with many full stack web developers is that it is simple yet comprehensive. The syntax for using jQuery is similar to JavaScript and, like JavaScript, jQuery enhances the content of a page rather than being directly integrated in it. jQuery is often cited as the best JavaScript library to start with, since it is not too far removed from the core JavaScript code, and JavaScript is often cited as the best first programming language to learn.

Additionally, the jQuery documentation is extensive and includes sample code that you can copy and paste, then modify. That documentation, jQuery tutorials, which are well worth reading, is available at https://api.jquery.com. You can find other jQuery tutorials online.

A large user community writes and supports jQuery. If you encounter a problem using jQuery, you will not be the first one to do so, and the answer to your question is most likely a short Internet search away.

Released under the MIT open-source license, jQuery is free to use for anyone who agrees to the terms of the license. You can read more about those terms at https://opensource.org/licenses/MIT. The open-source license means that you can explore, learn, and use jQuery without having to buy it or the tools used to create webpages with it.

Note

The MIT open-source license is the most popular of several open-source software licenses used throughout software development. The basic idea behind open-source software is that by building software as a community instead of as a for-profit corporation, both the software and the community benefit from a better product.

Users of open-source software are free to download the software and bundle it with their own intellectual property as long as they leave a copy of the original license intact in the code. This applies even if those users are creating a commercial product that will generate profits or unique intellectual property that will subsequently be licensed itself.

Getting Started

As you have done in the previous chapters, create a Chapter_6 folder inside of your existing folder structure for this course, and then create folders for the Samples and Projects in this chapter. Inside the Samples and Projects folders, create CSS and resources folders. Download a copy of the starting files for Chapter 6 and put the various file types in their respective folders.

Because this chapter compares the JavaScript work you did previously to the work that goes into using a JavaScript library, you will use the same three HTML pages as sample exercises, building a calculator, stoplight, and form validation, then adding the products.html page from the Totally Awesome Stuff website.

Note

It isn't necessary to write raw JavaScript exclusively in text files that have a .js extension and are saved in a separate folder. Raw JavaScript code can be embedded in the HTML of the webpage, just like you can embed CSS code in the webpage. However, keeping your JavaScript code files in a folder separate from your images, CSS, and HTML makes finding and updating those files easier and makes the JavaScript code available across multiple HTML pages.

JavaScript libraries can be considered resources instead of JavaScript code, since you won't be customizing them or modifying the code they contain. Creating a separate folder for your JavaScript libraries and calling it something like "resources" puts those libraries in a convenient place that isn't mixed in with your own custom JavaScript files, if you choose to add those.

Quick Check 6-1

1. Why do web developers prefer to use JavaScript libraries instead of writing their own code?

   a. JavaScript libraries are more flexible than writing your own code.
   b. JavaScript libraries are easier to use than writing your own code.
   c. JavaScript libraries are more important on a resumé than coding ability.
   d. JavaScript libraries offer more features with less time invested than writing your own code.

2. Why does using a JavaScript library help create uniformity of function across browsers?

   a. Different browsers use different libraries to perform the same task.
   b. The library will load any necessary code from the browser API to customize the code for that browser.
   c. The library includes browser-specific code blocks that have been tested against the supported browsers.
   d. JavaScript libraries use the HTML DOM in the browser to show updates and modifications within the browser.

3. What is open-source software?

   a. Software with the original source code visible to developers
   b. Software that is open to hacking and therefore unsafe to use without proper precautions
   c. Software that is available as a precompiled package of executables
   d. All software is open source, since somebody had to write it at some point

1) d. JavaScript libraries are preconfigured blocks of software that offer specific features with less coding necessary than writing your own code. **2) c.** JavaScript libraries include browser-specific code to create uniformity whenever necessary. **3) a.** Open-source software is code supported by the development community that created it and available for editing and improvement by that community of users.

6.2 Implementing jQuery

You can obtain a copy of jQuery to incorporate into your webpage in two ways. One is to download a copy to your local machine and create a reference to it from within your HTML page just like any other JavaScript file. This downloaded file would then become part of the files you move to the production web server when you launch your website.

The other is to use a previously uploaded version of jQuery that is hosted externally by a company like Google. Using this approach, you create an absolute link to that externally hosted library file that the webpage needs to function. Each approach has pros and cons that you will learn more about in this section.

Creating a Local Copy of jQuery

To download a local copy of jQuery, you can open the link at https://jquery.com/download and follow the instructions to get your own copy of the latest version.

If you have a list of project requirements and you therefore know exactly which jQuery components you need to complete your project, you can choose to include only those parts in a custom download. On the other hand, if you are exploring the jQuery functionality, you can download the entire build. For the purposes of this tutorial, you will need the entire uncompressed development build of the most recent version.

The development team that keeps jQuery updated releases new versions as bugs in older versions are reported and fixed and as new features are released. Major and minor version releases correspond to the version numbers. A major version change takes the current release number from 1.0 to 2.0, for example. A minor version change takes the build from 2.0 to 2.1. A bug fix or feature update moves the release from 2.1.0 to 2.1.1.

On the jQuery download page, find the link to the "uncompressed development build" of the most recent production jQuery build and download it into the resources folder you created earlier. You can do this by right-clicking or Ctrl+clicking the link and selecting an option like "Save Link As." Alternatively, you can open the .js file, and since it is just plain text, copy and paste it into a new text file that you save locally with the same name as the original file. In the next section, you add links to this file in the webpage you will be modifying.

The text of the code in the full development build includes many comments about the functions, bug fixes, and other interesting components included in the code. It is worth reading through the code, even if not all of it makes sense to you, since reading someone else's code is always an enlightening experience.

When you are done with your development on the website that includes jQuery, you can update the link to the compressed, or **minified**, version that corresponds to the uncompressed development build version. You must link to the corresponding minified version by matching the two version numbers exactly, since the features you used may be different if you change to a newer or older version of jQuery. However, the minified version is significantly smaller and therefore faster to load on all devices since most of the superfluous text like comments and whitespace have been stripped out.

Creating a Link to an External Library

One of the services that Google offers is a **content delivery network (CDN)** that includes many popular JavaScript libraries. A CDN is a group of high-speed web servers strategically located near major Internet traffic hubs that return resource files to the requests from web browsers. jQuery is included in the list of files that are offered. You can review the list at the Google Hosted Libraries page at https://developers.google.com/speed/libraries.

To use a CDN resource in your webpage, find the specific JavaScript library that you want to include and add an absolute link to it in the `<head>...</head>` section of your page. You will then be using Google's ultrafast web servers to deliver a part of your webpage content to your users.

The downside of this approach is that you may only use the general version that includes all features. While this ordinarily doesn't present any problems, it is something to be aware of if network bandwidth or file sizes are a concern.

Note

The Google Hosted Libraries page lists specific versions of those libraries. At one time, the jQuery section included a more generic link to a "latest stable build" without citing a specific version number. The advantage of using a link to the latest version was that as features were added, they could be included in the webpages under development by virtue of that generic link.

The disadvantage was that occasionally new features broke old functionality or changed the way the webpage behaved. Support for the generic link without a version number was dropped, and the only possibility now is to link to a specific version that has been released into production.

The Hybrid Approach

Some full stack web developers take both the download and the CDN approaches to using jQuery. They download the latest full development version to their local resources file, and then create a link to the CDN version when they move their website to a full production state. That provides the advantage of being able to explore the code locally while relying on the faster network speed of the CDN in a production application.

Quick Check 6-2

1. How can you acquire a copy of an open-source JavaScript library like jQuery?

   a. You buy a copy of it burned on a CD from any software outlet.
   b. You download it from wherever you can find it on the Internet.
   c. You view the source of someone else's webpage and download their copy.
   d. You visit the official documentation source for the library project and download it from there.

2. What is a downside of using a JavaScript library from a CDN?

   a. The CDN will be slightly slower to load the first time, since it is a different server from the web server that hosts the webpage.
   b. The CDN will charge for the use of network bandwidth.
   c. The CDN library can't be customized for a specific use case.
   d. The library on the CDN won't be updated to a newer version like a locally stored library will.

3. Why do web developers prefer to link to a specific version of a JavaScript library instead of the latest version?

   a. Because the latest version may include features or functions that break previous versions and therefore the webpage
   b. Because good web developers are strategically lazy and don't want to constantly update their code
   c. Because specific versions are more stable than the most recent version
   d. Because the code in the older versions has been tested and documented more thoroughly than the latest version

1) d. One of the two safe places to get a copy of an open-source JavaScript library is from the official site for the project. **2) c.** The version of the JavaScript library on the CDN contains all features of the library instead of just a few in a customized build since many developers link to the CDN version and use those different features. **3) a.** Linking to a specific version is less likely to result in broken webpages than linking to the latest version that is updated over time.

6.3 Using jQuery to Manipulate HTML

In the previous chapter, you wrote the JavaScript code and functions necessary to make a working webpage stoplight. In this section, you use the same starting file to compare the amount of code you wrote in that previous project to the amount of code that jQuery requires to accomplish the same tasks.

In the starting files for Chapter 6, open stoplight.html and light_style.css in your text editor and review the code in each. Then open the webpage in your browser. You should see the same blank stoplight with Red, Yellow, and Green buttons that you began with in the last chapter.

Linking to jQuery from the Webpage

In the <head>...</head> section of the stoplight.html webpage, add a link to the version of jQuery that you downloaded earlier and stored in your resources folder. The link should look something like the following, though your version number will differ:

```
<script src="resources/jquery-3.6.0.js"></script>
```

If you don't do this, you'll generate an error, since the code that jQuery uses is different from the JavaScript you have been working with in that it begins with a $. The specific error you see in the JavaScript debugger if jQuery can't be found looks like this:

Uncaught ReferenceError: $ is not defined

Finding a solution to that error is just like the differential diagnosis process for finding bugs described in the previous chapter. Start by viewing the source of your webpage that is generating the error, and then click the link to jQuery in the `<head>...</head>` section of the HTML code. If you don't have a link, add one, then refresh your page and check the debugger again for errors. If you do have a link but clicking it opens a "Page Not Found" error, check that the file path to jQuery and the file name are correct.

Writing jQuery-Specific JavaScript

Next, create an opening and a closing `<script>...</script>` tag set on separate lines inside the `<head>...</head>` section of your webpage. Add a blank line between those two tags, then add the following line of code:

```
$(document).ready(function(){});
```

This new code appears intimidating at first, and that single line has a lot to unwrap, but once you read a few lines of jQuery code, it will become easier to follow.

A dollar sign ($) begins every chunk of jQuery code. The actual function without the other code used in the previous example looks like this:

```
$();
```

Why does a jQuery function begin with a $? Strategic efficiency, also known as good programmer laziness. The dollar sign is a variable that replaces the name of the jQuery function. In fact, you can instead write every jQuery function like the following code and all of them will work equally well:

```
jQuery();
```

However, that's five more characters to type, and over the course of hundreds of lines of code, using just the "$" instead adds up to a significant savings in keystrokes and file space. It also avoids errors. It is nearly impossible to spell "$" incorrectly and, as you may recall, jQuery is not the same as Jquery or JQuery since JavaScript is case sensitive.

Whether you write `$();` or `jQuery();` you are passing to the jQuery library function the text in the parentheses, which means you are sending something for the `jQuery()` function to process. In the line of code you added, you are passing to the jQuery library the `document`, which is the DOM, or the HTML of the webpage loaded in the browser as an object model.

The `$(document)` code creates a jQuery **object**, which is a composite made up of the data from the webpage using jQuery and all the functions in the jQuery library for manipulating the DOM. You will see many examples of jQuery functions in the next several sections, but each is a block of code that runs using the data loaded in the object.

Another way to think about an object is as a self-contained code block prepopulated with data that the code itself can read and modify. It is also possible to load new data into the object if the user updates a form element, for example.

The `.ready()` function is an event that happens in the browser once the entire DOM has been loaded into the browser's memory. This is a safe starting point to begin executing the JavaScript that might manipulate the DOM, since all parts of the HTML page will exist and be positioned by the CSSOM. For more information on this function, you can read the jQuery documentation at https://api.jquery.com/ready.

> **Note**
>
> If you read the documentation for the jQuery API function `ready()`, you will find that the code you are writing has been deprecated. That means that it still works but won't be supported in the future. So much existing code uses the syntax `$(document).ready(function(){})`; that it is unlikely the statement will be replaced with the new preferred syntax: `$(function(){})`;.
>
> This chapter does not use the newer, shorter syntax because the documentation for jQuery and other software that uses jQuery still use the older syntax. While the new syntax is shorter, the older syntax is more thoroughly documented and easier to follow.

The full code of the `ready()` function is `ready(function(){})`. The parentheses contain an anonymous function: `(function(){})`. Anonymous functions are used extensively in jQuery since they let you avoid creating an actual named function.

Instead, you can tell the JavaScript engine to treat the code in the curly brackets after `function()` as if it were the body of a named function. Right now, the curly brackets do not contain any code, but you will add some shortly. As with a named function, the lines of code will execute in order and then exit the function when complete, returning the flow of the path to the code that started the function.

Notice that events are chained together with periods, or the dot operator, in this line of code. Reading from left to right, the `$(document).ready(function(){})`; chain tells the JavaScript engine that when the document is ready, call an anonymous function.

This pattern is used often in jQuery, where several operations or events are chained together to create an order of tasks or functions to complete on the same object. This syntax is usually of the form *selector.operation.property(value)* or *selector.property.operation(argument)*.

Each step in this process, separated by the dot operator, is connected to those that come before and after it, but each is also a unique operation or function. You will see many more examples of this pattern in the code that follows.

Add a new line of code between the curly brackets and on its own line, as shown in the following bold text:

```
$(document).ready(function(){
    $('input[type="button"]').click(function(){});
});
```

The new line of code is another jQuery `$()` function that follows the same pattern of *selector.operation* but passes different arguments to the selector function. In the first set of parentheses, `('input[type="button"]')` is a **jQuery selector**, which is used to find one or more elements in the DOM that was loaded in the first step that match the criteria passed to the `$()` function in the second step.

In this case, the outer quotes indicate that a string is passed to the function, telling jQuery to search for all `<input>` tags with a `type="button"` attribute. If you review the HTML code for the stoplight, you will find three `<input>` tags that meet the criterion, and so will jQuery. Notice, too, the combination of single outer quotes and double inner quotes, since matching the `type="button"` attribute requires both the name and quoted value of that attribute while the entire argument is also a string. To read more about selectors in the jQuery API documentation, follow the link https://api.jquery.com/input-selector.

The next operation chained to the selector is the `.click()` event handler in the code `.click(function(){})`. Inside those parentheses is a familiar pattern—another anonymous function. Reading from left to right on the complete line of code, the jQuery function will be passed a selector that will find all input buttons and assign a click function to each of them. For more about the assignment of a click event handler, follow the link https://api.jquery.com/click.

Using a single selector to match all input buttons and then update them all is where jQuery is so powerful. Because the entire webpage has been loaded before the `.ready()` event occurs, and jQuery is based in JavaScript and has access to the HTML, it takes over control from the basic functionality of the webpage and reassigns the click event to the lines of code between curly brackets following the click event. Each function in the operation will be between the curly brackets of the function above it. This means jQuery can replace the click event that the buttons ordinarily would perform with a click event that jQuery tells them to do instead.

Add a new line of code between the curly brackets of the anonymous function called by the `.click()` event handler. Insert the code (shown here in bold) on a new line for readability as follows:

```
$(document).ready(function(){
    $('input[type="button"]').click(function(){
        $('#' + $(this).val() + 'Light').css("background-color",
            $(this).val());
    });
});
```

This line of code is complex and powerful. It is a concatenation of operations performed from left to right. The resulting operation is assigned to the click event of buttons found by the selector in the previous function.

The first part of the new code is the following:

```
$('#' + $(this).val() + 'Light')
```

This code combines two concepts you have encountered before: string concatenation and jQuery selectors. The pound sign or `'#'` that begins the selector tells the jQuery function to search the DOM for an ID, and the text of the ID is composed of the string concatenation.

The code `+ $(this).val() +` appends to that jQuery ID search the value of the button that was clicked. Recall that the keyword `this` is used contextually, and here it refers to the button. The code `$(this).val()` uses the jQuery selector to find the button that was clicked, then retrieves the value from that clicked button. The values are Red, Green, or Yellow for these buttons. Not coincidentally, the IDs for the lights are RedLight, GreenLight, and YellowLight.

After the selector is the following chained function:

```
.css("background-color", $(this).val());
```

This function tells jQuery to update the background color of the selected object to the value of the clicked button. The `background-color` is a CSS property for an HTML element that the jQuery object can modify. The `css()` function takes two parameters—the property and the value—and sets them for the element selected in the preceding block of code. In this case, the property is `background-color` and the value is the `val()` from the button that was clicked. Just like regular JavaScript, jQuery has access to the full HTML and CSS of the webpage and can manipulate both of these parts of the webpage.

Reading back the entire block of code, the process starts when the document is completely loaded in the browser. The jQuery function then searches the elements in the document, filtering for `input` elements with the `type='button'`. To each of those `input[type='button']` elements, it adds a click action handler. The click action handler changes the `background-color` value of the HTML element with an ID (i.e., "RedLight") that matches the string made up of the value of the button (i.e., "Red") that was clicked plus the word "Light." The `background-color` is set to the `val()` of the button (i.e., "Red").

Save this set of changes, then refresh your webpage in the browser and click all three buttons. You should end up with all three lights lit. This is awesome, but not realistic. Only one light at a time should be lit. To fix this problem, the previous chapter required a complex function to create an array of objects found by a class selector, which then looped through each object and set the background color to nothing. That function was called before the rest of the light function ran to clear any previously illuminated lights.

A similar block of code is necessary here. Add the new line of code shown in bold:

```
$(document).ready(function(){
    $('input[type="button"]').click(function(){
        $( ".light" ).css( "background-color", "" );
        $('#' + $(this).val() + 'Light').css("background-color", $(this).val());
    });
});
```

The new line of code uses the jQuery class selector to find all HTML elements in the DOM with the class of `"light"` and set the `css` property of `background-color` to nothing (`""`). Similar to the jQuery ID selector that uses the pound sign, the class selector uses the *.classname* syntax to create this operation. That syntax is shorter and easier to follow than the corresponding JavaScript function you created in the previous chapter.

Save this change, refresh your browser, and click the buttons. You should have a properly functioning webpage stoplight now.

Adding Mouseover Events to HTML Elements

In the previous chapter, the second way to change the stoplight color was to move the pointer over each light. This behavior can be replicated with jQuery but with some changes similar to those you've already seen.

After the last line of jQuery code you added to stoplight.html, add the following code starting on a new line. The code will look both new and somewhat familiar:

```
$(".light").mouseover(function(){
    $( ".light" ).css( "background-color", "" );
});
```

Logically, the first step in this block of code is to clear the background colors of the lights. The only new part in this code is the `.mouseover` jQuery event, which is assigned to all HTML elements with the `.light` class in the DOM. As the name suggests, the `.mouseover` jQuery event is triggered when the user moves the pointer over an HTML object.

After the line that sets the `background-color` to nothing, add the new line of code shown in bold in the following block, inside the closing curly bracket and parenthesis that end the `mouseover()` action handler:

```
$(".light").mouseover(function(){
    $( ".light" ).css( "background-color", "" );
    let v_color = event.target.id;
});
```

If that line of code looks like regular JavaScript, that's because it is. Sometimes in the fancy new world of jQuery, a classic bit of JavaScript is the most efficient way to perform a task. Here, it captures the ID of a `mouseover` target. This line of code declares a variable `v_color` and sets its value to the ID of the HTML element that was the target of the event. In this case, the event is a mouseover, and the target is the light the pointer hovers over. Since the jQuery selector used the class selector `$(".light")`, the code adds this function to all of the lights in the stoplight.

Recall that the IDs of the lights are RedLight, GreenLight, and YellowLight. From those IDs, you need to extract a color to assign to the background. This takes two steps, which is why the ID is loaded into a variable. Add the two steps shown in bold to the code block:

```
$(".light").mouseover(function(){
    $( ".light" ).css( "background-color", "" );
    let v_color = event.target.id;
    v_color = v_color.replace("Light","");
    $(this).css("background-color", v_color);
});
```

The first new line of code, read from left to right, assigns to the variable `v_color` the value that comes from the `replace()` function, which is passed two arguments, `"Light"` and `""`. The JavaScript `replace()` function finds the first text string in parentheses for the variable it is attached to and replaces it with the second text string in the parentheses. Because that second string is empty, the string "Light" is replaced with nothing, so "RedLight" becomes "Red," for example.

The next line includes another use of the `$(this)` selector. The light that is the target of the `mouseover` event is the same one that has its `background-color` property set to the value in the `v_color` variable. That means the

.css() jQuery function is chained to the selector. In other words, the light with the event that starts the function running will be the light that is updated.

Save all of your changes. Your code should look like that in **Figure 6-1**, though your line numbers may differ.

Figure 6-1   The jQuery code for the stoplight webpage

```
11 ▼          <script>
12 ▼          $(document).ready(function(){
13
14 ▼              $('input[type="button"]').click(function(){
15                    $( ".light" ).css( "background-color", "" );
16                    $('#' + $(this).val() + 'Light').css("background-color", $(this).val());
17 ┗              });
18
19 ▼              $(".light").mouseover(function(){
20                    $( ".light" ).css( "background-color", "" );
21                    let v_color = event.target.id;
22                    v_color = v_color.replace("Light","");
23                    $(this).css("background-color", v_color);
24 ┗              });
25 ┗          });
26 ┗          </script>
27 ┗      </head>
```

Source: BBEdit

Next, refresh the stoplight webpage and check to see that all the functions you created are working. All three buttons should turn on their respective lights, and only one light at a time should be lit. Moving your pointer over each light should do the same thing.

jQuery Animation

You have one last thing to add to the webpage stoplight to set it apart from more pedestrian webpage stoplights. After the page loads, the webpage stoplight can float up from the bottom of the page through the use of the jQuery animate() function. You can read more about the jQuery animate() function in the API documentation, found at https://api.jquery.com/animate.

The animate() function is useful for any CSS property that can have a starting and an ending value expressed as numbers. Targets for the animate() function include properties like margins, padding, widths, and heights that can start at one value and end at a larger (or smaller) value. This function is most useful to smoothly reveal, hide, or move objects on the HTML page.

To include the animation, modify the light_style.css stylesheet. Start by changing the margin at the top of the stoplight so you can push the stoplight off the bottom of the page. The existing style for the div that contains the stoplight in light_style.css looks like the following:

```
#wrapper {
    text-align: center;
    width: 100%;
}
```

You need to make two changes to this style to incorporate the animate() function. First, include a position declaration to tell the browser how the wrapper fits on the page with the other HTML elements. Without this declaration, the target element (the wrapper) is just included in the flow of the other HTML elements relative to their positions, not to the web browser window.

You also need to add a much larger margin at the top to push the wrapper element down in the page and out of sight. Add the following two new lines of code shown in bold to the #wrapper style:

```
#wrapper {
    text-align: center;
    width: 100%;
```

```
        margin-top: 900px;
        position: absolute;
    }
```

Next, add a line of jQuery code that changes the top margin from `900px` to `15px` and includes a time interval over which to change the margin. Add the following jQuery code to stoplight.html as the first line after the `$(document).ready(function(){` statement:

```
    $('#wrapper').animate({'margin-top': '15px'}, 1500);
```

This is similar to other blocks of code you have seen before. First, the selector finds an element with the ID of `wrapper`. Chained to that ID selector is the `animate()` function, with the CSS property that will change (`margin-top`) and the ending value for the change (`15px`) inside curly brackets. In this case, the `animate()` function changes the `margin-top` property to `15px`, reducing the margin and creating the effect of the stoplight floating up the page. The last parameter is the number of milliseconds over which this change will occur. The default value is 400 milliseconds, which is too fast to look smooth for a webpage stoplight, so this operation specifies 1.5 seconds.

You added the new line of code in the `$(document).ready` block because this operation begins only after the entire page is loaded in the browser. The completed block of code will look like that in **Figure 6-2**.

Figure 6-2   Incorporating animation into the stoplight webpage

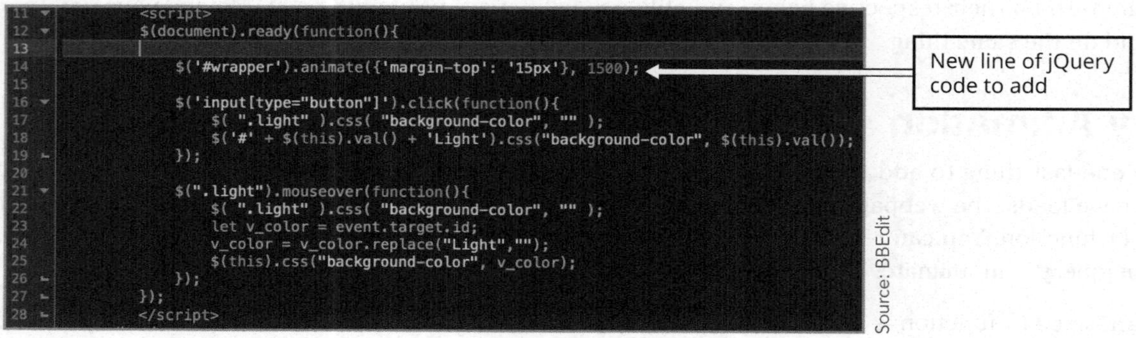

Source: BBEdit

```
11 ▾      <script>
12 ▾      $(document).ready(function(){
13
14            $('#wrapper').animate({'margin-top': '15px'}, 1500);          New line of jQuery
15                                                                          code to add
16 ▾          $('input[type="button"]').click(function(){
17                $( ".light" ).css( "background-color", "" );
18                $('#' + $(this).val() + 'Light').css("background-color", $(this).val());
19            });
20
21 ▾          $(".light").mouseover(function(){
22                $( ".light" ).css( "background-color", "" );
23                let v_color = event.target.id;
24                v_color = v_color.replace("Light","");
25                $(this).css("background-color", v_color);
26            });
27        });
28        </script>
```

Save your changes, then reload the stoplight webpage in your web browser. The page should open as blank and then show a stoplight float from the bottom of the page as the top margin shrinks.

Common Mistakes

Just because you can use jQuery to create some really awesome webpage magic doesn't mean you should. Consider what would happen to your webpage if no JavaScript were included in the page. Would it still be usable?

This is the situation that people who depend on screen readers encounter. The code that you have used so far adds value to the webpage by assigning click event operations to buttons and mouseover events to HTML elements that are already on the page. This type of code won't fundamentally change the content of the page since the buttons and HTML elements are part of the page when it is loaded.

However, jQuery can dynamically add new content that doesn't exist before an event triggers it. That is a problem for screen readers, since you would need to reload the page to pick up the new content and have it narrated to you.

You must carefully test critical page elements like date pickers and shopping carts with a screen reader before launching the website. jQuery is a powerful tool but can also create pages that don't work for all of your users.

> ## Quick Check 6-3

1. What does "Uncaught ReferenceError: $ is not defined" signify?

  a. JavaScript is not installed on the web browser you are testing.
  b. jQuery is not linked to properly in the HTML document.
  c. The version of jQuery you are trying to use isn't up to date.
  d. The version of jQuery you are trying to use is too new for the code you are writing.

2. What does `$('input[type="button"]')` do?

  a. Selects all buttons on a webpage
  b. Creates a click event for the buttons on a webpage
  c. Causes an error
  d. Updates all generic input elements to become buttons in the DOM

3. Is it acceptable to combine classic JavaScript with jQuery code?

  a. No, this is against the best practice of keeping those two types of code separate.
  b. Yes, but they need to be stored in separate files.
  c. No, this will cause an error.
  d. Yes, this is often necessary.

1) b. If the browser can't access the jQuery library file, it won't be able to execute the JavaScript code in that library. **2) a.** The selector in the parentheses first finds all input HTML elements, then further filters to select those with the type of `button`. **3) d.** jQuery is a JavaScript library that contains many useful functions but often requires you to use JavaScript functions as well.

6.4 Using jQuery to Make Interactive Webpages

In the previous chapter, you used simple JavaScript to create an interactive multifunction calculator. In this section, you recreate the same functionality using jQuery.

If necessary, copy calculator.html and calculator.css in the starting files for Chapter 6 to the appropriate directories in your folder structure. Open both files in your text editor and read the code.

In the <head>...</head> section of calculator.html, add a link to the version of jQuery you downloaded. Then add an opening and closing pair of <script>...</script> tags and insert a blank line between them.

Adding Functions Based on a Class

With jQuery, most of the buttons in the calculator will perform the same task as they did originally. When clicked, the button will put its value in the display. One easy way to differentiate the buttons that display their value from the buttons that create a more complex operation is to add them to a CSS class.

The buttons that display their value when clicked include the number buttons (0–9), the arithmetic operators (+, −, *, /), and the decimal point (.). To each of these buttons in calculator.html, add the attribute `class='show'` as in the example for the 1 button:

```
<input type="button" class='show' id="1" name="1" value="1">
```

Nothing is special about this class or the name chosen. It could have been called `'display'` instead, but that name is already used in the calculator for the display. The name `'show'` is used because that's what these buttons do—they show a value in the display.

Next, you need to create some jQuery code to add a click event to each button in this class. This is where the power of jQuery is once again clearly illustrated. Add the following code inside the `<script>`...`</script>` tags in the head section of calculator.html:

```
$(document).ready(function(){
    $("input.show:button").click(function(){
        $("#display").val($("#display").val() + $(this).val());
    });
});
```

This code begins with the familiar `$(document).ready` since this code should only add these click events to every button identified by the selector after the entire document has been loaded in the browser.

The next line of code follows the same pattern you have seen before, a selector followed by an operation. The selector in this case is `$("input.show:button")`, which tells jQuery to search for all inputs with the class of `show` that are buttons.

You could also have reversed the criteria and searched for all inputs that are buttons with the class of `show` and retrieved the same set. This selector is future-proofed against any new buttons added to the form that aren't of the class `show` and any other HTML elements that might have the class `show` added to them that aren't buttons.

The `.click(function(){` operation adds a click event to each of the selected items that match the search criterion, and the code in the curly brackets is what those buttons will run when they are clicked.

In the `$("#display").val($("#display").val() + $(this).val());` line of executable code, you might recognize a similarity to the function you wrote in JavaScript, with the syntactical differences that jQuery requires.

The first part of the code is the equivalent to an assignment operation. However, `$("#display").val()` is passed a value instead of being assigned the value. In jQuery, when you want to set the HTML element with the ID of `display` to a specific value, you pass that value in the parentheses. This is different from raw JavaScript where you had code like the following:

```
document.getElementById('display').value = 7;
```

The jQuery `.val()` function is similar, however, in that it can be used to set the value of the element or to retrieve a value from the element. If the parentheses in `.val()` are empty, this function will retrieve a value. If the parentheses contain a value, that will be the new value in the HTML element being modified. This is what the next part of the bold jQuery code does—it sets the value of the `display` element.

```
$("#display").val($("#display").val() + $(this).val());
```

As you recall, the + operator in JavaScript either adds two numbers together or appends a text string to another text string. In this case, the + operator appends one text string to another since the display holds text characters.

The `$("#display").val() + $(this).val()` code retrieves the value from the display using the empty `val()` function and appends to it the value from `$(this)`, which refers to whatever button was clicked to start running this code. The new value is composed of those two values appended to each other and is then sent back to the display using the same `val()` function, which now contains a value.

Reading the entire new line of code from left to right, the new value in the display is reset to the old value in the display plus the value of the button that was clicked. For example, if the value in the display is 1 and you click the 2 button, the inner `val()` function will retrieve the value 1 currently in the display and the outer `val()` will then put the value 12 into the display. You both retrieve and set the values using the same code, but the difference is in the contents of the parentheses that follow the `val()` function.

Save your changes, then load the calculator.html page in your web browser. You should be able to click all of the numbers and all of the mathematical operators and have those values appear in the display. However, you can't clear the display without reloading the page.

Adding Calculator Functions Using jQuery

The next block of code should clear the display. In the raw JavaScript version of this code, you updated the value of the display element, found by its ID, to nothing to clear the display. You will do the same thing with jQuery by adding the following code to the `script` section of calculator.html in the `$(document).ready()` function:

```
$("#C").click(function() {
    $("#display").val("");
});
```

This new code follows the same *selector.operation* pattern you have been using. First, jQuery selects the C button by its ID, adds a click event handler to the C button, and in the anonymous function that will be used when the button is clicked, sets the value in the HTML element that has the ID of `display` to nothing.

Save your changes to the HTML page, then refresh it in your browser. Click 1, 2, 3, and then click the C button. The display should clear and return to the default 0.

The next button to tackle is the sign switcher, labeled as the +/− button. This operation uses multiplication by −1 to change the sign of the number in the display. The jQuery code is identical, except for the selectors. Add the following code to the `script` section of calculator.html in the `$(document).ready()` function:

```
$("#sign_switch").click(function() {
    $("#display").val($("#display").val() * -1);
});
```

This is a close copy of the code used to append a value to the display and to clear the display. The new value in the display is assigned to the old value in the display multiplied by −1. Save your changes; refresh the webpage; click 1, 2, 3; and then click the +/− button. The value should change to −123. Click the C button to clear the display.

The next button that needs a click function is the % button. As you might recall, the math for this button is simple. The value in the display is divided by 100, then returned to the display. Add the following jQuery code to the `script` section of calculator.html in the `$(document).ready()` function:

```
$("#percent").click(function() {
    $("#display").val($("#display").val() / 100);
});
```

Save your changes and refresh the webpage in the browser. Test to make sure all of the numbers and functions work, including the % button.

The final piece to add to this calculator is the actual calculate button, which is labeled as the = button. The raw JavaScript code used the `eval()` function to accomplish the task of taking the numbers and symbols in the display and performing the mathematical operation specified. As you might guess, the basic concept translates here, too. Add the following jQuery code to calculator.html:

```
$("#equals").click(function() {
    $("#display").val(eval($("#display").val()));
});
```

Be careful counting the closing parentheses at the end of the line. This block of code assigns to the display the new value calculated from the old value that was in the display passed through the `eval()` function. Recall that the `eval()` function is discouraged from use since it can also be used by hackers to execute nonmath functions. In this specific case, however, it is the simplest solution and does not pose a substantial risk.

The completed code for this section looks like that in **Figure 6-3**.

Figure 6-3 The completed code for the calculator.html webpage

```
10  ▼              <script>
11  ▼                  $(document).ready(function(){
12  ▼                      $("input.show:button").click(function(){
13                              $("#display").val($("#display").val()+$(this).val());
14  ⌐                      });
15
16  ▼                      $("#C").click(function(){
17                              $("#display").val("");
18  ⌐                      });
19
20  ▼                      $("#sign_switch").click(function(){
21                              $("#display").val($("#display").val()*−1);
22  ⌐                      });
23
24  ▼                      $("#percent").click(function(){
25                              $("#display").val($("#display").val()/100);
26  ⌐                      });
27
28  ▼                      $("#equals").click(function(){
29                              $("#display").val(eval($("#display").val()));
30  ⌐                      });
31  ⌐                  });
32  ⌐              </script>
```

Source: BBEdit

The only button remaining is the M, or memory button. If you complete Project 2 at the end of this chapter, you will add the code to make the M button work.

If you compare the amount of code you wrote in the previous chapter to the amount of code you wrote in this one to make the calculator function, you will see why jQuery and other JavaScript libraries are so popular with full stack web developers. The more succinct wrapper functions that jQuery offers around the complex operations that JavaScript allows make a more manageable code base for a website.

Quick Check 6-4

1. How is the jQuery `.val()` function used?

    a. It is used to evaluate an expression that is passed to it in the parentheses.

    b. It is used to create a new value for a CSS property.

    c. It is used to set the `val()` property of an HTML element.

    d. It is used to either retrieve or set the value of an HTML element that has a value attribute.

2. Why is it a good idea to use a specific selector like `("input.show:button")`?

    a. To reduce the possibility that jQuery will mistakenly select the wrong HTML elements

    b. To be as specific as possible with the selector to prevent errors that might occur in the future following modifications

    c. To help the next developer identify what the selector is meant to select

    d. To prevent jQuery from creating a conflicting selector chain that interferes with the JavaScript selector

3. What does `$("#display").val("");` do?

    a. Initializes the HTML element with the ID of `"display"` to its starting value

    b. Clears the HTML element with the ID of `"display"` of any values

    c. Sets the HTML element with the class of `"display"` to whatever is chained next in the code

    d. Updates the HTML element with the class of `"display"` to the variable that it is assigned in the next step

> **1) d.** If the parentheses contain a value, `val()` is used to set the value of an element, and if the parentheses contain nothing, `val()` is used to retrieve the value from an element. **2) b.** Similar to using CSS selectors, the most specific jQuery selector necessary to find the correct elements helps to ensure that future developments won't introduce errors. **3) b.** The pound sign in a jQuery selector indicates a selection by ID, and the `val()` with the empty parentheses gets the value from that element.

6.5 Validating Form Data Using the jQuery Validation Plug-In

As you have seen, you can use jQuery (and JavaScript, for that matter) to modify the existing HTML of a webpage. Some widely used software packages extend the base functionality of jQuery. These are known as **software plug-ins**, which increase the capability of the original software by extending the functions.

In the previous chapter, you wrote numerous lines of JavaScript code to validate the form entry data in contact_us.html. This code was complex, looping through the form input elements to count how many were still invalid after each `onblur` event occurred.

jQuery offers a much-improved feature set for form validation, especially when combined with the jQuery Validation plug-in. To read the validation plug-in documentation (which in this case is more than a good idea—it is essential), follow this link to the jQuery Validation Plugin home page at https://jqueryvalidation.org. On that home page, you can watch a short tutorial video and find additional links to further information about the validation plug-in.

The documentation will start your journey to easier form validation. The jQuery Validation Plugin page lists links below headings that include the text "hotlinking welcome." This means you can use these links in your own website, which is what you will do for this section.

Open contact_us.html from the starting files for Chapter 6. Create a link in the <head>...</head> section of your contact_us.html page like you would to a local JavaScript file, but since it is an external file, it should look like the following:

```
<script src="https://cdn.jsdelivr.net/npm/jquery-validation@1.19.5/dist/jquery.validate.js"></script>
```

Note that the version on the jQuery Validation Plugin home page may be different from the previous link, so you'll need to update the version numbers as necessary. You will also need to create a link to your local copy of jQuery, since this is a plug-in that extends jQuery.

Use the following link to begin reading the jQuery Validation Plugin documentation: https://jqueryvalidation.org/documentation.

This page includes an example block of code that ends with the following statements:

```
<script>
    $("#commentForm").validate();
</script>
```

The first challenge with using this block of sample code without changes is that the ID of the form in contact_us.html isn't `commentForm` but `feedback_form`. That selector needs to be updated in the code you use on the contact_us.html page.

The second challenge is that your current implementation of jQuery requires you to wrap that validation code inside a `document.ready()` operation so it runs after the DOM has loaded but before the form is submitted. This is critical, since the form validation event handler will then connect to the form in the DOM before the user interacts with it and after each change in a validated form element value.

The First Pass: Providing User Feedback

In your text editor, add the following jQuery code to the `head` section in contact_us.html:

```
<script>
    $(document).ready(function(){
        $("#feedback_form").validate({
        });
    });
</script>
```

Save your changes, then open the page in your browser. Click the Submit button with no form data entered.

If your code is correct, you should see a form with error messages like those shown in **Figure 6-4**.

Figure 6-4   Form validation feedback created by the jQuery Validation plug-in

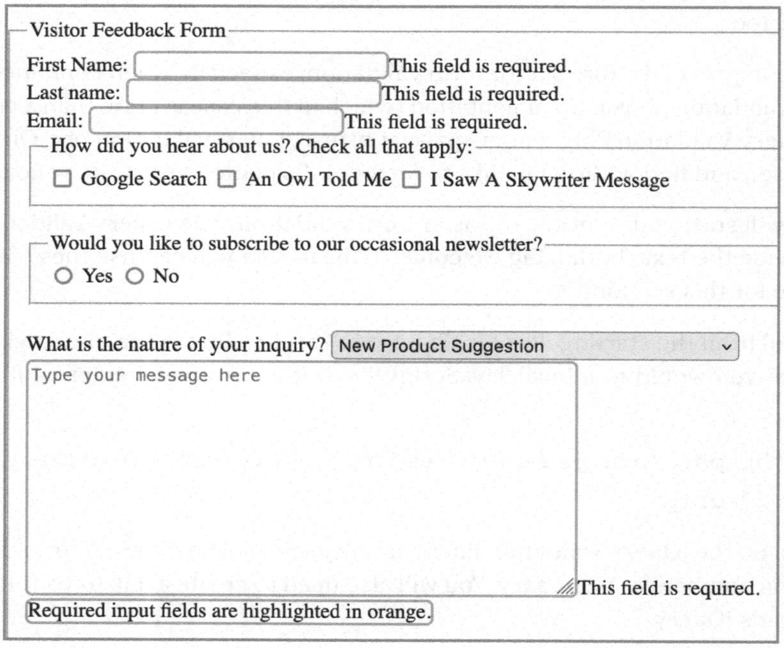

These are not just simple text messages added to the DOM with the form, however. In the browser, drag to select the first two fields and their associated error messages. Right-click (or Ctrl+click on a Mac) the selection, and then choose View Selection Source or a similar command such as Inspect on the shortcut menu to see that these messages are more complex.

The text of the error labels includes information for screen readers to identify missed fields for users who are hearing the pages read to them. **Figure 6-5** shows the text of the error labels.

Figure 6-5   Source code of the error labels from the jQuery Validation plug-in

```
<legend>Visitor Feedback Form</legend>
<label for="f_name">First Name:</label>
<input type="text" id="f_name" name="f_name" required="" class="error" aria-invalid="true"><label id="f_name-error" class="error" for="f_name">This field is required.</label>
<br>
<label for="l_name">Last name:</label>
<input type="text" id="l_name" name="l_name" required="" class="error"><label id="l_name-error" class="error" for="l_name">This field is required.</label>
<br>
<label for="email">Email:</label>
<input type="email" id="email" name="email" minlength="8" required="" class="error"><label id="email-error" class="error" for="email">This field is required.</label>
<br>
```

The important part of each error label is the `aria-invalid="true"` statement. Screen readers read that text and prompt the user to follow the text of the label that has been helpfully appended to this field with further instructions.

Next, you should test the validity checks for each field. Enter the letter *A* in the First Name field, *B* in the Last Name field, and *C* in the Email field, and then press Tab to exit the Email field. For the first two, the error messages will disappear since the jQuery form validation library is taking care of the `onblur` events for you.

That *C* in the email field changes the prompt, however, to "Please enter a valid email address." Change the entry to a valid email address and press Tab to dismiss the prompt.

One distinct advantage of using the jQuery validator is that older browser support is still intact. If you have a copy of Internet Explorer 6 (and if you do, it is a security vulnerability and you probably shouldn't use it anymore) the HTML5 validation that you saw previously in your new version of Chrome, Firefox, Safari, or Edge with the polite messages of "This field is required" won't work.

You can't guarantee that all of your users will be completely up to date with their web browsers, however, so it is better to have the multibrowser version support that jQuery brings by default. The error messages you are generating here will work with the older versions of most browsers.

The Second Pass: Counting the Missing Fields

In the last chapter, you wrote code to count the number of invalid fields. Using the jQuery Validation plug-in, you can just implement the function that performs this action for you instead of writing your own code. To find the documentation for this function, search online for "jQuery validation number of invalid elements" and then search the page of the documentation. The URL for the base documentation is https://jqueryvalidation.org/validate.

The following block of code is the sample provided by the authors of the plug-in to count the number of invalid elements and add them to a warning label:

```
$("#myform").validate({
  invalidHandler: function(event, validator) {
    // 'this' refers to the form
    var errors = validator.numberOfInvalids();
    if (errors) {
      var message = errors == 1
        ? 'You missed 1 field. It has been highlighted'
        : 'You missed ' + errors + ' fields. They have been highlighted';
      $("div.error span").html(message);
      $("div.error").show();
    } else {
      $("div.error").hide();
    }
  }
});
```

This is the starting point for your code but needs several modifications to work with your form. The code you need to use starts on the second line. You already have the first and last lines of code since you created those to implement the base functionality of the `validate()` method in the previous step where you added the starting code, so you can focus on the body of code between those lines.

The code you need to use and update starts on the second line with `invalidHandler: function(event, validator)`. Creating an `invalidHandler` event handler instructs jQuery, and JavaScript in the browser, what to do when the form is invalid. The `function` is anonymous but takes two parameters: the `event` that triggered the use of the `invalidHandler` and the `validator` object itself, which contains the form and its elements along with the valid/invalid state of those elements. The `validator` object also has functions that can be used on those elements.

A legacy comment (`// 'this' refers to the form`) that has been ignored over the years as the implementation has changed remains in the code. The code does not include a `this` anymore.

The next line is `var errors = validator.numberOfInvalids();`. You should recognize this code as JavaScript—the declaration of a `var` variable set to the value that comes out of the `numberOfInvalids()` function that the `validator` object has as one of its many functions. As you might guess, this function counts the number of currently invalid form elements and returns an integer value, which is then sent to the variable.

The next chunk of code to examine is the if-else block. The logic is that if the count of errors is greater than 0, then the label showing the number of errors is populated with text. Else (there are no errors), the warning label is hidden.

The original authors of this code also included JavaScript code to handle the grammatical difference in the error message between "You missed 1 field. It is highlighted." and "You missed 2 fields. They are highlighted." The supplied code can be more descriptively rewritten as follows:

```
if (errors)
{
    if(errors==1)
    {
        message = 'You missed 1 field. It has been highlighted';
    }
    else
    {
        message = 'You missed ' + errors + ' fields. They have been highlighted';
    }
    $("div.error span").html(message);
    $("div.error").show();
}
else
{
    $("div.error").hide();
}
```

While that code is longer, it is easier to read and follow logically, which reduces the possibility for errors from you or any future developer who needs to update this code.

The form on the contact_us.html page does not include a `div` element with the class of `errors`, but it does include two `span` elements with the class of `form_errors`. You can update to the name of the class of the elements that will be used to display the errors and add the `error` class to that element when there are errors. Add the following code inside the curly brackets of `$("#feedback_form").validate({ });` in contact_us.html:

```
invalidHandler: function(event, validator)
{
    var errors = validator.numberOfInvalids();
    var message = '';
    if (errors)
```

```
        {
            if(errors == 1)
            {
               message = 'You missed 1 field. It has been highlighted';
            }
            else
            {
               message = 'You missed ' + errors + ' fields. They have been highlighted';
            }
            $(".form_errors").addClass("required");
            $(".form_errors").html(message);
            $(".form_errors").show();
        }
        else
        {
            $(".form_errors").removeClass("required");
            $(".form_errors").html('');
            $(".form_errors").hide();
        }
}
```

Save your changes. You should have a body of code that reflects **Figure 6-6**.

Figure 6-6   Code for counting and displaying the number of invalid form elements

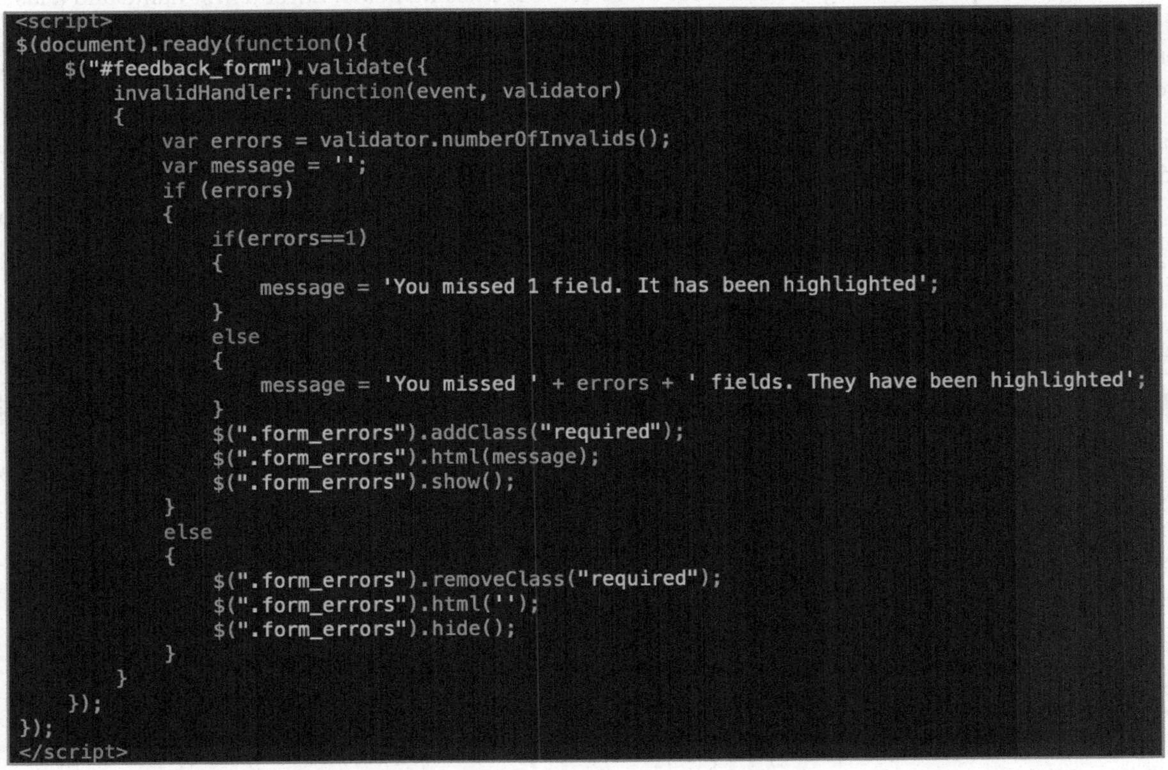

```
<script>
$(document).ready(function(){
    $("#feedback_form").validate({
        invalidHandler: function(event, validator)
        {
            var errors = validator.numberOfInvalids();
            var message = '';
            if (errors)
            {
                if(errors==1)
                {
                    message = 'You missed 1 field. It has been highlighted';
                }
                else
                {
                    message = 'You missed ' + errors + ' fields. They have been highlighted';
                }
                $(".form_errors").addClass("required");
                $(".form_errors").html(message);
                $(".form_errors").show();
            }
            else
            {
                $(".form_errors").removeClass("required");
                $(".form_errors").html('');
                $(".form_errors").hide();
            }
        }
    });
});
</script>
```

Source: BBEdit

Refresh the page in your web browser, then click the Submit button without entering any data in the form. You should see the error message at the top and bottom of the form, with the correct count of invalid form elements.

The Third Pass: Validating the Data with jQuery

As you read in the previous chapter, a valid email address that can be delivered by an email server using the Simple Mail Transfer Protocol needs to have at least two characters in each part of a valid email address, for a total of eight characters when the dot and ampersand are included. That is, a@b.c is not a valid email address, but aa@bb.cc is.

Note	Of course, someone could try to spoof the validation system by using an email address like aaaa@b.c if they know the required character count is eight, but the volume of code necessary to prevent creative users from bypassing all of the email validation would be cost prohibitive for the return on investment.
	A cost–benefit analysis is necessary in creating robust form validation. For forms that must gather critical data, the effort required to create more robust form validation is worthwhile. For newsletter subscriptions, a gentle prescreening with a functional character count is as much as is necessary. If people want to subscribe to the occasional newsletter, they most likely will try to use a correct email address.

The `minlength` property of an HTML input element is a reasonably good way to ensure this pattern is followed. The contact_us.html page provided in the starting files includes an email address field with a `minlength='8'` property to ensure that the field collects only valid email addresses.

Refresh the contact_us.html webpage form and click the Submit button. The required fields are highlighted, and the error message is displayed telling the user that there are four missing fields. Enter a first name and a last name in the first two fields. The form should remove the highlights from those two fields. Enter the invalid email address a@b.c in the email address field. The error message "This field is required" should be replaced by "Please enter at least 8 characters." Update the email address to aa@bb.cc to remove the error message.

This is out-of-the-box functionality that comes when you use the jQuery validation library. Without writing any new code, you used the properties of the form to validate the data entries. Additionally, since the authors of jQuery and the Validation plug-in actively accept feedback from their users, the errors and warnings are equally applied to visual browsers and screen readers so all of your users will benefit from the form validation.

Quick Check 6-5

1. What does the phrase "hotlinking welcome" refer to in the documentation of an online software library?

   a. You can download the library without paying a fee.
   b. You can include the library in your software without violating copyright laws.
   c. You can use the link provided in your webpage to access the library from that source.
   d. The link provided is hot, or prone to failure, so you should download the file before it fails.

2. What is the best way to learn about the features in a software plug-in?

   a. Read the comments about the features on a website like Stack Overflow.
   b. Find websites that are using the plug-in and copy that code to modify as your own.
   c. Read the documentation and examples provided by the plug-in authors.
   d. Start writing code to implement the features of the plug-in.

3. What is the `minlength` property used for?

    a. To create a minimum word length in a `textarea` element used for essays

    b. To create a minimum character length in an input element

    c. To create the minimum name or ID length for an HTML element

    d. To create the minimum size of an element in the CSS property it is assigned like `height` or `width`

1) c. Hotlinking refers to creating a link to the file stored in a CDN from your own webpage. **2) c.** The authors of a reliable software plug-in document the features and provide code samples for appropriate usage to help users adopt their product. **3) b.** The `minlength` property is used to create form validation for the minimum number of allowed characters in a form text input element.

6.6 Extending jQuery with the DataTables.js Plug-In

Another of the most useful plug-ins for jQuery is DataTables.js. You can (and should) read through the documentation at https://datatables.net. This plug-in will transform any properly formatted HTML table into an interactive webpage element that you can sort by the column headers, filter by entries in a Search box, or paginate by a record count. This plug-in seamlessly creates dynamic content from static HTML.

You will add this plug-in to modify the table on the products.html webpage.

Configuring the HTML Table

Before you can use DataTables.js, you need an HTML table that is formatted properly. The documentation is clear about what HTML table elements are necessary for it to work properly. For example, the documentation says, "the table must be valid, well-formatted HTML, with a header (`thead`) and a single body (`tbody`)."

To configure the HTML table:

1. Open products.html from the starting files in your simple text editor and review the HTML table in it.

2. To make a table ready for DataTables.js, you need to include an ID in the opening `<table>` tag. Change the existing tag to the following:

```
<table id='products'>
```

As you have seen in this chapter, jQuery is often used to select HTML objects by their ID. That pattern will be followed here as well, so the table will need this ID to be found and formatted by the plug-in.

Next, you need to include two more HTML tag sets that were not included in the original table. These are the `<thead>`...`</thead>` and `<tbody>`...`</tbody>` tag sets. The `<thead>`...`</thead>` tags are used to signify the table row that contains the `<th>` tags. In the products.html table, this is the first actual row after the `<colgroup>`...`</colgroup>` tags.

3. Add the opening `<thead>` tag before the `<tr>` tag that opens the row and add the closing `</thead>` tag after the closing `</tr>` tag that ends the row.

4. Add the opening `<tbody>` tag after the closing `</thead>` tag, since the `<tbody>` tag set will wrap around all of the rows of table data.

5. Before the closing `</table>` tag, add a closing `</tbody>` tag so all of the rows of data are inside the `<tbody>`...`</tbody>` tag set.

The updated HTML in the page will look like that in **Figure 6-7**, although the data in the rows in the table have been hidden so you can focus on the new tags.

Figure 6-7 Setting up the HTML table prior to the DataTables transformation

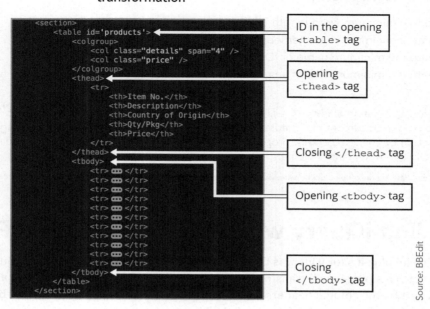

Source: BBEdit

Adding the Link Configuration

Now that the HTML table is set up to work with DataTables.js according to the documentation, you need to add links to the files that the plug-in requires. For these steps, you will link to the CDN that the authors of DataTables have created, but you could also download your own copies of their software if that was your preferred path. Note that you may need to update the version numbers for this plug-in if a newer version is available.

To add links to the plug-in files:

1. Add a link in the <head>...</head> section to your local copy of jQuery that you downloaded previously.

2. Add the following links in the <head>...</head> section of products.html:

   ```
   <script type="text/javascript" src="https://cdn.datatables.net/1.12.1/js/jquery.
   dataTables.min.js"></script>
   <link rel="stylesheet" type="text/css" href="https://cdn.datatables.net/1.12.1/
   css/jquery.dataTables.min.css" />
   ```

   The first link is the minified, or compacted, dataTables.min.js JavaScript file, and the second link is to the CSS file that DataTables needs to style the HTML table.

3. Finally, add an opening and a closing <script>...</script> tag pair and a block of jQuery code between them as follows:

   ```
   $(document).ready(function () {
       $('#products').DataTable();
   });
   ```

   Those two lines of code are all you need—along with all of the other configurations of the HTML and the links to the plug-in JavaScript and CSS—to transform your HTML table into a DataTable. Once the webpage is loaded in the browser, the jQuery plug-in transforms the table selected by the ID of 'products' into a DataTable object.

4. Save your changes, view the page in a browser, and, if all of the code and links are working correctly, you should see your HTML table transformed into a DataTable object in the DOM like that in **Figure 6-8**.

Figure 6-8   The HTML table transformed into an interactive webpage element via DataTables.js

Item No.	Description	Country of Origin	Qty/Pkg	Price
04509	Ab-Suey-Lutely Ab Roller for Potbellied Pigs	Vietnam	1 roller	$39.99
03965	Wing Floaties for Aquaphobic Ducks	Canada	1 pair	$29.99
86753	Ty-D-Paws Paw Sanitizer for Hygienic Raccoons	United States	64oz Pump Dispenser	$29.99
00008	Interrogatives For Curious Owls: A Primer	United States	1 book	$19.99
03965	Anger Management Techniques for Hornets	United Kingdom	1 paperback book	$19.99
00103	No-More-Snarls Shampoo and Conditioner for Curly Hedgehog Quills	South Africa	16 oz bottle	$19.95
00211	Revive-O-Possum Smelling Salts for Catatonic Marsupials	United States	144 individual packets	$13.99
00011	Low-fat Candy for Goldfish	Canada	10oz bag	$12.95
09000	Vanishing Cream for Introverted Chameleons	Madagascar	10oz Tube	$9.99
00059	Whisker Wax for Dapper Cats	United Kingdom	1oz jar	$3.99

Show 10 entries — Search:

Showing 1 to 10 of 11 entries — Previous 1 2 Next

Exploring the DataTables Feature Set

The default build of DataTables.js includes many useful features. In the upper-left corner is a total rows filter. You can use that selection list to filter the table to display a set number of rows and then use the page feature in the lower right to move to the next 10 rows.

The Search feature in the upper right filters the contents of the table to match whatever is entered into the search box. If you start typing "Candy" in the box, you filter the table for Low-Fat Candy for Goldfish, since that fine product is the only confection in the table.

In the lower-right corner, you can see the number of pages of table data for the number of rows being displayed. If the table had 100 rows of data and you set the row filter to 25 rows at a time, you would see four pages of data in the page buttons.

Finally, you can see the record count in the lower-left corner. This too helps identify which set of data in a multi-page presentation is being shown.

Inside the table itself, the header row has transformed into sort order buttons. If you click the Price header, the products table is sorted in ascending order by price. Click the Price header again to re-sort the table by price in descending order.

Common Mistakes

You can perform an interesting experiment in how jQuery and DataTables.js work by viewing the source of the page you are currently working with—in this case, products.html. Either right-click the page and choose View Page Source or use a menu option such as Page Source on the View menu if that is available in your browser. You then see that the original HTML remains unchanged after jQuery and DataTables modify the page contents.

On the other hand, if you drag across the DataTables features so that they are highlighted along with the original HTML table, and then right-click (or Ctrl+click on a Mac) and choose View Selection Source or Inspect on the shortcut menu, you will see entirely different HTML in the page source code. jQuery and DataTables.js manipulate the DOM, which is the in-memory representation of the HTML.

The reason this vignette about the behind-the-scenes operations is in a Common Mistakes box is that screen readers reading the HTML of the page won't see any updates to the DOM that occur where the screen reader is not currently reading the content aloud or transforming it into Braille. The code you just added by including the DataTables plug-in modifies the DOM right after the page is loaded but before a screen reader would start reading the webpage. This results in a webpage that can still be used with a screen reader. On the other hand, if a click event added this content, the screen reader would potentially miss that DOM change.

DataTables can also change the contents of the DOM being presented—like when you filter the table for "Canada." Changing the DOM presentation for someone who can't see the change happen would be confusing and frustrating if that was the only way to filter a long table for a specific item.

Be cautious when using JavaScript to modify the contents of a webpage. Critical functionality like search and filter that can only be used by visual browsers might make your webpages inaccessible for valued customers you also want to have a positive user experience.

Additional features and plug-in extensions can make DataTables even more powerful and useful, like the Buttons library. Adding a few lines of code to the JavaScript creates a set of buttons that will export or copy the filtered data from the HTML table into an Excel spreadsheet, CSV file, or PDF. To read more about these features, see https://datatables.net/extensions/buttons.

Quick Check 6-6

1. Why isn't it necessary to write the code for a JavaScript event like an `onblur` event when using a JavaScript library?

    a. Because the library already includes an `onblur` event handler
    b. Because the library replaces the primitive `onblur` event with a more complex event of its own
    c. Because the library doesn't need to use the `onblur` event since it has different code for each type of browser
    d. It is still necessary to write an `onblur` event of your own, but the rest of the code will be from the library.

2. Why does DataTables.js require `<thead>...</thead>` tags in a table?

    a. So it can create an interactive title for the table
    b. So it can create the clickable column headers from the `<th>...</th>` tags inside the `<thead>...</thead>` tags
    c. To use as placeholders for the Search field
    d. Because `<thead>...</thead>` tags are required by the W3C for a properly formatted HTML table

3. Why is using the Search function in DataTables not recommended as the only way to find a record in a table?

    a. Because users won't intuitively know how to use the Search feature without reading through the documentation
    b. Because the Search function won't work on smartphones or tablets
    c. Because the Search function doesn't refresh the page
    d. Because users who are listening to the page read to them with a screen reader might not be aware that the table gets updated

1) **a.** The JavaScript library comes with all of the functions that it will need to call the `onblur` event from inside the library. 2) **b.** DataTables replaces the static contents of the `<th>...</th>` tags with dynamic clickable header elements that sort the HTML table by that column. 3) **d.** The Search function doesn't trigger the screen reader to reread the contents of a page, so someone hearing the page read to them might not be able to use your website in the way that you intend if this is the only way to filter for records.

Summary

- JavaScript libraries are software packages that reduce the amount of raw JavaScript code web developers need to write to create interactive websites.

- JavaScript libraries are available as downloads or as links from the content delivery network servers that host them.

- JavaScript libraries are targeted at uses such as building user interfaces or complex graphics.

- jQuery is a good starting point for learning about JavaScript libraries because it is similar to JavaScript, well documented, widely used, and easy to learn.

- JavaScript objects are programmatic combinations of webpage data and functions that work with that data.

- jQuery provides shortened versions of JavaScript code functions to accomplish many routine tasks that would ordinarily require many lines of raw JavaScript code.

- Reading the documentation for a JavaScript library is the best way to learn about what the library can do and how to include the library code in a webpage.

- JavaScript library plug-ins are software packages that extend the original library functions in a specific way.

- Two of the many useful jQuery plug-ins are Validation and DataTables.

- The jQuery Validation plug-in contains functions to validate web forms in a simpler manner than writing raw JavaScript.

- The jQuery DataTables plug-in adds significant functionality to HTML tables, turning the static table into an interactive webpage element.

- Use caution when adding dynamic HTML DOM manipulation by jQuery and JavaScript so you keep the webpage accessible for all users.

Key Terms

content delivery network (CDN)	jQuery selector	object
JavaScript library	minified	software plug-ins

Review Questions

1. What is a JavaScript library? (6.1)

   a. A package of prebuilt JavaScript code that web developers can use to extend webpage functionality in the browser

   b. A list of all of the JavaScript functions that the web browser can perform

   c. The documentation for the web browser's JavaScript API

   d. A document from the W3C that describes how a web browser should use JavaScript

2. Why does jQuery remain popular with full stack web developers? (6.1)

   a. Because Facebook pays many developers a lot of money to keep it updated

   b. Because Google continues to support the development and maintenance of the code

   c. Because web developers are reluctant to adopt new technologies

   d. Because it is simple to learn, well documented, and includes many important and useful functions

3. What does a CDN, or content delivery network, do? (6.2)

   a. Delivers webpages over a network port

   b. Stores cached copies of webpages for faster download speeds

   c. Creates the routing for webpages to be delivered to web browsers

   d. Creates storage space for resource files like JavaScript and CSS

4. Why do full stack web developers use the compressed build of a JavaScript library after a website is launched? (6.2)

   a. To keep hackers from viewing the source code

   b. To speed up the download time for the file

   c. To make the file unavailable to other competing developers in other companies

   d. To speed up the runtime of the functions in the code

5. When does the `document.ready()` JavaScript event occur? (6.3)

   a. When the web browser is ready to load the HTML document

   b. When the web browser has finished creating the HTML DOM

   c. When the webpage form is ready to accept user input in the browser

   d. When the HTML document is ready for printing

6. What is the difference between `$();` and `jQuery();`? (6.3)

   a. Nothing, they both do the same thing.

   b. The first is an anonymous function; the second is a named function.

   c. The first won't work but the second will.

   d. The first is the new way of calling an anonymous function; the second is the old way of calling a named function.

7. What does the jQuery `animate()` function do? (6.3)

    a. Changes a numeric property incrementally from a starting value to an ending value over a specific duration to create the appearance of movement of the HTML element

    b. Changes the HTML element that is targeted in the DOM from one type to another over a specific duration to create the appearance of animation in a webpage

    c. Modifies the browser settings to speed up or slow down DOM/CSSOM transformations, creating the appearance of animation in a webpage

    d. Moves HTML elements around in the DOM over a specific duration to create the appearance of movement in the webpage

8. Can you combine more than one operation or function in jQuery? (6.4)

    a. No, each needs to be on a single line of code.

    b. Yes, but it is against best practices.

    c. No, this will cause errors because the operations will run out of order.

    d. Yes, you just separate them with the dot operator, creating a chain.

9. What is a software plug-in? (6.5)

    a. A package of software that adds features to another package of software

    b. A package of software that fixes bugs in another package of software

    c. A package of software that automatically updates another package of software

    d. A package of software that can be used in place of a deprecated software package

10. Why is the HTML attribute `aria-invalid="true"` important for screen readers? (6.5)

    a. Because it alerts the screen reader that the form element it has been applied to is invalid

    b. Because it highlights the field in the screen reader

    c. Because it applies the `error` CSS class to the field in the screen reader

    d. Because it stops the form from being submitted by the screen reader

11. Why is it necessary to format your HTML according to the requirements specified in the documentation of the library you are attempting to use? (6.6)

    a. Because the authors of the library write HTML their own way

    b. Because software developers have their own preferences for the HTML formatting

    c. Only valid HTML that conforms to the standards of the library will work with the default functions in the library.

    d. It isn't necessary; most new JavaScript libraries include code translations for different browsers and HTML coding standards.

12. Why is the configuration necessary for using a JavaScript library more complex than writing your own JavaScript? (6.6)

    a. JavaScript libraries are only written to work with some versions of browsers.

    b. It isn't more complex; using a JavaScript library is simpler than writing your own code as long as you follow the documented requirements.

    c. The authors of JavaScript libraries need to write more complex code to add functions and features that other libraries don't have.

    d. Because JavaScript libraries are so complex, the implementation is also very complex.

Programming Exercises

1. Using your favorite search engine, search for "most useful jQuery plug-ins." Read at least three of the references you find and summarize the commonalities in a one-page report. Include links to the pages you reviewed. (6.1–6.6)

2. Using your favorite search engine, search for "most common uses of jQuery." Read five of the articles returned in the results and summarize the most common uses and functions in a one-page report. Include links to the pages you reviewed. (6.1–6.6)

3. Add comments to each function you created in this chapter describing what each function does. (6.1–6.6)

Projects

1. Using jQuery, add a blinking red stoplight function to the webpage stoplight. This function will run only when the red light itself is clicked and leave the stoplight in a blinking-red state until another button is clicked to change the color of the light. (6.1–6.4)

2. Using jQuery, add the necessary code to make the M (Memory) button in the calculator work. The M button should put the value shown in the display into the hidden memory input element if no value appears in the display. If a value is shown in the display, the M button should append the value in memory to the value in the display. Also, add another line of code in the C button click event handler to clear the memory. (6.1–6.4)

3. Add a jQuery function to the `textarea` element in contact_us.html. The function will compare the `maxlength` attribute value from the `textarea` to the length of the value currently in the `textarea` and insert the text "You have X characters left" in a `span` element used as a warning label to the right of the `textarea` or just below it. (6.1–6.5)

Chapter 7

Scripting Frameworks: An Overview and Comparative Exploration

Learning Objectives

When you complete this chapter, you will be able to:

7.1 Compare the characteristics and uses of scripting frameworks and libraries.

7.2 Create a simple single-page app using Angular.

7.3 Create a simple single-page app using Vue.

7.4 Create a simple single-page app using React.

7.1 What Is a Scripting Framework?

As you now know, JavaScript can be used to update the contents of the DOM of a webpage based on user interaction. Clicking a button can change the text on a page, for example. Pushing this concept to a more extreme example, clicking a button can also change an entire section of the same webpage to show a new user interface (UI). You can even automate the updates so that users don't need to click a button for a feature like a news feed to update itself.

In static HMTL websites, each page is a set of HTML tags that present information and images styled with Cascading Style Sheets (CSS). A web server sends the HTML page as a complete unit to the browser. The organization of a website into logical blocks means that each webpage presents a different set of information. Navigating the static pages is the only way to discover new information.

Traditional data-driven web applications follow this same design. They crunch data from a database into an organized display in a completed webpage for a one-way transaction that the web server hands off to the browser in response to a user request. The access point to this data, such as a search or filter feature, is on one page, and the results are displayed on a second page.

Each user interaction such as clicking a Submit button or More Details link reloads the entire contents of the webpage. Reloading the page results in another round trip from the browser to the web server to the database server to retrieve the same set of data it supplied in the previous request. The web server recomposes the same page with updated data and sends it as a complete unit back to the browser where it is re-rendered.

As you probably noticed, it is inefficient to create webpages that have to be loaded and reloaded each time a user interacts with them. When this design pattern was formalized, the code that makes up these pages was the limiting factor. Although web programmers love shiny new technology, this pattern became the default design standard for many years.

The unfulfilled need is obvious for anyone who has recently interacted with the Internet. The better way to handle user interaction is to dynamically load just the parts of a webpage the user is interacting with. JavaScript and TypeScript frameworks and libraries make this possible in the browser. They update the dynamic component of the HTML/CSS/JavaScript technology stack.

A **scripting framework** is a body of code that uses JavaScript or TypeScript as its native language and extends the language to include features for building dynamic applications. The framework is designed in modules to include components a developer can use to satisfy common requirements for web applications.

This chapter includes code written for Angular, Vue, and React, three of the most popular scripting codebases currently in use. In a previous chapter, you wrote code using the jQuery library as a transition from raw JavaScript into more advanced work like this chapter presents. Now you pick up where jQuery leaves off.

Note	Scripting libraries and frameworks fundamentally change how you as a web developer interact with JavaScript and are worth in-depth study because they are the future of front-end web development. This chapter provides a brief overview of Angular, Vue, and React to give you an idea of how they work and what to expect when you use them to develop dynamic webpages. As with all the technologies explored in this course, a full course in any one of these website scripting libraries or frameworks would be appropriate to master the technology and understand the underlying concepts.

Is the Code JavaScript or TypeScript?

The descriptions and documentation for scripting frameworks and libraries reference JavaScript and TypeScript, which are two different scripting languages.

JavaScript is the original scripting language used in web browsers to create dynamic or interactive elements. However, it was not originally designed to support the robust and complex applications that populate the modern Internet. As you have seen, JavaScript works well for simple applications and is an easy programming language to learn.

TypeScript is the new arrival to the browser scripting realm. It includes all the syntax and features of JavaScript while providing a more robust feature set, including strongly typed variables. As you may recall, JavaScript variables are loosely typed, so the variable `myVar` could contain an integer, string, or object. Typescript requires that you declare `myVar` as an integer, for example, and only allows you to use integer values in that variable.

TypeScript is designed to build robust and complex dynamic applications that run in a web browser. However, TypeScript needs to be compiled before it runs. The TypeScript compiler translates the executable code into JavaScript that a browser can run.

All valid JavaScript is also valid in TypeScript. If you have a working JavaScript file with a .js extension and you change the extension to the TypeScript extension of .ts, your code compiles in a TypeScript compiler. The reverse is not true since TypeScript expands what JavaScript can do with additional functions and features that are not backward compatible.

React is written using JavaScript. Angular and Vue are written using TypeScript, although Vue still refers to itself as a JavaScript framework.

Is the Code a Framework or a Library?

React calls itself a JavaScript library, Vue declares itself to be a JavaScript framework, and Angular is referred to as a TypeScript framework. What's the difference between a library and a framework? Many people use the two terms interchangeably.

A library and a framework share some common features. They both allow you to write less raw code and often create less HTML to build a more feature-rich web application. Both allow you to write your own code using the features and following the syntax of the library or framework. Both create dynamic web applications by using the JavaScript interpreter in the browser.

However, a library is composed of functions you can use to make your pages dynamic or interactive. If you need an interactive calendar, for example, you can use one included as part of a library without needing to implement the rest of the library.

A framework, on the other hand, is a webpage development engine composed from a template. Your content is added dynamically to the template as the user interacts with the page. You can't choose which parts of the framework template to include in your webpages because your webpages are built from the template.

The fundamental difference is that you add contents from a library into your webpages and you add your own contents to the application structure created by a framework.

The Single-Page Application

Angular, Vue, and React are used to create a **single-page application**. In a single-page application, the contents of a webpage are dynamically changed as the user interacts with them. The page itself does not need to be reloaded. If the home page of a web application is index.html, the starting point for user interaction is the default welcome screen. The contents inside index.html are updated by the JavaScript/TypeScript framework or library depending on the actions the user takes on the page.

For example, when the user clicks a search icon, the search feature is loaded, replacing a placeholder or empty `<div>`...`</div>` tag pair on that page designated for the search feature. After the user enters text in the search box and clicks a search button, the results are appended to the contents of the same page. Clicking an item in the search results opens the details of that item, though still within the same page.

If the single-page application is a news feed, the initial load of the news articles is pulled from the most recent updates into a static page that serves as a framework. Scrolling down in the feed continuously retrieves older news articles in chronological order. Each set of news articles is appended to the previous set in the display, so scrolling back up allows you to move forward through time until you return to the most current article.

Many sites make money by displaying an advertisement pane on the right or bottom of the content pane that diverts the attention of website viewers with ads promoting content such as that one weird trick doctors hate. That advertising is targeted to the viewer based on search history. It begins with scripting code that accesses and reviews the browser's history and cookies, then heads to the ad-generation application, which returns ads as partial page contents to incorporate into the designated spaces.

A single-page application works by separating the traditional webpage presentation into its component parts. For example, in one design pattern for building web applications, the visual or auditory framework that the user interacts with is one component. Another component is the data feed that returns initial or updated data to append to designated places in the framework. The programmatic logic between these two is the third component. You learn more about this design pattern later in this chapter.

Common Framework Features

Web developers can use a scripting library or framework, including the ones discussed in this chapter—Angular, Vue, and React—to create dynamic websites and single-page applications. These technologies share common features, including syntax, terminology, outcome, and structure.

The scripting libraries and frameworks that create dynamic webpage elements use JavaScript or translate their TypeScript into JavaScript to run in the browser's native JavaScript engine. It bears repeating that no web browser can currently execute TypeScript. This does not mean, however, that writing raw JavaScript is a common feature of the TypeScript and JavaScript libraries and frameworks.

Each framework or library has its own syntax. Even though all of these frameworks and libraries devolve into JavaScript, the developers who built the original software had their own preferences for style and terminology. Learning this syntax is one of the challenges with using a new framework, just like learning any new programming language.

These libraries and frameworks also use specific terms to describe features and functions. The libraries and frameworks share some terms such as templates and components, but other terms are unique to a framework, such as directives in Angular. Part of learning a new framework or library is deciphering the jargon and understanding what those parts described by the jargon actually do.

Another common feature of these libraries and frameworks is the outcome. All the libraries and frameworks are purposefully written to reduce the amount of code required to create an application. You could write your own JavaScript to recreate the feature set of that application, but the mountain of code necessary would be an inefficient use of your time.

Teams of experienced developers have created and used these libraries and frameworks in thousands of projects. Throughout that process, the libraries and frameworks have been thoroughly tested and debugged. Reinventing the wheel with custom JavaScript you write and test yourself means significantly fewer developers and users interact with your code. Less testing and debugging increases the chances of an undocumented feature (also known as a bug) leaking into the production version of your application.

Finally, all the libraries and frameworks in this chapter are purposefully designed to create a **separation of concerns** between logical components. A separation of concerns divides blocks of code into different sections, typically the user interface, the processor, and the data components. The libraries and frameworks use different design patterns to accomplish a separation of concerns, but all follow the same basic model of how a user interacts with a computer to inform their separation of concerns into these sections. When you are using a computer, you interact with the user interface, which causes code to run in the processor and data to be stored in or retrieved from the hard drive. This is a separation of concerns in the computer.

Coding Samples and Examples

In the next three sections of this chapter, you examine the same two web applications written three ways. First, you examine the code in a Hello World example written for each scripting codebase. Next, you build a simple one-page application to dynamically convert Celsius temperatures to Fahrenheit (or the reverse) in two text boxes. An update to the temperature in one text box automatically recalculates the value in the other text box using the library or framework.

You use a pair of inverse formulas to convert temperatures. To convert from Fahrenheit to Celsius, you use the following formula:

$$C = ((F - 32) * (5/9))$$

To convert from Celsius to Fahrenheit, you use the following formula:

$$F = ((C * (9/5)) + 32)$$

The basic operations in Angular, Vue, and React are the same, but the code to complete the operations is different due to the syntax and rules for each library or framework.

Additionally, each section uses the library or framework from a content delivery network (CDN), so you do not need to install software locally. In practice, a developer using Vue, React, or Angular would install the library or framework locally. The library or framework organizes its code in a purposefully distributed file scheme with a specific set of files and folders.

Trying to thoroughly introduce the complexities of installation and configuration here would at least triple the length of this chapter to successfully cover the necessary details. For ease of introduction, this chapter compresses the use of the library or framework into a single HTML file for each example.

As you have in previous chapters, copy the Chapter_7 folder provided for this course to your directory structure. In the Chapter_7 folder, create a subfolder for Projects. Since each sample file is a standalone example, you don't need additional javascript or css folders.

Quick Check 7-1

1. Why are traditional static and data-driven websites considered inefficient compared to a single-page application?

    a. Because coding them takes more time than using newer innovations
    b. Because the web servers that serve the content are not as fast as dynamic webpage servers
    c. Because the entire webpages need to be loaded or reloaded for each user interaction
    d. Because the text files that make them up are large and require lots of network bandwidth

2. What is a JavaScript framework?

    a. Any JavaScript file that you link to from the `<head>...</head>` section of a webpage
    b. The JavaScript template into which you add your HTML, CSS, and JavaScript to create a dynamic webpage
    c. A JavaScript file that includes functions and features you can use in your own webpages to create dynamic features
    d. A high-speed server that returns links to JavaScript code files

3. What is the general purpose of JavaScript frameworks and libraries?

    a. To create job security for programmers since both are more complex than traditional web applications
    b. To create webpages that users can customize for themselves
    c. To replace older technologies that are slower at doing the same functions
    d. To write less code while creating more dynamic web applications driven by user interactions

1) c. Each user interaction in a traditional website results in the complete reloading of the webpage the user is interacting with. **2) b.** A JavaScript framework is the templating engine into which you add your own HTML, CSS, and JavaScript. **3) d.** JavaScript frameworks and libraries are intended to reduce the amount of code that needs to be written while creating more interactive web applications.

7.2 Exploring Angular

As is often the case with a new JavaScript framework, the history of Angular is rooted in an unmet need identified by one or more developers working at a large tech company. The unmet need in 2009 was a better way to develop new webpages and applications without having to recreate the entire infrastructure behind a webpage. The large tech company was Google, and the original developers were Misko Hevery and Adam Abrons.

Angular has been revised several times. The original framework was a JavaScript framework called AngularJS. As of January 1, 2022, Google dropped support and updates for AngularJS in favor of a new version, Angular, composed of TypeScript.

> **Note** | Why is the name of this framework "Angular" and not "Steve" or something else? According to the Frequently Asked Questions page on the Angular website, the original developers acknowledged that HTML tags are enclosed by angular brackets (< and >), and thus the name was born, since the Angular code is written inside those brackets.

The Angular website where you can learn more about this framework, explore the documentation, and examine the features is at https://angular.io. This is an updated site and different from the original AngularJS framework website, which is still available for legacy code support.

Using the Angular Model, View, and Controller

The original version, AngularJS, uses the **model-view-controller (MVC)** design pattern to create a separation of concerns. In this design pattern, the data is stored in a **model**, the **view** presents a UI to the user, and the **controller** serves as the processor, directing and responding to the activities that the user creates in the view. As a result, the model retrieves data to show in the view or returns data to store in the database as directed by the controller.

The MVC design pattern is used extensively throughout software programming because it clearly separates an application into three parts: the part a user interacts with, the part that needs to respond to user actions, and the data that comes from or is displayed to a user. This separation creates logical divisions between sections of the code with similar functions.

The new version of Angular, known as Angular 2, has strongly typed objects, which effectively behave like a model. Angular 2 uses templates, which equate to a view. The action of getting data into a model and associating the model with the view is done with a **component**, which is similar to a controller. A component is a reusable block of code that functions independently in the application, like a calculator or news feed.

However, the Angular 2 component is used with the design pattern concept known as a **viewmodel**. You can read more about the viewmodel in greater detail in the section on Vue. The differences between controllers and viewmodels with components are subtle, and the similarities are that both contain code used to create interactions between the data in the model and the user interface in the view.

Because the design patterns of AngularJS and Angular 2 are similar, this chapter takes advantage of the simplicity of MVC to demonstrate the separation of concerns.

Using a design pattern that separates concerns into logical groupings is useful because different people or teams can work on one component without affecting the other two as long as the team agrees on the connections among the three parts before coding.

Furthermore, the modularity of an application with three distinct parts means that one part can be updated in response to a change in technology or requirements without needing to update the other two parts.

You can visualize MVC in the context of a student record shown on a web application with editing enabled for that record. The data that makes up the student record, including the first and last names, student ID, birthdate, and cumulative GPA, are loaded into a data structure called the model. After the model is created in memory for one student by loading it from the database behind the web server, the view can access or update any part of that data using the properties and methods of the model.

The view in the MVC for Angular is the HTML that makes up the webpage, which is the user interface for presenting data from the model to the user. The boundaries for a view in a webpage are defined by an Angular-specific attribute, ng-app, that is added to a standard HTML tag. This attribute assignment also creates the outer boundary for manipulating the contents within the HTML DOM.

For example, if the Angular attribute is added to the `<html>` tag at the top of a webpage, the entire webpage is the view, or the user interface that Angular can modify. On the other hand, if the attribute is limited to one `<div>` tag, then that block alone is the location of the updates and modifications that the Angular framework can make.

Using the previous example of student data, the view is the HTML code that presents an interface containing a text box for each data element. Each text box contains one element from the model. The first name data from the model is loaded into the first name text box, and so forth.

The controller for Angular is the body of code that directs the activities of loading data from the model into the view. When the user interacts with the data and submits it from the view, the controller instructs the model on what to do with the data.

For example, when the user enters a new set of semester grades for a student, the controller binds each course grade stored in the model to the appropriate field in the view. When the user clicks the Save button, the controller directs the model to update the database with the new grades. In the UI, the controller displays an updated cumulative GPA for the student record.

Reviewing the Angular Hello World

In your simple text editor, open the angular_world.html file included with the course downloads. This file is the traditional first programming example developed using the coding style and syntax of a typical Angular application. Open angular_world.html in your browser as well to view the webpage as a working example.

While a robust web server is not creating dynamic content to load into the DOM of this webpage, the text you see when you view the angular_world.html page in a web browser doesn't actually exist in the HTML until the Angular framework creates it and adds it to the page.

Note that the Angular framework is being loaded from a content delivery network by your browser to eliminate the amount of time you would otherwise need to spend installing and configuring the framework. For the purposes of this tutorial, that exercise in strategic efficiency means you can compare three JavaScript frameworks instead of spending a significant amount of time installing and configuring one.

Typically, Angular is installed on the computer used to develop the web application. Setting up Angular involves first installing Node.js then the Node Package Manager (NPM). You can search for tutorials online to help you install and configure this software when you are ready to do it on your own.

The code for angular_world.html is shown in **Figure 7-1**.

Figure 7-1 Angular Hello World code

```
1     <!DOCTYPE HTML>
2     <html ng-app="hello">
3         <head>
4             <title>A Very Angular Hello World</title>
5             <script src="https://ajax.googleapis.com/ajax/libs/angularjs/1.6.9/angular.min.js"></script>
6         </head>
7         <body>
8             <h1 ng-controller="myCtrlr">{{message}}</h1>
9
10            <script>
11                var ngHelloApp = angular.module('hello', []);
12
13                ngHelloApp.controller('myCtrlr', function ($scope)
14                {
15                    $scope.message = "Hello World!";
16                });
17            </script>
18
19        </body>
20    </html>
```

Start examining this Angular code on line 2. Instead of the usual `<html>` tag, line 2 includes an extra attribute so the tag looks like the following:

```
<html ng-app="hello">
```

The `ng` is used as part of the namespace for this code due to the phonetic similarity to "ang" or Angular. The `ng-app` is one of many directives used in Angular. The complete attribute, `ng-app="hello"`, designates the root element, or starting point, for transforming standard HTML into an Angular application named `hello`.

The interesting thing about the approach Angular takes is that the HTML tags making up the starting point of an Angular application are the framework for the rest of the page contents. Thus, you need only a minimalist framework of valid HTML to build an Angular application.

For simplicity, the Angular framework used in this application is loaded from a CDN that makes a version of Angular available. You can see the link to the CDN in the `<script>` tag in the `<head>` section of angular_world.html on line 5.

The next line of code specific to Angular is on line 8, which looks like the following:

```
<h1 ng-controller="myCtrlr">{{message}}</h1>
```

The `h1` HTML element contains the `ng-controller` attribute. This attribute creates a designated space inside the HTML page where Angular can add its own contents by using the Angular directive `ng-controller`. A directive is an injection point to create a connection between the Angular view, which is made up of HTML, and the Angular controller, which is the code used to add contents to the view.

The `<h1>` tags contain another example of adding Angular-specific content—the variable `message` enclosed inside the double curly brackets. This code creates the shorthand for another Angular directive, `ng-bind`, using a variable from the controller, `message`, in the view. The `message` variable is referenced and updated from inside the controller, which is found in a block of code on lines 10 through 17, enclosed by opening and closing `<script>...</script>` tags. The following code appears between those `<script>` tags:

```
var ngHelloApp = angular.module('hello', []);
ngHelloApp.controller('myCtrlr', function ($scope)
{
    $scope.message = "Hello World!";
});
```

This code is more complex than what you have seen before and requires some unwrapping. However, some parts might look like the familiar JavaScript and jQuery.

When you read this code for the first time, look for its overall purpose. This block of code creates the object `ngHelloApp` using the `var` declaration. Recall that an object is a composite of code and data that work together to form a unique combination in computer memory. The `ngHelloApp` object is created by calling the Angular framework function `module()`. The object can then use its `controller()` method to access the contents of the `<h1>` tag inside its data and update the contents.

Read the code in more detail next. The first line—`var ngHelloApp = angular.module('hello', []);`—is similar in syntax to JavaScript and jQuery. It contains a reference to the `angular` framework that calls the `module()` function and passes two values to that function—`'hello'` and `[]`. The text string `'hello'` sends to the `module()` function the same name that was used with the `ng-app="hello"` attribute in the opening `<html>` tag.

The second parameter in the `angular.module('hello', [])` declaration is a pair of square brackets. These are necessary but empty since the `module()` function retrieves a specific module if only one parameter is sent to it but creates the object if two are sent in the parentheses. The square brackets are empty because the `module()` function doesn't need advanced options for a simple creation like this Hello World example.

An Angular module is an application that runs using Angular code. It includes individual components, which are the building blocks of the application and connections between those components.

The name used in this module creation (`"hello"`) is important because by matching the value used in the `ng-app` attribute, it defines the template, or boundaries of where the Angular framework can manipulate the contents of the webpage. If instead of the opening `<html>` tag, the scope was limited to a single `<li>` tag inside an ordered list, that would be the only part of the webpage the Angular library could modify with new contents. The HTML assigned to the object becomes part of the object's data that the object's functions can then modify.

In the next part of the code—`ngHelloApp.controller('myCtrlr', function ($scope)`—the `ngHelloApp` object calls its own `controller()` function. The `controller()` function attaches the controller named `'myCtrlr'` to the Angular object created on line 11 of Figure 7-1. The Angular controller directs the data loaded elsewhere into the view that is made up of the HTML in the webpage. The controller serves as the information traffic cop, pointing data from the model into the right parking stalls in the view. If this were the news feed section of a webpage, the data in the stream of news could be inserted dynamically into that HTML element.

Instead, the simpler code in this example just adds the text string "Hello World." The process used with more complex news feed data is nearly identical. The `controller()` function is passed two values. The first value is `'myCtrlr'`, the unique name of the section identified with the attribute `ng-controller`. The second value passed to the `controller()` function is the code to run against that section of the HTML. The second parameter begins on line 13 and ends on line 16.

This body of code is similar to the anonymous functions used in jQuery except that the code uses the Angular `$scope` object. The `$scope` object is another example of an object that contains both data and methods. It is used to transmit data between the controller and the HTML view. In the view, the `$scope` properties are accessed using the syntax `{{message}}` to retrieve a value from that property in the `$scope` object. This process is known as **data binding**, where a variable from the controller is added to the view and then is synchronized in both places so an update to one updates the other location.

On line 15, the `$scope` object's `message` property is set to "Hello World." On line 8, `$scope` isn't referenced but implied by the data binding, and `{{message}}` is displayed inside the view.

Building the Angular Single-Page Application

Make a new copy of the angular_world.html page in your Samples folder for this chapter and call it angular_temp_converter.html. The Hello World example is a convenient starting point for building the Celsius–Fahrenheit temperature converter since you know the code in the Hello World app is working.

The first line of code to modify is in line 2. Update the `ng-app` attribute value to `"converter"` since that describes the application more accurately than `"hello"`. Next, update the title of the page to `A Very Angular Temperature Converter`. Lines 2–4 should appear as follows:

```
<html ng-app="converter">
    <head>
        <title>A Very Angular Temperature Converter</title>
```

Remove the `<h1>...</h1>` tag pair and their contents on line 8 and replace them with the following code:

```
<div ng-controller="tempCtrlr">
    <h2>Enter a temperature in either input box to convert it to the
        corresponding temperature</h2>
    <div>
        Fahrenheit <input ng-model="f" ng-change="calculateC()" type='number'>
    </div>
    <div>
        Celsius <input ng-model="c" ng-change="calculateF()" type='number'>
    </div>
</div>
```

Because this application is more complex than the simple Hello World code, it needs to have a <div> wrapper around the application space, with the ng-controller attribute applied to name it as the container for the application. Note that the name of the controller isn't critical, and it could be called Steve instead of tempCtrlr and work equally well. However, as you have seen elsewhere, descriptive names help the next developer identify the unique parts of an application.

The ng-controller attribute on line 8 creates a connection between this HTML user interface and the code in the controller. This part of the plumbing is necessary to create the connections between the view and the controller.

The <h2>...</h2> tag pair on line 9 creates the standard HTML for a header.

The new code is wrapped in a pair of <div>...</div> tags. Line 11 starts with Fahrenheit in plain text and concludes with an interesting feature of the Angular framework. The code input ng-model="f" creates an input element that is plumbed directly to the data in the controller due to the ng-model attribute. The controller will have a direct link to this text box and any numbers entered into it.

The next attribute, ng-change="calculateC()", is also critical to create a **two-way data binding**. A two-way data binding uses the code of the library or framework to automatically update the value in a controller variable displayed in the view if the controller or model changes. The binding does the reverse if a user updates the value in the view. It is like having the same variable appear in two locations at the same time with a link between them so that an update to one location updates the other.

As you might guess by reading that small snippet of code, an ng-change event will be captured by the Angular framework if the value in the Fahrenheit input box changes. The calculateC() function runs when a value changes in the Fahrenheit box since this application accepts user input in one box and uses that new value to update another box.

The next pair of <div>...</div> tags on lines 13–15 contain the parallel input box for the Celsius value. This code is the inverse of the Fahrenheit code with all of the same pieces. When a new value is entered into the Celsius box, the Fahrenheit calculation runs to update the Fahrenheit input box.

Next, replace the Hello World code contents between the <script>...</script> tags with the following new code:

```
var ngConverterApp = angular.module('converter', []);
ngConverterApp.controller('tempCtrlr', function ($scope)
{
    $scope.c = 0;
    $scope.f = 0;
    $scope.calculateC = function()
    {
        $scope.c = Number((($scope.f - 32) * (5/9)).toFixed(1));
    }
    $scope.calculateF = function()
    {
        $scope.f = Number((($scope.c * (9/5)) + 32).toFixed(1));
    }
});
```

As with the Hello World app, the first line of code creates a new Angular object using the module() method. The first parameter again ties the module to the ng-app attribute value applied to the opening <html> tag.

The second line of code creates a controller for the new ngConverterApp function and ties it to the div element that forms the boundaries of the application with the correct ng-controller attribute value applied to it. The $scope object is created to pass values between the controller and the view.

The next lines of code are where this block gets interesting. The $scope object contains two properties or variables, c and f. These variables are directly connected to the view variables of the same name declared by using ng-model="f" and ng-model="c". The two variables are initialized to 0 to have starting values in the calculation.

This is as close to creating a model as this example will get, since it isn't using a database to store these values. The basic data structure only contains two values, C and F.

Next, two `calculate` methods are added to the $scope object along with the code the `calculate` methods should execute. The first method calculates the Celsius value for a change in Fahrenheit, and the second calculates the reverse. These two methods are tied to the view by the `ng-change="calculateC()"` and `ng-change="calculateF()"` code in the view.

However, because $scope is an object created by the Angular framework and accessed by both the view and the controller, it can use its own data inside its methods. That's what happens with the innermost line of code:

```
$scope.c = Number((($scope.f-32) * (5/9)).toFixed(1));
```

Working from the innermost parentheses out, the value of the $scope.f variable, which comes from the input box for the Fahrenheit value due to the `ng-model="f"` attribute, has 32 subtracted from it then 5/9 multiplied by it. The result of that operation, which could contain many decimal places, is rounded to one decimal place by the `.toFixed(1)` operator. The result is cast to a `Number` so the value in the c property is stored as a number.

The code in the controller assigns the results of this calculation to the $scope object's c property, and the value in the input box for Celsius is automatically updated due to the two-way data binding.

The other function is the parallel of this, but in reverse so that when a value is changed in the Celsius input box, the Fahrenheit value is calculated and then assigned to the $scope.f property, which updates `ng-model="f"`.

This code demonstrates the complexity of using the Angular framework and the simplicity of the code you can write since you are using a $scope object that Angular creates and manages, while adding a method and a property to that Angular object to customize it.

The finished code looks like that in **Figure 7-2**.

Figure 7-2 Angular temperature conversion code

```
1   <!DOCTYPE HTML>
2   <html ng-app="converter">
3       <head>
4           <title>A Very Angular Temperature Converter</title>
5           <script src="https://ajax.googleapis.com/ajax/libs/angularjs/1.6.9/angular.js"></script>
6       </head>
7       <body>
8           <div ng-controller="tempCtrlr">
9               <h2>Enter a temperature in either input box to convert it to the corresponding temperature</h2>
10              <div>
11                  Fahrenheit <input ng-model="f" ng-change="calculateC()" type='number'>
12              </div>
13              <div>
14                  Celsius <input ng-model="c" ng-change="calculateF()" type='number'>
15              </div>
16          </div>
17          <script>
18              var ngConverterApp = angular.module('converter', []);
19
20              ngConverterApp.controller('tempCtrlr', function ($scope)
21              {
22                  $scope.c=0;
23                  $scope.f=0;
24
25                  $scope.calculateC = function()
26                  {
27                      $scope.c = Number((($scope.f-32) * 5/9).toFixed(1));
28                  }
29                  $scope.calculateF = function()
30                  {
31                      $scope.f = Number((($scope.c*9/5)+32).toFixed(1));
32                  }
33
34              });
35          </script>
36
37      </body>
38  </html>
```

Source: BBEdit

Save your changes, then load the page in your browser. If everything is correct, you should see an interface like that shown in **Figure 7-3**.

Figure 7-3 Angular temperature conversion in a browser

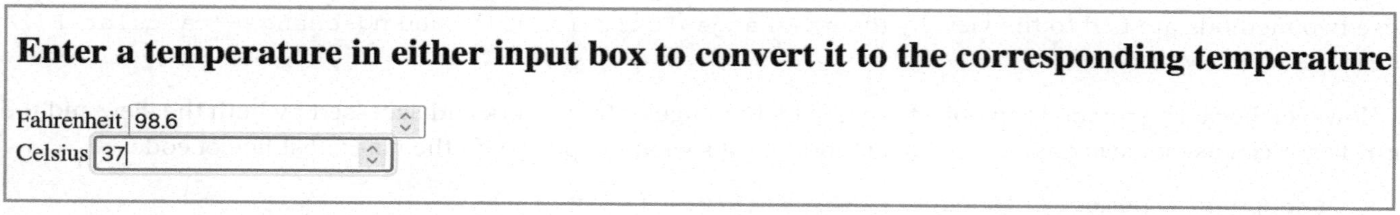

Enter a temperature in either input box to convert it to the corresponding temperature

Fahrenheit 98.6

Celsius 37

Update the value in the text box to automatically change the output. That's some mighty powerful Angular magic in a simple single-page application.

Quick Check 7-2

1. What is the model used for in the MVC design pattern?

    a. Creating the HTML contents of the web application page shown to the user
    b. Translating the inputs from the view back to the controller, which is used to talk to the database
    c. Creating a data structure that holds data coming from or heading to the database
    d. Creating a wrapper around the HTML used to dynamically render the framework components

2. Why is the MVC design pattern frequently used in web programming?

    a. It provides a clear separation of the user interface from the logic that runs the application and the data used in the application.
    b. Because it is what all the cool kids are doing these days
    c. Because most modern programming languages and frameworks require it
    d. To create simpler applications with fewer parts

3. What is the ng-app directive used for in an Angular application?

    a. A placeholder that is replaced with Angular code when the application is running in the web browser
    b. As the attribute used to designate an outer HTML tag that contains an Angular application
    c. As the key word used to create or name a controller in the MVC pattern
    d. As the Angular application constructor in the Angular framework script

1) c. The model is the data-bearing component in the model-view-controller design. **2) a.** The clear separation of three distinct parts of the application is useful for a team-based approach to development and to creating logical chunks of software with similar function. **3) b.** The ng-app directive is used as part of an attribute added to the outer HTML tag containing the Angular web application.

7.3 Exploring Vue

As with the Angular framework, Vue is a TypeScript framework for building dynamic web applications. However, the goal of Vue is slightly different from Angular. Vue was originally created to build user interfaces instead of comprehensive web applications. The project has evolved as additional components have been incorporated, and now it is a more comprehensive framework. However, the purposefully lightweight framework principles remain.

According to the documentation for the Vue project, Evan You started writing Vue in 2014 while working on the Angular project at Google. The syntax of Vue is inherited from and is similar to that of Angular, but the complexity of the code is reduced. In interviews, Evan has said that he tried to extract the best parts of Angular and compose them into a lighter-weight front-end framework that could more rapidly build user interfaces.

> **Note** | Why is the name of this framework "Vue" and not "View" or "Bilbo Baggins"? According to the lore of the Internet, Evan You originally wanted to call his framework Seed.js. However, that name was already taken by another framework, so Evan renamed it with the French spelling of view, vue, since it works primarily with the View in the Model-View-Viewmodel design pattern.

The Vue 3 website, where you can learn more about this framework, explore the documentation, and examine its features, is at https://vuejs.org. You can find tutorials and documentation on that page, along with other useful information about the differences between the most recent version of Vue and previous versions.

Using the Vue Model-View-Viewmodel Design

In the previous section, you learn about the MVC design pattern that AngularJS uses. Vue uses something similar, but because the framework is focused on building user interfaces, the design pattern used for Vue is **model-view-viewmodel (MVVM)**.

Like the MVC design pattern, the MVVM design pattern designates where parts of an application should be coded according to logical function. The MVVM design pattern separates components the same way as the MVC. The view is the same—it is the user interface, and in the case of web applications, it is composed of HTML. The model is also the same in that it is responsible for maintaining the data and handling data transactions.

The difference is that instead of a controller as in MVC, the MVVM uses a viewmodel. The viewmodel, as the name suggests, is a body of code in a separate file or between the `<script>...</script>` tags in a simple application that has direct links to the view and the model.

The viewmodel is used to control the displayed data from the model in the view and route the data that the user enters in the view back to the model through the processing of a component. The component takes care of any heavy lifting like that handled by the controller in MVC, whereas the viewmodel maintains connection between the model and the view.

This connection is advantageous for a lightweight front-end framework like Vue because either the user or the database could trigger an event that causes an update, so the viewmodel needs direct connections to both the view and the model. The viewmodel participates directly in the data translations between the view and the model in addition to responding to events in both.

Keep in mind that these design patterns are theoretical, whereas the real world is a messy place filled with pragmatic decisions about what functions go where in the code and which part updates first after an event. Whether it is called a controller or a viewmodel with components, the code still needs to be written to route data into a user interface and back to the database on a return trip.

Reviewing the Vue Hello World

In your simple text editor, open the vue_world.html file, which was included with the course downloads. This file is another example of the traditional Hello World first programming example developed using the coding style and syntax of a typical Vue application.

Open vue_world.html in a browser. While no robust web server is creating dynamic content to load into the DOM of this webpage, the text that you see when you view this page in a web browser doesn't exist in the HTML code until the Vue framework creates it and adds it to the page.

Similar to Angular, Vue is typically installed on the computer used to develop the web application, and the installation and configuration involves first installing Node.js, then the NPM. Many tutorials are available online to help you install and configure this software.

The code that generates the vue_world.html page is shown in **Figure 7-4**.

Figure 7-4   The Vue Hello World code

```
1    <!DOCTYPE HTML>
2    <html>
3        <head>
4            <title>A Very Vue Hello World</title>
5            <script src="https://unpkg.com/vue@3/dist/vue.global.js"></script>
6        </head>
7        <body>
8            <div id="display">{{ message }}</div>
9
10           <script>
11               var myVue = Vue.createApp({
12                   data() {
13                       return {
14                           message: 'Hello World!'
15                       }
16                   }
17               });
18               |
19               myVue.mount('#display');
20           </script>
21
22       </body>
23   </html>
```

Source: BBEdit

The coding style and functions in the Vue code are similar to code in the Angular framework, since the original author of Vue was on the team developing Angular and wanted to take the best parts to create a simpler tool. For example, on line 8, the structure of the directive {{message}} is identical to that used in Angular.

A major difference is that the Vue code works with the native HTML, using tag, ID, and class references as necessary. The opening <html> tag is a normal HTML tag. The page contains no additional attributes in the HTML specific to Vue.

The first line of Vue code in vue_world.html is on line 8: <div id="display">{{ message }}</div>. This line contains the same injection point for dynamic content that Angular has, the directive {{message}}. The body of Vue code that makes that dynamic content appear starts on line 11 inside the opening <script> tag:

```
var myVue = Vue.createApp({
    data() {
        return {
            message: 'Hello World!'
        }
    }
});
myVue.mount('#display');
```

The first line of code—var myVue = Vue.createApp({—calls on the Vue framework to create a new Vue object named myVue using the createApp() method. The last line of code—myVue.mount('#display');—attaches the myVue Vue object to the HTML element with the ID of 'display' using the mount() method. The mount() method has a parameter passed to it that names the HTML ID, class, or tag where the Vue application will run inside a webpage.

The createApp() method is similar to a new() method in other programming languages and frameworks. It creates a new instance of the Vue framework for the single-page application using the HTML it is mounted to as the template for the view. Only one instance of the Vue framework is necessary to run the single-page or dynamic web application.

In this pattern, the dynamic contents of the framework are attached to a specific spot in the HTML using the native HTML tags and attributes instead of introducing language-specific attributes as in Angular.

The empty data() method inside the createApp() method creates a store of variables containing data. Although this example is simple, the store of variables effectively creates a component. The code has one variable called message set to the value 'Hello World!' on line 14. This variable is tied to the HTML using the same syntax as in Angular. When the framework asks for the variable in the directive {{message}}, the value returned is Hello World.

As promised at the design of Vue, this is a simpler body of code to create the same result as the Angular framework. Vue works directly with the HTML itself instead of requiring its own attributes in the HTML tags and uses a simpler code pattern.

Building the Vue Single-Page Application

Make a new copy of the vue_world.html page in your Samples folder for this chapter and call it vue_temp_converter. html. The Vue Hello World example is another convenient starting point for building the next example of the temperature converter since you know all of the code in the Hello World app is working.

Update the title of the page to A Very Vue Temperature Converter.

Remove the contents of the existing <div id="display">...</div> tag pair and replace them with the following code:

```
<h2>Enter a temperature in either input box to convert it to the corresponding
    temperature</h2>
<div>
    Fahrenheit: <input type='number' v-model="f" @input="calculateC">
</div>
<div>
    Celsius: <input type='number' v-model="c" @input="calculateF">
</div>
```

The first line of this code is the standard <h2>...</h2> tag set for an h2 heading.

The next two div elements contain the first new chunks of Vue-specific code, included as attributes of the <input> HTML element for the Fahrenheit and Celsius text boxes. The second attribute of the Fahrenheit <input> element, v-model="f", is akin to the ng-model="f" attribute in the Angular example. This attribute creates a viewmodel binding of the variable f in the HTML view to the variable f in the component code you will create in the <script>... </script> tags.

The next attribute in the `<input>` element is `@input="calculateC"`. When the Fahrenheit input is updated, the `calculateC` function runs because of this `@input` **event listener**. An event listener is a block of code in the browser that waits for an event to occur, like a mouse click or value change, and then runs.

This `@input` attribute also connects any change in the input value in the view to a user-defined function named `calculateC` in the component. In other words, when the user enters a value in the Fahrenheit input box, the `calculateC` function runs. The next `div` element sets up a similar event listener for the Celsius input box. When the user enters a value in the Celsius input box, the `calculateF` function runs.

Next, you need to update the contents of the `<script>`...`</script>` tags. Remove the current contents and replace them with the following code:

```
var myVue = Vue.createApp({
    data() {
        return {
            f: '',
            c: ''
        }
    },
    methods: {
        calculateC(evt) {
            this.c = Number(((this.f - 32) * (5/9)).toFixed(1))
        },
        calculateF(evt) {
            this.f = Number(((this.c * (9/5)) + 32).toFixed(1));
        },
    }
});
myVue.mount('#display');
```

The first three lines of this code are the same as the Hello World app. On the next lines, the f and c variables are initialized to nothing instead of a text value like "Hello World" so that the user can provide a starting value. These are the same two variables the Vue view can access.

In addition to the empty `data()` method, which returns two empty variables, the `createApp()` method has a `methods:` operator. A comma follows the closing } bracket for the `data()` method to separate the `data()` method from the `methods:` operator. Inside the `methods:` block is the `calculateC(evt)` function that corresponds to the `@input=calculateC` event listener in the `<input>` element. This parallel code connects the view and the viewmodel for the updating function.

The `calculateC(evt)` function takes one parameter, `evt`, which is the input parameter pointing back to the event that caused the execution of the code. That event is the change of value in the `<input>` element.

The next line of code is where the magic happens in this application, just like it did in the Angular application. The Vue code uses the same JavaScript calculation to convert Fahrenheit to Celsius as in Angular. The next three lines of code in the `methods:` block runs the `calculateF` function and converts from Celsius to Fahrenheit.

This application code is an example of implementing the integral plumbing that makes a framework useful. You could have written all this code yourself using primitive JavaScript and HTML, but instead, with some new syntax, you write less code overall to achieve the same results in a user interface.

Figure 7-5 shows the completed code.

Figure 7-5   Vue temperature conversion code

```
1    <!DOCTYPE HTML>
2    <html>
3        <head>
4            <title>A Very Vue Temperature Converter </title>
5            <script src="https://unpkg.com/vue@3/dist/vue.global.js"></script>
6        </head>
7        <body>
8            <div id="display">
9                <h2>Enter a temperature in either input box to convert it to the corresponding temperature</h2>
10               <div>
11                   Fahrenheit: <input type='number' v-model="f" @input="calculateC">
12               </div>
13               <div>
14                   Celsius: <input type='number' v-model="c" @input="calculateF">
15               </div>
16           </div>
17
18           <script>
19               var myVue = Vue.createApp({
20                   data() {
21                       return {
22                           f: '',
23                           c: ''
24                       }
25                   },
26                   methods: {
27                       calculateC(evt) {
28                           this.c = Number(((this.f-32) * 5/9).toFixed(1))
29                       },
30                       calculateF(evt) {
31                           this.f = Number(((this.c*9/5)+32).toFixed(1));
32                       },
33                   }
34               });
35
36               myVue.mount('#display');
37           </script>
38
39       </body>
40   </html>
```

Source: BBEdit

The completed interface is shown in **Figure 7-6**.

Figure 7-6   Vue temperature conversion in a browser

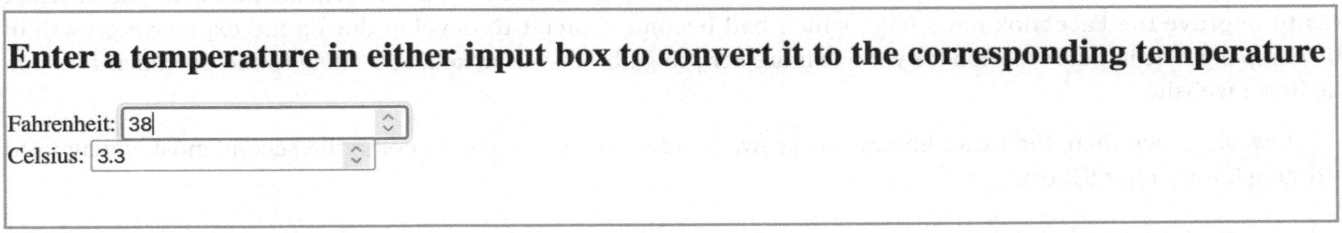

Enter a temperature in either input box to convert it to the corresponding temperature

Fahrenheit: 38

Celsius: 3.3

Quick Check 7-3

1. What is the MVVM design pattern useful for?

   a. Writing code that correctly connects the database to the HTML page
   b. Designing an accessible, standards-compliant user interface
   c. Implementing a TypeScript framework on a local computer
   d. Creating a logical separation of functions among the components of a web application

2. What is one difference between a controller and a viewmodel?

   a. The controller connects directly to the model and the view, whereas the viewmodel directs the activities of the model and the view.
   b. The viewmodel connects directly to the model and the view, whereas the controller directs the activities of the model and the view.
   c. The controller is written in script code, whereas the viewmodel is composed of valid HTML.
   d. The viewmodel is written in script code, whereas the controller is written in a server-side language like PHP or C#.

3. What does the `mount()` method do in the Vue framework?

   a. Attaches the code in the viewmodel to a specific HTML tag in the view
   b. Starts running the Vue application
   c. Creates an instance of a Vue object in the browser
   d. Attaches the Vue TypeScript framework to the browser's JavaScript interpreter

1) d. Like the MVC design pattern, the MVVM design pattern is a way of designating by logical function where different parts of an application should be coded. **2) b.** The viewmodel has code that corresponds to parts of the view and the model. **3) a.** The `mount()` method has a parameter passed to it that names the HTML ID, class, or tag where the Vue application will run inside a webpage.

7.4 Exploring React

At the 2013 JSConf, a conference held for JavaScript developers, a software engineer from Facebook named Jordan Walke announced the arrival of an open-source JavaScript library called React. The original intended use of React was to improve the Facebook news feed, which had become difficult to develop during the explosive growth of the company. The initial reception for yet one more scripting library was mixed, according to the documentation on the React website.

However, since then, the React library has grown in adoption and use to become the second-most widely used scripting library after jQuery.

Note Why is the name of this library "React" and not "Linear" or something else? According to their blog, the original developers, Jordan Walke and Tom Occino, gave their library the initial name "FBolt" while it was under development at Facebook. They later changed the name to React since the library would "react" to user inputs in a lightweight and responsive manner.

The React website where you can learn more about this library, explore the documentation, and examine the features is at https://reactjs.org. You can find tutorials and documentation on that page.

Reviewing the React Hello World

In your text editor, open the react_world.html file included with the course downloads. This file is an example of the traditional Hello World first programming example developed using the coding style and syntax of a typical React application.

Open react_world.html in a browser. When you do, the React library is loaded from a content delivery network to bypass the amount of time you need otherwise to spend installing and configuring React. Typically, the React library is installed on the computer used to develop the web application, and the installation and configuration involves first installing Node.js, then the NPM. Many tutorials are available online to help you install and configure this software.

The <head> section of the react_world.html page contains three links. The first is a link to the general React library. The second is to the React DOM library that allows for manipulating the HTML DOM. The third is to the Babel JavaScript library, which acts as a JavaScript compiler to efficiently translate text-based JavaScript into executable code.

For react_world.html, the Babel translator is used to convert the raw React code into executable JavaScript that the browser can run without having the complete React environment installed. This is helpful for this tutorial since installing and configuring the React environment is a complex task that is beyond the scope of this chapter.

The code for react_world.html is shown in **Figure 7-7**.

Figure 7-7 React Hello World code

```
1   <!DOCTYPE HTML>
2   <html>
3       <head>
4           <title>A Very React Hello World</title>
5           <script src="https://unpkg.com/react@16/umd/react.production.min.js"></script>
6           <script src="https://unpkg.com/react-dom@16/umd/react-dom.production.min.js"></script>
7           <script src="https://unpkg.com/babel-standalone@6.15.0/babel.min.js"></script>
8       </head>
9       <body>
10          <div id='display'></div>
11
12          <script type="text/babel">
13              ReactDOM.render(
14                  <h1>Hello, world!</h1>,
15                  document.getElementById('display')
16              );
17          </script>
18
19      </body>
20  </html>
```

Source: BBEdit

The React-specific code begins on line 12 with an addition of the `type="text/babel"` attribute to the opening `<script>` tag. This attribute replaces the standard `<script "type=text/javascript">` so that the browser doesn't attempt to interpret the code that follows as regular JavaScript. Instead, `type="text/babel"` indicates the Babel library should compile this code into JavaScript that the browser can then handle with its native JavaScript interpreter.

Lines 12 through 17 contain the following code:

```
<script type="text/babel">
    ReactDOM.render(
        <h1>Hello, world!</h1>,
        document.getElementById('display')
    );
</script>
```

You can probably figure out the purpose of this code by reading it. Line 13 calls the `ReactDom` library function `render()`. Lines 14 and 15 send the `render()` function two parameters. The first parameter is the text to inject into an HTML element, and the second is the standard JavaScript code to find an element in the DOM by its ID. Combined in the `render()` function, the two parameters modify the DOM of the HTML page much like jQuery did by adding the contents of the first parameter to the place identified by the second.

This code creates a virtual `h1` HTML element that is inserted into the contents of an actual HTML element with the ID of `'display'`. This process is a common pattern in React, creating a component to add to an HTML page that is used as the framework to display those components. While this code is simple, the complexity is handled behind the scenes by the libraries included in the `<head>` section of the page. This is a case of requiring much less code to create the same output as with Angular or Vue.

Building the React Single-Page Application

Make a new copy of the react_world.html page in your Samples folder for this chapter and call it react_temp_converter.html. The react_world.html example is another convenient starting point for building the next example of the Fahrenheit–Celsius converter since you know all of the code in the Hello World app is working.

Update the title of the page to A Very React Temperature Converter.

Because of how React injects its dynamic contents into the HTML DOM, the contents between the `<script>`...`</script>` tags are the only other updates this single-page application needs. The `<div id="display"></div>` tags are the home for this application in the HTML page.

Remove all the contents between the `<script>`...`</script>` tags used for the Hello World application.

Next, add the following new code between the `<script>`...`</script>` tags:

```
function Calculator()
{
    const [temp, calcTemp] = React.useState({ c_temp: 0, f_temp: 0 })
    const updateF = evt => calcTemp({
        f_temp: evt.target.value,
        c_temp: ((evt.target.value - 32) * (5/9)).toFixed(1)
    })
    const updateC = evt => calcTemp({
        c_temp: evt.target.value,
        f_temp: ((evt.target.value * (9/5)) + 32).toFixed(1)
    })
return (
    <div id="converter">
        <h2>Enter a temperature in either input box to convert it to the
corresponding temperature</h2>

        <div>
            Fahrenheit <input type='number' value = {temp.f_temp} onChange =
{updateF} />
        </div>
        <div>
            Celsius <input type='number' value = {temp.c_temp} onChange =
{updateC}/>
```

```
        </div>
      </div>
    )
  }
  const rootElement = document.getElementById('display')
  ReactDOM.render(<Calculator />, rootElement)
```

This is a lot of new code and code pattern to understand. Its complexity is one of the challenges of using React, since it is less like traditional JavaScript than other frameworks or libraries.

The first line of code should look familiar; `function Calculator()` is a function declaration like any other JavaScript function declaration, with the name `Calculator` for this one.

The code inside the `Calculator` function instantiates the React library via the `useState` method, which takes the variables `c_temp` and `f_temp` initialized to 0 as parameters. The output from this instantiation is the `temp` object, which has a `calcTemp` method. That's a lot of jargon to decipher to understand what is happening.

The React library function `useState` creates something similar to the Angular `$scope` object, except that you can name it anything you like. In this case, the code names it `temp`. The `temp` object has two properties and one method that are used to maintain the state of the user interface. The properties are variables that hold the values for Fahrenheit and Celsius in the input text boxes, and the method recalculates the temperature if one of the values changes.

The following lines of code are in one of the functions fired when an event triggers them in the user interface:

```
const updateF = evt => calcTemp({
  f_temp: evt.target.value,
  c_temp: ((evt.target.value - 32) * (5/9)).toFixed(1)
})
```

The `updateF` function handles updating the Fahrenheit temperature, which is initially set to 0. You can see that `updateF` is sent the `evt` event, calling the `calcTemp` function. The `calcTemp` function reevaluates the value of the `f_temp` variable and recalculates the `c_temp` variable using the data from the event. The code `evt.target.value` captures what was changed, sets `f_temp` to that value, and recalculates `c_temp` to a new value as a result of the update to the Fahrenheit temp.

The corresponding function for `updateC` performs the parallel update process for the Celsius text box. This effectively creates two-way binding in the React library, since an update in either text box where the temp object's properties are used updates the other value using the same `temp` object as an intermediary.

Data binding in this code uses the React `temp` object created as the first step in the function declaration as an intermediary to link the user interface and the data processing. This linkage requires an event to trigger an update, just like the `onBlur` event triggered an update in the standard JavaScript code.

The code following the `return` statement is the view, or UI, for this application. It is primarily composed of HTML with React library additions that provide hooks into the view from the viewmodel.

The following snippet provides an example of the React library code:

```
Celsius <input type='number' value = {temp.c_temp} onChange = {updateC} />
```

In this code, the `input type='number'` attribute is normal HTML that defines a field for entering a number. The remaining attributes are React code. The `value` attribute retrieves the `temp` object's `c_temp` property to set its value dynamically, and the `onChange` event handler calls the `updateC` method. The `onChange` event handler will be used when the text in the Celsius box changes so that the calculation runs and updates the contents of both input elements.

The first line of code after the closing curly bracket for the `Calculator` function is a variable declaration that captures a link to the HTML element with the ID of `'display'` to create an attachment point for the React library code in the HTML of the view:

```
const rootElement = document.getElementById('display')
```

The contents of the variable `rootElement` are used next in the last line of code, `ReactDOM.render(<Calculator />, rootElement)`.

This code calls the ReactDom library's `render()` function, passing to it the `Calculator` viewmodel object and the variable `rootElement` containing a handle to the HTML element with the ID of `'display'` found in the previous line. This attachment point in the `rootElement` variable is where the viewmodel is attached to the view, which in this case is a very simple HTML document.

The completed code is displayed in **Figure 7-8**.

Figure 7-8   React temperature conversion code

```
1    <!DOCTYPE HTML>
2  ▼ <html>
3  ▼     <head>
4              <title>A Very React Temperature Converter</title>
5              <script src="https://unpkg.com/react@16.14.0/umd/react.development.js"></script>
6              <script src="https://unpkg.com/react-dom@16.14.0/umd/react-dom.development.js"></script>
7              <script src="https://unpkg.com/babel-standalone@6.15.0/babel.min.js"></script>
8  ▙     </head>
9  ▼     <body>
10             <div id="display"></div>
11
12 ▼         <script type="text/babel">
13             function Calculator()
14 ▼           {
15                 const [temp, calcTemp] = React.useState({ c_temp: 0, f_temp: 0 })
16
17 ▼               const updateF = evt => calcTemp({
18                     f_temp: evt.target.value,
19                     c_temp: ((evt.target.value - 32) * 5 / 9).toFixed(1)
20 ▙               })
21
22 ▼               const updateC = evt => calcTemp({
23                     c_temp: evt.target.value,
24                     f_temp: (evt.target.value * 9 / 5 + 32).toFixed(1)
25 ▙               })
26
27 ▼               return (
28                     <div id="converter">
29                         <h2>Enter a temperature in either input box to convert it to the corresponding temperature</h2>
30                         <div>
31                             Celsius <input type='number' value = {temp.c_temp} onChange = {updateC} />
32                         </div>
33                         <div>
34                             Fahrenheit <input type='number' value = {temp.f_temp} onChange = {updateF} />
35                         </div>
36                     </div>
37 ▙               )
38 ▙           }
39             const rootElement = document.getElementById('display')
40             ReactDOM.render(<Calculator />, rootElement)
41 ▙         </script>
42 ▙     </body>
43 ▙ </html>
```

Source: BBEdit

The completed interface is shown in **Figure 7-9**.

Figure 7-9   React temperature conversion in a browser

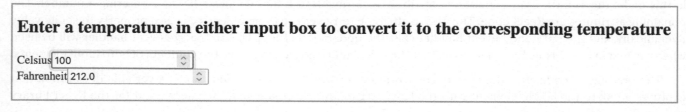

Enter a temperature in either input box to convert it to the corresponding temperature

Celsius `100`
Fahrenheit `212.0`

Quick Check 7-4

1. What does the tag `<script type="text/babel">` mean?

   a. The code enclosed by the `<script>` tags should be compiled by the Babel compiler.

   b. The code enclosed by the `<script>` tags is valid BabelScript.

   c. The browser should use its Babel interpreter to execute this code instead of the JavaScript interpreter.

   d. The browser should validate the code enclosed within the `<script>` tags using the Babel validator.

2. What does the syntax `{temp.c_temp}` create when used in a React view?

   a. A placeholder for injecting the React virtual HTML into the HTML DOM

   b. An expression that allows the `c_temp` variable in the `temp` object to connect to the corresponding variable in the viewmodel to set up two-way binding

   c. A function call that will run and return a value from the database to display in the `c_temp` variable in the view

   d. The instantiation of the object named `temp` with a variable named `c_temp`

3. What does the `ReactDOM.render()` function do?

   a. Loads the HTML DOM into the React object

   b. Creates a `render` object from the ReactDOM library

   c. Reloads the React webpage in the browser

   d. Adds the contents sent to the function to the location specified in the DOM

---

1) a. The `text/babel` value for the `type` attribute means that the code should be compiled using the Babel library. **2) b.** In the view, the code `temp.c_temp` is used to place the contents of the variable `c_temp` from the `temp` object of the viewmodel inside the view. **3) d.** The ReactDom library manipulates the DOM, and the `render()` method injects dynamic contents inside a specific HTML tag pair.

Summary

- A scripting framework is used to build dynamic web applications.

- JavaScript and TypeScript are two different scripting languages for building dynamic web applications.

- A scripting framework is different from a scripting library. Content is added to the framework, whereas library content is added to an HTML-based web application.

- Angular is a popular TypeScript-based web application development framework.

- Vue is a JavaScript framework for building dynamic, lightweight web applications.

- Vue has its origins in the Angular framework.

- React is a popular JavaScript library for developing dynamic web applications.

Key Terms

component

controller

data binding

event listener

model

model-view-controller (MVC)

model-view-viewmodel (MVVM)

scripting framework

separation of concerns

single-page application

two-way data binding

view

viewmodel

Review Questions

1. What is a JavaScript library? (7.1)

   a. A high-speed server that returns links to JavaScript code files

   b. Any JavaScript file that you link to from the `<head>`...`</head>` section of a webpage

   c. The JavaScript template into which you add your HTML and CSS to create a dynamic webpage

   d. A JavaScript file that includes functions and features you can use in your own webpages to create dynamic features

2. What is a single-page application? (7.1)

   a. A web application in which the contents are dynamically loaded into a single page based on user interaction

   b. Any web application that only has one page

   c. Any dynamic page in a static website that has links to the JavaScript libraries or templates in its `head` section

   d. A webpage that serves as the single directory with links to gain access to all of the other web applications on the website

3. What is the difference between JavaScript and TypeScript? (7.1)

   a. Nothing—they are just two different labels for the same type of code when running in different web browsers.

   b. JavaScript is the original in-browser programming language, and TypeScript is the newer, more expansive programming language.

   c. TypeScript is the original in-browser programming language, and JavaScript is the newer, more expansive programming language.

   d. JavaScript is used in the web browser, and TypeScript is used in the web server to create the same dynamic webpage features.

4. What is an Angular `module()` function used for? (7.2)

   a. Creating an Angular web application object

   b. Creating a link to the Angular library

   c. Creating a single modular function inside a dynamic webpage

   d. Creating an Angular model for the data

5. What is the `$scope` object used for in the Angular framework? (7.2)

   a. To transmit data between the controller and the view

   b. To transmit data between the model and the controller

   c. To transmit data between the model and the view

   d. To create the boundaries of the application inside the HTML document

6. What defines the boundaries of the view in an Angular web application? (7.2)

    a. The entire HTML page is the view.

    b. The view is added to the page dynamically by the controller when it adds content to the webpage.

    c. The boundaries of the view are established by the controller adding model data to the HTML tags that make up the view.

    d. The `ng-app` attribute is added to the tag that forms the outer boundary of the HTML view.

7. What is two-way data binding? (7.2)

    a. The real-time virtual connection between a web application's data stored in the model and the data stored in the database

    b. Creating a link between the data in the database and the data in the view

    c. The connection through intermediary code of a single variable shared in two parts of the web application

    d. The code for updating the database from the UI, or the UI from the database

8. What is an event listener? (7.3)

    a. A block of code that creates a user interaction point in an HTML page

    b. An application that the browser uses to load or reload webpages after an update occurs

    c. A block of HTML written to allow user input into a web application form in an interactive form element

    d. A block of code that is executed after an event such as a mouse click

9. What does the `methods:` operator do in Vue code? (7.3)

    a. Creates the list of events the viewmodel will respond to and identifies what code will execute for those events

    b. Lists all of the methods in a Vue object

    c. Creates an array of the functions the Vue object can perform in the view

    d. Creates a list of the events the view will respond to and identifies what code will execute for those events

10. Where is the viewmodel built in Vue code? (7.3)

    a. In an external script file or between the `<script>...</script>` tags in a simple example

    b. In the HTML page out of the HTML tags designated by the view

    c. In the PHP code that creates the backend

    d. In the data structure provided by the model when it is incorporated into the HTML that makes up the view

11. What is a React component? (7.4)

    a. A reusable block of user-generated code that is added to the HTML DOM

    b. A part of the React library that is used in the user-generated code

    c. An object created from the React library to perform a discrete task

    d. An attribute added to an HTML tag to create the wrapper around a React application that runs inside of it

12. How is user data from the React view transferred between the view and the viewmodel? (7.4)

    a. The data is stored in the database that both the view and viewmodel can access

    b. The event object causes a data hand-off from the view to the viewmodel

    c. The view object is accessed directly by the viewmodel to retrieve values

    d. The object that is created to maintain the state of the application is accessed by both

Programming Exercises

1. Using your favorite search engine, research the "Easiest JavaScript library or framework to learn." Review five articles and summarize the consensus among them. Include in your one-page summary a list of links to the articles you reviewed. (7.1–7.4)

2. Using your favorite search engine, research "Is Vue or Angular better than React?" Review five articles and summarize your findings. Include links to the articles you reviewed and state your opinion as to whether Vue is better than React and why. (7.1–7.4)

3. Using your favorite search engine, research "Why is React the most popular JavaScript library?" Review five articles and summarize your findings. Include links to the articles you reviewed. (7.1–7.4)

Projects

The Rule of 72 states that if you divide 72 by the interest rate for a savings account, bond, or other type of interest-earning asset, you will get the number of years required to double your initial investment, assuming the interest compounds annually. The formula looks like this:

years = (72/rate)

For example, if you are earning 3 percent interest on the preferred stock offered by Hieroglyphs, the parent company of Totally Awesome Stuff, it will take you 72/3, or 24 years, to double your initial investment assuming the stock price remains the same over that time period.

This same rule can be applied to a rate of inflation decreasing your purchasing power. If annual inflation is calculated as 8 percent, the time required to decrease the value of your dollar by half will be 72/8, or 9 years. That is, if you put $100 in a safe and pull it out after 9 years, you would only be able to buy the equivalent of $50 of low-fat candy for goldfish after that time period.

This legacy formula actually dates back at least as far as 1494, when Italian mathematician Luca Pacioli mentioned the rule in his math textbook *Summa de Arithmetica*. Of course, in 1494, single-page applications referred to a single page of paper, so the starting point for the user interface was even simpler than the Google search home page.

1. Using the Angular temperature converter as a starting point, create an application that has one input field and one `<h2>...</h2>` HTML element containing the output field to show the number of years it will take to double the initial investment using the Rule of 72. Name your application angular_calculator.html. (7.1–7.4)

2. Using the Vue temperature converter as a starting point, create an application that has one input field and one `<h2>...</h2>` HTML element containing the output field to show the number of years it will take to double the initial investment using the Rule of 72. Name your application vue_calculator.html. (7.1–7.4)

3. Using the React temperature converter as a starting point, create an application that has one input field and one `<h2>...</h2>` HTML element containing the output field to show the number of years it will take to double the initial investment using the Rule of 72. Name your application react_calculator.html. (7.1–7.4)

Chapter 8

Content Management Systems: An Overview

Learning Objectives

When you complete this chapter, you will be able to:

8.1 Describe a content management system.

8.2 Install WordPress on a local computer.

8.3 Build a simple webpage using WordPress.

8.4 Describe commonly used WordPress features.

8.5 Explain how to publish a website built using WordPress.

8.1 What Is a Content Management System?

You might have already worked with plug-ins, which are software packages that extend the functionality of an original piece of software, such as those you used with jQuery. If you have, you know that using software packages someone else wrote can improve the speed and simplicity of developing webpages by reducing the amount of code you need to write. The next step in this evolutionary process is to create webpages without writing any code at all.

A **content management system (CMS)** is a software application used to manage a website, including creating and modifying webpage contents and handling website layouts. Beginning web developers and experienced website managers use CMSs to be more efficient by creating page content and managing the plumbing of a website instead of writing all the code that makes up the pages and features.

Using a CMS is a logical extension of strategic efficiency. While it is fun to write raw code to create unique and innovative websites, most websites are practical tools for transmitting information to users and collecting data from them. A CMS still offers opportunities to exercise the creative mind, but it sets up the website structure and styles in advance to decrease the total amount of time and labor necessary to take a website from ideation to deployment.

CMS software applications have two parts. The **content management application (CMA)** is the interface the web developer uses to create the website content, configure the templates that display the content, and organize the plug-ins that extend the features of the website. The **content delivery application (CDA)** is the engine that combines the templates, software plug-ins, and website content to deliver completed webpages to the users on the Internet who want to consume them.

The webpage templates, plug-ins, and website content are stored as files and data that the CDA combines when the user asks for a webpage from the web server. The web server, following the user request, retrieves the templates, plug-ins, and webpage contents, merges them together as a discrete webpage, and returns the completed request.

Flavors of Content Management Systems

Many CMSs are available today, both open source and proprietary. Open source CMSs are developed by a community of web developers contributing their time and intelligence to a project that they will also use and benefit from. These open source CMSs are typically available for free with one of the standard open source licenses.

The original open source CMSs developed in the early 2000s and still recognizable today include WordPress, Joomla, and Drupal. These defined a CMS for web development as a web application for building websites that didn't require the user to know web coding and an engine to combine template, code, and content to create webpages on demand.

Proprietary CMSs are created by a for-profit company, often a web host, which sells the use of that software as part of its hosting service. These CMSs are offered with terms, conditions, and a warranty or agreement that the application will perform to specified standards.

Web hosting companies like GoDaddy, Wix, and Squarespace offer proprietary CMSs to people creating websites hosted by those companies. However, nearly every web hosting company has their own flavor of CMS. Most also allow using WordPress as an option.

Why WordPress?

The origin of WordPress as a CMS is in blogging, which is a way for someone to document or record their episodic thoughts in a webpage accessible to subscribers or the entire world. Blogging is the forebearer of today's social media but is dominated by text with a feature for comments rather than images or videos vying for likes or retweets. Additionally, blogs feature significantly fewer viral dances or pictures of meals people are about to eat.

When WordPress was introduced, most bloggers with thoughts to share were not web developers, so they needed an easy-to-use solution that could be configured and securely deployed with minimal technical knowledge. WordPress filled this niche, and many bloggers adopted it in the early 2000s.

WordPress evolved to become a webpage engine as the user community supporting it contributed updates to the platform. These visionary early users created the themes and plug-ins that make WordPress what it is today. It is by far the market leader in CMSs, with well over half of all webpages developed in a CMS built on the WordPress platform. The market share for all other CMSs is in the single digits by comparison.

What gives WordPress the advantage over all other CMSs? One reason for its popularity is that WordPress is easy to start using. The web application interface is simple and intuitive and there are numerous online tutorials. A large community of developers and users have generated an extensive amount of documentation, and most are willing to help a newbie by answering questions or giving technical guidance.

A second reason WordPress is popular is that while the on-ramp to creating a working website is not too steep, that ramp continues to climb since the development community has extended WordPress to include a vast array of options. By default, WordPress includes features that support Internet security, mobile-first design, and search engine optimization. You can also customize WordPress for specific use cases.

A third reason WordPress is popular is that it is designed to be secure by default. Novice web developers who don't know what they don't know might create a security vulnerability in their website without understanding how or why. The WordPress web development sandbox prevents the most common blunders and provides security audits and plug-ins that scan the website you are building for additional known vulnerabilities.

Even seasoned professional developers who practice good data hygiene (i.e., creating robust passwords and storing them securely) and follow the documentation carefully are well positioned for online security when using WordPress.

> **Note** The names of two websites start with "WordPress" but have different extensions. WordPress.com is the commercial web hosting site for web developers who want to use the software package offered at the website WordPress.org. The .org site is where the community of developers and users gather to share themes, create upgrades, fix bugs, and exchange information about the tool. You can download the WordPress software package from WordPress.org if you are hosting it on BlueHost or GoDaddy, but you can also use that same software on WordPress.com.

Local Hosting versus Remote Development

When you install WordPress and use it to create a local website, you transform your local computer into a web server and use the CMS tools in WordPress to build the webpages for your site. As you have read, WordPress is a website builder that uses a web application to create the websites. To use it on a computer, you must have a web server running on that machine.

Some web developers use this same process of local development to build websites professionally. After using a laptop or desktop as a local web server for the initial development, the web developers move the new website to a remote web server. Other web developers use the WordPress toolset exclusively on the remote web server to develop, test, and deploy the website.

The advantages of developing a site locally and then moving your completed work to a remote server are the following:

- Local development reduces the consequences for making a mistake. On your local machine, you discover that you made a mistake or installed the wrong plug-in or theme before you publish the website. Of course, this also means you need to thoroughly test your work before moving it to the remote server.

- Developing pages locally is faster than developing them on a web server. You do not need to cope with network latency or long wait times when the entire site is on your computer.

- It is safer to explore options. Your local web server is less likely to be hacked, so you can explore configuration options that would create vulnerabilities on a web server directly connected to the Internet.

- You can do your development work with or without a connection to the Internet. You can create your website masterpiece from a coffee shop, even if the "free Wi-Fi" is slow, spotty, or not secure.

The potential disadvantages of doing your development locally are also considerations. These include the following:

- You must create your own backup schedule and outside backups of your website. If your laptop is lost or stolen, or your desktop computer stops working, all of the web development that you haven't uploaded or backed up will also be lost.

- Keeping a remote site updated with local content takes more work than doing your development on the remote server. You need to transfer the new content and configuration from your local machine to the remote server. You can use software packages that make this process easier, however.

- You can't collaborate with other developers on the same website. Since your work is only accessible to you, nobody else can edit it or contribute content to it.

There isn't a right answer to the local versus remote development debate. You make the decision with an informed judgment of your circumstances.

For this chapter, you do only local development because the URL totallyawesomestuff.com is already claimed, and if everyone reading this chapter tried to publish their own version of the website, the Internet would be littered with products that are totally awesome.

Quick Check 8-1

1. Why do experienced web developers use a CMS instead of writing raw HTML, CSS, and JavaScript using a text editor?

   a. Because the CMS reduces the amount of HTML, CSS, and JavaScript you need to write, just like using a JavaScript library reduces the amount of JavaScript that is needed
   b. Because the CMS allows the developer to create the HTML, CSS, and JavaScript from starter templates and then add content like text and images to those completed templates
   c. Because the CMS prechecks the errors in the HTML, CSS, and JavaScript better than a simple text editor can
   d. Because the time to finish and deploy a website with a CMS is less than starting from an empty text file

2. What does the content delivery application refer to in the context of a CMS?

   a. The toolset used to build webpages that use themes and configure websites using plug-ins
   b. The engine that combines the templates and contents to deliver webpages requested by a browser
   c. The window in the CMS used to manage themes and plug-ins pulled from remote web servers that host them
   d. The integrated wrapper around the four applications that are necessary for a CMS to function

3. Which of the following is NOT a reason WordPress is the most popular CMS today?

   a. It is designed with security as a critical consideration.
   b. It is feature-rich and flexible.
   c. It is easy to use when first getting started.
   d. Googlebots will rank WordPress websites higher in the rankings.

> **1) d.** The total time to deployment is much less for both simple and complex sites when using a CMS. **2) b.** The CDA is the software that combines content with themes and plug-ins to render finished webpages. **3) d.** Googlebots evaluate the content and usability of the website, not the development platform that created the website.

8.2 Installing WordPress

If you already have an instance of WordPress on your computer and you are looking at the WordPress dashboard in your web browser while reading this, you might be thinking about skipping the next section on installation and configuration and heading directly to the WordPress Dashboard Tour section.

However, reading about how the installation of WordPress works gives you background information on WordPress and prepares you for installing it yourself in the future. These instructions refer to the online documentation recommended by WordPress, which will be the most up to date as the software continues to evolve.

Here's a quick overview of what is necessary. To turn your laptop or desktop into a fully functioning self-contained web server hosting the CMS, you need the following software:

- **Operating system:** Your current operating system also serves as the operating system for your local web server.
- **Web server software:** You need the web server software Apache, which is the application that serves webpages to browsers that request them.

- **Database:** You also need the MySQL database to hold the contents of the WordPress webpages.
- **Programming language:** Finally, you need a programming language to combine the templates with the content to render the webpages. For WordPress, that programming language is PHP.

WordPress is not a standalone web application. A CMA requires a website to build the contents that the CDA delivers to the web browser from the Apache web server. The CMA webpages that the CDA renders are composed of data from the MySQL database and PHP code. The CDA engine that composes finished webpages requires Apache, MySQL, and PHP running on an operating system.

That sounds like a lot of software to install and configure, but several software packages bundle these disparate applications into a cohesive unit that you can install and configure yourself. The next section walks you through the more technical way to install and configure these systems. The section that follows bundles these applications in a preconfigured Docker container that functions in nearly the same way but within a single preconfigured bundle. Both approaches are valid methods to install WordPress locally.

Installing and Configuring WordPress Manually

WordPress does not run alone as a single application like Adobe Photoshop or Microsoft Word. The three applications that run on the operating system can be conveniently bundled together in a desktop client called MAMP (for Macintosh/Apache/MySQL/PHP) or WAMP (for Windows/Apache/MySQL/PHP). You can also successfully install and run the MAMP server on a Windows machine.

To install WordPress in a MAMP or WAMP:

1. Use a web browser to go to one of the following links to open a webpage with instructions for installing a MAMP or WAMP:

   MAMP: **https://codex.wordpress.org/Installing_WordPress_Locally_on_Your_Mac_With_MAMP**

   or

   WAMP: **https://wordpress.org/support/article/installing-wordpress-on-your-own-computer/#wamp**

   You can also find the installation and configuration instructions in the WordPress documentation by searching for "WordPress MAMP (or WAMP if you are using Windows) installation instructions."

2. On a Mac, complete steps 1–3 on the MAMP webpage to download and install the MAMP. On a PC, use the **WAMP Server** or **WAMP Server at SourceForge** link to download the WAMP stack. Search for "WAMP server installation steps" and review the results. For additional instructions, watch WAMP installation tutorials on YouTube or search for text-based step-by-step instructions online, which are beyond the scope of this chapter. The following installation steps are for the versions of WAMP/MAMP available at the time this module was written. The most up-to-date installation steps are available at the URLs cited in step 1. Keep in mind that software developers publish updates frequently. Professionals who work with software on the job must become adept at adjusting to discrepancies in instructions and changes in software.

3. You must create a space for installing WordPress in a known location. On a Mac, make sure you have created the following folder structure: Users/UserName/Sites/wordpress/. On a Windows machine, create the following folder structure on the C drive: c:\wamp.

   The result of these steps is the starting point for installing WordPress itself on a running instance of the WAMP or MAMP application such as that shown in **Figure 8-1**.

4. Next, you need to create a MySQL database to host the contents of WordPress. On a Mac, type the following URL in your web browser:

   http://localhost:8888/phpMyAdmin/

   This may redirect to your specific version of the tool that your MAMP application is running such as http://localhost:8888/phpMyAdmin5.

   On Windows using the WAMP server, the URL for accessing the PHP interface is http://localhost/phpmyadmin. You may also be prompted for a username and password. The username is root, and there is no default password, although you should update this security flaw immediately by resetting the password to a secure value.

Figure 8-1 Running instance of the MAMP application

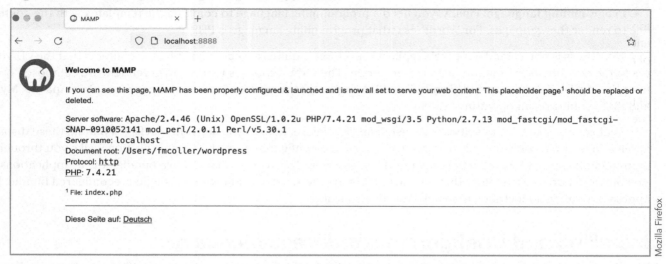

5. On the PHP administration page, click the Databases tab to display the Create database page.

6. Create a new database with the name of **wordpress** in lowercase letters. Check to make sure the Collation value is "utf8_general_ci" or the value closest to that in your list of Collation values, and then click the Create button shown in **Figure 8-2** to create the storage space for your installation of WordPress. If you choose to use a name other than wordpress, write down the database name because you need it in the next steps.

Figure 8-2 Create database page

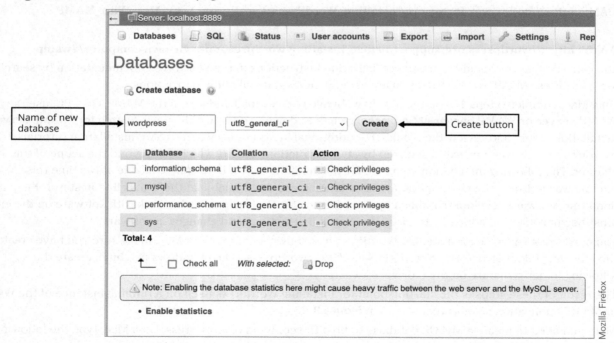

In the WAMP stack, you might be prompted to create a database user and password with full database Create/Read/Update/Delete privileges to use this user in the WordPress configuration in a future step.

7. On a new tab in your web browser, go to WordPress.org and then click Get WordPress. Download the most recent production release of WordPress as a zip file, and then extract the contents of that file into a convenient folder. Move contents of the extracted wordpress folder into the www folder you created earlier.

8. Enter the URL **http://localhost:8888** on the MAMP stack or **http://localhost/wordpress** on the WAMP stack to open the WordPress admin page. See **Figure 8-3**.

Figure 8-3 The WordPress admin page

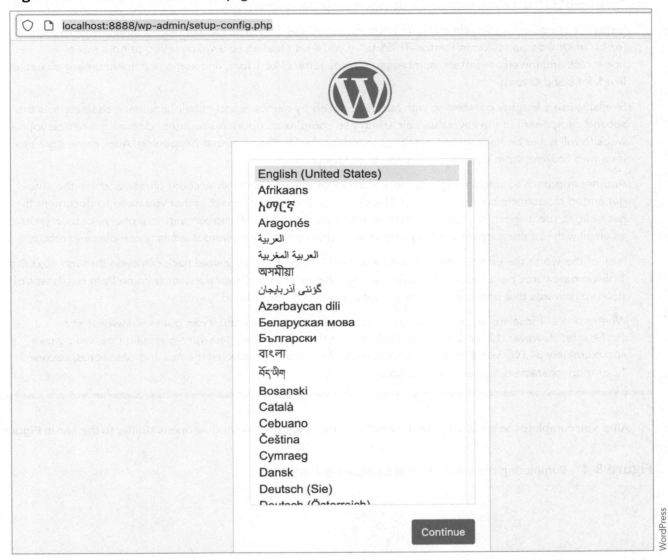

9. Select your language and then work through the next series of steps to configure WordPress while it is running on a web server. That's a little mind-bending to think about, but it's part of the web-centric nature of WordPress and WAMP/MAMP. If you are using WAMP and need to supply the user credentials to connect to the MySQL database that you created earlier, the screen to configure that user is available at http://localhost/wordpress/wp-admin/setup-config.php.

Common Mistakes

Two critical steps in configuring WordPress are creating an administrator login and password for the website and for the database.

The login/password combinations become the only way to access your website and database to make updates. You have probably read about the need to create secure passwords. You should also create a secure administrator name. If you think about these identifiers as key/value pairs, a complex key (the name of the administrator) and a complex value (the password) double the complexity of the key/value pair.

Using the login "administrator" or "admin" is convenient and memorable. Then again, so is using "password123" as a password. Neither is secure nor a good idea.

Instead, consider using an administrator account phrase like "1AmTheAweometAdmini$trator4Thi$$ite" (or "1@m@n@dequate@dmini$trator4Thi$$ite" if you aren't feeling so awe$ome yet) using a mix of uppercase and lowercase letters, numbers to replace letters like 1 for *l*, and some nonalphanumeric characters like $ for *s* and @ for *a*.

Similarly, use a lengthy passphrase with letters replaced by numbers and nonalphanumeric characters as the second component in the key/value pair. Using two complex components together doesn't guarantee your website will never be hacked, but it does help reduce the likelihood of that happening. Also, never agree to let a web browser store your account name or password.

Another approach to website login security is to create the administrator account phrase and use the auto-generated random characters password. The challenge with this approach is that you need to document the password to use it again. You can write it down, take a picture of it on the screen with your phone, or send yourself an email with just the password in it, as long as your email address password is similarly complex and robust.

Is all of this worth the effort? Consider the following. A brute-force password hack can cycle through 10,000 to 1 billion passwords per second depending on the network speed. Those passwords come from databases of stolen passwords that unsuspecting users have involuntarily contributed.

When none of those stolen passwords work, random character generators can guess passwords at a similar rate. However, 12 random characters, even at that astounding password-guessing rate, would take approximately 34,000 years to crack with current technology. Complex usernames and passwords, each with 12 or more characters, can double that time.

After you complete the initial steps in the configuration, a WordPress window opens similar to the one in **Figure 8-4**.

Figure 8-4   Completing the initial steps in configuring WordPress

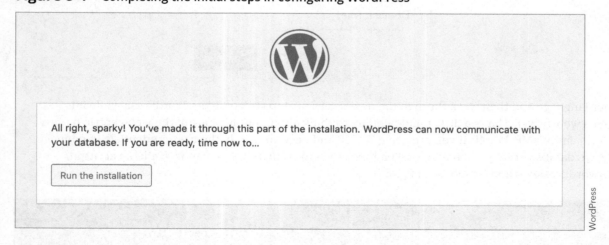

All right, sparky! You've made it through this part of the installation. WordPress can now communicate with your database. If you are ready, time now to...

Run the installation

WordPress

10. Click the Run the installation button to perform the installation, creating a secure site administrator account and password, and adding other important details to your new site when prompted. You should create a complex administrator name and password, since you access your WordPress website using the WordPress interface that is also available on your website. That means that your website is accessible to the entire Internet if someone else gets your password.

When you have successfully completed the installation, the WordPress Dashboard opens. You might need to log in to WordPress and the site first. **Figure 8-5** shows the Dashboard for Totally Awesome Stuff using the version of WordPress current when this module was written.

Figure 8-5   WordPress Dashboard

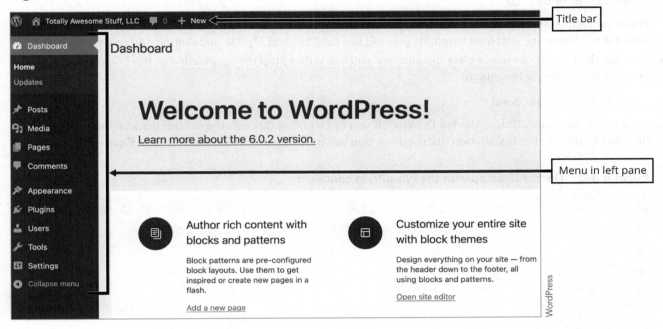

Using a Docker Container

In addition to installing WordPress on a MAMP or WAMP server bundle, you can also install it as part of a Docker container. Docker containers are preconfigured software bundles with all the software necessary to run WordPress on a virtual Docker desktop. Docker Desktop is a software application that runs like a self-contained operating system on your local machine. It can be used to run Docker containers of the software bundles.

To install WordPress in a Docker container:

1. Use a web browser to go to one of the following links to open a webpage for installing Docker Desktop on a Mac or PC:

   For Windows: **https://docs.docker.com/desktop/install/windows-install/**

   For Mac: **https://docs.docker.com/desktop/install/mac-install/**

   These links include the most recent download of Docker Desktop and the instructions for installing it on your machine. Follow the steps to install and start Docker. As you do, you create the space for a Docker container to run in Docker Desktop.

2. After you have Docker Desktop up and running, move the file named wordpress-docker.zip from the starting files for this chapter to a convenient directory on your local machine, and then extract the files it contains.

   The first file in the outer level of the folder is a configuration file called docker-compose.yml. Open it with your favorite text editor and review the contents.

3. If the computer you are using is already running IIS or Apache locally, you need to update the port the Docker container uses for its localhost. To do this, change the following line:

   ```
   ports:
       - '80:80'
   ```

   to this new value:

   ```
   ports:
       - '8080:80'
   ```

This change maps the port 8080 on the web server (also known as your local computer) to port 80 in the container so the application running in the container can connect through the localhost.

4. Open a terminal window or command line and navigate to the folder that contains the unzipped contents of wordpress-docker.zip. Enter the following command:

```
docker compose up
```

This command starts the Docker container, which then installs all the necessary parts of a local WordPress installation. If you are watching carefully, you will see the PHP and MySQL installation and update take place.

5. To close the Docker container after installation, you can either stop the application in the Docker interface or enter the following command:

```
docker compose down
```

6. Return to your installation of Docker Desktop. If you are working through the default installation outlined in the links to the Docker installation instructions, you see a Containers window like that in **Figure 8-6**.

Figure 8-6 Docker Desktop with the WordPress container

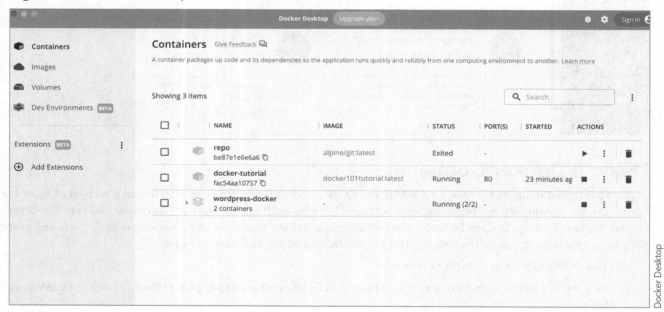

If your screen looks like Figure 8-6, your installation of Docker Desktop and the Docker container for WordPress is complete.

7. In a web browser, enter the following URL:

http://localhost:8080

You should be redirected automatically to the following URL:

http://localhost:8080/wp-admin/install.php

Except for the port number, you will see the WordPress admin page, shown earlier in Figure 8-3.

8. Select your language, and then work through the next series of steps using the WordPress window to configure WordPress.

9. When the window shown in Figure 8-4 appears, click the Run the installation button to install WordPress, create a secure site administrator account and password, and add other important details to configure your new site. You should create a complex administrator name and password, since you will access your WordPress website using the WordPress interface that is also available on your website. That means that your website is accessible to the entire Internet if someone else gets your password.

When you have successfully completed the installation, you should see a WordPress Dashboard window as shown in Figure 8-5.

Using a MAMP/WAMP or Docker are not the only ways to install WordPress locally, nor are you required to do this yourself if the computer you are using is already preconfigured. Your school might already have WordPress set up for you and you can simply log in and see a Dashboard window like that shown in Figure 8-5.

Many schools and employers have already installed and configured WordPress. To ensure that WordPress is installed correctly, most paid web hosts also offer a WordPress installation and default configuration as part of the startup for a new website. The typical starting point for a professional website is adding content to a WordPress installation, which is the next topic in this section of the chapter.

Common Mistakes

You may have read this warning before in this course, but it bears repeating. Setting up a web server appears to be a simple task. Configuring the localhost environment you performed earlier in this chapter is similar to that performed by a systems administrator on a production web server exposed to the Internet.

However, a web server exposed to the Internet needs to be carefully configured, patched, and protected from hackers so that it doesn't become a host for unintended webpages and webpage content. Moreover, an e-commerce website that handles credit card information needs even more security so that it doesn't become the vector for stolen information.

Leave the setup and configuration of the web server to the professionals. WordPress runs securely on a well-configured web server. Many web hosting companies offer a one-click installation of WordPress on one of their servers, freeing you to use the tools for what they do well—creating and configuring webpage contents—while letting the hosting company take care of configuring the hardware and software that make secure web servers functional.

Quick Check 8-2

1. Why is a database necessary for storing WordPress webpages?
   a. Because the contents and templates for the webpages are stored in the database
   b. Because webpages can't be stored outside of a database
   c. Because the localhost can't run successfully without the configuration stored in the database
   d. It isn't. WordPress will run without a database, just not as quickly.

2. Why is it important to use lengthy and complex passwords and account names to access your WordPress website?
   a. It's a requirement of the web server.
   b. Because you edit the website from the website itself, so the login is exposed to the Internet and can be hacked
   c. To avoid having to use captchas, which is the other preferred means of ensuring a human being is logging in
   d. To prevent web browsers from caching your WordPress login credentials

3. What are two ways to install WordPress on a local computer?
   a. As a standalone application and as part of a WAMP/MAMP stack
   b. As part of a WAMP/MAMP stack and in a Docker container
   c. As localhost or as a virtual web server
   d. The hard way and the easy way

1) a. WordPress stores the contents of its websites in the MySQL database it is connected to. **2) b.** The WordPress interface that you use to edit your site is stored in the same location on the same web server as your website, so it is available to you and anyone else who wants to try to edit it. **3) b.** Both the WAMP/MAMP stack and the Docker container can be used successfully for local WordPress development.

8.3 Creating a Website Using a CMS

If you already have WordPress installed on a computer that you can access, start WordPress now following the startup procedure you were given. This should also start a localhost web server so that you can use the WordPress interface as it runs on a web server.

This simulates the situation that many developers adopt where they build a website on their own laptop or desktop and, when local development is completed, export the new or updated site to the remote web server. As updates and improvements are needed, the developer makes those changes first on their local instance, then exports the changes to the remote server.

Before you begin work, download the starting files for Chapter 8 to a handy location on your computer so you can upload the images and access the other files easily.

The WordPress Dashboard Tour

The title bar of the WordPress window shown earlier in Figure 8-5 includes the following controls:

- **WordPress logo:** The logo appears as an icon. Move the pointer over the icon to open the WordPress menu, including the About WordPress option along with links to the online Documentation, Support, and Feedback pages that the WordPress community contribute to.

  Use the About WordPress page when determining the version number of WordPress that you have installed for compatibility with WordPress themes and plug-ins. WordPress themes are preconfigured styles and page layouts that include CSS code and designated places for displaying your page contents. WordPress plug-ins are similar to JavaScript library plug-ins. They are code bundles that extend the larger application, which in this case is WordPress.

- **Home icon and site name:** The site name is for the default site that this version of WordPress is connected to. If you don't have a site name, you can create one using the Appearance option in the left pane. The site name also serves as the link you click to review your most recent updates and changes to the website you are building as it is running on the local web server.

- **Speech bubble and counter:** In Figure 8-5, the counter is set to 0, which is the total count of comments that have been made about your site and the total amount of feedback you have received since you started your site. You can change this counter as soon as you have a site by leaving yourself site feedback.

- **+New button:** Move your pointer over the +New button to display a menu with options for creating a new post, media, page, or user. You use the Post option to create a new blog post. You select the Media option to upload pictures or videos. You use the Page option to create a new webpage and the User option to create a new user. Adding a new person to the authorized users allows you to add site content authors, editors, or administrators who can contribute content and modify the website. This won't be useful on your local machine, but it will on a remote server.

The commonly used features on the title bar are replicated as single items in the menu in the left pane, which includes the following options:

- **Dashboard:** This option takes you back home to the WordPress Dashboard. Additionally, clicking this link shows the content pane, which displays useful features to give you information about your site status.

- **Posts:** This option is specifically tailored to using WordPress as a blog engine. While outside of the scope of this course, the Posts option is an important feature for some people to incorporate a blog into a full-featured website.

- **Media:** Use this item to upload images and videos to your website and incorporate them into your webpages. Because WordPress is self-contained, you need to upload your images before you can incorporate them into your webpages. The Media handler also allows you to delete old or unused images and it tells you which images aren't currently being used in your webpages.

- **Pages:** As you may have guessed, this option is the primary means of managing the webpages that you need to create and update in WordPress. Click the Pages option to display the primary webpage management tools, shown in **Figure 8-7**. You use the Pages tools to add and delete webpages or access them directly for editing.

Figure 8-7   Pages tools

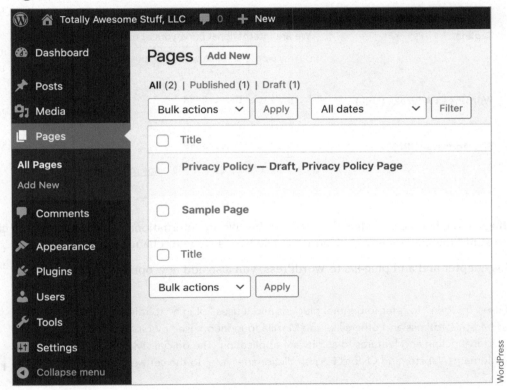

- **Comments:** This option displays feedback from your website users. Comments can help improve site usability, though some site administrators prefer to have a more formal process that requires a login, captcha, or email address so anonymous users don't post useless feedback.

- **Appearance:** The appearance of your WordPress website is controlled primarily by the WordPress theme you are using. As you have learned, WordPress themes are made up of styles and formatting for the webpages in the website. Many free WordPress themes are available online. When you have become an adept WordPress user and are comfortable modifying an existing theme, you can even create your own.

- **Plugins:** Use this option to open the page for managing the software extensions you have installed on your website. You can download free plug-ins using the tools in your dashboard or upload plug-ins you have purchased using the same toolset.

- **Users:** Select this option to manage users and assign them roles. User management is an important part of website maintenance if you are using a team-based approach, even if all members of your team are full stack developers. The division of tasks allows for greater creativity through collaboration. Assigning one person the Editor role helps to ensure uniformity in the wording of the webpage.

- **Tools** and **Settings:** These two options are the "And Everything Else" options of WordPress. Chances are, if you are wondering where to find an option that doesn't appear in the other menus, you will find it here.

When you select Settings, WordPress displays the General Settings page, which contains text boxes for setting or updating your site title and tagline. **Figure 8-8** shows entries for the Totally Awesome Stuff site.

Figure 8-8   General Settings page

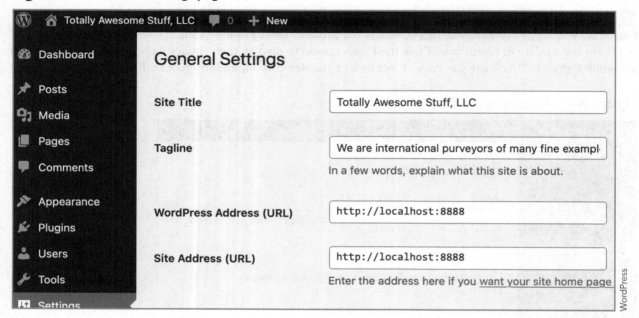

In WordPress, click Settings in the left pane, update the title and the "We are international purveyors of many fine examples of totally awesome stuff." tagline as shown in Figure 8-8, and then save your changes.

As you work through this chapter and add plug-ins to WordPress, you also add new options to these menus.

Note	This chapter uses "plug-in" to refer to general plug-ins and it uses "plugin" to refer to those labeled as such by WordPress. WordPress and others like the Mozilla foundation use "plugin" to refer to a software package that adds function and features to a software application. The official style guide from Microsoft and both the Merriam-Webster and Oxford English dictionaries refer to the software package as a "plug-in."
	Like other fantastically mundane controversies such as which make better pets, cats or dogs, this one has the potential to be debated for years to come. The current trend is toward using the nonhyphenated name to refer to all software that extends a base application, but the accepted standard is to include the hyphen.
	Because the author and editors of this text prefer to stay on the fence and out of the fray, we defer to the WordPress standard when referring to a tool, menu option, page name, or other part of the WordPress software labeled as a "plugin." Otherwise, this chapter and others use the hyphenated form of "plug-in."
	Also, the answer is clearly dogs, by a nose.

Choosing a Theme

You are not required to choose a theme before you use WordPress to begin constructing a website. However, it is sometimes useful to think about the possibilities and constraints created by the theme before building the site. An alternative approach is to build the contents of the core pages of a website, then try different themes to define the layout and appearance of your pages.

The advantage of choosing a theme first is that it provides a concrete template of where each major webpage component will appear while you are building your website. The theme you choose displays the header in a certain size and the navigation in a specific position, for example.

The advantage of creating the core pages before applying a theme is that after you gain experience with WordPress, you can visualize what makes for a good WordPress website, and then you can find or build a theme that matches your image.

Both are valid approaches. The first is more often used when novice users are exploring the WordPress options, while more seasoned WordPress users often adopt the second approach.

To select a WordPress theme:

1. In WordPress, click the Appearance option in the left pane to display the Themes management page.
2. At the top of the Themes management page, click Add New to display the Add Themes page.
3. On the Add Themes toolbar, click Feature Filter to open a page where you can filter for themes that will work with the Totally Awesome Stuff, LLC, e-commerce site in its WordPress version.
4. Check the boxes for the E-Commerce, Accessibility Ready, Grid Layout, and Left Sidebar in the Subject, Features, and Layout lists. Note that your list options may differ slightly from those in **Figure 8-9**.

Figure 8-9   Add Themes page with filter selections

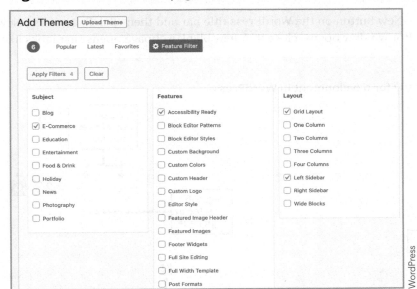

You are selecting the Grid Layout and Left Sidebar layout because the design of the Totally Awesome Stuff website uses a left sidebar for the menu along with a grid layout for some pages. You can explore other options, but keep in mind that these filters are additive, so as you include more criteria, you decrease the number of themes that match them.

5. Click the Apply Filters button and then review the themes in the search results. A theme called Neve appears to be worth further exploration for the future content of Totally Awesome Stuff. The figures in this chapter show the Neve theme, but you are also encouraged to choose your own theme to explore after completing this tutorial. Any of the themes for E-commerce and Accessibility fulfill the project requirements, regardless of the layout of the website contents.

   On the Appearance page, you can move your pointer over a theme thumbnail and then click the Details & Preview button to learn more about a selected theme. All of the new themes should include "responsive" in their list of descriptive words.

6. Click the Install button in the lower-right corner of the theme you have chosen. Then click the Activate button for the theme to make it the active theme for the next step in your WordPress webpage development journey. Finally, close the Details & Preview view, if necessary.

> **Note** While in the previous chapters you first built a full-screen website, then rebuilt it as a mobile-first design website, the authors of the WordPress themes you are exploring have addressed responsive design criteria in their themes to reduce your workload. The layout of the newest themes should be mobile-first by design, and since you are adding your content to that framework, you will be creating pages that are responsive simply by using the theme as it was intended.
>
> It is still a good idea to test your website using an emulator at the mobile, tablet, and full-screen breakpoints, however.

Building the Home Page

As you may recall, the home page for TotallyAwesomeStuff.com is a landing page that features the site branding and serves primarily as an introduction to other pages in the site. In WordPress, you need to build the contents of this page within the context of a WordPress template rather than from scratch using HTML and CSS.

The work of learning to use WordPress is not in becoming familiar with a new language with complicated technical details or syntax. Instead, it involves learning how to use the WordPress interface options.

To build the Totally Awesome Stuff home page:

1. Move your mouse pointer over the +New button on the WordPress title bar and then click Page on the New menu. If a Welcome to the block editor window opens, close it. A new blank webpage opens that looks like that in **Figure 8-10**.

Figure 8-10 Blank webpage ready for development in WordPress

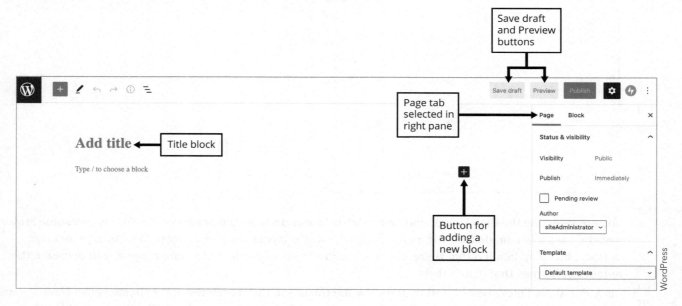

WordPress uses the concept of a **block** to create a page. Each block is a container for a specific type of webpage content including images, headers, tables, footers, sidebars, and menus. Each block contains a unique part of the webpage in the theme-based layout.

2. Click inside the title block where the default text is Add Title, and then type **Welcome to Totally Awesome Stuff, LLC!** as the title of the page. This title also becomes the default name of the page, though you can change the page name from within WordPress.

3. Click the [+] button to add a new block to your webpage, and then click Heading to display the default options on the Heading menu. Because this new block is made up of text to create a secondary heading, you can leave the heading size at H2.

4. Click inside the new heading block and type **We are international purveyors of many fine examples of totally awesome stuff.** as the heading.

5. Below the new heading block you just added, click the [+] button, expand the menu options by clicking Browse all, and then click the Columns option. On the Columns menu, choose two 50/50 columns to create two columns of equal width.

6. Repeat step 5 to add a total of two rows of two columns to replicate the foursquare look of the original home page. You should now have a page that looks like that in **Figure 8-11**.

Figure 8-11   Adding blocks to the home page for Totally Awesome Stuff

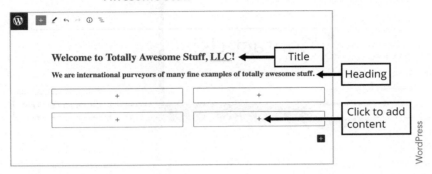

7. Inside each of the four cells you just created, click the + button and then click Image. On the Image menu, select the about_us.png, catalog.png, contact_us.png, and people_places.png image from the Chapter_8\ images folder as appropriate for each cell. For each image, add alt text using the options in the right pane.

8. Click the Save draft button in the upper-right corner of the window. You should get in the habit of clicking the Save draft button after you make a few major changes to each page so you have less work to make up if something breaks or stops working.

Note that in WordPress, you are always prompted to save your changes before leaving an editing page. If you try to move to a different page without saving your changes, WordPress reminds you that you have unsaved changes and asks you to confirm if you want to leave the page. If you choose to stay, you can continue editing or you can click the Save draft button to save your changes.

That's it! You've created your first WordPress webpage.

9. To the right of the Save draft button, click Preview. You can preview your work on a desktop, tablet, or mobile device. Click Mobile, since mobile-first design is a principle you want to follow in this website.

The mobile preview shows you that the images are stacked vertically, and the heading and subheading arrange themselves on the screen appropriately. Since the page does not have a navigation block with data in it yet, the navigation menu isn't visible. When you add pages to the navigation block, you can confirm that it is mobile-first by default by choosing the Mobile option on the Preview menu.

Note

Depending on the theme you are using, you may or may not recognize the page that you were just working on when it opens in the preview window. Some themes come bundled with a Search block by default, for example, and others come with many blocks that you didn't see when you were building the initial page. This is because a WordPress theme is an empty template that you add your content to. The page layout and some default blocks are already present in the theme before you start adding your own content.

If the theme you are using introduces extra blocks that you don't want in your page, you can remove them. To do this, change the preview from Mobile to Desktop so you can see the whole page. Click an extra or unwanted block, and then click the three dots button. On the menu, click Remove XXXX, where XXXX is the name of the block, as in Remove Search. This option is highlighted at the bottom of the menu in **Figure 8-12**.

Figure 8-12 Removing a block from a webpage in WordPress

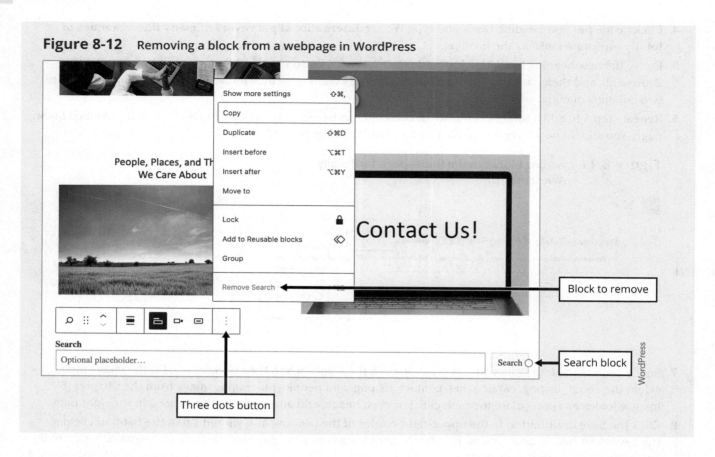

People, Places, and Th
We Care About

Show more settings   ⇧⌘,
Copy
Duplicate   ⇧⌘D
Insert before   ⌥⌘T
Insert after   ⌥⌘Y
Move to

Lock   🔒
Add to Reusable blocks   《》
Group

Remove Search

Contact Us!

Block to remove

Search
Optional placeholder…   Search ○

Search block

WordPress

Three dots button

10. Change to the Tablet preview. Notice that the images get larger and the header text rearranges itself.

11. Finally, change to the Desktop view to see the full-screen version of your new home page.

WordPress includes these three preview display sizes so you can test your webpages without having to use the browser's emulator. The developers of WordPress have included this handy preview feature, along with many others, because they are necessary in a mobile-first world.

Updating the Metadata

Your new home page by default has the name used in the Title field at the top of the page, which is Totally Awesome Stuff, LLC! For a page like this one where the title should be welcoming and the name should be Home, you need to update the data about this page. Information of this type is called **metadata**—data about the data on the page.

The right pane provides a menu of options that apply to the page or the block, depending on which is selected. In **Figure 8-13**, the pane includes the Permalink options, which apply to the page. (You might need to click the link in the URL box first.) Your screen may differ depending on the version of WordPress you are using.

The URL Slug box or the URL dialog box shows the link the WordPress engine will use to access the page. A WordPress **slug** is the short name used to create links to a blog post or webpage. (The origin of the use of the word *slug* comes from newspapers, where the short name for a news article was used to simplify the description of the article.) The slug is also used to create the WordPress **permalink**, which is the internal navigation name stored in the database for the website.

The only time it is a good idea to edit this webpage metadata in WordPress is before you publish your new webpage. If you edit the URL Slug value after you publish your webpage, the metadata for the website and webpage will not match, causing Googlebots to downgrade your website.

To update the metadata:

1. Click Permalink in the right pane to expand the section. (You might need to click the link in the URL box instead.)

Figure 8-13   URL Slug box for a webpage

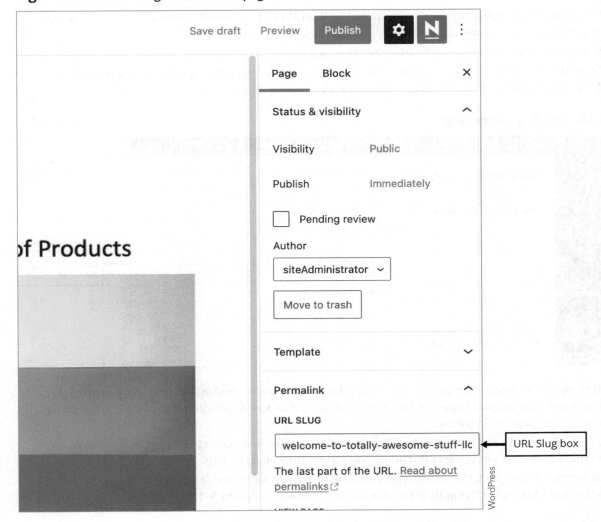

2. Update the link in the URL Slug or Permalink box to **home** in all lowercase text because the page you created is the home page for the Totally Awesome Stuff website. The slug text must be lowercase and should not use spaces as it becomes the basis for creating a link to the page in all of the menus. Close the URL dialog box, if necessary.

3. Click the Save draft button to save your changes.

4. Review your webpage, and then click the Publish button. (If a Publish pane opens, click the Publish button again.) Publishing makes the current version of the webpage available to anyone who has access to the URL. Because you are running this WordPress instance on your local machine, only you can view your published webpage. However, if you were running this website on a publicly visible web server, publishing your webpage would make your updates, including any mistakes, visible to the outside world.

Congratulations! You have just published your first WordPress webpage. You can bask in the warm glow of not having to write a single character of HTML, CSS, or JavaScript to create a well-formed, standards-compliant website with a mobile-first design.

Next Steps

The next task in setting up the WordPress version of Totally Awesome Stuff is to designate the home page in the WordPress site configuration. If a browser requests the URL https://totallyawesomestuff.com, the WordPress web server needs to know which page to return. This URL does not end with "default.html" or "index.html," which would specify the page. To set the default home page, you need to change the Reading settings.

To designate the default starting page:

1. Click the WordPress logo on the title bar to return to the WordPress Dashboard, and then click the Settings option to expand the Settings menu.

2. Click the Reading option to display the Reading Settings page.

3. Click the "A static page (select below)" option button in the "Your homepage displays" area as shown in **Figure 8-14**, and then select the home page you just created.

Figure 8-14 Reading Settings page

The other option shown in this pane—the "Your latest posts" option button—is useful if you are using WordPress as a blogging engine. However, since you are using it as a web development platform, the static home page will greet your site visitors.

4. If necessary, scroll down to the bottom of the Reading Settings pane and then click Save Changes to update the site metadata to always show users the home page when they visit the site.

5. To see what users will see, click the website preview link to Totally Awesome Stuff (the site name in the WordPress title bar) to display the mobile-sized home page shown in **Figure 8-15**.

Figure 8-15 Mobile-sized Totally Awesome
Stuff home page

Your fabulous new home page appears as it will to your website visitors, though WordPress tools are still available so you can navigate back to your editing screen. Since you are currently logged in to the web server as an authenticated site administrator, you are viewing a live version of your website using the same engine as your users, though with a higher level of permissions.

The home page for Totally Awesome Stuff should also include a menu and footer. Additionally, each image on the home page needs a link users can click to navigate to each content area. One quirk of WordPress is that you can't create links to pages that don't exist yet because navigation menu items are stored as data in the database, not as links. The database can't store empty values as placeholders for those pages. The navigation menu must link to pages you've already created.

If you add a menu at this point, it can link only to the home page, since that's the only page in the website. In the next section, you first create pages to link to from this home page, and then create the navigation menu for your pages.

Quick Check 8-3

1. What is one advantage of choosing a WordPress theme before you begin building a website?

   a. The theme will update itself as you add website contents to it during development.
   b. You can't update to a different theme if you are partway through the development process and realize the theme doesn't work with your website contents.
   c. The theme will use different plugins depending on the content you add to it.
   d. Choosing a theme first provides a concrete template of the webpage design and layout while you are building your website.

2. How do you publish your webpages when developing them in WordPress?

   a. You click the Publish button.
   b. You copy and paste the file or use FTP to transfer the newly completed webpage to the website folder on the WordPress web server.
   c. You click the Save button.
   d. You click the Preview and Post button.

3. What is a block in WordPress?

   a. A distinct part of one menu in the WordPress window
   b. A completed composition of webpage, theme, and plugin elements that becomes a single WordPress webpage
   c. One of the four applications that needs to be running to compose WordPress webpages in the CDA
   d. A container for one part of the webpage contents

1) d. If you know how a page will look before you start building it, you can think about how the content will appear in the theme. **2) a.** Clicking the Publish button finalizes your changes to a webpage and makes them visible to users. **3) d.** A block in WordPress is a container for content in a WordPress webpage.

8.4 Exploring WordPress Features

One purpose of the Totally Awesome Stuff website is to sell products. WordPress has plug-ins for e-commerce sites, which include product list and shopping cart widgets. The Totally Awesome Stuff website also has a Contact Us page to gather information from users in an organized way. WordPress provides plug-ins specifically designed to handle the contact form, since it is a common feature of many websites.

Using your favorite search engine, search for "WordPress e-commerce plug-in." The search results include a range of opinions about the best plug-ins, but a consistent consensus is that WooCommerce is better than the others. WooCommerce is the standard for WordPress e-commerce plug-ins.

Adding Your First Plug-In

1. Return to the WordPress Dashboard, if necessary. In the left pane of the WordPress window, click Plugins (or move the pointer over it), and then choose Add New. The Add Plugins window opens. See **Figure 8-16**.

Figure 8-16   WordPress Add Plugins window

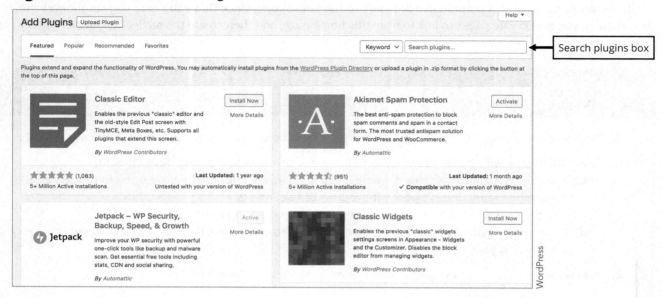

2. In the Search plugins box, type **WooCommerce** to search for the WooCommerce plug-in. After a short pause, WooCommerce appears in the search results.

3. Scroll down in the list to find plug-ins that refer to WooCommerce, such as the WooCommerce Google Analytics Integration plug-in. These plug-ins further extend the WooCommerce plug-in.

    Note that WooCommerce has more than 5 million active installations and thousands of positive reviews. These are key metrics to identify whether a plug-in is worth exploring. The wisdom of crowds indicates that WooCommerce is a good plug-in to use in your own site. Plug-ins with few users and few reviews should be treated with some skepticism.

4. Click More Details in the WooCommerce plug-in to display information the developers provided to describe WooCommerce features and integrations with other plug-ins. Note the list of contributors on the right side of the Details window. Actual people put their names on this plug-in—not because they want to get paid but because they are invested in the success of their software package.

5. Click the Installation tab to display installation details, including the required versions of PHP and MySQL. Note that automatic installation is possible. Not all plug-ins offer this easy integration with the standard WordPress installation. For some, especially those you are required to purchase, you must download the zip file containing the plug-in only after completing the purchase. You can then load the plug-in manually.

> **Note** If you need to buy a WordPress plug-in that doesn't offer an automatic installation, you can still use the WordPress Add Plugins window to successfully install it. Figure 8-16 shows the Upload Plugin button at the top of the Add Plugins window. Click the Upload Plugin button to select the zip file that you receive when you buy a plug-in. The automated installation proceeds from there.

6. Click the FAQ tab to display links to other helpful documentation, including the Getting Started guide and New WooCommerce Store Owner Guide. It is a good idea to read both guides, or at least open and bookmark pages to refer to later when you need help. Additionally, note the WooCommerce Support Forum. This is where the community of WooCommerce users provides help to each other and to new users.

    To return to these links after you have completed the installation, reopen the Add Plugins window and filter for the specific plug-in you need help with.

7. Close the Details window and then take a deep breath and click the Install Now button.

8. After the automated installation is complete, click Activate.

That's all you need to do to install WooCommerce. The "Welcome to WooCommerce" five-step configuration wizard guides you through the steps to use the plug-in successfully. You can stop completing the configuration steps if asked to set up the financial information, since you won't be accepting credit cards or attaching a digital account to the example used in this tutorial.

Note that the left pane in WordPress has now been updated to include WooCommerce along with the necessary submenus.

Exploring the Plug-In Features

WordPress plug-ins such as WooCommerce create webpages as necessary to add features to your WordPress website. As you explore WooCommerce, you create a Products page for the Totally Awesome Stuff website.

To explore WooCommerce:

1. Click the WooCommerce option in the left pane of the WordPress window.

2. Click a few options on the WooCommerce menu. These options include e-commerce configuration options, such as the shipping cost and local tax rate updates. Since you are running this website locally and not taking orders, those options do not apply to this tutorial.

   The next update to make is to load a list of products. This action creates the Products page, along with tools that allow users to add items to a WooCommerce shopping cart. Recall that you must create a page before you can create a link to that page in a navigation menu.

3. Click the Products option on the menu and then click the Import button to open the Import products from a CSV file window. See **Figure 8-17**.

Figure 8-17   Import products from a CSV file window

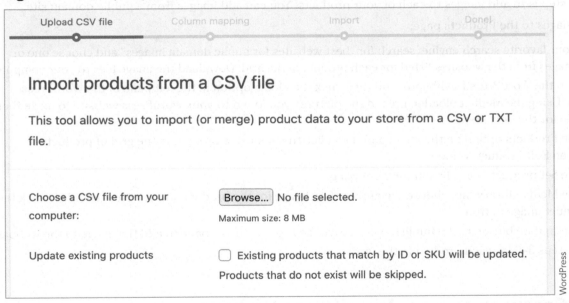

4. Click the Browse button or the Choose File button, choose TAS_Items.csv from the Chapter_8 folder, and then click Open. The file is a simple spreadsheet of comma-separated values for the products sold by Totally Awesome Stuff.

5. Click the Continue button to open a window that maps the data in the CSV file to the commonly used columns in the Products table. **Figure 8-18** shows which values in the Products table map to the values in the CSV file. Update the values as necessary.

   The column names from the CSV file are on the left and the closest matching column for the WooCommerce Products table are chosen from the boxes on the right. Since WooCommerce does not have a "Country of Origin" field, the Short description is the next best alternative, for example.

Figure 8-18 Mapping imported fields

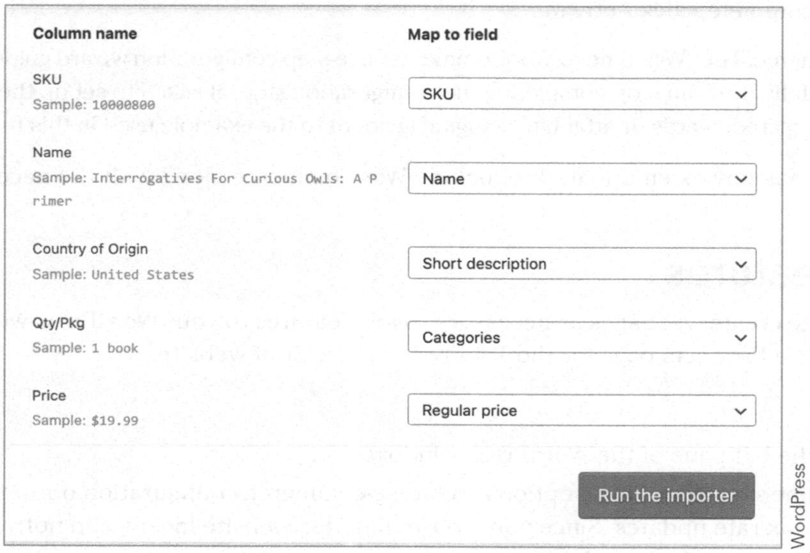

6. When you have set up the importer as it is in Figure 8-18, click the Run the importer button to import the fields and values from the CSV file.

7. Click the View products button to display the recently imported products in your Products grid. Click the View products option in the WordPress title bar to preview the layout of the products grid.

8. Click an item to display the details of that product. You can also add the product to the Shopping Cart and then view the shopping cart. The WooCommerce plug-in provides these features by default.

The next step is to add images to each of your products. You can add images from a public domain site.

To add images to the Products page:

1. Using your favorite search engine, search for "best websites for public domain images" and choose one or more images from the websites listed for each product in the grid. Download the image files to your computer.

2. Return to the WordPress Dashboard, and then click the Media option in the left pane of the WordPress window. Using the Media uploader, upload the pictures you found to your WordPress website to make them available for the next step.

3. Click the Products option on the menu and then click the name of a product in the grid of products to display an Edit Product window.

4. Click the Set product image link in the right pane.

5. Click the Media Library tab, choose the appropriate image for the product you selected, and then click the Set product image button.

6. Click the Update button in the Publish pane above the Product image pane to add the image to the webpage.

7. Repeat steps 3–6 for each product in the grid.

Adding Features to Your WordPress Website

After installing WooCommerce and creating the Products page, you need to update the navigation menu for the site. Each theme has its own style and location options for the navigation menu. This is key to remembering where you update the menu.

To update the navigation menu:

1. In the WordPress window, click Appearance and then click the Theme Details button for the active theme, such as Neve.

2. Click the Menus button to open the Menus window. **Figure 8-19** shows the window with menus added for the site.

Figure 8-19 WordPress Menus window

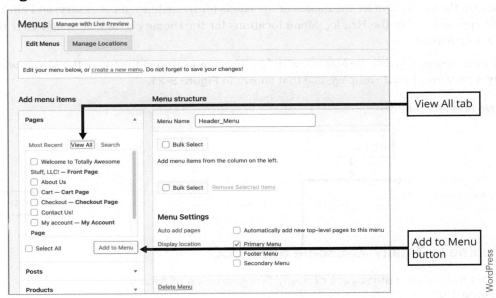

Make sure Header_Menu appears in the Menu Name box since that is the menu you want to update. (Add a menu with the name **Header_Menu** and the Primary Menu display location, if necessary.) Note that your Menus window may display fewer pages in the Pages section than the ones shown in Figure 8-19.

3. On the View All tab, check the boxes for the home page (called the "Front Page") and the Shop Page and then click the Add to Menu button to add links to the menu for the selected pages.

    The new menu items appear in the Menu structure box at the right, but the text does not accurately describe each item. These are the Home and the Products pages rather than the Front and Shop Pages.

4. Click the Front Page arrow button to expand the section and then change the text to **Home** in the Navigation Label box. Click the Shop Page arrow button and then change the Navigation Label text to **Products**, shown in **Figure 8-20**.

Figure 8-20 Renaming options on the navigation menu

5. Click the Save Menu button to create the navigation menu.

You follow the same steps to create any menu with WordPress—create the pages; check the boxes for the links to the pages that should appear in the menu; update the names of the labels for those links, if necessary; and click Save Menu. This same menu will appear in all of the Header_Menu locations for the theme chosen, although your theme may have a side or footer menu instead.

Another option to edit menu items is to use the Manage with Live Preview button at the top of the Menus window. Click that button to display a preview of your webpage like that shown in **Figure 8-21**.

Figure 8-21   Manage Live Preview window

The Home and Products links already appear in the navigation menu in the upper-right corner of the page. As you add menu items, they also appear in the navigation menu.

The navigation menu will work well on all of your pages, but the title and tagline shown in Figure 8-21 are too similar. The Neve theme repeats the title and tagline above the header, but since the page already contains this text, you can remove the title and tagline using the Manage Live Preview window.

To remove theme options, click the block in the header or point to the title and then click the pencil icon to select it. In the left pane, click the slider buttons for Show Site Tagline and Show Site Title to remove those elements. See **Figure 8-22**.

Figure 8-22   Removing the tagline and title

Click the Publish button to save your changes and then view your newly completed website in your browser.

Quick Check 8-4

1. How do you add plug-ins to a WordPress website?

    a. By copying and pasting the code of the plug-in into files stored in the resources folder of the website

    b. By downloading the plug-in code and then saving the file as a *filename*.pl file in the plug-ins directory for the website

    c. By clicking a button in the Add Plugins window

    d. By using a hotlink to the external file that contains the code for the plug-in

2. Why do some plug-ins have additional plug-ins in WordPress?

    a. To extend the features of the original plug-in

    b. To fix mistakes made in the original plug-in

    c. To add security or responsive display to the original plug-in

    d. To make more money for the developers of both plug-ins by selling twice as many products

3. How do you build the WordPress webpages that incorporate features provided by WooCommerce or another similar plug-in?

    a. You don't; the plug-in builds the webpages for you.

    b. You start with a blank page and drag and drop WooCommerce blocks into the sections where you want to display them.

    c. You choose the type of page from the menu in the theme that WooCommerce uses and the WooCommerce theme builds the page for you.

    d. Similar to other WordPress webpages, you use the Pages menu to choose the type of page to display and then configure the logical blocks into a completed page.

1) c. You use the Add Plugins window to manage new plug-ins. **2) a.** Plug-ins add features to the original software they are associated with. **3) a.** WordPress plug-ins like WooCommerce create webpages as necessary to add features to your WordPress website.

8.5 Publishing a Website Using a CMS

You have been using a localhost setup to create a functioning web server on your local computer. This works well to simulate the experience of creating content and publishing WordPress webpages that use themes and plug-ins. However, a laptop or desktop is not configured to be a fully functioning web server, nor should it be.

To make your webpages visible to the users of the Internet, you need to publish the pages to a web server that is open to the outside world. That web server can be hosted by your school, your employer, or a paid web hosting company. The web server has the necessary hardware and proper software configuration to securely handle the network traffic that hosting a website requires.

The alternative approach is to develop your website on the live web server. This approach avoids the challenges of remote server deployment but creates a more constrained sandbox for experimentation and development, since you are working on a live site while users are potentially interacting with it.

Even if you are careful about managing your development, the chances of making a mistake and unintentionally deploying it to production are greater using the approach of editing a live website. This option is best left to seasoned WordPress developers.

Finding a Web Host

You can use an Internet search to find any number of companies willing to take your credit card number and set you up with a login and a WordPress instance on one of their servers. Bluehost is the official partner of WordPress and offers several tiers of products, from free hosting for limited domains to high-throughput commercial sites with unlimited storage for a more significant price. Bluehost also offers well-regarded customer support. However, it is just one of many available hosts for WordPress websites.

If you use your favorite search engine to search for "best hosts for WordPress," you can review the rankings in the search results. Web hosts vary by price, levels of support, and customer service. It is worth reading the reviews of these hosts while considering the intended purpose of your WordPress website.

As with every online review, view with skepticism the overly enthusiastic positive comments and the unnecessarily negative ones. Most actual customers who use a product or service offer more moderate or nuanced reviews if they leave one at all. Pay attention to the number of reviews—the more reviews, the greater validity to the consensus.

Being an informed consumer of the web hosting service is an important part of being a full stack developer. The decision of where your website is hosted may be made for you when you are starting out in your tenure as a full stack web developer, but as you gain experience, you might consider a freelance web development career. You would then be responsible for finding the appropriate host for your customers' sites.

Established, well-known WordPress hosts like GoDaddy, Google Domains, and Amazon Lightsail are worth investigating. It might seem like a bargain to go with an inexpensive, little-known web host, but the software engineers who provide support for the larger domains are more likely to be available for the full lifespan of your WordPress website. You will get access to better hardware, networking, and software updates with an established host. In short, you get what you pay for.

Deploying Your Local Site to a Remote Web Server

A WordPress plug-in can automate exporting your WordPress site to an external host. You can also perform the migration manually and go through the gritty details of moving each component individually via File Transfer Protocol (FTP) using an FTP application.

If you use the plug-in route (and you would be smart to do this if you are allowed by your web host), you can use the Add Plugins window to search for the WordPress Duplicator plug-in. You can review the documentation at https://wordpress.org/plugins/duplicator.

Installing and using the Duplicator plug-in is similar to other plug-ins that perform the same tasks, but Duplicator is the most reviewed and downloaded of the plug-ins that transfer a WordPress website.

As you install the Duplicator plug-in, it adds a menu option to the WordPress dashboard. The Duplicator window that opens from that option walks you through creating a copy of your website and provides an installer that you use to reinstall your website on the remote web server.

You can also use the Duplicator plug-in to create backup copies of your website at periodic intervals so you can store those copies securely on a backup drive or in source control.

The documentation and videos on the Duplicator plug-in page explain how to use the plug-in to move a WordPress website from a local computer to a remote web server. The videos also show why many WordPress developers use Duplicator—because of its ease of use and variety of options.

The alternative approach is to use an FTP client to move the file contents of your local web server to the remote host. The FTP client will show two panes containing the files and folders of your local computer and the remote computer. You can either click and drag the files or select the files and then click a button to move your files and folders from the local to the remote server.

You also need to move the contents of the MySQL database that holds the data and configuration for your WordPress website to the remote web server to mirror your local configuration. You can read more about doing so by searching for "using FTP to transfer a WordPress website."

The steps are straightforward, but the technical details are more difficult to get right than using a plug-in to accomplish the same outcome.

Common Mistakes

Before you deploy your local website to a remote server, you should test the entire website or webpage depending on the scope of the changes you are moving. Small changes or updates to a plug-in, theme, block, or webpage can have unintended consequences to the page or website.

Changes to a shared element like a header or navigation should be tested sitewide. Changes that modify only part of one page should still result in testing the entire page.

Develop and use a testing plan for each incremental change. This testing plan should include what was changed, where it affects the website, and how to test to ensure that the website still meets the requirements.

It is always a good idea to have another website editor or web developer test your changes before moving something new into production. When you are developing your website, you will be focused on the change itself and you may easily miss the negative outcome related to your change on a different section of the same page or on a different page.

This course does not require you to perform the task of moving your website from a local to remote web server since you would need to register a domain and clutter the Internet with yet another copy of totallyawesomestuff.com.

Quick Check 8-5

1. What is an advantage of editing a live WordPress website on the web server hosting it?

    a. You can experiment with different themes and plug-ins without affecting the live site.

    b. You can check for mistakes you made or errors that the themes or plug-ins are creating in your actual production environment.

    c. You can avoid using a plug-in or FTP to move your local development to the remote server.

    d. The local setup doesn't usually match the remote web server configuration, so editing directly on the remote server bypasses potential configuration errors.

2. How can you identify a good web host for your WordPress website?

    a. Read the documentation provided by the hosts and look for the WordPress logo.

    b. Ask for recommendations from the WordPress authors.

    c. Move your website to a host and test it and the host yourself.

    d. Read the documentation provided by the web hosts for WordPress and then read the reviews by knowledgeable reviewers and website developers.

3. What is the best way to deploy a local WordPress website to a remote web server?

    a. Use a plug-in to automate the task.

    b. Use a theme to automate the task.

    c. Use a source control software application to automate the task.

    d. Use the command-line interface to automate the task.

1) c. Avoiding the need to use an automated tool to move your WordPress website doesn't outweigh the potential consequences of the other options to this question. **2) d.** The collective wisdom of many users of the services provided by web hosts is a good guide. **3) a.** Using a plug-in to automate the task of deploying a WordPress website from local computer to remote server is a web development best practice.

Summary

- A content management system (CMS) is a software application used to manage a website, including creating webpage contents and website layouts.

- WordPress is one example of an open source CMS.

- WordPress is the most popular CMS because it is easy to use and feature-rich.

- WordPress can be run on a local computer by installing it as part of the WAMP/MAMP stack or in a Docker container.

- The startup screen in WordPress is called the dashboard. It contains the base menu that is extended when plug-ins are added.

- WordPress themes are configuration files for styling webpages developed in WordPress.

- WordPress provides tools for downloading and installing themes and plug-ins.

- To make your webpages available on the Internet, you need to publish the pages to a web server that is open to the outside world, such as one hosted by your school, your employer, or a paid web hosting company.

- The local copy of a WordPress website can be uploaded to a remote web server using a plug-in designed for that purpose or using FTP and doing the transfer of the components manually.

Key Terms

block	content management system (CMS)	plug-ins
content delivery application (CDA)	metadata	slug
content management application (CMA)	permalink	themes

Review Questions

1. Why do both beginning and seasoned web developers prefer using a CMS to create websites? (8.1)

   a. A CMS allows the developer to translate concepts into pages faster and more easily than writing the raw code that makes up the webpages.

   b. The CMS allows for more seamless development of the HTML, CSS, and JavaScript that make up the webpages.

   c. A CMS allows the developer to write the HTML, CSS, and JavaScript used for the webpage on the web server itself.

   d. The CMS has a user-friendly interface that combines the code writing, storage, and webpage deployment into a single unit.

2. What does a CMA do in a CMS? (8.1)

   a. It is the webpage rendering engine in the CMS.

   b. It is the webpage development and website configuration engine of the CMS.

   c. It is the source control component to a CMS.

   d. It coordinates the different operations of the operating system, database, programming language, and web server software that make up a CMS.

3. Why does installing WordPress on a local computer also require installing a complete web server stack? (8.2)

    a. To use the CDA to manage the contents of your website in your web browser

    b. To use the CMA, deliver the contents of your website in your web browser

    c. To recreate the web server stack that will be used on the remote web server for testing the website prior to deployment

    d. Because doing website development on WordPress running locally requires your machine to provide the WordPress interface that uses the CDA and CMA in your browser

4. What is the difference between a WordPress theme and a WordPress plug-in? (8.3)

    a. Themes are software packages that extend the base functionality of WordPress, and plug-ins are the prepackaged styles and layout for the webpages that use them.

    b. Plug-ins are the software packages that extend the base functionality of WordPress, and themes are the prepackaged styles and layout for the webpages that use them.

    c. Themes and plug-ins are two different terms for the same tools in WordPress.

    d. Themes are used by the WordPress CMA to style the plug-ins that are used in the CDA.

5. Why is user management an important part of WordPress? (8.3)

    a. So that multiple developers and editors can collaborate on a website under development

    b. To track who made the mistakes so that they can be corrected

    c. To prevent too many people from working on the same project at the same time

    d. To keep the branches of the project organized in the version control system

6. What is the simplest way to test a WordPress site for responsive display? (8.3)

    a. Use the emulator that comes bundled in the WordPress CMA.

    b. Publish the WordPress website to a production server then open it using your mobile phone.

    c. There is no need to test, since nearly every WordPress theme uses a mobile-first or responsive design.

    d. Publish the WordPress site to a production server, then open it with a web browser and use its emulator to test the responsive design.

7. What is metadata in the context of a CMS webpage? (8.3)

    a. Data about the webpage that is used by the CMS but that doesn't appear on the webpage

    b. Data in the `<head>...</head>` section of the webpage that is used by the CMS

    c. Data about the webpage that tells the database used by the CMS how to store it

    d. Data that search engines use to index and crawl the webpages in the CMS

8. What is a WordPress slug? (8.3)

    a. The header on a webpage that is shown in the preview pane

    b. The short name for a webpage that is used in links

    c. The home link in a website that appears on every webpage

    d. The base URL for a site such as https://totallyawesomestuff.com

9. Why do you need to create webpages before you can create the menu that links to them in WordPress? (8.5)

    a. Because the menu object can't contain information that doesn't exist

    b. Because the links in the menu will not update if you modify the pages after you create the menu

    c. Because the default SEO engine won't crawl the pages if you create the navigation before the pages exist

    d. Because WordPress themes require you to build navigation blocks this way

10. Why do WordPress plug-ins install their own menus on the WordPress dashboard? (8.5)

    a. To create documentation of their features

    b. To make accessing and using the plug-in features easier

    c. To make the dashboard interface responsive to different display sizes

    d. They don't; WordPress just lists the plug-ins you have installed in the dashboard

11. Why are navigation menus stored as data instead of links on the page in WordPress? (8.4)

    a. Because that one menu will be reused everywhere the navigation block is added to the theme

    b. Because there is only one menu used and it is found on the home page

    c. Because the menu is used inside an iframe on all of the pages

    d. Because WordPress stores the individual block component together as completed webpages saved in the database

12. What does the WordPress Duplicator plug-in help with? (8.5)

    a. Creating a copy of a webpage in the same WordPress site

    b. Creating a copy of the WordPress theme you are using so you can modify the copy yourself

    c. Creating a copy of the complete WordPress website and transferring that to a different web server

    d. Creating a copy of a WordPress plug-in you are using so you can modify it yourself

Programming Exercises

1. Using your favorite search engine, research the "best proprietary CMS." Review five articles that are not advertisements for a web hosting company touting its own services and summarize the consensus among them. Include in your one-page summary a list of links to the articles you reviewed. (8.1–8.5)

2. Using your favorite search engine, research "best WordPress themes for (the topic of your new website)." You could search for e-commerce, authors, nonprofits, photographers, or whatever topic is interesting to you. You could also just search for "best WordPress themes." Review three articles and summarize your findings in a one-page report. Include links to the articles you reviewed. (8.1–8.5)

3. Using your favorite search engine, research "most useful WordPress plug-ins for (the topic of your new website)." You could search for e-commerce, authors, nonprofits, photographers, or whatever topic is interesting to you. You could also just search for "best WordPress plug-ins." Review three articles and summarize your findings in a one-page report. Include links to the articles you reviewed. (8.1–8.5)

Projects

1. Using your current WordPress site, install the WPForms plug-in. Then, create a Contact Us form using the previous Totally Awesome Stuff Contact Us page as a starting point. As you are building this form, make the appropriate fields Required. Add the links to the site menu that will appear at the top of every page and the image on the home page. Save and publish all of your changes. (8.1–8.4)

2. Add a new page to your WordPress site for "People, Places, and Things We Care About." You can use the previous page you created earlier in the course as a template or you can update the content as you see fit. Add a link to this new page from the home page and add a menu item with the short title "Causes" that will appear in the site menu at the top of every page. (8.1–8.4)

3. Using your current WordPress site, create the footer for your pages. You can recreate the simple footer from the static HTML pages you created previously or you can incorporate other details that you feel are appropriate. Add the footer block to all of your webpages, then publish your webpages. (8.1–8.4)

Chapter 9

WordPress Security, Themes, and Plug-Ins

Learning Objectives

When you complete this chapter, you will be able to:

9.1 Create a website security plan.

9.2 Explain the security features built into WordPress.

9.3 Customize a WordPress theme.

9.4 Create a simple WordPress child theme.

9.5 Create a simple WordPress plug-in.

9.1 Why Is Website Security Important?

All too often, the news reports a data breach, website hack, or website being held hostage by ransomware. As a full stack web developer, a significant part of your responsibilities in a development project is to prevent your products from being hacked and ensure that you and your customers can recover from malicious activities when they do occur.

Your customers will rely on your expertise as a security-conscious web developer to assess, plan, and implement comprehensive website security. You are not alone in this responsibility, as you will most likely share this duty with a database administrator and a systems administrator. If you are fortunate, you may even have a security administrator to help you with planning and assessing your website security.

Regardless of why hackers are targeting your website, being hacked disrupts the core business processes and costs you, the owners of the site, and potentially your website visitors,' time and money. Your customers may take their business elsewhere because of a security breach. Some visitors might even sue you for damages if your website is the vector for the theft of their credit card information or other significant financial consequences for them.

Furthermore, if your website gets hacked, you will be downranked in the Google search results to decrease your now-compromised site's profile because your site is a security vulnerability that Google does not want to recommend in its rankings.

It is more important to have a secure website and web presence than it is to have a finely polished CSS presentation or really neat JavaScript functionality. While those are worthwhile parts of the user experience of the website, they pale in comparison to having to deal with identity theft or a credit freeze with all three credit ratings agencies.

Why Are Websites Hacked?

To understand how to protect your website, you must know why websites are attacked in the first place. Websites are hacked not for a single reason but for several.

First, some hackers are in the business of making money from their "work," such as it is. If they can capture the credit card information going through your website, they can add phony charges on each transaction or make unauthorized purchases with the stolen card numbers. If they can hold your website hostage with ransomware and force you to pay to retrieve your website contents, they make money. If they can steal personal information like usernames and passwords and sell it, they also make money.

Second, some hackers are after proprietary information, intellectual property, or other data that has value. Even seemingly simple websites contain information attractive to hackers. Logins and passwords are useful because so many people reuse them with multiple access points. If you are so inclined, you can buy databases containing millions of usernames and passwords to use in an automated password-guessing software attack.

Third, some hackers are looking for a website they can take over to provide hosting for their own website contents or to use the server resources that would otherwise go to hosting the website. Sometimes this takes the form of injecting unnecessary links from your webpages to their site to make their site appear more popular in a search engine. Other times, defacement is meant to create or transmit a political message.

Finally, some hackers are just out to make mischief to prove they can. This is the least likely reason a website would get hacked, however.

What Are the Most Common Types of Exploits?

The Open Web Application Security Project (OWASP) maintains a list of the most critical security risks by calendar year. The data in this list changes as new security vulnerabilities are discovered and documented. You can view the top 10 list at https://owasp.org/www-project-top-ten.

The report includes some technical jargon but reading about the risks reported to OWASP by security professionals around the globe gives you a good idea of the most recent trends in security vulnerabilities.

The OWASP home page contains links to detailed pages for each of the top 10 items, including descriptions, examples, solutions, and additional suggestions for reading. Read these important security concerns so you are aware of them and avoid becoming part of their statistics.

Another worthwhile part of the OWASP top 10 list is the comparison with previous years. The useful lifespan for a website after deployment is about three to seven years. Over that time, different vulnerabilities may materialize or be discovered that weren't originally of concern during the development phase of the project. The OWASP comparison can help you identify old problems that were never addressed in the original design.

The Low-Hanging Fruit of Web Security

The most common attacks against a website are automated software attacks. These malicious bot attacks are similar to Googlebots crawling the web looking for new or updated site contents to index in the Google search results, except the malicious bots are looking for default admin accounts, default or nonexistent passwords, and settings that haven't been updated following a new installation of the website software.

An automated software attack probes a new website within minutes or hours of being exposed to the Internet. As a full stack developer, you should never put off creating a new, complex password for an administrator account, especially one with the username "administrator." Change the administrator account name, if you can, to double the difficulty of a brute-force password-guessing attack.

Additionally, you should always apply all offered software updates to the operating system on your web server, website software platform, database, content management system (CMS), and desktop or laptop computers. Enable the setting to "keep this software updated automatically" when you are offered the opportunity, and then monitor your software for successful update installations.

You should also allow only trusted users to set up credentials to access and create or modify your content. Make sure your fellow users are well trained about passwords and website security. People are the greatest source of security vulnerabilities in website development.

Don't cache your passwords in your web browser. While this is a convenient service offered by most web browsers, it also presents an easy target for malicious actors, since you are creating a database of your credentials in the most accessible tool they could hope for.

The software engineers of the major browsers are doing their best to create secure software. However, if you cache passwords in your browser, any vulnerability that hasn't yet been discovered and patched means the tool you use to access the Internet also stores the credentials you are using to secure your website.

Finally, make sure the local computers you use to access your website are patched, receiving automated updates, and used by security-conscious individuals who don't click links in emails promising riches from a Nigerian prince. Security training for yourself and your coworkers is an ongoing effort that shouldn't stop after new employee orientation. A compromised laptop or desktop is an open invitation to access everything that computer has access to, including your website.

Next-Level Web Security

Even if you are security conscious and follow a checklist of basic dos and don'ts, you need to follow additional steps to implement a comprehensive security stance as a full stack web developer responsible for building and maintaining websites.

You can realize significant dividends by paying more for an HTTPS URL if you need to purchase that service from your web host. Some web hosts include this service by default in their hosting packages, but you should look for the HTTPS component in the service listing if it isn't documented.

As you may have read previously, HTTPS stands for Hypertext Transfer Protocol Secure. This protocol is the "language" that web servers and web browsers use to communicate. As the secure version of HTTP, HTTPS encrypts data prior to sending it over the Internet rather than transferring it in plain text. Any information sent via plain text using HTTP can be read by any automated intercepting agent between the browser and web server.

What was previously called SSL, or Secure Sockets Layer, is now called TLS, or Transport Layer Security. HTTPS uses TLS to encrypt data prior to transmission and decrypt it upon receipt. The TLS protocol is what the S in HTTPS refers to.

Encrypting data prior to transmission in both directions—to and from a web browser and web server—means that any personally identifiable information, credit card information, or even usernames and passwords are transmitted as a hash of information instead of in plain text. Encryption makes the information significantly harder for a snooper of network traffic to find valuable information.

Another feature to look for in the services offered by your website host is **distributed denial-of-service (DDoS)** protection. A DDoS attack occurs when a malicious actor or group of actors creates a software system that requests a page from your website thousands of times per second from multiple computers. Sometimes, these computers are previously compromised websites, but they can also be desktops with fast network connectivity. The effect is the same as reloading the targeted webpage thousands of times per second, which quickly overwhelms the web server and takes your website offline.

One software-based solution that many web hosts offer to stop a DDoS attack is to block or ignore requests coming from the IP addresses making repeated requests after a relatively low number of requests within a short time interval. Some web hosts offer this service with the default hosting package, while others provide it as an additional service for a fee.

You should also perform routine website security audits using a tool like Mozilla Observatory. This tool performs a thorough and detailed security audit of your website and web infrastructure, creating a report with links to solutions for each of the known vulnerabilities that it can find. This tool is like those used by malicious actors who are probing your website for vulnerabilities, except that if you find the vulnerabilities first, you can fix them before they are exploited.

Note	Why is general website security a topic covered in a chapter primarily about WordPress?
	The chapter covers website security for two important reasons. First, WordPress is the go-to solution for rapid webpage development and the most commonly used CMS. In WordPress, taking a website from concept to deployment is nearly automated and apparently simple, even though it is complex and nuanced.
	Creating and publishing a non-WordPress website is more deliberate and involves greater technical barriers to overcome. WordPress is purposefully easy, but the downside of that streamlined deployment is that a first-time web developer can easily overlook critical security measures. The first website you publish and make visible to the Internet is likely to be a WordPress website.
	Second, the fundamentals of website security are universal, regardless of the platform. You are learning specific actions and preventative measures that WordPress simplifies through its configuration and software solutions. You would need to make these changes manually with a non-WordPress website. The website security concepts presented in this section and the next are universal, but the means of achieving them are more technical for non-WordPress websites.

Beware of Security Services for Sale

The history of the Internet is littered with examples of apparent security services that are actually **Trojan horses**. A Trojan horse is malware that hides the true intentions of the giver, who has malicious intentions. This is often in the form of "security software" that is anything other than that.

Naive but security-conscience people find and unwittingly download a "security package" that introduces a new vulnerability to their computer. Often this malware disables the common antivirus software and then blocks further access for downloading an update for the antivirus software that would be helpful to preventing or quarantining an infection.

Some pay-for-service companies function in nearly the same capacity as this malware. Advertising themselves as white knights, they ask users to turn over the administrator account to the local computer or website to sanitize it. As soon as they have the administrator credentials, they are off to the races in accessing and logging everything they can find.

Use only well-established security software. Do your own independent web search and look for recognized and trustworthy sources for information. Buy security software from a reputable online retailer. Install it, update it, and then run the scan that it offers. Configure the software to run a periodic sweep and to constantly protect your browser from malicious or noxious content.

Creating a Security Plan

Creating a security plan may seem like an unnecessary step in the complex process of building a new website, but the consequences for not doing so and for not following the plan are too costly to ignore. Like the complete checklist that pilots go through on an airplane before takeoff, each step in introducing a new website should be scripted and confirmed before officially launching.

In addition to applying patches, scheduling software upgrades, creating complex usernames and passwords, and other commonsense security best practices, other tasks are necessary to document in a security plan.

Your security plan should include a procedure for recovering from a website hack. A critical step in this planning is periodically creating an offsite and recent backup of your entire website to use as a new starting point. If the server hosting your website is disabled by an attack or hardware malfunction, you may not be able to recover your data from it. You might even need to move to a different web host. A robust backup system will help reestablish your website following a catastrophic loss or ransomware attack.

Always make backups of your website that you can access independent from your hosted website access credentials. A good web host also makes backups for you, but if the host itself is hacked, you may be out of luck retrieving your website from that compromised host. Test the backups to make sure you can restore them before you actually need to do so.

As part of your security plan, determine how much data and settings you and your customers are willing to lose and create a backup schedule accordingly. If you have a high-traffic site, you may need to back up the database contents every four hours and create an offsite backup every night. For lower-traffic sites, a nightly backup with a weekly offsite backup might be enough.

The components of a security plan can be organized into areas of vulnerability and responses. The U.S. federal government's Cybersecurity and Infrastructure Security Agency (CISA) has a Security Tip whitepaper at https://www.cisa.gov/uscert/ncas/tips/ST18-006 that provides a solid starting point for a security plan.

This document outlines the critical steps every systems administrator and full stack web developer should follow to create a security plan that all members of the software development team are trained on.

Another reason this security plan should be documented and signed by all parties involved, including your customers, is the legal coverage it provides for you and your team. If you do everything that you have documented is required of you, and your web host is the source of a data breach, you limit your legal liability. On the other hand, if you clicked the link promising untold wealth from that Nigerian prince, you may end up being forced to repay some of that untold wealth to your customers.

Note

Is a lot of money really at stake in website security vulnerabilities?

In 2013, the retail chain Target suffered a data breach, with over 40 million stored credit card numbers being stolen or compromised from their databases. Target customers who had saved their credit card information on Target's servers for easier future purchases found themselves the victims of a hack.

The total cost of the recovery, loss of revenue, and extended credit protection offered to customers for Target was over $300 million. The direct costs of the resulting lawsuits and making their customers safe was over $200 million, with another $100 million in lost sales.

Quick Check 9-1

1. Why should you apply software updates automatically, or as often as they are published by the authors of the software?

   a. Because the updates usually patch security vulnerabilities that have been recently discovered
   b. Because fixing broken software increases your job security since it ensures you have something to do
   c. Because using the most recent version of the software results in a better user experience
   d. Because of that delicious new software smell that comes bundled with each update

2. What is a Trojan horse in website security?

    a. A specific type of security software with an outer user interface that is different from the inner security functionality to hide it from hackers

    b. An FTP software package used to transport critical security updates across an unsecure network

    c. A type of malware that pretends to be security software or other valuable type of software

    d. Legacy security software originally written in Turkey but sold by Greek retailers

3. Why is it necessary to have a recovery plan component included in the security plan for a website?

    a. It is a software requirement of most CMSs during the initial setup.

    b. Because web hosting companies are notoriously unreliable

    c. To justify the cost of creating backups

    d. New vulnerabilities are being discovered all the time, and humans make mistakes.

1) a. Security-conscious software developers continuously update their products as vulnerabilities are found and documented. **2) c.** A Trojan horse is software that masks its true purpose behind a veneer of some kind. **3) d.** It is better to plan for something bad happening, even if it never does, so that you can recover from it more easily when it occurs.

9.2 Examining WordPress Security

With so many websites built on the WordPress platform, the common exploits of unpatched WordPress vulnerabilities are some of the first ones attempted by the automated bots trying to gain entry into a website. Simple math suggests that the platform with nearly half of the websites built on it is the most likely to have deficiencies to exploit.

Using WordPress can potentially increase your website hacking visibility and also decrease your website security vulnerability. Used wisely, WordPress is secure. Followed carefully, WordPress security protocols and procedures increase your overall site security. However, if you do not carefully follow the well-documented protocols for securing a WordPress website, you open the door to a website breach and effectively post a sign displaying the WordPress logo and the words "Please Come in and Help Yourself to a Free Sample of Our Customer's Personal Data" in the front window of the virtual storefront next to that open door.

The developers who contribute to the WordPress platform are proactive about implementing security and have thoroughly documented the steps for creating a secure WordPress website. Review the protocols for WordPress security on the WordPress security website at https://www.wpbeginner.com/wordpress-security.

The WordPress security site provides basic steps that are common sense, but not what you might think about if you are using WordPress for the first time. What you don't know about the new concepts you are still learning becomes the security vulnerabilities exploited by hackers. It is in your best interest to review a list of the critical vulnerabilities.

Default WordPress Security

The first step to make your WordPress website more secure is to set your WordPress app to receive updates from the WordPress developers.

As with many things WordPress, you can use a helpful plug-in to manage your updates. The plug-in is called the Easy Updates Manager.

To install and use the Easy Updates Manager:

1. On the WordPress dashboard, click Plugins.

2. Click the Add New button at the top of the Plugins page.

3. In the Search plugins box, enter the name **Easy Updates Manager**.

4. In the search results, install and activate the Easy Updates Manager.

5. To access the Easy Updates Manager from the WordPress dashboard, click Dashboard in the left pane and then click Updates options. The Easy Updates Manager window opens as shown in **Figure 9-1**.

Figure 9-1   The Easy Updates Manager window

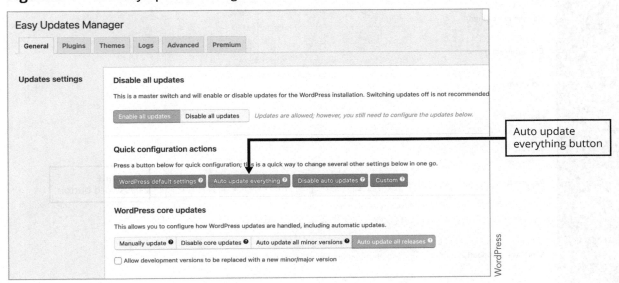

6. Click the Auto update everything button to apply all security upgrades to your WordPress website. This is the strategically efficient approach to ensuring that your WordPress website always stays as current as possible.

An update for a plug-in or theme might possibly cause a malfunction in your WordPress website, so another helpful step is to install the WP Rollback plug-in. This plug-in allows you to undo a specific update if it causes problems. Often, a subsequent version of the update fixes the bug introduced in the rollout of an upgrade, so you need to test and then redeploy the update if it restores your site and makes it functional. If you choose to use the Auto update everything option in step 6, install the WP Rollback plug-in before you need to use it to roll back an update.

The need for testing is another reason to keep a local copy of your WordPress website. Without exposing the site to the Internet, you can make sure a fix made to a broken plug-in really does fix a bug.

Another step in the default security stance of managing a WordPress website is to practice good user access hygiene, including for yourself. These practices include making users of your WordPress website create strong passwords. To enforce this requirement, you can generate a strong password on the Users page when you are creating the accounts for your website editors and content providers who have direct access to the WordPress administrative interface.

To generate a strong password with an account for new users:

1. On the WordPress dashboard, click Users, and then on the Users menu, click Add New to access the Add New User window shown in **Figure 9-2**.

2. Click the Generate password button to create a strong password. Your new user will need to use this password to access the WordPress account instead of their preferred password of "password123."

Additionally, be cautious about adding authors and editors to your WordPress website. If a user has a compromised desktop or laptop, the credentials used in the web browser on that machine may be captured, providing access to your website. While it is helpful to have more people contributing to a website, all your users should have a minimum level of security training to ensure none become the easy vector for a website hack.

Figure 9-2 Generating a strong user password

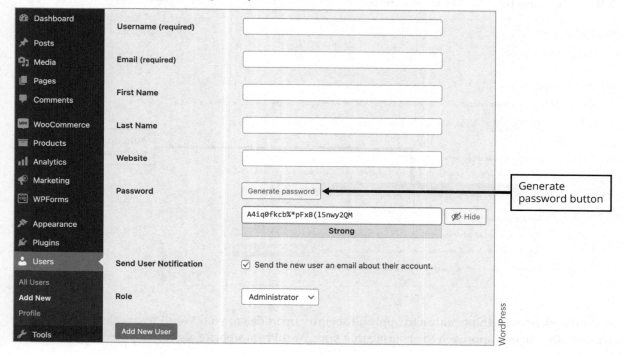

Additional WordPress Security Plug-Ins

Many WordPress plug-ins offer security services for WordPress users. As part of the security plan suggested in the previous section, you should document all plug-ins and the features you are using, including the security plug-ins and what vulnerabilities they are meant to address.

One of the most well-regarded WordPress security plug-ins is WPScan. The plug-in is maintained by the same cohort of WordPress developers who support WooCommerce. These developers and other users report vulnerabilities to a central database of the known issues for each version of WordPress. The development team also tracks the known security vulnerabilities in WordPress themes and plug-ins and finds those before a malicious actor can. Additionally, WPScan looks for poorly configured default setups and outdated or vulnerable themes and plug-ins.

Another highly recommended WordPress security plug-in is Wordfence. This plug-in offers additional proactive features that aren't available with WPScan, such as a firewall and enhanced login protection. The Web Application Firewall (WAF) is a Wordfence feature that blocks incoming traffic from known IP addresses used by hackers. WAF has a configurable interface that updates itself regularly in response to new hackers and techniques. Additionally, it has important security settings like blocking an IP address after three failed login attempts.

Most of the WordPress security plug-ins have a feature for hiding the WordPress version number. Select this feature (often a check box) to keep one piece of revealing information from hackers. Some security vulnerabilities for WordPress apply only to specific versions, so if you don't advertise the version on your WordPress website, hackers won't have an easy time identifying specific exploits to be attempted against your version.

The final piece of the security puzzle is to perform an automated security audit of your site security using a tool like Sucuri SiteCheck prior to launching your WordPress website. This plug-in scans the configuration of your website from the white-hat hacker perspective and catalogs all vulnerabilities it can find. This security audit automates the pre-launch checklist to help find and address human forgetfulness and mistakes prior to a hacker finding and exploiting them.

WordPress Backup Plug-Ins

A WordPress website backup system is a feature you hope you never need but will be grateful to have when you do. Backup systems create snapshots of your entire WordPress website, including the database, themes, and plug-ins you are using. If your web host is hacked and you have a copy of your current website stored on physical media in a safe location, you can restore your website from that backup within minutes.

If you make a batch of changes and then realize the old version was significantly better, you can restore the older version. Additionally, you can use the backup software to transfer your WordPress website from one web host to another if the web host is not meeting the requirements of your website.

Many web hosts offer a backup service, sometimes for free as an included line item in the base services offered. However, if the host is the target of a broader attack, your website becomes one of the innocent casualties. Retrieving a backup of your own intellectual property from a web host that can't bring its web servers back online is not a fun exercise.

One of the most highly rated backup plug-ins is called UpdraftPlus. The documentation of features and how to use them are at https://updraftplus.com. This plug-in allows you to connect your WordPress site to a cloud storage solution like Google Drive or Dropbox so you don't have to remember where you put a USB drive containing your last backup when things go sideways.

UpdraftPlus is freemium software, which means the base package is free but you pay for upgrades. For a small site, the free version is sufficient, but for larger sites with critical uptime constraints, the paid version is worth exploring. One beneficial component to the paid version is the use of incremental backups. Incremental backups store only the changes that you made since the last backup, saving far less data than a full backup so you aren't needlessly consuming network and storage resources.

Hardening Your Infrastructure

One line item you should check off prior to launching your WordPress website is to change the default login page name. Every new WordPress installation has the same login page, wp-login.php. Unless you change the default, anyone can access the login page for your website by appending /wp-admin/ to the end of the default URL for your website.

Since every WordPress website default configuration starts using this login page, hackers will try to access that page first in their automated attempt to hack your website. You can thwart this lazy scripted hacking by renaming the login page to anything other than wp-login.php. In fact, you can use a plug-in to rename the page and update corresponding changes to your WordPress website configuration.

The plug-in WPS Hide Login allows you to change the name of the default login page. Using an easy-to-guess name like login.php is not recommended. Instead, changing the page name to a random set of characters that end with .php or using a longer page name like this_is_not_the_page_you_are_looking_for.php makes accessing the default login page more complicated for lazy hackers. This seemingly small change makes your website more secure.

Another step to take in hardening your infrastructure is to stop brute-force password-guessing attacks after a number of failed attempts to authenticate. You may have inadvertently encountered this security precaution in other settings or applications if after three failed logins you were locked out of access until an administrator unlocks your account.

The iThemes Security plug-in offers this lock-out feature. After a set number of failed attempts, the IP address of the computer attempting to gain access is blocked from further access to the WordPress website. Adept hackers can switch to a different IP address (as you can if you forget your password for a number of attempts), but this change makes it more difficult for a bot to continually pound on your login page for thousands of login attempts.

Using Multifactor Authentication

Multifactor authentication (MFA) adds one extra step to the standard login process. After using a laptop, for example, to successfully log in to a site with your username and password, an MFA-enabled login process typically sends a text message with an authentication code to your phone as the second step. You must enter the authentication code on your laptop to gain access to the site as an administrator. You may have used MFA if you have an iTunes account or any other account that requires entering a code in addition to a username and password.

This style of MFA relies on the concept of something you know and something you have. You know your admin username and password. Your friendly neighborhood website hackers may also know your admin username and password if your desktop or laptop has been compromised. You also have a phone. The hackers do not have your phone (hopefully). By combining these two things, you decrease the ease of access for people who shouldn't have access, even if your user credentials are compromised.

If you haven't used MFA before, it may seem like extra annoyance for little gain, but it is a minor inconvenience and offers more robust security. MFA is a response to the ongoing challenge of managing users who are managing their own passwords. With MFA, a user who has "password123" as a password or who clicks a link in an email that compromises their desktop won't automatically grant access to the WordPress site, even if the browser they are using has the password cached.

As with many security improvements, you can use a plug-in specifically for MFA. Adding the Google Authenticator plug-in written by Ivan Kruchkoff leverages the Google Authenticator application you install on your phone to your WordPress website. Using this plug-in ensures that gaining access to the administrator interface is more challenging than guessing random usernames and passwords thousands of times. Other WordPress security plug-ins also offer MFA.

For the gain of an extra layer of security, the price is worth it. MFA is rapidly becoming not just a best practice but a necessity. It isn't the only solution, but it is a significant part of a comprehensive approach to WordPress website security.

Quick Check 9-2

1. What does a web application firewall like Wordfence do?

   a. It blocks all incoming Internet requests from accessing the login page for a WordPress website.
   b. It blocks all incoming Internet requests from accessing the WordPress admin interface.
   c. It allows only certain IP addresses to access the WordPress website.
   d. It blocks known hacker IP addresses from accessing the WordPress interface.

2. Why is changing the default login page name for WordPress a useful security practice?

   a. It makes bot attacks less likely to succeed, since the login page name is part of the hardcoded script those bots use.
   b. It keeps unauthorized users from guessing logins and passwords.
   c. It stops brute-force password hacks after a set number of attempts.
   d. It blocks the IP address of any bot that tries to access the default login page.

3. What is multifactor authentication?

   a. Using both a complex username and complex passphrase in a login
   b. Using something you know like a username/password and something you have like a mobile phone to create a second layer of security in the login procedure
   c. Logging in first to a website, then into the web server hosting that website to access the administrator's portal
   d. Logging into a website, then asking the administrator for permission to gain access to the editor role in WordPress

1) d. A web application firewall has a list of IP addresses that are used by hackers and prevents those IP addresses from accessing the WordPress website. **2) a.** All WordPress websites start with the same initial login page, so scripted bot attacks try to access that page by name first. **3) b.** Multifactor authentication involves an extra step of sending a number or token to a second device that is not the computer you are logging into to prove that it is you performing the authentication.

9.3 Customizing WordPress Themes

The WordPress theme you chose for your website comes complete with a preselected group of fonts, font colors, sizes, and other formats. You can accept these default values, but if you or your clients want to tailor your site, or you have a specific set of requirements to satisfy, you can update your theme using the theme editor.

Note	Each set of instructions in this section starts from the WordPress dashboard. You don't need to start from the dashboard each time you change your website, but it is useful to know how to navigate to each feature from a common starting point.
	Because WordPress is a complex CMS, it often provides multiple ways to navigate to a feature or menu. Navigating from the dashboard is a useful way to learn how to find the configuration options in WordPress. As you gain experience, you will learn your own shortcuts.
	Remembering where to find a specific menu or option in a menu can be a challenge when using WordPress. Learning where to find options is the equivalent to learning the syntax of a programming language, except that the debugger in this case is WordPress and the menus are visual representations of the syntax.

To access the WordPress theme editor:

1. On the WordPress Dashboard, click Appearance in the left pane to open the Themes page in the content pane. **Figure 9-3** shows two options that open the theme editor.

Figure 9-3   WordPress Themes page

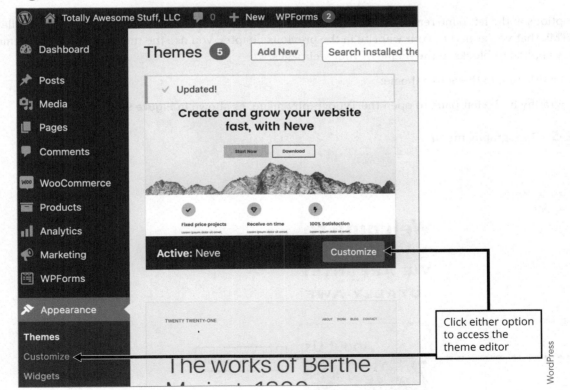

The first way to access the theme editor is to use the Customize button on the Neve theme banner in the content pane. The second way is the Customize link on the Appearance menu.

2. Click the Customize button or the Customize link to open the theme editor.

The WordPress Theme Customization Tools

You customize a WordPress theme using the tools shown in **Figure 9-4**.

Figure 9-4 Tools in the theme editor for customizing a theme

The menu options in the left pane represent the stylistic components that make up a WordPress theme. Similar to the blocks of HTML that you added to your website in the previous chapter, you use the theme editor menu items to modify the styles applied to blocks in the theme of your webpages.

To change the title font in the active theme:

1. Click Typography in the left pane to open the Typography menu, as shown in **Figure 9-5**.

Figure 9-5 Typography menu

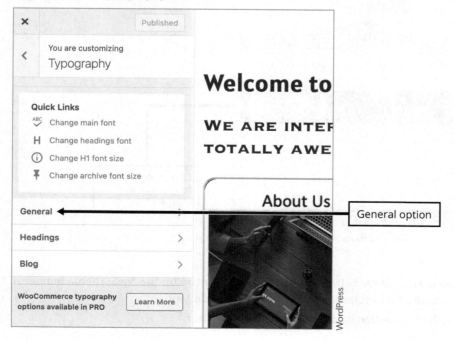

You use the options in the Quick Links section to perform common typography tasks, such as changing the font for headings, but it is worth examining the General and Headings options on the lower part of the menu.

2. Click General and then click Headings to review the available options.

General: This font styling applies to all of the webpage contents that are not in the headings, including the text, captions, bulleted lists, and other page contents. Updating the General font transforms the contents of your entire WordPress website. In the current theme, Neve, the default font is set to Arial, Helvetica, sans-serif. This cascade of fonts ensures that at least one will apply, with the preference being Arial.

Headings: This font styling applies to the title block, along with anywhere else using h1 or h2 tags. **Figure 9-6** shows the default settings for h1 headings.

Figure 9-6 Default settings for H1 headings

Note that the topmost menu item is the Font Family. You modify this option to change the font of the h1 and h2 headings. The Font Family style is currently set to Inherit, which means that it uses the same font as the rest of the site as specified in the theme. That font was set in the General menu as Arial, Helvetica, sans-serif for the Neve theme, but your value may be different if you are using a different theme.

3. Click the Font Family button and then click the font of your choice. The preview of your WordPress page in the right pane updates to reflect the font change. If the font you chose doesn't work with the default font of the rest of the website, you can choose a different headings font or change the default font of the rest of the site.

4. When you are satisfied with your updates, click the Publish button at the top of the menu pane to save your changes and republish your page.

5. If you have a Preview button in the upper-right corner of the window, click it to view your shiny new webpage with updated fonts.

Customizing with CSS

You are not limited to updating the WordPress theme using the available menu options. You can also modify the CSS code to customize a WordPress website.

To change the appearance of a WordPress website using CSS:

1. On the WordPress Dashboard, click Appearance and then click Customize on the Appearance menu.

2. Scroll down to the Additional CSS option. Your previously acquired CSS skills are useful here while working with WordPress.

   As you may recall from the previous version of Totally Awesome Stuff, the four images in the foursquare pattern on the home page should each have a border with rounded corners. The code to make those rounded corners is as follows:

   ```
   .four-square-border {
       border-style: solid;
       border-color: rgb(175,175,175) rgb(200,200,200);
       background-color: black;
       border-radius: 20px;
   }
   ```

3. Click the Additional CSS option, and then add the rounded-borders code to the input field. See **Figure 9-7**.

Figure 9-7 CSS code for rounded borders

4. Click the Publish button at the top of the left pane. You can now apply the new style to your WordPress website.

Adding Custom CSS to a WordPress Element

After creating custom CSS for a WordPress website, the only challenge remaining is finding the WordPress location where you can add that new style to the correct block containing the HTML element you want to style with it.

To style a block with the custom CSS:

1. On the WordPress Dashboard, click the Pages option.
2. In the content pane, click your home page (Front Page) to open it for editing.
3. Click the "Our Catalog of Products" image in the foursquare pattern to select it for editing and display the Page/Block editing menu. See **Figure 9-8**.

Figure 9-8 Changing the style of a home page image

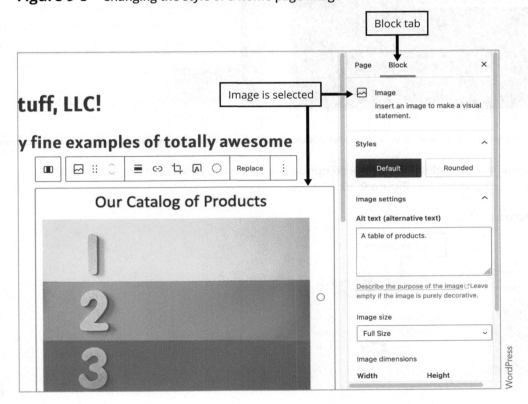

The Block tab has been activated because you clicked an individual block in the page. You need to click the block and the HTML element inside that block to apply a custom style. If a block contains more than one HTML element, you must carefully select the individual element you want to style, since you aren't looking through the HTML for a specific ID of that element. The WordPress user interface is your only way to ensure you are applying a style to the correct element.

Common Mistakes

You can add a custom CSS class to any block or HTML element in that block. The danger in this flexibility is that you can apply a CSS class to the entire block instead of the HTML element inside that block. Similarly, you can click the wrong HTML element in the editor and apply the style by mistake to that element. Always make sure the name of the element you are applying the custom CSS to is in the menu at the right below the Block tab.

As shown in **Figure 9-9**, the rounded-corner class has been applied to the container of the image, but not the image itself (which has been resized to make this mistake obvious).

Figure 9-9 Selecting the wrong block element for editing

4. Scroll the Block menu and then click the Advanced option to expand the Block menu and display the Additional CSS Class(es) section. See **Figure 9-10**.

Figure 9-10 Accessing the custom CSS class

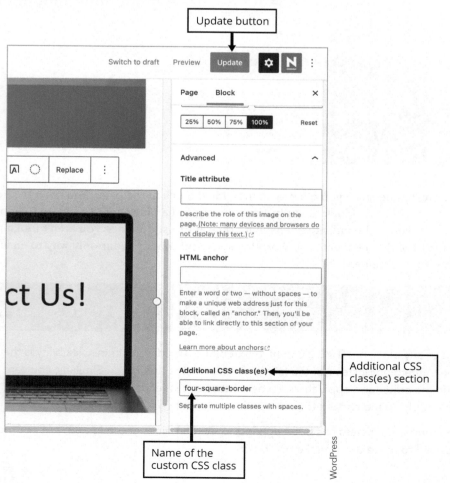

5. In the Additional CSS Class(es) text box, enter the name of the custom CSS class you created, such as four-square-border. You do not need to include the dot at the start of the name.

6. Repeat steps 3–5 for the other three images on the home page.

7. Click the Update button above the Block tab. Because the custom CSS is applied when the page is requested in the browser and composed by the WordPress engine, the preview doesn't show your modification.

8. To view the changes to the webpage, click the WordPress logo and then click the Visit Site link. Alternatively, click the Preview link in the upper-right corner of the dashboard. When the home page opens, you should see your foursquare images with the rounded corners style applied.

Quick Check 9-3

1. Where is the theme editor found in the WordPress interface?

   a. In the Theme Editor plug-in
   b. On the Appearances menu using the Customize link
   c. In the Themes Management window using the Edit Theme link
   d. In the contextual theme editing menu

2. How do you preview the results of your updates to the theme to ensure your customizations are correct prior to publishing them?

   a. You open the webpage in a browser and refresh the webpage.
   b. You use the View Source option in the browser to confirm your changes have been incorporated correctly.
   c. You use a plug-in such as Page Preview to confirm the changes have the desired effect.
   d. You use the WordPress Live Preview feature to view your changes as you make them.

3. How do you apply a new custom CSS style to an HTML element in WordPress?

   a. You use the Page/Block editing menu in WordPress.
   b. You use a plug-in designed for a custom CSS application.
   c. You edit the theme with a simple text editor to add the style to an element.
   d. You edit the HTML of the page directly in your text editor.

1) b. You can edit the theme by clicking Appearance and then Customize on the Appearance menu. 2) d. The Live Preview feature shows how your updates will look as soon as you complete them. 3) a. The Page/Block editing menu allows you to apply your new style.

9.4 Creating Your Own WordPress Child Theme

If you want to add more than one simple CSS element to a WordPress theme to customize it, you can create a **child theme** that includes all of those updates rather than incorporating them as individual CSS components.

The child theme inherits all the stylistic elements of the **parent theme** and overrides them individually as you customize the parent properties. For example, if the parent theme has a blue h1 heading on each page and you want a green h1 heading instead, you can specify a green h1 in your child theme to override the parent theme style. When the font family in the parent theme is updated by the original developers of that theme, your child theme inherits those updates for the font family, as long as that isn't included in your modifications.

One interesting note about child themes is that the WordPress rendering engine first loads the webpage using the child theme and adds the stylistic contents of the parent theme if the child theme doesn't override them. This feature is called the WordPress style queue. The rules of the WordPress style queue enforce using the child theme style over the parent theme style if there are duplicates between the two.

Adding a Child Theme Using a Plug-In

A plug-in is available to help develop a child theme. To be more specific, over 1,000 plug-ins are available to help you with creating a child theme.

To add a WordPress child theme:

1. On the WordPress Dashboard, click Plugins and then click the Add New button in the Plugin Manager pane.
2. In the Search plugins box, type **child theme** to search for child theme plug-ins.
3. Review the results, looking for the highest-rated and most-downloaded plug-in.

   The Child Theme Configurator is one of the most highly regarded plug-ins, with hundreds of reviews and hundreds of thousands of active users. Add this plug-in to your WordPress website and then continue with the next step.

4. In the left pane, click Tools and then click Child Themes to open the Child Theme Configurator window shown in **Figure 9-11**. Your version may differ.

Figure 9-11   Child Theme Configurator window

Analyze button

5. Click the Analyze button in the Step 2 area to check if the theme you are using supports creating a child theme. The Neve theme, used in this tutorial, does support child themes, so the Configurator window expands from three steps to show nine steps in setting up the Child Theme Configurator:

   Step 4 is naming the theme directory where the files created by this plug-in are stored in WordPress. You can rename this folder or use the default folder name.

   Step 5 involves determining where the new styles will be incorporated—either in the primary stylesheet or in a separate stylesheet. If you are only adding a few new styles and you won't need to roll back those changes to a previous state, you can choose the primary stylesheet. However, if you are making extensive changes, you may want to choose the separate stylesheet to preserve the original style. Similar to the multiple stylesheets you created in the adaptive display chapter, creating multiple stylesheets makes it easier to manage individual styles. For this tutorial, accepting the default of storing the styles in the primary stylesheet is the preferred option.

   Step 6 determines how to handle the child–parent theme interaction. Most new themes have a default configuration to handle the interaction, as the Neve theme does. The default option is "Do not add parent stylesheet handling" because the Neve theme already has the proper routing to handle it correctly. If your theme does not have this routing, the safe option is to "Use the WordPress style queue."

   Step 7 allows you to add information to the data supplied by the original developers of the parent theme. You can add your name as the theme author along with development notes in the Theme Description box. It is customary to append your personal data to the existing data created by the authors of the parent theme, since you are extending their intellectual property and citing your sources is helpful to the next developer who is trying to figure out why something is broken or looks odd.

   Step 8 allows you to copy the menus and widgets from the parent theme into the child theme. If you don't want to include those elements, leave the box unchecked. For this tutorial, check the box since the changes you'll make don't include overriding the menus and widgets.

   Step 9 provides a button to click to create the child theme.

6. Click the Configure Child Theme button to create the child theme and refresh the screen with a confirmation message like that in **Figure 9-12** if all goes smoothly.

Figure 9-12   Successfully creating a child theme

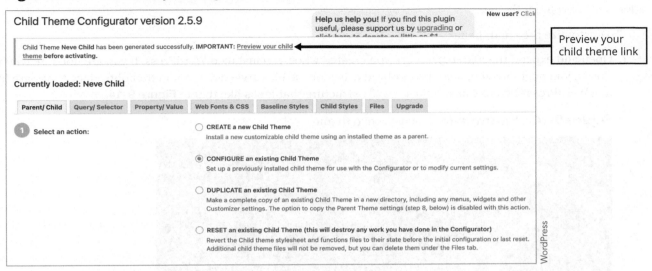

7. Click the Preview your child theme link to confirm you created the child theme successfully. The Live Preview window opens.

8. If you see the same WordPress website you started with, click the Activate & Publish button, as shown in **Figure 9-13**.

Figure 9-13   The Neve Child theme preview.

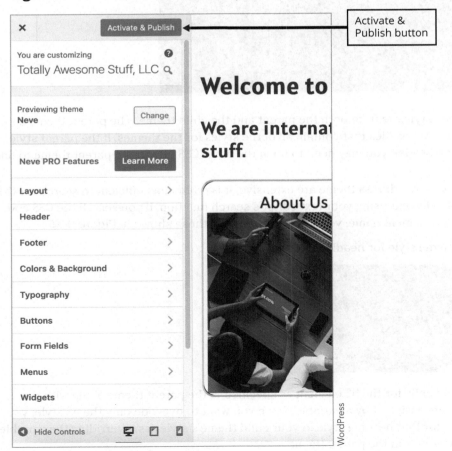

Adding Style to a Child Theme

The next part of creating a child theme is a familiar one if you've already worked through the samples and projects in the previous chapters. You need to create the new CSS code for the child theme that customizes it beyond what was offered by the parent theme.

To customize the child theme:

1. Open and expand the folder structure you created when you installed WordPress. If you are not sure where this is, you might need to search your hard drive for the files style.css and function.php, since those are files in a WordPress theme. You should see a file structure that looks like that in **Figure 9-14**.

Figure 9-14 File structure for a new child theme

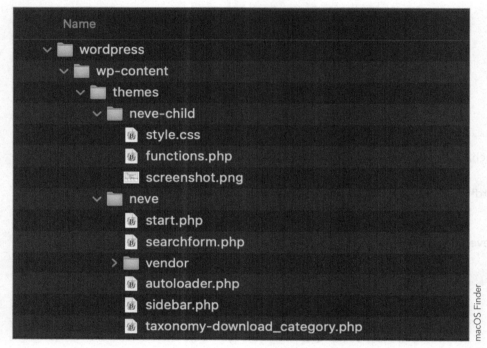

2. In your simple text editor, open style.css from both the parent and the child theme. The parent theme and the child theme have one or more CSS files that contain all of the styles for the themes. If the parent style .css file is empty except for the header, you may need to open the other CSS files in the parent theme to find the style you are looking for.

   Because the stylesheets for a WordPress theme are extensive, it is often most efficient to search for the name of the class, ID, or HTML element using your text editor's search function. If you search the CSS code for an individual class, ID, or HTML element name, you will find styles like those shown in **Figure 9-15**.

Figure 9-15 The parent theme style for headings in style.css

```
290
291    h1,
292    h2,
293    h3,
294    h4,
295    h5,
296  ▾ h6 {
297      margin-bottom: 30px;
298      font-family: var(--headingsfontfamily), var(--nv-fallback-ff);
299  ▸ }
300
```

BBEdit

This figure shows the font family for the h2 element as specified in the parent theme along with the other headings. These values are assigned by a variable. Since you want to override only the h2 style, you can specify a font family value for that heading style in your child theme's style.css, overriding the variable without changing the other headings in the parent theme.

Another way to find which theme style you need to override with your child theme is to view the page source of the parent-themed webpage in your browser. Using the browser's web developer's tools, click View on the menu bar and then click Page Source or right-click the page (Ctrl+click on a Mac) and choose View Source. In the source code that makes up the page, find the class or ID of the element you want to restyle or, if you are trying to restyle an HTML element like an h2 heading, you can just apply that style as you have previously.

3. Once you have identified which element selector you need to override, add the CSS in the child theme style.css to customize your child theme.

In this case, the previous use of the font faces Copperplate and Copperplate Gothic will be reapplied to the h2 selector everywhere it is used in the WordPress version of Totally Awesome Stuff. You are encouraged to add your own stylistic elements as well.

Add the following CSS code to your child theme style.css to make all h2 elements in the website use the same font face:

```
h2 {
    font-family: Copperplate, "Copperplate Gothic", serif;
}
```

4. Save the file. In your web browser, refresh the home page for Totally Awesome Stuff. The font of the h2 heading should change to one in the Copperplate font family.

While this example is short, the same steps are all you need to customize your child theme's style. You are encouraged to add as many new updates as you see fit to your own child theme, since everything that you have used previously in raw CSS applies here as well.

Quick Check 9-4

1. How do you create a child theme in WordPress?

   a. You find a suitable theme in the Themes Manager window and attach it to the parent theme as a child theme.
   b. You use a plug-in to create the child theme.
   c. You upload a CSS file.
   d. You append your own style to the parent theme using the CSS customization tools.

2. How does WordPress handle CSS conflicts if a parent and a child theme both specify a style for an element?

   a. The child theme style overrides the parent theme style.
   b. The parent theme style overrides the child theme style.
   c. The WordPress default style is used in case of a conflict.
   d. WordPress shows a CSS error in the debugger.

3. How can you find where a style for an HTML element is set in the parent theme?

   a. Search the MySQL database for the parent theme by file name.
   b. Search the WordPress themes for the name of the parent theme.
   c. Open the parent theme's functions.php file with a text editor and use the Find feature.
   d. Open the parent theme's CSS files in your text editor and search for the style by name or ID.

1) b. The easiest way to create a child theme is to use a plug-in designed for this task. **2) a.** The rules of the WordPress style queue enforce the child theme style over the parent theme style. **3) d.** The parent theme has one or more CSS files that contain all of the styles for the theme.

9.5 Creating a WordPress Plug-In

Until this point in your journey through WordPress, you have been downloading and using plug-ins created by other developers without looking at the source code. Often, you can find a plug-in that does exactly what you want it to do, so you don't need to build your own.

At its core, a plug-in is a simple text file that includes the important information required for the WordPress plug-in engine to recognize and process it as a valid plug-in. Plug-ins are written using a programming language called PHP, which is more complex than JavaScript but includes the same conceptual components.

The developers who contribute to the WordPress project have created a series of tutorials and documentation to help you create your own plug-in. You can review that information at https://developer.wordpress.org/plugins.

In a world filled with negativity, strife, and inferior remakes of movie sequels, it would be nice to have a daily affirmation appear on a WordPress website. However, the site has not had an Affirmation Easter Egg plug-in. Until now.

The Affirmation plug-in goes beyond a simple Hello World plug-in, and further than even a Hello Exoplanet plug-in, in that it displays an affirmation of kindness to the reader of the Totally Awesome Stuff website that was entered in the data entry form created by the plug-in.

Reading the Plug-In Text File

Using your simple text editor, open the affirmation.php text file included with the course downloads for Chapter 9. This plug-in starts as a text file, written in the programming language PHP. **Figure 9-16** displays an example of the PHP code as shown in BBEdit on a Mac.

Figure 9-16 PHP code of the Affirmation Easter Egg plug-in

```php
1    <?php
2    /* Part 1 — the comments that are used to create the Plugin documentation in the WordPress interface
3     * The Affirmations Easter Egg Plugin
4     *
5     * @package Affirmations Easter Egg
6     * @author (your name)
7     * @license GPL-2.0+
8     * @link https://totallyawesomestuff.com/affirm_me/
9     * @copyright 2023 Totally Awesome Stuff, LLC. All rights reserved.
10    *
11    * @wordpress-plugin
12    * Plugin Name: Affirmation Easter Egg Plugin
13    * Plugin URI: https://totallyawesomestuff.com/affirm_me/
14    * Description: Affirmation Easter Egg Plugin creates an input box to update the affirmation hidden in plain sight on the website.
15    * Version: 1.0
16    * Author: (your name)
17    * License: GPL-2.0+
18    * License URI: http://www.gnu.org/licenses/gpl-2.0.txt
19    */
20
21    /* Part 2 — create the hook to the wordpress footer for the function show_affirmation */
22    add_action( 'wp_footer', 'show_affirmation' );
23
24    /* Part 3 — the function used to show the affirmation */
25    function show_affirmation()
26    {
27        $textvar = get_option('affirmation_variable', 'You are Totally Awesome!');
28        echo "<em id='affirm'>".$textvar."</em>";
29    }
```

BBEdit

This code is provided as a file instead of instructing you to build it block by block because this chapter is about WordPress, not PHP coding. Two other chapters in this course are dedicated to PHP. However, WordPress plug-ins are built using PHP, so this section includes a brief discussion of the PHP coding necessary to create the Affirmation Easter Egg plug-in.

- **Line 1:** This line contains the opening PHP declaration, `<?php`. This token tells the PHP processor that everything between the opening `<?php` and the closing `?>` tokens should be processed as PHP code. In this file, the first closing `?>` token occurs on line 51.

- **Lines 2–19:** Starting with the text "Part 1" is a series of comments. Unlike ordinary code comments in JavaScript or HTML that are only for the person reading the code, the WordPress engine transforms the comments in the opening of plug-in code into useful information displayed in the plug-in manager. Multiline comments are surrounded by a /* and a */. A block of these comments extends from line 2 to line 19.

  In your text editor, update the values in the parentheses in this block, such as your name. Read the key/value pairs in these comments. You will see them again in the plug-in manager when you install this plug-in.

- **Lines 21–22:** Part 2 is where operational PHP code begins. The first part of the code on line 22 is add_action(), which assigns a PHP function to a part of the WordPress display. This code is known as a **hook**. A hook is a designated location in WordPress where the developer can add customizations. The function called by the add_action() hook is show_affirmation. Calling on the hook puts the text in the function immediately before the closing </body> tag rendered by the WordPress engine. Note that calling this PHP function does not require the use of parentheses.

- **Lines 24–29:** Part 3 in the plug-in code is where the value stored in the WordPress option uncreatively named "affirmation_variable" is displayed for the website visitor. The PHP variable used for this process is $txt_affirm. In PHP, variables don't need to be declared before using them, just like in JavaScript. Using the variable creates it. The value assigned to this variable comes from the function get_option() on line 27.

  An option in WordPress is a variable used to store a block of text, a setting, or other important piece of information that isn't part of a theme, plug-in, or other type of data. The option values are stored in the database to ensure they exist even if the website is updated in other ways. Options have a name and a value.

  The second parameter in the get_option() function is a hardcoded default value to ensure that some value is displayed if one has not been stored previously. The code on line 28 starting with the command echo prints the contents of the PHP variable between an opening and closing <em> tag with an ID of affirm. The ID for the <em> tag will be useful later when you need to apply additional style to its contents.

- **Lines 31–32:** Part 4 adds another hook for this plug-in to the WordPress admin_menu section, which is the menu in the WordPress dashboard. The hook uses the PHP function called my_admin_menu, which can be found in Part 5.

  The PHP function my_admin_menu calls another function, add_management_page, which is a WordPress function used to create the details of the options you have been using when you clicked menu items in the WordPress Dashboard.

  You can read more about the add_management_page function in the developer documentation at https://developer.wordpress.org/reference/functions/add_management_page. That link is also useful for the other WordPress-specific functions referenced in this section.

  The function add_management_page takes five parameters. In order, they are the page title, menu title, capability, menu slug, and callback function. The name of the callback function is affirmation_updater, which is the PHP function found in Part 6 of this code.

- **Lines 40–67:** Part 6 is the longest block of code, and it is composed of PHP and raw HTML. These lines are part of an extended PHP function called affirmation_updater, which creates the user interface you use to update the affirmation.

  The first block of code in this function checks to see if the affirmation data entry form has been submitted with a new value and, if it has, updates the WordPress option variable affirmation_variable to the text that was entered in a text box later in the code. A user can update the option by storing it in the MySQL database, where it is retrieved and shown in the footer when the webpages load.

  The token ?> on line 51 ends the PHP code so that a block of HTML can be used to display a simple web form. This web form contains HTML and PHP operators to retrieve values from the PHP variables used in this code. In this way, standard HTML can be mixed with PHP to use the values of the variable set elsewhere, in code like the following:

```
value="<?php echo $txt_affirm; ?>"
```

That line of code is on line 57 for the value of the input text box to retrieve the PHP variable $txt_affirm and show it in the HTML text box.

The final five lines of code close the PHP function affirmation_updater. The closing curly bracket is on line 65 by itself to make it easy to find.

Uploading Your Plug-In to a WordPress Website

You can convert the affirmation.php plug-in file you have been examining to an uploadable plug-in that WordPress accepts if you add it to a zip file. The plug-in upload feature in WordPress only accepts files with a .zip extension.

To upload the plug-in to a WordPress website:

1. Using Finder on a Mac, Ctrl+click the file and then click Compress affirmation.php on the shortcut menu. Using File Explorer in Windows, right-click the file and then use the shortcut menu to compress (zip) the file. Either method creates a new zipped file named affirmation.zip.

2. On the WordPress Dashboard, click Plugins, then click Add New on the Plugins menu or click the Add New button on the Plugins page to open the Add Plugins page.

3. Click the Upload Plugin button on the Add Plugins page to open a dialog box like the one shown in **Figure 9-17**.

Figure 9-17 The Add Plugins dialog box

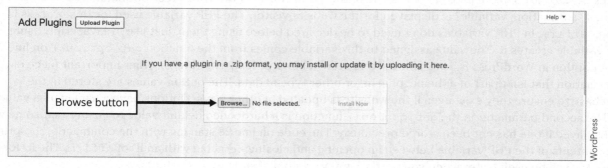

4. Click the Browse button. (Your button may be labeled Choose File.) Navigate to the folder that contains the zip file you just created, click the zip file to select it, and then click Open.

5. Click the Install Now button on the Add Plugins page to display a confirmation window like the one shown in **Figure 9-18**.

Figure 9-18 Installing a plug-in from an uploaded file

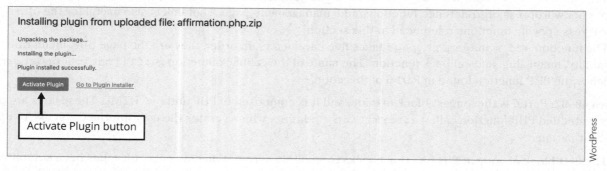

6. Click the Activate Plugin button. On the Plugins page, the Affirmation Easter Egg Plugin is listed with your installed plug-ins. The data you added to the comments at the beginning of the PHP code is used to display data about the plug-in.

Using Your Plug-In

To use the new plug-in on a website:

1. On the WordPress Dashboard, move your pointer over Tools to display the Tools menu shown in **Figure 9-19**.

Figure 9-19   Tools menu with new plug-in

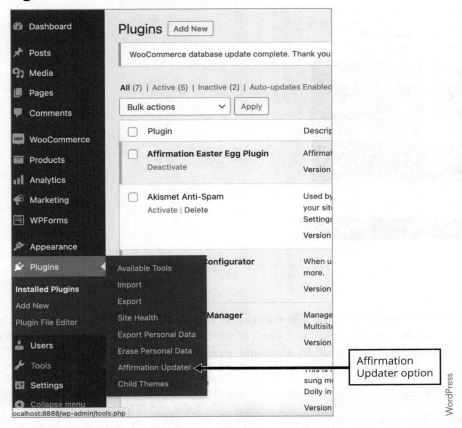

WordPress

2. Click Affirmation Updater to open the Affirmation Easter Egg Changinator window shown in **Figure 9-20**.

Figure 9-20   Affirmation Easter Egg Changinator
window

WordPress

3. Update the text in the text box to an affirmation you would like your site visitors to find and then click the Update Affirmation button. The code that stores your affirmation in the MySQL database runs so the affirmation text can be retrieved when WordPress loads the website.

4. Reload the home page for Totally Awesome Stuff, then scroll to the bottom of the page to display the new affirmation as shown in **Figure 9-21**. (Depending on your theme, you may see something slightly different.)

Figure 9-21 Affirmation text in the footer

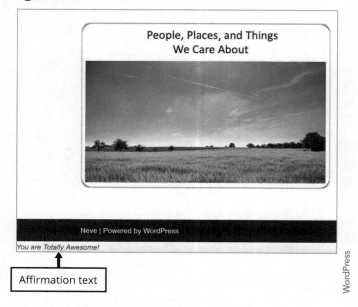

In Project 3 for this chapter, you add style to make the affirmation text appear as part of a black banner, which is the proper Neve theme footer for the Totally Awesome Stuff website. For now, you have completed the task of creating your own plug-in, uploading it, and running it. That's a totally awesome accomplishment.

Quick Check 9-5

1. What is a hook in WordPress?

   a. A headline or text that grabs the reader's attention
   b. A discrete part or block of the webpage like a header or column
   c. A specific place in the WordPress webpage where a developer can add custom code, functionality, or other elements
   d. A link between the HTML page and the CSS file that WordPress uses to create the completed webpage

2. What does `<?php` represent in a plug-in or PHP file?

   a. The opening token to create the start of the PHP code
   b. A PHP variable
   c. The closing token to end the PHP code
   d. The start of a PHP function

3. What is the required file extension for a plug-in uploaded to WordPress?

   a. .txt
   b. .php
   c. .js
   d. .zip

1) c. A hook is a designated location in WordPress where the developer can add customizations. 2) a. The `<?php` token tells the PHP interpreter where the PHP code begins. 3) d. The plug-in upload interface only accepts files with a .zip extension.

Summary

- Websites are hacked because they contain value and the hackers can make money from their effort.

- The OWASP maintains a list of the top 10 security vulnerabilities by calendar year that is useful for review by security-conscious web developers.

- The cost of not implementing robust website security is much greater than the initial expense of setting up a secure website.

- The most common website hacks are automated and are looking for easy points of entry like poorly configured or default-configured login pages.

- Creating a security plan is an important step in full stack web development.

- WordPress provides built-in security features, but because the default configuration is easily available it is also more likely to be probed by hackers.

- WordPress plug-ins to enhance security are widely adopted by WordPress users and make increasing your website security easier than doing it yourself.

- Adding multifactor authentication is a recommended security best practice.

- You can customize a WordPress theme and add your own CSS code to a WordPress theme using WordPress tools.

- Creating a child theme based on a parent theme is an effective way to incorporate a batch of customizations to the parent theme.

- Plug-ins start as PHP code files written in plain text.

- You can upload and incorporate your own plug-in on a website using WordPress tools.

Key Terms

child theme	hook	parent theme
distributed denial of service (DDoS)	multifactor authentication (MFA)	Trojan horses

Review Questions

1. What is the most common type of website hacking? (9.1)

    a. Automated bot attacks probing common security vulnerabilities

    b. Ransomware holding websites hostage

    c. Password-guessing attacks

    d. Bored nerds making mischief

2. Which of the following is NOT a valid component of a security plan? (9.1)

    a. User management best practices

    b. Data and website backups

    c. Using HTTP in the URLs

    d. Sharing the security plan with all people it affects

3. Why is security so important when using WordPress as a CMS? (9.2)

   a. WordPress is buggy software because it has had so many different developers.

   b. Open source software is always less secure because anyone can look at the source code to find vulnerabilities.

   c. WordPress is still being developed so it isn't completely finished.

   d. Because so many websites are published using WordPress

4. What is an automated security audit? (9.2)

   a. A bot that checks your website for vulnerabilities but reports them back to you instead of exploiting them.

   b. A bot that checks your website for vulnerabilities and exploits them instead of reporting them back to you.

   c. Software that performs automated updates to all of the other software packages in a stack used for webpages.

   d. A service offered by security companies who hire white-hat hackers to check for security vulnerabilities in a client's infrastructure.

5. What is a common mistake made when trying to apply a custom CSS to a WordPress website using the visual editor? (9.3)

   a. Applying the style to the whole page instead of a specific HTML element

   b. Applying the style to the block or incorrect HTML element by mistakenly clicking the wrong thing

   c. Not naming the CSS class properly to conform to WordPress naming conventions for custom CSS

   d. Saving the custom CSS file in the wrong place and therefore not making it accessible to the production website

6. What does the key word "inherit" mean in the context of customizing a WordPress theme? (9.3)

   a. An individual style takes its features from the global settings in the theme.

   b. The CSS style being referenced takes its setting from the default browser setting for that element.

   c. The styles applied by the theme's global CSS will ignore any customization for a specific element's local style.

   d. The global style specified by the theme should not be overwritten by a user attempting a local customization.

7. How do you add a custom CSS property to WordPress? (9.3)

   a. You use a plug-in.

   b. You edit the original theme using a text editor.

   c. You use the CSS customization interface.

   d. You can't add a custom CSS property to a WordPress theme.

8. When should you consider creating a child theme in WordPress? (9.4)

   a. When you have more than a few minor changes to the WordPress theme you are using

   b. Any time you want to modify a WordPress theme so that you can keep your changes separate from the original source code

   c. When you can't find a theme that fits the requirements of the website you are building, since all themes are child themes of the WordPress parent theme

   d. When you are ready to start building your own theme from scratch

9. What is the WordPress style queue? (9.4)

   a. The way WordPress tells the browser to handle the cascade of styles applied to HTML elements

   b. The loading process for retrieving first the HTML, then the CSS from the MySQL database when rendering a webpage

   c. The step in rendering a page before sending it to the browser requesting the page where the CSSOM is combined with the HTML DOM to create the page for the browser

   d. The priority application of CSS specifiers in order starting with a specific local CSS style, then the child theme style, and finally the parent theme style

10. Where are child theme styles stored? (9.5)

    a. In a location similar to where the parent theme styles are often stored—in a file called style.css

    b. In the MySQL database table called child_styles

    c. In a configuration section appended to the parent theme in the my_styles.css file

    d. As a separate CSS file called child_styles.css

11. What programming language are WordPress plug-ins written in? (9.5)

    a. JavaScript

    b. A WordPress-specific JavaScript library

    c. PHP

    d. jQuery

12. How do you add your own plug-in to a WordPress website? (9.5)

    a. You use a plug-in to manage your plug-ins.

    b. You save the custom plug-in directly in the MySQL database table my_plugins.

    c. You use the WordPress Dashboard FTP client.

    d. You use the WordPress plug-in manager.

Programming Exercises

1. Using your favorite search engine, research the "most common reasons WordPress websites are hacked." Review five articles in the search results. Write a one-page summary of the reasons and include a list of links to the articles you reviewed. (9.1–9.2)

2. Using your favorite search engine, research the "most useful WordPress security plug-ins." Review five articles in the search results. Write a one-page summary of the security plug-ins and include a list of links to the articles you reviewed. (9.1–9.2)

3. Using your favorite search engine, research "how to create a WordPress plug-in." Review five articles and summarize your findings in a one-page summary. Include links to the articles you reviewed. (9.5)

Projects

1. Create a security plan for your WordPress website. Include in your plan the important items you learned in Sections 9.1 and 9.2 of this chapter. (9.1–9.2)

2. Add and configure the plug-ins WPScan and Wordfence in your WordPress website. Read the documentation for both plug-ins and use the tools they provide to review your website security and harden your WordPress website against hackers. (9.1–9.2)

3. Add the style to your child theme necessary to display the affirmation text you created in this chapter in the footer of your website. If you chose the Neve theme, move the affirmation to the black banner and float it to the right. Update the color of the text to white so that it shows on the black background. If you chose a different theme, update as necessary to incorporate your affirmation text into the footer. (9.3–9.5)

Chapter 10

Building Dynamic Webpages with PHP

Learning Objectives

When you complete this chapter, you will be able to:

10.1 Explain the purpose of PHP.

10.2 Create and use PHP variables in code.

10.3 Create and use user-defined PHP functions.

10.4 Create and use a PHP object.

10.5 Create a PHP web form.

10.1 What Is PHP?

PHP is a programming language created in 1994 by Rasmus Lerndorf. The original acronym PHP stood for Personal Home Page tools but was refactored to stand for PHP: Hypertext Preprocessor.

PHP is a server-side interpreted language, meaning that the code you write is executed by the web server instead of in the web browser. Interpreted languages like PHP are not compiled into executable code—the PHP interpreter executes your code on the web server. Running the PHP code on the web server is different from JavaScript, which is a client-side programming language executed by the web browser.

You can use PHP code to create dynamic webpages composed of HTML and PHP. Thus, your previous experience with HTML will be helpful in creating PHP webpages. The logic of PHP is similar to JavaScript, so your previous experience with JavaScript is also helpful.

Although the syntax of PHP is basic, it is a robust and versatile programming language for creating dynamic webpages. It is similar enough to other programming languages that it is considered one of the best server-side languages to learn at the start of a journey toward becoming a full stack web developer.

What Is PHP Used for?

PHP is primarily used to build dynamic webpages, the contents of which change based on user interaction and input. A simplified use case might be familiar to anyone who has used the Internet—you enter your name, email address, and other demographic information in a web form, click the Submit button, and receive a confirmation message on a new webpage stating that your information has been saved. This use case requires the following steps:

1. A web browser requests the page that contains the data entry form from the web server.
2. The web server composes the page containing the data entry form and sends it to the browser.
3. The browser displays the data entry form in the webpage.
4. The user enters data into the form and clicks the Submit button.
5. The web browser sends a payload of user data from the form to the web server.
6. Code stored on the web server processes the user data.
7. The web server composes and returns a confirmation message and a new page customized to include the user data it received in Step 5.
8. The web browser displays the confirmation message in the second webpage.

Handling user data from a web form is one of three types of tasks that PHP can perform. The other two tasks are command-line scripting and creating desktop applications. Command-line scripting is used for tasks like processing bulk database information on a nightly schedule. Desktop applications are similar to those you are familiar with and use every day. However, developers use PHP for web form processing more often than for other tasks. Other programming languages are better at efficiently managing the details of command-line scripting and creating desktop applications.

Why Learn PHP?

PHP is one of many programming languages you can use to build dynamic webpages. While it was introduced near the beginning of the modern Internet, it has been reinvented and refactored since then to remain a useful programming language for the task it does well—creating dynamic webpages.

PHP has remained in the top 10 list of most in-demand programming languages because it is easy to learn and use. It has a large community of developers contributing time and energy to keeping it relevant as technology continues to evolve. The documentation those PHP developers create is key to helping the new programmers learn PHP.

This course uses PHP instead of another programming language because WordPress is built on PHP. Like WordPress, PHP is also open source. The WordPress plug-ins used in previous chapters are built using PHP.

The fundamentals of programming that you learn by writing code in PHP also apply to the next programming language that might be more complex.

Using MAMP or WAMP

If your school or college has installed the MAMP or WAMP stack on your computer, you are ready to begin working in PHP. If you didn't install the MAMP or WAMP stack when you worked with WordPress, please review and install one of those packages now.

As you may recall, MAMP stands for Macintosh/Apache/MySQL/PHP, and WAMP stands for Windows/Apache/MySQL/PHP. Both are bundles of software preconfigured to run on the operating system that begins the acronym, although MAMP also runs on Windows.

The MAMP or WAMP stack comes bundled with everything you need to begin learning PHP, which you need to complete this tutorial. You also need the Apache web server running to review the dynamic webpages you create. WordPress is not necessary for this tutorial.

If you are reusing the configuration you set up previously to use WordPress on MAMP or WAMP, you need to update the **document root** location from the folder where you installed WordPress to the folder where you store your other chapter projects. The document root is the folder the web server uses as the starting point for finding and running PHP and other files.

On a Mac, complete the following steps:

1. Create a chapter_10 folder in the folder you created for your course files.
2. Create a samples and a projects folder inside the chapter_10 folder. You store the PHP files you create for Chapter 10 in these folders.
3. Open the MAMP application.
4. Click the Preferences button on the toolbar to display the configuration settings shown in **Figure 10-1**.

Figure 10-1   Configuration settings for the MAMP server

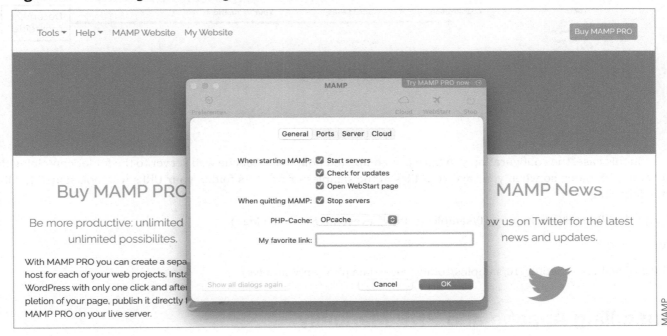

5. Click the Server tab.
6. Click the Choose button, then open the parent folder that contains the Chapter 1 through Chapter 10 folders for this course. The parent folder is the new document root.
7. Save your changes.

On a Windows machine, complete the following steps:

1. Search for the www folder in the WAMP folder created when you installed WAMP.
2. Create a chapter_10 folder inside the www folder.
3. Create a samples and a projects folder in the chapter_10 folder. You store the PHP files you create for Chapter 10 in these folders.
4. Open a web browser then type **localhost** in the address bar to display WAMP server configuration settings like those shown in **Figure 10-2**. The Your Projects section lists the document root folder.

The web server uses the document root as the starting point for finding files to serve and run when web browsers request the files. As you may recall, a web server functions like an Internet-accessible file server locked down to only the directories it can access.

Figure 10-2   **WAMP server configuration settings**

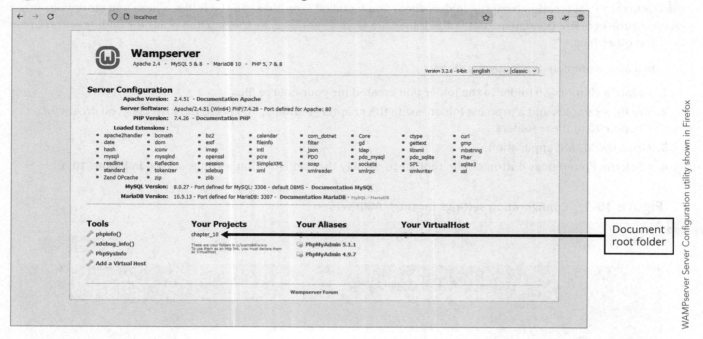

WAMPserver Server Configuration utility shown in Firefox

In this case, the configuration you have just completed points the Apache web server to the folder containing the chapter_10 folder, so when you save your files in the samples or projects folder, your URLs will look something like the following:

http://localhost:8888/chapter_10/samples/totally_awesome.php (on a Mac)

or

http://localhost/chapter_10/samples/totally_awesome.php (on Windows)

Installing Apache and PHP Manually

If you previously installed MAMP or WAMP, you are all set. Those stacks include Apache and PHP, which you need for the steps and exercises in this chapter. If you did not install MAMP or WAMP, you can install and configure Apache and PHP individually.

To download and install PHP, follow the instructions found here:

https://www.php.net/manual/en/install.php

Be sure to choose the documentation that matches your operating system and the most recent production version of PHP. For a more detailed tutorial on installing PHP on your operating system, search online for a tutorial that matches your local setup.

To download and install Apache, follow the instructions found here:

https://www.apache.org

> ## Common Mistakes

One of the most common mistakes made when installing and configuring Apache and PHP manually is storing these applications in folders with path names that contain spaces.

For example, if you install the applications in a folder named My Documents in Windows, errors appear when you try to start Apache because the My Documents folder name contains a space. A quick Google search for the errors provides a common solution: Reinstall everything in a folder structure that doesn't contain folders with spaces in their names.

You'll also need to choose the documentation that matches your operating system. Many tutorials are available online for installing Apache.

After installing PHP and Apache, you need to configure Apache to run PHP. Search online for instructions and demonstration videos.

Writing PHP Code

When you have a computer with the WAMP or MAMP bundle or individual applications for Apache, MySQL, and PHP installed and configured, it's time to write some PHP code. As is traditional, the first code you write displays "Hello, World!" to make sure PHP is working on your machine.

To create a PHP document:

1. In your samples folder, use a text editor to create a new document called hello.php and add the following text to it:

```
<html>
    <head>
        <title>Hello World</title>
    </head>

    <body>
        <h1>
            <?php echo "Hello, World!"; ?>
        </h1>
    </body>
</html>
```

The new PHP code mixed in with the familiar HTML is the line between the `<h1>` and `</h1>` tags. The `<?php` and `?>` opening and closing tags mark the beginning and ending of the contents the PHP interpreter handles.

The `echo` command tells the PHP interpreter to print the contents inside the quotes. The semicolon marks the end of a complete line of code, like the period at the end of a sentence.

2. Save your changes to hello.php.

3. Open your web browser and enter one of the following URLs:

http://localhost:8888/chapter_10/samples/hello.php (on a Mac)

or

http://localhost/chapter_10/samples/hello.php (on Windows)

You should see the standard Hello World application. This tells you more than what you might think—if the text "Hello, World!" is printed on the screen, you know that PHP is installed and configured successfully, Apache is installed and configured successfully, the Apache link to the PHP interpreter is configured properly, and you should be able to successfully complete the next several sections. If you don't see the text "Hello, World!", check your code to find bugs or reexamine your installation and configuration of Apache and PHP.

Finding Bugs in PHP Code

Unlike JavaScript and HTML, the web browser does not tell you what is broken in your PHP code unless one of the following is true:

- The broken PHP code is also generating incorrect HTML or JavaScript errors.
- The settings for your Apache/PHP configuration in the php.ini file allow errors to be sent to the browser.

The reasons PHP errors aren't shown in the web browser by default are twofold.

First, errors aren't occurring in the browser—they are being generated in the web server when it attempts to run your code. The web server can be configured to send these errors to the browser to see them, though this setup creates the second problem.

PHP error messages are very useful for your code development on a local web server like WAMP/MAMP because they tell you why your code isn't working but should never be shown for code that is running in production.

If you configure the production web server to send the text of an error message to the browser about a bug in the PHP running on that web server, you create a potential security vulnerability that a hacker can exploit. Using different configurations to show errors on development servers and hide them on production servers is critical to web security.

For example, if your PHP code has a bug in the process used to access the database and the full description of the error includes the username and password or even the database name, displaying that error gives a hacker valuable information.

Instead, use the default setting that writes errors in production PHP to a log file stored where the Apache web server can access it. This log file is called php_error.log and is typically stored inside a logs folder. The php_error.log file lists all the errors created when your PHP code is running incorrectly.

If you see errors in the web browser when you accidentally or purposefully create an error in PHP code, your configuration is set to use the development setup. This is helpful as you are diagnosing and fixing errors. When you move your code to production, you may need to update your php.ini file on the production server to not show errors in the browser. You can see an error in an example file called hello_world.php shown in **Figure 10-3**. This error was purposefully created by misspelling "echo."

Figure 10-3   Intentional PHP error displayed in the browser

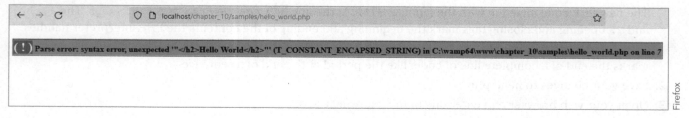

You can turn the error display on and off if you have access to the php.ini file in your Apache/PHP setup. If you do, search the text of the file php.ini for the following setting:

```
error_reporting = on
```

When "on," the error_reporting setting shows the errors in the browser. When it is set to "off," the browser does not show errors, but they are still added to the error log.

Learning what the errors mean is part of learning how to write and fix PHP code. If an error in the log file is not clear, search the Internet to determine what the log is telling you about the error and what you need to do to fix it.

Quick Check 10-1

1. What does PHP stand for?

   a. Program Helpers Perl
   b. Personal Home Page
   c. Percussive Helping Processors
   d. PHP: Hypertext Preprocessor

2. Where is PHP code executed?

   a. In the web browser
   b. In the web server
   c. In the database
   d. In the OS of the web client

3. What is PHP most frequently used for?

   a. Creating dynamic webpages
   b. Creating interactive desktop applications
   c. Creating command-line scripts that run on a schedule
   d. Creating apps that run on mobile devices

1) d. PHP is a recursive acronym for PHP: Hypertext Preprocessor. **2) b.** PHP is a server-side programming language, so it runs on a web server. **3) a.** PHP is used most frequently to create dynamic webpages.

10.2 Creating PHP Variables

As with every modern programming language, PHP has variables to contain data used in the code. Just like JavaScript, variables in PHP are loosely typed, which means the variable called $myVal can contain a string, an integer, or an object. Loosely typed variables have a type only when a value is assigned to them.

Declaring Variables

Unlike JavaScript where variables can begin with any letter or an underscore, all variables in PHP must begin with the same symbol, a dollar sign. This syntax is similar to Perl, which informed the early development of PHP.

Like JavaScript, variables are case sensitive, so $firstName is a different variable from $FirstName.

Also like JavaScript, you can declare your variables by using them. This practice creates the same challenge as in JavaScript. The PHP interpreter considers a new variable valid even if it is unintentionally introduced by misspelling an existing variable. PHP does not have a Let or Var declaration syntax as JavaScript does, however.

Following the starting character of the dollar sign, PHP variable names can use either the underscore or a letter to begin the name. The characters that follow can be any combination of letters and numbers, along with the underscore. For example, `$firstName`, `$_firstName`, and `$first_name` are valid PHP variable names.

A word of caution about naming variables: using descriptive names for your variables is helpful to the next developer who picks up your code. Using the variable `$x` is perfectly acceptable from the PHP interpreter's standpoint but doesn't help you or the next developer identify what that variable `$x` is used for. Instead, if you call that variable `$firstName`, you and anyone else reading the code knows exactly what data type that variable should contain and what value should be found in it.

Types of Variables

As with most programming languages, PHP variables can contain any of the important types of data that might be used in code. Integers, text strings, decimal values, arrays, or PHP objects can all be stored in PHP variables. You create examples of some of these types in the next section.

Variable typing is important when using and processing variable contents. If you attempt to add two integers using the mathematical + operator, you will get the results you expect. On the other hand, if you attempt to add an integer value to a string using the + operator by mistake, you will get an unexpected result.

For example, if a PHP string variable contains the value "hello" and an integer variable contains the value "34," adding the string and integer variable values results in 34. However, if the string variable value is set to "321 Baltic Avenue" and you add it to the integer variable value "34," the result will be 355 because the PHP interpreter will convert the string value "321 Baltic Avenue" to the integer value 321 and then add the 34.

This would not be something most programmers would do on purpose, of course, but PHP doesn't generate an error like other strongly typed languages will, so that mistake is not easy to diagnose.

Using Variables

You can practice writing PHP code by creating a PHP file that demonstrates using variables.

To use PHP variables:

1. Begin by saving a copy of the hello.php file as variableinator.php. Change the contents of the first few lines so they match the following code:

```html
<html>
    <head>
        <title>Variableinator</title>
    </head>

    <body>
        <h1>Variable Demo</h1>
        <p>
```

2. On a new line below the opening `<p>` tag, enter the beginning of the PHP code:

```php
<?php
// integer variables
$integer1 = 12;
$integer2 = 34;
```

The first line of the new code is a PHP comment. The next two lines of code declare two PHP variables ($integer1 and $integer2) and assign them integer values of 12 and 34, respectively. Because those values are integers, the variables are treated by the PHP interpreter as integer variables.

3. Add the following code after the first two variable declarations:

```
// string variables
$string1 = "first string";
$string2 = "second string";
```

After the // string variables comment, the PHP variables $string1 and $string2 are assigned string values. Contextually, the PHP interpreter treats these variables as strings, so using any mathematical operators like addition or subtraction won't work with the variables.

4. Add the following code after the previous two variable declarations:

```
// float variables
$float1 = 1.23;
$float2 = 4.56;
```

The $float1 and $float2 variables are two floating decimal point variables, or float variables. They are different from integers because they contain a decimal point. If you need to create a floating point variable but use an integer as the starting value, you can assign a value like 4.0 to a PHP variable.

5. Add the following code after the two float variable declarations:

```
// a Boolean variable
$bool1 = true;
```

This is a Boolean variable used to hold a value of true or false. In this case, the $bool1 variable will evaluate to true in any if() or while() conditional test. You have used conditional tests in the chapters on JavaScript and jQuery, and PHP follows the same logic and syntax.

Note

In addition to Boolean variables, PHP has Boolean expressions like the one in the following example that evaluates to true:

```
$myInt = 10;
if($myInt > 5) //evaluates to true
```

The first line of this code is the declaration of an integer variable. The second compares the variable $myInt and the value 5 using the PHP operator for evaluating greater than (>). The evaluation of the $myInt variable occurs inside the parentheses of a conditional, if. Because this conditional evaluates to true, whatever follows the conditional statement is run next.

The previous code is an example of the use of a Boolean expression in PHP—you don't need to add it to your code.

---

6. Add the following code after the Boolean variable declaration:

```
// array variables
$arr1 = array("one","two","three");
$arr2 = array(4,5,6);
```

The $arr1 and $arr2 variables are examples of the array variable declaration in PHP. An array is one variable that contains multiple items of the same type that can be accessed using the index of the item in the array.

All arrays start with an index of 0 for the first item. A convenient way to think about arrays is like a row in a spreadsheet that contains values, with the first column having a header label of 0 and the second column having the header label of 1 and so forth.

In this case, $arr1[0] will retrieve the value at the first position in the array, or "one".

Arrays are a useful data structure when you need two or more of the same type of data stored in a single location. You could create different variables to hold each data element, but that would be inefficient.

7. Add the following block of code to display all the variables when the PHP interpreter runs this PHP page and the Apache web server returns the results to the browser:

```
echo "integer addition: ".($integer1 + $integer2);
echo "<br/>";
echo "string concatenation: ".$string1." ".$string2."!";
echo "<br/>";
echo "float division: ".($float1 / $float2);
echo "<br/>";
echo "bool evaluation: ";
var_export($bool1);
echo "<br/>";
echo "array display: ".$arr1[2];
echo "<br/>";
echo "array display: ".$arr2[2];
```

Each line of code will display the contents listed after the echo statement, with some evaluation in the case of the variables. Every other line is a line break rendered as a string. These line breaks are sent to the browser as valid HTML. The browser uses the line breaks to create a new line after the PHP interpreter processes it through the Apache web server.

The first line of code (echo "integer addition: ".($integer1 + $integer2);) uses string concatenation to append the sum of two integer variables to a string with the dot operator. This is another instance where reading the code from right to left yields the procedure the code follows.

First, the $integer1 and integer2 variables in the parentheses are added together. The PHP interpreter uses the integer contents of those variables to perform integer addition, and the parentheses suggest the order of operations. To the left of the opening parenthesis, the dot operator appends the results of the calculation to the "integer addition: " string, which comes before it. Finally, the echo command puts the entire result on the output stream to display in the HTML of the webpage that the Apache web server returns to the browser.

Following the line break is an example of string concatenation using string variables: echo "string concatenation: ".$string1." ".$string2."!";. This is a common operation in dynamic applications, where data like a user's first and last names are retrieved from a database and then added to an HTML page for display. In this case, the code concatenates the three text strings in quotes to the values of $string1 and $string2 using PHP string concatenation operators.

After the next line break is PHP code performing floating point, or decimal division: echo "float division: ".($float1 / $float2);. This operation will display a long decimal number on the webpage. Since the operation does not include rounding, the full extent of the allowed decimal places will be shown.

The bool evaluation in the echo "bool evaluation: "; and var_export($bool1); lines is different from the rest of the code because it uses the native PHP function val_export() to turn the Boolean variable value into a text string. Boolean variables contain either a true or a false value—not the word *true* or *false*. To retrieve the value and convert it to the text string "true" or "false," you use the val_export() function. The

$bool1 variable is sent to the val_export() function to convert the value to a string. The val_export() function is a convenient way to examine the contents of any variable, but it is especially useful with Boolean variables.

The next two lines of PHP are echo "array display: ".$arr1[2]; and echo "array display: ".$arr2[2];. They retrieve values from the $arr1 and arr2 variables using the index to retrieve a specific value from each array.

Note that the arrays used in this section store three values each. The code $arr1[2] retrieves the third element, which is stored at the index position of 2 because positions are numbered starting with 0.

8. If necessary, add the following closing tags to complete the code:

```
?>

        </p>
    </body>
</html>
```

9. Save your changes to variableinator.php. The code in a text editor should look like that shown in **Figure 10-4**.

Figure 10-4   Completed code in variableinator.php

```
1   <html>
2       <head>
3           <title>Variableinator</title>
4       </head>
5
6       <body>
7           <h1>Variable Demo</h1>
8           <p>
9               <?php
10              // integer variables
11              $integer1 = 12;
12              $integer2 = 34;
13              // string variables
14              $string1 = "first string ";
15              $string2 = "second string ";
16              // float variables
17              $float1 = 1.23;
18              $float2 = 4.56;
19              // a boolean variable
20              $bool1 = true;
21              // array variables
22              $arr1 = array("one","two","three");
23              $arr2 = array(4,5,6);
24
25              echo "integer addition: ".($integer1+$integer2);
26              echo "<br/>";
27              echo "string concatenation: ".($string1." ".$string2)."!";
28              echo "<br/>";
29              echo "float division: ".($float1/$float2);
30              echo "<br/>";
31              echo "bool evaluation: ";
32              var_export($bool1);
33              echo "<br/>";
34              echo "array display: ".$arr1[2];
35              echo "<br/>";
36              echo "array display: ".$arr2[2];
37              ?>
38          </p>
39      </body>
40  </html>
```

BBEdit

10. Open the page variableinator.php from your localhost. The results in a browser should look like **Figure 10-5**.

Figure 10-5 The variableinator PHP code displayed in a browser

Variable Demo

integer addition: 46
string concatenation: first string second string !
float division: 0.26973684210526
bool evaluation: true
array display: three
array display: 6

Mozilla Firefox

Variable Scope

A PHP variable has a **scope**, or the limits of where it is valid. The scope prevents the PHP interpreter from confusing variables with the same name in different blocks of code. The scope also prevents variables from continuing to exist beyond the flow of the code they belong in.

Variables declared inside a function can't be used outside that function unless they are purposefully sent to another function using the syntax like the following:

```
doStuff($myVar);
```

This code calls the function `doStuff` and sends it the variable `$myVar`.

Similarly, variables declared outside a function can't be used in the function unless they are passed into that function via the parentheses at the end of the function name, as in the following example:

```
function doStuff($myVar){
}
```

In this code, `$myVar` is being sent into the function `doStuff` so the function can use the variable. You will see a more tangible example of this important concept in the next section on PHP functions.

Quick Check 10-2

1. What is meant by variables being loosely typed in PHP?

    a. Loosely typed variable names are not case sensitive.

    b. Loosely typed variables don't have any required character pattern that they need to follow.

    c. Loosely typed variables can contain any type of value and become that value type when the value is assigned.

    d. Loosely typed variables are easier to use than strongly typed variables.

2. How do you create a variable in PHP?

    a. By using it in the code

    b. Declaring it with a data type and size limit

    c. Using the `Dim` variable declaration statement

    d. Using the `Var` or `Let` variable declaration statement

3. Why is $x not a good name for a variable in PHP?

    a. Because it doesn't follow the PHP rules for naming variables.

    b. Because it will cause an error when the code is executed by the PHP interpreter.

    c. Because it is too few characters to be a valid variable name.

    d. Because it is not self-descriptive.

> **1) c.** Loosely typed variables only have a type when a value is assigned to them. **2) a.** Just like JavaScript, PHP variables are created when you start using them in the code. **3) d.** Variable names should be self-descriptive to make it easier to see what they are used for.

10.3 Using PHP Functions

Functions in PHP are similar to functions in every other programming language, including the JavaScript functions you have created and used previously. Functions are blocks of code with a distinct name and a clearly defined beginning and end.

Programming theory suggests that each function should perform one discrete task, like opening a file. In the real world, functions often combine a group of related tasks into one block of code such as opening a file, reading its contents, and then printing the contents to the screen.

Programming in the real world is composed of a set of pragmatic judgments that you make as a developer. Programming theory about functions is clean and elegant, whereas the real world is messy and disorganized. Often, the deciding factor in determining what makes a function complete is the judgment you make to avoid repeating yourself in your code.

For example, suppose you are writing code for a business process and you need to create a function containing two or more tasks that always occur together in the same order. The simplistic approach to coding this solution is to write two sequential tasks in one function.

On the other hand, suppose you need to reuse a specific task from that composite function elsewhere in your code. The rule of Don't Repeat Yourself suggests extracting the reusable task into its own function so you can reduce the amount of code you need to write. You will gain experience in making this judgment as you write more code and recognize where a reusable task can be created.

Functions in PHP come in two flavors—built-in functions and user-defined functions. The PHP programming language has more than 1,000 built-in functions. You saw an example of one built-in function earlier when you used `var_export()` to echo the contents of a Boolean variable to the screen.

User-defined functions are those PHP programmers write to perform a task that fulfills a specific requirement. Like built-in functions, user-defined functions combine variables and logic to produce an output.

Built-In PHP Functions

More than 1,000 functions are listed in the documentation at the home page of PHP: https://www.php.net/manual/en/indexes.functions.php.

These built-in functions form the foundational layer of operations that PHP can perform. For example, you can use the predefined `filemtime()` function to determine the date and time a file was last modified, without having to create your own code that would accomplish that task. You can find the full documentation of how to use the `filemtime()` built-in function at https://www.php.net/manual/en/function.filemtime.php.

This PHP documentation provides a full description of what each function does, how to use it, and a sample block of code that uses the function.

It is always a good idea to see if PHP has a built-in function before creating your own user-defined function, since using someone else's tested code saves you significant development time.

Additionally, because the PHP development community is well supported by subject-matter experts, you can have confidence that the built-in function is significantly less prone to error than a function you create when you are first starting to write PHP code for yourself.

User-Defined PHP Functions

User-defined functions are those a programmer creates to perform discrete tasks that the built-in PHP functions cannot complete successfully. User-defined functions can be composed of built-in PHP functions, user-defined code, and user-defined variables.

The syntax of a user-defined function in PHP is similar to JavaScript. To begin exploring this new code, complete the following steps:

1. Create a copy of the variableinator.php file and save it as functionator.php. Remove the contents between the `<?php` and `?>` tags, change the page title to **Functionator**, and update the text of the h1 tags to **Function Demo**.

   PHP functions have two components—the **function declaration** and the **function body**. The function declaration is the first line of the function that begins with the word `function`. The function body is the block of code that follows, beginning with the opening curly bracket and ending with the closing curly bracket. The **function call** is the block of code found outside of the function but within the PHP tags that tells the PHP interpreter to run the code in the function. Without a function call, the function itself won't execute.

2. Inside the opening `<?php` tag, add the following function:

```
// display a value using a function
function showValue() {
    echo "This is a value<br/>";
    return;
}
```

   This function performs one discrete task. The task is to show a value on the page when it is rendered in the browser.

   The function begins with the keyword `function` and has a descriptive name, `showValue`. The opening curly bracket signifies the beginning of the contents of the function code.

   The first statement (line of code) uses the PHP `echo` directive to display the string that follows on the screen. This is similar to what you have done with the Hello World example. The statement concludes with a semicolon to complete the line.

   The last line of code, `return;`, is not necessary for this function to run since no value is being returned. The flow of processing from the calling function through this function and back to the calling function will follow an implicit return path without the explicit code `return;`, but using `return;` is helpful to identify the path where that flow occurs.

3. Add the following calling function after the closing curly bracket of the `showValue` function:

```
// run all of the functions from a single function
function runFunctions()
{
    showValue();
}
```

The `runFunctions` function will call each function you create in this tutorial so that they run in order.

4. Add the following lines of code to call and run the `runFunctions` function.

```
// call the function so it runs
runFunctions();
```

The code at this point is shown in **Figure 10-6**.

Figure 10-6   Adding a function to functionator.php

```
1  ▼  <html>
2  ▼      <head>
3             <title>Functionator</title>
4  ⌐      </head>
5
6  ▼      <body>
7             <h1>Function Demo</h1>
8  ▼         <p>
9  ▼            <?php
10                // display a value using a function
11 ▼             function showValue() {
12                    echo "This is a value<br/>";
13                    return;
14 ⌐             }
15                // run all of the functions from a single function
16                function runFunctions()
17 ▼             {
18                    showValue();
19 ⌐             }
20                |
21                // call the function so it runs
22                runFunctions();
23 ⌐         ?>
24 ⌐      </p>
25 ⌐      </body>
26 ⌐  </html>
```

BBEdit

5. Save your changes and open the page functionator.php in your web browser. You should see the text of the function `showValue` displayed on the page.

The flow of code that makes this possible starts from the bottom and runs upward through the code. It starts with the last line of code containing the name of the first function to run, `runFunctions();`. This function calls the only other function currently on this webpage, `showValue`, which displays a string.

6. Add the following new function right after the `showValue` function and before the `runFunctions` function:

```
// display a value sent to the function
function showInputValue($inVal) {
    echo "input value: ".$inVal."<br/>";
    return;
}
```

This new function takes a parameter (the `$inVal` variable) that the function call sends to it. The next two lines of code are similar to code you have used before. They concatenate string values to show a string on the page and then return the programmatic flow to the original calling function.

7. The calling function is the same as before, so add the following code immediately below the `showValue();` line inside the curly brackets of the `runFunctions()` function:

```
showInputValue("I like cheese!");
```

If you do not actually like cheese, or you are not from Wisconsin (where it is against state law to dislike cheese), you are welcome to update that declaration to something that you do like instead.

8. Save your changes, then refresh the page in your browser. You should now see the declaration from `showInputValue` displayed on your page in addition to the previous value being shown.

9. Add another function after the `showInputValue` closing curly bracket and before the `runFunctions()` function:

```
// return the value of a calculation
function returnVariableAddition($inVal1, $inVal2)
{
    return ($inVal1 + $inVal2);
}
```

This function is a new wrinkle on the parts of PHP code that you have already seen. The `$inVal1` and `$inVal2` parameters are expected in the call of this function, sending two values into the function for processing. The line of code between the curly brackets returns the result of a simple calculation—in this case, addition of the two values.

10. Add the following line of code inside the `runFunctions` code before the closing curly bracket:

```
echo returnVariableAddition(2,2);
```

Other functions in this set perform the echo operation to display text on the screen. This example performs a calculation and returns a result to the calling function, which then performs the echo.

11. Save your changes. The functionator.php file in a text editor looks like **Figure 10-7**.

Figure 10-7 Completed functionator.php code

```
1  <html>
2      <head>
3          <title>Functionator</title>
4      </head>
5
6      <body>
7          <h1>Function Demo</h1>
8          <p>
9              <?php
10                 // display a value using a function
11                 function showValue() {
12                     echo "This is a value<br/>";
13                     return;
14                 }
15                 // display a value sent to the function
16                 function showInputValue($inVal) {
17                     echo "input value: ".$inVal."<br/>";
18                     return;
19                 }
20                 // return the value of a calculation
21                 function returnVariableAddition($inVal1, $inVal2)
22                 {
23                     return ($inVal1 + $inVal2);
24                 }
25                 // run all of the functions from a single function
26                 function runFunctions()
27                 {
28                     showValue();
29                     showInputValue("I like cheese!");
30                     echo returnVariableAddition(2,2);
31
32                 }
33                 // call the function so it runs
34                 runFunctions();
35             ?>
36         </p>
37     </body>
38  </html>
```

BBEdit

12. Refresh your browser to display results like those shown in **Figure 10-8**.

Figure 10-8   The functionator PHP code displayed in a browser

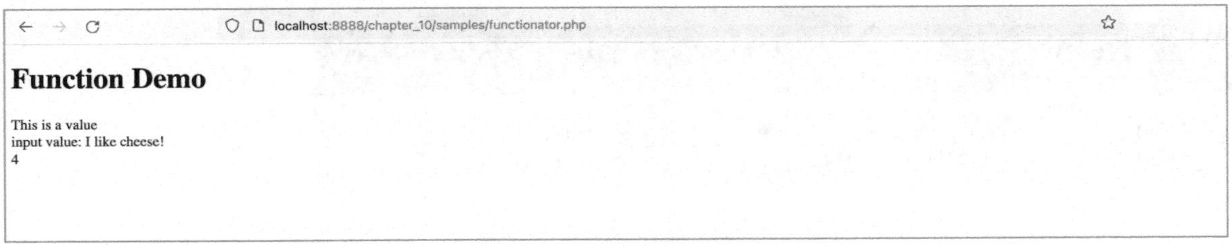

Variable Scope in PHP Functions

If a variable is defined inside a function, its scope is defined by the bounds of that function. The scope of a variable is defined by the code where it is still valid. Recall that a PHP variable can be created just by using it. Consider the following code:

```php
<?php
    // global variable
    $myValA = "A";
    function testVariables()
    {
        //local variable
        $myValB = "B";


        echo "A= ".$myValA;
        echo "B= ".$myValB;
    }
    testVariables();
?>
```

This code has two variables. The $myValA variable is declared inside the PHP tag, and $myValB is declared inside the function testVariables(). Both variables are then printed to the screen inside the testVariables() function using echo statements.

Figure 10-9 shows the results of this code, including an undefined variable error, on the PHP page created by the local WAMP server.

The reason for this error is that while the variable $myValA is declared and used outside of the function testVariables() as a global variable, inside the function it is no longer in scope so it effectively doesn't exist. Global variables are declared outside of any function in PHP.

Figure 10-9 Error from variables being used outside of scope in PHP

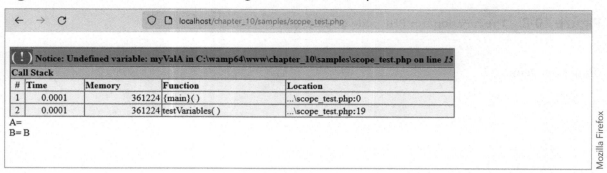

Common Mistakes

It is possible to create global variables in PHP, but it isn't a programming best practice to use them in PHP. Instead, using function-scoped variables with parameter passing is a better way to create and use variables in PHP. Function-scoped variables are declared and used within the same function.

If you need to get data into a function by using a variable, use parameter passing to send the variable in through the parentheses at the end of the function declaration. If you need to send data out of a function to another function, also use parameter passing to accomplish this task.

The result is tidier code that creates less opportunity for making mistakes.

Quick Check 10-3

1. What are user-defined functions in PHP?

   a. Any code that is written in PHP is by definition a user-defined function.
   b. Functions written in PHP by a programmer to accomplish a single task in a business process.
   c. PHP code in the code library that you can use.
   d. Functions that begin with the keyword `_UDFunction`.

2. What is a variable's scope in PHP?

   a. The size of the data it can contain.
   b. The types of data it can contain.
   c. The length of the name of the variable.
   d. The bounds in the PHP code of where the variable is valid.

3. What are global variables in PHP?

   a. Variables that only hold round objects.
   b. Variables that are declared inside of a function.
   c. Variables that are declared outside of any function.
   d. Variables with names that start with a `$g_` prefix.

1) b. User-defined functions are those functions written by a PHP programmer. **2) d.** A variable's scope is the body of code where it is recognized by the interpreter as valid. **3) c.** Global variables are declared outside of any function in PHP.

10.4 Writing Object-Oriented PHP

As you may recall from JavaScript, you can create a class by writing code that serves as a container for a bundle of variables and functions composing a set of related information. The class is a template containing the variables and functions that will be populated by a unique set of data pulled from a database or entered by a user. When the variables and functions in a class receive data while the program is running, an instance of the class is created. That instance is called an object.

Objects and object-oriented programming are part of the vocabulary you need to learn to pass the secret handshake test to be a full stack web developer. Programmers use certain terminology when they are referring to object-oriented programming. Knowing how to translate these terms into concepts you already know is the secret to learning technology like object-oriented programming.

Object-oriented PHP is code written to create and manipulate PHP objects. PHP objects are created when the code using PHP classes is executed. PHP classes are code templates composed of variables and functions that make a logical group. It may sound complex, but it is not that different from what you already know about coding.

Creating Classes in PHP

A typical Student class defines a student as having properties (variables) such as name and grade-point average. A Student class also has methods (functions) that establish and update the properties. For example, one method sets the student name and another gets, or retrieves, the name.

To create a PHP class:

1. Make a new copy of the functionator.php file and call it classinator.php. In a text editor, update the title to **Classinator** and update the heading to **Class Demo**. Remove the contents of the `<?php` and `?>` tags.

2. Add the following code to your classinator.php file between the `<?php` and `?>` tags to create a class in PHP:

```php
class Student {
    // Properties (also known as variables)
    private $name;
    private $gpa;

    // Methods (also known as functions)
    function set_name($name) {
      $this->name = $name;
    }
    function get_name() {
      return $this->name;
    }
     function set_gpa($gpa) {
      $this->gpa = $gpa;
    }
    function get_gpa() {
      return $this->gpa;
    }
  }
```

The class declaration `class Student` signifies that this code will be used to create a class. The name of the class is `Student` because this class holds student data. When you use the `class` declaration followed by a name, you create a class.

Two variables make up the data in a student: `$name;` and `$gpa;`. Because the variables are in a class, they are known as **properties** of the class. When you see the word *properties* used with a class or object-oriented programming, remember they are just variables used inside the class. The keyword `private` declares that the two properties are used by the class and can only be accessed by code inside of the class.

Similar to the concept of variable scope, a `private` declaration for a property means that the scope of the variable is limited to the bounds of the class. The property can't be updated by any code outside of the class. The only way to update private properties is through the public functions of the class that have access to those private properties. The public functions can update private properties because the functions are in the same class as the properties. When the functions are in the same scope as the properties, the functions can update the properties.

The next four functions are `set_name`, `get_name`, `set_gpa`, and `get_gpa`. Functions that set and get are common to classes and object-oriented programming and are collectively known as getters and setters. However, because these functions are in a class, they are also known as **methods**. When you read about methods in the context of object-oriented programming, remember that methods are just functions of the class or object. The difference between a function and a method is that methods are included within the code of the class, and functions are written outside of the code of a class.

The methods in the `Student` class are used to update or retrieve the private properties of the class. Because the properties are declared as `private`, the only way to set them to a value or retrieve a value from them is through the getters and setters. Using setters allows for validating or preprocessing the inbound values that are sent to the class before they are assigned to the properties. Using getters lets PHP translate the values on the outbound path.

The `Student` class does not require much processing to get or set a name or GPA. If another class requires processing, the get and set methods can be used to further process the data before it is sent to or retrieved from the properties. Additionally, the data coming in can be validated before it is set. For example, the string `name` property cannot be set to a numeric `gpa` value by mistake elsewhere in the code.

Note the syntax differences between the `get` and the `set` methods. The `set` methods take a parameter, or value sent to the function, such as `$name` in `function set_name($name)`. They then set the property to that value using the `$this->` signifier, as in `$this->name = $name;`. As you learned in JavaScript and jQuery, `this` is a keyword that refers to the thing itself—in this case, the `Student` class, which becomes the object.

The `get` method returns the appropriate value from the property being accessed by the method. For example, the `get_name` method uses `return $this->name;` to return the name value. Because the `Student` class has only two properties, it needs only four methods to update and retrieve all of the properties. This code is the bulk of the body of the `Student` class and serves as a template for holding a simple set of student data. However, it isn't a student object yet.

Creating Objects in PHP

When a class is filled with a unique record while the code is being executed, the class becomes an object. With a few additional lines of code, object will be created from the `Student` class in classinator.php as the PHP code is running.

First, you should create a **constructor** method for the `Student` class. A constructor is a method in the class that builds an instance of the class, making it an object. Constructors can be written to take in parameters that will fill properties of the object with data. In PHP, constructor functions start with a double underscore, as in `__construct()`. Using the constructor syntax is optional in PHP, but it follows the pattern that other object-oriented programming languages like Java use.

To add a constructor function to the Student class:

1. Add the following code after the get_gpa() function but before the closing curly bracket that marks the end of the class:

```php
function __construct($name, $gpa) {
    $this->name = $name;
    $this->gpa = $gpa;
}
```

This constructor will fill the Student object with the specified data when you create a new student.

2. Add the following printMe() method after the __construct function. The printMe() method lets the Student object print its own name and GPA.

```php
function printMe() {
    echo $this->name." has a GPA of ".$this->gpa;
}
```

3. Add the following code after the closing curly bracket for the Student class:

```php
// create an instance of the Student class
$aStudent = new Student("Roberto Saunders",4.0);
```

The code after the comment creates an object from the class. It declares the variable $aStudent and fills the Student class with two specific pieces of data—a name and a GPA—that the object in $aStudent can manipulate with its methods. The code new Student() calls the __construct() method in the class to properly route those starting values into the properties of the class while creating an object in the variable $aStudent.

4. Add the following code to display the properties of the Student object:

```php
// print the properties of the Student object on the screen
$aStudent->printMe();
```

This line of code calls the printMe() method from the $aStudent object.

Figure 10-10 shows the completed code.

5. Save your changes, then open the page classinator.php in your browser. You should see the results shown in **Figure 10-11**.

Using Classes and Objects

If the classinator.php code to create a Student object seems like a lot of work for minimal gain, consider the following. With the most recent lines of code, you created an object containing two distinct data elements. That object can now be referred to using a single handle, the name of the object $aStudent. Any properties can be retrieved from the object using an appropriate method, like $aStudent->get_gpa(); or $aStudent->get_name();.

The effect of creating a Student object is some fantastic strategic efficiency. By creating the code that encapsulates the important data elements and the functions necessary to process those elements, you create a single chunk of code that can be reused over and over again. That chunk of code is the class. Each time you reuse a class to create another object, the object includes a unique set of data that the methods in the object can manipulate.

The next strategically efficient use of the Student object could be to create a Course object composed of many Student objects. Each Course object would also have an instructor, a room number, title, and so forth unique to that course, along with the set of students who have signed up for the course.

Figure 10-10 PHP code for the `Student` class

```
1    <html>
2        <head>
3            <title>Classinator</title>
4        </head>
5        <body>
6            <h1>Class Demo</h1>
7            <p>
8                <?php
9                    class Student {
10                       // Properties (also known as variables)
11                       private $name;
12                       private $gpa;
13
14                       // Methods (also known as functions)
15                       function set_name($name) {
16                           $this->name = $name;
17                       }
18                       function get_name() {
19                           return $this->name;
20                       }
21                       function set_gpa($gpa) {
22                           $this->gpa = $gpa;
23                       }
24                       function get_gpa() {
25                           return $this->gpa;
26                       }
27                       function __construct($name, $gpa) {
28                           $this->name = $name;
29                           $this->gpa = $gpa;
30                       }
31                       function printMe() {
32                           echo $this->name." has a GPA of ".$this->gpa;
33                       }
34                   }
35                   //create an instance of the Student class
36                   $aStudent = new Student("Roberto Saunders",4.0);
37                   //print the properties of the Student object on the screen
38                   $aStudent->printMe();
39                ?>
40            </p>
41        </body>
42    </html>
```

BBEdit

Figure 10-11 The classinator PHP code displayed in a browser

Mozilla Firefox

By breaking down each logical chunk of data into a building block, you realize a great deal of coding efficiency. Additionally, if you need to update the `Student` class to include a `Photo_ID_Number` property, you only need to update the code in one place—the class. All the other uses of that student object in your code will reflect the change. You will then be able to use that `Photo_ID_Number` property everywhere you use a student object.

By working harder at the beginning of a project, you can save time later when you need to use the classes you create. This is, of course, strategic efficiency.

Quick Check 10-4

1. How does the code of a PHP class become an object?

  a. When the code is being executed
  b. When the code containing it is compiled
  c. When the Apache web server sends it to the browser
  d. When the developer enters and saves the class code

2. How is a class created in PHP?

  a. By using the `class` declaration in front of a name
  b. By declaring a valid PHP variable with the `$_Class` prefix
  c. When an empty object is filled with data as the code is executed
  d. Any valid PHP variable will be used as a class by the PHP interpreter.

3. What is the difference between a function and a method?

  a. Functions are blocks of code outside a class, and methods are functions inside a class.
  b. Methods are declared using the `Method` operator, and functions are declared using the `Function` operator.
  c. Functions are a special type of method used in a class.
  d. Methods can only be used outside of a class, and functions can only be used inside of a class.

1) a. Classes become objects when they are in running code. **2) a.** Using the `class` declaration tells the PHP interpreter that the name and code that follows is to be treated as a class. **3) a.** The only difference between functions and methods is that functions are outside of a class, and a function used inside of a class is called a method.

10.5 Creating Dynamic HTML Pages Using PHP

In this section, you create a web form that gathers data in the web browser and then sends it to the server. On the web server, the server-side code processes the data and then returns it to the browser in another page. This is the essence of building dynamic webpages.

Recall that static webpages are sent from the web server to the web browser in a one-way handoff of the file. Dynamic webpages accept user input to create a unique page for each two-way transaction between the browser and the web server. The web server can create dynamic pages from database contents before the user interacts with them, or the user can enter form data that is routed first to the web server then to a database.

Building the Web Form

Web forms with PHP are similar to the HTML forms you created in other chapters. To create a basic web form:

1. Make a new copy of the classinator.php file and call it my_form.php. In a text editor, remove the content between the `<body>`...`<body>` tags, update the title to **My First PHP Form**, and insert an h1 element with the same text between the `<body>`...`</body>` tags.

2. Add the following code after the h1 element:

```
<form action='name_reflector.php' method="post">
    <label for="fname">First Name:</label>
    <input type="text" id="fname" name="fname" /><br>
    <label for="lname">Last Name:</label>
    <input type="text" id="lname" name="lname" /><br>
    <input type="submit" value="Submit" />
</form>
```

This is similar to the HTML you used when building webpages, except for the two new attributes in the `<form>` tag. The `action` attribute tells the browser what webpage on the web server to send the data gathered by the form to (name_reflector.php, in this case), and the `method` attribute tells the browser what method to use to send that data (post).

3. Save your changes to my_form.php.

The two basic `method` operators are GET and POST. The GET method sends the form data in plain text as part of the page request, effectively creating the following URL:

name_reflector.php?fname=bilbo&lname=baggins

The POST method creates a data structure that is passed to the web server as a set of key/value pairs. If the URL uses HTTPS, the data structure is encoded prior to sending, which further helps with web data security.

Processing the Submitted Values

The web form you just created is the first step of form submission and reflection. The second step is writing the code that runs on the web server to handle the submitted data.

In the following steps, you reflect the submitted data onto a new webpage to see how the web server cycle works. In the real world, the data would be stored in a database or processed in a more complex manner.

To process the form data:

1. Make a new copy of the classinator.php file and call it name_reflector.php. Update the title and heading text to **Name Reflector**, and then remove the code between the `<?php` and `?>` tags.
2. Add the following code between the `<?php` and `?>` tags:

```
if ($_SERVER["REQUEST_METHOD"] == "POST")
{
    $fname = $_POST["fname"];
    $lname = $_POST["lname"];
}
echo "<h2>Hello ".$fname." ".$lname."!</h2>";
```

This new PHP code runs on the web server to capture the data sent in the POST request from the web browser to the web server. First, the `if ($_SERVER["REQUEST_METHOD"] == "POST")` code checks to see if the browser is using the correct method for this form to capture the data. If the sending form is using the right method (POST), the rest of the code will run properly. If the sending form is using the GET method, this code will not run, nor will it create an error. This data processor is tightly coupled to the POST method.

Next, two string variables are created (`$fname` and `$lname`) to capture parts of the `$_POST` values. The key/value pairs in a POST request correspond to the keys (the names of the input elements in the form) and the values the user enters before clicking the Submit button.

The keys have to match the web form input names exactly because POST uses the names from the input form elements as the first part of the key/value pairs. If you are debugging a web form or data processing script that isn't working properly, check whether you are misspelling a key/value in your data transaction if the rest of the values are working properly.

3. Save your code in name_reflector.php, then open the webpage my_form.php in your browser. Type a first name and last name, then click the Submit button. The name_reflector.php page loads and reflects the data you entered in the form.

This, in a nutshell, is how web form data processing works. But there's a problem.

Web Form Security with PHP

The problem involves web security. To test the security of the web form:

1. Reload the web form my_form.php in the browser. Enter `<a href='https://www.lego.com/'>Click Me!!!</a>` in the First Name box. Enter `<script>alert(document.cookie)</script>` in the Last Name box.

2. Click the Submit button in the form, click OK if necessary, and look carefully at the results displayed in the name_reflector.php page. The link you just created to lego.com actually works and will take you to the fun of buying Legos. However, this link could also take an unsuspecting user to a malicious site. This is bad.

The second line of code entered into the Last Name text box creates an executable script that, when added to a webpage, captures and displays any cookies in the user's browser. When you submitted the form, you should have seen an odd-looking pop-up like that shown in **Figure 10-12** because the script you typed into the input text box became part of the code in the page that the browser dutifully executed.

Figure 10-12   Adding scripting code to input fields in a non-secure PHP web form

That is really bad.

This pop-up code results in displaying a custom cookie with the text "this is a delicious chocolate chip cookie" that was added manually to the other cookies in the browser. Your display will be different depending on what other cookies have been set on your browser. You can use the Web Developer tools in your browser to create your own custom cookie if you would like to recreate this pop-up exactly.

Although displaying the custom cookie in an alert is not actually malicious, a different script easily could be. Loading an external script that can run in the browser requires only the additional webpage code that the browser executes. The code `<script>alert(document.cookie)</script>` did exactly this.

You can solve this critical problem by validating form input and filtering data. As you saw in JavaScript and jQuery, form validation prior to submission is an integral part of good data hygiene. You can add HTML5 attributes to your form input elements like `"required"` and `"type='email'"` or `"type='number'"` to ensure non-malicious users supply the necessary data in the proper format when they use your form.

If your web form allows only specified types of data and includes length limits that prevent users from adding long script tags, you create a first layer of defense. This is not a guarantee of complete protection, however, since an adept hacker can post malicious code using other tools like the JavaScript debugger in the browser. The next and more effective layer of web security occurs at the web server.

You need additional PHP functions in your web server code to filter out bad data. PHP has several built-in functions to help address this concern.

1. Update the two variable assignments in name_reflector.php to reflect the following bold code:

```
$fname = filter_var($_POST["fname"],FILTER_SANITIZE_STRING);
$lname = filter_var($_POST["lname"],FILTER_SANITIZE_STRING);
```

The built-in PHP function `filter_var` is designed to prevent malicious code injection like you just created. It does so by filtering the contents of variables that might contain malicious content. The parameter `FILTER_SANITIZE_STRING` identifies what type of data is expected so that an email address or a date is not corrected by the `filter_var` function inappropriately.

To read more about the `filter_var` function, including additional parameters, see https://www.php.net/manual/en/function.filter-var.php.

The name_reflector.php code should look like **Figure 10-13**.

Figure 10-13 The name_reflector.php code updated for security

```
1   <html>
2       <head>
3           <title>Name Reflector</title>
4       </head>
5       <body>
6           <h1>Name Reflector</h1>
7           <p>
8               <?php
9                   if ($_SERVER["REQUEST_METHOD"] == "POST")
10                  {
11                      $fname = filter_var($_POST["fname"],FILTER_SANITIZE_STRING);
12                      $lname = filter_var($_POST["lname"],FILTER_SANITIZE_STRING);
13                  }
14                  echo "<h2>Hello ".$fname." ".$lname."!</h2>";
15              ?>
16          </p>
17      </body>
18  </html>
```

2. Save your changes, refresh the web form, and reenter the semi-malicious script and link in the First Name and Last Name boxes.

3. Click the Submit button and review the results. Plain text and no pop-up should appear on the page.

This is now the beginning of securely processing a web form that completes the cycle from web server to browser, back to the web server, and finally back to the browser. This is how dynamic webpages work.

Quick Check 10-5

1. Why is server-side data validation important even if you have robust client-side data validation?

    a. Hackers can bypass client-side validation.

    b. Web form validation doesn't work on mobile devices.

    c. Server-side data validation is not important if you have robust client-side data validation that prevents malicious content from making it to the server.

    d. Client-side data validation only catches missing data from required fields.

2. What is the first step in preventing malicious content from being submitted by a hacker?

    a. Client-side data validation

    b. Server-side data validation

    c. Robust encoding of strictly typed variables

    d. Testing your code for vulnerabilities

3. What does the `filter_var` function do in PHP?

    a. Filters variables for those in scope of the current function

    b. Filters variables for those that contain the correct data type

    c. Filters the contents of variables for the correct data type

    d. Filters the contents of variables that might contain malicious content

1) a. Client-side data validation can easily be bypassed by an adept hacker. **2) a.** Client-side validation is the first step, but not the only step, in preventing malicious activity. **3) d.** The built-in function `filter_var` is used to replace malicious content in form data submitted from the web.

Summary

- PHP is a popular programming language used to create dynamic webpages.

- PHP is similar to most other programming languages in its use of variables, functions, and code.

- PHP is considered a good first server-side programming language to learn because it is robust, well documented, open source, and easy to learn.

- PHP variables are loosely typed and declared by using them. PHP variables begin with the $ prefix.

- PHP functions are blocks of code that perform a single task or a group of related tasks that always occur together.

- PHP functions are declared using the `function` declaration.

- PHP classes are logical groupings of variables and functions that encapsulate a body of code.

- A variable inside a class is known as a property. A function inside of a class is known as a method.

- A web form with `action` and `method` attributes can send its data to a block of code on the web server that will process it.

- PHP has built-in functions to prevent malicious activity from occurring when web form data is entered by hackers.

Key Terms

constructor	function call	properties
document root	function declaration	scope
function body	methods	

Review Questions

1. What is the document root in PHP? (10.1)

   a. The folder containing the PHP code that runs to create dynamic PHP pages

   b. The folder containing the PHP interpreter

   c. The folder containing the WAMP/MAMP stack

   d. The folder containing the configuration files for PHP

2. How do you find bugs in PHP code? (10.1)

   a. Look at the error log in the browser.

   b. Look at the errors displayed on the screen of the browser.

   c. Look at the error log on the web server.

   d. Look at the error logs stored in the database.

3. What are float variables used for in PHP? (10.2)

   a. To create a variable that can float between two or more values

   b. To create a variable that can contain a number with a decimal point

   c. To create a variable that can contain any type of value including text or a number

   d. To create a variable that doesn't get a value until it is used in a calculation

4. If the array `$arr1` contains the following data: ("eenie", "meenie", "mienie"), what would the code `$arr1[2]` display? (10.2)

   a. An error

   b. "eenie"

   c. "meenie"

   d. "miene"

5. What is a code statement in PHP? (10.3)

   a. A complete line of code that performs one action and ends with a semicolon.

   b. A complete function with a beginning function declaration and an ending curly bracket.

   c. All code written in PHP is a statement.

   d. A complete line of PHP code that ends with a period.

6. What are parameters used for in PHP functions? (10.3)

   a. To create a single line of code that performs one task

   b. To send values to the function from the function call

   c. To return the value of a variable used within the function

   d. To mark the beginning and end of the function body

7. When should a programming task become its own function instead of remaining a part of a larger function? (10.3)

    a. When it will be used again elsewhere in the code

    b. When the task becomes too long to be completed as part of a larger function

    c. When the code no longer compiles

    d. When the name of the function no longer fits the description of what the task does

8. What are private properties used for in a class? (10.4)

    a. As variables that contain the data of the class

    b. As functions inside the object created by the class

    c. As constants that are not updated

    d. As labels for the object created when using the class

9. What is the difference between a property and a variable? (10.4)

    a. There is no difference between a property and a variable.

    b. JavaScript uses properties and PHP uses variables.

    c. Properties are variables used inside of a class, and variables are used outside of a class.

    d. Variables are properties used inside of a class, and properties are used outside of a class.

10. What does the form `action` attribute tell the browser? (10.5)

    a. What page to send the `POST` or `GET` request to

    b. What server to send the `POST` or `GET` request to

    c. What the URL of the current page is

    d. What to do when the user reloads the webpage

11. What is the data structure created by a `POST` request composed of? (10.5)

    a. An array of the form values

    b. An array of the form elements containing the values

    c. A set of key/value pairs, one for each element in the form

    d. A set of key/value pairs, one for each variable in the form processing code

12. What does the PHP function `var_export()` do? (10.5)

    a. Exports the variable in the parentheses to a text file

    b. Shows all variables used in a PHP function on the screen

    c. Sends the results of the calculation to the browser

    d. Displays the type and contents of a PHP variable

Programming Exercises

1. Using your favorite search engine, search for "most employable or in-demand programming languages." Read at least five of the references you find and summarize the commonalities in a one-page report. Include links to the pages you reviewed. (10.1–10.5)

2. Using your favorite search engine, search for "most common uses of PHP." Read five of the articles returned in the results and summarize the most common uses in a one-page report. Include links to the pages you reviewed. (10.1–10.5)

3. Using your favorite search engine, search for "what websites are built using PHP." Read five of the articles returned in the results and summarize the most common sites in a one-page report. Include links to the pages you reviewed. (10.1–10.5)

Projects

1. Create a PHP class that when executed creates an object that contains data representing important things about you. Your object should contain at least five properties along with their associated getters and setters, an instantiation, and a `printMe()` method that when called displays your information on the screen. Use the classinator.php file as a starting point for your own class. (10.1–10.4)

2. Create a PHP web form that gathers all of the data elements present on a mailing label, and another PHP page that shows those data elements as a properly formatted HTML mailing label when the first web form is submitted. (10.1–10.5)

3. Create a PHP `Address` class that contains all of the properties necessary to be a valid mailing label. Add this class to the mailing label code in Project 2, replacing any code that is no longer necessary. Include a constructor and a `printMe()` method that prints the mailing label. Create an instance of the class, populate it with the `POST` data, and print the object using its own `printMe()` method. (10.1–10.5)

Chapter 11

Database Basics with MySQL

Learning Objectives

When you complete this chapter, you will be able to:

11.1 Define a database and how it is used.

11.2 Create a MySQL database.

11.3 Create MySQL table structures from a data dictionary.

11.4 Build MySQL Create, Read, Update, Delete (CRUD) procedures.

11.5 Create an ad-hoc MySQL query.

11.1 What Is a Database?

If you have used spreadsheet software like Microsoft Excel, you are familiar with the concept of organizing data into tables. A spreadsheet program like Excel uses tables to organize each **field** of a dataset into columns with a row for each **record**. The fields represent individual data elements like those you gather in a web form, such as first name, middle initial, last name, and birthdate. The records represent a single person described by those pieces of data.

A **database** is a structured set of data, typically stored in a computer. A database uses tables as its foundational element with rows and columns that store data in an organized format. However, the difference between a database and a collection of spreadsheets is that the software, structure, and function of the database software extend beyond those foundational tables.

A database is composed of **database objects**, which are the building blocks that web developers and database administrators use to create an instance of a database. Database objects include the following:

- **Tables** contain the rows and columns of data in the database. Tables are the foundational elements upon which all other objects in the database are built or reference.

- **Views** are built from database code to create a table-like structure displaying a subset of the data from one or more of the actual database tables.

- **Stored procedures** are blocks of database code similar to functions in other programming languages and are used to perform repeated tasks like adding, updating, and deleting the data in a table.

- **Indexes** are used to identify the unique piece of information for each record in a table.

- **Sequences** are used to keep a running counter of the next value to be used when a new record is added to a table.

In addition to database objects, you also use a programming language to write the code the database engine can execute. The general database language is called **Structured Query Language (SQL)**.

You use SQL to perform the basic operations of a database: **Create, Read, Update, and Delete (CRUD)**. These four operations are the building blocks of data management:

- Creating a record adds data elements to the columns in the database table.

- Reading a record requests the data elements from the table using criteria to match one or more logical filters.

- Updating a record modifies the data of an existing record.

- Deleting data removes data from a table according to the criteria specified in a delete statement.

You also use SQL to perform the managerial tasks of the database such as creating, reading, updating, and deleting tables and the relationships between them and to create the subprograms that can automate repetitive tasks such as batch updates.

Each brand of database, including MySQL, Oracle, SQL Server, and PostgreSQL, has its own syntax, but the basic SQL structure is similar in these products.

What Is a Database Used For?

The fundamental purpose of a database is to store pieces of data in an organized way so that they can be used together as information. That means a single piece of data like "$12.95" needs to be stored so that it can be accessed, updated, and related to other pieces of data. As a record in a Products table that also contains data such as "Low-Fat Candy for Goldfish" and "10 oz bag," the combined pieces of data become information about the product.

A record in the Products table needs to be displayed in a webpage so it can be useful information for the customers of Totally Awesome Stuff. The record therefore needs to be retrieved by the PHP code that dynamically constructs the webpage on the web server when a browser requests the page to show the product data in an HTML table.

Additionally, the data stored in each table needs to be maintained. Prices can go up or down, products can go out of stock, and new products can be introduced. Maintaining data is significantly easier in the organized storage scheme of a well-designed database.

As another example, consider the pieces of your individual data to store in a Students table for a database for your school. You need to store your first and last or family names and, if you have one, a middle initial. You also need to store a Student ID number, or a Photo ID number if that's how your school uniquely identifies you. Combined, these pieces of data form a one-of-a-kind record that represents you in the Students table.

The Students table for your school will contain many hundreds or thousands of records. You also need to create other tables for other types of data, such as a Class table listing all the classes for a semester. In the Class table, you store data about each class that makes it unique, including Class Name, Class Number, Start Date, End Date, and Number of Credits.

The Students and Class tables contain data representing logical objects for people and classes. Each table has an ID field that uniquely identifies each record. The ID field can contain the value from a running counter of the records added since the table was created. For example, the first record has the ID of 1 and the tenth record has the ID of 10. The unique ID number identifies each record in the database, but it is merely a number that increments each time a new record is added.

To list the students enrolled in classes, you need a third table in the school database. This Enrollment table will contain only the record number for each student enrolled in a class and the record number for the class. You use the Enrollment table to create relationships between students and classes.

You can see an example of how this works in **Figure 11-1**.

Figure 11-1 Design layout for a relationship between students and classes

Students				
ID	Last Name	First Name	Middle Initial	Photo ID Number
234	Chen	Mina	K	999000723
235	Rodriguez	Tony	A	999000204
236	Hollings	Jordan	M	999000349

Classes				
ID	ClassName	Class Number	Start Date	End Date
5872	Macroeconomics	301	09/01/2025	12/21/2025
5873	Thermodynamics	482	09/01/2025	12/21/2025
5874	Full Stack Web Development	201	09/02/2025	12/22/2025

Enrollment		
ID	Student ID	Class ID
523	234	5872
524	235	5872
525	236	5872
526	234	5873
527	235	5873
528	236	5873
529	234	5874
530	235	5874
531	236	5874

An alternative is a flat storage scheme. One table contains every student in every class. Each enrollment record contains all the information about each student and each class. The problem with this approach is one of simple math. If you have 20 students enrolled in five classes each semester, that makes 100 unique rows. Each row contains redundant information about each student and the classes the student is enrolled in. Redundant data leads to errors, inefficiencies, and inconsistencies.

A flat storage scheme violates the notion of Don't Repeat Yourself, since each full student record is repeated up to five times, once for each class the student is enrolled in. Each class is also repeated up to 20 times, once for each student enrolled in it. **Figure 11-2** shows a simplified example of three students enrolled in three classes creating nine rows of redundant data.

Figure 11-2 Design layout for a flat storage scheme of all students enrolled in all classes

ID	Last Name	First Name	Middle Initial	Photo ID Number	Class Name	Class Number	Start Date	End Date
99	Chen	Mina	K	999000723	Macroeconomics	301	09/01/2025	12/21/2025
100	Rodriguez	Tony	A	999000204	Macroeconomics	301	09/01/2025	12/21/2025
101	Hollings	Jordan	M	999000349	Macroeconomics	301	09/01/2025	12/21/2025
102	Chen	Mina	K	999000723	Thermodynamics	482	09/01/2025	12/21/2025
103	Rodriguez	Tony	A	999000204	Thermodynamics	482	09/01/2025	12/21/2025
104	Hollings	Jordan	M	999000349	Thermodynamics	482	09/01/2025	12/21/2025
105	Chen	Mina	K	999000723	Full Stack Web Development	201	09/02/2025	12/22/2025
106	Rodriguez	Tony	A	999000204	Full Stack Web Development	201	09/02/2025	12/22/2025
107	Hollings	Jordan	M	999000349	Full Stack Web Development	201	09/02/2025	12/22/2025

Adding, updating, and deleting records is a challenge when using the flat storage scheme shown in Figure 11-2. If Mina Chen needs a new Photo ID, you need to update her Photo ID number in three rows. If the start date for Thermodynamics is mistyped, three records need to be updated. That's a significant amount of extra work that isn't necessary when you use relationships in a well-designed database. In that case, you could update one piece of data in one row for each change.

Grouping data logically makes a more efficient approach. Each student is stored in one row in one table. Each class is stored in one row in a different table. A third table stores the relationships between unique students and unique classes. This storage scheme minimizes repeated information.

A database composed of tables of related data in this manner is called a relational database. The relationships between the data in the tables is formalized in the code that the database uses. Relationship maintenance is a critical component of relational databases.

Why Learn MySQL?

The database management software included in the WAMP/MAMP stack is called MySQL. It is technically a relational database management system (RDBMS) because it is designed to create and manage database tables and the relationships between those tables.

MySQL is an open-source database management system (DBMS) used throughout the full stack web development ecosystem. It is well documented, and the community of developers who exchange knowledge about using MySQL are helpful in sharing that knowledge with new users.

Other DBMSs are also available. Oracle, Microsoft SQL Server, PostgreSQL, and MongoDB are widely used. Each has a slightly different user interface and set of features. However, if you learn how to use one DBMS successfully, you can transfer that knowledge to the others.

MySQL is primarily used to build the data storage behind dynamic web applications. In this chapter, you focus only on the data structure itself, however, to reduce the complexity of new things to learn.

Using WAMP/MAMP

If your school has installed the WAMP/MAMP stack on your computer, you are ready to begin working with MySQL. If you want to do your own systems administration on your computer and you didn't install the WAMP/MAMP stack when you worked through the units on WordPress and PHP, please review and install one of those packages now.

The WAMP/MAMP stack comes bundled with everything you need to begin learning MySQL. This is the most efficient and simplest way to begin working with MySQL. To complete this tutorial, you also need to run the Apache web server to use the MySQL management interface to create and manage the database. WordPress is not necessary for this tutorial.

Installing MySQL

Installing and configuring MySQL on its own are cumbersome and time-consuming tasks best left to system administrators. You are encouraged to use the WAMP/MAMP stack instead.

If you want to learn about installing and configuring MySQL on its own, use your favorite search engine to search for "MySQL installation guide." The instructions you need depend on your operating system and the version of MySQL you are installing.

If you choose to install MySQL outside of the WAMP/MAMP stack, you also need to use a MySQL Integrated Development Environment (IDE) as the user interface for interacting with the DBMS. This chapter provides instructions for using the PHP-based IDE in the WAMP/MAMP server, which is called phpMyAdmin. You can use alternatives to phpMyAdmin for a MySQL IDE, including dbForge and MySQL Workbench. You can find tutorials for installing and using these alternatives online.

The MySQL Interface

To open the starting screen of the WAMP/MAMP stack, start the WAMP/MAMP application, open a browser, and then enter the localhost URL. On a MAMP, the URL is similar to **http://localhost:8888/phpMyAdmin/**. On a WAMP, enter **http://localhost/phpMyAdmin/**.

Figure 11-3 shows the starting screen for phpMyAdmin in the MAMP interface. The WAMP interface is nearly identical. If you are reading the chapters of this course in sequential order, you used this interface briefly when working with WordPress. If necessary, you can review those chapters to get accustomed to the WAMP/MAMP interface in phpMyAdmin.

Figure 11-3   Setting up MySQL on a MAMP server

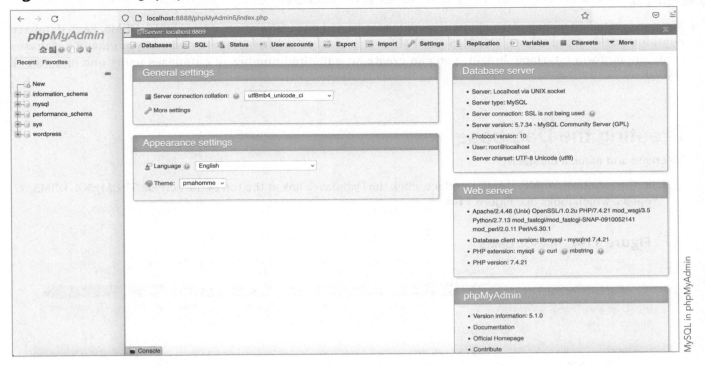

MySQL in phpMyAdmin

Quick Check 11-1

1. What is the foundational element of a database?

   a. One or more tables with rows and columns of data
   b. Excel spreadsheets stored in a collection of spreadsheets
   c. The database management software itself
   d. The columns and rows that organize the data

2. Why is it important to follow the rule of Don't Repeat Yourself in a database?

   a. To reduce the total number of tables necessary to store the data
   b. To make it easier to manage the total number of rows of data in any one table
   c. To group information logically into tables without storing redundant data
   d. To be consistent with the code of the dynamic webpages

3. What is a relational database?

   a. A database used to store the relationships in a flat structure like a spreadsheet
   b. A database composed of tables of related data
   c. A database composed of data in rows with columns that contain the relationships between the rows
   d. A database composed of data in columns with rows that contain the relationships between the columns

1) a. Tables of data are the foundational elements of databases. **2) c.** Storing data without unnecessary repetition avoids errors, inefficiencies, and inconsistencies. **3) b.** A relational database stores and provides access to data in tables that are related to one another.

11.2 Creating a MySQL Database

You can create and manage many individual databases using one installation of the MySQL DBMS. Each database contains one or more tables. The MySQL DBMS is designed to help you create and maintain many databases from one uniform interface. In fact, you can create an unlimited number of databases using one instance of MySQL.

Creating the Database

To create and name a database:

1. In the localhost WAMP/MAMP interface, click the Databases link at the top of the screen. The MySQL DBMS opens, which looks like **Figure 11-4**.

Figure 11-4 MySQL DBMS

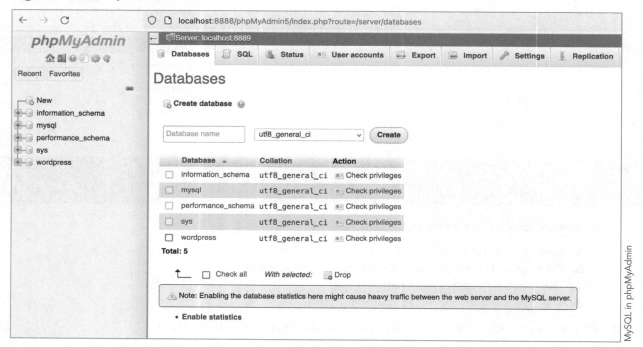

MySQL in phpMyAdmin

2. In the new Database name text box, enter **taus_data** to name the database for Totally Awesome University that you are building in this tutorial. Make sure the selection list to the right of the Database name text box shows utf8_general_ci character encoding or the closest value to that in the list you are provided.
3. Click the Create button to open the Create table window shown in **Figure 11-5**.

One way to see what is possible in the MySQL DBMS is to review a database someone else has already built.

If you completed the section on WordPress, you already have a well-composed and complex example of a MySQL database to learn from. If you didn't complete that section prior to starting this one, you can skip the next section and move directly to creating new tables.

Figure 11-5   Creating a table in MySQL

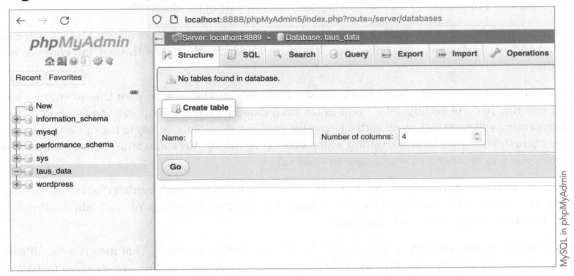

MySQL in phpMyAdmin

Exploring the MySQL DBMS

The left pane of the MySQL DBMS contains links to each database active in the DBMS. Begin your exploration using the wordpress database. (WordPress uses all lowercase for the name of the database.)

To explore the wordpress database:

1. In the left pane, click the plus icon next to wordpress to display the database objects used in the wordpress database.

   The WordPress convention is to prohibit spaces and changing the case in object names, so WordPress uses an underscore to separate words in the names of tables and other database objects. This convention is known as snake_case, which uses all lowercase with underscores to separate words, whereas CamelCase capitalizes the first letter of each word. Neither convention allows spaces in names.

2. In the expanded list of tables in the left pane, click the wp_options table. The wp_options table opens in the right pane, as shown in **Figure 11-6**.

Figure 11-6   The table wp_options in the WordPress database

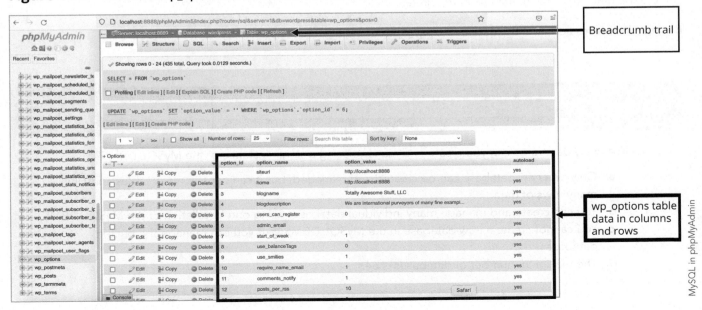

MySQL in phpMyAdmin

You use the left pane to find individual parts of the database. Use the right pane to manipulate those parts. Across the top of the right pane is a breadcrumb trail displaying the selected part of the database.

Below the breadcrumb trail are tabs you click to perform actions on the open database object. The SQL tab changes depending on what part of the database you have open. If you are working with a table, the SQL tab contains actions that apply to a table.

The wp_options table stores WordPress settings and site information. The structure for this WordPress website information uses one row per site setting with columns for both data and database operations like Edit, Copy, and Delete. The data represents site settings, each with a key/value pair. For example, one key in the option_name column is blogname. The corresponding value in the option_value column is Totally Awesome Stuff, LLC. To add a new site setting in this table, you add another row with a new key and value.

A key to a good database design is future-proofing your work, even when you can't predict that future. Storing key/value pairs as the wp_options table does is a time-tested approach to future flexibility. You can add another key and value when necessary by adding a new row to the table.

You can easily maintain the contents of a table like wp_options from a webpage. That means a WordPress site administrator doesn't need to access the database table directly to add a new record for a new key/value pair.

In a database table, each column is a field, or category of data. In the wp_options table, the option_id column contains unique ID values for the records, the option_name column contains the names of the WordPress options, and so on. The column names are short and descriptive. As with naming variables and functions when writing PHP or JavaScript code, short, descriptive column names are helpful to you and the next developer when identifying which column contains the data necessary for a new database operation.

The option_id values are a significant part of the table structure. Rather than row counters, the values in the option_id column are unique ID numbers for each WordPress setting. In the wp_options table, this column is designated as the **primary key**. A primary key is the identifier for unique data that makes one record different from all other records in a table. The primary key can be one number, as in the option_id column, or a combination of data that uniquely identify the record.

The links to the left of the data are provided for the following tasks:

- Edit: Change a value. You can also click a value to edit it.
- Copy: Copy a row of data to add to a new record.
- Delete: Remove a row of data from the table.

Because WordPress created the data in the wp_options table, do not update any keys or values.

Quick Check 11-2

1. How many databases can you create and manage using a single instance of the MySQL DBMS?

    a. Only one new database can be created and managed, but it can contain many tables containing many rows of data.

    b. You can create and manage many individual databases using one installation of the MySQL DBMS.

    c. You cannot create a new database in the MySQL DBMS, but you can manage the built-in databases.

    d. The maximum number of databases is 64.

2. How should you name columns in a database table?

    a. Use names that contain five characters at most to minimize typing later on.

    b. Use numbers as column names since you are just identifying the important part of the table—the data in the columns.

    c. Use a common name and unique number derived from the table name like Student_Data_1, Student_Data_2, and Student_Data_3.

    d. Use short, descriptive names similar to variable or function names in a programming language.

3. In the wordpress database table wp_options, what is the column option_id used for?

    a. To store a unique number used to identify each record

    b. To store a counter of the total number of records in the table

    c. To store the row number for each record in the table

    d. To store the page number that the option is used on in the WordPress website

1) b. There is no limit to the number of databases you can create using one instance of MySQL. **2) d.** Column names should be short and descriptive like first_name or start_date. **3) a.** The option_id column is used as the identity column and contains the unique ID for each record in the table.

11.3 Creating MySQL Tables

As you have seen, MySQL tables are the containers for information stored in a row-and-column format. Tables can store key/value pairs or a longer set of data elements identifying a person or street address.

Creating a table in MySQL can be fun. However, you must perform some necessary design work before the fun begins. The design work involves planning for how to access, analyze, and relate the data in the table. Creating tables according to a plan is more efficient than figuring out what you need as you build.

Planning Before You Build

If you have ever built anything—a Lego set, a piece of Ikea furniture, a small skyscraper, or a lunar rover—you probably followed a plan to assemble the parts in a series of steps. Planning before you begin building helps to make the construction as smooth as possible. One aspect of your job as a full stack web developer is creating the plan that you and others will follow for assembling the structure of the components in a data-driven website.

The following are common steps in planning a new database that supports a web application:

1. **Determine the purpose and scope of the database.** You can start this assessment by sketching a workflow of the logical objects in the database and the processes that interact with the data.

    If you are building a web application for selling products, for example, you need a Products table. You also need a Customers table and an Orders table that stores the data about products sold to customers. In this example, the customers and products are the logical objects, and sales are the process the objects pass through. Each table stores the data for only one type of object or process. A Returns table would store data about products returned from customers, rather than attempting to reuse the Orders table for a second process.

2. **Identify the data elements stored in each table.** Logical objects like customers have data elements such as first and last names, street addresses, cities, states, and postal codes. Products have data elements such as names, descriptions, prices, and SKU codes. You may have tangible examples of these data elements, like the components of a mailing label used to send products ordered to customers. Other data elements like the date/time the order was shipped are less concrete but are still important to capture.

3. **Choose the primary key.** Each record needs to be uniquely identified in the database. For example, each customer needs a Customer ID in the Customers table. The ID number is the primary key for the Customers table. Each product needs a Product ID used as the primary key for the Products table. The Orders table also has a unique Order ID for each order but uses one Customer ID and one or more Product IDs to create a relationship between the customer and product logical objects to complete the ordering process.

4. **Document your plan in a data dictionary.** A **data dictionary** is an external document that contains the plan for building the complete data structure for a database, including the names and types of the data elements in each table and how the data tables relate to each other in the relational database structure.

At a minimum, a data dictionary should contain the following information:

- A list of the data tables, including a name and description of use
- A list of the data elements inside each table, including properties such as the **data type** and size and whether those fields are a unique identifier or index value
- A list of the data validation rules for each data element, such as minimum or maximum length allowed
- An entity-relationship diagram that documents how the tables are related to each other

A data type determines the type of data to store in a table column. Common data types include integer, text, decimal, and date/time. When you construct a table, you must set the data type for each column. The data type is one of the column's **properties**, or characteristics.

Also consider how the data might be used outside of the CRUD operations. For example, you could store customer names in your Customers table in a single Full_Name column. However, with that design, you could not search, sort, or filter the records based on only the customer's last name. If you store the first and last names in separate columns, you could search, sort, or filter records to list customers in alphabetic order by last name, for example, or to display all customers whose last name begins with the letter *C*.

Storing data in a properly formatted and organized structure also addresses **data normalization**. Data normalization applies a uniform set of rules to the structure of a database so that data is organized to reduce redundancy and increase accuracy and performance. Normalization rules include the following:

- Minimize redundant data.
- Break each piece of data into its smallest useful parts.
- In each table, include a column or set of columns that uniquely identifies each row.
- Store data of the same type, format, and quality in a column.

One rule of data normalization is minimizing redundant data (Don't Repeat Yourself). For the student enrollment database, the Students table has one record for each student, and the Classes table has one record for each class. The Enrollment table is a join table used to create the relationships between students and classes, with one record for each unique student/class combination. This is the most efficient way to store this data without repetition.

Data normalization also encourages you to store your data in its smallest logical parts. For example, instead of storing the full mailing address of a person in one column, you should store the street address, city, state, and postal code in separate columns to make it easier to create, retrieve, update, delete, sort, and filter by each data element. It is easier to reassemble data stored granularly with a logical pattern than it is to try to disassemble a long string of data stored in a single column.

Another rule for data normalization is to use a primary key as the unique identifier for a row of nonredundant data. In each row, a primary key is the unique identifier that differentiates the data in the row from any other data. The primary key can be a single identifier like an ID number, Social Security number, or driver's license number, or it can be a combination of several columns that identify a unique record. The primary key is also used to join the row of data with other rows of related, nonredundant data in other tables. The unique identifiers from the other tables are called **foreign keys** and are used to create relationships between tables.

Data normalization also dictates the consistent use of the same type, format, and quality of data. For example, U.S. zip codes are made up of numbers but are used as text since they cannot be used in calculations. Additionally, zip codes can contain five or 10 characters. A zip code column in any table in a single database should therefore have a 10-character VARCHAR data type to create consistency in type, format, and quality.

In the taus_data database, you will build three tables. The following is an outline of a simple data dictionary listing the name of the table, the fields (columns) it contains, and the properties (characteristics) of each field:

- tbl_student
  - id—INT, not null, auto increment, primary key
  - first_name—VARCHAR(100), not null
  - mi—VARCHAR (1)
  - last_name—VARCHAR(100), not null
  - photo_id_number—INT, not null
- tbl_class
  - id—INT, not null, auto increment, primary key
  - class_name—VARCHAR(100), not null
  - start_dt—DATE, not null
  - end_dt—DATE, not null
  - class_number—INT, not null
- tbl_student_class
  - id—INT, not null, auto increment, primary key
  - student_id—INT, not null, foreign key (id column from tbl_student)
  - class_id—INT, not null, foreign key (id column from tbl_class)

The names of the three tables each begin with the tbl_ prefix to identify them as tables. This convention isn't necessary, but it does help to identify database objects. Some MySQL developers prefer to use a shorter t_ prefix or no prefix at all as long as the tables have short, descriptive names that identify the data stored in the table.

The tbl_student table has five columns: id, first_name, mi, last_name, and photo_id_number. The id column contains an integer (INT) that can't be null because it is used as the primary key for this table. The auto increment property means that each time a new row is added, the counter for the id column goes up by one and that new value is added to the id column.

The data type VARCHAR is used for storing less than 100 variable characters in a field, as in the first and last names in tbl_student. The first and last names are required, or "not null," but the middle initial is not. Finally, the photo_id_number is the number on the ID card Totally Awesome University assigns to each student. This could be used as the unique identifier for a student. However, because the loss of a student ID card or re-enrollment may mean the school must issue a new ID card, this property is not used as the singular unique identifier for this table.

The tbl_class table also has five columns in this simplified example: id, class_name, start_dt, end_dt, and class_number. Similar to the id field in tbl_student, the id field in tbl_class will contain integers that can't be null values since this column contains the primary key in the table. The start and end dates are stored in DATE fields so that calculations using MySQL date functions are possible. Finally, the class_number is an integer with a value such as 101 or 461.

The third table, tbl_student_class, contains the data that creates the relationships between the student data and the class data stored in the other two tables. It has a simpler structure than the other two—just three integer fields—but contains the power of foreign keys. Recall that foreign keys are the unique identifiers from a different table stored in the table used to create relationships.

Each primary key field from the tbl_student and tbl_class tables is used as a foreign key in the join table, tbl_student_class. Although not specified in the data dictionary, the tbl_student_class table also has a validation rule that says each pair of foreign keys in tbl_student_class needs to be unique so that one student isn't enrolled in the same class twice.

The tbl_student_class table provides a relationship between one student who is enrolled in many classes. It also provides a relationship between one class and the many students enrolled in the class. Each relationship is a **one-to-many relationship**, in which one record in a table is associated with one or more records in another table.

The direct relationship between students and classes is conceptually a many-to-many relationship because many students take many classes, and many classes have many students enrolled in them. As in the database for Totally Awesome University, you use a join table to create a many-to-many relationship out of two one-to-many relationships.

Be aware that records in the join table can become orphaned. If you delete a student record because the student drops out of school, you remove their id value and other field values from the tbl_students table. The student's id value must also be deleted from the tbl_student_class table. Otherwise, the tbl_student_class table will contain student id values that don't match any students.

The MySQL DBMS has a feature to prevent orphaned records called "cascade delete." You can configure the join table to cascade the deletion of the foreign keys if a primary key is deleted in the related table. In this case, the database deletes all instances of the student id value from every table where it was used.

> **Note**
>
> There are different schools of thought about naming conventions for id fields. Some database administrators and full stack web developers believe student_id or class_id is the proper name of the id field for records representing a logical object like a student or class. These same names are then reused in the join table to create relationships between students and classes. The wordpress wp_options table uses this approach with the option_id field.
>
> Another approach is to use "id" as the name of the first column in each table. The id column contains unique id values. For the foreign keys in the join table, you use a more descriptive name that matches the logical objects being joined. As in the data dictionary for the Totally Awesome University database, you rename the id field from tbl_students as student_id and rename the id field from tbl_class as class_id in the join table.
>
> Each approach has costs and benefits. Use a method that makes sense to you and the other members of the development team you are working with and do so consistently.
>
> Field names help people using the database identify and use the data in the database. The DBMS prohibits only the use of duplicate field names in the same table and the use of a SQL keyword as a field name.

Assigning Appropriate Data Types

The data type defines the type of data stored in each column. Assign a data type appropriate for the data to ensure data integrity and determine the interactions the data can have. If you store all data containing dates in a column with the DATE data type, you can search or filter for dates within the last 30 days, 1 year, or first quarter of the first year of each decade, for example. Assigning a numeric data type to a column lets you use a mathematical MySQL function such as `average()` to average the column values.

Common MySQL data types include INT, DECIMAL, VARCHAR, and DATE. INTs are whole numbers without decimals, and DECIMAL numbers include a decimal point. The VARCHAR data type is used to store variable characters, or text strings. A DATE data type column can contain only valid dates.

Choose your data types carefully. Numbers should be stored as a numeric data type, dates as dates, and so forth. The more restrictive the data type, the more normalized that data will be. Data such as postal codes, Social Security numbers, and phone numbers contain numbers but should be assigned a text data type. For example, if you use a numeric data type for U.S. zip codes, the database drops the leading zero in zip codes such as 02301. Use a numeric data type only for data that can be used in calculations.

Besides choosing the appropriate data types for columns, assign field sizes that fit the data. Using appropriate field sizes improves database performance and accuracy. For example, if you set a field size of 20 characters to a field containing last names, you might generate errors when entering names of people with names containing more than 20 characters.

Available field sizes depend on the data type for a column. MySQL measures the field size of a numeric data type such as TINYINT, a small integer, as a whole number in a specified range such as –128 to 127. A text (or string) data type such as VARCHAR is measured in characters.

Selecting Primary Keys and Table Indexes

When you store data in a table, you are organizing it to be useful information. However, storing the information is only one part of the task. You must also plan how to retrieve the correct records from a growing mass of information so you can make sense of data and use it in a meaningful way.

Retrieving the right record from a database depends on a table having unique identifiers for its unique records. For example, people stored in a Students or Customers table often have similar or even the same names. The given names Sophia and Mohammed are among the most common in the world. Two of the most common family names are Wang and Li. That means millions of people might be named Sophia Wang and Mohammed Li. These full names are only useful pieces of information if an individual Sophia Wang and an individual Mohammed Li can be identified to serve the goals of a particular task, such as sending a package or bill to a customer.

At least one more piece of information is necessary to identify the Sophia Wang who lives on Drury Lane and the Mohammed Li who lives at 333 Third Street. Given how common these names are, two Sophia Wangs could live on Drury Lane and three Mohammed Lis could live on Third Street. A database table might also need to store their birthdates or another unique number such as a driver's license number. Together, this data can be used to create one unique record for one unique person.

These unique identifiers are known as **natural keys**. A natural key is an external value that uniquely identifies a record in the database, like a driver's license number or a Social Security number. Natural keys originate outside of the database but are used as unique identifiers for records in the database.

A caution when using natural keys is that some will change. A stolen Social Security number might need to be replaced. A driver's license number needs to be updated if the holder of that natural key moves to a different state.

One way to plan for future change is to assign a unique number to each record in your table, as specified for the tables in the taus_data database. In this way, any single part of a unique record can change, including a natural key like a Social Security number. However, the record ID in your database remains the same and can be used to uniquely identify that object in the table. The ID number is a running counter assigned to each unique record when the record is created.

You can assign additional meaning to a column of unique record numbers by making it the primary key field. Recall that the primary key in a table is the distinct piece of data that uniquely identifies a record. A primary key can be a single value such as 909 or it can be composed of multiple values.

When working with large sets of data, the next step in making a database more efficient is to add a **table index**. A table index is an internal identifier the DBMS uses to uniquely identify records in the table so it can find and retrieve them faster. The DBMS uses the index to optimize its internal algorithm for searching, sorting, filtering, and querying. The table index helps to speed up data retrieval, not to ensure the uniqueness of the row of data in the table.

The test of uniqueness is performed by the primary key, which is a **constraint** on the table. A constraint is a rule for the data in a table, similar to a data type. If you set a column containing Social Security numbers as the primary key for the table, you are creating a rule that the column can never have duplicates. Whereas a database uses the table index for speed and efficiency, it uses the primary key to ensure uniqueness of your data as you add it to the table.

Creating Your First MySQL Tables

With the data dictionary at the ready, it is time to build your first MySQL table. Using the MySQL phpMyAdmin DBMS makes this task easier than typing the commands manually. Note that it is possible, and in some cases necessary, to create tables using only SQL programming code.

To create the tbl_student table in MySQL:

1. In the phpMyAdmin DBMS, click taus_data in the left pane to open the database. The contents of the database are shown in the right pane, although this database does not contain any objects yet.
2. In the Table name box, enter **tbl_student** as the name of the first table.
3. Change the Add columns setting to **5** then click Go.
4. Enter the values as shown in **Table 11-1** to set up the five columns in the tbl_student table.

Table 11-1 Columns in the tbl_student table

Name	Type	Length/Values
id	INT	
first_name	VARCHAR	100
mi	VARCHAR	1
last_name	VARCHAR	100
photo_id_number	INT	

5. Check the Null box for the mi column since null values are allowed in that column but nowhere else in the table.
6. Check the A_I box for the id row to add the Auto Increment property to the id column. For each new record, the Auto Increment property creates a counter for the table that adds a unique value one greater than the last number used.
7. Click the Index selection list to open it for the id row. The settings and index options should look like those in **Figure 11-7**.

The entries in Figure 11-7 correspond to the details of the data dictionary. Each row in the table creation window represents a column in the table.

Figure 11-7 Adding columns and data types for the tbl_students table

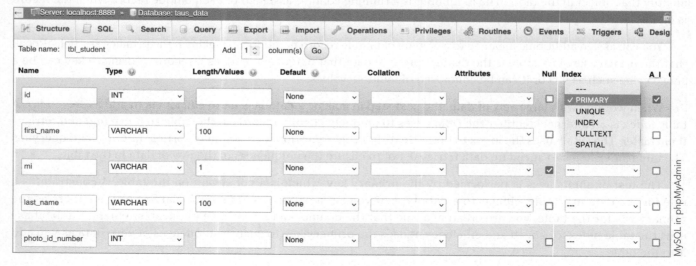

MySQL in phpMyAdmin

8. In the list of Index options, click the PRIMARY property, if necessary, to set the id column as the primary key. The Add index dialog box opens as shown in **Figure 11-8** so you can provide additional details about the primary key for this table. You might need to click the PRIMARY link below the Index list to open the Add Index dialog box in WAMP.

Figure 11-8   Add Index dialog box

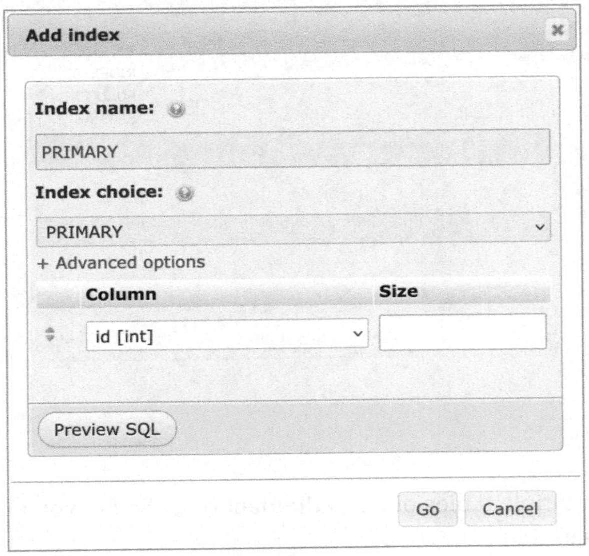

MySQL in phpMyAdmin

9. Accept the defaults in the Add index dialog box and create the primary key for this table by clicking the Go button.

10. At the bottom of the window for the tbl_student table, click the Save button to create the table.

To create the tbl_class table in MySQL:

1. Create another new table named **tbl_class**.

2. Create each type of column used for each data element to reflect the values in the data dictionary including the primary index as shown in **Table 11-2**.

Table 11-2   Columns in the tbl_class table

Name	Type	Length/Values	Index
id	INT		PRIMARY
class_name	VARCHAR	100	
start_dt	DATE		
end_dt	DATE		
class_number	INT		

3. Check the A_I box for the id column and choose the primary key for this field from the Index list, if necessary, as you did for tbl_students.

The table structure for tbl_class is shown in **Figure 11-9**.

4. Save the table structure, and then click the Database: taus_data link in the breadcrumb trail at the top of the pane to return to the database management screen.

Figure 11-9   Creating the tbl_class table

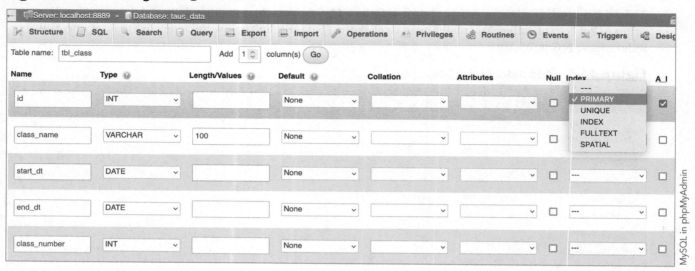

Joining Tables

If you follow the rules of data normalization, you will create multiple tables of nonredundant data. So far, you created a table with only student data and another table with only class data.

You also need a table that provides the relationships between the students and the classes at Totally Awesome University. This table doesn't store the student data, nor does it store the class data. It only specifies the relationships between students and classes. That is, it is a join table that stores student record ID numbers and class record ID numbers for the classes the students are enrolled in.

Storing data in this way makes each element of the relationships independent. You can update a student's name in one place (the tbl_student table) without updating the classes they are enrolled in. You can update the name of a class in one place (the tbl_class table) without affecting the students taking that class. You can create a new relationship for a student with a class or delete a relationship if a student drops a class.

To create the tbl_student_class table in MySQL:

1. Create a new table named **tbl_student_class**.
2. Add three columns to this table: id, student_id, and class_id. Assign the INT data type to all three columns. Check the A_I property for the id column. Make the id column the primary key for this table, if necessary.

The completed table structure for tbl_student_class is shown in **Figure 11-10**. Save the table.

Figure 11-10   Creating the tbl_student_class table

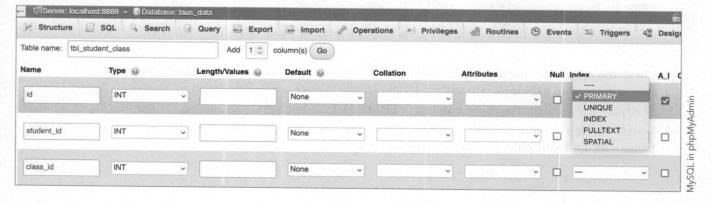

To create the table relationships:

1. In the left pane of the MySQL Management window, expand the taus_data database if it isn't already expanded, and then click the Tables link, if necessary, to list the tables in the database.

2. Click the tbl_student_class table to display the table management window for the table in the right pane.

3. Click the Structure tab at the top of the window to show the table structure.

4. Click the Relation view button to display the relationship information for this table. If you don't have a Relation view button, you may need to change your database storage engine type to InnoDB.

   You use the Relation view to set and display table relationships. The tbl_student_class table is intended to store the relationships between the tbl_student table and the tbl_class table. The primary keys from each table will be used as a foreign key in the tbl_student_class table. Using Relation view, you will add two constraints to create two foreign keys.

5. In the first empty row of the Foreign key constraints section, type **fk_class** since it is a foreign key on the class table. Confirm that the ON DELETE value is RESTRICT and the ON UPDATE is also RESTRICT. This setting prevents a class from being deleted if students are enrolled in it. Since the tbl_student_class table contains the id values for students enrolled in classes, any class with students in it is represented in the table.

6. Choose class_id as the column this foreign key constraint will be enforced on, choose taus_data as the database, if necessary, choose tbl_class as the table, and choose id as the primary key field.

7. Click the Add constraint link to display a new blank row.

8. Add a second constraint named **fk_student** to be the foreign key from the id field in the tbl_student table.

   The foreign key for tbl_student is different from the one for tbl_class. Students drop classes without affecting the class. If a student drops out of school and is removed from the database, the delete should cascade to include all records associated with the student's current enrollment to keep the records from being orphaned.

9. To enforce this behavior, choose CASCADE for the ON DELETE and choose RESTRICT for the ON UPDATE property.

10. Choose student_id as the column this foreign key will be enforced on, choose taus_data as the database, if necessary, choose tbl_student as the table, and choose id as the primary key field. You can see a completed version of the foreign keys in **Figure 11-11**.

11. Click the Save button to save your constraints for the table tbl_student_class.

Figure 11-11   Creating foreign keys for tbl_student_class

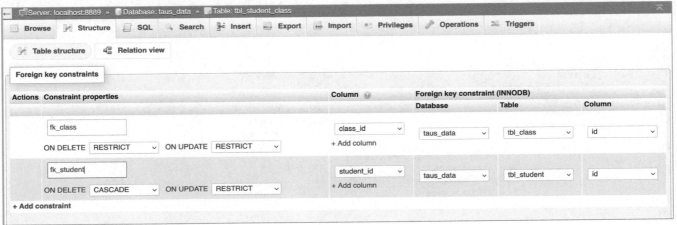

You specified two types of constraints because two types of updates are possible. The first rule prevents the deletion of a class with students enrolled in it. At Totally Awesome University, canceling a class that still has students enrolled in it would annoy the students, so this foreign key constraint prevents that from happening.

On the other hand, students leave Totally Awesome University for various reasons, so deleting a student from the database should cascade that deletion to all of the classes that the student was enrolled in. In this way, student ID numbers aren't orphaned in the join table of students and classes.

The final necessary modification is to add a constraint requiring a unique combination of values for the tbl_student_class table. The same student can't be enrolled twice in the same class, nor would you want to list a class twice with the same students enrolled. Either situation would double the tuition charged for the class and increase the number of credits awarded.

The uniqueness of this constraint is in the combination of student_id and class_id, since the tbl_student_class table holds the same student_id and the same class_id more than once but should never have the same student_id and class_id stored together in a record more than once.

To add this constraint to the table, you use a SQL programming statement.

To modify the tbl_student_class table:

1. Click the Database: taus_data link in the breadcrumb path and then click the SQL tab.
2. Type the following into the text box in the SQL pane:

```
ALTER TABLE 'tbl_student_class' ADD UNIQUE 'unique_index' ('student_id',
'class_id');
```

This line of code begins with two SQL keywords. ALTER TABLE tells the SQL processor to find the specified table and update it with the code that follows the name. That code is ADD UNIQUE, which adds the constraint named unique_index. The unique_index constraint is based on the combination of the columns student_id and class_id.

3. Click the Go button to run this code and modify the table.
4. To see how these tables are now related to each other, click the Designer tab at the top of the window. You should see a display like that shown in **Figure 11-12**.

Figure 11-12   Designer view of the taus_data database

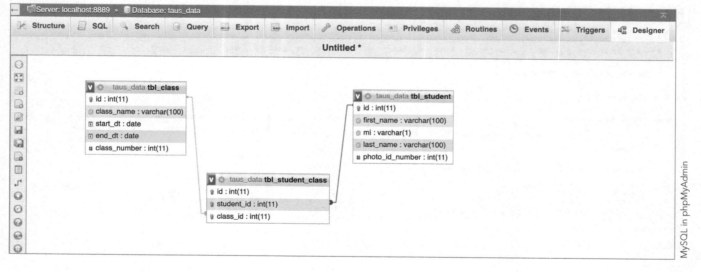

MySQL in phpMyAdmin

The lines between the tables represent the relationships you just created. This confirms that the intent of the relational design has been fulfilled.

You can also create the same constraint when creating the tbl_student_class table. In the Index selection list for the student_id column, select the UNIQUE constraint, which opens a similar dialog box to the Add index dialog box.

Create the UNIQUE constraint, naming it something like unique_index. Next, add a UNIQUE constraint to the class_id column, but choose the option to create a composite constraint, choosing the unique_index constraint you created for student_id as the constraint to make into a composite.

Quick Check 11-3

1. Why is it important to create a plan for the database before creating tables?

   a. It is faster and more efficient to build tables that are well defined.
   b. If you make a mistake while creating a table, you must delete all the tables in a database before you can create a new one.
   c. The relationships between the tables need to be defined before the tables can be completed.
   d. You can translate the plan into actual tables using the automated table creation interface.

2. What is a data dictionary?

   a. A table in the database that contains the names and data types of all of the data elements used in the database
   b. A set of key/value pairs defining the data elements used in a database
   c. A document defining every type of data that can be used in a database
   d. A document describing the tables and the type of data elements stored in those tables, including foreign keys to create the relationships between the tables

3. What is data normalization?

   a. A database function that normalizes data being saved in a table
   b. Creating a table structure for storing data in a database according to a set of rules
   c. Combining data stored in separate columns according to a set of rules
   d. Removing the unnecessary punctuation and whitespace from data being saved in a database

1) a. Building tables according to a plan is more efficient than figuring out what you need as you build. **2) d.** A data dictionary is the plan for creating tables and data elements in a database. **3) b.** Data normalization specifies a set of rules that are used to create uniform table structures in a database.

11.4 Creating MySQL Stored Procedures

After you create the foundational table structure for a database, you need to build the database objects that supply data to and retrieve data from your tables. Because you need to run the same database CRUD operations repeatedly, you can save each of the input/output operations as a self-contained body of SQL code called a *stored procedure*.

Stored procedures are named blocks of SQL code that can accept input values, use variables, modify table values, perform database functions, and return results. A stored procedure in a MySQL database looks and acts like a function in PHP or JavaScript code. The body of SQL code inside the stored procedure is contained within curly brackets and is composed of one or more SQL programming statements. You should create a procedure for each CRUD operation on each of your database tables.

Using Stored Procedures

It is a web development best practice to create a layer of separation between the code that handles the webpages and the code that interacts with the data in the database tables. This intermediary layer of data-handling code may seem redundant at first glance. You may see examples of PHP code for a dynamic web application that contains SQL code. However, the extra work of creating stored procedures instead of this in-code SQL is worth the extra effort for two reasons.

First, using stored procedures to create an interface between the PHP code and database makes a logical separation of concerns. The code for interacting with the database belongs in the database. The data processing included in stored procedures should logically be part of the contents of the database itself. Additionally, the data input/output operations performed in a stored procedure are significantly more efficient since the database is optimized for running the code of stored procedures.

Second, and more importantly, using stored procedures exclusively for data input and output increases the security of your data and data transactions. Through the use of stored procedures, you restrict the path of data flow in and out of the database tables. This restriction helps prevent data hygiene errors, since the variables you use require integers, text strings, or dates as the strongly typed parameters for the data elements going into the tables. You can also prevent some malicious database attacks such as SQL injection by using these strongly typed parameters instead of raw SQL statements written in PHP to insert or update data into your tables.

> **Note**
>
> Another option is available for creating a more efficient and secure database interaction layer than in-code SQL. Parameterized queries are functionally equivalent to stored procedures and create a greater level of security than in-code SQL.
>
> However, parameterized queries still require you to compose database-specific SQL code in the PHP code instead of in the database where it belongs. Using parameterized queries doesn't create the layer of abstraction between the PHP code and the SQL code that using stored procedures does.
>
> Programming code belongs in the web application, and database code belongs in the database.

Preventing SQL Injection Attacks

A poor alternative to using stored procedures is to write the SQL code in plain text inside the web application code, such as PHP, Ruby, Perl, C#, or Java. This is called *string concatenation SQL*, or *in-code SQL*. String concatenation SQL creates a major security vulnerability because it is an open invitation to create a SQL injection hack. SQL injection attacks are one of the most common hacks for websites.

In a SQL injection hack, a hacker inserts extra SQL code into a data entry text box in a web form, attempting to modify the text of the statement so that when it runs on the web server, it discloses sensitive data or disrupts the business processes of the website.

String concatenation SQL built as a text string on a web server begins with a statement similar to the following stored in the web application code such as PHP:

```
select * from tbl_student where last_name = '
```

This SQL statement selects all records from the tbl_student table where the last_name field matches the text string the user enters in the web form. Text values used in SQL as an input value are surrounded by single quote marks so they are treated as string literals.

The input value from the web form's text box is appended to the in-code text string. Nonhackers would use the text box as it is intended and enter a value such as Smith or Li, which completes the SQL statement properly as in the following statement:

```
select * from tbl_student where last_name = 'Smith';
```

This SQL statement filters the tbl_student table for all records containing a last_name equal to the value Smith and returns those records to the user.

A hacker could add a short block of SQL code such as `Smith' or 1 = 1'` to the end of the input value in the web form text box. The result is the following line of code:

```
select * from tbl_student where last_name = 'Smith' or 1 = 1'';
```

This code, including the apostrophes, completes the SQL statement with an additional criterion for selection that matches every record in the tbl_student table. The hacker doesn't have to know anything about the table or the format of the data. The statement returns all records because 1 = 1 is always true.

If a hacker used the text string `Smith' or 1 = 1'` with a stored procedure, no results would be returned because the tbl_student table does not contain a last name with the character string `Smith' or 1 = 1'`. Because a stored procedure takes in the entire text string as a single value for the selection criterion, using stored procedures thwarts this type of SQL injection attack.

However, this is a simple example of a SQL injection attack. Others are more complex and even more dangerous. Because it is possible to use the SQL programming language to manipulate data, or even the database objects, a hacker could include SQL code to delete tables or update all data in a table to be empty.

Later, you create stored procedures to delete individual records from the database using the record ID value. The criteria for deletion are similar to those in the `select * from tbl_student where last_name = '` statement. If a hacker appended `or 1 = 1` to the end of a delete statement, every record in the table would be selected and then deleted.

Most SQL injection attacks are thwarted by sanitizing user input at both the client side and the server side and through the use of stored procedures. All three of these steps are critical. Additional steps are recommended in the OWASP SQL Injection Prevention Cheat Sheet (https://cheatsheetseries.owasp.org/cheatsheets/SQL_Injection_Prevention_Cheat_Sheet.html).

Writing Insert Procedures

You should write a separate stored procedure for each of the CRUD operations to maintain the records in a database.

> **Note**
>
> While each step in the database CRUD operation is treated in this chapter as a separate transaction, you often need to combine these logical operations in one stored procedure.
>
> For example, you might need to delete an older record before inserting a new record. You might also need to test whether the database contains a record with a unique natural key or keys. If the database does contain the record, update the data in it; otherwise, insert a new record. This is called an *upsert operation*, for the update-if-possible-otherwise-insert record processing.
>
> Stored procedures are like other programming language functions that can be written to handle multiple operations. Like Legos, these logical blocks connect to each other to form a larger creation.

To create a record, you use the SQL INSERT command. This command saves a new record in the table it references. The phpMyAdmin DBMS contains a utility to help you create stored procedures.

To create a stored procedure for inserting records in the tbl_student table:

1. In the Database Management window, click the Routines tab and then click the Add routine link at the bottom of the Routines pane to open the Add routine dialog box.

   The first procedure you create adds a student to the tbl_student table. The procedure is called sp_insert_student. The name of the procedure begins with the letters *sp* so you know this database object is a stored procedure. The procedure takes four parameters, each with names beginning with p_ so you can tell in the

SQL code that they are parameters. The four parameters correspond to the four columns in tbl_student that are not the id field. As you recall, the id column automatically adds a new ID number for each new record, so the sp_insert_student stored procedure only needs to insert a record composed of the other four data elements.

The four parameters for this stored procedure are p_first_name, p_mi, p_last_name, and p_photo_id_number. The data types for these parameters should match the data types of the columns in the table that the procedure references.

2. Enter **sp_insert_student** in the Routine name box, press Tab, click the Type arrow, and then select PROCEDURE.

3. Enter the parameters shown in **Table 11-3** and accept the other defaults.

Table 11-3 Parameters for the sp_insert_student procedure

Direction	Name	Type	Length/Values
IN	p_first_name	VARCHAR	100
IN	p_mi	VARCHAR	1
IN	p_last_name	VARCHAR	100
IN	p_photo_id_number	INT	

The Add routine dialog box should look like that in **Figure 11-13**.

Figure 11-13 Creating the sp_insert_student procedure

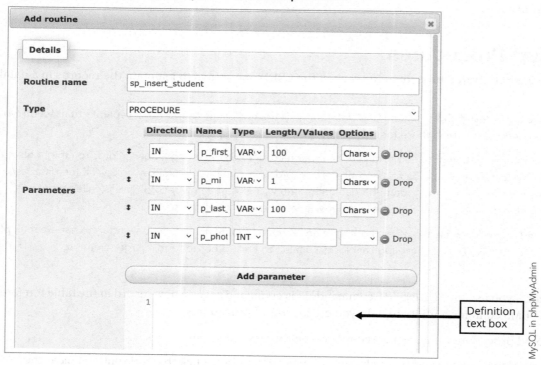

MySQL in phpMyAdmin

You enter the body of the stored procedure in the Definition text box. This text box provides prompts as you type to help you identify and use keywords and other objects in the database. For example, as you type the prefix of a table name, a list of tables in the database appears, as shown in **Figure 11-14**.

Figure 11-14   Using prompts provided to enter a stored procedure

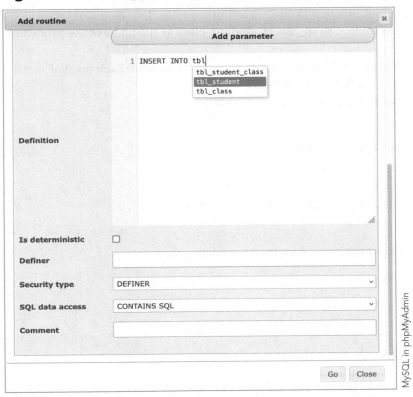

4. In the Definition text box, enter the following SQL code, which is the SQL programming code that performs the work of this stored procedure:

```
INSERT INTO tbl_student (
    first_name, mi, last_name, photo_id_number
    )
VALUES (
    p_first_name, p_mi, p_last_name, p_photo_id_number
    )
```

The `INSERT INTO tbl_student` statement tells the SQL processor which table to use. The `first_name, mi, last_name, photo_id_number` code specifies into which fields to insert data. The statement uses a comma-separated list of field names in parentheses.

Following the VALUES keyword is a list of the parameters you created for the sp_student_procedure. The parameters are used to insert the data into the columns specified in the first part of this code. Note that the columns and parameters have to match exactly in order and number.

This code shows why it is helpful to use parameter names that begin with p_ and otherwise match the names of the fields in the table. Larger insert procedures can have tens or hundreds of parameters, making this proper naming even more important.

Also note that keywords such as INSERT are in uppercase text. The MySQL DBMS suggests uppercase as you type the first few letters for each keyword.

Recall that this stored procedure doesn't have a value for the id field. Because you added the AUTO_ INCREMENT property to the id field when building the table, the field value will be entered when you add the other data using this procedure.

5. Click the Go button. The stored procedure utility parses your code and parameters and displays errors if it finds any or a validation screen if it does not.

To create stored procedures for inserting records in the other tables:

1. Using the previous set of steps as a model, create two more insert procedures. Use **sp_insert_class** as the name of the procedure for the tbl_class table. Use **sp_insert_student_class** as the name of the procedure for the tbl_student_class table.

   Each procedure needs an input field for all the fields in the table except the id field. Each must also match the data types of the input parameters to the columns in the table.

2. Enter the following SQL code in the Definition box for sp_insert__class:

   ```
   INSERT INTO tbl_class (
        class_name, start_dt, end_dt, class_number
   )
   VALUES (
        p_class_name, p_start_dt, p_end_dt, p_class_number
   )
   ```

3. Enter the following SQL code in the Definition box for sp_insert_student_class:

   ```
   INSERT INTO tbl_student_class (
        student_id, class_id
   )
   VALUES (
        p_student_id, p_class_id
   )
   ```

It is always a good idea to test your new procedures by using them to insert data into the associates tables.

To test the new procedures:

1. Click the Routines tab in the Database Management window and then click the Execute link for sp_insert_ student to display the Execute routine 'sp_insert_student' dialog box shown in **Figure 11-15**.

Figure 11-15 Execute routine dialog box for the sp_insert_ student procedure

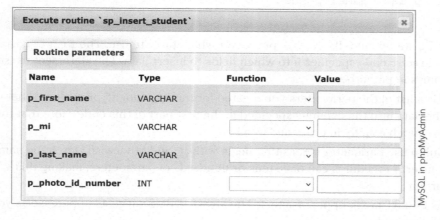

MySQL in phpMyAdmin

2. In the Value box for each parameter, enter your name and a nine-digit photo ID number of your choosing and then click the Go button.

3. Add four more records using the values specified in **Table 11-4**.

Table 11-4   Parameter values for the sp_insert_student procedure

p_first_name	p_mi	p_last_name	p_photo_id_number
Keeley	T	Naidoo	999000123
Ramona	D	Malindi	999000124
Tram	K	Pak	999000125
Florentino	A	Chiros	999000126

4. Display the Execute routine dialog box for the sp_insert_class procedure and then add the three classes to the class list of Totally Awesome University that correspond to **Table 11-5**. Update the year in the start and end dates to the current year.

Table 11-5   Parameter values for the sp_insert_class procedure

p_class_name	p_start_dt	p_end_dt	p_class_number
Thermodynamics	2025-09-04	2025-12-22	549
Intro to Western Existentialism	2025-09-05	2025-12-21	438
Pickleball	2025-09-04	2025-12-20	119

5. Enroll your students in Totally Awesome University classes by running the sp_insert_student_class procedure manually 15 times, adding the five students to each of the three classes.
6. Open each table to make sure all the data you entered was inserted successfully.

Writing Update Procedures

The next set of procedures to create are another component of CRUD. Update procedures modify records.

To create an update procedure for the tbl_student table:

1. Click the Routines tab in the Database Management window, and then click the Add routine link.
2. Name the new stored procedure **sp_update_student**. Create an input parameter for each column in the tbl_students table that matches the data type and size for that column.

   Unlike the Create procedure, the Update stored procedure has a parameter for each field in the table, including the id field. Because the id is always unique for every record in the table, using the id value to identify which row to update ensures that you update only the correct record.
3. Add the following code to the Definition text box for the sp_update_student stored procedure:

```
UPDATE tbl_student
SET first_name = p_first_name,
    mi = p_mi,
    last_name = p_last_name,
    photo_id_number = p_photo_id_number
WHERE id = p_id
```

   You should have a body of code that reflects **Figure 11-16**.

   This code will update each field in the tbl_student table that matches the id sent to the procedure in the p_id parameter.
4. Click the Go button and then fix any errors, if necessary.

Figure 11-16 Creating the sp_update_student procedure

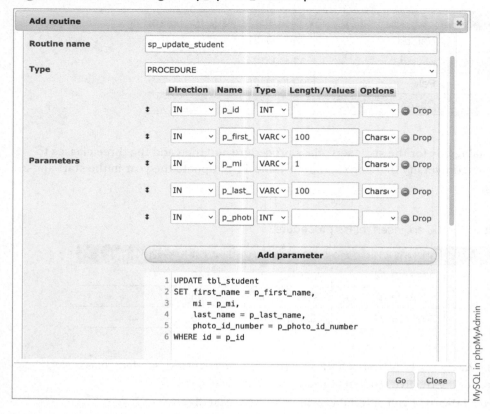

To create update procedures for the other tables:

1. Click the Routines tab in the Database Management window and then click the Add routine link.
2. Use **sp_update_class** as the name of the procedure for the tbl_class table. Use **sp_update_student_class** as the name of the procedure for the tbl_student_class table. Create an input parameter for each column in the table that matches the data type and size for that column.
3. Enter the following SQL code in the Definition box for the sp_update_class procedure, which takes five parameters, one for each field in the table:

```
UPDATE tbl_class
SET class_name = p_class_name,
    start_dt = p_start_dt,
    end_dt = p_end_dt,
    class_number = p_class_number
WHERE id = p_id
```

4. Enter the following SQL code in the Definition box for the sp_update_student_class procedure, which takes three parameters, one for each field in the table:

```
UPDATE tbl_student_class
SET student_id = p_student_id,
class_id = p_class_id
WHERE id = p_id
```

5. Test these procedures by executing them. Update your name to an incorrect spelling, then open tbl_student to make sure your change was successful. Update one of the classes as well.

Writing Delete Procedures

You may need to expire or delete some data in a database from time to time. Developers typically take one of two approaches to deleting data stored in database tables.

Some developers believe that once data is stored successfully in a table, it should never be removed. In this scenario, you add an extra column to a table, named something like "deleted." The stored procedure for deleting records adds a value to this column, such as "Yes." All other procedures that access the data in the table and any joined tables would exclude any record with a value in the "deleted" field.

This approach is useful if you need to maintain data beyond the data expiration date. Public records and data warehouses are two examples of this legitimate business need. Public record laws may require you to retain all data stored in your database for a period such as seven years. Data warehouse business rules with a similar time requirement may apply to your data as well.

On the other hand, for a lightweight application with no need to maintain records for legal or posterity reasons, deleting the data from the table is adequate.

To delete a record from a table, you need to specify matching criteria so you don't mistakenly delete the wrong record or records. In the following steps, the id of the record in all three tables is the unique identifier used for this purpose.

To create the delete procedures:

1. If necessary, click the Database: taus_data link in the breadcrumb path, click the Routines tab, click Go, and then in the Routines pane, click the Add routine link.
2. Use **sp_delete_student** as the name of the new procedure. Specify one parameter named **p_id** with an INT data type.
3. Enter the following SQL code in the Definition box:

```
DELETE FROM tbl_student WHERE id = p_id
```

   The body of this procedure is also shown in **Figure 11-17**.

   Note that because you set up the foreign keys and cascade constraint on tbl_student_class, deleting a student from tbl_student also deletes all the corresponding rows in the tbl_student_class table to keep the database tidy with no orphaned rows.
4. Click the Go button to create the procedure.
5. Add another procedure named **sp_delete_class** that takes the **p_id** parameter. This procedure will delete a class that has no students enrolled using the parameter p_id for the id of the class. Note that because of the constraint you created in tbl_student_class, any class with enrolled students cannot be deleted from the table tbl_class.
6. Enter the following SQL code in the Definition box and then click Go:

```
DELETE FROM tbl_class WHERE id = p_id
```

7. Add a third procedure named **sp_delete_student_class** that takes the **p_id** parameter. This procedure deletes records from the tbl_student_class table that match the specified id.
8. Enter the following SQL code in the Definition box and then click Go:

```
DELETE FROM tbl_student_class WHERE id = p_id
```

Before deleting a class from tbl_class using the procedure sp_delete_class, you must run the sp_delete_student_class procedure for all the enrolled students to delete all student and class records.

Figure 11-17 Creating the sp_delete_student procedure

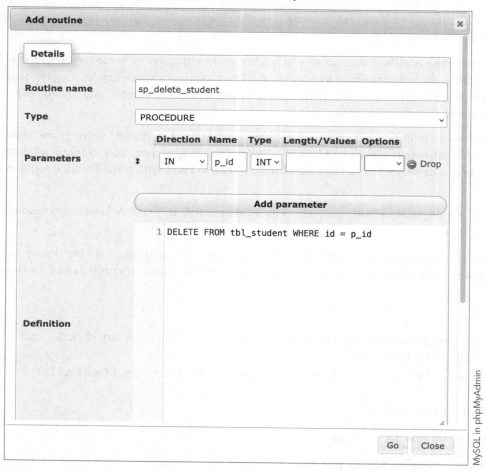

Writing Read Procedures

The last set of procedures find and return an individual record for an ID that is passed to each procedure. While the CRUD acronym refers to this as the Read operation of the data, the SQL term for this is "select." The SELECT SQL command retrieves data from the database that matches the specified criteria.

To create the select procedures:

1. If necessary, return to the Routines tab and in the Routines pane, click the Add routine link.
2. Use **sp_get_student** as the name of the new procedure. Specify one parameter named **p_id** with an INT data type.
3. Enter the following SQL in the Definition box:

```
SELECT first_name, mi, last_name, photo_id_number
FROM tbl_student
WHERE id = p_id
```

The body of this procedure is shown in **Figure 11-18**.

4. Click the Go button to create the procedure.
5. Create another procedure named **sp_get_class** that takes the **p_id** parameter.

Figure 11-18   Creating the sp_get_student procedure

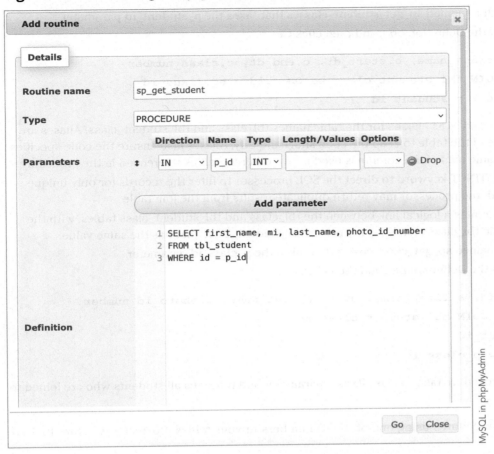

6. Enter the following code in the Definition box and then click Go:

```
SELECT class_name, start_dt, end_dt, class_number
FROM tbl_class
WHERE id = p_id
```

7. Create another procedure named **sp_get_student_class** that takes the **p_id** parameter.

8. Enter the following code in the Definition box and then click Go:

```
SELECT student_id, class_id
FROM tbl_student_class
WHERE id = p_id
```

Finally, you need to create two more procedures that retrieve the data you have entered in all three tables. First, you need to retrieve all the classes one student is enrolled in. Second, you need to retrieve all the students enrolled in one class. Each procedure takes one ID number for either the student or the class being retrieved.

To accomplish this, you must join the tables. When you join two or more tables, you specify the criteria for matching records between the tables.

When these stored procedures are used from a user interface like a dynamic web form, the student's name is already displayed, but you would want to retrieve a list of classes for the ID that corresponds to the student's name. In other words, the procedure doesn't need to retrieve more information than you already have.

To retrieve records from the tables:

1. Create another new procedure named **sp_get_student_classes** that takes the **p_student_id** parameter.
2. Enter the following code in the Definition box, and then click Go:

```
SELECT DISTINCT c.class_name, c.start_dt, c.end_dt, c.class_number
FROM tbl_class c JOIN tbl_student_class sc ON c.id = sc.class_id
WHERE sc.student_id = p_student_id
```

This code uses the letters *c* and *sc* as **aliases** for the table names tbl_class and tbl_student_class. Aliases are shorthand for the full name of the table to keep the code short and tidy. Aliases also ensure the code specifies the correct column if the same name for a column is used in two different tables referenced in the procedure.

The procedure uses the DISTINCT keyword to direct the SQL processor to filter the records for only unique rows. Without this keyword, the processor may return duplicate results from the join table.

The SQL code for the join creates a logical link between the tbl_class and tbl_student_class tables, with the criterion of the id number in tbl_class matching any row in tbl_student_class that has the same value.

3. Create another procedure named **sp_get_class_roster** that takes the **p_class_id** parameter.
4. Enter the following code in the Definition box and then click Go:

```
SELECT DISTINCT s.id, s.first_name, s.mi, s.last_name, s.photo_id_number
FROM tbl_student s JOIN tbl_student_class sc
ON s.id = sc.student_id
WHERE sc.class_id = p_class_id
```

The sp_get_class_roster procedure takes a class ID as a parameter and retrieves all students who are joined to it by the join table.

Test each of these new stored procedures using one of the ID numbers in your tables. Correct any errors that are reported.

This group of stored procedures represents the starting point for a comprehensive set of database operations. In your journey toward full stack web development mastery, you will encounter many more business process requirements that require other procedures. However, those procedures will be branches off of the CRUD tree, and the work you just did is the trunk of dynamic website construction.

Quick Check 11-4

1. What is a stored procedure?

   a. A named block of SQL code that performs a database function
   b. SQL code that is saved in a database table so it can be executed anytime
   c. A menu option in the database management interface that is used to create database objects
   d. A block of SQL code with a discrete function inside a larger body of SQL code

2. Why should you use stored procedures instead of string concatenation SQL to perform database operations from a dynamic webpage?

   a. To prevent SQL injection hacks
   b. To save the data with the correct data type in the table the procedure interacts with
   c. To translate raw text from a dynamic webpage into other more appropriate data types prior to storage in a database table
   d. To store SQL code in the webpage that uses it for greater coding efficiency

3. What is SQL injection?

    a. Storing SQL code to a database table

    b. Adding new SQL code to a stored procedure

    c. Appending criteria to a SQL statement to filter the results

    d. Adding SQL code to a piece of data in order to try to get the code to run

1) a. A stored procedure is similar to a function in other programming languages, with a name and a block of code to run. **2) a.** The most important reason to use stored procedures is to prevent SQL injection hacks. **3) d.** SQL injection is the malicious addition of SQL code into a valid piece of data.

11.5 Querying MySQL Data

In addition to the standard input/output functions for the logical objects and processes stored in your database, you may need to filter your database to display a subset of data that you did not create an input/output procedure for. To handle this scenario, you can write a **query** to retrieve a subset of the data in your database. A query is composed of SQL programming code and uses a combination of the database objects and SQL keyword operators to extract a new set of information from the existing data.

Building an Ad-Hoc Select Query

As with other programming languages, SQL has the equivalent of nouns, verbs, and adjectives. To complete a SQL programmatic statement, you combine the name of a database object with an action and sometimes a modifier. You have seen this type of code in context for each of the stored procedures you created. INSERT, UPDATE, DELETE, and SELECT are SQL keywords that represent actions associated with tables and the data in them.

A stored procedure is a named block of SQL code in the database that you run repeatedly. You run an ad-hoc query once or twice to find a unique result for a specific requirement or request. For example, an ad-hoc query is useful if you want to find all students enrolled in classes that begin on or before September 2 of the current year.

If you need to run an ad-hoc query more than a few times, create a stored procedure or a view to save the query logic as part of a database object. A view is a database object composed of a saved query that returns rows of data from one or more tables that match the conditions of the query.

All SQL queries begin with an action keyword. Typical action commands include SELECT, UPDATE, and DELETE. Note that MySQL is case insensitive with these action commands and other keywords, but the DBMS will politely offer to change the words to all uppercase.

You have already seen the syntax for a SELECT query in the stored procedures used to retrieve a record. However, you use an ad-hoc query to retrieve a different dataset than a stored procedure.

In the following steps, you create an ad-hoc query to retrieve all students with the last name starting with the letter *C* enrolled in a class with a name starting with Thermo.

To create an ad-hoc query:

1. In the SQL tab text box for the taus_data database, enter the following query:

```
SELECT s.first_name, s.last_name, c.class_name
FROM tbl_student s JOIN tbl_student_class sc ON s.id = sc.student_id
    JOIN tbl_class c ON sc.class_id = c.id
WHERE s.last_name LIKE 'C%'
    AND c.class_name LIKE 'Thermo%';
```

Your query should look like that shown in **Figure 11-19**.

Figure 11-19 Creating an ad-hoc query

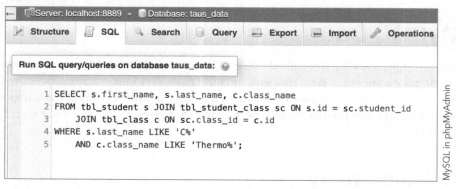

2. Click the Go button to display a dataset returned like that shown in **Figure 11-20**. (Your dataset may differ.)

Figure 11-20 Results of the ad-hoc query

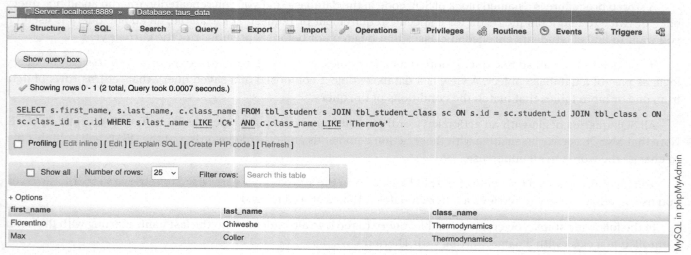

Starting with the first line, the SELECT statement is one you have seen before in your sp_get stored procedures. This statement is followed by a list of the fields to retrieve from two different tables, tbl_student and tbl_class.

The next line is a FROM clause. This clause identifies the data sources for this query, starting with the keyword FROM. The first table is tbl_students with an alias of "s" appended to it. The JOIN keyword tells the SQL processor to attempt to collate the data between the table on the left (tbl_student) and the table on the right (tbl_student_class). The table on the right, tbl_student_class, is aliased as "sc."

The join criteria come next, starting with the keyword ON. The SQL engine uses the join criteria to try to match rows in the left table with rows in the right, retrieving records that match the join criteria. In this query, the criteria are `s.id = sc.student_id`, so when the query finds an id in tbl_students that matches a student_id in tbl_student_class, all matching records are included in the results.

The next JOIN statement is `JOIN tbl_class c ON sc.class_id = c.id`. This statement adds another set of records to the same logic, creating a connection between the table tbl_student_class and the table tbl_class using the matching ids. The join criteria is `sc.class_id = c.id`, so when the query finds an class_id in tbl_student_class that matches an id in tbl_class, it retrieves the record.

The query results include every record that matches both of these join criteria.

Finally, the criteria are specified in the next two rows of the query to include only some of the records. This inclusion begins with the keyword WHERE. The conditions both use LIKE statements to retrieve rows that match the partial text strings "C%" and "Thermo%." The percent sign is used as the wildcard symbol, so that any text string beginning with the letter *C* or any text string beginning with the letters *Thermo* are included in the query results.

Note	LIKE searches are case sensitive. In SQL, a class name beginning with "thermo" is not the same as a class name beginning with "Thermo."

When you set up a database, you used the default character encoding for MySQL for your region, which is mostly likely UTF-8. In the UTF-8 character formatting, the letter q has a different value from the letter Q. Expressed as a hexadecimal, q is 71 and Q is 51. The SQL processor uses the UTF-8 values for letters to perform the query match, and obviously 51 is not equal to 71.

If you want to search a text column without worrying about the case of the letters, you would transform the text using the UPPER function. The following is new criteria in the previous query:

```
WHERE UPPER(s.last_name) LIKE 'C%'
AND UPPER(c.class_name) LIKE 'THERMO%';
```

This is not truly a case-insensitive search because you are translating the data in the columns into all uppercase letters so that the match is independent of the actual case of the letters in the data.

Creating a View from an Ad-Hoc Query

If you need to run an ad-hoc SELECT query more than once or twice, you can save it as a view. A view is just a saved query that behaves like a read-only table. The view is composed of a set of SQL statements used to extract or compose a new set of information from one or more of the tables in the database. Views compose the queried data into a table-like structure that becomes a database object. Note that views can only be used to select data, unlike a stored procedure, which can modify data.

The first step in creating a view in MySQL on the WAMP/MAMP stack is building the query itself. When building a query, the outcome defines the process. First, you add the columns you need to display, then specify how the tables containing the columns relate to one another, select the data to include or exclude if you have criteria, and finally, include an addendum like a preferred order of the data in the display or how to group redundant records.

To create a view:

1. In the SQL tab of the taus_data database, type the following SQL code:

```
SELECT DISTINCT c.id AS c_id, c.class_name, c.start_dt, c.end_dt, c.class_number,
sc.id AS s_c_id,
    s.id AS s_id, s.first_name, s.mi, s.last_name, s.photo_id_number
FROM tbl_class c JOIN tbl_student_class sc ON c.id = sc.class_id
JOIN tbl_student s ON sc.student_id = s.id
ORDER BY c.class_name, s.last_name
```

Many parts to this code should look familiar to you, like the SELECT statement used to retrieve records. The DISTINCT keyword is used to only retrieve unique records. Following the SELECT DISTINCT keywords are a list of the fields from the three tables that make up the contents of the database, so this query will retrieve a collated set of all the records.

Because this query includes data from multiple tables, each with an id field, the id fields are re-identified uniquely in the query using the AS keyword to rename the displayed column.

The FROM clause lists the tables and indicates how to join them via their relationships in the database. Finally, the ORDER BY clause tells the SQL processor in which order to display the data.

2. Click the Go button to display the results. The dataset is large since it shows all records. Scroll down to the bottom of the pane to see a set of results that reflects **Figure 11-21**.

Figure 11-21 Results of a query to save as a view

c_id	class_name ▲ 1	start_dt	end_dt	class_number	s_c_id	s_id	first_name	mi	last_name	photo_id_number
2	Intro to Western Existentialism	2025-09-05	2025-12-21	438	7	4	Florentino	A	Chiweshe	999000126
2	Intro to Western Existentialism	2025-09-05	2025-12-21	438	11	5	Max	Q	Coller	999000555
2	Intro to Western Existentialism	2025-09-05	2025-12-21	438	4	2	Tram	K	Iwuchukwu	999000125
2	Intro to Western Existentialism	2025-09-05	2025-12-21	438	2	1	Ramona	D	Malindi	999000124
2	Intro to Western Existentialism	2025-09-05	2025-12-21	438	18	3	Keeley	T	Naidoo	999000123
3	Pickleball	2025-09-04	2025-12-20	119	16	4	Florentino	A	Chiweshe	999000126
3	Pickleball	2025-09-04	2025-12-20	119	12	5	Max	Q	Coller	999000555
3	Pickleball	2025-09-04	2025-12-20	119	14	2	Tram	K	Iwuchukwu	999000125
3	Pickleball	2025-09-04	2025-12-20	119	13	1	Ramona	D	Malindi	999000124
3	Pickleball	2025-09-04	2025-12-20	119	15	3	Keeley	T	Naidoo	999000123
1	Thermodynamics	2025-09-04	2025-12-22	549	6	4	Florentino	A	Chiweshe	999000126
1	Thermodynamics	2025-09-04	2025-12-22	549	10	5	Max	Q	Coller	999000555
1	Thermodynamics	2025-09-04	2025-12-22	549	3	2	Tram	K	Iwuchukwu	999000125
1	Thermodynamics	2025-09-04	2025-12-22	549	1	1	Ramona	D	Malindi	999000124
1	Thermodynamics	2025-09-04	2025-12-22	549	17	3	Keeley	T	Naidoo	999000123

MySQL in phpMyAdmin

Although the dataset has repeated values for the class and student information, this query represents a starting point for creating the view that retrieves all unfiltered records. (Your data may differ.)

3. Click the Create view button at the bottom of the results pane. A view creation dialog box opens that looks like that in **Figure 11-22**.

4. In the VIEW name box, enter **v_all_student_class_data** as the name for this view and then click the Go button. In the left pane, a new database object is created under the Views tree item.

5. Click v_all_student_class_data in the left pane to open the view in the right pane.

Figure 11-22   The view creation dialog box

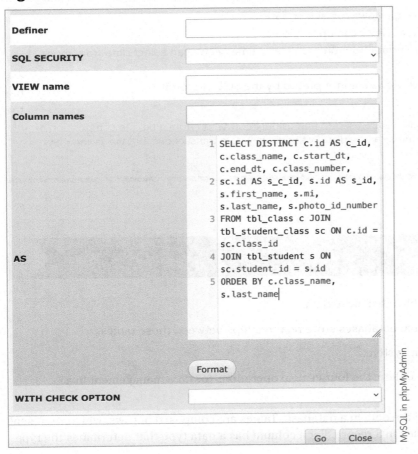

Definer

SQL SECURITY

VIEW name

Column names

```
1 SELECT DISTINCT c.id AS c_id,
  c.class_name, c.start_dt,
  c.end_dt, c.class_number,
2 sc.id AS s_c_id, s.id AS s_id,
  s.first_name, s.mi,
  s.last_name, s.photo_id_number
3 FROM tbl_class c JOIN
  tbl_student_class sc ON c.id =
  sc.class_id
4 JOIN tbl_student s ON
  sc.student_id = s.id
5 ORDER BY c.class_name,
  s.last_name
```

AS

Format

WITH CHECK OPTION

Go   Close

MySQL in phpMyAdmin

This view represents a saved query that will automatically show updated data when it is opened (or otherwise refreshed) to include a new student or class, to show that a student dropped a class, and so forth. That is, the data in the view changes as the data in the tables that make up the view are updated. Furthermore, you can search, sort, and filter the data in the view using the tools in the MySQL DBMS.

Quick Check 11-5

1. What is a view in a database?

   a. A panel in the database management interface
   b. A saved query that shows a set of data stored in the database
   c. A subset of data shown in a filtered table
   d. The user interface for a stored procedure

2. When would you use an ad-hoc query in a database?

   a. When you need to extract a composition of data from one or more tables that meet specific conditions
   b. When you want to run a stored procedure
   c. Any time that you need to add new values to a table
   d. When you want to create an index on a table

(continued)

3. What is one difference between a view and a stored procedure?

    a. Stored procedures can update data; views can select data.

    b. Stored procedures can select data; views can update data.

    c. Stored procedures can only select data from one table at a time; views can select data from more than one table.

    d. Stored procedures are compiled; views are interpreted by the SQL interpreter.

1) b. A view is a saved query. **2) a.** Ad-hoc queries are used to find useful information from a unique composition of the data in the database. **3) a.** Stored procedures can be used with two-way data transactions, but views can only select data from one or more tables for display.

Summary

- Databases are composed of one or more tables that store data.

- In addition to storing data in tables, relational databases store relationships between those tables.

- MySQL is one type of database management system.

- CRUD stands for Create, Read, Update, and Delete, the four critical operations for data management in a database.

- Tables are database objects that contain all the data in a database. Tables are composed of rows, which represent records, and columns, which represents fields in a record. Each column has a data type that determines the type of data it can store.

- Stored procedures consist of blocks of SQL code that can be run repeatedly to perform the CRUD operations of a database. Stored procedures help prevent SQL injection hacks.

- Data can be queried and retrieved using ad-hoc queries.

- Ad-hoc queries that will be run repeatedly can be used to create views of data.

Key Terms

aliases	field	relational database
constraint	foreign keys	sequences
Create, Read, Update, and Delete (CRUD)	indexes	stored procedures
data dictionary	natural keys	Structured Query Language (SQL)
data normalization	one-to-many relationship	
data type	primary key	table index
database	properties	tables
database objects	query	views
	record	

Review Questions

1. What does CRUD stand for in terms of database functions? (11.1)

   a. Create, Read, Update, Delete

   b. Create, Rewrite, Update, Drop

   c. Columns, Rows, Update, Data

   d. Columns, Rows, Uniformity, Data

2. What is SQL used for? (11.1)

   a. Manipulating data in a database

   b. Documenting the logic of a database

   c. Building the connection to the database from the webpage

   d. Creating the user interface used to manage a database

3. What is MySQL? (11.1)

   a. A specific type of SQL programming language with unique syntax

   b. The software application that PHP uses to connect to a database

   c. The name given to an instance of a logical table structure in a database

   d. A relational database management software application

4. What information is contained in the left pane of the MySQL DBMS? (11.2)

   a. The contextual menu of options available for a particular database object

   b. The breadcrumb trail showing the user which part of the database is being manipulated

   c. The list of databases and database objects

   d. The table of contents for the data dictionary

5. Which of the following is NOT a valid part of the data dictionary? (11.3)

   a. The names of the tables

   b. The names of the columns in each table

   c. The names of the people stored in the table

   d. The data type and size for each column in a table

6. What are join tables used for in a relational database? (11.3)

   a. To store the text of the join queries used to create connections between data tables

   b. To store the foreign keys from two or more tables to create relationships between the data they contain

   c. To store the data dictionary describing how the database tables are joined together

   d. To store the unique data that would be repeated in a nonjoined table structure

7. What does the AUTO_INCREMENT property do when applied to a column of data in a table? (11.3)

   a. Creates a validation rule ensuring each new value added to a column is unique in the table

   b. Creates a number column that can be used to store integers or decimals

   c. Creates the sort order for the column as data is being added to it

   d. Creates a counter on a field that increments by one each time a new row is added so the field will contain unique row numbers

8. What is a natural key? (11.3)

   a. A specific data type used in a database column

   b. A unique record identifier that originates outside of the database

   c. A record identifier that is incremented in the database to ensure each row has a unique number

   d. The unique combination of several nonunique identifiers that identify a single record

9. What is an alias used for in a SQL statement? (11.4)

   a. To mask the identity of a table in a query for better data security

   b. To prevent SQL injection from being successful

   c. To make a query run faster

   d. To shorten the length of the text of a query and clarify which columns are used in the query

10. In addition to greatly enhancing security, what is another reason using stored procedures for data transactions is a database best practice? (11.4)

   a. The code used to manipulate data within a database belongs in the database.

   b. The names of the parameters in the procedure will match the columns of the table.

   c. The SQL of the stored procedures is stored in the tables the procedures modify.

   d. The data dictionary is considered complete when it contains stored procedures.

11. What does the following SQL code do in a stored procedure? (11.4)

```
INSERT INTO tbl_records (id, record_id)

VALUES (p_record_id)
```

   a. Causes an error

   b. Creates a new record in the table tbl_records

   c. Updates the value in record_id using the value in p_record_id

   d. Automatically increments the ID field and inserts the value stored in p_record_id into the column record_id

12. How do you create a view in the MySQL DBMS? (11.5)

   a. Create a query, then save it as a view.

   b. Create the view, then add the query it runs.

   c. Use the View Builder interface.

   d. Use a stored procedure to build the view.

Programming Exercises

1. Using your favorite search engine, search for "websites built using MySQL." Read at least five of the references you find and summarize the commonalities in a one-page report. Include links to the pages you reviewed. (11.1–11.5)

2. Using your favorite search engine, search for "preventing SQL injection." Read five of the articles (including the OWASP SQL Injection Prevention Cheat Sheet) returned in the results and summarize the most common recommendations in a one-page report. Include links to the pages you reviewed. (11.1–11.5)

3. Using your favorite search engine, search for "mysql database security best practices." Read five of the articles returned in the results and summarize the most common recommendations in a one-page report. Include links to the pages you reviewed. (11.1–11.5)

Projects

1. Create a new table in the database for Totally Awesome University to contain the email addresses of the students. The data dictionary entry for this table is as follows (11.1–11.5):

   - tbl_email
   - id—INT, not null, primary key, AUTO_INCREMENT
   - email—VARCHAR(100), not null, unique value only
   - student_id—INT, not null, foreign key on id in tbl_student, cascade delete if student id deleted from tbl_student
   - preferred_email—TINYINT, holds the value 1 if the email address is flagged as preferred

2. Create four stored procedures for the table tbl_email created in Project 1, one for each part of the CRUD operations. Name these stored procedures appropriately. Then, create another stored procedure called sp_get_student_preferred_email. This procedure will only retrieve the email address flagged with the preferred field value of 1 for a student id. (11.1–11.5)

3. Using the stored procedures you created in Project 2, add two email addresses for each of the five students attending Totally Awesome University. Mark one of the email addresses as Preferred. Then, update the view you created in the chapter to include the preferred email address for each student in the query behind the view. (11.1–11.5)

Chapter 12

Building a Dynamic Webpage with a MySQL Database

Learning Objectives

When you complete this chapter, you will be able to:

12.1 Explain how PHP connects to a MySQL database securely.

12.2 Execute MySQL stored procedures from PHP.

12.3 Build PHP data-driven pages from MySQL data.

12.4 Build an interactive data grid using an HTML table.

12.1 Connecting PHP to MySQL

In the previous two chapters, you learned about the basics of writing PHP code and how to create and maintain data and objects in a MySQL database. The missing element from these two chapters was creating the relationship between PHP and MySQL. Like the join table in a database, this chapter connects the code of PHP with the data management of MySQL.

The connection between PHP and MySQL, and more broadly between any web programming language and a database, is how dynamic data-driven webpages are built. PHP and MySQL are convenient representative examples of a language and a database for this process.

Before you begin performing the steps in this tutorial, copy the Chapter_12 folder provided for this course to your local folder structure that you used as the document root when setting up PHP in Chapter 10.

Securely Creating a New User Account

The first step in creating a secure connection between the PHP application and the MySQL database is to create a dedicated user with what is referred to as least privilege. The **Principle of Least Privilege (PoLP)** means that all database users should be granted only the rights and access to the absolute minimum parts of the system that are required for each user to interact with the database successfully.

In the taus_data MySQL database you constructed for Totally Awesome University, implementing the PoLP suggests that you should first create a new user account to use in the PHP code to connect to the taus_data database.

When you were building the taus_data database, you were doing so as the root user with complete access to every table, view, stored procedure, and other database object. You also had full create, read, update, and delete rights on those objects and the data stored in the tables. This permission set is what a typical database administrator needs to do the job, so your rights fit the spirit of PoLP.

However, a web user accessing the database from PHP code should be granted rights only to a limited set of database objects to keep the data secure. This security-first approach to design is a necessary restriction for creating a robust approach to data security. The web user account credentials should be used only for the dynamic webpage database connection string stored in the PHP code. The web user credentials should also be granted rights only to execute stored procedures in the MySQL database.

To create a new user:

1. Start the MySQL DBMS as you did in Chapter 11, and then click the Privileges tab. You should see a window like that shown in **Figure 12-1**. Your screen may differ.

Figure 12-1 The Privileges tab in the MySQL DBMS

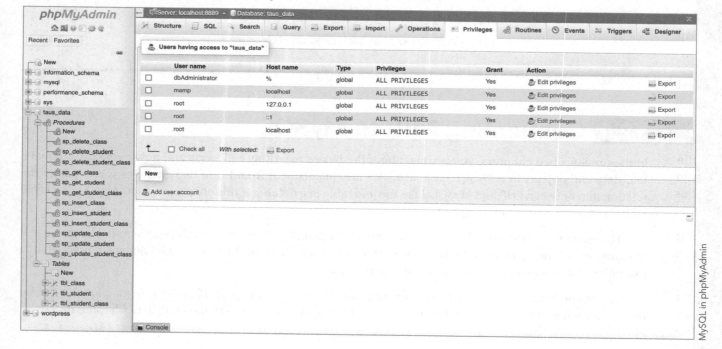

2. Click the Add user account link to open the Add user account window.
3. In the User name text box, enter **taus_web_user**. This user will access the taus_data database from the web interface you create in PHP. Use a descriptive username like this one because it is included in MySQL database and PHP code. If another developer looks at the DBMS catalog of users and wonders why taus_web_user has restricted permissions, the name alone helps to identify the reason.

4. Click the Generate button to create a strong password with random characters. **Figure 12-2** shows a random password, but yours will be different. Copy the password by pressing Ctrl+C or Cmd+C.

Figure 12-2   Generating a password for a new user

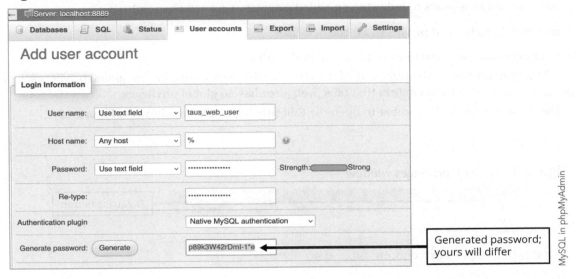

Generated password; yours will differ

MySQL in phpMyAdmin

5. Open the data_handler.php file in the Samples folder for this chapter, which is shown in **Figure 12-3**.

Figure 12-3   The starting code in data_handler.php

```php
1    <?php
2        class DataHandler {
3            // Properties
4            private $db_conn;
5
6            // Methods
7            public function __construct() {
8                //Create the database connection.
9                $this->db_conn = MySQLi_connect(
10                   "localhost", //Server Name
11                   "taus_web_user", //Username.
12                   "p89k3W42rDmI-1*e", //Password.
13                   "taus_data" //Database Name
14               );
15               //Test the connection
16               if (MySQLi_connect_errno()) {
17                   die("Connection failed: " . MySQLi_connect_error());
18               }
19           }
20
21           public function get_student($s_id) {
22               //stored procedure to run.
23               $query = "CALL sp_get_student('".$s_id."')";
24
25               //stored procedure preparation
26               $exec_query = MySQLi_query($this->db_conn, $query);
27
28               //Fetching result from database.
29               $q_results = MySQLi_fetch_array($exec_query);
30
31               return $q_results;
32           }
33       }
```

BBEdit

6. Find the "//Password" comment (line 12 in Figure 12-3), which indicates where to paste the new password you just generated for the MySQL database. Replace the commented password with the random password generated when you performed step 4 and then save the data_handler.php file.

7. In the Add user account window in the MySQL DBMS, scroll down and uncheck any checked boxes. All options listed in the Global pane apply to every database, not just to taus_data, so these options violate the PoLP and unchecking them removes the global permissions.

8. At the bottom of the pane, click the Go button to create a new user account with no global permissions. A confirmation message appears to indicate you added a new user named taus_web_user.

To set the appropriate rights and privileges for the new user:

1. Click the User accounts tab. Your new user is listed in the table.

2. Click the Edit privileges link on the right side of the table for this user to display the global privileges. Leave all the privileges unchecked and confirm that taus_web_user has no global privileges.

3. Click the Database button on the toolbar to open the Edit privileges window shown in **Figure 12-4**.

Figure 12-4   Edit privileges window

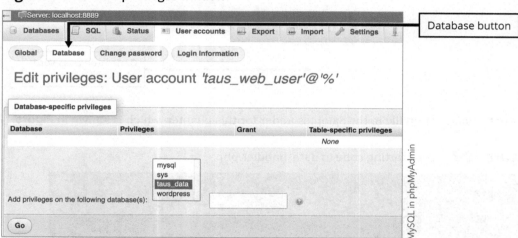

4. Choose taus_data from the list of databases the user taus_web_user can access, and then click the Go button to assign permission to the taus_web_user only for the taus_data database. Another Edit privileges window opens.

5. Check the Execute check box in the Structure list as shown in **Figure 12-5**. Selecting this option means the user taus_web_user can only execute stored procedures. No other privileges are allowed for the taus_data database or for any other database.

6. Scroll down to the bottom of this page and click the Go button. A confirmation message appears indicating that you updated the privileges for the user taus_web_user.

Note The database user account you just created and assigned restricted privileges to is the account Internet-based hackers would have to use to gain access from the Internet through the PHP code and into the MySQL database. Performing the extra step of restricting the exposed user to only executing the stored procedures in one database makes any future malicious activity more challenging for hackers. It is not a guarantee that your website will never be successfully hacked, but every step you take to harden your infrastructure is to your advantage.

Figure 12-5   Granting only Execute privileges to a user

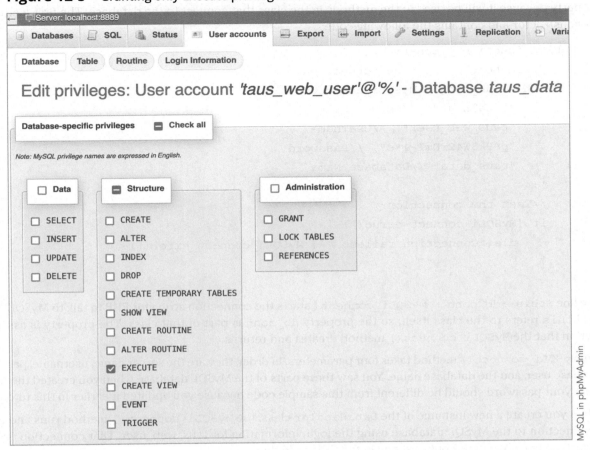

MySQL in phpMyAdmin

Creating the Database Access Point

To connect webpages to a database, you next create the PHP code that accesses the MySQL database. PHP can use two different software packages to make this connection: MySQLi and PDO. MySQLi is included with the default installation of PHP, so you can use it in your PHP code like any other built-in PHP function.

In addition to the connection software, you must make programming choices about how to establish the connection. Often in the past and in some current web applications, PHP developers have written code to create a new connection to the database each time they needed it on every PHP page built to display or interact with data from a database. That is, each page contained a complete block of the full connection information along with the MySQL code necessary to access the data. You may inherit PHP pages that use this approach.

As you may be thinking, this is a lot of repeated code. It is inefficient to update all the connection strings stored in multiple pages if a new username or password is required. A better way creates one PHP file as the database access point for the entire web application. In this file, you write all the code that interacts directly with the database. You also create a class that has methods for each data transaction in the system. All the code that interacts with the database goes in this class, and PHP data objects come out from these methods. You can think of the PHP database class as the translator between the PHP and the database. No database code such as SQL statements or connection strings should be in any of the other PHP pages that make up the web application.

If necessary, open the data_handler.php file containing the new password for taus_web_user. The PHP code you have written previously mixed PHP with HTML code to create a webpage. The data_handler.php file has no HTML because its purpose is to serve as the singular point of contact for all database interactions for the dynamic webpages.

At the top of the page is a class declaration and one property, the connection to the database. This connection is a property because it will be used in the methods in the class that connect to the database. The first method is the default constructor and contains the following code:

```
public function __construct() {
    //Create the database connection
    $this->db_conn = MySQLi_connect(
        "localhost", //Server Name
        "taus_web_user", //Username
        "p89k3W42rDmI-1*e", //Password
        "taus_data" //Database Name
    );
    //Test the connection
    if (MySQLi_connect_errno()) {
        die("Connection failed: " . MySQLi_connect_error());
    }
}
```

The line $this->db_conn = MySQLi_connect(starts the connection string for PHP to talk to MySQL. The PHP keyword this refers to the class itself, so the property db_conn is part of that class. The property is assigned the connection that the MySQLi_connect() method creates and returns.

The MySQLi_connect() method takes four parameters. In order, they are the server name, username, password for the database user, and the database name. You saw these parts of the MySQL database when you created the database. Note that your password should be different from this sample code because you updated it earlier in this tutorial.

When you create a new instance of the DataHandler class, the MySQLi_connect() method runs and creates a fresh connection to the MySQL database using the login information for taus_web_user. That connection ends when the DataHandler object goes out of scope in the PHP code that uses it.

The final block of code in this method tests the new connection to make sure it is working properly before any database interactions begin. This test uses the MySQLi_connect_errno() method to ask the MySQLi connection for any error numbers associated with the attempted connection. If there are any errors, the if() statement is true and the PHP die() method runs. The die() method ends all running PHP code so that no further code functions or processes continue to run.

The exit is important because the DataHandler class serves as the single pathway into and out of the database. If a connection can't be made successfully, nothing else will (or should) work. However, before this block of code is moved into a production capacity, the die() method should be updated to display only the "Connection failed" message and not the actual connection error. The error number created by an intrusion attempt shown to a hacker is a useful piece of information that you don't want to provide.

For this tutorial, however, you should know error details if the connection to the database is not working. You will also find detailed error messaging helpful when you are doing development work in PHP prior to a production launch.

The other method in this class is called get_student() and is the starting point for building the functionality of the DataHandler class. The code for the get_student() method begins on line 21 in data_handler.php:

```
public function get_student($s_id) {
    //Stored procedure to run
    $query = "CALL sp_get_student('".$s_id."')";

    //Stored procedure preparation
    $exec_query = MySQLi_query($this->db_conn, $query);

    //Fetching result from database
```

```
        $q_results = MySQLi_fetch_array($exec_query);


        return $q_results;

    }
```

The `get_student()` method has a descriptive name and takes one parameter, the record ID number identifying a unique student record to retrieve from the database. The `get_student()` method name will also be used in the PHP code of the dynamic webpage that needs this data, so a descriptive name helps you use the right method at the right point in the code.

The statement `$query = "CALL sp_get_student('".$s_id."')";` is the first line of code after the opening curly bracket of the method. It creates a `$query` variable containing the text of the SQL command that needs to run. The contents of this variable concatenate the text and the value passed into the method, which is stored in the `$s_id` parameter.

The code `$exec_query = MySQLi_query($this->db_conn, $query);` runs the query text generated in the `$query = "CALL sp_get_student('".$s_id."')";` line. It does so using the connection to the database established when the `DataHandler` object was created. The `MySQLi_query()` function takes two parameters: the connection to use and the SQL query to run. The results of the query are returned to the `$exec_query` object.

Finally, the `MySQLi_fetch_array()` function extracts the first row of data (and the only row, if the query is working correctly) that matches the query parameters into an associative array. Executing the query on the database connection creates the database results returned to the `$exec_query` object.

An associative array is useful here because it recreates the column names from the table or query with an associated value in each column, except the data structure is created in PHP code instead of the database code. The PHP associative array is also the data structure returned from this function to the PHP webpage that called it.

This `get_student()` method illustrates what using a method from a `DataHandler` class should create—the interaction between PHP code and the SQL code that runs in the database. The results returned from the database are then translated back into PHP code.

Using the DataHandler Class in Code

Open the check_connection.php file included with the starting files for this chapter. This file is intended to test whether the database connection is working and serves as the starting point for building the code in the remainder of this tutorial. You can see a copy of this file in **Figure 12-6**.

Figure 12-6   The code in check_connection.php

```
1    <!DOCTYPE html>
2    <html>
3        <head>
4            <title>Check Connection</title>
5            <link rel="stylesheet" type="text/css" href="css/my_styles.css" media="screen, print" />
6        </head>
7        <body>
8            <h1>Check Connection</h1>
9            <p>
10               <ul>
11               <?php
12                   include "data_handler.php";
13
14                   $dh = new DataHandler();
15                   $results = $dh->get_student('1');
16
17                   echo "<table class='fullborder'><tr><th>First Name</th><th>MI</th><th>Last Name</th><th>Photo ID Number</th></tr><tr>";
18                   echo "<td>".$results['first_name']."</td>";
19                   echo "<td>".$results['mi']."</td>";
20                   echo "<td>".$results['last_name']."</td>";
21                   echo "<td>".$results['photo_id_number']."</td>";
22                   echo "</tr></table>";
23               ?>
24               </ul>
25           </p>
26       </body>
27   </html>
```

BBEdit

The HTML of this page is straightforward. The following new code occurs inside the PHP tags:

```php
<?php
    include "data_handler.php";
    $dh = new DataHandler();
    $results = $dh->get_student('1');
    echo "<table class='fullborder'><tr><th>First Name</th><th>MI</th><th>Last
Name</th><th>Photo ID Number</th></tr><tr>";
    echo "<td>".$results['first_name']."</td>";
    echo "<td>".$results['mi']."</td>";
    echo "<td>".$results['last_name']."</td>";
    echo "<td>".$results['photo_id_number']."</td>";
    echo "</tr></table>";
?>
```

The first new PHP code inside the opening tag is the `include "data_handler.php";` statement. In PHP, as with other programming languages, an `include` statement tells the PHP interpreter that the code in the file named in the quotes should be included, or inserted in this file.

This statement demonstrates the rule of Don't Repeat Yourself. You will use the database connectivity code from the data_handler.php file throughout the pages of this dynamic website. When you need the database connectivity code, you can use it by inserting the `include` statement.

The next two lines are `$dh = new DataHandler();` and `$results = $dh->get_student('1');`. In these two lines, you create an instance of the `DataHandler` class called `$dh` and then use one of its methods to retrieve an associative array from the database. The `$results = $dh->get_student('1');` line creates a variable named `$results` that contains the associative array returned from calling the `$dh` object's `get_student()` method, sending the value 1 to that method as the student record ID number to use in the query. This method calls the stored procedure named `get_student` to retrieve the record with a value of 1 in the id column from the tbl_student table.

The `echo` statements illustrate the convenience of using an associative array. First, the beginning structure of an HTML table is printed to the page using the `echo` command. Then, a series of HTML `<td></td>` tag pairs are created around each named element of the associative array, beginning with the `$results['first_name']` element. This PHP code searches the associative array for a key called `first_name` and returns the value associated with it.

Save your new MySQL password in data_handler.php if you have not previously done so. Then, start your MAMP/WAMP application and open one of the following URLs depending on whether you are using MAMP or WAMP:

For MAMP, open a URL similar to http://localhost:8888/chapter_12/starting_files/check_connection.php

On WAMP, open a URL similar to http://localhost/chapter_12/starting_files/check_connection.php

You should see a webpage that looks like **Figure 12-7**.

Figure 12-7 The webpage displayed after successfully executing the PHP code

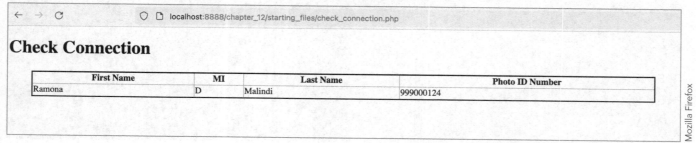

First Name	MI	Last Name	Photo ID Number
Ramona	D	Malindi	999000124

Your record for the student with the ID of 1 in your MySQL database may be different from the one shown in Figure 12-7. Your objective is to successfully retrieve a record from the database and display it in a webpage.

If a record is not shown in the PHP page, perform a differential diagnosis similar to other debugging you have done during this course. First check whether your WAMP/MAMP application is running by opening the phpMyAdmin interface in your web browser.

Next, check the PHP error log that you examined previously in Chapter 10. If you generate a PHP error, it appears in the log where you can see more details about why the PHP code isn't working.

If the PHP error log does not contain any errors, check the Apache error log stored in the same folder as the PHP error log.

Finally, check to make sure the stored procedure named `get_student` is working when you send it a value of 1 by using the MySQL DBMS to execute the procedure directly, following the instructions from Chapter 11.

You may need to search for help on the error text you find, but an advantage of using an open source and widely used technology stack like WAMP/MAMP is that someone else has most likely created and documented the error you find in the logs.

Quick Check 12-1

1. What is the Principle of Least Privilege?

    a. An approach to database security that allows only the minimum access required for each user to interact successfully with the database

    b. A permission set in the MySQL database using the PoLP pane to assign access to a user

    c. The object-oriented approach to secure database connectivity between a programming language like PHP and a database like MySQL

    d. An approach to database security that allows full access to users unless they prove they are untrustworthy or unable to safely use the tools and access they are granted.

2. According to PoLP, what database object should a web user be granted access to?

    a. Full CRUD access, but only on specific tables in the database

    b. Full CRUD access on everything except the tables in the database

    c. Full CRUD access, but only on the specific database the user should have access to

    d. The stored procedures necessary to perform the CRUD operations on the data stored in the tables

3. What is a disadvantage of using one PHP file as the single point of access to the database in a web application instead of including the database connectivity in every page that needs it?

    a. This is not a disadvantage but an advantage.

    b. The code is more complex in the user interface.

    c. The code is more complex in the PHP database file.

    d. Having all of the code in one file creates an efficiency bottleneck since you don't have a distribution of concerns across each of the pages that use it.

1) a. PoLP is a security-first approach to assigning database privileges that allows users to access only the parts of the database they need. **2) d.** Web users should only be allowed to interact with the database through stored procedures. **3) a.** Creating a single point of access to the database simplifies the web application and the code that makes it up.

12.2 Creating an Interactive Webpage Using PHP and MySQL

In the previous section, you created a simple data transaction using PHP and MySQL. The value used to retrieve a record from the MySQL database was hard-coded into the query. The PHP code then sent the value to the database through the data_handler.php file.

Hard-coding a value into the function while testing is a useful start to an incremental build. By reducing the complexity of the operation, you can limit the sources of malfunctions or bugs in the code. Using a known value also decreases development time. The written code can then be tested with a single unit test to determine if the code does what it was designed to do.

To create an interactive webpage, however, you need to replace the hard-coded value with an HTML form for entering data. The user submits this form to the web server, which processes the form and data. You've used these PHP components previously, so you only need to update the existing code.

Creating an Interactive Search Page

To update the PHP file:

1. Save a copy of check_connection.php as a new file called show_student.php.
2. Update the HTML `title` and `h1` values for the page to **Student Lookup**.
3. Add the following HTML code after the `<h1>`...`</h1>` tags:

```
<form action='show_student.php' method="post">
    <label for="s_id">Student Record#:</label>
    <input type="number" required id="s_id" name="s_id" /><br/>
    <input type="submit" value="Submit" />
</form>
```

The action for this form is the same page that loads the form, the show_student.php page. The method is `post`. The form has three elements: a label for the text box, the text box itself, and a submit button. Users can type a value into the Student Record# text box (or click an arrow to increase or decrease the value, since it is a number field) and then click the Submit button to display a record returned from the database.

You need to add the PHP code to handle the POST request that results from submitting the form you just created, which is also code you've seen before.

4. Update the PHP code between the opening and closing PHP tags to reflect the following bold code:

```
include "data_handler.php";
if ($_SERVER["REQUEST_METHOD"] == "POST")
{
    $s_id = filter_var($_POST["s_id"],FILTER_SANITIZE_STRING);
    $dh = new DataHandler();
    $results = $dh->get_student($s_id);
    echo "<table class='fullborder'><tr><th>First Name</th><th>MI</th><th>Last
Name</th><th>Photo ID Number</th></tr><tr>";
    echo "<td>".$results['first_name']."</td>";
    echo "<td>".$results['mi']."</td>";
    echo "<td>".$results['last_name']."</td>";
    echo "<td>".$results['photo_id_number']."</td>";
    echo "</tr></table>";
}
```

With these additions, you have created an interactive page. The highlighted code reflects the parts necessary to run this entire block only when the user clicks the Submit button and the page is submitted to the server. Additionally, you are sanitizing the value submitted to help prevent possible malicious activity like a SQL injection.

5. Save your changes. Your file should look **Figure 12-8**.

Figure 12-8 The updated show_student.php for loading data dynamically

```
1   <!DOCTYPE html>
2   <html>
3       <head>
4           <title>Student Lookup</title>
5           <link rel="stylesheet" type="text/css" href="css/my_styles.css" media="screen, print" />
6       </head>
7       <body>
8           <h1>Student Lookup</h1>
9           <form action='show_student.php' method="post">
10              <label for="s_id">Student Record#:</label>
11              <input type="number" required id="s_id" name="s_id" /><br/>
12              <input type="submit" value="Submit" />
13          </form>
14          <p>
15              <?php
16                  include "data_handler.php";
17
18                  if ($_SERVER["REQUEST_METHOD"] == "POST")
19                  {
20                      $s_id = filter_var($_POST["s_id"],FILTER_SANITIZE_STRING);
21
22                      $dh = new DataHandler();
23                      $results = $dh->get_student($s_id);
24
25                      echo "<table class='fullborder'><tr><th>First Name</th><th>MI</th><th>Last Name</th><th>Photo ID Number</th></tr><tr>";
26                      echo "<td>".$results['first_name']."</td>";
27                      echo "<td>".$results['mi']."</td>";
28                      echo "<td>".$results['last_name']."</td>";
29                      echo "<td>".$results['photo_id_number']."</td>";
30                      echo "</tr></table>";
31
32                  }
33              ?>
34          </p>
35      </body>
36   </html>
```

BBEdit

6. Open the file in your web browser. When you first load it, only a blank form appears in the webpage. The code you added makes a POST request, but you haven't yet executed the new POST method that builds the table with data from the database.

7. Enter the number 1 in the text box then click Submit. You should see a webpage that looks like that in **Figure 12-9**, though your data may be different.

Figure 12-9 Updated Student Lookup webpage

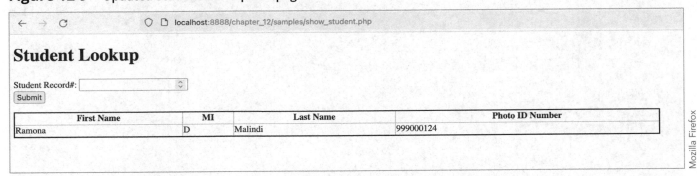

localhost:8888/chapter_12/samples/show_student.php

Student Lookup

Student Record#: [   ]
[Submit]

First Name	MI	Last Name	Photo ID Number
Ramona	D	Malindi	999000124

Mozilla Firefox

8. Use the Student Record# text box to quickly run through the records in your database. If you enter a number that doesn't return any results, however, you see an error message like "trying to access array offset on value of type null" or only the header of the table. You do not see the rest of the data if your PHP is configured not to display error messages, as described in Chapter 10.

This could easily cause confusion for your users, so a "No Records Found" message would improve the user experience. That's the next step in improving the user interface.

Improving the User Interface

When no records are found, a helpful message should be displayed. The user then knows the result is normal behavior rather than an unknown error. To display a helpful message, you need to add a test that checks for records.

To add an error message:

1. In show_student.php, on the line before the first `echo` statement that begins the printing of the HTML table structure, add the following code:

```
if($results != null)
{
```

This uses the PHP "not equal" comparison to null to test whether the `$results` object contains any values. If the associative array contains values, the statement is true. The rest of the code then runs to build table using those values.

2. Following the last echo statement, add the following code:

```
}
else
{
    echo "<p>No Records Found</p>";
}
```

This second section of the code runs if the `$results` is null, which means no results were found. Save your changes. The completed updates are shown in **Figure 12-10**.

Figure 12-10 Improved show_student.php file

```
1    <!DOCTYPE html>
2    <html>
3        <head>
4            <title>Student Lookup</title>
5            <link rel="stylesheet" type="text/css" href="css/my_styles.css" media="screen, print" />
6        </head>
7        <body>
8            <h1>Student Lookup</h1>
9            <form action='show_student.php' method="post">
10               <label for="s_id">Student Record#:</label>
11               <input type="number" required id="s_id" name="s_id" /><br/>
12               <input type="submit" value="Submit" />
13           </form>
14           <p>
15               <?php
16                   include "data_handler.php";
17
18                   if ($_SERVER["REQUEST_METHOD"] == "POST")
19                   {
20                       $s_id = filter_var($_POST["s_id"],FILTER_SANITIZE_STRING);
21
22                       $dh = new DataHandler();
23                       $results = $dh->get_student($s_id);
24
25                       if($results != null)
26                       {
27                           echo "<table class='fullborder'><tr><th>First Name</th><th>MI</th><th>Last Name</th><th>Photo ID Number</th></tr><tr>";
28                           echo "<td>".$results['first_name']."</td>";
29                           echo "<td>".$results['mi']."</td>";
30                           echo "<td>".$results['last_name']."</td>";
31                           echo "<td>".$results['photo_id_number']."</td>";
32                           echo "</tr></table>";
33                       }
34                       else
35                       {
36                           echo "<p>No Records Found</p>";
37                       }
38                   }
39               ?>
40           </p>
41       </body>
42   </html>
```

BBEdit

3. Refresh the page then test the new code by entering a student ID number that exceeds the current number of students enrolled in Totally Awesome University, such as 30. When you click the Submit button, you should see the message "No Records Found."

One more polishing touch is in order for this webpage. The look of this application is stark. A border around the data entry part of the webpage will draw the user's attention to the text box. Aligning the Submit button with the lower-right corner of the data entry area helps the user follow the intended flow of the webpage from top left to bottom right.

To enhance the appearance of the webpage:

1. Open the my_styles.css file in the css folder inside your samples folder and then add the following style to the end of the file:

```css
#searchBox {
    border: 2px solid black;
    border-radius: 5px;
    width: 25%;
    padding: 5px;
}

#searchBox input[type=submit] {
    margin-top: 5px;
    margin-left: 80%;
}
```

2. In show_student.php, add a div element with the ID of searchBox around the input form.
3. Save your changes to the CSS and PHP files and then refresh the webpage in your browser. The updated Student Lookup page looks like that in **Figure 12-11**.

Figure 12-11   Updated Student Lookup page

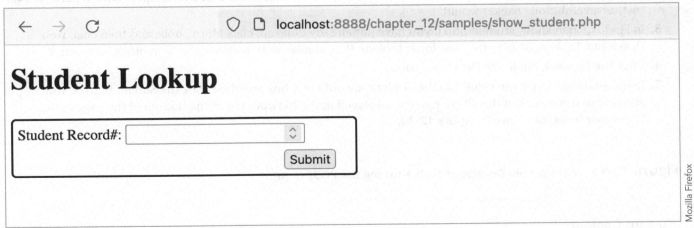

Mozilla Firefox

Testing for SQL Injection Resistance

It is useful to do your own ethical hacking on your website. Recall that SQL injection involves a hacker injecting additional SQL commands into normal data. Including a text box on your webpage that Internet users can access creates a new attack vector for your web application.

The first ethical hacking test is an easy one. You have been testing the Student Lookup webpage nonmaliciously using numeric values. You've also added code that informs the user that no records are found if an ID value is entered that doesn't correspond to a record in the database.

You use quasi-numeric data to test for SQL injection resistance. To test for SQL injection resistance:

1. In the Student Record# text box on the Student Lookup webpage, enter the following attempted SQL injection value, if your browser allows the entry:

   ```
   1' or 1=1'
   ```

2. Click the Submit button. Because this input text box has a `type="number"` attribute, you should receive a client-side validation prompt like "Please enter a numeric value" as shown in **Figure 12-12**.

Figure 12-12 Client-side validation prompt

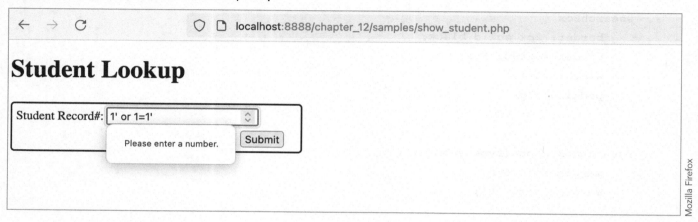

This is good! Client-side validation is a good first step to prevent lazy hackers, or those with only an automated script accessing these text boxes, from performing a simple SQL injection.

The next step in testing for SQL injection resistance is to bypass the client-side validation and inject a payload of data directly into the POST request. You can use the browser's web developer tools to perform this test, as an ambitious hacker would.

3. In Firefox, open show_student.php if you have not already done so, click More Tools, and then click Web Developer Tools to display the Developer toolbar. (Use similar web developer tools in other browsers.)

4. Click the Network tab in the Developer tools.

5. In the webpage, enter the value **1** in the Student Record# text box and then click the Submit button. You should see the results of this POST request displayed in the Network tab at the bottom of the page in the Developer tools, as shown in **Figure 12-13**.

Figure 12-13 Firefox Web Developer tools showing the POST request

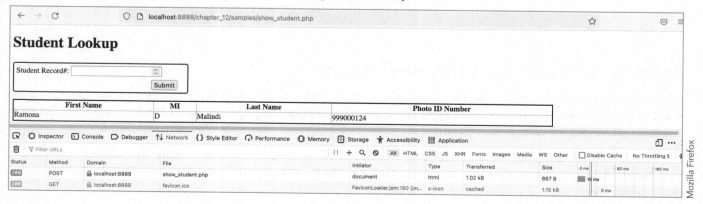

6. In the list of requests on the Network tab, click the POST request to open the request details pane. You can see an example of this view in **Figure 12-14**.

Figure 12-14 The Network details pane showing the POST request

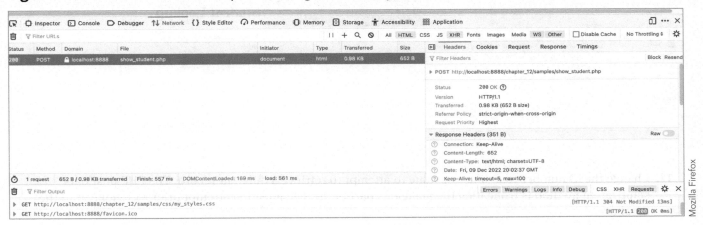

7. In the upper-right corner of the request details pane, click the Resend button if your browser has one to open the New Request pane, which you can use to resend the POST request.

8. Scroll down to the bottom of the New Request pane to show the Body area, shown in **Figure 12-15**, along with an edited payload of data—the SQL injection attempt. Your browser might not include this pane.

Figure 12-15 New Request pane with edited POST data

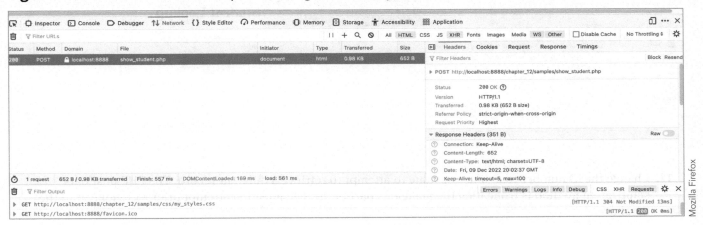

9. Update the data in the Body area to use the pattern `1' or 1=1'` and make it an attempted SQL injection and then click the Send button.

10. To review the response sent from the web server, click the Response tab on the right of the Network Request pane. (Your browser might have a Preview tab instead.) You should see a response similar to that shown in **Figure 12-16**.

The data displayed in Figure 12-16 is the unstyled webpage returned from Apache following the request you made via the Developer tools.

Figure 12-16 Results of the POST request after resending data

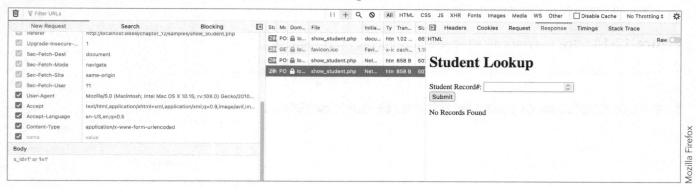

11. Change the ID number to a different value to attempt to retrieve a different record. The PHP post data sanitization method is truncating the malicious part of the SQL injection attempt prior to sending it to the database.

12. Continue testing by moving the single quotes to different positions to attempt different ways of injecting SQL into the POST request. Use the input value `1 or 1=1` in case no single quotes were used in the query to identify the input as a text string and numeric values were used instead.

You are bypassing the client-side validation using this method, but because your code sanitizes the input and only calls a single stored procedure with one purpose and one input allowed, you retrieve only the payload of data as intended, or "No Records Found" if your attempted SQL injection includes data that can't be sanitized.

Making the User Interface More Realistic

The initial testing conditions for building the Student Lookup webpage uses the easiest parameter in the database to test the continuity of the PHP webpage POST request, the ID for a record. That POST request containing the ID number is sent through the stored procedure to retrieve a record from the database table with an ID number that matches the number the user entered. The record is then sent back through the same plumbing to create a table containing that record and display it in the webpage.

However, having users enter a record ID number is not realistic. It is unlikely you know your row or record ID number in the table of students in the school database. However, you probably know your last name and student ID number (or photo ID number if that's what your school calls it). A more robust user interface would accommodate those two search criteria.

To make the user interface more realistic, you need to create a new stored procedure that takes two parameters for a photo ID number search or a last name search. The first parameter is an integer that will be used for the photo ID stored in the photo_id_number column in the table of students. The second parameter will be the first few letters in the text string of a last name stored in the same table.

To change the requested search criteria:

1. Open the MySQL DBMS, if it is not already open, and then create a new stored procedure named **sp_get_students**.

2. Assign two parameters to the new stored procedure, **p_photo_id_number**, which is an INT data type, and **p_last_name**, which is a VARCHAR with a maximum length of 10 characters.

3. In the Definition box, enter the following code as the text of the query and then click Go:

```
SELECT s.id, s.first_name, s.mi, s.last_name, s.photo_id_number
FROM tbl_student s
```

```
WHERE (s.photo_id_number = p_photo_id_number
    AND p_last_name = '')
OR
    (UPPER(s.last_name) LIKE CONCAT(UPPER(p_last_name),'%')
    AND p_photo_id_number = 0)
```

The first line of this query is for retrieving the record ID and the other student data. The student data will be used in the PHP code to identify a unique record.

The WHERE clause has two parts joined by an OR operator. The OR means that either part can be true, so if the first condition is true, the query stops and returns a record without attempting the second part. Because the most efficient database search is one for a distinct value like 999000123, that's the first part of the query to evaluate.

The first part of the WHERE clause (before the OR) compares the values in the photo_id_number column to the value in the p_photo_id_number parameter, as long as the p_last_name parameter is empty. The AND operator means both parts of the condition must be true. Thus, the photo_id_number column value in the table of students must match the value in the parameter p_photo_id_number AND the parameter p_last_name must be empty for this search to be true and return a record.

The second part of the WHERE clause follows the OR. The statement makes a more complex comparison between the uppercase value in the last_name column of tbl_student and the uppercase value of the p_last_name parameter. It uses a LIKE search to compare the first few letters of a last name in both the input parameter and the last_name column.

The second part of the WHERE clause is less efficient (and more complex) in terms of database processing. Searching for a partial match of a last name is an inexact search. It requires parsing the partial text of each value stored in the last_name column and comparing it to the partial text of the input parameter for as many values appear in each row of the table.

This LIKE search uses the % wildcard to tell the SQL processor to match the value in the p_last_name parameter to the starting letters in all the names in the last_name column. That is, if you enter the letter c in the user interface, the p_last_name parameter will contain the letter c changed to uppercase by the UPPER() function. Next, the CONCAT() function appends to the letter C the % symbol, which is the wildcard telling the database to compare C% to any value in the last_name column starting with the uppercase letter C.

The AND p_photo_id_number = 0 statement means the comparison is valid only if the p_photo_id_number parameter is equal to 0. The 0 value is necessary because integer parameters must not be null in stored procedures. However, no record has a photo ID of 0, so this statement tests whether the p_photo_id_number parameter contains a valid photo ID number.

The completed stored procedure is shown in **Figure 12-17**.

Test your new stored procedure before moving on to the PHP database class to ensure that any bugs you find later in development are only in the PHP and not in the stored procedure.

To test the sp_get_students stored procedure:

1. In the list of stored procedures, click the Execute link for sp_get_students.
2. Enter the first letter of the last name for a student in the taus_web_user database, such as **c**, enter **0** for the photo ID, and then execute the procedure. You should return a record.
3. Execute the stored procedure again, entering a photo ID number (a value like **999000123**) and nothing in the last name field to see if that search works correctly.

These incremental build steps are useful so that you aren't testing the entire data path from start to finish. Similar to other stepwise builds like those in HTML, CSS, JavaScript, and WordPress, isolating each step reduces the number of variables to make it easier to identify the source of a bug.

Figure 12-17 Code for the sp_get_students stored procedure

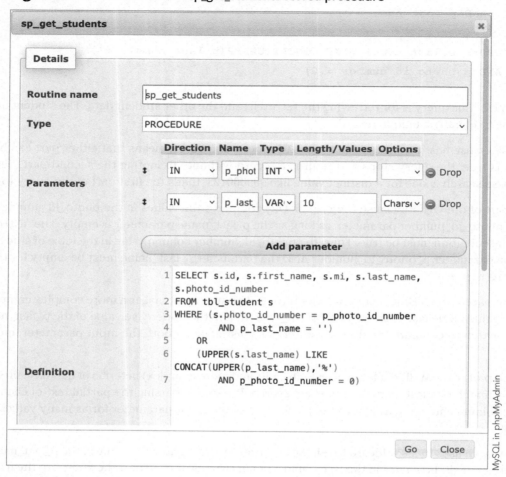

Next, you need to update the `DataHandler` class to use this new stored procedure. The code will be similar to code you have created and used previously, but with a modification since it is possible to return more than one record with a LIKE search.

To update the data_handler.php file:

1. Open data_handler.php, if necessary, and then add the following new function declaration, opening comment, and null value replacement:

```
public function get_students($photo_id, $last_name)
{
    // check to see if the photo id is empty
    // assign it the default value 0 if it is
    // this is necessary because this stored procedure
    // requires a value for the integer input parameter
    if($photo_id == '')
    {
        $photo_id = 0;
    }
}
```

The parameters `$photo_id` and `$last_name` are now passed into this method. The comments tell the next developer why you need to test to see if a parameter is empty.

The `if` statement code is a simple test and update for the `$photo_id` parameter. Although the test could also be accomplished in the UI, the `DataHandler` class is the intersection between the content the database requires, like a 0 value in integer input parameters, and the PHP code used to create the UI, so the class is a logical place to perform this operation.

2. Add the following code to explicitly declare an array to contain the associative arrays returned from the MySQLi library following the successful query:

```
//declare the array variable
$my_arr = array();
```

This array, as with all arrays, will contain 0 or more of the same type of data. In this case, the array will contain all rows of returned data, so it functions like a PHP version of the filtered database table. In the webpage, this array will need to be processed with a loop going through each row to retrieve each associative array, which can then be used create a row in the HTML table.

3. Add the next two PHP statements to the code:

```
//stored procedure to run
$query = "CALL sp_get_students('".$photo_id."','".$last_name."')";


//stored procedure preparation
$exec_query = MySQLi_query($this->db_conn, $query);
```

The first statement builds the query to run a specific stored procedure, sp_get_students, in this case. The second statement runs the stored procedure using the database connection property of the class.

4. Add the following code to the body of the function to build an array of associative arrays, one associative array for each row of data returned from the query. This array is useful (and necessary) because a LIKE search can return 0 or more records, so you need a loop to add as many rows as are returned by the query.

```
//loop through the results, building the array of associative arrays
while($row = mysqli_fetch_array($exec_query)) {
    $my_arr[] = $row;
}
return $my_arr;
}
```

The `while()` function in PHP will run as long as the conditions in the parentheses are true. The result from the stored procedure is a null value when no records are found or no more records are found. In Boolean terms, a null value evaluates to "false," ending the loop. The `$row` variable is assigned the associative array from the `mysqli_fetch_array()` function. The `mysqli_fetch_array()` function parses the results of the `$exec_query` object one row at a time. The `$row` variable that holds the associative array is added to a new row in the `$my_arr` array, translating the database data structure into a PHP data structure.

The `return $my_arr;` statement returns the `$my_arr` array to the calling function in the PHP webpage, which you now need to create to take advantage of this new database class functionality. Save your changes. You can see an example of this completed code in **Figure 12-18**.

5. Save a copy of show_student.php as a new file called show_students.php.

6. Update the form at the top of the page to match the following updated code:

```
Search for a student by:
<form action='show_students.php' method="post">
    <label for="photo_id">Photo ID#:</label>
    <input type="number" id="photo_id" name="photo_id" /> -or-<br/>
    <label for="last_name">Last Name Starts With:</label>
    <input type="text" id="last_name" name="last_name" maxlength='10'/><br/>
    <input type="submit" value="Submit" />
</form>
```

Figure 12-18 DataHandler class updated to call the new stored procedure

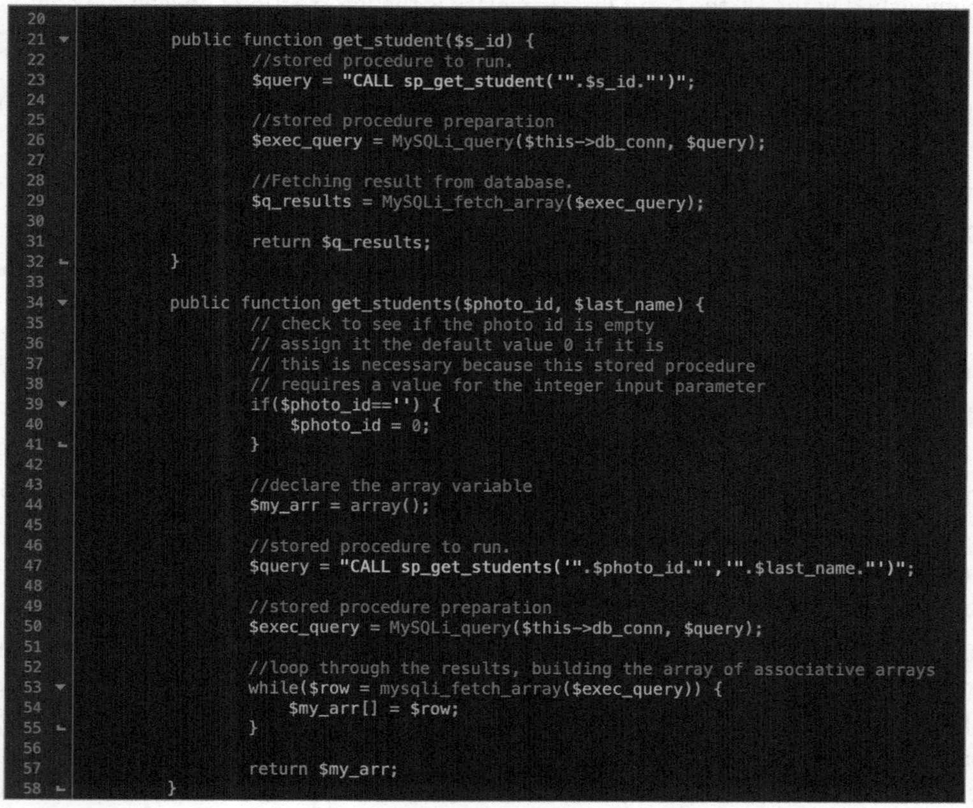

```
20
21  ▾    public function get_student($s_id) {
22           //stored procedure to run.
23           $query = "CALL sp_get_student('".$s_id."')";
24
25           //stored procedure preparation
26           $exec_query = MySQLi_query($this->db_conn, $query);
27
28           //Fetching result from database.
29           $q_results = MySQLi_fetch_array($exec_query);
30
31           return $q_results;
32  ⌐    }
33
34  ▾    public function get_students($photo_id, $last_name) {
35           // check to see if the photo id is empty
36           // assign it the default value 0 if it is
37           // this is necessary because this stored procedure
38           // requires a value for the integer input parameter
39  ▾        if($photo_id=='') {
40               $photo_id = 0;
41  ⌐        }
42
43           //declare the array variable
44           $my_arr = array();
45
46           //stored procedure to run.
47           $query = "CALL sp_get_students('".$photo_id."','".$last_name."')";
48
49           //stored procedure preparation
50           $exec_query = MySQLi_query($this->db_conn, $query);
51
52           //loop through the results, building the array of associative arrays
53  ▾        while($row = mysqli_fetch_array($exec_query)) {
54               $my_arr[] = $row;
55  ⌐        }
56
57           return $my_arr;
58  ⌐    }
```

The first change this code makes is the form action, so the form is posted to the new show_students.php page instead of the old PHP page. Next, the s_id, which was used to denote the ID field in the tbl_student database table, is changed instead to correspond to the photo_id_number field. This continuity between the names of the columns and form elements isn't necessary, but it is helpful to remember which input field corresponds to the appropriate column in the table or query.

Finally, the last name filter field has a new label and input text box. Note that the maxlength value for the last_name field matches the maximum length on the stored procedure. Because the query uses the LIKE search, only the first 10 starting letters of a last name are necessary to use as a filter criterion.

The next set of changes are more complex. Since an array of associative arrays is possible with the LIKE search if more than one record is returned, you need to loop through the array to print each associative array as another row in the table of results.

The same starting if ($_SERVER["REQUEST_METHOD"] == "POST") code block used previously is used here because the form will be posted to this PHP page.

7. In show_students.php, add the following new content inside the curly bracket that follows the if() statement, replacing the previous code:

```
$photo_id = filter_var($_POST["photo_id"],FILTER_SANITIZE_STRING);
$last_name = filter_var($_POST["last_name"],FILTER_SANITIZE_STRING);
$dh = new DataHandler();
$results_arr = $dh->get_students($photo_id,$last_name);
```

This block of code includes the necessary updates to use two filter criteria and send them to the data handler. The results returned are 0 or more rows in an array of associative arrays.

8. Add the following code to handle looping through the array.

```
if(count($results_arr)>0) {
    $results = "<table class='fullborder'><tr><th>First Name</th><th>
MI</th><th>Last Name</th><th>Photo ID Number</th></tr><tr>";
```

This code begins by checking whether the count of the rows in `$results_arr` is greater than zero. If so, the webpage should build a table to display to the user.

9. Add the following code to loop through the array of associative arrays, extracting one associative array each time through the loop and then extracting the values from the associative array to build the cells in the HTML table for that row of the data:

```
foreach($results_arr as $row){
    $results .= "<tr>";
    $results .= "<td>".$row['first_name']."</td>";
    $results .= "<td>".$row['mi']."</td>";
    $results .= "<td>".$row['last_name']."</td>";
    $results .= "<td>".$row['photo_id_number']."</td>";
    $results .= "</tr>";
}
```

This code specifies that for each element in the `$results_arr` array, extract one associative array element into the `$row` object. The `$row` object will hold the next associative array from the `$results_arr` array until none remain. The loop then ends, and no more rows are added to the table.

10. Add the following code to complete the HTML table, close the starting `if()` statement that tests whether the array contains any rows, and displays the final results:

```
    $results .= "</table>";
}
else {
    $results = "No Records Found";
}
echo $results;
```

You can see a completed copy of this code in **Figure 12-19**.

To test the show_students.php file:

1. Save your changes and then open show_students.php in a web browser.

2. In the Last Name Starts With text box, type the first letter of your last name and then click the Submit button. If you added yourself as a student to the roster of Totally Awesome University in the previous chapter, you should see an HTML table that looks like **Figure 12-20**, although your data will be different.

3. Next, enter a nine-digit photo ID number such as **999000123** or the one you assigned to your student record and then click the Submit button to test the photo ID part of the query.

4. Enter both a last name and a valid photo ID for the same student, such as **n** and **999000123** for Keeley Naidoo in this sample data set, and then click Submit to test whether the stored procedure is properly performing mutually exclusive tests as it was designed to do. You should see no results returned, since this is not what the interface allows the user to do.

Figure 12-19 Completed copy of show_students.php

```
1    <!DOCTYPE html>
2    <html>
3        <head>
4            <title>Student Lookup</title>
5            <link rel="stylesheet" type="text/css" href="css/my_styles.css" media="screen, print" />
6        </head>
7        <body>
8            <h1>Student Lookup</h1>
9            <div id='searchBox'>
10               Search for a student by:
11               <form action='show_students.php' method="post">
12                   <label for="photo_id">Photo ID#:</label>
13                   <input type="number" id="photo_id" name="photo_id" /> -or-<br/>
14                   <label for="last_name">Last Name Starts With:</label>
15                   <input type="text" id="last_name" name="last_name" maxlength='10'/><br/>
16                   <input type="submit" value="Submit" />
17               </form>
18           </div>
19           <p>
20               <?php
21                   include "data_handler.php";
22
23                   if ($_SERVER["REQUEST_METHOD"] == "POST")
24                   {
25                       $photo_id = filter_var($_POST["photo_id"],FILTER_SANITIZE_STRING);
26                       $last_name = filter_var($_POST["last_name"],FILTER_SANITIZE_STRING);
27
28                       $dh = new DataHandler();
29                       $results_arr = $dh->get_students($photo_id,$last_name);
30
31                       if(count($results_arr)>0) {
32                           $results = "<table class='fullborder'><tr><th>First Name</th><th>MI</th><th>Last Name</th><th>Photo ID Number</th></tr><tr>";
33                           foreach($results_arr as $row){
34                               $results .= "<tr>";
35                               $results .= "<td>".$row['first_name']."</td>";
36                               $results .= "<td>".$row['mi']."</td>";
37                               $results .= "<td>".$row['last_name']."</td>";
38                               $results .= "<td>".$row['photo_id_number']."</td>";
39                               $results .= "</tr>";
40                           }
41                           $results .= "</table>";
42                       }
43                       else {
44                           $results = "No Records Found";
45                       }
46                       echo $results;
47                   }
48               ?>
49           </p>
```

BBEdit

Figure 12-20 Updated Student Lookup webpage

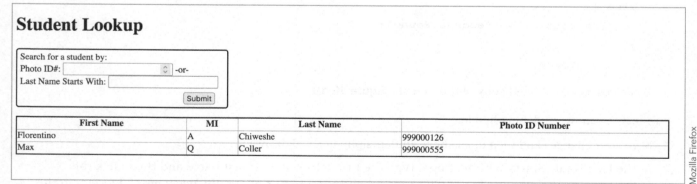

Mozilla Firefox

Quick Check 12-2

1. Is hard-coding a value into the code you are writing a useful practice in programming?

    a. No, hard-coding values in code is never a good practice.

    b. Yes, it is useful to create a test of progress with a known value to decrease the complexity of the operation.

    c. No, hard-coding values into the code is a bad idea since those will get forgotten and become permanent parts of the code.

    d. Yes, this is a good way to create job security, since you'll need to update the code with new values any time those hard-coded values need to be updated.

2. Is a "No Records Found" message necessary in a user interface?

    a. Yes, it is a standard expectation that an appropriate message is displayed if a search finds no records.

    b. No, it is not required, but if you have time when doing the development, the message is nice to have.

    c. Yes, the code won't work properly unless all return paths from the database are paired with a response to the user interface.

    d. No, users will know that a search for something that doesn't exist doesn't return results, so nothing should be displayed.

3. How can you help your users identify and use the interactive elements of a web form?

    a. Put the form in the middle of the screen so the users can find it easily.

    b. Highlight the background of the interactive elements with a bright color.

    c. Write instructions on the form telling the user how to interact with it.

    d. Add a border around the grouping of interactive elements, place it near the top of the UI, and arrange the elements in a logical flow from top left to bottom right.

> **1) b.** Hard-coding a value as part of a test is a useful part of the development process but should not be done in production code. **2) a.** Users expect to know if no records are returned from a search. **3) d.** Following conventions of the Internet by grouping interactive elements of a web form inside a border and arranging them in a logical flow is part of creating a positive user experience.

12.3 Creating a Data Entry or Update Form

The interactive website for Totally Awesome University needs a data entry form for creating a new student record. The data entry form can also be used to update a student record retrieved from the database. Updating a record involves first retrieving the current values in the record from the database, then saving the new data updated by the user in the same record. You can also use the data entry form to delete a student record.

You have already created stored procedures for creating a student record (sp_insert_student), retrieving a student record (sp_get_student), updating the data (sp_update_student), and deleting a student record (sp_delete_student). The remaining tasks are creating a new set of functions in the `DataHandler` class and providing a new user interface that requests data from or passes data to the new functions in the data handler.

Open and review the four CRUD stored procedures sp_insert_student, sp_get_student, sp_update_student, and sp_delete_student.

You also have the code in the `DataHandler` class to retrieve a student from the database using an ID number of a student record. You can use this code in the data entry form page to retrieve a specific record and populate the web form elements with data.

Creating the Data Entry Form

To create the form:

1. Save a copy of the original show_student.php (not show_students.php) as add_student.php.

2. Update the `title` and `h1` elements to use the text **Add/Update Student** and change the form action to **add_student.php** to correspond to the new file name.

3. Replace the input boxes with those necessary for adding a student record: first_name, mi, last_name, and photo_id_number.

4. Include a hidden form element that will contain the ID for the student record. This hidden field will be used for updating a student record, so it shouldn't be displayed to the user. The completed code looks like the following:

```
<form action='add_student.php' method="post">
    <label for="first_name">First Name:</label>
    <input type="text" required id="first_name" name="first_name" /><br/>
    <label for="mi">Middle Initial:</label>
    <input type="text" id="mi" name="mi" /><br/>
    <label for="last_name">Last Name:</label>
    <input type="text" required id="last_name" name="last_name" /><br/>
    <label for="photo_id">Photo ID Number:</label>
    <input type="text" required id="photo_id" name="photo_id" /><br/>
    <input type="hidden" id="s_id" name = "s_id" />
    <input type="submit" value="Submit" />
</form>
```

The hidden field is a convenient means of storing data that users do not need to update and should not update by mistake.

> **Note**
>
> Just because a web form field is hidden doesn't mean that it is secure. Anyone can view the source of the add_student.php HTML page to see the data elements in the form, including the value in the hidden field you just created.
>
> Furthermore, as you saw previously, the data from the hidden ID field can be altered with a POST request sent from the browser's developer tools.
>
> The hidden field is useful only for storing values such as record IDs that normal users shouldn't have access to. It is not secure, and confidential or private data such as passwords or credit card numbers should not be stored in a hidden field in an attempt to create a more secure operation with that data.

To add the new functions in the `DataHandler` class:

1. In add_student.php, add the following code to replace the contents between the `<?php` and `?>` tags:

```
include "data_handler.php";
if ($_SERVER["REQUEST_METHOD"] == "POST") {
    $first_name = filter_var($_POST["first_name"],FILTER_SANITIZE_STRING);
    $mi = filter_var($_POST["mi"],FILTER_SANITIZE_STRING);
    $last_name = filter_var($_POST["last_name"],FILTER_SANITIZE_STRING);
    $photo_id = filter_var($_POST["photo_id"],FILTER_SANITIZE_STRING);
    $s_id = filter_var($_POST["s_id"],FILTER_SANITIZE_STRING);

    $dh = new DataHandler();
    $message = $dh->add_student($first_name, $mi, $last_name, $photo_id);
    echo $message;
}
```

This code will run the `DataHandler` method `add_student()`, which you create next. It passes in all four parameters that make up a student record in the table of students. The `add_student()` method returns a success or error message, which this code displays to alert the user of a successful save.

2. Save your changes. The completed code in add_student.php looks like that in **Figure 12-21**.

Figure 12-21   Completed add_student.php code

```
1    <!DOCTYPE html>
2  ▼ <html>
3  ▼     <head>
4           <title>Add/Update Student</title>
5           <link rel="stylesheet" type="text/css" href="css/my_styles.css" media="screen, print" />
6  ╘     </head>
7  ▼     <body>
8           <h1>Add/Update Student</h1>
9  ▼         <div id='searchBox'>
10 ▼             <form action='add_student.php' method="post">
11                  <label for="first_name">First Name:</label>
12                  <input type="text" required id="first_name" name="first_name" /><br/>
13                  <label for="mi">Middle Initial</label>
14                  <input type="text" id="mi" name="mi" /><br/>
15                  <label for="last_name">Last Name:</label>
16                  <input type="text" required id="last_name" name="last_name" /><br/>
17                  <label for="photo_id"">Photo ID Number:</label>
18                  <input type="text" required id="photo_id" name="photo_id" /><br/>
19                  <input type="hidden" id="s_id" name = "s_id" />
20                  <input type="submit" value="Submit" />
21 ╘             </form>
22 ╘         </div>
23 ▼         <p>
24 ▼             <?php
25                  include "data_handler.php";
26
27                  if ($_SERVER["REQUEST_METHOD"] == "POST")
28 ▼                 {
29                      $first_name = filter_var($_POST["first_name"],FILTER_SANITIZE_STRING);
30                      $mi = filter_var($_POST["mi"],FILTER_SANITIZE_STRING);
31                      $last_name = filter_var($_POST["last_name"],FILTER_SANITIZE_STRING);
32                      $photo_id = filter_var($_POST["photo_id"],FILTER_SANITIZE_STRING);
33                      $s_id = filter_var($_POST["s_id"],FILTER_SANITIZE_STRING);
34
35                      $dh = new DataHandler();
36                      $message = $dh->add_student($first_name, $mi, $last_name, $photo_id);
37
38                      echo $message;
39 ╘                 }
40 ╘             ?>
41 ╘         </p>
42 ╘     </body>
43 ╘ </html>
```

BBEdit

3. Update the data_handler.php file with the corresponding code to the previous method call from the user interface by adding the following code for the add_student() method to the DataHandler class:

```php
public function add_student($first_name, $mi, $last_name, $photo_id)
{
    $message = "";
    //build query
    $query = "CALL sp_insert_student('".$first_name."','".$mi."','".$last_name."','".$photo_id."')";
    //query execution
    $ExecQuery = MySQLi_query($this->db_conn, $query);
    if($ExecQuery == '1')
    {
        $message = "Success!";
    }
    else
```

```
        {
            $message = "Save Operation Failed";
        }
        return $message;
    }
```

In other methods of this class, you have retrieved one or more associative arrays of data to build an HTML table. In this code, you are instead inserting a record into the database. The result of this insert procedure is a success or failure code returned from the database. The `if...else` block handles the success/failure code, translating the database code of 1 to a "Success!" message and anything other than 1 to a "Save Operation Failed" message.

"Save Operation Failed" is intentionally vague so you can use it to investigate if your code is not working without specifying the error. Not revealing to users why a save operation failed is another small but important measure of web security.

4. Save your changes. The completed code in data_handler.php looks like that in **Figure 12-22**.

Figure 12-22   Completed code in data_handler.php for the add_student method

```
64
65          public function add_student($first_name, $mi, $last_name, $photo_id)
66      ▼   {
67              $message = "";
68
69              //build query.
70              $query = "CALL sp_insert_student('".$first_name."','".$mi."','".$last_name."','".$photo_id."')";
71
72              //Query execution
73              $ExecQuery = MySQLi_query($this->db_conn, $query);
74
75              if($ExecQuery == '1')
76      ▼       {
77                  $message = "Success!";
78      ⌐       }
79              else
80      ▼       {
81                  $message = "Save Operation Failed";
82      ⌐       }
83              return $message;
84      ⌐   }
85
```

BBEdit

5. Open the add_student.php page in a web browser to display an interface like that shown in **Figure 12-23**.

Figure 12-23   The completed Add/Update Student webpage

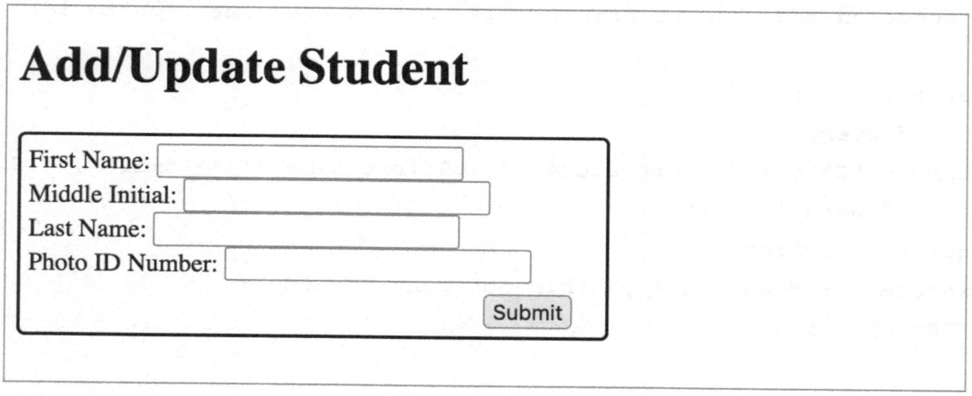

Add/Update Student

First Name: _____
Middle Initial: _____
Last Name: _____
Photo ID Number: _____

Submit

Mozilla Firefox

6. Enter the required data into the form using sample data of your choice and click the Submit button. If the code is working properly, you should see a "Success!" message.

7. Review the table in the taus_data MySQL database to see your new row of data.

8. Open the show_students.php page in a browser and search for the person you just added. You should be able to retrieve the student record you just added.

This completes the Create and Read operations for student data. When performing the successful save operation, however, you may have noticed one flaw. When you receive confirmation that the save operation was successful, the form data disappears. This is not a desirable behavior, even though it is the default behavior of a web form processed by PHP.

The data does not remain displayed because the form action points to the same file used to enter the data, which reloads the page after it is processed by the web server. The reloaded page doesn't contain the data entered in the form anymore, so it appears blank. This can be disconcerting to your users, so in the next section, you add code to keep the data in the form.

Retrieving Student Data into the Form

To add code to use the data entry form for updating:

1. Save a copy of the add_student.php file as add_student2.php.

2. Update the form action to point to **add_student2.php** instead of add_student.php. This new page is the starting point for the next stage of development for this web application.

You are creating a lookup-and-update web application like those you may have used before. The Photo ID and Last Name search function that you created in show_students.php is a good start to a search form that creates a grid of search results. However, that grid of results needs a way to connect to the data add/update form you just created. Users typically want to first identify a record in the table of results that needs to be updated, and then click a link in that record to open the update form.

To use this add/update web form to update student data, you need to send the ID number of the record you want to retrieve to the code in the add/update page. You have already created code similar to this operation, first with a hard-coded value and then with the text box input value that was posted to the PHP code. Both functions successfully retrieved a specific record from the database, including all the data for that record. This is useful behavior that will be repeated here so you can update the data as it was stored in the database.

However, the previous code retrieved an associative array and used it to build an HTML table of results. The new code will retrieve an associative array and assign the values to the input boxes of the data entry form. To retrieve the data from a link in the HTML grid of students, you need a new way of handling web form data.

In addition to the POST method, you can use a GET method to create interactions between a PHP webpage and a database. You use the GET method to pass information from an HTML link into a PHP page through a **query string** in the URL requesting the page from the server. A query string is the text after the normal URL that begins with the question mark. The query string passes information into a webpage. The format for an information-passing query string is as follows:

add_student2.php?s_id=7

Unlike the hidden POST data, the information in the query string is shown in plain text in the URL. This means that it is not a secure means of transmitting information. It is, however, convenient and easy to code.

You need to add the code that runs when the PHP page receives a GET request with a query string. The add_student2.php file already has the code for the POST request, which is made when a form is submitted using the method="POST" declaration in the web form used to save form data. However, add_student2.php needs more code to run with the GET request.

The POST code is contained in an if() block used to identify the type of request. It is located toward the bottom of the add_student2.php page. PHP code is interpreted from top to bottom, so any variables need to be declared and given a value before they are used in the HTML, as when you put PHP variables into the HTML form values.

To update add_student2.php:

1. Select the entire block of PHP code from the opening `<?php` tag to the ending `?>` and move it to the line below the `<h1>`...`<h1>` tag pair. The location of the PHP code doesn't affect its interpretation or execution, but it is critical to the use of the PHP variables in the HTML form.

2. Update the code inside the opening `<?php` tag by inserting the following lines shown in bold:

```php
<?php
    include "data_handler.php";
    $first_name = "";
    $mi = "";
    $last_name = "";
    $photo_id = "";
    $s_id = "";
    $message = "";
    $dh = "";
```

This is a variable declaration block, which is not a requirement of valid PHP code. To create a variable in PHP, you can simply start using it. However, these variables will be assigned values in one of two ways, depending on whether the page receives a GET or a POST request. Declaring them at the beginning of the code creates a single starting point with empty values before any other code runs.

3. Add the following code immediately after the variable declarations:

```php
if ($_SERVER["REQUEST_METHOD"] == "GET")
{
    if (isset($_GET["s_id"]))
    {
        $s_id = filter_var($_GET["s_id"],FILTER_SANITIZE_STRING);
        $dh = new DataHandler();
        $results = $dh->get_student($s_id);
        $first_name = $results['first_name'];
        $mi = $results['mi'];
        $last_name = $results['last_name'];
        $photo_id = $results['photo_id_number'];
    }
}
```

This code is similar to the code you created previously for retrieving a record from the database using the stored procedure sp_get_student via the `get_student()` data_handler method. The difference is that first line uses GET instead of POST.

In the second line of code, the built-in PHP function `isset()` is used to determine if the GET request is passed a value for the parameter s_id. The `isset()` function returns either true or false. A true value means that the GET request has a value for s_id, causing the next block of code to run. In it, the `$s_id` variable is assigned the value from the `$_GET[]` array of values, similar to the POST version of this retrieval.

This code will run for both the GET that initially loads a blank page and the GET that initially loads a student record from the database when a parameter is passed in via the GET request. It uses a test to see if the `$_GET["s_id"]` value exists to determine whether a trip to the database to retrieve the student data is necessary.

4. After the GET block, change the `if()` code for the POST block to `else if()`, as in the following example and shown in **Figure 12-24**.

```php
else if ($_SERVER["REQUEST_METHOD"] == "POST") {
```

Figure 12-24 The completed code for handling the GET request

```
1    <!DOCTYPE html>
2    <html>
3        <head>
4            <title>Add/Update Student</title>
5            <link rel="stylesheet" type="text/css" href="css/my_styles.css" media="screen, print" />
6        </head>
7        <body>
8            <h1>Add/Update Student</h1>
9            <?php
10               include "data_handler.php";
11
12               $first_name = "";
13               $mi = "";
14               $last_name = "";
15               $photo_id = "";
16               $s_id = "";
17               $message = "";
18               $dh = "";
19
20               if ($_SERVER["REQUEST_METHOD"] == "GET")
21               {
22                   if (isset($_GET["s_id"]))
23                   {
24                       $s_id = filter_var($_GET["s_id"],FILTER_SANITIZE_STRING);
25
26                       $dh = new DataHandler();
27                       $results = $dh->get_student($s_id);
28
29                       $first_name = $results['first_name'];
30                       $mi = $results['mi'];
31                       $last_name = $results['last_name'];
32                       $photo_id = $results['photo_id'];
33                   }
34               }
35               else if ($_SERVER["REQUEST_METHOD"] == "POST") {
36
```

The code in this block will stay nearly the same as it was previously because the POST request is the same as before. However, you add a small difference next so the form on this page can be used for creating and updating a record.

5. Use the following code to replace the two lines of code after the instantiation of the DataHandler class in the $dh variable:

```
if($s_id != '') {
    $message = $dh->update_student($s_id, $first_name, $mi, $last_name,
$photo_id);
}
else {
    $message = $dh->add_student($first_name, $mi, $last_name, $photo_id);
}
```

This if...else block uses the existence of a value in the $s_id variable to determine whether the PHP code should update or add a student. The initial GET request for a single student's data will include a record ID value to populate the form. If the data includes an ID value, a value has been added to the s_id hidden form field in the form sent with the POST request data. That means the form should be used to update the record in the database.

If this ID value is absent, then the form is being used as a blank data entry form, and a record should be inserted using the values entered by the user.

You also need to change how the PHP code renders the form. Throughout this chapter, you used the PHP echo command to print one line of text to display in the browser. You need a more efficient way to print a multiline HTML form from within PHP code.

6. Use the following PHP code to replace the remainder of the code up to but not including the closing ?> tag:

```
echo <<< THE_END
    <div id='searchBox'>
        <form action='add_student2.php' method="post">
            <label for="first_name">First Name:</label>
            <input type="text" required id="first_name" name="first_name"
value="$first_name" /><br/>
            <label for="mi">Middle Initial:</label>
            <input type="text" id="mi" name="mi" value="$mi" /><br/>
            <label for="last_name">Last Name:</label>
            <input type="text" required id="last_name" name="last_name"
value="$last_name" /><br/>
            <label for="photo_id"">Photo ID Number:</label>
            <input type="text" required id="photo_id" name="photo_id"
value="$photo_id" /><br/>
            <input type="hidden" id="s_id" name = "s_id" value="$s_id" />
            <input type="submit" value="Submit" />
        </form>
    </div>
    <p>
        $message
    </p>
THE_END;
```

Note the first line echo <<< THE_END and the very last line, the corresponding token, THE_END;. This block of code includes only one PHP echo command, but it is followed by the PHP **heredoc** syntax. The PHP heredoc syntax creates a multiline string of text. The heredoc identifier is made up of the echo statement to start, three less than (<) symbols, and a token repeated at the end of the block of text to be printed by the single echo statement. This command is like telling PHP "print everything from here to there." The tokens used can be any combination of letters or underscores. The PHP block ends with a semicolon to complete the statement.

Using heredoc syntax to print a long block of preformatted HTML output has another advantage. The HTML block is within the PHP code, so the variables in the code above it are still in scope and contain values. This is useful in this example because of the value= HTML code in each input element. The variables used for the actual values set in these HTML attributes are PHP variables. Mixing HTML and PHP only works if the PHP variables are still in scope and contain values.

7. Save your changes.

The final step in adding this new code is in the update_student method in data_handler.php.

To update the data_handler.php page:

1. Add the following code to the end of the data_handler.php file:

```
public function update_student($s_id, $first_name, $mi, $last_name, $photo_id)
{
    $message = "";
    //build query
    $query = "CALL sp_update_student('".$s_id."','".$first_
name."','".$mi."','".$last_name."','".$photo_id."')";
```

```
    echo $query;
    //query execution
    $ExecQuery = MySQLi_query($this->db_conn, $query);
    if($ExecQuery == '1')
    {
        $message = "Success!";
    }
    else
    {
        $message = "Save Operation Failed";
    }
    return $message;
}
```

2. Save your changes and then open the page add_student2.php in your browser. You should see a page that looks like add_student.php.

   Next, test to see if this page still works with a simple POST.

3. Add a new student to Totally Awesome University. You should see the Success! message displayed and the student data you entered persist in the web form after you save it because of the `value=` PHP variable code you added. That's already a big improvement over the previous form.

4. In the browser's address bar, add the query string to the end of the URL using the following format:

   add_student2.php?s_id=1

   This should open record #1 in the web form using the GET request.

5. Update part of the student data for record #1 and then click the Submit button. Again, your data should persist after the update is completed and you should see the Success! confirmation message.

6. Update the query string value to 2 to review record #2 and then consider the security implications. You just opened another record simply by incrementing the query string value.

Common Mistakes

The s_id key in the query string tells the browser that the value after the equal sign will be used in the webpage code to retrieve a record from the database. This value can be used to identify records uniquely by their ID number as stored in the table. For this example, the s_id key and the value of 1 or 7 is sufficient, but the design has a fundamental flaw.

If you want to view or edit every record in the database, you can change the query string in the URL from add_student2.php?s_id=7 to add_student2.php?s_id=8, for example. Allowing such an entry is an open invitation for anyone who can access the URL to retrieve every record in the database, one at a time. That's a significant data security problem if you want to restrict access to only specific records.

A slightly better solution is to create a query that uses two pieces of unique information, such as the ID number and a natural key like the photo_id_number field. The query string would look like the following:

add_student.php?s_id=1&photo_id=999000123

However, a malicious person could still loop through the records by incrementing each ID value one at a time to snoop on records they shouldn't be viewing.

(continues)

The best solution is to use at least a 32-bit hash key stored in the same table as the other data to retrieve sensitive records via the query string. A 32-bit hash of the ID number 1 and photo_id number of 999000123 is 4abb5003a60aad036b97d243567eb85d. The 32-bit hash of the ID number 2 and student_id record of 999000456 is 92f7f493881dc99ee193b84991a3d526. The query string that would result from this would look like the following:

add_student.php?s_id=4abb5003a60aad036b97d243567eb85d

Even the most motivated snooper will have trouble guessing hash values like this one. You can't simply add 1 to the record anywhere in that long list of characters to increment it.

Hash values can be stored as text in an id_hash column in the same table as the rest of the data. These unique values are the best way to retrieve rows using a query string when you don't want someone snooping through each row in a table.

You can create hash values using the MD5 hash function built into MySQL by running the following query in the SQL pane of the MySQL DBMS and examining the values that it creates:

```
SELECT MD5(CONCAT(s.id, s.photo_id_number)) FROM tbl_student s
```

To use this function to populate the column of values in tbl_student, you would add a new column to the table tbl_student named something descriptive like id_hash, then update the values in that column by setting that value to the results of a database operation like the one in the preceding select statement. The code to do that would look like the following:

```
UPDATE tbl_student s SET s.id_hash = MD5(CONCAT(s.id, s.photo_id_number))
```

This statement concatenates values from the id and photo_id_number fields, then runs the result through the MD5 hash function. The result of that hash function is added into the row for each student to produce a hash stored in the id_hash column for your use in query strings. You would retrieve this new value as part of each student's record in the stored procedures used to manipulate student data.

Linking the HTML Table Data to the Update Form

Now that you have the query string working for the data entry form, you can create links to it from the HTML table you built earlier in this tutorial. You create the links in two parts—the link and the query string.

To link to table data in the form:

1. Return to the show_students.php file. A convenient place to create a link is around the Student ID data in the table. Update the row of PHP code that adds the table cell containing the Photo ID Number data to reflect the following code:

```
$results .= "<td><a href='add_student2.php?s_id=".$row['id']
."' target='_new'>".$row['photo_id_number']."</a></td>";
```

This code uses PHP string concatenation to construct an HTML link to the page, with a query string containing the unique value in the associative array element $row['id']. The attribute target='_new' is added to this link to open the form in a new page.

2. Save your changes and then open or refresh the page show_students.php in a browser.

3. Filter for a student record to display a new version of the HTML table with a link to the update page included for each photo ID number.

4. Click a photo ID number to open the Update interface and load that student's data into the web form, where you can update it.

That now completes the CREATE, READ, and UPDATE processes. There is more work to do in the next section to make this user interface complete.

> ## Quick Check 12-3

1. What is a hidden form field used for?

    a. Storing confidential form values you don't want your users to see

    b. Storing form values you don't want your users to update

    c. Storing login credentials like passwords and usernames

    d. Storing the form name or form ID

2. What is an example of a useful return type from a save function in a data handler class?

    a. A success or failure message

    b. The associative array of values that were successfully saved

    c. The database code returned from the stored procedure

    d. A 1 or a 0 to show to the user after the save function runs

3. Why does the HTML form become empty by default after a successful POST data save operation in PHP?

    a. Because it is designed to be cleared for the next record to be entered and saved

    b. Because it is more secure to clear the data so there isn't a repeated save operation

    c. Because the POST method used with this form specifies that the form action be directed back to the same page, which reloads the page in the browser

    d. Because this behavior is a holdover from when HTML forms were first being used that browsers still have to support

1) b. Hidden form fields are useful for storing values you don't want your users to update. **2) a.** The data handler class is the transition point between PHP code and database code, so a success or failure message in PHP would be useful to present to the user. **3) c.** The POST request that is directed to the same page refreshes the page, and the web form is emptied when the page is reloaded.

12.4 Completing the CRUD Cycle

The user interface for managing student data for Totally Awesome University is growing in both functionality and complexity. This progress follows the typical arc of developing a new application. To complete the CRUD cycle, however, you need to do additional engineering of the user experience for the interactive elements in the application.

Lumping all the CRUD elements of the typical UI into one page would make that page challenging to use but convenient to find and bookmark. The goal of a data application is to create an easy user experience where users can access all functions with three clicks or less. However, the technical details of merging multiple distinct functions into a single cohesive application make this task more challenging.

Creating a record should be as easy and accessible as possible since users will perform the task often, and the consequences of adding a new student by mistake are not profound. A link to a data entry form for new student records creates a direct on-ramp to the new data.

On the other hand, deleting a student record should be more difficult because the consequences of deleting a student by mistake are significant. The application should prevent users from inadvertently deleting a student record by presenting a data confirmation off-ramp to the user before deleting the record.

You will add both elements of the user experience to the application in the next sections.

Adding the Create New Record Functionality

To allow users to add a new record:

1. Review the code in show_students.php and then display the page in a browser. This page needs a link to the new user creation data entry form as part of a more robust application.

   The placement of the link to open the New Student interface affects the user experience of the application. The link could go inside the search box, but that cross-functionality might confuse the user about the purpose of the search box.

   On the other hand, if the top banner of this page contains different functions grouped by logical block, the user experience would be consistent with other web applications. Users have been trained by countless interactions with software to expect access to functions in a banner or toolbar across the top of the page.

2. In show_students.php, change the h1 tag set to **h3** tags and change the text between the tags to **Student Enrollment Management**.

3. In add_student2.php, update the h1 tag to an **h3** to reduce the size of the text in that heading as well.

4. In show_students.php, change the div with the id of searchBox surrounding the search form to a **span** instead. As you may recall, a div is a block-level element, whereas a span can be placed on the same horizontal plane as another span. This change will allow more menu items to appear side by side in the banner menu at the top of the page.

5. Inside the `<span id='searchBox'>` tag but before the opening form tag, add the following text to help your users identify what they should do:

   ```
   <p>Search for a student by:</p>
   ```

6. Add another span after the searchBox span and give it the id of menuOptions. Inside that span, add the following code:

   ```
   <a href="add_student2.php" target="_new">
       <figure>
           <img src="images/student.png" alt="add student"/>
           <figcaption>Add Student</figcaption>
       </figure>
   </a>
   ```

   This code will create an image icon to help your users identify how they can add a new student to the student management application. The student.png file should be stored in the images subfolder for this chapter.

7. Add a div with an id of banner that contains both of the new spans you just created. When you are done, you should have a body of code that looks like that in **Figure 12-25**.

8. Open the my_styles.css file in the css folder and update the style for searchBox to include the following declaration, which modifies the span so it behaves like it should to display the HTML:

   ```
   display: inline-block;
   ```

9. Update the style for the submit button in the #searchBox style to reflect the following declarations:

   ```
   margin-top: 2%;
   margin-left: 80%;
   ```

10. Add a new style declaration for the #menuOptions style using the following code:

    ```
    #menuOptions {
        text-align: center;
        display: inline-block;
    }
    ```

    This style declaration will center the image and caption in the way a toolbar icon should be presented to the user.

Figure 12-25   The updated code in show_students.php

```
1   <!DOCTYPE html>
2   <html>
3       <head>
4           <title>Student Lookup</title>
5           <link rel="stylesheet" type="text/css" href="css/my_styles.css" media="screen, print" />
6       </head>
7       <body>
8           <h3>Student Enrollment Management</h3>
9           <div id='banner'>
10              <span id='searchBox'>
11                  <p>Search for a student by:</p>
12                  <form action='show_students.php' method="post">
13                      <label for="photo_id">Photo ID#:</label>
14                      <input type="number" id="photo_id" name="photo_id" /> -or-<br/>
15                      <label for="last_name">Last Name Starts With:</label>
16                      <input type="text" id="last_name" name="last_name" maxlength='10'/><br/>
17                      <input type="submit" value="Submit" />
18                  </form>
19              </span>
20              <span id='menuOptions'>
21                  <a href="add_student2.php" target="_new">
22                      <figure>
23                          <img src="images/student.png" alt="add student"/>
24                          <figcaption>Add Student</figcaption>
25                      </figure>
26                  </a>
27              </span>
28          </div>
29          <p>
30              <?php
31                  include "data_handler.php";
32
33                  if ($_SERVER["REQUEST_METHOD"] == "POST")
34                  {
35                      $photo_id = filter_var($_POST["photo_id"],FILTER_SANITIZE_STRING);
36                      $last_name = filter_var($_POST["last_name"],FILTER_SANITIZE_STRING);
37
38                      $dh = new DataHandler();
39                      $results_arr = $dh->get_students($photo_id,$last_name);
40
41                      if(count($results_arr)>0) {
42                          $results = "<table class='fullborder'><tr><th>First Name</th><th>MI</th><th>Last Name</th><th>Photo ID Number</th></tr><tr>";
43                          foreach($results_arr as $row){
44                              $results.="<tr>";
45                              $results.="<td>".$row['first_name']."</td>";
46                              $results.="<td>".$row['mi']."</td>";
47                              $results.="<td>".$row['last_name']."</td>";
48                              $results.="<td><a href='add_student2.php?s_id=".$row['id']."' target='_new'>".$row['photo_id_number']."</a></td>";
49                              $results.="</tr>";
```

BBEdit

11. Save your changes in all the files and then reload the page show_students.php in your web browser. You should see an updated user interface like that shown in **Figure 12-26**.

Figure 12-26   Updated Student Enrollment Management webpage

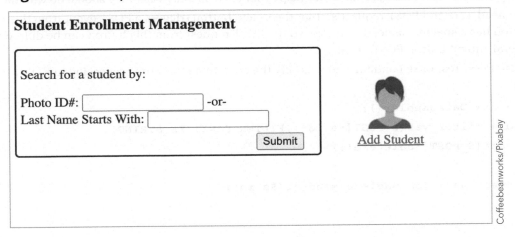

Coffeebeanworks/Pixabay

This is the start of a web application for managing students enrolled in Totally Awesome University. As you add functions to the application, the menu will expand to the right with additional icons for activities like enrolling students in classes.

Adding the Delete Functionality

While the delete procedure is technically simple, it should be more complex to use. People make mistakes, and the application should help users identify potential mistakes before they occur.

You could add a simple Delete button to each row in the HTML table loaded in show_students.php after a successful search. This would be convenient, but the rows are narrow, and repeating the Delete button or link introduces the possibility of deleting the wrong record by mistake.

On the other hand, users expect a confirmation prior to deleting the data, which is helpful to avoid an accidental deletion. You may have seen a web application that displays a pop-up message asking, "Are you sure you want to delete the Internet?" with OK/Cancel buttons for the response.

Showing the user the complete record in the Update interface also creates a double confirmation of the entire student data prior to deletion. A blank form confirms the record was deleted successfully. This helps create a more exacting user experience with the application.

To allow users to delete a record:

1. Open add_student2.php in your text editor. Add a new $delete_button variable to the starting declaration of variables. Set it to an empty string as the starting value.

2. Add the following code inside the GET method code block, after the $photo_id variable is assigned its initial value:

```
$delete_button = <<< END_BUTTON
<button type="submit" name="deleteMe" onclick="return confirm('Do you really
want to delete $first_name $last_name?');">Delete</button>
END_BUTTON;
```

Note the heredoc syntax again to contain the compound quotes nested in the code that creates the Delete button. This code also uses the values returned from the database in the GET block to create a delete confirmation message.

3. Add the $delete_button variable to the form in the search box after the Submit button. The Delete button will only be displayed when a GET request passes data into the form, since a Delete button isn't necessary for a new blank record. This dynamic behavior helps to unclutter the user interface because a delete operation isn't useful unless the record contains data. Clicking the Delete button when there is nothing to delete won't cause problems, but a simplified and contextual user interface helps your users identify what they should do with the UI.

You also need a second POST request so that the Delete button triggers a POST event from this form. However, this button has a specific name, deleteMe, so the POST request from this button can be differentiated from the general Submit button POST event.

4. In the PHP POST response handling code, modify the code that starts the processing to reflect the following new code:

```
$dh = new DataHandler();
$s_id = filter_var($_POST["s_id"],FILTER_SANITIZE_STRING);
if(isset($_POST['deleteMe']))
{
    $message = $dh->delete_student($s_id);
}
else
{
```

The code first instantiates the DataHandler class so it can be used for either the general or the specific POST request. Then, the $s_id variable is set to the value passed in the POST request because it too will be used for both the general and specific POST requests.

Next, the test is performed to see if the value deleteMe is included in the POST request. Because the Submit button is part of the submitted form, it is included in the POST data sent from the request. The if() block detects if the deleteMe button triggered the POST request and then calls the delete_student() method from the DataHandler class. If the Submit button triggered the POST request, this code would be bypassed and the normal save process for updating or inserting a record would run instead.

5. Add one more closing curly bracket to the end of the POST processing block to end the `else` condition and then save your changes. You should now have a body of code that reflects **Figure 12-27**.

Figure 12-27   Updated POST code

```
24 ▼        {
25               $s_id = filter_var($_GET["s_id"],FILTER_SANITIZE_STRING);
26
27               $dh = new DataHandler();
28               $results = $dh->get_student($s_id);
29
30               $first_name = $results['first_name'];
31               $mi = $results['mi'];
32               $last_name = $results['last_name'];
33               $photo_id = $results['photo_id'];
34 ▼             $delete_button = <<< END_BUTTON
35               <button type="submit" name="deleteMe" onclick="return confirm('Do you really want to delete $first_name $last_name?');">Delete</button>
36 ▙ END_BUTTON;
37 ▙           }
38 ▙       }
39 ▼       else if ($_SERVER["REQUEST_METHOD"] == "POST") {
40
41               $dh = new DataHandler();
42               $s_id = filter_var($_POST["s_id"],FILTER_SANITIZE_STRING);
43
44               if(isset($_POST['deleteMe']))
45 ▼             {
46                   $message = $dh->delete_student($s_id);
47 ▙             }
48               else
49 ▼             {
```

BBEdit

6. In data_handler.php, add the following code to the `DataHandler` class to create the method used to delete students:

```php
public function delete_student($s_id)
{
    $message = "";
    //build query
    $query = "CALL sp_delete_student('".$s_id."')";
    //query execution
    $ExecQuery = MySQLi_query($this->db_conn, $query);
    if($ExecQuery == '1')
    {
        $message = "Success!";
    }
    else
    {
        $message = "Delete Failed";
    }
    return $message;
}
```

This method takes one parameter, the student record ID number, and calls the sp_delete_student stored procedure. It also returns a success or failure message to the calling function.

7. Save your changes and then open or refresh the page add_student2.php in your browser. With no record returned from the initial GET request, the Delete button should not be displayed. Confirm that the data entry process is still working properly for the first test of this new functionality by adding a new student.

8. Add a query string to the end of the URL such as **add_student2.php?s_id=5**. This should open a record, populate the form fields, and display the Delete button. Update a value in the student data and click the Submit button. The update functionality in this page should work as expected.

9. Append the query string to the end of the URL for this page again and then refresh the data in the form. Click the Delete button. You should see a confirmation message asking if you are sure you want to delete a specific student by name. Click the Cancel button to test to make sure that function works. Then click the Delete button again, this time clicking the OK button to run the delete stored procedure. A blank form and a Success! message should be displayed.

Next Steps to a More Robust Application

While the tutorial for this chapter ends in this section and the guided application development stops with this paragraph, you are encouraged to use the tools described in previous chapters to continue to explore full stack web development.

For example, to turn the code you have built into a more robust application, you would need to incorporate a scripting library or framework. Including jQuery, for example, would allow you to turn the HTML table into a DataTable that you can search or filter dynamically. You could also use the jQuery popover function to show the contents of the data entry form in a small window that appears over the top of the primary page. You could also use any of the scripting frameworks you have explored previously.

This application is limited only by available time and ambition. You are well on your way to becoming a full stack web developer if you have the interest.

Quick Check 12-4

1. Why should your users be able to access primary functions of your web application in three clicks or less from the starting interface?

   a. It's a W3C rule for Internet applications.
   b. It's a W3C best practice for Internet applications.
   c. It's a good way to create a positive user experience so users continue using your web application.
   d. Users like to click things in web applications.

2. In the user experience of a web application, why should deleting be more difficult than adding data?

   a. The stored procedure for deleting is more complex to run than the stored procedure to save data.
   b. Saving data by mistake is more consequential than deleting data by mistake.
   c. Adding data to a database makes the storage space used more expensive while deleting data to keep the database tidy is important.
   d. Adding data by mistake is easier to fix and has fewer consequences than deleting data by mistake.

3. Why is it a good idea to hide the Delete button when no data can be deleted?

   a. To prevent database records from being deleted by mistake
   b. To keep users engaged with the user interface by making them guess what to do next
   c. To reduce the complexity of the code on the page
   d. To show options that can be used in the interface when they should be used

1) c. Keeping your application simple and making the UI approachable are best practices for web development. 2) d. Once a record is deleted from the database, it is gone, whereas adding data by mistake can be solved by deleting it. 3) d. Customizing the UI to narrow the options available for a user makes the choices of what to do next easier to make.

Summary

- Accounts used to log into the database from a dynamic web application should be created using the Principle of Least Privilege.

- The Principle of Least Privilege states that only the parts of a database that are critical to the function of a user should be granted to that user.

- Web user accounts used for accessing a database should only be granted rights to execute stored procedures.

- Putting all of your database interaction code into one file creates an efficient singular interaction point between the PHP code and the database code.

- You use an `include` statement to further the principle of Don't Repeat Yourself by importing the functionality of one PHP file into another.

- Designing a user interface to be more user friendly is part of creating a positive user experience.

- A browser's developer tools can and should be used to test a web application for SQL injection resistance.

- A GET request can use a query string to retrieve a specific record from the database.

- The data in a query string are visible to anyone viewing the request, so it is not a secure way to retrieve a record.

- Deleting data from a database via a web application should include a confirmation prior to deletion to help the user catch mistakes that can't be reversed.

Key Terms

heredoc   Principle of Least Privilege (PoLP)   query string

Review Questions

1. Why should you hide the connection error details from the users of your PHP web application and display only a generic error message instead? (12.1)

    a. To keep your users from becoming worried about the problems they are causing in your system
    b. To prevent hackers from gaining useful information about the success or failure of their attempted hacking
    c. To keep users from knowing that your system contains errors or bugs
    d. To prevent hackers from trying to hack your database, since they won't know if a web application is using one

2. What is an associative array? (12.1)

    a. A data structure containing multiples of the same type of data like integers or strings
    b. A data structure with key/value pairs
    c. A data structure used to hold other data structures in an association
    d. A data structure that shouldn't be used anymore since newer and more efficient structures have rendered it obsolete

3. What does the use of an `include` statement in PHP accomplish? (12.1)

   a. Inserts the contents of one row from a table in the database into one row in an associative array in PHP

   b. Makes the contents of the file named after the `include` command available to the code in the page where the command is used

   c. Imports the text of the file named after the `include` command into the file where the command is used

   d. Exports the functions in the file where the command is used into the file named after the command

4. How can you bypass client-side validation to test a web form for SQL injection resistance? (12.2)

   a. You can't—client-side validation is too robust to bypass in modern browsers.

   b. Use the mobile emulator built into the browser.

   c. Use the web developer tools to create a POST event.

   d. Use PHP code to bypass the web browser.

5. What is the LIKE SQL operator used for? (12.2)

   a. To test for a match between partial strings

   b. To test for a match between uppercase strings and lowercase strings

   c. To test for a match between partial numbers

   d. To test for a match between numbers and text strings

6. Why is the order of search matching important when using an OR operator to join two or more searches in a SQL query? (12.2)

   a. Because the OR search runs until all searches are completed

   b. Because the OR search runs until the first TRUE result is found

   c. Because the OR search runs from bottom to top in the code

   d. It isn't important; the OR search runs all searches simultaneously for efficiency.

7. What is a query string used for? (12.3)

   a. Identifying which part of the SQL statement the database should run

   b. Passing information into a GET request

   c. Identifying which page to load in a web application

   d. Telling the web browser which part of the PHP code on the webpage to execute

8. If query string data is visible to anyone visiting a webpage and thus not secure, why is it used? (12.3)

   a. Because it is a simple and convenient way of transmitting information as part of a GET request

   b. Because web programmers are slow to abandon old technology

   c. Because the code needs to work with older browsers so both GET and POST requests must be supported

   d. Because data security is overblown and not a primary concern for web developers who aren't security experts

9. What is the PHP heredoc syntax used for in code? (12.3)

   a. To create a multipart query string

   b. To create the text document in PHP code

   c. To create a multiline string in code

   d. To create a PHP document out of multiline text

10. Can you create more than one type of POST request from a web form? (12.4)

    a. No, only one POST and one GET request are possible in the web browser.

    b. Yes, but you need to create a different form for each type of POST request.

    c. No, creating more than one type of POST request will create errors.

    d. Yes, but you need to identify which button created each POST request.

11. Why is it important to confirm that all previous functionality is still working when completing a new function in a web application? (12.4)

    a. Because unintended consequences or mistakes may change a previously completed function

    b. Because the user interface will look different with each change, so the user experience needs to be retested

    c. Because that's what is suggested by the Agile approach to project management

    d. It is a good idea when you are first starting out as a programmer, but can be dropped when you become a good programmer

12. Do you feel like you can be successful as a full stack developer now that you've completed this entire book? (12.4)

    a. Nope, not a chance. It's way too complicated.

    b. No, this stuff is very boring and unfulfilling.

    c. No, full stack web developers are all comp sci geniuses.

    d. Yes! (This is the correct answer, by the way.)

Programming Exercises

1. Using your favorite search engine, search for "build a single-page application using PHP." Read at least five of the tutorials you find and summarize the commonalities in a one-page report. Include links to the pages you reviewed. (12.1–12.4)

2. Using your favorite search engine, search for "Is PHP and MySQL development still relevant?" Read five of the articles returned in the results and summarize the opinions in a one-page report. Include links to the pages you reviewed. (12.1–12.4)

3. Using your favorite search engine, search for "PHP application development best practices." Read five of the articles returned in the results and summarize the most common recommendations in a one-page report. Include links to the pages you reviewed. (12.1–12.4)

Projects

1. Using show_students.php as a starting point, create a new component to the data management interface that will display an interactive HTML table of the classes at Totally Awesome University. Name the new page show_classes. php. Include in the show_classes.php page all of the same functionality as show_students.php. Note that you will need to create a new stored procedure in the MySQL database called sp_get_classes, along with the PHP code that calls it. (12.1–12.4)

2. Using add_student2.php as a starting point, create a new data management interface for the class data in taus_data. Name the new page add_class.php. Add the necessary functions to add, update, and delete classes. (12.1–12.4)

3. Connect the data management interface in Project 1 to the data entry/update interface in Project 2. Add to the h3 tags at the top of each page a middot and the name of the other major section in each management interface so that it contains text like the following:

Student Enrollment Management * Class Management

Then turn the text of each h3 heading into a link so users can switch between managing classes and managing students. (12.1–12.4)

Glossary

A

absolute links   An HTML link that includes the full file path to the webpage, including the server that hosts that page.

Agile project management   An approach to managing a project that involves breaking the project down into a series of smaller steps, each with a timeline and deliverable unit in the larger project.

aliases   The shorthand versions of the full name of the table in SQL code. Aliases keep code short and tidy and ensure the code specifies the correct column if the same name for a column is used in two different tables referenced in the procedure.

anonymous function   A function written in programming code that doesn't have a proper name like `doStuff()` or `validateInputs()` but instead uses the `function()` declaration alone.

application programming interface (API)   A software application built to create an interaction point between two different types of software, such as a database and the dynamic webpages that need to pull data from or send data to the database.

array   A data structure represented by a single variable that holds multiple values of the same data type.

attribute name   The key used as the first part of an attribute before the equal sign.

attribute value   The value assigned to the key in the second part of an attribute, after the equal sign.

attributes   HTML code added to the interior of HTML tags that is composed of a name and a value pair separated by an equal sign and used to modify or extend the properties of the tag.

block   A WordPress container used for one part of the webpage contents, such as images, headers, tables, footers, sidebars, or menus. Each block contains a unique part of the webpage in the theme-based layout.

B

block-level elements   HTML elements that make space for themselves in the text display of a webpage from the left margin to the right, moving all other text out of the way.

breadcrumb trail   A list of the navigation items or pages accessed to get to the current page being viewed, typically displayed as links near the header of the page.

breakpoints   The critical widths, measured in pixels, of the screen sizes that cause changes in the CSS source file in responsive design.

business analyst (BA)   A project role for a person tasked with both documenting the inputs, processes, and outcomes of an organization or software application and creating recommendations for process efficiency or cost savings.

C

Cascading Style Sheets (CSS)   A set of display formatting rules that tell the browser how to present the content of the HTML document.

Cascading Style Sheets Object Model (CSSOM)   A data structure created by the rendering engine in a web browser that the browser uses to style the HTML of a webpage using the CSS code that the web developer created.

child element   An HTML element nested inside an outer, or parent element.

child theme   A WordPress theme that inherits all the stylistic elements of the parent theme and overrides the elements individually to customize the parent theme properties.

class selector   A CSS selector that begins with a period and specifies the HTML elements with the corresponding class name that will be styled by the CSS code that follows the selector.

client-side   Code written to run in the web browser used to create interactivity and dynamic web elements.

cloud storage   A way of using file space on a remote web server through websites such as Google Cloud, Microsoft Azure, and Amazon Web Services as if it were your own local hard drive, without having access to a specific computer.

code debugger   Software used to find bugs in programming code with features that assist with the debugging process.

comment   Text used to provide information about the code or page to the person reading it that is ignored by the code interpreter or compiler.

compiled programming language   A programming language that is converted into executable form by a compiler prior to being run by a computer.

component   A reusable block of code that functions independently in the application, like a calculator or news feed.

conditional   A block of code used as a programming expression that resolves to true or false.

constraint   A rule about the data stored in a table, like NOT NULL or UNIQUE.

constructor   A method in the class that builds an instance of the class, making it an object.

containership   The composition of HTML tags that are contained within other tags. The outermost tag pair that contains all other tags in an HTML page is `<html>...</html>`.

content delivery application (CDA)   The CMS engine that combines the templates, software plug-ins, and website content to deliver completed webpages to the users on the Internet who want to consume them.

content delivery network (CDN)   A group of high-speed web servers strategically located near major Internet traffic hubs that return resource files to the requests from web browsers.

content management application (CMA)   The CMS interface the web developer uses to create the website content, configure the templates that display the content, and organize the plug-ins that extend the features of the website.

content management system (CMS)   A software application used to manage a website, including creating and modifying webpage contents and handling website layouts, rather than writing the HTML, CSS, and JavaScript code manually.

controller   One part of the model-view-controller design pattern used to create a separation of concerns. The controller serves as the processor, responding to the events that the user creates in the view by directing the model to handle the data transactions.

Create, Read, Update, Delete (CRUD)   The four database operations that are the building blocks of data management.

CSS framework   A prebuilt set of CSS files used to style a webpage or website.

D

data binding   A method of connection in the code framework for an application that links the user interface with the data model and is displayed in the user interface so that an update to one also updates the other.

data dictionary   An external document that contains the plan for building the complete data structure for a database, including the names and types of the data elements in each table and how the data tables relate to each other in the relational database structure.

data normalization   The application of a uniform set of rules to the structure of a database so that it organizes

data to reduce redundancy and increase accuracy and performance.

data packets   Small units of digital information from a larger message or webpage sent from a web server to a web browser—or the reverse—over the Internet.

data type   A database rule that determines the type of data to store in a table column. Common data types include integer, text, decimal, and date/time.

database   A structured set of data, typically stored in a computer; uses tables as its foundational element with rows and columns that store data in an organized format.

database objects   The foundational building blocks of a database that web developers and database administrators use to create the structure of a database; examples include tables, stored procedures, and views.

deprecated   A feature or programming code that is no longer recommended for use but still works as originally designed.

description lists   HTML tags used to create a series of key terms and their definitions.

distributed denial of service (DDoS)   A malicious software system that requests a page from a website thousands of times per second from multiple computers to cause a malfunction.

Document Object Model (DOM)   The in-memory data structure created by the browser's rendering engine from the HTML that makes up a webpage.

document root   The folder the web server uses as the starting point for finding and running the code used for building webpages and any other necessary files.

Domain Name System (DNS)   A global network of servers, each with a copy of the database of all known human-friendly web addresses, such as www.google.com, and their corresponding IP addresses that are used to access the webpage contents at those addresses.

dynamic webpage   A webpage composed by a web server executing code to build the page when it is requested by the web browser.

E

em units   A relative sizing unit measured by the size of a capital letter *M* in the default display text size.

embedded style sheet   Styling information written in the top portion of an HTML page.

event listener   A block of code in a webpage that waits for an event to occur, like a mouse click or value change, and then runs.

events   Actions that happen in a browser.

external style sheet   A text file separate from the HTML files that store the CSS style information for a website.

F

fetch request   A general term for both GET and POST requests used by a web browser to retrieve information from a web server.

field   The individual data elements stored in database table columns like those you gather in a web form, such as first name, middle initial, last name, and birthdate.

flexbox   A CSS value that creates a flexible container out of the HTML element it is assigned to and shows content that expands, contracts, and rearranges itself depending on the screen size.

for loop   A programming structure used to repeat a code operation for a specified number of times.

foreign keys   The unique identifier columns from tables that are used to create relationships between tables in a separate table.

function body   The block of code after the function declaration, beginning with the opening curly bracket and ending with the closing curly bracket, that contains the code the function runs when it is called.

function call   The line of code located outside of the function but within the other code used for an application that causes the function named in the call to run.

function declaration   The function declaration is the first line of the function that begins with the word *function*.

functions   Units of code with a defined structure that perform discrete tasks.

G

GET request   A specific type of request made by a web browser using the HTTP protocol to ask a web server to return a webpage.

Googlebots   Self-contained applications that use the desktop and mobile versions of Google Chrome to replicate how a human user interacts with a website as they crawl and index website contents for the Google search engine database.

graphical user interface (GUI)   The visual component of a software application that creates the display of objects such as windows, icons, and buttons.

H

heredoc   A PHP coding syntax element used to create a multiline string of text.

hexadecimal color   A color value in the format #XXXXXX, with the first two Xs specifying the amount of red to use, the second two Xs specifying green, and the last two Xs specifying blue.

hook   A named location in a WordPress page used to add custom code to the WordPress code that makes up a webpage.

Hypertext Markup Language (HTML)   The programming language used to build webpages.

Hypertext Transfer Protocol (HTTP)   The networking language browsers use to communicate with web servers.

I

ID selector   A CSS selector that begins with a pound sign and specifies the single HTML element with the corresponding ID that will be styled by the CSS code following the selector.

image map   An HTML tag set used to create links inside specified shapes in an image.

indexes   Structural components of the database added to one or more columns in a table and used by the database engine to efficiently search the table rows for a specific record or records.

inline style   Styling information for an HTML tag that is written inside of, that is, inline with, the HTML tag as a set of attributes.

instantiation   Programming code written to create a variable or object so the rest of the code can use it.

internal style sheet   Styling information written in the top portion of an HTML page.

InterNic   The international agency responsible for maintaining the directory of the Internet to ensure each website has a unique address.

interpreted programming language   A programming language that uses the processing power of the code interpreter to run the code as written by the programmer without converting it into executable form first.

J

JavaScript   An interpreted programming language that is primarily used for creating interactive effects in web browsers.

JavaScript library   A package of prebuilt JavaScript code that web developers can use to extend webpage functionality in the browser.

JavaScript Object Notation (JSON)   A plain-text data structure used to create nested key/value pairs.

jQuery selector   A block of code used to find an HTML element that matches the criteria passed to the jQuery selector function.

just-in-time compiler   A component of most modern browsers that creates compiled code from an interpreted language such as JavaScript for greater speed and efficiency the second time the code is executed.

L

list item   A `<li>...</li>` tag pair used to create a list item, which the browser then displays as a bulleted or numbered item in a list in a webpage.

logical error   An error in the programming logic of code that otherwise follows the basic rules of the programming language and does not include misspelled variables or functions.

logical operators   Keywords or symbols used to test conditions like equal to, not equal to, greater than, or less than to create decision points in the code flow.

M

meta tag   An HTML tag added to the head section of a webpage that supplies information to the browser about the HTML in the webpage that follows. Meta tags are not shown when the user views the webpage in a browser.

metadata   Data about the data on a webpage.

methods   Functions included inside the code that makes up a class.

minified   The compressed version of code, which is not as easily human readable as the non-minified version due to the removal of white space and comments.

mobile device emulators   An interface component of most web browsers used to show a webpage on a screen that is the same size (width and height) as a mobile device.

mobile-first design   An approach to webpage design that begins with identifying the site's most critical components to display on the small screen of a mobile device, and then adds less critical elements as more screen size is available with larger devices.

model   One part of the model-view-controller and model-view-viewmodel design patterns used to create a separation of concerns. The model retrieves data to show in the view or returns data to store in the database as directed by the controller or viewmodel.

model-view-controller (MVC)   A software design pattern used to create a separation of concerns. In this design pattern, the data handling occurs in a model, the view presents a user interface to the user, and the controller serves as the processor directing the interactions between the view and the model.

model-view-viewmodel (MVVM)   A software design pattern used to create a separation of concerns. In this design pattern, the data handling occurs in a model, the view presents a user interface to the user, and the viewmodel has direct links to the view and the model, maintaining the state of the application instead of directing the actions as the controller does in model-view-controller.

multifactor authentication (MFA)   An authentication process used for logging into a website or application that has multiple steps to create greater security. After using a computer to successfully log in to a website with a username and password, an MFA-enabled login process typically sends a text message with an authentication code to a user's phone as the second step. The user must then enter the authentication code on the computer to gain access to the site.

N

natural keys   External values that uniquely identify a record in the database, like a driver's license number or a Social Security number; they originate outside of the database but are used as unique identifiers for records in the database.

nested   Arranged in a hierarchical structure like inner HTML tags that occur between other opening and closing HTML tag pairs.

O

object   A logical software structure composed of data, variables, functions, and programming logic.

one-to-many relationship   A relationship in the data stored in a database where one record in a table is associated with one or more records in another table.

ordered lists   HTML tag sets used for series of items in a ranked order, like the steps in a recipe or the eras in geology.

P

parent element   An outer HTML tag pair that contains an inner or child HTML element.

parent theme   A WordPress theme that contains all of the necessary style and layout components for a website that a child theme then modifies by overriding specific elements.

permalink   The internal navigation name stored in the database for a webpage or blog post created in the WordPress website.

PHP   An interpreted programming language designed for web application development.

plug-ins   Code bundles that extend the WordPress application to incorporate additional features or functions.

POST request   A specific type of request made by a web browser using the HTTP protocol to send data to a web server from a webpage.

primary key   The identifier for unique data that makes one record different from all other records in a table.

Principle of Least Privilege (PoLP)   A database administrator's approach to data security that suggests all database users should be granted only the rights and access to the absolute minimum parts of the system that are required for each user to interact with the database successfully.

project manager (PM)   A professional planner responsible for planning, organizing, leading, and controlling the people, resources, and processes that make up a project.

properties   Variables included inside the code that makes up a class.

pseudo-class   A CSS class that only exists when the HTML element it modifies is in a conditional state, such as when the pointer is moved over it.

pseudocode   A written description of the programming flow without using actual programming language syntax and code.

pseudo-element   A keyword added to a CSS selector used to style a specific part of the selected HTML element as if it were a different HTML element.

Q

query The SQL programming code that uses a combination of the database objects and SQL keyword operators to extract a new set of information from the existing data.

query string The text beginning with a question mark that appears after a URL and passes information into a webpage.

R

record A collection of fields about the same person, item, or object in a database.

relational database A database composed of tables of related data where the relationships between the data in the tables is formalized in the code that the database uses.

relative links Links that include a file path to another file stored in the same file system on the computer.

relative size A measure of font size given in proportion to the size of the font of the parent element.

rendering engine A component of the browser software application that is responsible for composing the text, images, and other content for display as a webpage.

responsive design An approach to building webpages that creates a flexible framework for webpage content and shows different content depending on the screen size of the device accessing the webpage.

runtime error A coding error that appears when the code is being compiled or executed due to calling a function or using a variable that doesn't exist, such as when a function name is mistyped.

S

scope The bounds in the code containing a variable of where the variable can be used.

scripting framework A body of programming code that uses JavaScript or TypeScript as its native language and extends the language to include features for building dynamic applications. The framework is designed in modules to include components a developer can use to satisfy common requirements for web applications.

search engine A website that lists other websites categorized by search terms or keywords that users might type while looking for information.

search engine optimization (SEO) Creating webpage contents that conform to the standards set by search engines to ensure your web content is visible to the search engine and ranked as highly as possible in the index database.

self-closing tag An HTML tag that does not use a closing tag but instead ends with a slash, like `<br/>`.

separation of concerns Dividing a software application into sections to handle different operations, typically the user interface, the processor, and the data handling components.

sequences Database objects that keep a running counter of the next value to be used when a new record is added to a table.

server-side A programming language or code written to run on a web server.

sibling element The next HTML element that occurs within the same enclosing HTML element.

single-page application A webpage that changes dynamically as the user interacts with it. The page itself does not need to be reloaded because the contents of the page are changed.

slug The WordPress term for a shortened name for a blog post or webpage that is used to create links.

software plug-ins Software packages that increase the capability of the original software by extending functions.

statement A complete line of programming code, similar to a sentence in a written or spoken language.

static webpage A text file that is transformed into a webpage the same way each time it is displayed by the browser.

stored procedures Database objects composed of database code for performing repeated tasks like adding, updating, and deleting the data in a table.

strongly typed A variable with a specific data type such as a number, date, or text string.

Structured Query Language (SQL) The programming language used to write the code that a database engine can execute to perform database operations.

syntax The logic and rules that make any type of language—spoken, written, or computer—understandable by a human.

syntax error A coding error that breaks the rules of the programming language, preventing the code from running.

T

table index An internal identifier a database management system uses to uniquely identify records in the table to find and retrieve them faster.

tables The foundational elements upon which all other objects in the database are built or reference; they contain the rows and columns of data in the database.

technology stack A list of the software used to complete an application or technical process from start to finish.

text strings One or more characters.

themes Preconfigured styles and page layouts in WordPress that include CSS code and designated places for displaying your page contents.

Trojan horses   Malware that hides the true intentions of the software developer, who has malicious intentions. A Trojan horse is often a form of "security software" that is anything other than that.

two-way data binding   A feature of the scripting frameworks that uses the code of the scripting library or framework to automatically update the value in a controller variable displayed in the view if the controller or model changes.

U

Uniform Resource Locator (URL)   The address, or "name," of a webpage, like www.google.com.

unordered lists   HTML tag sets used to create bulleted lists of similar items that belong together but don't occur in a specific order, like the ingredients in a recipe or lifeforms of a geologic era.

user experience   The overall impression or emotion created by a website, including the look and feel, color scheme, navigation, fonts, and information presented.

user interface (UI)   The portion of the software used to create the space where users interact with software.

V

variable   In programming code, a designated container of data used to store a value.

variable declaration   A programming command used to create a variable so the rest of the code can use it.

version control   Software used to create a series of code backup milestones at convenient points during development.

view   One part of the model-view-controller and model-view-viewmodel design patterns used to create a separation of concerns. The view represents the user interface.

viewmodel   One part of the model-view-viewmodel design pattern used to create a separation of concerns. In this design pattern, the data handling occurs in a model, the view presents a user interface to the user, and the viewmodel has direct links to the view and the model, maintaining the state of the application.

viewport   The screen width, measured in pixels, on a web browser running in a device.

views   Database objects built from database code that create table-like structures displaying a subset of the data from one or more of the database tables.

void tag   An HTML tag that does not use a closing tag but instead ends with a slash, like `<br/>`.

W

waterfall project management   An approach to project management where the entire project is tested and then launched into production (or goes over the edge of the waterfall) only after all development is completed.

web browser   A software application used to access, search, and interact with the Internet.

what you see is what you get (WYSIWYG)   A type of webpage editing software application that displays a visual representation of the webpage instead of showing the text of the code that makes up the page.

WordPress   An open-source content management system used for a majority of CMS web development.

World Wide Web Consortium (W3C)   The committee that makes the rules for how information travels on the Internet and how web servers and web browsers should communicate with each other to display webpages.

Index

A

Absolute links, 38
Ad-hoc query, 355–359
Agile project management, 18, 19
Aliases, 354
`align-items: center;`
    property, 119
`alt` attribute, 70
Angular, 211–212
    Hello World example, 213–215
    module, 214
    MVC for, 212–213
    `ng-app` directive, 214
    temperature conversion,
        215–218
Angular 2, 212
AngularJS, 212
`animate()` function, 187
Animation, in jQuery, 187–188
Anonymous function, 170, 184
Apache web server, 10, 13,
    298–299
Application programming
    interface (API), 20–21, 143
`<area>` tag, 73
Array, 159
`<a>...</a>` tags, 37
Attribute name, 37
Attributes, 37
Attribute value, 37
Automated software attack, 266, 267
Automating responsive design,
    131–132

B

BA. *See* Business analyst (BA)
`background-color:`
        `rgb(175,175,175)`
        property, 67
`background-image` property, 76
Bare Bones Edit, 30
`<base/>` tag, 49
Block, 248, 249
Block-level elements, 35
Blogging, 234
Bluehost, 260
`<body>...</body>` tags, 35
`bold` attribute, 68
Boolean expression, in PHP, 303
Bootstrap, 132
`border-collapse` property, 83
`border-color` property, 72
`border-radius` property, 72
Borders
    image, 72
    table, 82–83
`border-style` property, 72
Box, 31
Breadcrumb trail, 128
Breakpoints, 101
    in JavaScript debugger, 154–155
Browser. *See* Web browser
`<br/>` tag, 49, 55
Bugs, 104
Business analyst (BA), 17, 18

C

C++, 160
Cache, 6
Cascading style sheet (CSS), 4
    creating external style sheet, 47
    hexadecimal color values, 52
    link information, 107–108
    printer-friendly, 129–130
    resizing images, 71
    selectors, 53
    style effects, 67
    syntax, 48
    WordPress theme customization
        with, 278–281
Cascading Style Sheet Object
    Model (CSSOM), 6, 48
CDA. *See* Content delivery
    application (CDA)
CDN. *See* Content delivery
    network (CDN)
CERN, 2
`checkValidity()` function,
    165–166
Child element, 113
Child theme
    adding style to, 284–285
    plug-ins, 282–283
    in WordPress, 281
Chrome, 102
`class` attribute, 52–53
Classes, in PHP, 313–317
    methods, 314
    properties, 314
Class selectors, 51–52, 55
`clearLights()` function,
    158–159
`Click Here` text, 37
Client-side data validation, 321
Client-side programming, 138
Cloud storage, 31
CMA. *See* Content management
    application (CMA)
CMS. *See* Content management
    system (CMS)
Code debugger, 137
`<col/>` tag, 49
Column's properties, 334
`<command/>` tag, 49
Comment, 48
Compiled programming languages,
    21–22
Component, 212
Conditional, logical `if` test, 147
`confirm()` function, 170, 171
Constants, 159
Constraint, 337
Constructor, 314
Containership, 36
`content` attribute, 107, 112
Content delivery application
    (CDA), 234, 236, 237
Content delivery network (CDN),
    181, 182
Content management application
    (CMA), 234, 237
Content management system
    (CMS), 8, 233. *See also*
    WordPress
    open source, 234
    proprietary, 234
    publishing a website using,
        259–261
Controller, 212
`createApp()` method, 221, 222
Create, Read, Update, and
    Delete (CRUD), 326, 345,
    397–402

D

Database
    defined, 325
    purpose of, 326–328
    relational, 328, 329
Database management system
    (DBMS), 328, 331–332
Database objects, 325
Data binding, 215
Data dictionary, 334
Data entry/update form, 387
    creation of, 387–391
    GET request, 391–393
    linking with HTML table data,
        396
    POST request, 388, 391–393, 397
    retrieving data, 391–395
`DataHandler` class, 371–373
`data()` method, 222
Data normalization, 334–335
Data packets, 4
Data storage, 6
DataTables.js plug-in, 199–202
Data type, 334
Data validation. *See also* Form
    validation
    with JavaScript, 162, 169–170
    with jQuery, 198
Debugger, JavaScript, 150–156, 168
Deprecated tags, 91
Description lists, 40, 41
`die()` method, 370
`display: flex;` property,
    116, 119
`display: grid;` property,
    111, 125
`displayMe()` function, 141–144
Distributed denial-of-service
    (DDoS) attack, 267–268
`div` element, 55
DNS. *See* Domain Name System
    (DNS)
Docker containers, 241–243
`doctype` declaration, 36
Document Object Model (DOM),
    5–6, 48, 139, 202
Document root, 297
Document tree building, 4–6
Dollar sign ($), 183
Domain Name System (DNS), 2, 3
Dot operator (.), 184
Dropbox, 31
Duplicator plug-in, 260
Dynamic webpage, 3, 4, 12–15,
    296, 317–321

E

Easy Updates Manager, 270–271
Edge, 102
`else if()`, 147, 148

CSS.

CSS. *See* Cascading style sheet
    (CSS)
CSS framework, 131
`css()` function, 185
CSSOM. *See* Cascading Style Sheet
    Object Model (CSSOM)
Cybersecurity. *See* Web security
Cybersecurity and Infrastructure
    Security Agency (CISA), 269

Embedded style sheet, 45
`<embed/>` tag, 49
Emulators
    mobile device, 102
    testing with, 102–105
Em units, 44
Encryption, 267
Equal sign, in JavaScript,
    144–146, 148
Errors
    File Not Found (404), 11, 12
    JavaScript, 150, 151–156
    logical, 150, 153–156
    message, 152
    in PHP code, 300
    runtime, 150–152
    style, 46
    syntax, 150, 153
    webpage, 34
`eval()` function, 145, 191
Event listener, 222
Events, 139
Excel, 325
External style sheets, 45, 47–48

F

Fetch request, 2–4
Field, 325
`fieldset` element, 88–89, 93
`figcaption` element, 74
File extension, 70
File Not Found (404) error,
    11, 12
File Transfer Protocol (FTP), 260
Firefox, 2, 102, 138
Flexbox, 116
`flex-direction: row;`
    property, 119
`float` property, 66
`font-weight` property, 68
Foreign keys, 334
`for` loop, 160
Forms
    creation of, 317–318
    elements, 91–92
    email field, 88
    feedback, 91
    HTML, 87–92
    with PHP, 317–321
    processing the submitted
        values, 318–319
    security, 319–320
`form` tag, 87–88
Form validation, 139, 162
    with JavaScript, 162–163
        counting the missing fields,
            164–169
        data validation, 169–170
        highlighting, 163–164
        `required` attribute, 163, 171
        `validate_form()` function,
            166–167
        warning labels, 165, 168
    with jQuery
        counting the missing fields,
            195–198
        data validation, 198
        error labels, 194–195
        user feedback, 194–195
        using jQuery Validation
            plug-in, 193
404 error, 11, 12